Seasonal
SUNDAYS
SORTED
BOOK 1

Rachel Summers
Eleanor King

Illustrations by Eleanor King

INCLUDES
DOWNLOADABLE
RESOURCES

kevin
mayhew

The material in this book has been taken from *Sunday Sorted Book 1.*

kevin
mayhew

First published in Great Britain in 2019 by Kevin Mayhew Ltd
Buxhall, Stowmarket, Suffolk IP14 3BW
Tel: +44 (0) 1449 737978 Fax: +44 (0) 1449 737834
E-mail: info@kevinmayhew.com

www.kevinmayhew.com

9 8 7 6 5 4 3 2 1 0

ISBN 978 1 83858 033 9
Catalogue No. 1501627

Cover design by Rob Mortonson
© Images used under licence from Shutterstock Inc.
Illustrations by Eleanor King
Edited by Linda Ottewell
Typeset by Angela Selfe

Printed and bound in Great Britain

LINK TO
DOWNLOADABLE
RESOURCES

http://bit.ly/2mj1BG0

CONTENTS

ABOUT THE AUTHORS

Rachel Summers

Rachel lives in a vicarage in East London with her husband, their five kids, and a veritable menagerie of pets.

A teacher by trade, Rachel moved from teaching in primary schools, through doing work one-to-one with excluded teens, to retraining as a forest school practitioner. She now delivers forest school sessions to nurseries, schools, and the general public.

Sharing the magic of all things slimy and interesting, watching the seasons shift and the weather change, finding the beauty in the commonplace and insignificant, holding space for others to explore: these are some of the things which get Rachel excited.

Eleanor King

Eleanor lives by the seaside in Essex with her husband and three children, and buckets and spades on the doorstep.

She spends a lot of time running different groups in the community, both inside and outside the church, but when she is not doing this she likes to make biscuits, go walking and knit or crochet things that are not too big or complicated.

INTRODUCTION

Seasonal Sundays Sorted is a resource for the whole church family. From vicars looking for sermon inspiration, to the person preparing the intercessions, from the children's work team, to those looking to support the worship of families with young children in church, all will breathe a sigh of relief to get Sunday sorted. It ensures that everyone in church, from the youngest to the oldest, will be exploring and praying through the same themes, ideas, and scriptures. As the family of God we all have things to learn from each other and this book will enable such conversations to happen.

Each Sunday includes the following elements:

Thoughts on the Readings: This pulls Sunday's readings together, unpicking the common themes between them, and listening to how they speak into our context.

Discussion Starters: Some churches like to talk in a small group about the readings before the Sunday service. Others might use these discussion starters as part of a café church style sermon slot.

Intercessions: Offering up prayer on behalf of the worshipping church is an important job but one that often doesn't come with much support or training. The intercessions here will support you in that role, giving you confidence as you make the prayers your own.

Children's Prayer: Sometimes a shorter and simpler form of prayer is useful, either in a children's group, or in the main service to make sure prayer is more readily accessible for all.

Other Ideas!: Something to display, create, or do, that sets the scene for this Sunday and draws people of all ages into worship.

Children's Corner: Most churches have a children's corner, with books and soft toys. This provides suggestions for a simple activity to set out each Sunday, so that very young children and their parents or carers are able to join in the worship with the rest of the church community. It is also a good way of making some kind of provision for children if you are in a church where your numbers don't make a Sunday School viable, as the activities are open-ended enough for children to explore them at their own level.

All-age Talk: A talk suitable for everyone doesn't have to dumb down theological concepts or spiritual insight. These all-age talks allow everyone to understand the scriptures at a level they can understand.

Little Kids' Sunday School and **Big Kids' Sunday School:** Deliberately flexible on age grouping, these suggestions for children's activities keep things playful and explorative, as research shows that children learn best through playing. Some churches may be in the position to offer different activities for different age groups, with the younger kids' sessions including lots of gentle creative fun, and the older kids' sessions encouraging questions as much as giving answers. Other churches may find that they glance over both sessions and either run with a different one each week, or take inspiration from both to fit their group. You will know what will suit your group best.

Colouring Page: Each Sunday there is a downloadable/photocopiable colouring sheet, inspired by the readings. It is suggested that this is available in the children's corner in church, but many young people and adults also find colouring to be something that supports their faith development and aids their worship.

THE FIRST SUNDAY OF ADVENT

Readings

- Jeremiah 33:14-16
- Psalm 25:1-9
- 1 Thessalonians 3:9-13
- Luke 21:25-36

Thoughts on the Readings

A king is coming. A king of love. A king who is honest, who will bring both peace and justice. Jeremiah spoke out God's promise of a king who would come from the family of David, and we can look back now and see that he was talking about Jesus. Jesus was descended from King David on his father, Joseph's side.

We often hear people complaining that politicians are not 'honest' or 'fair' – this seems to have been a theme dating back to Jeremiah's time, as the thing that makes this king different is that he would rule with honesty and justice. And I'm sure that people then, as now, had misgivings about leaders who seemed to be in it for their own fame and glory. There's a lovely saying that sums this up: 'Those who actively seek power are the least suitable to receive it.'

And as we begin Advent, and look forward to the coming of Jesus, born as a human baby, this certainly rings true. As a baby, Jesus was not seeking fame and glory – but we also know from his life that this was never on his agenda. He rode an ordinary donkey, made friends with fishermen, spent time with tax-collectors and had no time for people who were religious show-offs.

As we also look forward, in the Gospel reading, to Jesus' second coming, we think about that wonderful promise at the end that 'you will soon be set free'. Often references to these signs of the end times are suitably vague, that we could always find something that sounds like it is happening now. But perhaps this is a good thing, because it keeps us alert, helps us keep things in perspective, and remember that whatever is happening in our world, God will be there for us and we do not need to be afraid. His values of love, peace and justice are ones that will endure.

Discussion Starters

- **Do we need justice to have peace?**
- **And what is God's justice like?**
- **How could we make things more just in our local community and our world?**
- **Think of one action to do this week.**

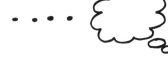

Intercessions

God of justice,
bring your kingdom of peace.

As we look forward to celebrating Jesus' kingly birth at Christmas,
may your kingdom come in our lives.

For those who are oppressed
through poor labour standards
or who do not feel appreciated or valued
for the unpaid caring work they do every day;
for those trapped by debt,
made to feel unworthy by glossy advertising campaigns.
God of justice,
bring your kingdom of peace.

May our churches at Christmas
be open and welcoming,
friendly, warm and non-judgemental,
ready to listen,
full of prayer,
anointed by the Holy Spirit,
showing love to our neighbours.
God of justice,
bring your kingdom of peace.

For those who are suffering
with things that will pass
or things that will last;
for those who have top of their Christmas list
'freedom from pain' or 'being able to cope',
we ask for your presence,
your love, and your healing,
and know that you've been there, too.
We name before you today . . .
God of justice,
bring your kingdom of peace.

Be near to those people
who are nearing the end of their lives here on earth;
bring comfort, peace, and a knowledge
that your kingdom is not far away.
We remember today . . .
God of justice,
bring your kingdom of peace.

Lord, we look forward to the time
when we will see justice and peace take root and flourish.
Show us this week where we can make a difference
and help to establish your good, honest and loving kingdom.
Amen.

Children's Prayer

With you, Lord Jesus,
we won't be afraid
of stormy weather
or crashing waves.
And if the world around
seems stormy too,
we'll hold your hand
and be safe with you.
Amen.

Other Ideas!

Adults or children could bring forward symbols of Jesus' kingly reign and place them on a cut-out shape of a crown at the front of the church. This could include a dove for peace, a rainbow to show everyone is welcome, a hand for caring and a heart for love.

All-age Talk

Bring in a large branch or two that you've pruned from a tree. It's a good time of year to do pruning, after all. Secure them with one end inside a bucket of soil or sand, and display at the front of church. Have prepared a good bunch of leaf shapes, cut out of paper, hole punched at one end, with string threaded through ready to tie.

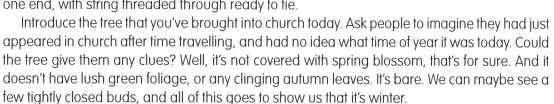

Introduce the tree that you've brought into church today. Ask people to imagine they had just appeared in church after time travelling, and had no idea what time of year it was today. Could the tree give them any clues? Well, it's not covered with spring blossom, that's for sure. And it doesn't have lush green foliage, or any clinging autumn leaves. It's bare. We can maybe see a few tightly closed buds, and all of this goes to show us that it's winter.

Just as Jesus speaks in the parable about how we can tell from the leaves on the trees when summer is here, it should also be obvious to us to tell from other signs around us when the kingdom of God is here.

In Jeremiah, the Lord speaks of raising up a 'righteous branch' who will 'execute justice and righteousness in the land' (33:15, NRSV). Well, here's another branch! What might the signs of God's kingdom be that we can see? How do we notice Jesus bringing justice and righteousness?

Offer the leaf shapes for people to contribute the signs of the kingdom that they have noticed. They can either write on the leaves, and tie them on to the branches themselves, then you can read them out and sum them up at the end, or they can call out suggestions for you to write on the leaves and tie on the tree for everyone to see.

Now here we have a tree, as in the parable, full of leaves. It is telling us that the kingdom of God is near. Over the next week, keep your eyes open. See what other signs you can spot, pointing to the coming kingdom.

Children's Corner

Have a tray with sand or salt, and a fork and a paintbrush. Display next to this the words, **Make me know your ways, O Lord; teach me your paths. Psalm 25:4** (NRSV).

With their parents, the children can explore making paths, and whisper about what God's path looks like.

The colouring sheet shows a path in the countryside, with those words from the Psalm written to be coloured in also.

Little Kids' Sunday School

Prepare some picture signs to hold up, maybe a green/red man from a road crossing, a sign from a fast food place they'll recognise, a sign from a motorway advertising beds for the night. Play a game where you hold up a sign, and they do what it shows (walking, stopping, eating, sleeping).

Signs are useful. They show us things. Sometimes signs are pictures so that we can all understand them even if we can't read yet.

Jesus spoke about how we look at signs to find things out. Show a picture of a tree in the summer time, full of leaves. Can the children tell from this sign what time of year it might be? What clothes they might choose to wear? What fun things they might do with their family? Show a picture of a tree in the winter time, bare and empty. Can they tell from this sign what time of year it might be, what clothes they'd wear, what fun things they might do? Jesus said, you are all so good at seeing the signs around you, the signs the trees give you about the seasons. Now you need to get looking for other signs too. The signs of the kingdom of God. What might these signs look like? Love? Peace? Kindness? Joy?

Decorate a road sign on card, with two eyes on it, to remind you to look for the signs of God's coming kingdom through this next week.

Big Kids' Sunday School

Play a game of musical emotions. Write slips of paper with emotions on them (happy, sad, angry, jealous, frustrated, suspicious, hungry, sleepy, bored, enthusiastic etc.) and put these folded up in a hat. As the music plays, pass the hat around. When the music stops, pull out a slip and act it out. Can the others read the signs of how you're feeling?

Our faces are very expressive. They have to be – as a species we don't have all the hair or feathers that other animals use for signalling how they feel, and our sense of smell isn't terribly acute to help us out either. Reading emotions on faces is a key skill that's helped us to function in societies through the millennia.

Jesus talks of us reading the signs. He speaks of how the people who surrounded him were expert in reading the signs that summer was on the way, by looking at the leaves beginning to grow on the trees.

We need to get better at reading the signs. The signs of God's coming kingdom of love, justice, and peace. What might we spot in our lives and in our community? Have a chat about the things going on around you – maybe a soup kitchen, a food bank, carol singing at a care home, a lollipop road crossing person who always smiles at every child. On a cut out 'road sign' circle, the children can write 'God's Kingdom' in the centre, and decorate it. Over the next week, can they add in the signs of this coming kingdom that they spot?

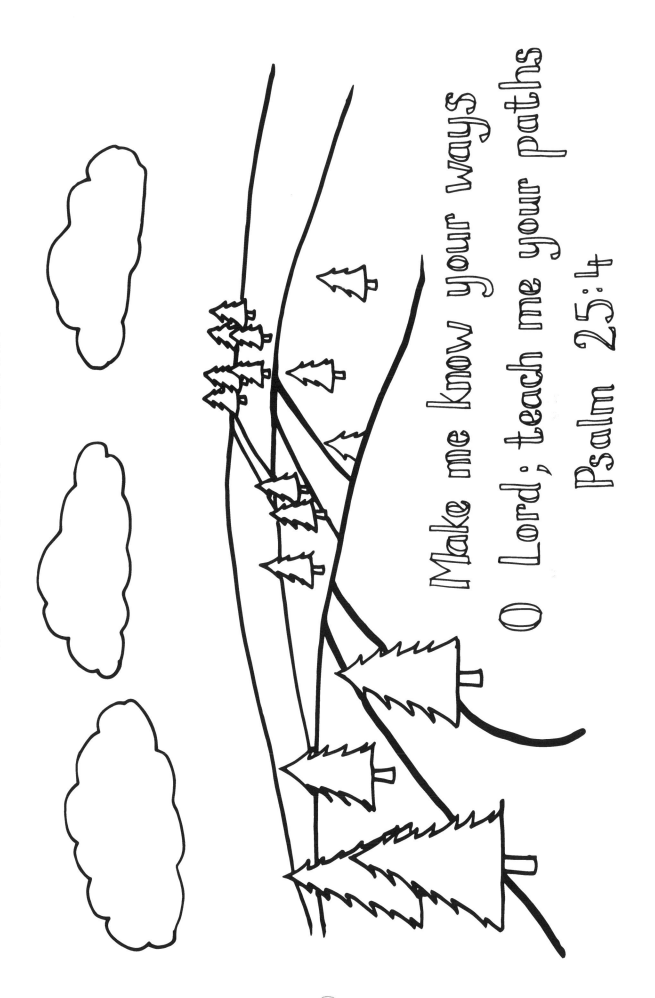

Make me know your ways
O Lord; teach me your paths
Psalm 25:4

THE SECOND SUNDAY OF ADVENT

Readings

- Malachi 3:1-4
- Canticle – Benedictus
- Philippians 1:3-11
- Luke 3:1-6

Thoughts on the Readings

God is preparing us for Jesus' coming. At this time of year many people are very busy preparing for Christmas, and in spite of all the advertising around us focusing on spending money, at heart our preparations are often in keeping with the way God wants us to prepare ourselves. Some people like to give money to a homeless charity or to buy 'alternative gifts' to send to friends and family, which are often practical things like seeds, compost, educational materials or clean water, delivered by a charity working in areas of need. Perhaps we have helped with a church fair or have one coming up, building community and welcoming people in to our buildings, while raising a bit of money for God's work in our local churches. And as we choose presents or write cards for those who are close to us, we think of them and try to put ourselves in their shoes, finding a picture on a card or a present that will make them happy. And of course, Christmas is a good time to catch up with people, to offer and accept hospitality, to listen to others and to share our news with them.

So perhaps Advent is not so different to the preparations that many of us are making, both inside and outside the church, and we should welcome this. But maybe, as we make some time to reflect as we come to church this Advent, we can also take a breather and allow God to do his work in us. Perhaps we can have a think during a quiet time in church about what qualities, what treasures we would like to receive from our good, kind and generous Father in heaven. He wants us to have beautiful, pure and shining lives, and if we have done things we regret, he is always ready to listen and to forgive.

Discussion Starters

- **What qualities would you like God to develop in you this Advent? Maybe wisdom, grace, peace, understanding or patience? Maybe something else? Think of two each, and as you go through the week, imagine receiving one in each hand from your heavenly Father.**

- **Are there any practical ways we in the church can support each other at this time? Perhaps posting letters for those unable to get out easily, swapping childcare to get a few Christmas jobs done, or giving a lift to someone to get to a Christmas event or concert?**

Intercessions

God of glory,
make us pure like you.

Lord, we are starting to be surrounded
by sparkly and glittery decorations.
May this remind us of Advent
and your promise to make us shine too
like pure gold and silver.

We bring you our local churches,
their fairs, Christingles and services,
their links with local schools
and their outreach.
May we work together
to show your love and
welcome others Into your family.
God of glory,
make us pure like you.

As we pray for our world
we think of the people who have made
the things we have bought as Christmas presents.
We think of the farmers who have been busy
growing our Christmas dinners.
And we think of everyone in the factories, bakeries and shops
who have helped to make the lovely things we eat at this time of year.
We thank you for them, Lord, and pray for a sustainable and ethical system
which is fair for everyone who lives in our world.
God of glory,
make us pure like you.

We pray for those who are ill at the moment,
for those waiting at A&E,
for those wondering whether to book doctors' appointments,
and those in hospital.
May they know your presence, peace, love and healing.
We remember those known to us and name before you now . . .
God of Glory,
make us pure like you.

We bring to you those who have recently died,
their family and friends;
for those who are at the point of death.
Thank you for your promise
that you will do your good work in us
and prepare us to live in heaven with you.
We particularly remember today . . .
God of glory,
make us pure like you.

Thank you, dear Lord,
that you will not leave us
unfinished or incomplete.
You already treasure the things in us
that chime with your way of doing things
and want to help us build on those
as we go through our lives.
Amen.

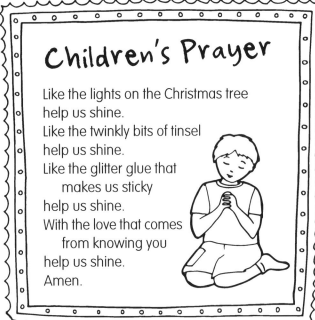

Children's Prayer

Like the lights on the Christmas tree
help us shine.
Like the twinkly bits of tinsel
help us shine.
Like the glitter glue that
    makes us sticky
help us shine.
With the love that comes
    from knowing you
help us shine.
Amen.

Other Ideas!

People can hand round a basket of shiny 'gems' or sequins to help everyone think about how God can make our lives shine with his love.

All-age Talk

Prepare a length of cloth (a bedsheet will do, cut in half to make a longer strip would be even better) to be a 'red carpet'. Clutter up the space leading towards the front of the church with chairs, kneelers, microphone stands, whatever you have hanging around your building, so it'll look like authentic, believable clutter!

Begin to prepare a special seat for a special visitor. Hang some fairy lights around a chair, maybe drape it in posh fabric offcuts. Talk about how excited you are about this important person who is coming, and how you can't wait to see them. How you want everything just perfect up here.

There's a bit of commotion at the back of church. Someone looking a bit disreputable comes crashing in, maybe wearing ripped jeans, or a tatty coat, their hair looking scruffy. 'Get ready! There's a special visitor coming! Why aren't you ready?' they shout as they come.

You are a bit taken aback. But you are preparing, aren't you? You've got this lovely chair ready. It looks really posh, don't you think? They're going to love what you've done with the fairy lights.

The disreputable messenger starts noisily moving away the clutter, exclaiming as they do so, 'What is all this doing here? How is the special visitor even going to get in?'

Oh. You suddenly realise that there's no point you fussing about the details up at the front, if there isn't even a clear passageway for the visitor to come through. Together you begin to clear away the mess and the muddle until it's clear enough to roll out a red carpet leading unobstructed to the posh chair.

John the Baptist came as a messenger, as prophesied in the scriptures, to tell people to make a path ready for the Lord to come. We are preparing for Jesus to come at Christmas, born into our lives and our hearts as our Saviour. But there's no point us just spending all our time and effort making that one day beautiful and special – we need to think about what mess, muddle and clutter we need to clear away out of our lives, so that Jesus can enter in.

Children's Corner

Make a sign asking the children to sort through the mess and muddle of the children's corner. They can try out the pens and throw away the ones that have run out of ink. They can sharpen the pencils. They can find the old colouring sheets stuffed down the back of the toy tub and throw them away. They can put all the cuddly toys in one place, and stand the books up the right way round. As they do so, they can whisper with their parents about what other things they can do in their lives to get ready for the coming of Jesus.

The colouring sheet has a picture of children preparing for Christmas by decorating their house, baking, and wrapping presents, and the verse from **Luke 3:4** (NRSV) written to be coloured in: **'Prepare the way of the Lord'**.

Little Kids' Sunday School

Fill a builder's mixing tray with sand or compost. Get the children to shape it into hills and valleys, and try 'walking' some toy people and animals from one side to the other. How can we make their journey easier? Go with everyone's suggestions and try them out. If nobody suggests it, you can also suggest flattening the mountains, and filling in the valleys. Give it a try and see how much easier the toys find it to cross the terrain.

Our reading from the Bible talks of lowering mountains and filling in valleys to prepare the way of the Lord. You can read it to them if you like – it's really pictorial language so not totally inaccessible. We are waiting for Jesus, waiting for Christmas. How are we preparing for Jesus to come again, to come into our lives?

Provide some cut out mountains, trees, buildings etc, glue sticks and cardboard. The children can stick along the bottom flap of the mountains and other obstacles, and attach them to the cardboard so that they stand up. When you say 'Prepare the way of the Lord!' they can push them down so they lie flat.

Big Kids' Sunday School

Set up an obstacle course for the children to try out, travelling from one side of the room to the other. Once everyone's had a couple of goes, they can help to clear it away, and see how much faster they travel from one side of the room to the other without all those obstacles in the way.

In the Bible we hear of how John the Baptist is telling people to get ready for the coming of Jesus. It's a bit like our race. Sometimes there are things in the way that we have to clamber over or climb through, that make it really difficult to get from one place to another. Sometimes we have invisible obstacles in our lives. Not tables and chairs, tunnels and beanbags, but selfishness and greed, hatred and laziness.

Provide each child with a clothes peg and attach a square of card to it with strong tape or a glue dot. Allow them to decorate the card with 'Prepare the way of the Lord!' on it. They can peg this to the side of their bin, so that every time they are tidying and clearing away their own physical clutter, they can remind themselves to clear away those things that are invisible obstacles in their own lives.

Prepare the way of the Lord

THE THIRD SUNDAY OF ADVENT

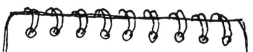

Readings

- Zephaniah 3:14-20
- Isaiah 12:2-6
- Philippians 4:4-7
- Luke 3:7-18

Thoughts on the Readings

John's message was challenging, but was not complicated. The things he told people must have been pretty obvious to them if they thought about it. The kingdom of God is not something mysterious which is hard to understand – all humans have somewhere inside them the ability to work out what is the right way to live. This is true for people inside and outside the church, of all religions and none. But what is not always so easy is to listen to these common-sense messages from the human conscience, and act on them. It is a case of valuing others as we value ourselves, and we also seem to have a very strong instinct that makes us want to value ourselves, and others who are similar to us more highly than people who are 'different'.

This is not God's way. In the first reading from Zephaniah, it talks about the lame and outcasts being praised instead of despised. This is certainly something we can think of as a church – how can we be welcoming to both adults and children with disabilities, to value them as God does and see them as an asset? And what about those groups who are excluded in our society – is there a way that we can let them know that they, too, are loved and valued?

A good start is to pray. We are told that 'this peace will control the way that you think and feel' (Philippians 4:7, CEV). As we rest in God's presence, as we know and accept his love for us, he will give us that peace which forms our attitudes to others. Our judgemental attitudes and prejudices will melt away, and we will naturally start to see the good in others. Perhaps we will also start to see what we have in common, and be able to work together for a better world.

Discussion Starters

- **What difference can thankfulness make to our attitudes?**

- **Can 'thankful' prayer make more of a difference than 'asking' prayer?**

Intercessions

Lord God,
bless us with your peace.

Thank you, Lord, that we do not have to worry about anything;
you have told us to bring it all to you when we pray.

Dear Lord,
thank you for the peace that no one can understand,
peace in the strangest of circumstances.
May your peace fill our churches
so that everyone who comes in over Christmas,
whether they're used to church or not,
has a surprising and pleasing encounter with you,
going home feeling filled with your special gift of peace.
Lord God,
bless us with your peace.

As we pray for our world
we think of areas of conflict
where people can't sleep
because of the sound of shells and gunfire.
We bring them to you now,
and ask for a peaceful resolution to the violence.
Lord God,
bless us with your peace.

We think of those who are debilitated
by anxiety or depression.
We remember those
waiting for medical test results
or for a procedure to take place.
We pray that your surprising and unexpected peace
may visit them today as we pray.
Lord God,
bless us with your peace.

And as we think of those who are near the end of their lives,
we ask that your peace would wash over them,
taking away any fear
and covering them with your love.
We remember those who have recently died,
and those whose anniversaries of death fall this week, especially . . .
Lord God,
bless us with your peace.

Thank you, dear Lord,
for the way you draw near to us,
the way you listen to us
and the peace you give us.
Amen.

Children's Prayer

For all you give us
we say 'thank you!'
For the world around us
we say 'thank you!'
For our friends and family
we say 'thank you!'
For your love that
surrounds us
we say 'thank you!'
Amen.

Other Ideas!

People can pass around some blank cards for members of the congregation to add their 'thank yous' to, either with words or pictures.

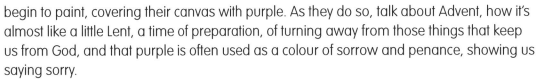

All-age Talk

Place an easel where everyone can see it, or string up a large piece of white paper, an opened-up cardboard box, or even a large white sheet.

Squirt some purple paint into a clear container. Invite some volunteers to come and begin to paint, covering their canvas with purple. As they do so, talk about Advent, how it's almost like a little Lent, a time of preparation, of turning away from those things that keep us from God, and that purple is often used as a colour of sorrow and penance, showing us saying sorry.

Our Gospel reading today has John the Baptist at his most caustic. 'You brood of vipers!' he calls his audience, who lap it up, and ask for more. His suggestions of how they can live better are hardly earth shattering – share what you have if you have more than you need, be content, don't take what's not yours – but he's pointing to the one who will come after him, who will come with a totally mind-blowing agenda.

The other readings contrast with this. 'Rejoice!' they say. They are readings full of joy. Begin to pour in some white paint into the pot of purple. Get a volunteer to mix it around and begin to paint with it. Today, with a little added expectation of the glory of Christmas, our purple of sorrow is tempered. It's changed. It's lightened to pink. To rose, if we're being liturgically correct!

We haven't cast off our purple of penance. We are still firmly in Advent, looking over our lives and changing them for the coming of Jesus. But as we rejoice, we are changed. We are lightened. God's saving power lives within us, totally changing us, so that even our darkness is made bright.

Children's Corner

Provide a basket of purple and pink objects to play with – baubles, tinsel, ribbons, feathers. Try to find a variety of textures and steer clear of plastic toys where possible. Parents and children can enjoy playing with these Advent colours, maybe making patterns with them on the floor.

The colouring sheet has baubles that can be stuck together back-to-back then hung on trees at home, with the words **'Rejoice!'** on each bauble in a variety of fonts.

Little Kids' Sunday School

Give one child a large box of bricks, sit down all the children, and ask them to each make you a brick tower. The child with the large box of bricks will have to share these out – see if they come to this conclusion themselves before you suggest it. As they're building, give one child loads of cosy scarves, and another a large bag full of some kind of edible snack (be careful with allergies). See if they notice that some children don't have these, and watch out for how they begin to share, and how they make sure they're sharing fairly.

In our Bible reading today, we hear John the Baptist telling people to share. If they have two coats, they are to give one to someone who needs it. If they have more than enough food, they are to share it. We know that sharing is caring.

Give each child a piece of card, with 'sharing is caring' written on it, and a hole punched in both ends. They can colour it in, then use scissors to cut it in half, thread each half on a length of wool or string, wear one as a necklace and give the other away. This looks a bit like a friendship necklace, reminding both parties to share.

Big Kids' Sunday School

Have a few different newspapers from this week, and lots of pairs of scissors. Get the children to scour the newspapers for good news stories, cut them out, and put them in a pile in the middle of you all.

I'm betting this pile won't be very large. Newspapers thrive on negativity, on the whole. Partly that's because, thankfully, bad things that happen are rare enough to become news. But it can skew our thinking. We can forget to see the positive things around us.

In today's New Testament reading we are told to rejoice. Sometimes that's easy and sometimes it's more difficult. But the fact that God loves us is enough for rejoicing.

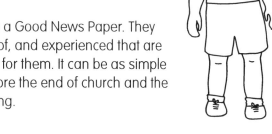

Get the children to work together to produce a Good News Paper. They can write articles of things they've seen, heard of, and experienced that are causing them to rejoice in what God's provided for them. It can be as simple as they like. If you're able, photocopy these before the end of church and the children can give them out to share their rejoicing.

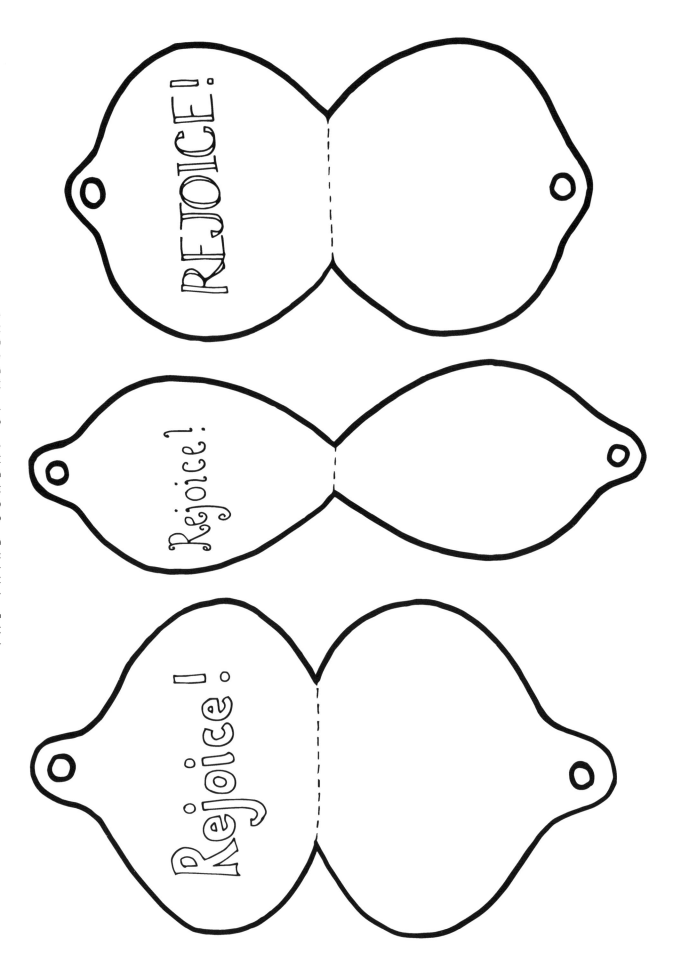

THE FOURTH SUNDAY OF ADVENT

Readings

- Micah 5:2-5a
- Psalm 80:1-7
- Hebrews 10:5-10
- Luke 1:39-45 (46-55)

Thoughts on the Readings

Today, the readings again show us about a different sort of king to what people usually expect. Micah tells us about a shepherd king, from a tiny town with humble origins – 'one of the smallest towns in the nation of Judah' (Micah 5:2, CEV). This king will care for and look after his people, and will bring peace – something that was desperately needed then, as it is now. And it is through that peace that the whole world will know his greatness – not through wealth, might, power, weapons or violence.

We, as Christians, see these passages as referring to Jesus – at the time, of course, no one knew exactly when or where this king would arrive on the scene. This picture of a caring shepherd, leading his sheep to safety, would have been a contrast to the way that many leaders held power at the time, just as it is now.

And in the passage from Hebrews, we are told how Jesus shows us a gentler way. We do not need to sacrifice animals to find freedom from our sins, but simply need to look to Jesus, who has already offered himself 'once and for all'.

As faithful, prayerful Elizabeth met with her young cousin Mary, she became full of the Holy Spirit and acknowledged Jesus as her Lord even before he was born. At this early stage in Mary's pregnancy, Jesus was very tiny indeed, a very small king with no earthly wealth or status at all. But this meeting was so significant that even Elizabeth's own unborn child, John the Baptist, knew something amazing was taking place! Elizabeth recognised God's blessing on everyone who was there – a remarkable encounter and certainly nothing she would have expected!

As we get near to Christmas, may we, too, be open to encounter Jesus in unexpected places.

Discussion Starters

- **What is the job of a shepherd?**
- **What would a 'Shepherd King' be like?**

Intercessions

Shepherd King,
thank you for your care.

Dear Lord, we come to you
knowing that you are always there
to lead us, guide us
and keep us safe in your love.

We pray for our Church,
for our leaders both locally and nationally,
that they would know you
as their loving Shepherd,
looking after them
and showing the way.
Shepherd King,
thank you for your care.

We pray for our world,
for the leaders of different countries,
for those trying to work for peace.
We pray for peace-building initiatives
bringing different groups together,
whether this is on a national scale
or in a local community.
Shepherd King,
thank you for your care.

We bring you our friends and families,
people we will see over Christmas
and people we will not.
May your peace and love
be in all our words and actions.
We pray for those who lose sleep
with discomfort, worry, sadness or pain.
Be with them, and bring your comfort, hope and love.
We name before you now those known to us, including . . .
Shepherd King,
thank you for your care.

We pray for the families of those who have recently died
and for those who are reaching the end of their life here on earth.
We particularly bring to you those for whom Christmas
brings bittersweet memories of loved ones they have lost.
May they be aware of your comforting presence
and feel at home with you.
We remember this week . . .
Shepherd King,
thank you for your care.

We know, dear Lord, that you love us
and that you want the best for us.
Lead us in your ways
so that we are nourished and strengthened
and stay close to you.
Amen.

Children's Prayer

A king is going to be born
but he won't have an army,
he won't have a palace,
he won't have a
    golden throne,
or even a crown.
This king is Jesus.
He will be a kind king.
He will look after us.
He will come and show us
how to live in peace.
Amen.

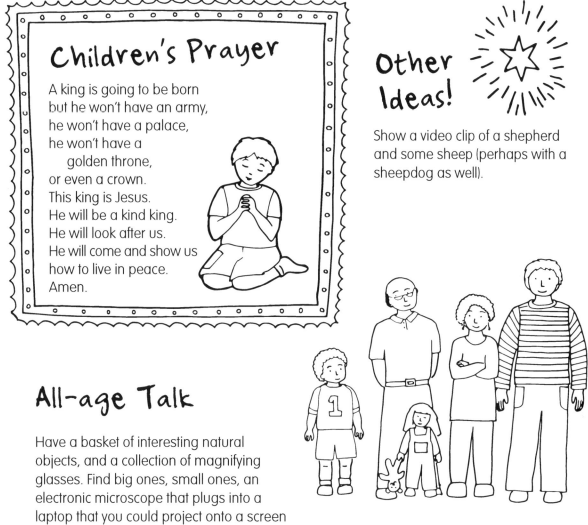

Other Ideas!

Show a video clip of a shepherd and some sheep (perhaps with a sheepdog as well).

All-age Talk

Have a basket of interesting natural objects, and a collection of magnifying glasses. Find big ones, small ones, an electronic microscope that plugs into a laptop that you could project onto a screen for everyone to see, or a microscope that you clip onto the camera of your phone.

Invite people up, or walk around offering them to people, to have a go looking closely at the different objects. What do they notice that they hadn't before?

Today we hear Mary's song, the Magnificat. She speaks of magnifying the Lord. Now, God is quite great enough already. He doesn't need us to make him any bigger! He doesn't have a fragile ego, that needs us to tell him how great he is, either. So what does she mean, 'My soul magnifies the Lord' (Luke 1:46, NRSV)?

As we look through the microscopes or magnifying glasses, we notice things we hadn't seen before. And so it is with God, as we focus on him, we become aware not only of his greatness and power, but of his compassion and mercy, of his strength and justice, as Mary sings.

In these last few days before Christmas, let us take a little time out from our frenetic last-minute preparations of presents, food, decorations, and social events, and magnify God, so that he comes better into focus for us, as we prepare to celebrate him being born among us.

Children's Corner

Provide magnifying glasses and a basket of objects for the children and parents to look at closely, and they can whisper together about how we focus on God at Christmas.

The colouring sheet has Mary and some of the words from the Magnificat to colour.

Little Kids' Sunday School

Get the children in a circle. They can take it in turns to walk round the circle, greeting each member of the group in turn. Each child can choose their own way of greeting – a little wave, a high five, a fist bump, a bow etc.

In the Bible today, we hear how Jesus' mum, Mary, went to visit her cousin, Elizabeth. When they greeted each other, the baby inside Elizabeth leapt about to greet the baby Jesus inside Mary. You might like to read them out the song Mary sang.

We can try to greet everyone with joy, knowing that we are all made in the image of God. Mary's song talks of this topsy-turvy kingdom that her son, Jesus, would bring about. An act of greeting other people, no matter who they are, as loved children of God, fits in well with this song.

The children can draw around their hand on card and attach it to a lolly stick – if their arm gets tired with all the waving they're going to do this week, they now have an extra arm to greet people with and share God's blessings!

Big Kids' Sunday School

Show the children some photos of ordinary objects taken under a microscope. Can they guess what the objects are? You could make this a quiz if your children like that kind of thing. Do they notice details they'd never seen before even though they're on objects they see every day?

As Mary sings about her soul magnifying the Lord, she reminds us to focus on God even amongst all our busy last-minute things before Christmas. The more we focus on God, the more we see – and we see his greatness and his power, his compassion and his mercy.

Give the children a small square of card. Make a hole in it, by resting it on some sticky tack and poking a pencil or pen through. Cover over this hole with sticky tape, and then carefully drop one drip of water over the hole. The bulge of the water will act as a magnifying glass, helping them focus on whatever is shown underneath the hole. As they practise using their magnifiers, this can remind them to focus on God this week.

MY SPIRIT REJOICES IN GOD MY SAVIOUR ... THE MIGHTY ONE HAS DONE GREAT THINGS FOR ME ... HE HAS BROUGHT DOWN THE POWERFUL AND LIFTED UP THE LOWLY ...

CHRISTMAS DAY

Readings
- Isaiah 9:2-7
- Psalm 96
- Titus 2:11-14
- Luke 2:1-14 (15-20)

Thoughts on the Readings

Well, here we are – on Christmas Day! We have been looking forward to this time and now it has arrived. We all have our favourite things about Christmas (and maybe a few things we don't like too!) but for now let's think about the amazing truth about God coming to earth.

A small baby, wrapped in strips of cloth, as babies were at the time, and laid in the hay (when he eventually fell asleep) as a makeshift cot. But such an amazing baby that God's glory lit up the whole sky when the angels told the shepherds the good news.

It is completely in keeping with what we have heard about God's kingdom over the past few weeks that the angel would first give this exciting news to the shepherds on the hillside. Surprising, breaking convention, putting the least important people in the world's eyes to the front of the queue to see the baby king – this event has God's fingerprints all over it. The birth of a member of royalty would usually be announced officially, through the 'proper' channels. There might be an authorised portrait issued to the public, while the great and good visited the new arrival in strict order of status. But Jesus' birth has none of this. It is the ordinary shepherds, out at work, who are visited by the angel. We have no idea how 'religious' these shepherds were in terms of how often they visited the Temple, whether they gave a proportion of their earnings, or whether they knew many prayers or passages of scripture by heart. But this was not a requirement for them to be a part of this momentous event. They just needed to be themselves, to listen to the angel, and to humbly come and visit Jesus. The rest is history.

As we come before God today, let's just come as we are – we have not done anything to earn the privilege of knowing Jesus. It is a gift. We can receive that today, just as the shepherds came before Jesus on that first Christmas night. God has come to earth, and he wants us to know him.

Intercessions

Glory to God in heaven!
Peace to us all here on earth.

As we think of Jesus, born as a human baby,
a humble start, small and helpless,
we give thanks that our God
has chosen to come close to us
so that we can know him.

We think of our brothers and sisters
celebrating Jesus' birth today around the world.
Different languages,
different customs,
different foods,
but the same joy in knowing
that God has come to earth.
We pray for them today,
as they remember us too.
Glory to God in heaven!
Peace to us all here on earth.

We pray for our world,
for a shifting of focus
to what is really important.
Behind the shiny wrapping paper of Christmas celebrations
we pray for your gifts of
peace, love, understanding and kindness.
Glory to God in heaven!
Peace to us all here on earth.

We bring before you now
anyone who is weighed down
by the expectations that this season can bring.
Expectations that they feel they cannot live up to
of personal appearance, gifts given, food prepared and guests entertained.
We also pray for those
who have painful or difficult memories
of Christmas in the past.
Be with them, dear Lord,
reassure them of your constant love,
your unconditional acceptance, and the true treasures that are found in you.
We also remember those who are sick or in need at this time, especially . . .
Glory to God in heaven!
Peace to us all here on earth.

As we remember those who have been welcomed into your heavenly kingdom
and are now at rest with you,
we thank you for your promise of eternal life
and your wonderful gifts that never fade or wear out.
We remember this week . . .
Glory to God in heaven!
Peace to us all here on earth.

Thank you for this day of celebration,
thank you for Jesus' birth,
thank you that you understand us as humans;
be with us in all we do today.
Amen.

Children's Prayer

Dear Lord,
Mary wrapped Jesus
in nice soft sheets.
She laid him in hay
to go to sleep.
A special King
so tiny and small,
bringing peace
and hope to us all.
Amen.

Other Ideas!

Give out chocolate coins as a sign of God's good gifts to us at Christmas.

All-age Talk

Dress up a volunteer as someone important, with maybe a smart jacket and cool sunglasses. Dress up another volunteer as someone 'religious' – use whatever cues this for your congregation (serving robes, vestments, guitar and mike for worship band leader).

Dress up yet another volunteer as a shepherd – you can bring out your tea towel to use as a headdress for this one!

We have all been waiting for God's promised Messiah to be born. Waiting for God to work in the world to bring about our salvation. And at the point where God is born into our world as a tiny human baby, as Jesus, who will God tell the news to first?

You might think that this important person deserves to know first. After all, if they hear, and tell others, everyone will listen and believe them. They are important and respected. But – and they can be sent off to 'sleep' on a chair – they were sleeping this night.

You might think God would choose to tell this religious person first. After all, they've spent hours in the temple praying and worshipping God. He must like them best. But no, they're sleeping this night, too.

What about this shepherd? They're not important. They're not religious. But they are awake, looking after their sheep. When God sends angels to tell them that Jesus is born, not only do they listen, but they hear and rush off to worship. The shepherd can rush off to your crib scene, if you have one in your church, and kneel in front of Jesus.

So also for us. What is important isn't how important we are, or how religious we are. What is important is that we are alert to listen to what God has to tell us, and that when we listen, it moves us to worship, and to kneel before that baby, God made man, lying in the manger.

Children's Corner

Provide a selection of Nativity sets for the children to enjoy playing with, and leave a children's Bible open on the story of the birth of Jesus.

The colouring page shows Jesus lying in the manger, watched over by Mary and Joseph, as the shepherds burst in, one kneeling in worship, one holding a lamb.

Little Kids' Sunday School

Have some time sharing news of what presents the children have been given. Get the children to remind each other of the rules of Good Listening – look at the person speaking, think about what they are saying, don't interrupt.

It's good to share good news. And even better to share good news with people who are ready and willing to listen to us. You can role play telling a child about one of your presents, while the child yawns, or looks out of the window, or tries to talk over you.

When Jesus was born, God was so excited to share this news with the people on earth that heaven broke open and the angels streamed out singing 'Glory to God in the highest!' Luckily, the shepherds who were watching were ready to listen, and caught the excitement, running straight away down to Bethlehem to worship the baby Jesus.

They can make a model shepherd out of a cardboard tube, with a face drawn on it, and a rectangle of fabric stuck over its head as a teatowel headdress, to remind them to listen to God's good news, just like the shepherds did.

Big Kids' Sunday School

Line the children up in pairs, one at each end of the room. Their task is to pass on their good news about their favourite Christmas present to their partner. However, they're only allowed to whisper! On the count of three, each child tries to tell their partner about their favourite Christmas present. After the whispering cacophony has died down, ask if anyone has succeeded.

Passing on good news can be difficult. No matter how amazing the news is, the person we are telling has to listen really well. Sometimes there are obstacles in the way to them hearing, sometimes there are other voices, sometimes it is very quiet compared to the noisy world outside.

When Jesus was born, the angels came to tell the shepherds. Luckily the shepherds were listening very carefully. They heard, and they acted on what they heard, rushing straight away to Bethlehem to worship the baby Jesus.

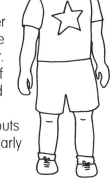

We need to copy the shepherds in our listening. Sometimes we hear other voices that tell us other things – things about how if we have more, we'll be happier. How if we look like this or dress like that, we'll be more popular. Sometimes the voice of God can sound very faint compared to the clamour of our world. But we need to listen, to hear God's voice, to hear that we are loved for who we are, not for what we have.

The children can make a sign that reads 'Remember to listen', using cut outs from Christmas wrapping paper, then hang it somewhere they'll see it regularly in their house.

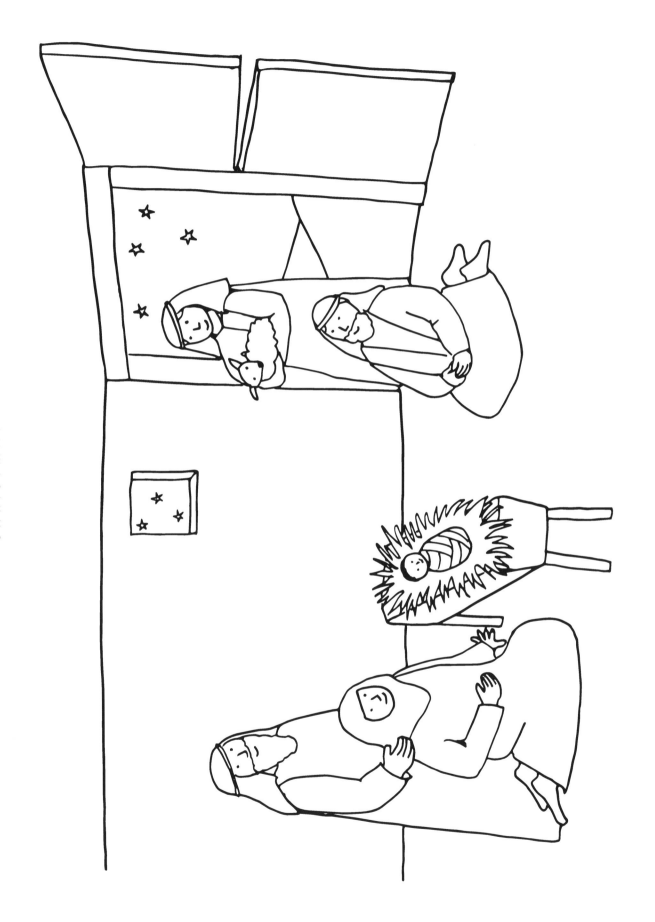

THE FIRST SUNDAY OF CHRISTMAS

Readings

- 1 Samuel 2:18-20, 26
- Psalm 148
- Colossians 3:12-17
- Luke 2:41-52

Thoughts on the Readings

We don't hear much about Jesus' childhood at all – so this story is particularly interesting. Jesus gets himself lost for four whole days, he doesn't seem to even have thought about how much this must have worried his mum and dad, and then gives a very strange answer when Mary asks him to account for what has happened.

If we think of Jesus as 'perfect', or 'sinless', how does this all add up? Poor Mary and Joseph – they must have been out of their minds with worry. Anything could have happened to their lovely boy. But perhaps God's idea of being perfect is bigger than the one we have of never making a mistake or unintentionally upsetting anyone through our actions.

It is comforting for us to see Jesus as a human – he had done what he thought was right, at 12 years old – he knew he was safe and he wanted to learn. Like many nearly-teenagers, he had completely forgotten to think about what effect this might have on his parents.

Maybe this shows us we can be a bit gentler on our teenagers, our children, ourselves and each other. Sometimes the things others do upset us, but this was not their intention. If we can find a way to sort this out together, with love, then we can all grow in understanding.

Being a teenager isn't wrong. Being a stressed parent isn't wrong. These things are part of our humanity. The end of our reading tells us that after this 'Jesus became wise, and he grew strong' (Luke 2:52, CEV). Let's keep looking to God, who loves us so much. He will surround us in his loving arms and will help us grow in wisdom every day as we go through our lives.

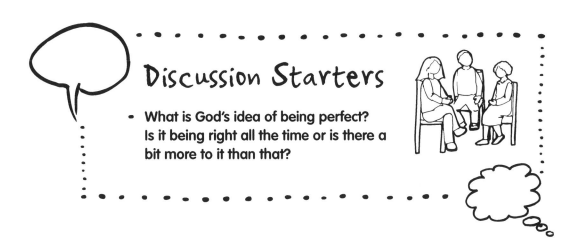

Discussion Starters

- **What is God's idea of being perfect? Is it being right all the time or is there a bit more to it than that?**

Intercessions

Loving God,
may we grow more like you.

Thank you that we can come to you
just as we are;
we may not get everything right all the time
but we know your wisdom is always available to us.

We pray for our church here,
for our relationship with other local churches
and places of worship.
We pray that you would help us all to understand each other,
speaking to each other with love and respect.
Loving God,
may we grow more like you.

We bring you those situations
which are hard to understand,
groups of people, nations or cultures
that are vilified and despised.
Help us to value and recognise
the humanity of all people
and help us work for the common good
in a loving and respectful way.
Loving God,
may we grow more like you.

We pray for those who are searching
for family members who are missing;
we pray for those who have decided
to make themselves 'invisible', for whatever reason.
We bring these people to your loving care
and pray that you would give them the strength they need.
We also name before you today those known to us who are sick or in need at the
moment, especially . . .
Loving God,
may we grow more like you.

We bring to you the families of those who have recently died
and those who are on the point of death.
May your peace and presence surround them
and may they know that heaven is nearby.
We remember before you today . . .
Loving God,
may we grow more like you.

Thank you, dear Lord,
that you love us and have chosen us.
May we become gentle, kind,
humble and patient
like you.
Amen.

Children's Prayer

Every day we grow,
we get taller,
we get stronger,
we get cleverer.
And every day we grow
with you, Lord,
we get wiser,
we get kinder,
we get gentler
and you fill us with your
peace.
Amen.

Other Ideas!

Have some 'Where's Wally?' books
for people to look at.

All-age Talk

Prepare a few labels that can be hung around people's necks – parcel labels on string are fine, or you might want to use A5 or A4 card so they can be readable from a distance.

Who is the wisest person in church today? I think that's probably me. After all, I have a degree or two, I've done lots of studying about the Bible and theology, I'm not daft. Write a list of your wise attributes on a label and hang it around your neck.

But what about Joyce? Or Beverley? They are wise, as they have so many years' experience of living. Maybe they've lived in different countries or different places. They've had different jobs, and brought up a family, and looked after grandchildren. They've got lots of wisdom. Write a label and put it round their neck.

Noah and Grace are pretty wise. They're studying hard for GCSEs or A levels. What they don't know about science or maths or history isn't worth knowing. They're wise too about how to deal with friendship issues, and they never need to ask for help to change the time on their phone and know instinctively how snapchat works. Write a label and put it round their neck.

Emmanuella and Ty are always wanting to find out new things. They're learning new things every single day, at school and at home. Their search for knowledge makes them wise. Hang a label around their neck.

And what about Cole and Elsie-May? They can't even talk properly yet. Are they wise, too? Well, yes. They're wise about knowing how to love and be loved. They're wise in that they trust the people who care for them with their whole lives. Hang a label around them (or their carers) too.

We hear today about a young Jesus, astounding those in the temple with his wisdom – and terrifying his parents with his disappearance in the process! We hear of a young Samuel, growing in stature and in favour with the Lord and with the people. Our idea of wisdom is sometimes pictured only in terms of adult academic achievement, but these Bible readings remind us that in God's economy, wisdom is never the preserve of only those that people would expect. Wisdom comes in many forms. Our Psalm today talks of old and young together praising God, and the reading from Colossians asks us to teach and admonish one another in all wisdom. That means that all of us have wisdom to share. We need to listen and learn from each other, the old from the young, and the young from the old. Nobody is too young or too old to be wise.

Children's Corner

Provide a model of a little boy, a mum, and a dad, and some other grown-ups. Lay these out on a tray or a table with a coloured sheet on. If you have a children's Bible with the story of the boy Jesus in the temple, open it up to that page and leave it next to the characters. Otherwise write a note, suggesting that parents listen carefully to the Gospel story and act it out with the characters provided.

The colouring sheet has Jesus in the temple, listening to and talking with the priests and teachers of the law, with Mary and Joseph just appearing at the edge of the scene looking relieved to have found their child. It has the Bible reference written at the bottom so parents can look this up again later if their child wants to talk about the picture more.

Little Kids' Sunday School

Share with the children a story of when you were lost as a child, or when one of your children got lost. Have they ever been lost? Let them talk about their experiences.

Today we hear one of the few stories we know of Jesus when he was a child. And it's a story of Jesus getting lost. Get up and walk the children through the journey of Jesus and his friends and family all around the space you meet in; walking to Jerusalem with all your bags, visiting the temple, eating together, celebrating together, heading home. Realising that Jesus is missing – you thought he was with them! They thought he was with you! Running back to Jerusalem to find him . . . where? Not where we slept. Not where we ate. Not in the market. In the temple, and there he is, listening to the teachers of the law. And they are listening to him! 'Didn't you know that I would be in my father's house?', Jesus asks (Luke 2:49, CEV).

The children can stick down flaps over a piece of card. Under one flap, they can draw the boy Jesus. They can give their lift-the-flap puzzles to each other – can they find Jesus? Jesus was like us; growing and exploring, searching and learning, wanting to read and to talk about the scriptures, and to be close to God.

Big Kids' Sunday School

Chalk or tape a line along the floor. Get the children to go and stand on it. Challenge them to re-order themselves in order of height/shoe size/age/alphabetical order without wobbling off the line. This may prove to be rather tricky and should result in some giggles.

What would have happened if you'd asked them to line up in order of cleverness? Of intelligence? Of wisdom? Sometimes we think that wisdom is something that we get more of as we get older, and of course growing older does bring with it the wisdom that comes with experience. Tell them the story of the boy Jesus in the temple, talking with the priests and teachers of the law on an equal footing. We all have wisdom to share, no matter how old or how young we are. That's why God has put us together in a community, so we can learn from each other.

Write a list of questions together about faith. What does your faith mean to you? Has God ever answered a prayer and how? Which Bible story do you love best and why? What's your biggest question you'd like to ask God? How has following Jesus changed you? You and your group can probably think of others. Make some kind of easy no-bake snack, maybe ice biscuits or make crispie cakes with melted chocolate. After church, the children can share their snacks, their questions, and their wisdom with the other members of their church community, on an equal footing.

LUKE 2:41-52

THE SECOND SUNDAY OF CHRISTMAS

Readings

- Jeremiah 31:7-14
- Psalm 147:12-20
- Ephesians 1:3-14
- John 1:(1-9), 10-18

Thoughts on the Readings

There is a message of hope this week – a message of God rescuing his people and bringing them back. Jeremiah the prophet tells us God's message about the great crowd of people, including pregnant women, the blind and the lame, who will celebrate as they are brought home. He talks of springs of water, dancing, and plenty of food for everyone.

We also hear in the Gospel reading those familiar and wonderful words about the 'Word', who had been there from the very beginning, becoming a human being and living among us. This is the means by which God will bless us. And in the reading from Ephesians, we hear that we are adopted as God's own children, and our sins are forgiven.

Sometimes we hear these words so often in church that they just wash over us, without the enormity of the truth of it all making an impact on us. But maybe today, as we think about the readings and the blessings that are promised to us, we can understand it in a fresh way.

We do not need to feel lost – we have a family in Christ. We do not need to worry about our status or whether others think we are 'good enough' – our identity is as one of God's children. And we can stop feeling trapped by our sin, resentment, and perceived inadequacies – because of Jesus, our sins really have been forgiven. Right from the start, Jesus was there. He came to earth to show us all the kindness of God, and we can know him and know that kindness now.

Discussion Starters

- **Have another look at the reading from John's Gospel. What verses stand out most for you today? Write them down and take them home with you.**

Intercessions

**Word of God,
live among us today.**

Thank you, dear Lord,
that you want to bless us,
that you love us
and that you accept us.
We are glad to be part of your family.

We pray for our church,
that you would dwell with us,
your presence would be in our buildings
and in the encounters we have with others.
Thank you for everyone
who helps lead our worship;
may they know your love
and refreshment.
**Word of God,
live among us today.**

In our world
we need your light in many ways.
We pray for those
without access to education
or electricity for radios and lightbulbs.
We also pray for those
who have shut their eyes
to the good things in the world around them
and live in their own sort of darkness.
**Word of God,
live among us today.**

We bring to you anyone
who is unwell at this time
and particularly think of those
whose sight is failing
or who have had to learn to live
with poor vision.
We also pray for anyone who is searching
for the way out of a difficult situation
and pray that you would bring your light to them.
We pray particularly for those known to us
who are in need at the moment, including . . .
**Word of God,
live among us today.**

We remember those who have recently died
and those who left their earthly life behind
many years ago, but are still in our thoughts.

40

We think of them
surrounded by your heavenly light.
We particularly remember today . . .
Word of God,
live among us today.

Thank you, Lord,
for your message of hope;
shine on us with your light
so that we may bring this with us
wherever we go.
Amen.

Children's Prayer

Lord, you were there
right from the very start
    of things
and you are with us now.
Thank you for the love
    you bring to us
and thank you that we
    are part of your family.
Amen.

Other Ideas!

Shine torches during the Gospel
reading for the verse, 'The true light
that shines on everyone is coming
into the world' (John 1:9, CEV).

All-age Talk

Set up two boxes and beanbags/rolled-up
socks. Ask for ten volunteers to come up to the
front. Choose two people to be team captains –
they take it in turns to pick four team members
each. Build up the 'who is getting chosen next'
thing. As you set them off doing a 'throw the beanbag in the box' relay challenge, talk about
our experiences of being chosen.

   Some of us may have bad memories of always being picked last for sports teams at school
– always being the reluctant choice of the team captain. Sometimes we are chosen to be part
of a prestigious new team at work, set apart from those we've worked with due to our talents
and experience.

What about that saying – 'Friends are family you've chosen'? Many of us, especially if we live away from our extended family, have special friends who share our lives and know us at our worst and at our best, and love us all the same. Friends who share our values, and who treat us with kindness.

Well, today our Bible readings show us that all of us here have been chosen. We have been chosen by God not as sports team members, not for a new team at work, not even as friends-that-become-family, but as his children. And God chooses us, not because of anything we have done, or anything we can do, not because we're the best of a bad bunch as in this unlikely beanbag crew, or because of how talented we are, but he chooses us because he loves us.

And he chooses us for that most messy, most intense relationship of all – he makes us his children. He doesn't choose us to slot us into only one part of his life. He doesn't choose us for only one particular role. But he chooses us as his children, to care for us, to worry about us, to love us even when we're at our most unloveable, and no matter how bad we are at throwing beanbags in a box!

Children's Corner

Provide some cuddly animals or other toys to play families with – these can be as varied as you like. One of my children loved to find a small, medium, and large fire engine to be a family!

The colouring sheet shows a wide variety of different happy people, from different cultures, different ages, differently abled. The writing to colour in says **'We are all children of God'**.

Little Kids' Sunday School

Give out cards with pictures of animals on them (maybe from a game of animal snap). You need several of each animal, so a few pigs, a few sheep, a few cats. The children don't show their card to anyone, but when you say 'go', they begin to make the noise of their animal. They walk around the space trying to find the rest of their family, and once they've found them, they hold hands. You may like to play this game several times.

Everyone is part of a family. A family is the group of people who love us, who care for us, and accept us for who we are. You could show some photos of different families – large ones, small ones, diverse ones – to help the children realise that family comes in many forms.

We are also part of God's family. He has chosen us to be his children. Make badges out of circles of card, with a safety pin taped to the back, and write on 'Child of God'. The children can make two – one to wear and one to give to someone else in church, to remind them that they too are chosen as God's children.

Big Kids' Sunday School

Have a number of different tasks – some physical (throwing a ball through a hoop/beanbags into a box), some more fiddly (making a house of cards/sewing a piece of fabric), and some more cerebral (times table questions/spellings/quiz questions). The children have to work together to choose a different child to put forward to have a go at each different task.

We all have different talents and skills, and that's just as well, as there's lots of things we need to get done, so it's good that there are lots of people to do them. Sometimes we get chosen because of our skills. We get chosen for the football team or the chess team. We get chosen as a class prefect. We get chosen to lead the line into the lunch hall.

God chooses us. He chooses us to be his children. But we're not chosen because of something great that we can do, we are chosen because he loves us. Does being chosen impact on how we behave? If we are chosen for the football team, sometimes that makes us show better sportsmanship. If we are chosen to lead the line into lunch, we walk tall and sensibly, showing a good example. If we are chosen as God's children, how does that make us want to live?

The children can make badges cut out of cardboard with a safety pin taped to the back to remind themselves that they are chosen. You could make them like a prefect's badge in shape, and write 'chosen' along the scroll.

THE EPIPHANY

Readings
- Isaiah 60:1-6
- Psalm 72:(1-9) 10-15
- Ephesians 3:1-12
- Matthew 2:1-12

Thoughts on the Readings

In the light of the story about the wise men who came to visit Jesus, that reading from Isaiah makes sense. It talks about people on camels coming and bringing gold and spices to the Lord, which certainly sounds very familiar when we are used to hearing the Christmas story. When we hear the readings in church, it is easy to forget that some of these familiar Old Testament prophecies were written a long time before Jesus was born. The Jewish people would have been very familiar with them, as would the Gospel writer Matthew have been. They would have naturally made the link and seen the visit of the wise men to Jesus as fulfilling this prophecy from long ago. But would the wise men themselves have known about these ancient Scriptures? We know they must have been wealthy and well-educated, but if they were from a completely different part of the world with a different culture and different religious practices, they may not have done. They just knew that a special baby was going to be born, a new king, and they wanted to bring gifts to honour and worship him.

The passage in Matthew talks about how excited and delighted the wise men were to see the star, and to find that it had stopped somewhere – their search was finally over. But they do not seem at all surprised (unless this part of the story has been lost in the mists of time) that this little king and his lovely family were living somewhere very simple. We do not know if Mary and Joseph were still in the stable at this time, or had found somewhere more appropriate to stay with their newborn, but as a carpenter Joseph may well have found a little place that was 'ideal for renovation'. The wisdom of those men who had travelled so far meant that they knew true kingship was a completely different thing from the power that comes through wealth.

And what did Mary and Joseph do with those gifts? We are not told what happened to them – perhaps they burned the incense on special occasions, and used the myrrh for Jesus when he was teething. The gold would have certainly been useful when the family had to flee to Egypt – both for their journey and to set up some sort of home when they got there. Those wise men had listened to God, and had played their part in keeping Jesus safe. They would have had no idea quite how far-reaching an effect their actions would have had. And if we listen to God, and take action for good where we can, what we do may have a positive effect far beyond what we could have imagined.

Discussion Starters

- In the wise men's tradition and culture, the stars would reveal significant events that were to happen. This led them to Jesus. How does this fit with our ideas about both astronomy and astrology?

- Could people be led to Jesus through ways which are not considered part of Christian culture and worship?

Intercessions

As we seek
may we find Jesus.

The wise men would not let anything
get in the way of their search for Jesus.
They carried their gifts over all different terrains
for many days
until they found him.
May we never give up in our search
to know Jesus better too.

We pray, Lord, for our Church,
for the wise women and wise men
who lead us in our prayer and worship
and the wise men and the wise women
who build our community
and help to make our churches
into welcoming places to be.
As we seek
may we find Jesus.

We pray for our world,
for wise leaders
and wise citizens
who will live your values
and make ethical choices.
We pray for the babies and toddlers
who will one day be in charge of things;
that you would equip, anoint and inspire them
to lead in a way that is in keeping with your kingdom.
As we seek
may we find Jesus.

We bring to you those who are in pain,
who would love someone to turn up on the doorstep
with myrrh for their sores
or incense to lift their spirits.
Make us aware of those around us
and show us the little ways where we can make a difference.
We particularly remember today those who have asked for our prayers . . .
**As we seek
may we find Jesus.**

We think of those who have come to live with you
in your heavenly kingdom
and those who are nearing the end
of their time here on earth.
We remember this week . . .
**As we seek
may we find Jesus.**

Lord, as the wise men listened to what God told them
and acted on it,
may we listen to you,
learn from you, and take action, wisely.
Amen.

Children's Prayer

Dear Lord,
we will follow you,
we will listen to you,
we will learn from you;
we want to get closer
    to Jesus.
Amen.

Other Ideas!

Hang up a string of stars across
the church, perhaps with some
sort of pulley system.

All-age Talk

Get four volunteers up to the front, and pass
them a sign to hold that says, 'We want to find
Jesus!' Talk about how the wise men were
searching for this baby king who had been born,

and the way that they found him was by following the star. Get someone to come up and carry a star over to a Nativity set, while one of the volunteers follows them. When they reach baby Jesus in the manger, they can kneel in worship.

We don't have a star here for people to follow to find Jesus, so how are they going to find him? Get someone to come over and put their arm around one of the volunteers, and lead them over to the manger where they kneel in worship. Sometimes we can be someone's friend, and our friendship, the way that we value them as beloved children of God, can lead them to Jesus.

Get someone to come over with an armful of greenery from the garden. Someone can follow them over to Jesus, and kneel in worship. Sometimes people can find a strong sense of spirituality through creation, and as they enjoy the world God has given them, maybe we can help them discover the creator who made it and gives it to them as a gift.

Get someone to come over with a large teapot and a cup for tea. Someone can follow them over to Jesus, and kneel in worship. Sometimes it's the things we do for others, rather than the things we say, that will lead them to Jesus. By showing God's love through what we do, our acts of love and service, people will be drawn to see God's love in the person of Jesus.

Just as the star led the wise men to Jesus, so we too can lead people to Jesus. There are lots of ways we can do this, and probably the best way for you, is the way that feels most comfortable, most authentically 'you'. That's the way God can use you to help all his people find their way home to him.

Children's Corner

Lay out a black or navy towel or sheet, and provide plenty of stars cut from shiny card for the children to make a night sky with. If you have a Nativity set that includes the wise men, you could also provide this for them to play with, alongside a children's Bible showing the visit of the wise men.

The colouring sheet shows the wise men pointing towards the star, with Bethlehem lying below them in the distance.

Little Kids' Sunday School

Hide some stars around the room, and send the children to search for them. When they have found them, they can bring them back into the centre of the group, and lay them out on a black or navy sheet or towel to be the night sky.

Talk about how when it's dark at night time they can look up and see the stars. The light from each star has travelled a long, long way to reach us. The wise men travelled a long, long way following a star to reach baby Jesus. We travel to Jesus too, not by camel or by walking, but by loving. Other people throughout our life will see our loving, and this will lead them to Jesus, too.

The children can make stars and stick them on the front of a strip of card to wear around their heads, to remind themselves and everyone in church that we are like the star that led the wise men to Jesus, and we can lead others to Jesus by the way that we show love.

Big Kids' Sunday School

Make the room as dark as possible, and use a really powerful torch to shine on the floor. You may need to stand on a step stool so you can point the torch beam down onto the floor. The children can take it in turns to follow the 'star' – the torch light – as you wave it around the floor, sometimes slowly, sometimes fast.

Get the children to pair up, to come up with some questions they'd like to ask the wise men about their journey following the star to baby Jesus. If they're confident at writing, you can give them pens and paper to write these down. Share all the questions, and see what answers you might come up with together. Some things we know, and some things we can only guess at, but that's fine.

What things in our lives lead us to Jesus? How can we help to lead others to Jesus?

Using an empty tin can, open end on the floor, the children can hammer holes in with a nail, then shine the torch through to show constellations. They can shine these in their homes at night, and think about how they are being led to Jesus, and how they have led others to Jesus today.

MOTHERING SUNDAY

Readings

- Exodus 2:1-10
- Psalm 34:11-20
- 2 Corinthians 1:3-7
- Luke 2:33-35
- John 19:25-27

Thoughts on the Readings

Each of the different readings today looks at either different mothers in the Bible, or at the motherly qualities that God shows us, and that he wants to show to others.

First of all, we see Moses' brave and inventive mother hiding her beautiful baby boy in her house as long as she could, and then making him a strong, watertight basket which would float in the water so that he would be hidden among the reeds. We have no idea whether any other Israelite mothers had done the same, or whether it was common to make floating cradles to lull babies to sleep in the Nile. This sort of thing, made out of natural materials, would not have survived long enough for archaeologists to find. But the story that has come down to us through all these years records this particular event, which has captured our imagination.

The next mother we see is the kind-hearted Egyptian princess. She finds the baby floating in the water and chooses to adopt him, meaning an instant ticket to a palace childhood. She then asks around for someone to care for and breastfeed the baby, and quick-thinking Miriam runs off to find her own mum.

Then we hear about Hannah, who had prayed and longed for a child for years. When her little boy Samuel is born, she dedicates him to God, keeping him at home with her until he had stopped breastfeeding. After this, she takes him to the temple to be an assistant to the wise Eli, and carefully makes clothes for him every year. She has no doubt at all that Samuel will grow up to be someone holy, with a close relationship with God. We can imagine that she continued to pray for him every day as he grew up.

The reading from Corinthians talks about God's nature, the way that he comforts us and cares for us, so that we can also comfort and care for others who are in need, while the reading from Colossians tells us how God has chosen us as his special people, as his family, and the qualities of kindness and compassion that he wants us to develop.

Then, as we move to the Gospel readings, we hear two stories about Mary. First, in Luke's Gospel, Simeon blesses Mary but also tells her that she will feel as if she has been stabbed by a dagger – not an easy thing to hear!

And the reading from John's Gospel tells us about when Jesus, on the cross, cares for Mary, putting her in the position of being a mother to his disciple, John. John then took her into his own home, providing for her, and no doubt she looked after him too. This shows how in the family of God we do not have to be blood relations. We can care for each other and look out for each other, especially for those who do not have family around them.

So although we celebrate mothers today, and all the things they do, we also celebrate the mothering qualities of God, and the kind and caring qualities that the Holy Spirit develops in us. We also thank God for adoptive mothers and adopted children, and those who do not have paperwork to say they are family, but the way they care about each other is a stronger tie than genetics. We know that God wants to help us in all our relationships, helping us to forgive each other, support each other, put up with each other and love each other. And we thank God for all of this today.

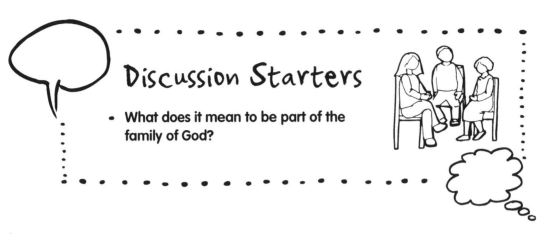

Discussion Starters

- **What does it mean to be part of the family of God?**

Intercessions

Caring God,
help us to show your kindness.

Thank you, Lord,
that we are part of your family,
that you care for us
and we will never be alone.

We pray for our church,
that it would be a place of welcome
where people feel they can belong
and be themselves,
accepted, and accepting others.
We pray that it would be a place
where those whose families are far away
or are not in contact
would find a community
where they can feel at home.
Caring God,
help us to show your kindness.

We pray for our world,
for families who become separated
when fleeing conflict.
We also pray for children
without parents to look after them
and those who have to take on
caring roles themselves.
Caring God,
help us to show your kindness.

We bring to you all women
who are pregnant at this time,
especially those who have additional health issues
or who have extra caring or work responsibilities to juggle.
We also think of those
who are in labour, or who have recently given birth
and pray that you would be with them, and their little ones.
We pray that you would bless newly adoptive parents
and we particularly remember those
who are unable to have children for any reason.
We also bring to you anyone who is unwell or in need, and name before you now . . .
Caring God,
help us to show your kindness.

We thank you for our own mothers
who brought us into this world.
We particularly think of those who have now gone
to live with you in heaven.
We also remember the women in our
unbroken line of female ancestors
and thank you for all the caring that went on
over thousands of years.
We remember today . . .
Caring God,
help us to show your kindness.

Lord, we thank you
for those mothers
and adoptive mothers
in the Bible
who were so faithful to you.
May we be faithful to you
as we seek to care for others.
Amen.

Children's Prayer

Dear God,
you are like a mummy kangaroo
with a Joey safely in its pocket.
You are like a daddy penguin
with the egg snuggled on
    its feathery feet.
You love us,
you look after us
and you will keep us safe.
Thank you, dear God.
Amen.

Other Ideas!

Often churches give out daffodils
or something similar on Mothering
Sunday. People can be involved
in preparing these, and can give
them out to everyone in church.

All-age Talk

You've brought along some mothers to introduce to the church today. First of all, meet this Hebrew woman. Invite up a volunteer, and throw a shawl over her head. When her baby was born, he was already in great danger. She bravely hid him in her home, and then when he became too big to hide, she hid him in a basket in the reeds of the river. Give her a clap.

Next meet this Egyptian woman. Invite up a volunteer, give them a white sheet, and black eye liner if they're up for it. She was going for a wash in the river, when she found a baby in a basket. Rather than ignore it and pretend she hadn't seen what was going on, she rescued the baby and brought him up in safety. Give her a clap.

Next I'd like to introduce Hannah. Invite up a volunteer, and give her a scarf to wear over her head. Hannah had longed for a baby for years, and when she is finally blessed with a child, she dedicates him to God, brings him to old and holy Eli in the temple to be his assistant, and carefully sews him new clothes every year. Give her a clap.

Finally, here's Mary. Invite up a volunteer, and give her the blue Nativity set Mary headdress. After all the joy and pain of being mother to Jesus, as she stood at the foot of the cross, Jesus gave her a new son to look after, his friend John. Give her a clap.

And, what's this? Pull out a tea-towel type headdress. Invite up a man or boy to wear it. Here's John. At the foot of the cross, as he watched his friend Jesus die, he was given a new mother to mother. He took her into his home, loved her, and cared for her. Give him a clap too.

Mothering takes many different forms. Sometimes this holy work of caring is done by people we are genetically related to, and sometimes it isn't. Looking at all these caring people up here, I'm sure we can all find more than one who reminds us of someone who has mothered us, in one way or another. We give thanks for them and their mothering care today, and remember that, as the church, we are all called to care for each other.

Children's Corner

Dig out your baby Jesus and his Moses basket from your Nativity play cupboard. Place him inside the basket, and lie it on a blue towel or blue sheet. Leave a children's picture Bible open on this story, so the children can play the story out with their parents or carers.

The colouring sheet shows baby Moses in his basket, with the princess holding out her arms to pick him up, and Miriam hiding, peering out from between the reeds.

Little Kids' Sunday School

Bring along a big blue sheet and a baby doll. The children can hold the edges of the blue sheet and bounce the baby about. If the baby falls off, they can pick it up and put it back on again.

Bouncing around on the water doesn't seem a very safe place for a baby, does it? But when baby Moses was born, there wasn't anywhere that was a safe place for a Hebrew baby boy. The Egyptians were scared of these foreigners living in their land, and wanted to get rid of them. Moses' mummy hid him in her house as long as she could (hide the baby under a table/in the cupboard/behind the cushions), and then when she couldn't keep him hidden any more she put him in a basket and floated it on the river (put the baby down on the still blue sheet). Moses' big sister Miriam hid, to see what would happen. And what did happen was this: a princess came down to the river to bathe, and she found the baby. She picked him up and decided to bring him home to the palace, and to bring him up as her own little son. But first she needed someone who could give him his milk as he was only a tiny baby. She looked all around, and Miriam stepped out. 'Would you like me to find a woman who can give the baby his milk?' she asked. The princess was happy that this little girl would help her. Miriam ran off and came back with baby Moses' very own mummy, who looked after him and fed him his milk until he was old enough to go and live in the palace with the princess, safe from the Egyptians even though he was a Hebrew.

The children can make a model of baby Moses in his basket, using a rolled-out blob of modelling clay wrapped up in white tissue, and placed inside a cake case that's been coloured in with brown and yellow to make it look like it's been woven from reeds. They can talk as they make it about the ways that the people who care for them look after them.

Big Kids' Sunday School

Play Hunt the Baby – someone hides a small baby doll somewhere in the room while the rest of you close your eyes. Once the baby has been found, the finder gets to do the hiding.

Sadly, there have been times in history when hiding a baby hasn't been a game. Sometimes there have been people who have had to hide their babies to keep them safe. When Moses was a baby, his people, the Hebrews, lived in Egypt. But the Egyptians were a bit scared of the foreigners, they didn't want to share their country with them. They made a law that all the Hebrew baby boys had to be killed! When Moses was born, his mum was determined to keep him safe. She kept him hidden in her house when he was tiny, until she wasn't able to hide him any longer. Then she wove a basket from reeds, put the baby inside, and floated it on the river. She sent the baby's big sister, Miriam, to go and keep hidden, watching to see what would happen. Along came the Egyptian princess, down to the river to bathe. She found the baby, and decided to bring him up as her son, in the palace. Miriam offered to go and find a woman to nurse the baby until he was old enough, and ran off to bring back Moses' own mum! So, that was how Moses was able to grow up, a Hebrew in the middle of Egypt, in safety.

Caring for others is a holy thing to do. It's not limited by who we are related to, or whether the people we need to care for or be cared by look like us, talk like us, or dress like us. Provide some card-making materials for the children – cards, pens, stickers, stampers etc. – so they can make a card for people who care for them, to say thank you. As they do so, they can think of the times that they have shown this holy caring to others, and see what opportunities they can find to do more of this in the next week.

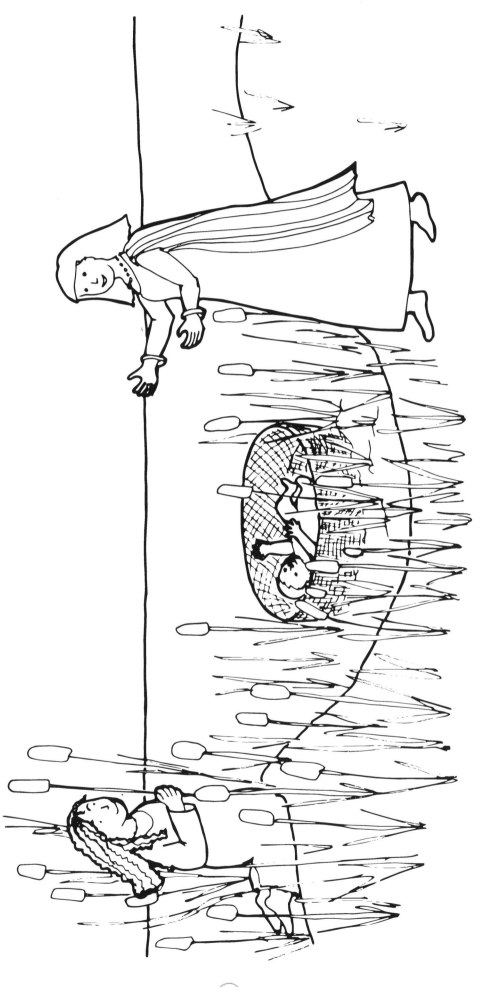

PALM SUNDAY

Thoughts on the Readings

Readings

Liturgy of the Palms
- Luke 19:28-40
- Psalm 118:1-2, 19-29

Liturgy of the Passion
- Isaiah 50:4-9a
- Psalm 31:9-16
- Philippians 2:5-11
- Luke 22:14–23:56 or Luke 23:1-49

Even though these stories are so familiar, when we listen to them on Palm Sunday we can often hear something new.

First, we hear the story of Jesus' entry into Jerusalem. He sends his disciples to borrow a young donkey – we presume its owner had heard of Jesus and recognised the disciples, as he did not hesitate to agree for them to lead the donkey away. As we know, there were already people who were plotting to get rid of Jesus and all that he stood for, but Jesus must have known that this ordinary donkey-owning village dweller was not one of these people. Jesus honours this loyalty by choosing the donkey to ride into Jerusalem – now one of the most well-known events of Jesus' life.

Jesus made a point by choosing a donkey to ride on – just in case anyone was still hoping or expecting him to be a military leader, this made Jesus' position absolutely clear. No expensive horse or chariot, no gilded saddle, shining sword or glamorous entourage travelling with him. Just an ordinary donkey, with clothes on its back to make the ride more comfortable. Jesus was a different sort of leader – one of us, who understands us, and had no interest in wealth, status or fortune.

Then today's Psalm echoes the crowd of disciples' words of praise – 'Blessed is the one who comes in the name of the Lord!' (Psalm 118:26, NRSV).

As we move on to the readings for the Liturgy of the Passion, the reading from Isaiah sets the scene for the suffering servant – the one who was insulted, beaten and spat upon, although he had done no wrong. The Psalm, too, tells the story of someone whose whole body aches, and who has been rejected by others who are planning to kill him, but turns to God in his distress, placing his trust in God to rescue him.

The reading from Philippians talks about the way that Jesus gave up everything, suffering terribly, and that he did not seek status. But because of this God honoured him and we now worship him.

Last of all, we hear the long Gospel reading, telling that well-known story of Jesus' passion. One thing after another culminates in Jesus being put to death on the cross. We feel sad as we think about the people who could have spoken out and put a stop to this senseless killing of a man who did no wrong, and the terrible habit of human beings to follow the crowd to fit in, even if this means causing suffering to others. We know, too, that we sometimes do these things. We do not always speak out and take action when there is an injustice, leaving it to others or hoping that things will resolve themselves without our intervention. We also see the temptation to want to please the group we are part of, even if that means excluding or judging others.

However, we also hear the voices of some people who understood something of who Jesus was, and the good that he can bring. Although one thief crucified next to Jesus made fun of him, the other recognised him as Lord, and Jesus honoured this by assuring him that today he would be with him in paradise. The Roman officer overseeing the crucifixion was also amazed by the events that happened at the time of Jesus' death, praising God and acknowledging that Jesus really was a good man.

So, as we hear these sad but wonderful stories again, we think about human nature – both Jesus' humanity as he suffered and was insulted, but also the humanity of those who were involved in any way. Jesus shows his godly nature as he speaks with compassion towards even those who crucify him 'Father, Forgive these people! They don't know what they're doing' (Luke 23:34, CEV).

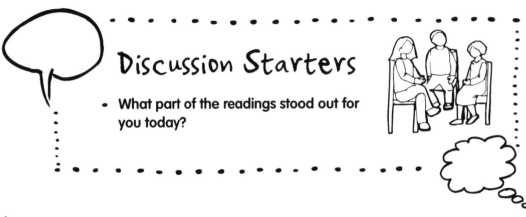

Discussion Starters

- **What part of the readings stood out for you today?**

Intercessions

**Peace in heaven
and glory to God.**

Lord, as you made the choice
of a donkey for your transport,
may we make choices
that reflect your humility,
simplicity and love of peace.

We pray for our church,
especially this Holy Week,
that you would help us to
draw closer to you,
to look at our lives
and become more like Jesus.
**Peace in heaven
and glory to God.**

We bring you our world
and pray for its leaders,
that they would know your true values
and work together for peace.
We also pray
for the leaders of large companies
who also hold power in our world,
that you would help them

to make good choices
in humility and wisdom.
**Peace in heaven
and glory to God.**

We bring to you anyone who is suffering,
whose bodies ache
and who feel they have no one to turn to.
Be with them, dear Lord,
may they know your comfort
and realise that you have been there too.
We especially pray for those known to us who are ill or in need at the moment, including . . .
**Peace in heaven
and glory to God.**

We bring before you
those who are near the end of their life.
Be with them, and assure them of your love
and your promise of an eternal home.
We also remember those who have died,
and name before you today . . .
**Peace in heaven
and glory to God.**

We thank you that
you value whatever we offer.
You are not looking for things
which are of high monetary value or status
but you will accept, treasure and use us
just as we are.
Amen.

Children's Prayer

Clip, clop, clip, clop,
I can hear a donkey coming,
clip, clop, clip, clop,
with long and furry ears.
Clip, clop, clip, clop,
I can see it's Jesus riding!
Clip, clop, clip, clop,
everybody cheers!
Amen.

Other Ideas!

Collect some donkey pictures,
toys or models to look at.

All-age Talk

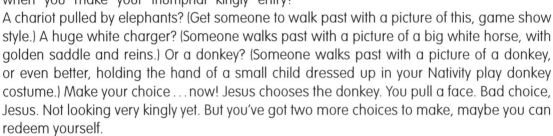

Welcome to today's episode of 'So You Want to be a King'. Our contestant today is an ex-carpenter from Galilee, please welcome Jesus! (Invite a volunteer up to the front, and maybe pay lip service towards dressing them up a bit.)

So, you're about to enter Jerusalem, the city of kings. You're going to have three choices, and we'll see whether you're king material.

Number One: What are you going to ride on when you make your triumphal kingly entry? A chariot pulled by elephants? (Get someone to walk past with a picture of this, game show style.) A huge white charger? (Someone walks past with a picture of a big white horse, with golden saddle and reins.) Or a donkey? (Someone walks past with a picture of a donkey, or even better, holding the hand of a small child dressed up in your Nativity play donkey costume.) Make your choice . . . now! Jesus chooses the donkey. You pull a face. Bad choice, Jesus. Not looking very kingly yet. But you've got two more choices to make, maybe you can redeem yourself.

Here's Number Two: What are you going to ride over when you make your triumphal kingly entry? A red carpet? (Someone flaps a red cloth.) A pavement made of gold, encrusted with jewels? (Someone walks past with a sign that reads, 'Sorry, no prop, budget doesn't stretch this far.') Or palm leaves ripped off the trees, and old cloaks. (Someone walks past with a palm branch.) Make your choice . . . now! Jesus chooses the palm leaves and cloaks. You pull a face again. Not doing too well at this, Jesus, are you? One more choice to make – let's see if you can do better this time.

So, finally here's Number Three: Who is going to welcome you when you make your triumphal kingly entry? A group of royal trumpeters? (Someone walks past blowing a trumpet fanfare.) A troop of cheerleaders? (Someone walks past waving pom poms.) Or all the ordinary people who live in the ordinary little houses near Jerusalem? (Someone walks past, looking as ordinary as possible.) Make your choice . . . now! Jesus chooses the ordinary people.

Oh, what a shame. Looks like you're not cut out to be a king after all, Jesus. You'd better go back into your dad's carpentry business.

But Jesus isn't like an ordinary king, is he? Everything about his life shows us that. His priorities are so wildly different from the priorities of our world that we can sometimes find them quite shocking. Jesus has come to be a king, he has come to be our king, but a king who rides a donkey, a king who is humble, a king who comes alongside the ordinary people and is not interested in wealth or status. This is what a real king looks like. This is the king we follow, and following him means that we become more like him, seeing the priorities of the world for the nonsense that they are, seeing the worth and value in ordinary people and loving them.

Children's Corner

Cut out tiny tunics and cloaks from scraps of fabric, and snip green and yellow paper into tiny palm branches. Lay these out at the edge of a tray, and provide a figure on a 'donkey' (small world figure on a horse), so the children can play at laying out clothing and palm branches to provide a path for Jesus to ride over on his donkey. Leave an illustrated children's Bible open on this story.

The colouring page shows Jesus riding on a donkey into Jerusalem as the crowds wave palm branches and throw their cloaks on the ground in front of him.

Little Kids' Sunday School

Split the children into two teams. They have to dress up in a donkey costume, run to the end of the room, then come back, take off the donkey costume, and pass it on.

When the children were wearing the donkey costume, could they go fast? Donkeys aren't the speediest of animals. They're not large, and people wouldn't ever use a donkey to show off how important they are. Donkeys are good at working hard, and are strong and tough, good at clambering over rocky places, and working well with people.

When Jesus was about to enter Jerusalem, the city of kings, he didn't choose a big king's horse to ride on. He chose a donkey. (Stand a child up, and dress them as a donkey. 'Jesus' can walk with her/his hand on the donkey's shoulder rather than riding them.) Everyone came out to cheer when Jesus went past – not an organised group of people wearing smart costumes and playing instruments, but the ordinary people, who came out of their homes and their places of work, because they were happy to see Jesus. (The other children can stand up and create two lines at the sides of the 'road' Jesus will come down.) They didn't have flags to wave, but made do with waving branches they tore off the trees, and although Jesus didn't have a posh red carpet to walk down, the people took off their coats and put them on the ground for his donkey to walk over. (The children can be passed a couple of palm branches to wave if you have them, and can take off their coats and jumpers and put them on the floor.) The people all cheered and shouted, 'Hosanna! Save us now!' (You all cheer and shout.)

Jesus isn't an ordinary king. He isn't interested in being important or having lots of money and rich things. But he's interested in loving people, ordinary people, just as they are. The children can make a palm branch to remember this story. Give them an A3 piece of green paper, and get them to roll it round and round into a thin tube. Tape all the way down the edge. Use scissors to make lots of cuts from the top to about halfway down. Hold the cut end in the middle, and gently tug. You'll find it telescopes out, and becomes like a palm branch.

Big Kids' Sunday School

Sit the children in a circle, and place a crown in the middle. When you call out two names, those children have to run around the circle, back in through their space, and try to get the crown on their head first.

Becoming a king has sometimes been a bit of a race, a bit of a competition, a bit of a scramble. Wannabe kings would fight each other, to try to become the most important, to be the one to wear the crown. But when we hear about our King Jesus in the Gospel reading today, he isn't fighting to wear a crown, to look important, to show off his status. Jesus doesn't ride in on a showy, expensive horse fit for a king. He rides to Jerusalem on a humble donkey, a working animal. He doesn't get the red carpet treatment, but the people who are coming to cheer him throw down branches they pull off the trees, and the cloaks off their backs, onto the ground to make a path. He doesn't have a trumpet fanfare, or outriders wearing luxurious costumes, but simply the crowds of ordinary people, who have come from their homes and their places of work, just as they are. Jesus is a different sort of king. He is a king who is humble, who values every ordinary person, who isn't interested in showing off wealth or status.

The children can make a simple biscuit dough by mixing 250 grams of butter with 140 grams of caster sugar in a bowl. Add one egg yolk and two teaspoons of vanilla essence. Mix in 300 grams of plain flour and use their hands to squash it into a ball. Roll out and use a cutter shaped like a donkey to make donkey biscuits. Bake at 160°C for about 15 minutes, and share with everyone after church, to remind them of the kind of king we follow.

EASTER DAY

Thoughts on the Readings

Readings

- Acts 10:34-43
- Isaiah 65:17-25
- Psalm 118:1-12, 14-24
- 1 Corinthians 15:19-26 or Acts 10:34-43
- John 20:1-18 or Luke 24:1-12

On this wonderful day of celebration, we hear the story of Jesus' resurrection and the empty tomb. If we are using the reading from Isaiah, we also think about the amazing kingdom of God, where there will be peace and happiness beyond belief. We could say that in recent history a lot has been done to bring about that kingdom of God, both here and around the world – reducing infant mortality, increasing life expectancy, improving health, and eliminating infectious childhood diseases. This is certainly something to celebrate, and is a great example of people working together from all backgrounds and religions to achieve a shared goal of making the world a better place. Of course, there is still a long way to go, and that image of peace where people are growing their own crops and living in their own houses, while the wolves and lambs graze quietly together, is not with us yet.

The reading from 1 Corinthians talks about Jesus' victory over death, so that we can live with him forever. Death is no longer to be feared, so it has lost its power over us.

As we listen to the Gospel reading, we imagine the shock and surprise of those first visitors to Jesus' tomb, who found that the stone was rolled away, with just the burial clothes inside. No one had expected this – although Jesus had given hints at what was going to happen to him, it did not fall into place in people's minds until they realised that he had actually come back to life.

It is interesting that in the account from John's Gospel, both Peter and 'the disciple whom Jesus loved' run to the tomb. This person is generally considered to be John, the writer of the Gospel. But perhaps John left the description ambiguous on purpose, in order that we could imagine ourselves living through the story of Jesus' life – as if we were there, experiencing it. After all, we are followers of Jesus and we know we are loved by him too.

So maybe, this Easter, we can imagine ourselves on that wonderful, strange, emotional, joyful and confusing morning, coming to the tomb and realising that our friend Jesus really had risen from the dead.

Discussion Starters

- **How does our knowledge of eternal life with Christ inform and affect our relationship with others, our use of our possessions and our time?**

Intercessions

**Risen Christ,
live in us today.**

As we hear the Easter story
and celebrate together,
we give thanks
that you have conquered death
and that we can live with you
forever.

Dear Lord,
we thank you for our Church
and for the Gospel stories
that have been carefully passed down to us,
so that we can know
about the life of Jesus.
We also thank you
for our brothers and sisters in Christ
around the world
and pray that you would bless them
as we celebrate your resurrection together.
**Risen Christ,
live in us today.**

We pray for our world,
anywhere that needs your light,
your hope, and your life.
We thank you for the new life you bring
as new plants sprout up from the earth.
We pray for reforestation projects
and where neglected areas of land
are being restored
so that nature can thrive.
**Risen Christ,
live in us today.**

We bring to you anyone who is suffering
with a condition that is difficult to treat
and those who may have reached a good age
but are struggling with dementia or chronic pain.
We pray that you would help us all
to work together for your kingdom,
to bring relief and comfort to those who need it.
We bring into your presence . . .
**Risen Christ,
live in us today.**

We bring to you anyone
who is close to the end of their life's journey
and ask that you would fill them with
the peace and hope of your resurrection.
We remember those who have recently died
and those who are missed at this time of year.
We name before you today . . .
Risen Christ,
live in us today.

May your presence be with us,
may we be filled with your joy
and may we know more of your new life in us
as we go through our lives.
Amen.

Children's Prayer

As we think of the tomb
with the stone rolled away,
we know our friend Jesus
is here to stay.
He went up to heaven
so we all could see
his love and his kindness
for you and for me.
Amen.

Other Ideas!

Involve others in preparing and
setting up an Easter garden.

All-age Talk

Ask for some help to look for things you've lost.
Send someone off to find your special Star Wars
mug (pick your own special mug!) – where
are they going to look? Probably at the back of
church, where you have coffee after the service.
That's where you'd expect it to be, and look! Here
it is. Brilliant. Send someone else off to find a spare hymn book – where are they going to
look? Over in the cupboard where all the church books are kept. That's where you'd expect to
find it, and look! Here is is. Thank you. Now send someone off to find your pink teddy – where

are they going to look? Over in the children's corner, where the church teddies live, and look! Here it is. That's great.

We know where we expect things to be. Normally when I lose things, the place I find them is the place I knew they would be all along, even if I've missed it the first time I check. The women in our Gospel story today knew where they expected to find Jesus' body. His body had been taken off the cross on that sad Friday, and laid in a tomb, too rushed for them to prepare his body for burial in the way that they needed to do. So today, they were heading back, to the last place they'd seen it, the place they knew it would be.

But to their shock and surprise, his body wasn't there! Because it is only dead bodies that belong in a tomb. That's where you'd expect to find them, and where they stay. But an alive Jesus, that's a different matter. Why would they be looking for the living among the dead, these dazzlingly clothed men ask them. And the women remember this impossible promise, they believe this impossible story, and rush back to tell the others.

And here we find something else that we've lost. So often we have lost the voice of women in the Bible. Half of the population, yet we seldom hear their story and seldom hear them speak. And here, as when the birth of Jesus was told not to those of power, but to the shepherds, his resurrection is proclaimed to these women. The first glad tidings of the resurrection of Jesus are proclaimed to us by these women, and no matter how much the disciples disregard what they have to say, 'these words seemed to them an idle tale', the good news comes down to us through the ages from the mouths of these women. Jesus always surprises us. We need to learn to look for him everywhere, including the places we least expect.

Children's Corner

Create an Easter garden for the children to explore, with a path, and an empty tomb, with a stone in front that they can roll away. Leave a children's Bible open on the story of the resurrection.

The colouring page shows the empty tomb, with spring flowers, and the three crosses empty in the background.

Little Kids' Sunday School

Collect enough pebbles so that there will be enough for one for each child, with a few left over so they can all get a choice. You're looking for pebbles of about fist size if possible, nothing too tiny. Find a slope outdoors or make one inside using a propped-up board or furniture. The children can take it in turns to roll their pebbles down the slope. See whose pebble travels furthest.

These pebbles look a bit like eggs, don't they? We use eggs at Easter partly because an egg doesn't look like it has any life inside it, but hidden inside is a chick, and when it is time the chick will peck its way out, full of life. They remind us of how life can burst out to surprise us from the most dead and hopeless of places. Even Jesus, dead on the cross, can come back to life in a new and glorious way. They also remind us of the stone that was used to cover over the entrance to Jesus' tomb. After he had died on the cross, his body was carried to the tomb, and a huge stone rolled across the entrance. Early on the Sunday morning, some women who had been his close friends came to say goodbye to his body. But as they arrived at the tomb, they discovered that the huge stone had been rolled away from the entrance, and that his body was gone. They realised that some men, who looked dazzlingly bright were there. The men asked them why they were looking for Jesus where the dead bodies are. 'Don't you remember?' asked the men. 'Don't you remember what Jesus said would happen?' The women did remember. They remembered how Jesus had promised that he would die but would come alive again, and full of joy and wonder they ran to tell the others.

The children can paint their pebbles to show how something that looks dead can become bright and alive. Use acrylic paint as this will show up better, or sharpie pens covered with nail varnish.

Big Kids' Sunday School

Let the children try out that trick with three cups and a ball, where you place the ball under one of the cups, and muddle them around to see if the children can work out where the ball is hiding. You could make it more Easter-themed by hiding a small chocolate egg under a cup instead. The children can take it in turns to have a go at being the hider and the seeker.

Sometimes we know exactly where to find something. Sometimes it's more difficult but if we concentrate we can work out where to look. After Jesus had died on the cross, and his body had been carried to the tomb, the women had run out of time to look after his body in the way that they wanted to. On that Sunday, very early in the morning, they went to find Jesus' body. They knew just where to look. Jesus had been buried in the tomb. That's where dead bodies are meant to be. But when they got there, his body was gone! The women were shocked. But then they saw some men who dazzled them by their appearance, and who asked them, 'Why are you looking for the living among the dead?' They remembered all that Jesus had told them, of how he would die and rise again, and realised they were looking in the wrong place. Of course Jesus wouldn't be in the tomb. He was alive, and that's not where to look for someone who's alive. They ran straight home to tell their friends that Jesus was alive.

The children can make an Easter garden in a foil food dish, using compost, moss, gravel, pebbles and tiny plants.

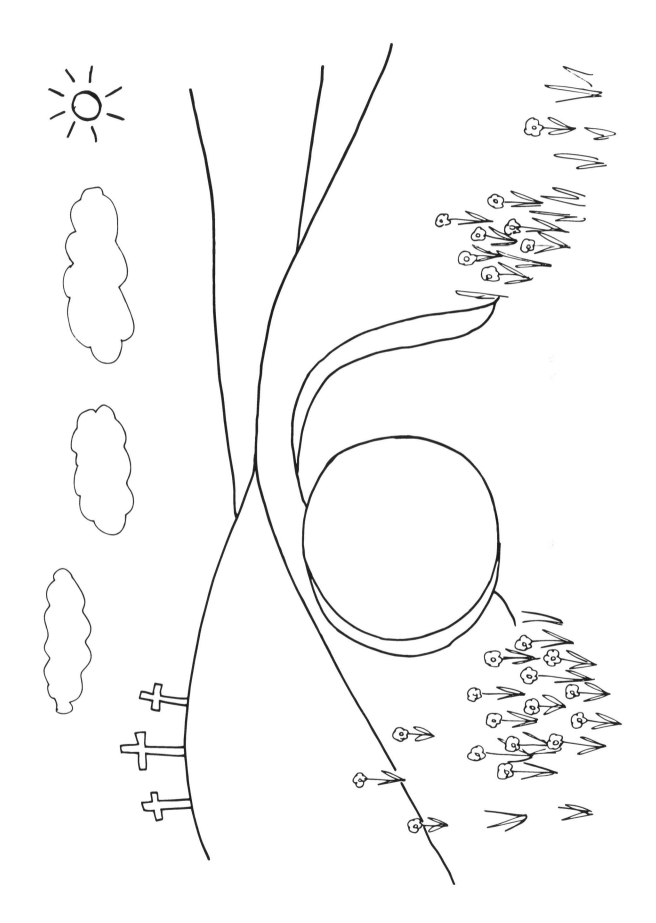

THE SECOND SUNDAY OF EASTER

Readings

- Acts 5:27-32
- Psalm 118:14-29
- Revelation 1:4-8
- John 20:19-31

Thoughts on the Readings

As Jesus appears to his disciples, they must have been delighted but confused – how could their friend Jesus appear in the middle of them, when they had locked all the doors? It wasn't even as if he had unlocked the doors and walked through. This was something that they could never have expected – Jesus was physically there with them, but in a new resurrection body which was not limited in the same way as our bodies.

It is interesting, then, that Jesus makes a point of showing his disciples the wounds in his hands and his side – he wanted them to know that he was not just a vision, a ghost, or a product of their imagination. It really was him. He breathed on them too – visions don't have warm, human breath. And as he did this, they received the Holy Spirit.

Thomas, as we know, was not there on the first occasion. The other disciples' account must have sounded very strange to him, and Thomas tells them that he wants to actually touch Jesus' hands and side. Perhaps he thought that it had just been a vision of Jesus the first time, since nobody else had touched Jesus.

Then, just a week later, Jesus appears among them again, and Thomas is with them this time. Thomas does not need to ask – Jesus knows just what he needs, and invites him to touch the wounds caused by his crucifixion. It seems strange that neither of them consider that this might be painful – after all, the wounds were deep and jagged. But maybe Thomas has a feeling that Jesus' risen body is somehow stronger and different than his body was before. The wounds have become something beautiful, a sign of his victory over sin and death. They are no longer painful but triumphant.

This makes us think about the wounds we sometimes live with in our lives. Perhaps we have been hurt in the past, let down by someone, or badly treated. We can carry these wounds with us, and they can be painful for years. But if we come to Jesus, he can bring us healing in a way we never expected. The wounds themselves never disappear – the events cannot be forgotten – but they can be transformed into something victorious. Then they no longer cause us pain, but can become beautiful, as we grow in wisdom, love and understanding.

Our reading from Revelation, a beautiful blessing, also echoes the theme of Jesus' victory over death, while the reading from Acts talks about the gift of the Holy Spirit that has been promised to us by Jesus. And the Psalm for today sings the praise of God who is kind and merciful, and who gives us power and strength.

These blessings are available to us all. Jesus knows what we need even before we ask him, and we just need to be ready to receive it.

Discussion Starters

- Is there a time that you have been aware of Jesus' presence when you least expected it?

Intercessions

Risen Jesus,
we put our trust in you.

Jesus, as you appeared in the middle of the disciples,
taking them by surprise,
we pray that you would
come and surprise us today.

We bring you our Church
and thank you for those first disciples
who spread the good news
about Jesus' victory over death.
We also thank you for those
who have followed in their footsteps
through the years,
starting new church communities
and caring for those
which are already established.
Risen Jesus,
we put our trust in you.

We bring to you anyone in our world who is afraid,
who feels they have to lock themselves away to be safe.
We pray for those who are persecuted
because of their faith or their political views
or because they belong to a particular group.
We pray that you would appear amongst them,
bringing your peace and strength,
so they know they are not alone.
Risen Jesus,
we put our trust in you.

We pray for those who are in pain
with physical wounds or wounds to their spirit;
we pray that you would bring your healing
and your comforting presence.
We bring before you today those known to us
who have asked for our prayers, especially . . .
Risen Jesus,
we put our trust in you.

As we think of Jesus and his resurrection body,
we pray for those who are in the last stage
of their life here on earth.
We pray that you would be with them,
and fill them with joy and hope
in what your resurrection promises.
We also remember in thankfulness and love
those loved ones who have now died,
now dwelling with you
in peace and without pain.
We name before you today . . .
Risen Jesus,
we put our trust in you.

Jesus, may your presence be with us
in our homes
and as we go about our daily lives.
Fill us with your Holy Spirit
so that we can be strengthened
to live for you.
Amen.

Children's Prayer

Jesus, you are with us,
Jesus, you are near.
You will never leave us,
we don't need to live
    in fear.
Amen.

Other Ideas!

Colour in or decorate a banner
which says 'Jesus is here'.

All-age Talk

Hold up a poster of an inspirational scene. Sometimes people come back from a beautiful place and try to tell us about it. They tell us how special it was and how it made them feel. But we can't really experience it until we visit it ourselves, a bit like Thomas in our reading today – he couldn't really understand what the disciples were saying about Jesus coming alive again until he could see for himself, and put his hands where Jesus' wounds were.

Talking of wounds . . . Rip the poster from the top to halfway down. Sometimes things get damaged. Sometimes people get damaged. Jesus, in his resurrection body, was still carrying his wounds.

Get some volunteers up and provide them with some differently coloured gaffer tape to fix the poster. No matter how well they fix it, the damage is going to be visible. The poster won't look the same. But it looks beautiful in a different way now. Not only is there the beauty of the original scene, but now there's also the beauty showing of someone who's spent time and effort to fix it. This fixed part is probably stronger than the rest of the whole poster now.

When Thomas finally got to see the resurrected Jesus, the wounds of Jesus were still there. Still there, defining him and his suffering, but healed and made beautiful, through his resurrection. And that's how God's healing works on all our wounds. We carry wounds through our lives, in our hearts and our minds. God doesn't erase them. That's not what healing looks like. But the glory of his resurrection, his promise of new life to all of us, in the now as well as in the kingdom to come, heals them. Like our poster, the beauty is in the fact that God has loved us enough to mend our wounds. And sometimes, indeed often, it is our healed wounds that God can use as our greatest strengths.

Children's Corner

Provide a selection of fans – paper fans and hand-held electric fans. The children and their parents and carers can listen out for Jesus breathing on his disciples, and whisper about how sometimes things can be there even when we can't see them, like the invisible air we can feel moving.

The colouring sheet shows Thomas meeting Jesus, and reaching out his hand to touch Jesus' wounds.

Little Kids' Sunday School

Play Grandmother's Footsteps. One child is chosen to be grandmother, and stands with their back to the rest of the group. The rest of the group have to sneak up and tap her on the shoulder before she spots them. Grandmother can turn around at any point. If she turns around, everyone has to freeze. If Grandmother sees them move, she can send them back to the start.

When you were being Grandmother, could you tell when there was someone right behind you? It's difficult to tell when you can't see someone, isn't it? Our Gospel story today is about Thomas. He was one of Jesus' friends, and after Jesus had come alive again, Thomas kept missing out on the times Jesus appeared to his friends. Thomas hadn't seen Jesus alive since that terrible Friday when Jesus had been killed on the cross. Thomas couldn't really believe the stories his friends were sharing. He thought that maybe they were making it all up, or it was wishful thinking. One day, Thomas was with his friends and he said to them, 'If I could just see him myself, I'd believe you. If I could see him, and touch him. If I could put my hands in his hands, and in the wound on his side, to know for sure.' A week later, Jesus appeared to his friends again, and this time Thomas was there. Thomas got to see Jesus, to touch him, and he believed everything was true. It was all so obviously true now that Jesus was there in the room, that he couldn't doubt it any more.

The children can draw around their hand onto card, and cut it out. They can write the words Thomas said when he saw Jesus and believed: 'My Lord and my God', one word on each finger. They can remember how Jesus held his hand out for Thomas to touch when he needed to be able to believe that Jesus was really there. And Jesus still reaches out to us, to fill us with faith, today.

Big Kids' Sunday School

Collect a tray full of different small objects – pencil, toy car, plastic animal, cotton reel, etc. Provide two tea towels – one to cover the objects and one placed on top of another tray or a table. Show the children the tray of small objects and then cover it over. One child can remove one object from the tray and hide it under the tea towel on the table, while the other children close their eyes. When they open their eyes, the hider can tell them which object they've hidden. The other children have to decide if they believe them!

It's really hard to believe what we can't see. No matter how much we know and trust the person telling us, we want proof for ourselves that something is true. And that's a good thing – it's good to keep asking questions and trying to find out more. Tell them the story of Thomas, how he'd missed seeing the risen Jesus when the others had, and how when they told him this extraordinary thing, he just couldn't believe it. How he said he wouldn't be able to believe it until he could touch his hands, and the wounds in his sides. And then how Jesus appeared again, a week later, and held his hands out to Thomas to touch. And how Thomas believed, and proclaimed, 'My Lord and my God!'

The children can make dice to help them to ask questions and think about their faith, like Thomas. Draw or print out a net for a cube, then before the children put it together, they can draw a question mark on two of the sides, an ear on two of the sides, and thumbs up on two of the sides. When they roll the dice, if it lands on a question mark, they can share a question they have about God or their faith. If it lands on an ear, they can share something they've heard about God or their faith, that they know the person telling them believes. If it lands on a thumbs up, they can share something they know for sure about God or their faith. Remind them that questions are a good thing, because the more we ask, the more we are interested to discover.

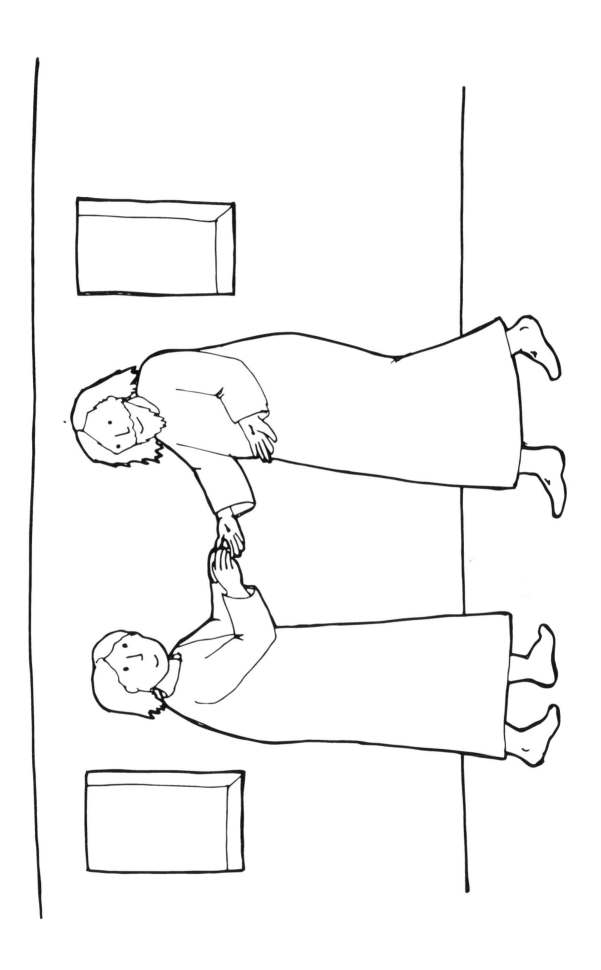

HARVEST FESTIVAL

Readings

- Jeremiah 2:4-13 or Ecclesiasticus 10:12-18
- Psalm 81:1, 10-16 or Psalm 112
- Hebrews 13:1-8, 15-16
- Luke 14:1, 7-14

Thoughts on the Readings

In our Gospel reading today, Jesus is invited to the home of a very important Pharisee, to have dinner. No doubt this was a lavish occasion, designed to impress the guests, and Jesus had been chosen as an interesting, popular and contemporary speaker.

What Jesus went on to say, however, was challenging and was probably not what people were expecting. With typical warm observation of human nature, Jesus pointed out how people jostle for the best seats at the banquet, when they would actually impress others more by taking a more humble position and not showing off.

Jesus then challenges, with good humour, the man who invited him, suggesting that he could invite the poor, the crippled, the lame and the blind to his next feast – they won't be able to invite him back, but God will reward him in heaven.

This powerful picture, of a banquet of the most expensive and luxurious food being served to those who are marginalised and disadvantaged, makes us think, too, of God's heavenly banquet, where everyone is invited. It is unlikely that the Pharisee in the story stopped inviting his friends and family over to dinner, and Jesus would not have meant that. But after hearing Jesus' words, we can imagine that he was inspired to share the food from his banqueting table with those who most needed it, and to use his wealth in a way that would benefit everyone.

This is Jesus' challenge for us too – we may not be having elaborate banquets with famous dinner guests, but we can find ways to share the blessings that God has given us. This might be something like giving to charity at birthdays or Christmas, or offering a couple of our chocolate biscuits to someone who is homeless. It may be that if there is food left over after an event or meeting, we could offer to take it to the homeless shelter or offer it to those people sitting on the pavement outside. It doesn't have to be complicated.

The reading from the letter to the Hebrews also continues this theme. We are told not to forget to help others, and to share our possessions with them. We are also warned not to fall in love with money – this can lead us to focus on the wrong things and hold us back from being generous towards others. And we are to welcome strangers into our homes – this can be more of a challenge for some people than others, but it could be as simple as being friendly and welcoming to the builders who we have booked to do some work, or as big as hosting a refugee family on a long-term basis. We might also be able to get involved with a community lunch or street party, providing a way for people to get to know each other who live in the same road.

In the reading from Jeremiah, God warns the people that they have turned away from him, even though he had blessed them and brought them to a land 'where food is abundant'. This blessing was intended to be shared and used to help others, but the people had forgotten God and had started to worship idols instead. In a time of plenty it is easy to forget that not that long ago, and not that far away, people are struggling to get by. It is easy to take God's blessings for granted.

In Psalm 112 we hear how God blesses those who share what they have, and are kind and compassionate. God will always give us enough to be generous to others. He will give us the finest bread and the best honey – what a wonderful picture of God's blessings! We do not need an elaborate banquet, but just need to stop and appreciate the simple things in life. Then there will be plenty for us to share with everyone.

Discussion Starters

- **What 'simple things' do we particularly feel blessed with? And how can we help others to share in these too?**

Intercessions

**As you have blessed us
may we bless others.**

Thank you, Lord,
for the wonderful things that you give to us.
Help us to appreciate them
and share them with those around us.

Father, we bring you our church
and pray that you would help us
to invite people in
to share your heavenly banquet.
Help us to make our church
a welcoming and inviting place
where nobody is excluded.
**As you have blessed us
may we bless others.**

We pray for our world
and we thank you
for any initiatives which are helping
to share food and resources with those most in need,

providing nutritious meals for those who are hungry,
clothes, toiletries, housing and other services.
As we look to follow your ways, we pray
that we would be open to see
any opportunities that we can help, too.
As you have blessed us
may we bless others.

Lord, we bring to you those who have any kind of difficulty in their life,
for those living with disability or limited mobility,
for those with long-term health conditions or addictions
and particularly for those
who do not have a family or community to support them.
We know that these are the people
you want to come and join in your banquet
and we pray that we would show your love and generosity too.
We particularly pray today for those known to us, including . . .
As you have blessed us
may we bless others.

Father, we remember with love
those who have died
and give thanks that they are able to join with you
in your heavenly feast.
We also pray for anyone who is nearing the end of life's journey
and ask that you would be with them at this time.
We name before you today . . .
As you have blessed us
may we bless others.

As we receive from you today
and experience your wonderful presence as we pray,
we ask that you would enable us
to show others your love
and that sense of belonging
that comes from being part of your family.
Amen.

Children's Prayer

Dear Lord,
thank you for the way
you never leave anyone out
and you welcome us all
into your family.
We know you love it too
when we ask people to
      join in,
when we share
and when we use
      kind words
to show your love.
Amen.

Other Ideas!

If you do not already have one, start a collection box for items to give to the local food bank or homeless shelter.

All-age Talk

Bring along some paper plates, or a toy tea set. Spread a blanket or tablecloth on the floor. Ask the children to come up and help you set out a tea party – this can either be for the church teddies, if you have such things, or for the other children. Tell them to make sure that no one is left out!

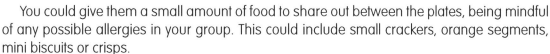

You could give them a small amount of food to share out between the plates, being mindful of any possible allergies in your group. This could include small crackers, orange segments, mini biscuits or crisps.

While the children are doing this, talk about how Jesus went to a very nice meal, with some very important people. They had some wonderful food (maybe even nicer than the children are setting out today!) and plenty of servants to look after them. The other guests were all interested to hear what Jesus had to say.

This wasn't what they expected! Jesus noticed that some of them were trying to get the most important seats, so that everyone would think they were special. (Are any of the teddies trying to do that? No, that's good . . .) He also told the man who had invited everyone to his banquet that he should not always invite other rich and important people to have dinner with him. God's way is to invite the people who do not think they are important, and are not always listened to. When we make sure that everyone is included, then we are doing God's work.

Have a look at the tea party – have all the teddies got something to eat? This is the sort of party that Jesus likes. One where everyone is included, nobody is left out, and all the good things are shared fairly. The children can now help the teddies eat their party food – making sure, of course, that they are being fair to others too!

Children's Corner

Make some playdough and put it on a tray alongside small plastic plates, with instructions for the children to create amazing food for a banquet to share. They can whisper about how they share what they have with others and that this is following Jesus.

The colouring sheet shows a heavily laden table for a banquet, with rich people and poor people all sitting around it to share the food.

Little Kids' Sunday School

Play musical chairs, with the chairs set out around a table, laid for dinner. Each time the music stops, take one chair away, until just the chair at the head of the table is left.

This leftover chair is the important one. This is where the host of our dinner party will be sitting. Choose a child, put some posh robes on them, and lead them to the chair at the head of the table. Put the other chairs back around the table, and let the children one at a time choose where to go and sit. Did most of them try to sit as close to the host of our dinner party as they could? These seats would show that you were important, too, because you were near to the host. Jesus was invited to a meal like this, and he noticed how everyone was jostling to try to get the best seats. He told the people listening, 'Don't try to show off, and appear important. Be humble. Take a seat lower down the table. It may be that then the host will invite you to come and sit near him, and you will be honoured.' Jesus said to the host, 'Next time you have a party, don't just invite your friends and family, because they will give you an invitation to come to a party at their house, and then you'll be repaid! Invite the poor, the crippled, the lame, and the blind. They won't be able to repay you with a party invitation, but you'll be rewarded in heaven.'

As the children share out the party food on the table (be aware of any allergies, and of providing food without a choking risk) they can talk about how they share the good things in their lives. They can have a paper plate each, and decorate it with pictures of some ideas of how they can do holy sharing.

Big Kids' Sunday School

Get the children to stand on a log, a low bench, or just a strip of masking tape on the floor. They have to get themselves into order of age, then alphabetical order, then height, then shoe size, all without falling off the log/bench/line.

There's a lot of jostling going on in that game! Jesus noticed a lot of jostling going on when he was invited to a dinner party. People weren't trying to get in age order, or height order, but were trying to get into importance order. They wanted to get close to the host of the party to show how important they were. Read out the Gospel reading, and get the children to imagine it happening, in their mind's eye.

What does being humble mean? Does it mean telling people how rubbish we are? Does it mean not being pleased about the things we are good at?

Use a yellow pool noodle to make 'Be Hummmmble' bees. Chop the noodle up into short sections, and draw stripes around them with a black pen. Cut out white wings from foam sheets and glue to the top. Cut out a round circle from a black foam sheet and glue this to the front to be the face. Add googly eyes and a smiley mouth. As their bees hum around, it will remind them to be humble.

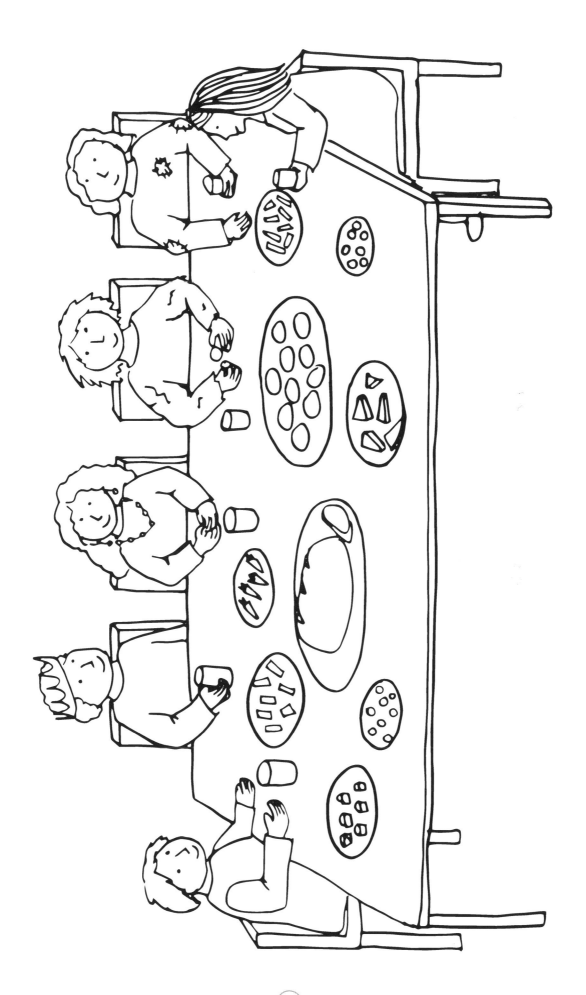

CHRIST THE KING

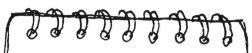

Readings

- Jeremiah 23:1-6
- Psalm 46
- Colossians 1:11-20
- Luke 23:33-43

Thoughts on the Readings

Jesus, on the cross, is in a position of utmost weakness and vulnerability, but it is here that his kingship is shown. The words, 'The King of the Jews' were put on a sign above him, demonstrating invincible Roman power, but Jesus' true kingship was acknowledged by the thief on the cross next to him, who asked Jesus to remember him when he came into power. This man, who had been arrested and was being punished for a crime that he had committed, knew in his last hours that Jesus was really someone special.

Our reading from Colossians tells of the way that Jesus reigns in power, as God's Son. He was there from the very beginning, being part of the process of creation, and how now he is the head of the Church, which is his Body. As part of that Body, we are in Jesus' kingdom of light, where our sins are forgiven and we are set free.

Psalm 46 describes how God is more powerful than any other kingdoms – these will fight against each other and fall, but God has the authority to end these conflicts, destroying their weapons of war. When all the nations of the world acknowledge God's authority, they will stop fighting each other and will be drawn together to worship him instead.

The reading from Jeremiah looks forward in hope to God's promise that he will appoint a good king, descended from King David, who will rule the world with justice. He will bring peace, and everyone will be safe. We can now see this prophecy as being fulfilled in the kingship of Jesus, who looks after his people like a real shepherd.

Discussion Starters

- **What characteristics do we see in some of our human leaders which reflect Jesus' way of being a king?**

Intercessions

**Jesus, our King,
reign in power.**

Jesus, we thank you
that you are a good king,
caring for us like a shepherd
and ruling with mercy and justice.
We come before you now
in thankfulness that we are part of
your good kingdom.

We bring you, Lord, our Church,
both here and around the world
and spanning across many different traditions.
We pray that we would be drawn together
by the acknowledgement of your kingship
and a shared goal of bringing your love
and peace to the world.
**Jesus, our King,
reign in power.**

We pray for our world
and its leaders,
that you would fill them with your wisdom
and guide them in your ways.
We also pray for those future leaders,
now teens, children, toddlers or babies,
that you would lead, teach,
encourage and inspire them
as they grow.
**Jesus, our King,
reign in power.**

We bring to you those
who are suffering with mental or physical illness
or are going through a time of pain or distress.
Good Shepherd, we pray
that you would hold them in your arms
and care for them,
so that they may know your love.
We remember before you today
those known to us who have asked for our prayers, including…
**Jesus, our King,
reign in power.**

We remember with love
those known to us who have died,
both recently and in years gone by.
We also pray for those
who are nearing the end of their journey of life
and we thank you for the promise
of a home in heaven with you.
We particularly name before you today . . .
Jesus, our King,
reign in power.

As we go out into the world,
may we know the reality
of living under your kingship.
May this knowledge inform
our choices, our words,
our thoughts and our actions.
Amen.

Children's Prayer

Jesus, you are our King
and you are our friend.
You care for us
and look after us,
you keep us safe
and bring us peace.
Amen.

Other Ideas!

Print out or show some
pictures of Jesus as king.

All-age Talk

Prepare some paper or cardboard crowns for
the children in your church. Two strips from the
long side of an A4 piece of paper, taped together,
should fit around a child's head. Label them
with different characteristics of Jesus' kingdom
– for example, peace, kindness, justice, mercy,
compassion, caring, love, and joy.

Explain that today is the celebration of Christ the King, and we think of Jesus' kingdom.

Some kings have a lot of money and some lovely jewels and gold, but we are going to think about the sort of treasure that Jesus' kingdom is rich in.

Ask if any children would like to come and wear a crown. Show them the crown you have chosen for them, and ask them to read out (or repeat after you) what it says on it. Then they can wear it.

All these good things are part of Jesus' kingdom. He is a good king, like a shepherd who looks after his sheep and cares for each one of them.

As his church, we are his people and we are part of his kingdom too! As we show God's love, kindness, compassion, caring etc. it is like we are wearing a crown on our head to show to others what Jesus' kingdom is like.

Children's Corner

Provide cut-out crowns (a piece of A4 paper, cut longways in half in a zig zag, then stuck together to make a long strip), glue, and small pieces of shiny paper. The children can make their own crowns to wear to celebrate how Jesus is our King.

The colouring page shows Jesus wearing a crown and dressed as a king. The writing to colour in reads: **'Jesus is our King!'**

Little Kids' Sunday School

Play King Dress Up. Put a robe, a crown, and an orb and sceptre (if you can bodge them out of something?!) in the centre of the circle. Pass around a dice – when the children throw a six, they have to come into the centre of the circle and dress up as a king.

Kings in stories are powerful and rich. They own jewels and fine clothes. They live in palaces. They order people about and command things to be done. Sometimes they are good kings, using their power wisely to make their subjects happy. Sometimes they are bad kings, using their power to make them more and more rich, with no thought for the happiness of their subjects.

But Jesus is a king quite unlike any others. In our Gospel reading today, we hear of Jesus on the cross, labelled the King of the Jews. Despite all appearances, his pain and agony, the sweat and the grime, his lack of power, Jesus was a king. One of the men crucified with him asked, 'Remember me, when you come into your kingdom'. Even in the midst of this awful situation, his true kingship shone out.

The children can make a cross out of lollipop sticks tied together with wool, and stick on a cut-out crown on the top, to remember that it is in this most hopeless and desperate of situations where Jesus' kingship is most obvious.

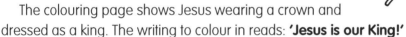

Big Kids' Sunday School

Make an orb from an orange with two cocktail sticks tied together to form a cross inserted in the top. Pass it round to music. When the music stops, the child holding it has to say a word that they think of when they hear the word 'king'.

Pass round a cross to music. When the music stops, the child holding it has to say a word they think of when they hear the word 'cross'.

We've got the juxtaposition of two very different things today, as we celebrate Christ the King. The words around kingship seem a world away from those around the cross, and yet in our Gospel reading today, this is precisely where we come across our King Jesus. Have someone read Luke 23:33-43. Here is Jesus on the cross, and amidst all this pain, suffering and defeat, the person being crucified next to him recognises his kingship.

Draw their attention back to the orb. This is something given to kings and queens in many countries at their coronation. It's a sign of authority. But of whose authority? The orange here, the globe, represents the world. But the world is crowned by the cross. It's this king, who suffered and died on the cross, who rules the world.

The children can make their own orbs to take home, out of oranges, with two cocktail sticks tied together to make a cross inserted in the top. As they make them, they can talk about what difference it makes to live in a kingdom ruled by a king who suffered, died, and rose again, rather than a kingdom ruled by an earthly king who lives within the trappings of wealth and status.

Jesus is our King!

MACROECONOMICS

Second Edition

R O G E R   E . A .   F A R M E R

University of California
Los Angeles

SOUTH-WESTERN

™

THOMSON LEARNING

Australia · Canada · Mexico · Singapore · Spain · United Kingdom · United States

Macroeconomics, 2nd edition, by Roger E. A. Farmer

Vice President/Publisher: Jack Calhoun
Acquisitions Editor: Michael Worls
Developmental Editor: Bob Sandman
Production Editors: Amy Gabriel and Deanna Quinn
Production House: Pre-Press Company, Inc.
Media Technology Editor: Vicky True
Media Developmental Editor: Peggy Buskey
Media Production Editor: John Barans
Internal Design: Jennifer Lambert/Jen2Design, Cincinnati
Cover Design: Paul Neff Design, Cincinnati
Cover Photos: ©Edwin Remsberg/Stone; ©EyeWire, Inc.
Marketing Manager: Lisa Lysne
Manufacturing Coordinator: Sandee Milewski
Printer: Quebecor World

Photo Credits:
Page 86 (from top to bottom): ©Bettman/CORBIS; © Stock Montage; ©Stock Montage; *Page 87 (from top to bottom):* ©CORBIS; ©Stock Montage; *Page 101 (from top to bottom):* Reprinted with permission of *The Region* magazine; Reprinted with permission of Edward Prescott; Reprinted with permission of Yale University; *Page 113:* ©CORBIS; *Page 114 (from top to bottom):* ©Bettman/CORBIS: ©Stock Montage; ©Bettman/CORBIS; *Page 174:* ©Hulton-Deutsch Collection/CORBIS; *Page 293:* ©CORBIS; *Page 398:* ©CORBIS; *Page 419:* Reprinted with permission of University of Chicago.

Printed in the United States of America
1 2 3 4 5   04 03 02 01

For more information contact South-Western, 5101 Madison Road, Cincinnati, Ohio, 45227
or find us on the Internet at http://www.swcollege.com

For permission to use material from this text or product, contact us by
- **telephone: 1-800-730-2214**
- **fax: 1-800-730-2215**
- **web: http://www.thomsonrights.com**

Library of Congress Cataloging-in-Publication Data

Farmer, Roger E. A.
      Intermediate macroeconomics / Roger Farmer.--2nd ed.
         p. cm.
      Rev.ed. of: Macroeconomics. c1999.
      Includes bibliographical references and index.
      ISBN 0-324-06971-5 (package)
      ISBN 0-324-14964-6 (book)
      ISBN 0-324-12058-3 (CD-ROM)
       1. Macroeconomics. I. Farmer, Roger E. A. Macroeconomics. II. Title.
      HB 172.5 .F36 2002
      339--dc21

                                                                      2001034860

To My Son, Leland Edward Farmer:

"If I were to own this countryside
As far as a man in a day could ride,
And the Tyes were mine for giving or letting . . .

. . . I would give them all to my son
If he would let me any one
For a song, a blackbird's song, at dawn."*

*Edward Thomas. "If I Were to Own." *Collected Poems*. New York: Thomas Seltzer, 1921.

Roger E. A. Farmer is a Professor of Economics at UCLA, where he has been teaching graduate and undergraduate macroeconomics since 1988. Prior to coming to UCLA, he held appointments at the University of Toronto and the University of Pennsylvania and visiting positions at Cambridge University, the Innocenzo Gaspirini Institute in Milan, and the European University in Florence, Italy. He is a Fellow of the Center for Economic Policy research, and a Fellow Commoner of Churchill College, Cambridge.

Professor Farmer is internationally known for his work on macroeconomics. His 1999 book, *The Macroeconomics of Self-Fulfilling Prophecies,* is widely used in graduate programs throughout the world. He has written extensively on macroeconomic and monetary theory, and is an associate editor of *Macroeconomic Dynamics,* and the *Journal of Economic Growth.*

A Consensus View of Macroeconomics

Until recently, there was much disagreement about the way to go about *doing* macroeconomics. Keynesians analyzed the economy using a theory developed by John Maynard Keynes in the 1930s. Others argued for a classical approach based on *general equilibrium* theory. This disagreement made it hard to teach the subject to undergraduates because a macroeconomics course would vary depending on the point of view of the instructor. Recently, this disagreement has begun to fade as economists recognize that many of the ideas central to Keynesian economics can be understood using the language of equilibrium theory. A consensus is emerging in which most economists recognize that the right language is that of general equilibrium, but that this language is capable of being used to express many different ideas. This book is based on this emerging consensus.

The core of most undergraduate macroeconomics courses is the IS-LM model, which has not been taught in graduate schools for 20 years. Graduate students of macroeconomics learn models that are dynamic; undergraduate students are taught models that are static. Graduate students learn general equilibrium theory; undergraduates are taught Keynesian economics. Many undergraduate treatments of macroeconomics have lost touch with data from the real world that our subject was developed to explain (this is also true, to a regrettable extent, of many graduate programs). *Macroeconomics* attempts to address each of these issues by providing a grounding in macroeconomics that undergraduates can understand while incorporating the major developments introduced in the last two decades. Because most journalists and policy makers still think in terms of the IS-LM model, the topic cannot (and should not) be ignored in a book of this kind; however, our emphasis lies elsewhere. *Macroeconomics* presents the subject from the viewpoint of general equilibrium theory; it introduces the tools of basic dynamics, and in every chapter, it relates theories to data.

WHAT'S NEW IN THE SECOND EDITION

The main changes in the second edition are in Parts A through C. These three parts of *Macroeconomics* have all been extensively rewritten and expanded in addition to routine updating of the data tables and appendices. In response to reviewer feedback, I have added two new chapters. The first edition chapter on unemployment, and aggregate supply has been completely rewritten and has been expanded into two chapters, one on unemployment and one on aggregate supply. The first of these, Chapter 7, develops an efficiency wage model that explains how unemployment can exist in equilibrium. The second, Chapter 8, adds a theory of sticky wages to explain how unemployment can deviate from its natural rate, possibly for long periods of time.

I have also extensively reworked the chapter on IS-LM from the first edition by expanding it into two chapters. Chapter 11 develops the IS curve from capital market equilibrium and Chapter 12 develops the IS-LM apparatus and the new Keynesian theory of aggregate demand.

The chapter on debt and deficits (now Chapter 14) has been revised as national economic events. In the first edition, I stressed the "problem" of the budget deficit. This problem has now transformed itself into four years of record budget surpluses. I have rewritten the chapter to reflect these changing events.

DISTINCTIVE FEATURES OF THIS BOOK

There are many books on the market aimed at intermediate students but none quite like this one. Here are some of the exciting features that make *Macroeconomics* stand out from its textbook competitors.

1. Data is emphasized in every chapter. Chapter 2 explains income and wealth accounting and how they are related to each other. It teaches students the magnitudes of wealth, income, and the components of income by presenting figures for the wealth and income of an average American and the relative wealth of different countries and different regions of the world. Chapter 3 shows how to remove the trend from a data series and how to construct scatter plots of one detrended series against another. These scatter plots are used extensively in later chapters to check the implications of simple theories against facts from the historical record.

2. Ideas are introduced in historical context. The theoretical section of the book begins, in Part B, with a classical model based on the idea that demand and supply are always

equal. Using this model, it explains data from the 1973 and 1979 recessions. Part C contrasts the Keynesian and classical models by demonstrating that data from the Great Depression can be more easily explained as an aggregate demand shift than as a shift in aggregate supply. Part D introduces the student to dynamics and explains the budget deficit, growth, the debate over the shifting Phillips curve, and rational expectations.

3. Every chapter uses the tools of demand and supply with a consistent theme running throughout—namely, that macroeconomics and microeconomics are both based on the idea that households and firms pursue their own self-interests subject to constraints. This theme is employed even in the chapters on Keynesian economics, in which unemployment is shown to result from an information problem that prevents firms and workers from trading at prices that exhaust all of the gains from trade.

4. The book brings dynamics to the intermediate market. It explains difference equations using a graphical framework and with a simple example that students can understand and relate to—that is, the economics of the government budget. It also uses difference equations to explain growth and the modern approach to monetary policy.

5. Much of modern macroeconomics has been directed at the causes of growth, and a major paradigm—endogenous growth theory—has absorbed the attention of many of the best minds in the profession. *Macroeconomics* has two chapters on growth and an entire chapter explaining endogenous growth theory, using the tools of modern dynamics.

6. The book contains a modern treatment of rational expectations and the constraints that it imposes on monetary policy, using examples from the speeches of Alan Greenspan to illustrate the relevance of the theory to the real world.

7. Extensive reference to Internet sites is made and information from the Internet is used to illustrate examples or to provide sources for additional research material.

8. Each chapter is illustrated with boxed examples that draw on practical problems to illustrate important concepts.

HOW TO TEACH FROM *MACROECONOMICS*

Macroeconomics is designed to allow you to teach at a number of different levels. A knowledge of some basic microeconomics is helpful, although it is not essential. Algebra, in the core chapters, is relegated to boxes or appendices, although there is a section on economic dynamics that makes more extensive use of equations.

NAVIGATING THROUGH THE BOOK

	Difficulty Level	Status
PART A: INTRODUCTION AND MEASUREMENT		
1. What This Book Is About	1	Required
2. Measuring the Economy	1	Required
3. Macroeconomic Facts	1	Required

EXPLANATIONS OF LEVELS

Level 1: This material is self-contained. Chapters can be covered in one lecture if students have already studied microeconomics. Analytic material is covered in graphs, with some algebra in appendices.

Level 2: These chapters are similar to Level 1 chapters but they introduce new ideas. Examples include the theory of efficiency wages, (used to explain unemployment in Chapter 7), and simultaneous determination of equilibrium in more than one market (the basis of the IS-LM model). Often these chapters will require two lectures for a complete understanding.

Level 3: Level 3 chapters are similar in difficulty to those in Level 2 and may also require two lectures per chapter. They differ from Level 2 chapters because they involve some simple dynamic analysis and the idea of a random variable. Conceptually, this material is no more difficult to convey to students than the ideas underlying IS-LM analysis, although the material is not usually covered at the intermediate level.

Level 4: These are the most demanding chapters in the book. They involve a discussion of difference equations, taught with graphs and demonstrated with examples. Of the three chapters in this group, two (Chapters 15 and 16) deal with economic growth and the third (Chapter 14) deals with the economics of the budget deficit. Chapter 14 is included at Level 4 because it uses difference equations, but it is easy to teach and students are usually highly motivated to learn the material.

WHAT'S IN EACH PART OF THE BOOK

PART A: INTRODUCTION AND MEASUREMENT

Part A consists of three chapters. Chapter 1 introduces three major questions that are covered in more detail later:

a. Why has GDP per person grown at an average rate of 1.9% per year since 1890?
b. Why does GDP per person fluctuate around its trend growth rate?
c. What causes inflation?

Chapter 2 explains how to measure GDP and its component parts and it relates the measurement of GDP to the measurement of wealth. Students learn how to attach numbers to the United States and the world economies. How big is GDP? How wealthy is the average American? How large is the United States economy relative to the rest of the world? Finally, Chapter 3 explains how to measure time series. What are the regularities that characterize business cycles and how can these regularities be quantified?

PART B: THE CLASSICAL APPROACH TO AGGREGATE DEMAND AND SUPPLY

Chapters 4, 5, and 6 move from a *description* of data to an *explanation* of it. They introduce a classical model of the whole economy that has developed over the course of 150 years. The classical model makes some strong simplifications that are too simplistic to enable it to capture all of the features of a modern industrial economy. There are, however, still features of the data that can be understood with the classical model, and it is useful as a framework for understanding how more complex theories work.

Chapter 4 constructs a model containing all of the features that determine output and employment in an economy operating at full employment. Chapter 5 adds money to this model and explains how inflation and prices are determined. Chapter 6 describes how the capital markets channel funds from savers to investors. By the end of Part B, students will have learned how to construct models using the equilibrium method—the idea that demand equals supply in each of several markets simultaneously. They will also have seen how equilibrium methods are applied in practice to real-world economic problems: the causes of business cycles; the cause of hyperinflation; and the determination of savings and investment with applications to current issues, such as the aging of the population and the funding of Social Security.

PART C: THE MODERN APPROACH TO AGGREGATE DEMAND AND SUPPLY

Part C contains five chapters that go beyond the classical model and incorporate insights from Keynesian economics. Chapter 7 explains unemployment as a market friction in which search is costly. It introduces students to the natural rate of unemployment, which is explained as an equilibrium in which no firm can profit from offering a lower wage or by searching more intensively for the right employee. Chapter 8 introduces the Keynesian theory of aggregate supply through a nominal wage rigidity that allows the level of unemployment to differ from its natural rate.

Chapters 9, 10, 11, and 12 explain the modern theory of aggregate demand that was developed from ideas in Keynes's *General Theory*. It is presented as a generalization of the classical model of aggregate demand, which recognizes that the propensity to hold money is not independent of the interest rate. This leads to a theory that explains why the position of the aggregate demand curve depends on factors other than the quantity of money.

Chapter 9 generalizes the quantity theory of money by allowing the propensity to hold money to depend on the interest rate. Chapter 10 explains how the Federal Reserve Board controls the money supply. Chapter 11 explains the derivation of the IS curve and Chapter 12 develops the IS-LM model and uses it to derive an aggregate demand curve similar to that of the classical model. The payoff to this generalization is presented as a theory of business cycles, in which recessions may be caused by shifts of both the aggregate demand curve and the aggregate supply curve. Because many variables can shift aggregate demand, including changes in investors' beliefs and changes in fiscal policy, the complete Keynesian model is seen to account for both the pre–World War II experience as well as for recessions in the postwar period. It also provides policy makers with an understanding of how government behavior can influence output and employment over the business cycle.

The last chapter in this part, Chapter 13, explains how demand management must be modified in an open economy. The chapter concentrates on the different kinds of exchange rate regimes and explains the constraints on monetary policy in a world of fixed exchange rates.

Chapters 9 through 13 contain ideas that were extremely influential in macroeconomics from 1940 through the 1970s. *Macroeconomics* takes the position that these ideas are important but not *essential* to an understanding of what has been happening *since* 1970. Their main contribution is to explain the interaction between the capital market and the demand and supply of money that, in turn, helps explain what shifts the aggregate demand curve. The more important recent ideas deal with the dynamics of aggregate demand and supply. These ideas can be understood using the classical theory of aggregate demand based on the quantity theory of money. For this reason, Chapters 9 through 13 are optional and instructors may choose to omit them and jump to the modern theory of expectations and dynamics covered in Part D.

PART D: DYNAMIC MACROECONOMICS

Part D contains five chapters that are united by their concern with economic dynamics. Chapter 14 introduces a graphical representation of a difference equation and uses it to explain the economics of the government budget. This chapter is the least demanding of the five and it can be taught in isolation from the others. It explains why, in the 1980s and early 1990s, policy makers were concerned with balancing the budget. It also explains changes in the mid-1990s that have turned the "problem of the budget" into a debate over how to spend projected surpluses.

Chapters 15 and 16 use difference equations to understand economic growth. Although these chapters are relatively advanced, they are also rewarding because they bring students to the frontier of knowledge on a topic that has absorbed some of the finest minds in economics over the past 20 years. Chapters 17 and 18 extend the neoclassical model to a dynamic setting. Chapter 17 introduces dynamics to the neoclassical model by allowing the nominal wage to change from one period to the next and by adding technical progress. Chapter 18 goes one step further by allowing expectations of future inflation and the nominal wage to be determined endogenously. This chapter introduces the theory of rational expectations and uses it to interpret a speech by Alan Greenspan about the role of monetary policy. Chapter 19 wraps up the book with a summary of the current state of economic research.

Suggested Course Outlines

The following suggestions represent different ways in which the material could be organized in a course.

1. **Short traditional course:** Parts A, B, and C. Part C ends with the IS-LM model and aggregate demand. It could be followed with Chapter 14 (the budget deficit) or Chapter 17 (the Phillips curve). Chapter 10 on the money supply and Chapter 13 on the international economy could be omitted.

2. **Longer traditional course with expectations:** Parts A, B, C, and Part D, Chapters 17 and 18. This is the same as course 1 but adds material on the dynamics of inflation and unemployment and on modern theories of economic policy. Chapter 14 also fits well with this course. Once again Chapters 10 and 13 are optional.

3. **Short course stressing equilibrium theory with rational expectations:** Parts A, B, Chapters 7 and 8 from Part C, Chapters 14, 17, and 18 from Part D. This course deals with the Keynesian theory of aggregate supply but skips the IS-LM model and goes straight to expectational dynamics. Chapter 14 is included as an introduction to dynamics. Even though it is a Level 4 chapter, Chapter 14 is easy to teach and fits well as an introduction to discussing inflation and unemployment in Chapters 17 and 18.

4. **Long course stressing equilibrium theory with rational expectations:** Parts A and B, Chapters 7 and 8 from Part C, and Part D. This is the same as course 3 but adds growth theory. Chapters 15 and 16 require at least four lectures and perhaps more depending on student abilities.

5. **Year-long course at leisurely pace:** Parts A through D. The entire book could be taught in a two-quarter (or two-semester) course.

Supplementary Items

To support the *Macroeconomics* text, the following supplementary items are available:

- A Study Guide, written by Jang-Ting Guo of the University of California, Riverside, provides a variety of review materials and problems that will help students master macroeconomics. Solutions are provided. (ISBN 0-324-12059-1)

- An Instructor's Manual/Test Bank, written by Todd Knoop of Cornell College, provides instructor support. For each chapter in the text, the Manual includes suggested answers to all of the end-of-chapter problems. The Test Bank includes 30 multiple choice and numerical problems per chapter to use in constructing in-class examinations. (ISBN 0-324-12060-5)

- A CD-ROM with interactive exercises, written by Eugene Kroch of Villanova University.
- All of the figures from the text are available in the form of PowerPoint slides, available for downloading at http://farmer.swcollege.com/.
- Both instructors and students will want to visit the *Macroeconomics* Web site. It can be accessed by using http://farmer.swcollege.com/.

ACKNOWLEDGMENTS

I would like to especially thank those people who have worked with me on producing supplemental materials for the book. Todd Knoop for producing the end of chapter questions and instructor's manual, Jang-Ting Guo for his work on the study guide, and Eugene Kroch for producing the CD-ROM. In addition, countless colleagues, students, and friends have given me suggestions and advice in the development of this book. Thanks to all of them. Thanks also to the following reviewers who worked with me on the second edition. Their criticism and feedback has enabled me to improve this latest version.

John Abell   *Randolph-Macon Women's College*

James Ahiakpor   *California State University, Hayward*

David Bivin   *Indiana University-Purdue University, Indianapolis*

David Black   *University of Toledo*

David Bunting   *Eastern Washington University*

Yongsung Chang   *University of Pennsylvania*

Minh Quang Dao   *Eastern Illinois University*

William Ferguson   *Grinnell College*

James Hartley   *Mt. Holyoke College*

Kenneth Jameson   *University of Utah*

Todd Knoop   *Cornell College*

Eugene Kroch   *Villanova University*

Tony Lima   *California State University, Hayward*

Michael Loewy   *University of South Florida*

G. Dirk Mateer   *Grove City College*

John Morley   *Marist College*

Salvador Ortigueira   *Cornell University*

Kerry Pannell   *DePauw University*

Lisa Surdyk   *Seattle Pacific University*

Mark Wohar   *University of Nebraska, Omaha*

I would like to thank everyone at South-Western for their help with the second edition. Dennis Hanseman was especially helpful during the development of the project. Also thanks to Bob Sandman, Amy Gabriel, Deanna Quinn, Mike Worls, and Lisa Lysne. Several generations of graduate students at UCLA helped me as teaching assistants. My biggest debt is to my family and friends, especially to my mother Kathleen, my wife Roxanne, and my son Leland.

Roger E. A. Farmer
Los Angeles, California
March 2001

CONTENTS

PART C THE MODERN APPROACH TO AGGREGATE DEMAND AND SUPPLY   171

Chapter 7 Unemployment   173

Chapter 8 The New-Keynesian Theory of Aggregate Supply   193

Chapter 16 Endogenous Growth Theory   357

Chapter 17 Unemployment, Inflation, and Growth   381

PART A

Introduction and Measurement

Part A consists of three chapters. Chapter 1 introduces the three major questions that we study throughout the book: Why has gross domestic product (GDP) per person grown at an average rate of 1.9% per year since 1890?; why does GDP per person fluctuate around its trend growth rate?; and what causes inflation? Chapter 2 explains how we measure GDP and relates the measurement of GDP to the measurement of wealth. This chapter covers the size and scope of GDP and the size of the U.S. economy relative to the rest of the world. Finally, Chapter 3 explains how economists measure economic time series, focusing on the regularities that characterize business cycles and how these regularities can be quantified.

CHAPTER 1

WHAT THIS BOOK IS ABOUT

INTRODUCTION

A UNIFIED APPROACH TO MACROECONOMICS

This book is about macroeconomics and about the debates between economists who study macroeconomics. The idea of distinguishing between macroeconomics and microeconomics did not take shape until the 1930s when John Maynard Keynes wrote *The General Theory of Employment Interest and Money.* Keynes tried to explain the working of the economy as a whole. He asked how employment related to prices, how prices and employment were influenced by government policies, and, above all, what the government could do to maintain full employment. Keynes used methods that were very different from those used by the microeconomists of his day, and the novelty of his approach led to the development of two separate subjects, macroeconomics and microeconomics, which remained disconnected for 30 years. More recently, economists have recognized that the methods used to study the behavior of individual producers and consumers in markets—**microeconomics**—can also be used to study the working of the economy as a whole—**macroeconomics**. This book explains the modern approach, which treats macroeconomics and microeconomics as different parts of one subject using a single method of analysis.

The Three Major Questions

The most important macroeconomic event in the twentieth century was the Great Depression. The Depression affected the entire world economy, although its magnitude and timing differed from country to country. In America, the Depression began in 1930; in the course of three years, unemployment reached 25% of the labor force and the output produced by U.S. workers fell 20% below trend. The economy did not recover from the Depression until 1941 when the United States entered World War II. The Depression was an event of such importance in people's lives that it shaped the way macroeconomists thought about their subject for the next 50 years. The generation of economists who lived through this era became concerned with a single overriding question: What causes economic booms and recessions? The study of this question is called the economics of **business cycles**.

Understanding business cycles is still one of the most important goals of macroeconomics. But although business cycles are important, they are not the most important determinant of living standards. The quantity of goods and services produced by the residents of a country is measured by its real gross domestic product (**real GDP**). Although fluctuations in real GDP are important, a more significant factor affecting economic welfare is the fact that capitalist economies have been experiencing sustained growth in real GDP for the past 200 years. Recently, economists have begun to see the Great Depression as reflecting a large fluctuation in the growth rate, and they search for a common explanation for business cycles and growth. The theory of growth focuses on why economies produce more each year on average, whereas the theory of business cycles explains why real GDP and employment fluctuate from year to year.

Figure 1.1 graphs real GDP per person in the United States from 1890 through 2000.[1] There are two features of this graph that you should notice. First, real GDP per person has followed an upward trend since 1890, the first date for which we have reliable estimates. Second, real GDP per person is subject to very big fluctuations around its long-run trend. These two features define the first two questions that we are concerned with in this book.

The cause of inflation is the third question we will study. **Inflation** is the average rate of increase of prices, and, occasionally in some countries, inflation has reached astronomical proportions. For example, at the end of World War I, several European countries experienced inflations of very high magnitudes, called **hyperinflations**. Prices in Germany in 1923 increased at a rate of 230% per month, which means that every day commodities cost 4% more than they had the day before;[2] workers were forced to spend their pay the day they received it, before the money became worthless. Currently, episodes of hyperinflation feature in the economic life of a number of countries. Examples of countries that have experienced recent hyperinflationary episodes include Israel, where prices increased 400% in 1985; Argentina, where they went up by 700%; and Bolivia, where the annual price increase in 1984 was a staggering 12,500%.

Although we have not experienced hyperinflation in the United States, there have been episodes of sustained inflation of a more moderate magnitude. For example, in the 1970s,

---

1.   The scale of the vertical axis on Figure 1.1 measures GDP using logarithmic units and the horizontal axis measures time. We call a graph of this form a logarithmic graph. Logarithmic graphs are a useful visual aid for understanding the behavior of rapidly growing variables because they can be used to plot the variable of interest as a straight line. The growth rate of a variable is the slope of this line.

2.   Mathematical Note: To compute a daily rate from the monthly rate, I used the formula $(1+2.3)^{1/30} - 1 = 0.04$.

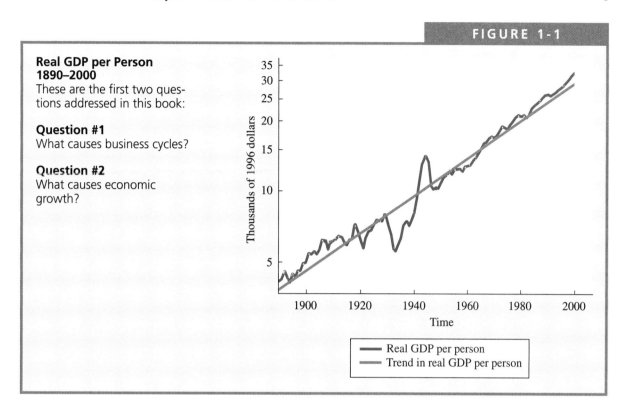

FIGURE 1-1

**Real GDP per Person
1890–2000**
These are the first two questions addressed in this book:

Question #1
What causes business cycles?

Question #2
What causes economic growth?

inflation reached 12%, and from 1973 through 1975 it stayed above 7% for three years in a row. On average, inflation has been equal to 4.0% per year since 1946, a little higher than the prewar rate of 1.7% per year.

Figure 1.2 shows the average price of commodities in the United States for each year since 1890 as a percentage of the average price level in 1996. The blue line on this figure measures the prewar trend in the price level and the red line measures the postwar trend. The pre- and postwar average inflation rates are equal to the slopes of these two lines. Notice that inflation is higher, on average, after World War II. This is reflected by the red line being steeper than the blue line. Because of inflation, a cup of coffee in a restaurant that had cost $0.12 in 1946 costs $1.00 today.

The third question we will study in this book is: What causes inflation? We will also examine how inflation is related to business cycles and growth.

ECONOMIC GROWTH

Economic growth is a sustained increase in a nation's standard of living. It is measured by the average rate of change of the real gross domestic product per person.

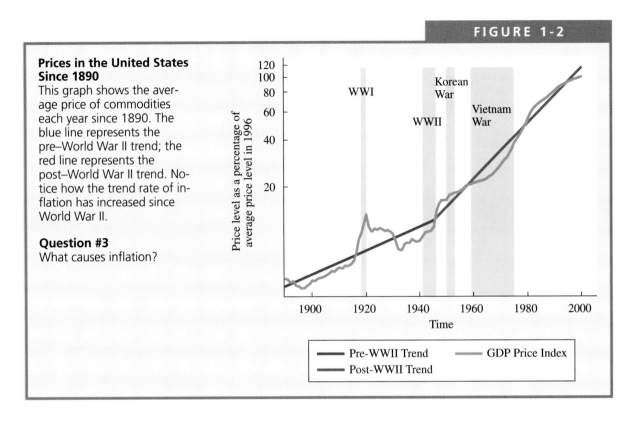

FIGURE 1-2

Prices in the United States Since 1890
This graph shows the average price of commodities each year since 1890. The blue line represents the pre–World War II trend; the red line represents the post–World War II trend. Notice how the trend rate of inflation has increased since World War II.

Question #3
What causes inflation?

SUSTAINED ECONOMIC GROWTH IS A RECENT PHENOMENON

The United States has been experiencing economic growth of about 1.9% per person for the past 100 years, but this kind of sustained increase in living standards is a relatively recent phenomenon in the span of human civilization. The collapse of the Roman Empire in the third century A.D. was followed by a period of stagnation and decline in living standards that did not substantially improve in the Western World until the beginnings of modern capitalism in the eighteenth century. Since that time, real GDP per person in most capitalist countries has grown at a rate of 1% to 2%.

The economic historian Angus Maddison has identified three periods in capitalist development.[3] Maddison argues that the seeds of capitalism were sown in the fifteenth century with the invention of movable type and the advent of printing. The early sixteenth century represents the beginning of a precapitalist period, during which European countries began to develop the modern institutions that are essential to the functioning of a market economy. It was during this period that the standard of living in Europe first began to overtake that of China. During the period from 1540 through 1810, the region today consisting of Belgium and the Netherlands was the most technologically advanced coun-

3.   Angus Maddison. *Dynamic Forces in Capitalist Development,* Oxford University Press, 1991.

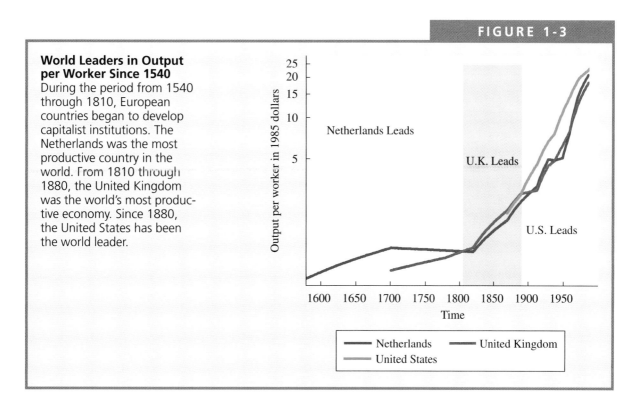

FIGURE 1-3

World Leaders in Output per Worker Since 1540
During the period from 1540 through 1810, European countries began to develop capitalist institutions. The Netherlands was the most productive country in the world. From 1810 through 1880, the United Kingdom was the world's most productive economy. Since 1880, the United States has been the world leader.

try in the world. Around 1810, Great Britain took over as the world's most productive economy and, in 1880, Britain itself was overtaken by the United States. Today, the United States enjoys the world's highest standard of living. The relative productivity of these three economies is illustrated in Figure 1.3, which graphs output per worker for the Netherlands, the United Kingdom, and the United States.

MEASURING ECONOMIC GROWTH

Economists measure the output available to an entire community with an index of the goods and services produced, called the real gross domestic product (real GDP). To measure the **standard of living** in a country, we divide real GDP by the number of people to arrive at GDP per person. Although GDP per person is an imperfect index of the standard of living of a community, it is highly correlated with a number of other indices that have been proposed as measures of economic well-being. Table 1.1 shows that countries with a high real GDP per person also consume more energy and more food, and have better access to physicians.

Although the use of per-capita GDP as a measure of economic well-being is widespread, it has been criticized as imperfect since the changes in our living patterns that are associated with growth are multidimensional. For example, increased production is often accompanied by increased pollution or increased crime. Countries like Sweden and Denmark

TABLE 1.1

Standard of Living Indicators for Selected Countries

	Per-Capita GNP, 1994	Per-Capita Annual Consumption (Kg.), 1994	Per-Capita Daily Intake	Population per Physician
	Dollars of Equivalent Purchasing Power	Energy (oil equivalent)	Calories	1988 – 1991
India	1,280	243	2,395	2,439
Japan	21,140	3,825	2,921	610
USA	25,880	7,905	3,642	420
Singapore	21,900	6,556	3,121	725
South Korea	10,330	3,000	3,298	1,205
Mexico	7,040	1,577	3,181	621
Russia	4,610	4,038	3,380	210
China	2,510	647	2,729	730
Pakistan	2,130	255	2,316	2,000

Source: The India Times, http://www.india-times.com.

have a lower level of real GDP per capita than the United States, but they also have lower crime rates.[4] These countries have a relatively equal distribution of income paid for with high tax rates. In Denmark, the income tax rate is 50% for mid-level to low earners and as high as 64% for those in top brackets. This compares with 30% and 42% in the United States, respectively.[5]

Any single number that represents the quantities of commodities produced in two different countries will miss quality-of-life differences that cannot be measured by market activity. Some people prefer to earn less money and live in an area or country with other attractions—for example, less crime or more equality of incomes. For this reason, you should be careful not to assume that because a country has a higher standard of living that its citizens are better off in other dimensions.

---

4. According to official Danish statistics (http://www.dst.dk), violent crimes in Denmark averaged 187 per 100,000 people in the 1990s, whereas the FBI (http://www.fbi.gov) reported violent crimes in the United States at 611 per 100,000 people in 1998.
5. Taxpayers Association of Europe: http://www.taxpayers-europe.com.

REAL AND NOMINAL GROSS DOMESTIC PRODUCT

There are two measures of GDP, real and nominal. **Nominal GDP** measures the average dollar value of the goods produced in any year, but it is not a good way to measure differences in the average quantities of goods and services produced over time. Nominal GDP can go up from year to year for either of two reasons. First, it may increase because a country produces more goods and services; we call this increase growth. Second, it may increase because goods and services cost more money on average; we call this increase inflation. To separate the increase in GDP that comes from growth from the increase that comes from inflation, we measure the value of GDP in two consecutive years using a common set of prices. These prices are the ones that prevailed in one year, called the **base year**. GDP measured using current prices is called nominal GDP, and GDP measured using base-year prices is called real GDP. Increases in living standards are measured by changes in real GDP per person.

COMPARING ECONOMIC GROWTH AND STANDARDS OF LIVING ACROSS COUNTRIES AND ACROSS TIME

Just as real GDP per person can be used to make comparisons across time, it can also be used to compare living standards across countries. The standard of living in most countries grows at a rate of 1% to 2% per year, although the range of growth rates across countries varies from -1% in some sub-Saharan African countries to 7% or 8% in Japan, South Korea, and mainland China. Cross-country differences in growth rates may seem like small numbers, but they can have quite a big impact on the standard of living because the increase each year is compounded.

If you have a bank account that earns compound interest, you are already familiar with compound growth. To get a feel for the importance of compounding, consider the **rule of seventy**, which can be used to gauge how fast a quantity will double in size. To use the rule of seventy, take the growth rate of a variable that is experiencing compound growth and divide it into 70. The result is (approximately) equal to the number of years it will take for that variable to double. For example, suppose that you put $100 into a bank account that pays 5% annual interest. In (70/5 =) 14 years, you will have $200 in your account.

The effects of compound growth on the living standards of different countries is illustrated in Figure 1.4, which compares the growth performance of the United Kingdom, India, Japan, and South Korea to that of the United States over the period from 1960 to 1992. The vertical axis of this graph measures GDP per person relative to GDP per person in the United States; the horizontal axis measures time. Notice the tremendous differences in living standards across the countries. The average American citizen earns 10 times as much as the average citizen of India and a third as much as a resident of the United Kingdom. This difference in living standards has persisted over long periods of time for countries such as the United Kingdom and India. Their position relative to the United States has not changed much in 30 years, and the growth rate of per-capita GDP has been (roughly) 2% per year in all three countries since 1960. Using the rule of seventy, we can establish that the time needed for the standard of living to double in any of these countries is

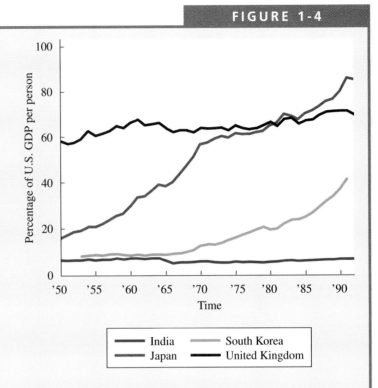

FIGURE 1-4

GDP per Person as a Percentage of U.S. GDP per Person in Four Selected Countries, 1960 to 1992[1]
Many countries grow at about the same rate as the United States, but the level of GDP per person in these countries is often much lower. The United Kingdom and India are examples of countries in this group. Other countries have experienced rapid growth relative to the United States, and their level of GDP per person, relative to the United States, has increased substantially in 30 years. Japan and South Korea are examples of countries in this group.

[1] The data in Figure 1.4 is taken from the Penn World Table by Alan Heston and Robert Summers. The Heston-Summers data is explicitly designed to make international comparisons of this kind by taking into account the cost of living in different countries and by using a price index in each country for a comparable basket of commodities. At the time of writing, the most recent revision of the Penn World Table included data through 1992, although by the time you read this book, more recent data may be available. The data is available at http://www.pwt.econ.upenn.edu.

$$\frac{70}{2} = 35 \text{ years.}^{6}$$

Although many countries have grown at about 2% per capita, another group of countries has grown at much faster rates since World War II. A leading example of this second group is Japan, which increased its standard of living at an average rate of 5.5% per year between 1960 and 1992. When we apply the rule of seventy to Japan, it follows that the time it took for the GDP per person to double in Japan was just

---

6.   Mathematical Note: If $1.00 is compounded at rate g, it will be worth $1(1 + g)^n$ dollars n years later. To find out when it has doubled, set $(1 + g)^n = 2$ and take natural logarithms: $n\ln(1 + g) = \ln(2)$. Since $\ln(1 + g)$ is approximately equal to g for small g (i.e., $g < 0.05$), and since $\ln(2) = 0.693$ is approximately equal to 0.7, we get that $ng \cong 0.7$, where $\cong$ means "is approximately equal to." Hence, $n \cong 100 \times (0.7)/g = 70/g$, where the factor of 100 is necessary if we express the growth rate g as a percentage.

$$\frac{70}{5.5} = 12.7 \text{ years.}$$

The difference in the growth rate between the Japanese and the U.S. standard of living may not seem very big, but small differences in growth rates have very big effects when compounded over 30 years. In 1960, the average Japanese citizen earned just 20% of the income of an average American; by 1990 this gap had narrowed to 80%. More recently, South Korea, Taiwan, Hong Kong, and Singapore have all grown rapidly, and the quality of life of their citizens has increased accordingly. The fastest-growing country in the world during the 1990s was China, where the GDP grew by more than 10% per year during the first half of the decade, and in some years it grew by as much as 14%. Although growth in China has since slowed to a more leisurely 7%, China is still growing more than twice as fast as the United States.

In the 1990s, the United States was the richest and most powerful country in the world, but this has not always been the case. In the fifteenth century, Europe overtook China as the world's most advanced civilization. The recent growth of China can be attributed to Deng Xiaoping's program of reform, which opened up the Chinese economy to the outside world. Since 1978, China's economic performance has brought about one of the biggest improvements in human welfare in the history of mankind. If China meets its self-imposed targets, by 2002 its GDP will have increased eightfold and, if China continues to grow at this rate, it will soon overtake the United States as the world's richest economy.

The startling growth of Asian economies has not yet challenged the United States' position because rapidly growing economies, like those of China and Japan, began from a much lower base. But there is no reason to assume that the United States will always be the richest country in the world. If a country can maintain even a small difference in its growth rate over a long period of time, its standard of living will inevitably outstrip those of other nations. Economists are interested in the reasons why economies grow at different rates, and they are actively studying the role of government policies in promoting the economic miracles of Japan, South Korea, Singapore, Hong Kong, and China.

THE BUSINESS CYCLE

The business cycle is an irregular, persistent fluctuation of real GDP around its trend growth rate, which is accompanied by the highly coherent co-movements of many other economic variables. Let's look more closely at this definition by precisely defining the terms "economic variable," "persistent," "coherent," and "co-movement."

MEASURING THE BUSINESS CYCLE

Macroeconomists measure the business cycle by first measuring the values of macroeconomic **variables**. These are measurable quantities that record the values of economic concepts, such as real GDP or unemployment, at different points in time. A collection of values of an economic variable recorded at regular intervals over a period of time is called a **time series**. Business cycles are irregular, persistent movements in many different economic time series.

Some time series measure economic activity; others measure prices or trade statistics. The most important measure of economic activity is real GDP, since movements in GDP and its relationships to other variables define the business cycle. When GDP is below trend for a number of time periods in a row, we say the economy is in a **contraction**, or a **recession**. When it is above trend for a number of time periods in a row, we say that the economy is in a **boom**, or an **expansion**.

TRENDS AND CYCLES

Many of the time series that economists are interested in display upward trends. GDP, prices, and consumption are examples of variables in this class. Other variables, such as interest rates and unemployment, show no tendency to grow. In order to separate the relationship between the long-run trends in two or more time series from the relationship between their business-cycle fluctuations, we need to define what we mean by trends and cycles. The process of separating the observations on a single time series into two components, a trend and a cycle, is called **detrending** a series.

Figure 1.5 illustrates the decomposition of GDP into a trend and a cycle that results from detrending per-capita GDP by drawing the best straight line through the points. This technique is called **linear detrending** and is one of three popular methods of breaking a time series into a trend and a cycle. (We examine two other methods in Chapter 3.) Figure 1.5 shows GDP per capita (the blue line) and the deviation of per-capita GDP from its linear trend (the red line). Notice that the red line is above zero when per-capita GDP rises above its trend and below zero when GDP falls below its trend.

RECESSIONS, EXPANSIONS, AND THE NBER

The National Bureau of Economic Research (NBER), an organization founded in 1920, dates recessions and expansions.[7] The NBER is a private, nonprofit, nonpartisan research organization dedicated to promoting a greater understanding of how the economy works. Many of the most influential economists in North America are members of the NBER, including 10 of the past 29 American Nobel Laureates in economics and three of the past chairmen of the President's Council of Economic Advisors.

Figure 1.6 plots unemployment and deviations of GDP from trend since the end of WWII. The shaded areas on this graph represent recessions. These are determined by a group of economists called the NBER Business Cycle Dating Committee. The NBER Business Cycle Dating Committee defines a recession as a recurring period of decline in total output, income, employment, and trade, usually lasting from six months to a year, and marked by widespread contractions in many sectors of the economy. Sometimes growth may slow down, but GDP will not decline. Periods like this are called "growth recessions." Slowdowns also may occur without a recession, in which case the economy continues to grow, but at a pace significantly below its long-run growth rate. A depression

---

7.   You can find out more about the NBER at http://www.nber.org.

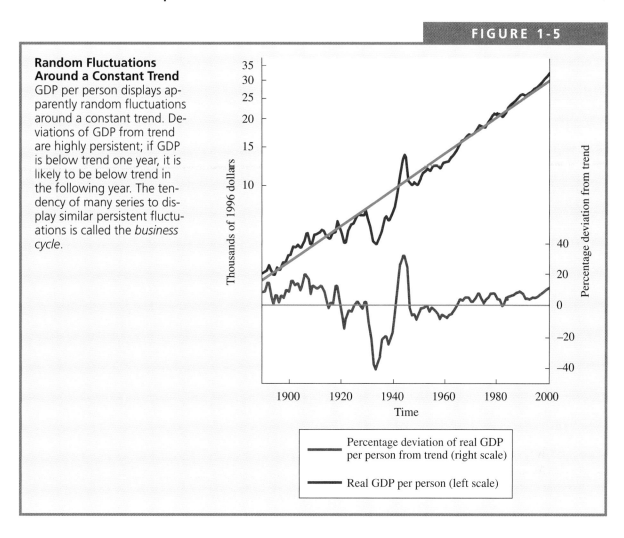

FIGURE 1-5

Random Fluctuations Around a Constant Trend
GDP per person displays apparently random fluctuations around a constant trend. Deviations of GDP from trend are highly persistent; if GDP is below trend one year, it is likely to be below trend in the following year. The tendency of many series to display similar persistent fluctuations is called the *business cycle*.

Percentage deviation of real GDP per person from trend (right scale)

Real GDP per person (left scale)

is a recession that is major in both scale and duration.[8]

COHERENCE AND THE BUSINESS CYCLE

When economists talk about business cycles, they are not referring to the regular periodic motion of physical systems. The business cycle is not a cycle in the same sense; it has an important random component. But although economic variables move in an irreg-

---

8.   Further discussion of these concepts can be found in the NBER book: *Business Cycles, Inflation and Forecasting,* 2nd ed., Geoffrey H. Moore, Ballinger Publishing Co., Cambridge, MA, 1983.

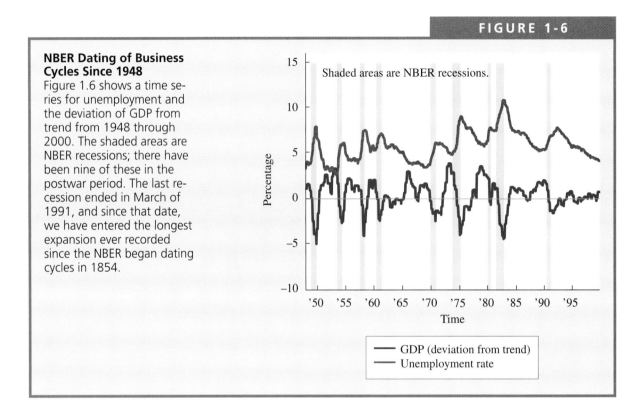

FIGURE 1-6

NBER Dating of Business Cycles Since 1948
Figure 1.6 shows a time series for unemployment and the deviation of GDP from trend from 1948 through 2000. The shaded areas are NBER recessions; there have been nine of these in the postwar period. The last recession ended in March of 1991, and since that date, we have entered the longest expansion ever recorded since the NBER began dating cycles in 1854.

ular way through time, many of them move very closely in tandem. This co-movement is called coherence. Coherence is the relationship between variables that accounts for many of the important characteristics of booms and recessions; for example, when GDP is below trend, coherence implies that unemployment is likely to be high and consumption is likely to be low.

Figure 1.7 illustrates the coherence between consumption and GDP per capita in panel A and between unemployment and GDP per capita in panel B. In each case, the cycle in consumption, unemployment, and GDP has been constructed by removing a linear trend. The cyclical component of consumption is plotted against the cyclical component of GDP per capita in panel A, and the cyclical component of unemployment is plotted against the cyclical component of GDP per capita in panel B. Variables like consumption, which move in the same direction as GDP over the cycle, are said to be **procyclical** because they move (pro) with the cycle. Unemployment, in panel B, is an example of a variable that tends to be high when GDP is low. Variables like unemployment that move in the opposite direction to GDP over the cycle are said to be **countercyclical** because they move (counter) against the cycle.

FIGURE 1-7

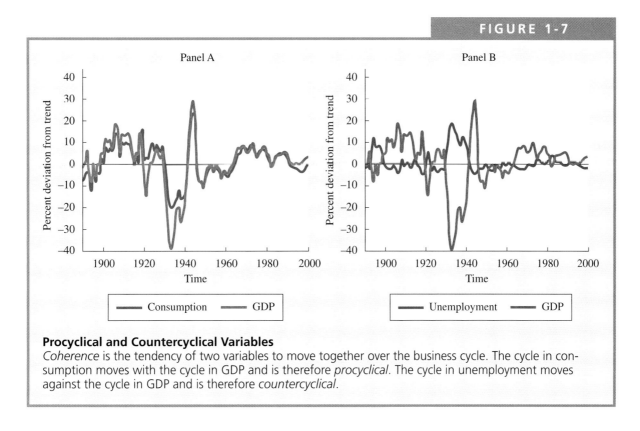

Procyclical and Countercyclical Variables
Coherence is the tendency of two variables to move together over the business cycle. The cycle in consumption moves with the cycle in GDP and is therefore *procyclical*. The cycle in unemployment moves against the cycle in GDP and is therefore *countercyclical*.

PERSISTENCE AND THE BUSINESS CYCLE

A second distinguishing feature of economic variables is their high degree of inertia through time; a recession in one year is very likely to be followed by a recession in the following year. The tendency of economic variables to display inertia is called **persistence**. Persistence provides a degree of predictability to economic forecasting. Persistence and coherence together make up the distinguishing characteristics of economic fluctuations that we refer to as business cycles. By identifying the reasons for the coherence of a set of economic time series at a point in time and for the persistence of each of these variables at different points in time, economists hope to be able to explain why recessions occur and how they can be controlled.

THE SOCIAL DIMENSION OF BUSINESS CYCLES

Although the economic dimension of the business cycle is important, there are many other social indicators that have a business-cycle dimension. Figure 1.8 illustrates the effect of

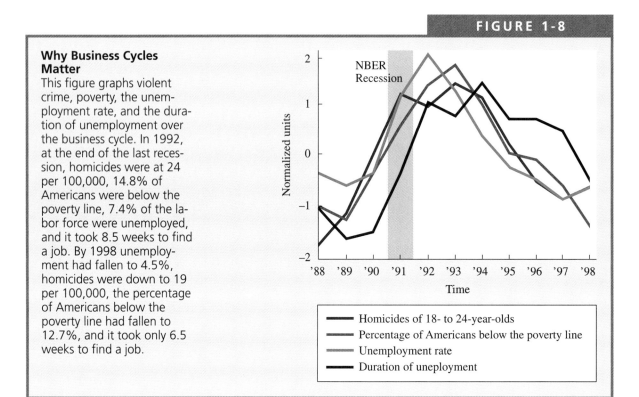

FIGURE 1-8

Why Business Cycles Matter
This figure graphs violent crime, poverty, the unemployment rate, and the duration of unemployment over the business cycle. In 1992, at the end of the last recession, homicides were at 24 per 100,000, 14.8% of Americans were below the poverty line, 7.4% of the labor force were unemployed, and it took 8.5 weeks to find a job. By 1998 unemployment had fallen to 4.5%, homicides were down to 19 per 100,000, the percentage of Americans below the poverty line had fallen to 12.7%, and it took only 6.5 weeks to find a job.

the economy on violent crime, poverty, the unemployment rate, and unemployment duration. Crime is measured by the number of homicides per 100,000 people among 18- to 24-year-olds. This is the blue line on the figure. The red line measures the percentage of Americans below the poverty line. The green and black lines measure the unemployment rate and the number of weeks on average that an unemployed person must spend looking for a job. The shaded area defines the last NBER recession. Notice how all of these time series move with the business cycle. During expansions there are fewer homicides, fewer Americans live in poverty, there is less unemployment, and it takes less time to find a job. For all these reasons, the study of business cycles is important; by studying the causes of recessions, economists hope to prevent them or reduce their magnitude, and thereby alleviate poverty and increase the welfare of the average citizen.

INFLATION

Inflation is a sustained increase in the average price level, measured by the percentage rate of change of one of several commonly used price indices.

MEASURING INFLATION

To measure inflation, we first must choose an index of the average price level. Several indices are in common use. They differ according to the bundle of goods and services that they include:

1. The **consumer price index (CPI)** measures the average cost of a standard bundle of consumer goods in a given year. The price of each good in the bundle is multiplied by a fraction, called its weight, and the weighted prices are added up to generate a single number, called the consumer price index. For the CPI, the weight of each good in the bundle is its share in the budget of an average consumer.

2. The **producer price index (PPI)** is also a weighted average, but the bundle of goods is selected from an earlier stage in the manufacturing process. For example, the producer price index includes the producer price of wheat and pork, as opposed to the consumer price of bread and bacon.

3. The **GDP deflator** is the most comprehensive price index. It includes all of the goods and services produced in the United States weighted by their relative values as a fraction of GDP.

4. The **GDP price index** is similar to the GDP deflator in that it includes all of the goods and services produced in the United States. It differs from the GDP deflator in the way it weights different commodities.

5. The **PCE price index** is like the GDP price index, but it contains only consumer goods and not producer goods. PCE stands for "personal consumer expenditure."

In this book we typically refer to the rate of change of the GDP price index when we talk about inflation.[9] The history of the GDP price index is graphed in Figure 1.9 as the red line and is measured on the right axis. Figure 1.9 also illustrates the history of inflation. Inflation is related to the GDP price index in the following way: When the GDP price index is higher in one year than in the previous year, inflation is positive; when the GDP price index is lower than in the previous year, inflation is negative. Although inflation has been positive every year since the end of World War II, there have been significant episodes in U.S. history when the price level fell. The Great Depression is the most striking example, although there have been other deflationary episodes, such as at the end of the nineteenth century and in 1920 when prices fell by 20% in a single year. A negative inflation rate (a fall in prices like the one that occurred in 1920) is called **deflation**.

INFLATION AND THE CENTRAL BANK

Inflation is widely accepted as being caused when a country increases its money supply faster than the rate of increase of money demand. Since the quantity of money in a country is controlled by its central bank, the control of inflation is viewed as a problem for the central bank. In the United States, the central bank is the Federal Reserve system; in the

---

9.   Recently, the Commerce Department has moved to the GDP price index as its price index of choice. There is now updated data available on the GDP price index going back to 1929.

FIGURE   1-9

Inflation and the Price Index

This figure illustrates how inflation is related to the GDP price index. The price index is graphed in red and measured, on the right scale, as a percentage of the average price level in 1996. Inflation, graphed in blue, is the annual percentage rate of change of the price index and is measured in units of percent per year on the left scale.

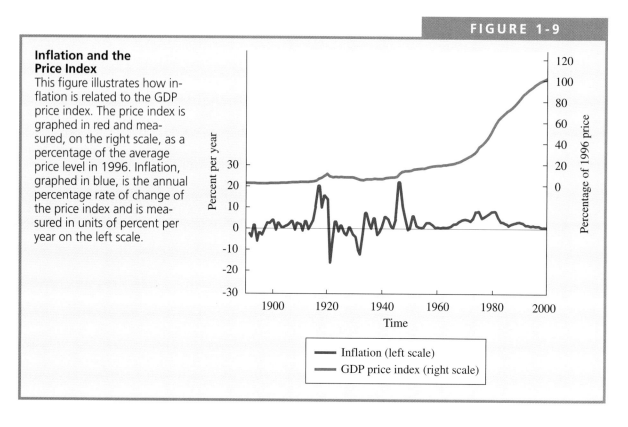

European Union, it is the European Central Bank; and in most other countries there is an equivalent national central bank that has (more or less) power, depending on the particular political system. Some central banks, like the Federal Reserve system, try to influence not only inflation but also unemployment. Other central banks, such as those of Sweden, the United Kingdom, New Zealand, and Canada, try to target the inflation rate over the medium term, and they do not attempt to influence employment or growth over the business cycle.

THE BENEFITS OF LOW INFLATION

Inflation goes hand in hand with price volatility. When inflation is low, most prices do not change very often and households and firms can easily estimate future relative prices. But in times of moderate or high inflation, not all prices change at the same rate. When the general level of prices is comparatively stable, changes in dollar prices can be interpreted as accurate signals on which to base decisions. In free market economies, clear, reliable signals from prices help people make choices that are best for them. And the best way to keep price signals clear is to keep inflation low and, in principle, to eventually eliminate it.[10]

---

10.   For an excellent discussion of the benefits of low inflation, see the speech by Thomas C. Melzer, former president of the Federal Reserve Bank of St. Louis, http://www.stls.frb.org/general/speeches/971028.html.

The problem of high, volatile prices is worse for high rates of inflation than for low rates. As inflation increases, prices also begin to fluctuate more, and the price system begins to function less accurately. Prices convey less information. For very high inflation rates, the problem is so bad that some markets break down completely. In hyperinflations, there is typically very high unemployment and very little output is produced as firms and households spend all their time trying to buy and sell goods and services by barter (the process of trading one good for another without using money).

In order to lower the inflation rate, the central bank must raise the interest rate. (A policy of lowering the inflation rate is called **disinflationary.**) A higher interest rate causes inflation to decrease by reducing aggregate demand for goods and services. But it has the unpleasant side effect of increasing unemployment and slowing the growth rate of real GDP. If the central bank does not raise the interest rate when signs of inflation appear, the problem may become worse, and a low to moderate inflation rate may develop into a medium to high inflation rate, or even into a hyperinflation. The process of removing inflation from the economy causes a loss in output; and the higher the output loss, the higher the inflation. For this reason, central banks throughout the world are committed to sustaining a low and stable rate of inflation by preventing inflation from occurring at an early stage.

ECONOMIC THEORY AND ECONOMIC FACTS

Economic theory does not develop in a vacuum. Instead, new economic theories are driven by the inadequacy of existing theories to explain contemporary problems. This book will trace the development of modern macroeconomic theory by placing it in historical context.

CLASSICAL ECONOMICS AND THE QUANTITY THEORY OF MONEY

Our study begins with the classical economists, from Adam Smith in the eighteenth century through Jevons and Walras in the late nineteenth century. These economists were concerned with the functioning of the price system, and their theories are embodied in the familiar ideas of supply and demand. To the extent that macroeconomics existed as a separate subject, it was concerned mainly with explaining inflation and its relationship to the contemporary monetary systems. Microeconomics provided an understanding of the determination of the level of GDP through the theory of the laws of supply and demand. Monetary theory in the form of the Quantity Theory of Money provided an explanation of inflation and the general level of prices. The classical explanation of output and inflation is explained in Chapters 4, 5, and 6.

INVOLUNTARY UNEMPLOYMENT AND THE GREAT DEPRESSION

Macroeconomics as a discipline was born after the Great Depression, which began in the United States in 1929 and lasted until 1941 when the U.S. entered World War II. Because contemporary theory could not provide an adequate explanation for the Great Depression, Keynes developed the concept of involuntary unemployment, and it is his book, *The*

General Theory of Employment Interest and Money, that marks the beginning of a separate discipline of macroeconomics.

Keynes was mainly concerned with trying to explain sustained high levels of unemployment and, as a consequence, the method he developed was static. He thought of the economy as a sequence of snapshots, each of which represented an equilibrium, or rest point of the economy. Because he was primarily concerned with unemployment, the methods developed by Keynes were not well suited to understanding growth or inflation.

In the 1960s, economists began to struggle with the problem of understanding unemployment and inflation with a single theory, and they realized that the Keynesian model was incomplete. Nobel Prize winner Milton Friedman starkly posed the problem by pointing out that the Keynesian model could either explain the price level for a given level of output or determine output for a given price level. But the model could not explain both the price level and GDP. Friedman called this problem the "missing equation." A search for Friedman's missing equation caused economists to synthesize the classical ideas of Smith through Jevons with the theories of Keynes. According to this synthesis, explained in Chapters 7 though 12, the classical theory applies in the long run, but the Keynesian theory applies over shorter periods.

POSTWAR MACROECONOMICS AND THE PHILLIPS CURVE

Soon after Friedman raised the issue of the missing equation, New Zealand economist A.W. Phillips noticed that in more than a century of data from the United Kingdom there had existed a remarkably stable relationship between inflation and unemployment. When unemployment was high, money wages tended to fall, and when unemployment was low, wages rose. The relationship between inflation and unemployment is called "the Phillips curve," and soon after its discovery, the Phillips curve became accepted as a fact to be explained by economic theory. The Phillips curve was adopted by contemporary macroeconomists as the missing equation that could complete the Keynesian system and allow it to explain both output and employment.

Although there appeared to have been a stable Phillips curve since 1880, not all economists were happy with the theoretical explanations that were offered for its existence. In two separate articles, Milton Friedman and Edmund Phelps pointed out that even if historically high inflation is observed to accompany low unemployment, do not expect this kind of relationship to be sustainable over long periods of time.

The Phelps-Friedman theory was called the "natural rate" hypothesis because they argued that the unemployment rate should be determined by the factors that determine the supply and demand for labor. They called the unemployment rate "natural" because they did not believe that it should be something that could be influenced by monetary policy. The central bank could not choose to lower the unemployment rate by increasing inflation as some economists had previously argued might be possible.

RATIONAL EXPECTATIONS AND MODERN DYNAMIC THEORY

The Phelps-Friedman theory was put to the test in the late 1970s and early 1980s as the U.S. economy concurrently experienced a period of high unemployment and high inflation. The Phillips curve, which had been stable for over 100 years, no longer seemed to apply. Phelps and Friedman argued that inflation would be associated with lower unemployment only if the inflation was unanticipated, and their argument brought the idea of expectations to the forefront of modern business-cycle theory.

Initially, economists modeled inflation by assuming that households and firms used mechanical rules to forecast the future, but this explanation was soon found lacking. It was replaced by the theory of rational expectations, championed by Robert E. Lucas, Jr., according to which households and firms use all available information to form the best possible predictions of future prices. In 1995, Lucas was awarded the Nobel prize for his work on rational expectations, and his ideas now form a central part of the modern theory of inflation and unemployment that will be explained in Chapters 17 and 18.

The Resurgence of Growth Theory

As economists began to concentrate on the relationship of unemployment to inflation, they also became concerned with understanding economic growth. Once again, economic events were responsible for a shift in emphasis in economic theory, since in the postwar period the high unemployment that had concerned an earlier generation of economists receded into the past. Since World War II, unemployment has never exceeded 10%, and the business cycle has been less of a problem than in previous decades.

Some economists argue that business cycles are currently less of a problem because governments have learned to control them, although it is possible that we have just been lucky; a major depression could reoccur. But for whatever reason, modern experience has caused us to turn our attention to the question of why some countries, such as Japan, Singapore, Taiwan, and (more recently) China, have grown so much faster than others. We study these questions in Chapters 14 through 16, in which we introduce the methods necessary to understand not only growth but also the modern approach to business cycles and inflation.

CONCLUSION

Three main issues are addressed in this book: What determines economic growth? What are the causes of business cycles? What determines inflation? Economic growth is a sustained increase in a nation's standard of living. Business cycles are irregular, persistent fluctuations of real GDP around its trend growth rate, accompanied by highly correlated co-movements in many other economic variables. Inflation is the rate of change of the average level of prices.

Economic growth is important because small differences in the growth rate can have very big differences in the standard of living when growth is compounded over several years. Business cycles are important because during recessions unemployment increases, and there are associated increases in a variety of social problems, such as homicides and poverty. It is important to avoid inflation because high inflation is associated with loss of output and related social problems. In practice, central banks usually act to remove inflation before it reaches this stage, but the policies required to do this may generate a recession.

Although the economics of growth, business cycles, and inflation are separate topics, the factors that cause one are related to the factors that cause the others. Economic theory has evolved in response to historical events. This book introduces macroeconomic ideas in a historical context and explains how they evolved and why they are important.

KEY TERMS

Base year	Linear detrending
Boom (expansion)	Macroeconomics
Business cycles	Microeconomics
Consumer price index (CPI)	Nominal GDP
Contraction (recession)	Persistence
Countercyclical	PCE price index
Deflation	Procyclical
Detrending	Producer price index (PPI)
Disinflationary	Real GDP
Gross domestic product (GDP)	Rule of seventy
GDP deflator	Standard of living
GDP price index	Time series
Hyperinflations	Variables
Inflation	

QUESTIONS FOR CHAPTER 1

1. Carefully define each of the following, making sure to explain why each of these concepts is important to the study of macroeconomics: *economic growth*, *business cycles*, and *inflation*.

2. What is the difference between *real GDP* and *nominal GDP?* Explain how each is calculated.

3. Explain why GDP is not a perfect measure of economic well-being. If it has these problems, why do economists use GDP?

4. Using annual data on real GDP from the back of the book, draw a graph of the logarithm of real GDP against time for the period from 1890 to the present. Using a ruler, draw the best straight line through the points. What years would you classify as recession? If you had used only the data from 1950 onward to draw the best line, how would your answer change?

5. Assume that Chinese real GDP per capita is approximately 12.5% of real GDP per capita in the United States. If Chinese real GDP per capita grows at 7% per year and U.S. real GDP per capita grows at 2% annually, how many years will it take for China to catch up with the United States?

6. U.S. real GDP in the year 2000 was approximately $9 trillion. If real GDP grows by 3% per year for five years, what will real GDP be in 2005? (Hint: Use a calculator to solve the equation $y_{t+1} = 1.03 \times y_t$ five times, beginning with $y_1 = 9$.

7. Explain the difference between *economic growth* and an *expansion*.

8. If business cycles are temporary, why should economists worry about them?

9. When is a variable procyclical? When is it countercyclical? Provide an example of each.

10. Consider the following time series: *unemployment, employment, consumption,* and *investment*. Which are procyclical? Which are countercyclical?

11. What are the costs of inflation? Provide at least two examples.

CHAPTER 2

MEASURING THE ECONOMY

INTRODUCTION

The goal of macroeconomics is to understand how real-world economies operate. We seek to understand the links between variables like growth and inflation, unemployment and interest rates, and government spending and taxes. Our hope is that by understanding these links, we can design policies that improve people's lives. But before we can begin to understand how the world operates, we must measure the data that we want to explain. This chapter covers the measurement of two kinds of data: flow variables, such as gross domestic product (GDP) and income, and stock variables, such as capital and wealth. We learn how stocks and flows are measured and how flows measure the way that stocks change through time.

This chapter begins by showing how to decide whether a particular economy is open or closed and how to subdivide it into sectors. We then turn to the measurement of flows, the most important example of which is GDP. A large part of this chapter is concerned with the measurement of GDP and its components. Next, we focus on measuring the most important example of a stock—national wealth. Finally, wealth accounting and national income will be linked.

BOX 2-1

FOCUS ON THE FACTS
North America and the World Economy

How big is the North American continent (United States and Canada) relative to the rest of the world? That depends on what you mean by size. If big means number of people, North America is relatively small. Its population in 1988 was 270 million, or 5% of all of the people in the world. But, although the United States and Canada are relatively small in terms of population, they make up by far the world's largest economic region when measured by goods produced. Combined U.S. and Canadian GDP in 1988 was $4.89 trillion, close to a quarter of the world GDP.

The fact that the United States produces a large fraction of the world GDP means that North American living standards, as measured by per-capita GDP, are the highest in the world. Per-capita GDP in North America was $17,600 in 1988 as opposed to $1,300 in Africa. North Americans produced nearly 14 times as many goods and services on average as did Africans, and North Americans are correspondingly much richer. The most important reason for higher productivity in North America is that North America has more capital. This is true of both physical capital (highways, railways, roads, airports, factories, and machines) and human capital. High human capital means that the average North American is better educated and in a better position to produce commodities that require a high degree of skill than people of many other regions. Human capital commands high income in the modern world marketplace.

This data is taken from the Heston-Summers data (http://www.pwt.econ.upenn.edu/).

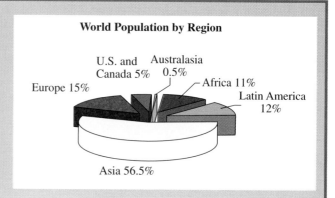

World Population by Region

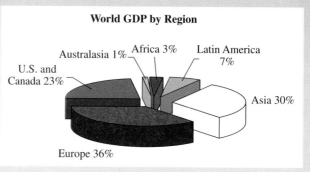

World GDP by Region

DIVIDING UP THE WORLD ECONOMY

OPEN AND CLOSED ECONOMIES

The world consists of many different national economies, and although we are sometimes interested in looking at how these economies interact with each other, in many cases we may want to study a single, isolated country. We call the economy of that country the "domestic economy," and we refer to the collection of all other economies as the "rest of the world." When a **domestic economy** is studied in isolation from the rest of the world, it is called a **closed economy**. When we explicitly consider interactions with other countries, we call it an **open economy**. Because all countries in the modern world engage in international trade, there are no real closed economies. But sometimes it is useful to ignore the effects of foreign trade in order to understand how a single economy works.

W E B W A T C H

Check out the Commerce Department on the Web at http://www.doc.gov.

This was the front page of the Commerce Department Web site on August 24, 2000. The site is updated daily, and it contains information on current events and on business news related to the U.S. economy.

The Commerce Department Web site also contains links to a fountain of useful information compiled by the Bureau of Economic Analysis at http://www.bea.doc.gov, the Bureau of the Census at http://www.census.gov, and many other related agencies.

This is an example of the data available at the BEA Web site. The table, in its entirety, contains annual and quarterly data on GDP in current dollars and in 1996 dollars, although we have presented only a small selection in this panel.

The BEA site contains much more. You can download the entire NIPA accounts in spreadsheet form, articles documenting how the data was constructed, and a host of other information, including wealth estimates, state-by-state GDP, and articles discussing how the data was constructed.

EXERCISE

Using your Web browser, click on http://www.bea.doc.gov and find the historical annual GDP for 1929 through the present. Highlight the current and real GDP data, and copy it into a word-processing program such as Microsoft Word or Wordperfect. Print out the data as a table.

Bureau of Economic Analysis
National Income and Product Accounts
Gross domestic product,
in current dollars and in chained (1996) dollars

	GDP Current dollars (billions)	Chained (1996) dollars (billions)
1929	103.7	822.2
1930	91.3	751.5
.	.	.
.	.	.
.	.	.
1998	8,790.2	8,515.7
1999	9,299.2	8,875.8

The United States and Canada together make up only 5% of the world population, but they produce 23% of the world output. Box 2.1 illustrates the tremendous differences between population and GDP by region. Understanding these differences is one of the central tasks of the theory of economic growth, which will be covered in Chapters 15 and 16.

SECTORS OF THE DOMESTIC ECONOMY

We often treat the entire U.S. domestic economy as though aggregate variables were chosen by a single decision maker. Treating the entire domestic economy as a single unit is useful when we want to know, for example, how the United States allocates its resources between consumption and investment. For other purposes, we break down the economy further into its component parts. One such division is between the **public sector** (government sector) and the **private sector**. This distinction is useful when we want to know how government affects the division of resources between consumption and investment.

Another useful division breaks the private sector into **households** and **firms**. Firms produce commodities and services, and they own land, factories, and machines. Ultimately, firms are owned by individuals who belong to households. Households buy and sell commodities, supply services to firms, and borrow and lend from the government, to firms, and to other households. The distinction between households and firms is important in models of income determination.

MEASURING GROSS DOMESTIC PRODUCT

INCOME, EXPENDITURE, AND PRODUCT

GDP is the most important indicator of the productive capacity of an economy. A comprehensive set of data on GDP and its components is recorded in the system of **National Income and Product Accounts (NIPA)**, published by the Bureau of Economic Analysis, a branch of the U.S. Commerce Department. The Commerce Department arrives at the GDP using three methods: the income method, the expenditure method, and the product (or value-added) method. To understand how these approaches work in practice, we first need to understand three concepts: final goods, intermediate goods, and value added.

GDP is the value of all final goods and services produced within the United States in a year. **Final goods** are those that are sold directly to end users, as opposed to **intermediate goods** (or inputs), which are produced by one firm and used as an input by another. Some firms produce final goods directly from capital and labor, but most firms also use intermediate goods. A firm that uses intermediate goods adds value because the goods it produces have a greater value than the intermediate goods purchased. The **value added** is the difference between the value of the output that a firm sells and the value of the intermediate goods used to manufacture that output.

THE CIRCULAR FLOW OF INCOME

Income and output flow around the economy like water through a pipe; this idea, illustrated in Figure 2.1, is called the **circular flow of income**. The blue arrow on the left tracks the flow of **domestic expenditure** by households; the green arrow on the left tracks the flow of commodities and services that households purchase. The blue arrow on the right represents the flow of **domestic income** from firms to households; the green arrow on the right represents the flow of **factor services** that households supply to firms in exchange for this income.

FIGURE 2-1

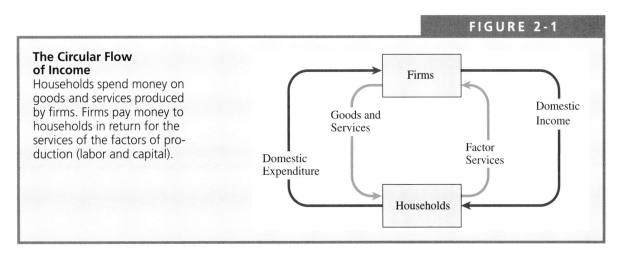

The Circular Flow of Income
Households spend money on goods and services produced by firms. Firms pay money to households in return for the services of the factors of production (labor and capital).

Factor services include labor, the services of land and factories, and the entrepreneurial skills supplied by managers of corporations and owners of small businesses. In reality, firms use many kinds of services in the production process. But for our theory-building purpose, we divide these services into just two types: labor and capital. We call the income that is earned by the supply of labor services **labor income** and the income that is earned from supplying the services of capital **rent**. By adding up all of the income earned by the factors of production, we arrive at the **income method of computing GDP**.

Domestic expenditure on final goods and services refers to the purchase of final goods by households and firms. By adding up all of the expenditures on final goods and services, we arrive at the **expenditure method of computing GDP**. Pursuing the analogy of water flowing through a pipe, the income and expenditure methods of computing GDP correspond to measuring this flow at different points in the pipe.

Box 2.2 illustrates the third method for computing GDP, the product or **value-added method**. For each firm in the economy, the product method computes the difference between the value of the firm's output and the cost of its expenditures on intermediate inputs; this difference is called the firm's value added. GDP is the sum of the values added over all firms in the economy.

CONSUMPTION AND INVESTMENT

For many purposes, we may want to measure the composition of goods that make up GDP. To compute GDP in a closed economy, we must add up the values of private consumption expenditure, private investment expenditure, and total government expenditure (on both consumption and investment goods). To compute GDP in an open economy, we must also add the value of exports (goods produced domestically but sold abroad) and subtract the value of imports (goods consumed domestically but produced abroad).

We begin by differentiating between consumption and investment goods. **Consumption goods** are commodities like haircuts, movies, beer, and pizza, which meet our

BOX 2-2

A CLOSER LOOK
Measuring GDP

The household buys bread from the baker and flour from the miller; these are expenditures on final goods. The baker buys flour from the miller; this is an expenditure on intermediate goods.

Only final goods production counts as part of the GDP. The miller pays $40 to households for the services of labor and $10 for

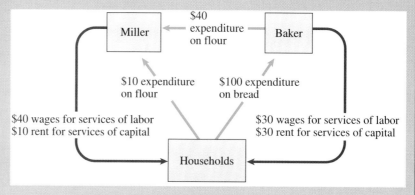

the services of capital, and uses these services to produce flour worth $50. Because the miller does not use intermediate inputs, its value added is equal to $50—the same as the value of its product. Because the miller sells its product both to final users (the household) and to intermediate users (the baker), flour is both an intermediate good and a final good. The value of the flour sold to the baker is $40; this part of the production of the miller is an intermediate good because the baker uses it to produce bread. The value of the flour sold directly to households is $10; this part of the production of the miller is a final good.

The baker combines the $40 of flour that it buys from the miller with $30 of labor services and $30 of capital services that it purchases from households. Using the flour and the services of labor and capital, the baker produces final goods worth $100. Because the intermediate goods purchased by the baker cost only $40, the value added by the baker is $60.

Recall that there are three methods for calculating the value of GDP. The expenditure method adds up the value of all expenditures on final goods and services. Because the household spent $10 on flour and $100 on bread, the expenditure method yields a figure of $110:

Expenditure = $10 + $100 = $110

Using the income method, we compute GDP by adding up the income earned by all of the factors of production. The household received $70 in wages and $40 in rent, also yielding a figure of $110:

Income = $70 + $40 = $110

To compute GDP using the product method, we sum the value added by every firm in the economy. The miller adds $50 in value and the baker adds $60. Once again, this approach yields a GDP value of $110:

Product = $50 + $60 = $110

Productive activity in the domestic economy is a flow that can be measured in three different ways.

immediate needs. **Capital goods** are commodities like tractors, power plants, roads, and bridges, which help us to produce more goods in the future. In any given year, the members of a society will enjoy a higher standard of living if they increase their consumption. But to consume more in the present we must produce fewer investment goods. Since capital goods are used to produce future goods of all kinds, additional current consumption can be gained only by giving up future consumption.

THE CAPITAL MARKET

Although society as a whole requires capital goods to produce output, households do not directly invest in capital. Instead, they save money by abstaining from consumption and lending resources to banks and other financial institutions. Firms invest when they purchase new capital goods. To raise money for investment, firms either borrow directly from banks or issue new shares that are sold to households or to other financial institutions in the capital market. Alternatively, firms may finance investment from retained earnings. Retained earnings are profits that are used to purchase new capital instead of being returned to shareholders as dividends. Whether a firm finances its investment through retained earnings or through new borrowing, the net effect is the same. Some of the income that could otherwise have been used to purchase consumption goods has instead been channeled into investment. Financial institutions that channel savings from households to firms are collectively referred to as the "capital market." They include banks, the stock market, pension funds, and savings and loan institutions.

SAVING AND INVESTMENT

It is very important to recognize the distinction that economists make between saving and investment. In common usage these words are used interchangeably, but economists use them to mean very different things. **Saving** is the act of abstaining from consumption. **Investment** is the result of purchasing a new capital good.

Households save by putting money in the bank or by lending it to the government or to firms. A loan to the government may occur directly if a household buys a government bond, or it may occur indirectly if the household puts money into a savings account and the bank uses the household's funds to buy government bonds. Similarly, the household may lend directly to a firm by purchasing corporate bonds or shares in a corporation, or it may lend indirectly if household savings held by pension funds or life insurance companies are used to purchase shares. These are all examples of saving, and they do not constitute investment, even though the word "investment" is commonly used when referring to some of these activities in everyday language.

Investment occurs when a household or a firm purchases a piece of capital equipment. For example, if a household buys a new house, this is investment. If a company buys a machine, a factory, or a new office building, this too is investment. If the government builds a new school or a hospital, this is investment. Saving occurs when the household decides not to spend some of its income on goods and services. Investment occurs when a household, a firm, or the government decides to add to the capital stock.

SAVING AND INVESTMENT IN THE CIRCULAR FLOW

In Figure 2.2, the circular flow model is amended to show the purpose of the capital market. Households divide their income between consumption and saving. When they fail to spend all of their income on consumption commodities, they channel the funds through the capital market to borrowers who use the money to buy factories and machines. The

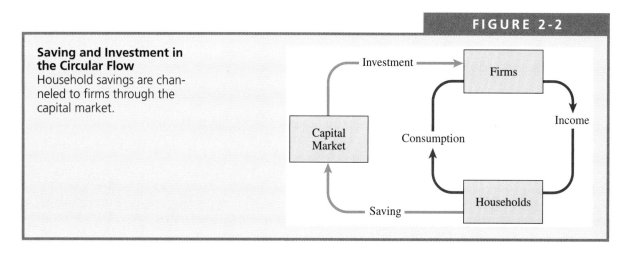

FIGURE 2-2

Saving and Investment in the Circular Flow
Household savings are channeled to firms through the capital market.

amount of income that is invested as opposed to that consumed is an important determinant of economic growth because the more resources a society invests now, the more commodities it will be able to produce later.

WAGES AND RENT

Because every commodity earns income for the factors that produced it, the GDP of a closed economy is equal to the income earned by its residents. In the NIPA, the income earned by the factors of production is broken down into several components. The largest component represents payments to the services of labor; this is called compensation to employees and consists of wages and other elements of employee benefits, such as the value of health care packages and pension benefits. Other categories include net interest, rent, corporate profit, and proprietor's income. In this book, we build very simple models in which land and capital are interchangeable, and labor is not separated into skilled and unskilled categories. In these simple models, we will distinguish only two types of income: labor income (wages) and capital income (rent). In the United States, the share of income earned by labor is approximately 60% of GDP, and the share earned by capital is approximately 40%. Box 2.3 illustrates the history of the shares of labor and capital as percentages of GDP in the United States since 1929, along with the shares of consumption and investment.

THE COMPONENTS OF GROSS DOMESTIC PRODUCT

Although individuals may save more or less than they invest, in a closed economy saving and investment are always equal.[1] In open economies, this idea extends to relationships among the government budget deficit, the trade deficit, and private saving.

---

1.   Remember, investment means the accumulation of physical capital, not the purchase of financial assets.

BOX 2-3

FOCUS ON THE FACTS
How Big are the Components
of the U.S. Economy?

National consumption (government plus private consumption) has remained roughly constant at 80% of
GDP since 1929. National investment has remained
constant at 20% of GDP. In other words, society as a
whole uses one-fifth of its resources (the services of labor and capital) to build new factories and machines
and to replace old ones.

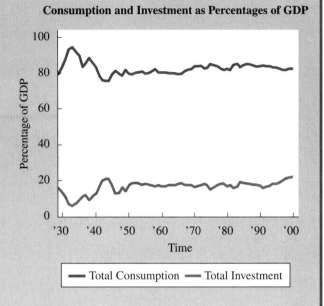

Consumption and Investment as Percentages of GDP

GDP produces income for the factors of production.
Ever since we have kept good records, the share of GDP
earned by labor has been approximately equal to 60%
of GDP. The remaining 40% generates income that
compensates the owners of land and capital.

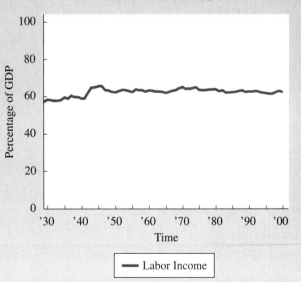

Labor Income as a Percentage of GDP

Data is from the BEA, http://www.bea.doc.gov. National consumption is the sum of private consumption, federal consumption of defense goods, nondefense goods, and state and local consumption. National investment is the sum of private investment, federal defense plus nondefense investment, plus
state and local investment.

SAVING AND INVESTMENT IN A CLOSED ECONOMY

Expenditure can be divided into three categories: private consumption expenditure, private investment expenditure, and government expenditure on goods and services. Equation 2.1 defines the relationships among these categories using the symbol Y to represent GDP, C for private consumption, I for private investment, and G for government purchases of goods and services. This equation is called the "GDP accounting identity."

2.1
$$Y = C + I + G$$

We can further divide government purchases into government spending on investment goods, I^{GOV}, and government spending on consumption goods, C^{GOV}.[2] Using these terms, we can rewrite the GDP accounting identity as follows:

2.2
$$Y = C^{NAT} + I^{NAT}$$

where $C^{NAT} = C + C^{GOV}$ is national consumption (the sum of government and private consumption), and $I^{NAT} = I + I^{GOV}$ is national investment.

In common usage, the words "saving" and "investment" refer to the same thing. In economics, we define saving as the part of income that is not consumed and investment as additions to the stock of capital goods. Using this definition, national saving is defined as:

2.3
$$S^{NAT} = Y - C^{NAT}$$

If we combine the definitions of the components of GDP from Equation 2.2 with the definition of saving from Equation 2.3, it follows that national saving and investment must be equal in a closed economy:

2.4
$$S^{NAT} = I^{NAT}$$

SAVING AND INVESTMENT IN AN OPEN ECONOMY

Although saving and investment are always equal in a closed economy, this is not true in the real world because countries sometimes invest more than they save by borrowing from abroad. This can lead to an interesting connection between two concepts that are frequently discussed in the news: **budget deficit** and **trade surplus**. The amount that the government borrows from the public can have a significant impact on goods imported from abroad.

---

2.   Government investment and government consumption statistics are available at http://www.bea.doc.gov. The series I^{GOV} and C^{GOV} used in the text is the sum of federal investment defense expenditure plus federal investment nondefense expenditure plus state and local investment expenditure. Similarly, government consumption is the sum of federal defense plus nondefense plus state and local consumption expenditure. The nominal quarterly data series were deflated by the GDP price index and converted to annual series by averaging.

TABLE 2.1

Concepts Used in Budget Accounting

Concept	Symbol	Definition	Category
Imports	IM		
Exports	EX		Foreign Trade
Trade Surplus (Net Exports) (Balance of Trade)	NX	$NX = EX - IM$	
Trade Deficit (Net Imports)	$-NX$	$-NX = IM - EX$	
Government Purchases	G		
Transfer Payments	TR		
Government Revenues (Taxes)	T		Government Budget
Government Budget Deficit	D	$D = G + TR - T$	
Government Budget Surplus (Government Saving)	$-D$	$-D = T - G - TR$	

What are deficit and surplus? A deficit is an excess of expenditure over income. When a government spends more than it earns, the excess expenditure is the government's budget deficit. When the nation as a whole spends more on foreign goods and services than it earns by selling exports, the excess of expenditures over income is the nation's trade deficit. Because the nation earns income by selling exports and spends accumulated assets by purchasing imports, the trade deficit is equal to imports minus exports.

In the years from 1970 through 1996, the government typically spent more than it earned; accumulating debt made up the difference. This has not always historically been the case, and neither is it true today. Since 1996, government revenues have exceeded expenditures, and when this happens, we say that the government budget is in surplus. Because a budget surplus results in an accumulation of government assets, we also refer to a budget surplus as government saving.

When exports exceed imports, we say that the nation enjoys a trade surplus. Because the trade surplus is equal to the difference in exports over imports, we also call this **net exports.** The value of net exports is also commonly referred to as the balance of trade. Table 2.1 lists these definitions and their mathematical relationships to each other. Notice in particular that a deficit is just a negative surplus; we often use the terms deficit and surplus interchangeably.

To study the relationship between saving and investment in an open economy, we begin by amending the national income accounting identity to allow for the fact that some of the expenditure of U.S. residents is on imported goods and some of the goods produced in the United States are sold to foreign countries. This leads us to add an additional term to Equation 2.2 to account for the difference between the value of the goods sold abroad and the value of the goods imported:

2.5
$$Y = C^{\text{NAT}} + I^{\text{NAT}} + NX$$

where NX represents net exports and is defined as exports, EX, minus imports, IM. Putting this equation together with the definition of national saving (Equation 2.3) produces an equation that relates saving to investment in an open economy:

2.6
$$S^{\text{NAT}} - I^{\text{NAT}} = NX$$

Equation 2.6 means that when a country saves more than it invests at home, saving results in a flow of commodities out of the country; that is, exports exceed imports. These resources can either be invested abroad in new factories and machines, or foreigners who incur a debt that must be repaid in future years may consume them.

GOVERNMENT AND THE PRIVATE SECTOR

National saving can be divided into government and private saving. To define private saving, we first need to introduce the term "disposable income"—the income that is available to the private sector after the government takes out taxes and puts back transfer payments to individuals and firms. Disposable income is defined as

2.7
$$YD = Y + TR - T$$

where YD is disposable income, TR is transfer payments, and T is taxes. We can now define private saving as

2.8
$$S = YD - C$$

If we put the definitions of private saving and disposable income back into Equation 2.6, and use the earlier definitions of national saving and national investment, we arrive at the following breakdown of saving and investment between public and private sectors:[3]

2.9
$$(S - I) + (T - TR - G) = NX$$

This equation tells us about the interaction of the government, the private sector, and the rest of the world. In Figure 2.3 we amend the circular flow diagram to include government and foreign trade.

---

3.   From Equations 2.7 and 2.5, we have $YD = C + I + G + NX + TR - T$. But from the definition of private saving, Equation 2.8, $YD = S + C$. Putting together these two expressions and rearranging terms gives us Equation 2.9.

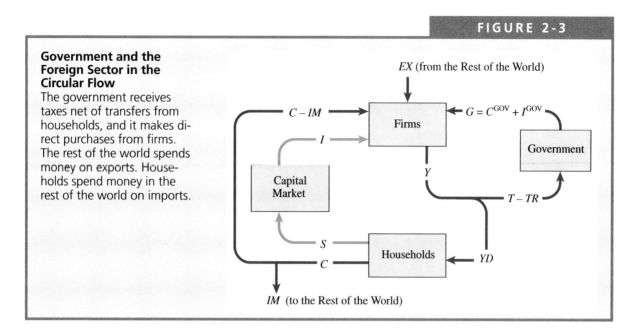

FIGURE 2-3

Government and the Foreign Sector in the Circular Flow
The government receives taxes net of transfers from households, and it makes direct purchases from firms. The rest of the world spends money on exports. Households spend money in the rest of the world on imports.

BUDGET DEFICIT AND TRADE SURPLUS

The term $(S - I)$ represents private saving; $(T - TR - G)$ is government saving. From 1970 until the late 1990s, the U.S. government budget was in deficit every year (government saving was negative) because the government spent more than it received in taxes. Equation 2.9 demonstrates that there are two ways the government can generate a surplus. It can borrow from U.S. residents—this happens when private saving, S, is greater than private investment, I; or it can borrow from the rest of the world—this happens when imports, IM, are greater than exports, EX; and hence net exports, NX, are less than zero. If the government borrows mainly from domestic residents, we expect private saving to be greater than private investment because domestic residents save to buy newly issued government bonds. If, on the other hand, domestic residents are unwilling to supply all of the resources required to fund government expenditure, we would expect to see a negative trade surplus, $NX < 0$, because the economy as a whole imports goods to fuel its excess demand for commodities. Box 2.4 shows how the relative importance of government and trade in the United States has increased since 1929.

THE HISTORY OF THE BUDGET SINCE 1970

Figure 2.4 shows the history of the budget deficit and the trade surplus in the United States since 1970. In the 1980s, the Reagan administration, in conjunction with Congress, cut taxes and increased defense expenditures, thereby raising the budget deficit.

BOX 2-4

A CLOSER LOOK
How Big Is Government and How Important Is Trade?

The federal government buys 6% of the goods and services produced in the U.S.; state and local governments account for an additional 12%. These percentages have grown considerably since 1929 when the federal government purchased 2% of GDP, and state and local governments accounted for an additional 9%.

If government is measured by its share of taxes in GDP, the numbers have grown still more rapidly. In 1929, Americans paid 3.7% of GDP in taxes to the federal government, and they paid 7% to state and local governments. In 1999, the federal share of taxes in GDP had grown to 19%, and the state and local share had grown to 17%.

In 1999, government as a whole took 36% of GDP in the form of taxes. Government spent 18% of GDP directly on goods and services, mainly on education and defense. What accounts for the difference between taxation and government purchases? Most of it is accounted for by transfer payments to individuals, such as in Social Security, Medicaid, and Medicare payments. Interest on the national debt is also an important expenditure item.

In 1929, foreign trade accounted for only 4% of GDP; in 2000, the figure was closer to 15%. In 1929, it was possible to argue that, for most purposes, the United States was a closed economy. The growing importance of foreign trade makes this assumption less tenable in the twenty-first century.

The Growth of Government Spending Since 1929

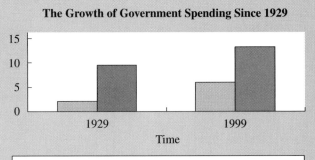

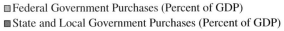

The Growth of Taxation Since 1929

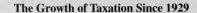

The Growth of Trade Since 1929

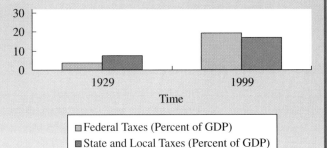

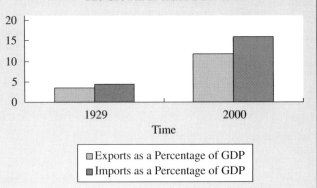

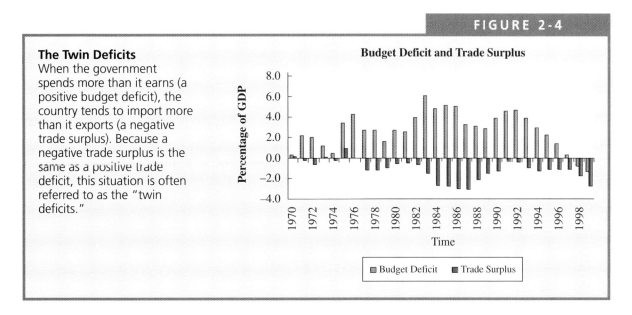

FIGURE 2-4

The Twin Deficits
When the government spends more than it earns (a positive budget deficit), the country tends to import more than it exports (a negative trade surplus). Because a negative trade surplus is the same as a positive trade deficit, this situation is often referred to as the "twin deficits."

Budget Deficit and Trade Surplus

Borrowing in the capital market paid for this increase in the budget deficit: The government sold bonds to the public. If U.S. citizens had responded to the increase in government debt by saving more, there would have been no adverse consequence for the trade surplus. However, foreigners purchased much of the increased government debt. This shows on Figure 2.4 as a larger negative trade surplus at about the same time as the increase in the budget deficit. Partly because Americans cannot endlessly borrow from abroad without eventually repaying the debt, large government budget deficits are perceived to be a problem.

In the second half of the 1990s, the government budget moved into surplus. There were two reasons for this. One was that the Clinton administration, in partnership with Congress, increased taxes and began to reduce public expenditures. The second and more important reason was that economic growth began to pick up in the 1990s and unemployment fell. As more people became employed, the government's share of national income increased as households and firms paid more in taxes. Figure 2.4 shows the effect of increased growth on the budget deficit, which has fallen every year since 1992. From 1970 through 1992, the budget deficit and the trade surplus moved in opposite directions. Since then, the budget deficit and the trade deficit have both fallen. Because the sum of the budget deficit and trade surplus is equal to the difference between saving and investment, we can infer from Figure 2.4 that since 1992 private investment has exceeded private saving. This additional investment in the United States occurs as foreigners, taking advantage of the buoyant U.S. economy, choose to channel their savings through the United States capital market rather than through the capital markets in their own economies.

TABLE 2.2

The Credit Card Statement of Jane Chavez

	Excess of Charges Over Payments (Flow)	Credit Card Balance (Stock)
Beginning Balance		$0
January	$100	$100
February	$100	$200
March	$100	$300
April	$100	$400
May	$100	$500

MEASURING WEALTH

The concepts used to measure GDP and its component parts are examples of flows. We will now look at the measurement of wealth. Wealth is a stock and is measured by a system of balance sheet accounting.

STOCKS AND FLOWS WITH AN INDIVIDUAL EXAMPLE

There are two kinds of economic variables: stocks and flows. A stock is a variable measured at a point in time; a flow is a variable measured per unit of time. A flow is often the rate of change of a stock. An important economic example is the relationship of government debt, a stock, to the government budget deficit, a flow. If the government deficit is equal to $100 billion per year, the government debt will grow bigger by $100 billion each year. Table 2.2 illustrates the relationship between a stock and a flow using the example of Jane Chavez, an economics student who spends more each month than she earns by borrowing against her credit card.

At the beginning of the year, Jane has a zero balance on her credit card. Every month she runs up bills that exceed her repayments to the credit card company by $100. Jane's deficit is $100 per month. This is a flow. Each month that her deficit equals $100, Jane's debt to the credit card company increases by the amount of the deficit. Jane's debt is a stock. Jane runs a constant deficit, so the stock of her debt grows each month, and by the beginning of May she has accumulated a debt of $500.

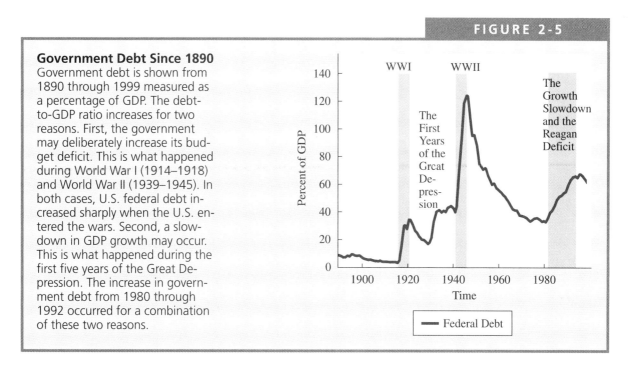

FIGURE 2-5

Government Debt Since 1890
Government debt is shown from 1890 through 1999 measured as a percentage of GDP. The debt-to-GDP ratio increases for two reasons. First, the government may deliberately increase its budget deficit. This is what happened during World War I (1914–1918) and World War II (1939–1945). In both cases, U.S. federal debt increased sharply when the U.S. entered the wars. Second, a slow-down in GDP growth may occur. This is what happened during the first five years of the Great Depression. The increase in government debt from 1980 through 1992 occurred for a combination of these two reasons.

U.S. GOVERNMENT DEBT AS AN EXAMPLE OF A STOCK

The budget of the U.S. government works just like Jane Chavez's credit card. When the United States spends more than it receives in taxes, we say that there is a budget deficit. This is like Jane spending more than she earns, and most federal deficit spending occurs as a result of unforeseen events, such as wars. Figure 2.5 shows the history of the federal debt in the United States measured as a percentage of GDP. Debt increased sharply to finance World War I (1914–1918) and World War II (1939–1945). The Korean War in the 1950s was relatively small in scale and did not have a large impact on debt. The Vietnam War in the 1960s and 1970s was largely financed by the Treasury printing money, and some observers believe that this was largely responsible for the increase in inflation that occurred during the 1970s and early 1980s.

At the ends of both world wars, the United States slowly reduced debt as a percentage of GDP by running small budget surpluses. A relatively rapid growth resulted that caused GDP to increase faster than debt. In 1929, however, growth slowed dramatically as the United States entered the Great Depression. During the period from 1929 through 1935, debt once again increased as a percentage of GDP, although this time the increase was not due to a deliberate increase in deficit spending, but to a dramatic drop in GDP. In the period from 1970 through 1992, debt once again increased, this time as a result of both increased budget deficits and a slow-down in growth. The budget deficit increased as the Reagan administration, in conjunction with Congress, lowered taxes and increased spending. At the same time, growth slowed down, possibly as a result of steep increases in the price of oil that occurred in 1973 and 1979. This combination of events was not reversed until the late 1990s when deficits fell and growth increased. Some economists believe that there is a causal link between low deficits and high growth, although this link has not been clearly established; it is difficult to sort out whether low deficits cause high growth, or vice versa.

REAL AND FINANCIAL ASSETS

The capital owned by an individual or firm is called a real asset. The wealth of an individual can consist not only of capital goods but also of less-tangible items, such as a promise by someone to repay resources in the future. Promises to deliver resources in the future are called "financial assets."

An individual who promises to deliver goods in the future incurs a financial liability. The individual who buys the promise gains a financial asset. An example of a financial asset is a mortgage on a house. A household borrows money from a bank by signing a mortgage. The mortgage represents a financial liability to the household, but to the bank the mortgage is a financial asset. An important feature of financial assets is that in a closed economy every financial asset is someone else's financial liability. One implication of this feature is that although a financial asset represents wealth to an individual agent, it does not represent wealth to the whole economy. In a closed economy, the sum total of all financial assets and liabilities is zero.

In an open economy, financial debts and liabilities do not equal zero because some individuals and firms borrow or lend abroad. In 1998, for example, U.S. financial assets in foreign countries were equal to $21,800 per person, whereas the value of U.S. assets owned by foreigners amounted to $27,800 per person. As a nation, we were in debt to the rest of the world to the tune of $6,000 per person.

BALANCE SHEET ACCOUNTING

The total wealth (net worth) of an agent is the sum total of his assets (both real and financial) minus the sum of his financial liabilities. The method used to keep track of the assets and liabilities of the households and firms in an economy is called "balance sheet accounting." Table 2.3 shows how balance sheet accounting is used to record the assets and liabilities of John Chen, a professor of economics. John has two real assets, a house worth $250,000 and a car worth $25,000. He also owns a bank account, which is an example of a financial asset because it represents a loan to the bank. On the liability side of his balance sheet, John has a mortgage and an auto loan.

It is conventional to separate a person's real and financial assets by drawing a horizontal line across the balance sheet. Above the line we record the real assets and below the line we record the financial assets. John's real assets (his house and his car) are worth $275,000, and his financial asset (a bank account) is worth $5,000. Offsetting these assets, he has financial liabilities in the form of a mortgage on his house for $150,000 and a loan on his car worth $15,000. Subtracting his liabilities from his assets, we arrive at John's net worth, which is equal to $115,000. By convention, net worth is recorded on the liabilities side of the balance sheet—it is a liability that you owe to yourself—guaranteeing that the total value of assets and liabilities add up to the same amount. John's assets and liabilities each add up to $280,000.

TABLE 2.3

An Example of Balance Sheet Accounting

The dashed line separates real assets from financial assets.

John Chen			
Assets		Liabilities	
House	$250,000		
Car	$ 25,000		
Bank Account	$ 5,000	Mortgage	$150,000
		Auto Loan	$ 15,000
		Net Worth	$115,000
	$280,000		$280,000

AMERICAN NATIONAL WEALTH

We have seen how to apply balance sheet accounting to an individual; now we apply it nationally to the United States. National wealth consists of the value of the country's land and natural resources, its accumulated physical structures in the form of houses, factories, machines, roads, bridges, and other public infrastructure, and the skills and knowledge of its people. Collectively, we refer to all of the tangible physical resources as physical capital and to the skills and knowledge of the people as human capital. Because the value of human capital is difficult to measure, it is often ignored in measuring wealth. In the rest of this book, unless stated otherwise, the term "capital" refers exclusively to physical capital.

How great is our national wealth? In 1998, the value of the nation's capital stock plus the value of all of the land in the United States was equal to $22.31 trillion. Because there are approximately 270 million Americans, the share of the nation's wealth that was owned by the average American was $97,000. Of course there is no such person as the "average American," and no individual owns exactly $97,000 at every stage of life, but this figure makes the wealth of the U.S. economy much easier to comprehend. The balance sheet of the average American, obtained by adding up the real assets and liabilities of the entire population and dividing by the number of people, is reported in Box 2.5.

THE LINK BETWEEN GROSS DOMESTIC PRODUCT AND WEALTH

Wealth accounting measures stocks, and income accounting measures flows; the NIPA can be used to show how the stocks of real and financial assets for different sectors of the economy change from one year to the next. The key to this relationship is that a flow can be used to measure the change in a stock.

BOX 2-5

FOCUS ON THE FACTS
The Wealth of the Average American[1]

Table A shows the balance sheet of the average American in 1998. The average American had a net worth of $91,000. This included physical assets of $97,000, such as land, housing, and machines. Offsetting these physical assets were net debts of $6,000 to the rest of the world.

Tables B and C break down the balance sheet of the Average American into assets and liabilities accumulated by the public and private sectors. Table B shows that the private sector owned $77,800 of physical assets in the United States: land, houses, factories, and machines. In addition to owning U.S. assets, Americans invest around $21,000 per person overseas, shown in Table B as ownership of foreign financial assets. In addition, foreigners invest in the U.S. economy. Foreign ownership of private U.S. assets is now larger than U.S. ownership of foreign assets. Americans also lend to their government to the tune of $3,700 per person.

Table C shows that about one-fifth of U.S. physical assets are publicly owned. These assets consist of roads, schools, government enterprises, public parks, and other government capital. The extent of these assets is a little more than twice the value of government debt. In 1998 the United States owned assets of around $19,200 for each American. Its debt was roughly equal to $8,500, of which $3,700 was owed to U.S. citizens and the remaining $4,800 was owed to foreigners.

Table A
The Balance Sheet of the Average American in 1998

	Assets	Liabilities
Physical assets	$97,000	
Net debt to foreigners		$6,000
Net worth		$91,000
	$97,000	$97,000

Table B
U.S. Private Sector

	Assets	Liabilities
Physical assets	$77,800	
U.S. ownership of foreign assets	$21,000	
Foreign ownership of U.S. assets		$23,000
Loans to U.S. government	$3,700	
Net worth		$79,500
	$102,500	$102,500

Table C
U.S. Government

	Assets	Liabilities
Physical assets	$19,200	
Govt. ownership of foreign assets	$800	
Debt to U.S. citizens		$3,700
Debt to foreigners		$4,800
Net worth		$11,500
	$20,000	$20,000

[1] Data for government debt and the international investment position of the United States in the tables is from the *Economic Report of the President 2000*, Tables B-87 and B-105 (available at **http://www.access.gpo.gov/usbudget**). Data on private wealth is from the April 2000 issue of the *Survey of Current Business* (available at **http://www.bea.doc.gov** in the section on industry and wealth data.) All figures are in current dollars and have been divided by 270 million, the approximate population of the U.S. in 1998. These figures are lower than those reported in the first edition of the book due to the release of a new set of estimates of private wealth by the Bureau of Economic Analysis.

TABLE 2.4

Gross Versus Net Domestic Product in 1999

Per Capita Expenditure in Billions of 1996 Dollars		Per Capita Flow ($ per Year)	Percent of GDP
Consumption (Government Plus Private)		$28,100	82%
Gross Investment (Government Plus Private)		7,400	22
Net Exports		(–1,250)	(–4)
Gross Domestic Product per Person	$34,250	34,250	100
Gross Investment		7,400	22
Depreciation	(–3,950)	(–3,950)	12
Net Investment		3,450	10
Net Domestic Product per Person	$30,300		88

GROSS VERSUS NET DOMESTIC PRODUCT

We can invest in new capital by producing new capital goods, such as factories, houses, and machines, but not all investment creates new capital; some investment is necessary each year to offset the deterioration through normal wear and tear of the existing stock of capital. The portion of gross investment that contributes to increases in the stock of capital is called "net investment." The portion devoted to replacing worn-out capital is called "depreciation."

The idea of net investment is linked to net domestic product (NDP), which is a measure of the maximum output of the economy that is available for consumption without running down the stock of capital. Table 2.4 shows the connection between GDP and NDP. From this table, we can see that in 1999 the average American produced goods and earned wages and rents equal to $34,250, spent $28,100 on consumption goods, and spent $7,400 on investment goods. These investment expenditures are divided into two parts: replacement of worn-out capital (depreciation) equal to $3,950, and creation of new capital goods (net investment) equal to $3,450. Because the average American must invest at least $3,950 to maintain the existing capital, the maximum income that he can produce on a continuing basis is $30,300, the measure we call "net domestic product."

STOCK AND FLOW ACCOUNTING

We have described the way that investment is related to changes in the stock of physical assets. In this section we will demonstrate by means of an example how the flows recorded in the NIPA accounts show up as changes in the balance sheets of the U.S. economy from one year to the next. The example we will use is a summary statement of the U.S. private sector and public sector balance sheets in December 1998 and December 1999, together with the NIPA flow accounts for the year beginning on January 1, 1999 and ending on December 31, 1999. These three sets of accounts are collected together in Table 2.5.

The top panel of this table represents the balance sheet of Ms. Average American in December of 1998. This balance sheet illustrates that in 1999 she began the year with assets of $97,000 in the form of physical capital but her net worth was only $91,000. The discrepancy arises from the fact that in December of 1998 Ms. Average American had net foreign liabilities of $6,000 arising from the fact that she has borrowed from abroad to finance past expenditures.

The middle panel of Table 2.5 shows that between December 1998 and December 1999 Ms. Average American produced goods worth $34,250, which she allocated between consumption and investment goods. She chose to allocate $28,100 to consumption goods and $7,400 to investment. Since $3,950 of gross investment was used to replace depreciated capital, this investment resulted in a net increase in the capital stock of $3,450. This net increase in capital is reported on the bottom panel of Table 2.5, where it shows up as an increase in real assets owned by Ms. Average American from $97,000 in 1998 to $100,450 in December of 1999. The 1999 balance sheet also shows that Ms. Average American's net worth increased from $91,000 in 1998 to $93,200 in 1999. The increase in net worth is less than the increase in real assets because part of the increased capital was purchased with borrowed funds.

SAVING, INVESTMENT, AND WEALTH

It might help to understand the relationship between stocks and flows if we return to the analogy of the circular flow of income. Figure 2.6 shows how to use this analogy when visualizing how investment and depreciation are related to changes in the capital stock. Using the fluid analogy, gross investment is like water flowing into a tank and depreciation is like a leak in the tank. The capital stock is the level of water in the tank. As long as gross investment exceeds depreciation, the capital stock will keep increasing. In this case net investment is positive. But if gross investment is smaller than depreciation, then the level of the capital stock will fall. This happens when net investment becomes negative.

The Science Museum of London, England, houses a complete, physical model of the circular flow of income. The model, which consists of fluid flowing around a complicated system of tanks and pipes, was created by A.W. Phillips, a New Zealand economist and former professor of economics at the London School of Economics. Phillips began his career as an engineer, and he used his knowledge of engineering to create the working model of the circular flow now on display in London. He is best known in economics for his work on the empirical relationship between wage change and unemployment, the so-called "Phillips curve" that we will learn more about in Chapters 17 and 18.

TABLE 2.5

How Balance Sheets are Linked to the National Income and Product Accounts

Balance Sheet of the Average American on December 31, 1998		
	Assets	Liabilities
Real Assets	$97,000	
Net debt to foreigners		$6,000
Net worth		91,000
	97,000	97,000

This balance sheet represents the net asset position of the average American at the end of 1998.

Income and Expenditure of the Average American, 1999	
Total Income	$34,250
Consumption	28,100
Saving	6,150
Net foreign borrowing	−1,250

This income statement shows how the average American allocated income during the year.

The average American consumed $28,100, saved $6,150, and borrowed $1,250 from abroad. Gross investment was equal to $7,400, but only $3,450 represented a net addition to the capital stock. The difference was the result of the $3,950 of gross investment that was used to replace worn-out capital.

Capital Accumulation of the Average American, 1999	
Beginning-of-year real assets	$97,000
Depreciation	−3,950
Gross investment	7,400
End-of-year real assets	100,450

Balance Sheet of the Average American on December 31, 1999		
	Assets	Liabilities
Real Assets	$100,450	
Net debt to foreigners		$7,250
Net worth		93,200
	$100,450	$100,450

This balance sheet represents the net asset position of the average American at the end of 1999. Notice that U.S. capital is greater than in 1998 by the addition of $3,450 net investment. Net worth is less than real assets because part of the capital stock is owned by foreigners.

GROWTH RATES AND PERCENTAGE CHANGES

Many of the variables measured in economics grow larger with time. The capital stock is one example; GDP is another. When a series grows, we measure its growth rate as a percentage change. To compute the percentage change in a series, we take the difference from one year to the next, divide by the level in the previous year, and multiply by 100. If y_t represents GDP in year t and y_{t-1} is GDP in year $t-1$, then the formula to compute a percentage change is given by:

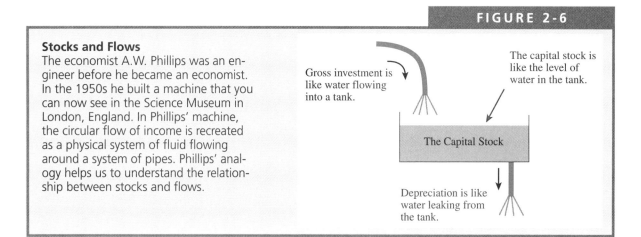

FIGURE 2-6

Stocks and Flows
The economist A.W. Phillips was an engineer before he became an economist. In the 1950s he built a machine that you can now see in the Science Museum in London, England. In Phillips' machine, the circular flow of income is recreated as a physical system of fluid flowing around a system of pipes. Phillips' analogy helps us to understand the relationship between stocks and flows.

Gross investment is like water flowing into a tank.

The capital stock is like the level of water in the tank.

The Capital Stock

Depreciation is like water leaking from the tank.

$$\text{Growth rate of GDP in year } t = \left(\frac{y_t - y_{t-1}}{y_{y-1}} \right) \times 100$$

For example, suppose that in the country of Lilliput real GDP equals $11 billion in 2000 and $10 billion in 1999. Lilliput's GDP growth rate in 2000 was equal to

$$\left(\frac{11 - 10}{10} \right) \times 100 = 10\%.$$

Table 2.6 uses this formula to compute GDP growth rates for the U.S. economy for the years 1996 through 1999.

CONCLUSION

The world economy is a collection of national economies, each of which can be analyzed as open or closed. The domestic economy can be further divided into a public sector; and the private sector can, in turn, be divided into households and firms.

The most important measure of the productive capacity of an economy is GDP, which can be measured in three ways: the income method, the expenditure method, and the value-added method. The GDP of a closed economy is equal to consumption plus investment. In an open economy it equals consumption plus investment plus net exports. GDP, consumption, investment, and net exports are examples of flows—that is, variables that are measured per unit of time. U.S. GDP in 1999 was $34,250 per person, of which 82% was consumed and 22% invested. The extra 4% came from abroad as foreigners chose to invest in the U.S. economy rather than in their own countries.

The wealth of an economy is a stock, a variable measured at a point in time. Wealth consists of real assets and financial assets. A real asset is a tangible commodity, such as land or a machine; a financial asset is a promise by someone to deliver commodities in the future. U.S. national wealth in 1998 was equal to $97,000 per person.

TABLE 2.6

How to Compute Percentage Growth Rates

Year	GDP	Formula	Percentage Growth Rate
1995	7537.1		
1996	7813.2	$(7813.2 - 7537.1)/(7537.1) \times 100 =$	3.7
1997	8165.1	$(8165.1 - 7813.2)/(7813.2) \times 100 =$	4.5
1998	8516.3	$(8516.3 - 8165.1)/(8165.1) \times 100 =$	4.3
1999	8861.0	$(8861.0 - 8516.3)/(8516.3) \times 100 =$	4.0

There are two kinds of investment: gross and net. Gross investment is net investment (additions to capital) plus depreciation (replacement of worn-out capital). Wealth and net investment are related to each other because net investment is an addition to wealth.

KEY TERMS

Budget deficit
Capital goods
Circular flow of income
Consumption goods
Domestic economy
Closed economy
Domestic economy
Domestic expenditure
Expenditure method of computing GDP
Factor services
Final goods
Firms
Household
Income method of computing GDP

Intermediate goods
Investment
Labor income
National Income and Product Accounts (NIPA)
Net exports
Open economy
Private sector
Public sector
Rent
Saving
Trade surplus
Value added
Value-added method

1. Discuss the differences between each of the following sets of concepts:

closed versus *open economy*

public versus *private sector*

government budget deficit versus *government debt*

aggregate income versus *aggregate expenditure* versus *aggregate production*

2. a. What equation defines the expenditure method of calculating GDP? Use this equation to derive the relationship between private saving, public saving, investment, and net exports in an open economy.

b. Given your answer to part (a), what is the most obvious explanation as to why the U.S. has consistently run trade deficits for more than 20 years, with the largest deficits occurring during the mid- to late 1980s?

c. According to your answers in parts (a) and (b), what should have happened to the trade deficit during the late 1990s? Looking at Figure 2.4, what actually happened to the trade deficit? Can you explain why?

3. The following data are for the year 2002:

Private consumption	5,000	Gross investment	1,000
Government budget deficit	200	Government taxes	500
Government transfers	200	Exports	600
Imports	800	2001 capital stock	10,000
Depreciation	200		

a. How much was government spending on goods and services in 2002?

b. Calculate GDP for 2002. What method did you use to calculate GDP?

c. Is this country a net foreign lender or borrower? By how much?

d. What share of GDP was devoted to consumption and what share to investment?

4. Discuss the difference between *stock* and *flow* accounting. Why are both important in order to get an accurate view of the economy?

5. Which of the following concepts are stocks and which are flows?

consumption	transfer payments
gross domestic product	capital
government debt	interest payments on the debt
government budget deficit	net domestic product.

6. The following balance sheets record the wealth of an average citizen of a small country in 2001 and 2002.

2001		2002		Per Capital National Income and Product: 2001:	
Assets	Liabilities	Assets	Liabilities	GDP	$5,000
Capital $10,000		Capital $ ____		Consumption	$2,000
Government Debt $7,000	Net worth $ ____	Government debt $____	Net worth $ ____	Government spending	$1,200

    a. What was the per-capita gross investment in this country in 2001?

    b. Economists have estimated that 10% of capital depreciates each year. What was per-capita net investment in 2001?

    c. What was per-capita net domestic product?

    d. What was the value of the capital stock at the beginning of 2002?

7. The following figures represent gross investment in a small economy during the 1990s. All figures are measured in U.S. dollars. (This nation uses 1990 as the base year for its GDP calculations.)

1995	$1,000
1996	800
1997	1,200
1998	500
1999	900

At the end of 1994, the stock of capital was valued at $5,000. Assuming depreciation of 10% per year, what was the capital stock in 2002?

8. John Brown owns a car worth $20,000 and a bank account worth $2,000. John lent his wife, Joan, $17,000. Joan owns a car worth $11,000 and a piano worth $2,000. Between them, John and Joan own a house worth $100,000 and have a mortgage valued at $90,000. Joan has $1,000 in her bank account and has credit debt of $700. Using this information, prepare balance sheets for John, for Joan, and for the Brown family as a whole. (You may assume that the house and the mortgage are divided equally between Joan and John.)

9. An economy has two firms. Households own all of the labor services and all of the capital, which they rent out to firms. Firm A produces sugar using labor services worth $10 and capital services worth $20. It sells $5 worth of sugar to households and $25 worth of sugar to Firm B, a bakery. The bakery produces cakes worth $80, which it sells directly to households. Households earn $30 in wages from firms A and B combined.

    a. What is the value of GDP in this economy?

    b. What is value added by Firm A?

c. What is value added by Firm B?

d. How much do the households earn in profit from Firms A and B, combined? (Recall that households are the ultimate owners of all firms.)

e. What is the total value of intermediate goods produced in this economy?

10. In 1999, country A's GDP was $200,000, and its population was 1,500. Country B had a GDP of $18,000, and its population was 175.

a. What measure would you use to compare the standards of living between these two countries?

b. Which country has the higher standard of living? Why?

c. If the world consists of only these two countries, what fraction of the world's GDP does each country produce?

11. Using the data in the tables at the back of the book and the growth rate formula, calculate the inflation rate as measured by the GDP price index between 1994 and 1999.

CHAPTER 3

Macroeconomic Facts

Introduction

Unlike many of the natural sciences, experiments cannot be conducted in macroeconomics. Instead, data must be collected by recording observations of variables as they occur. If enough data is collected, we may uncover regular patterns of behavior by averaging observations over many instances of similar events. For example, we could average the unemployment rates and the inflation rates during recessions. Although each recession is different, the average relationship between unemployment and inflation during a set of recorded recessions may display a pattern.

There are two kinds of regularities in economic data: relationships between the growth components in different variables and relationships between the cycles. We differentiate growth from cycles by removing the trend from a variable. Then we use three methods to uncover hidden patterns in the data: linear detrending, flexible detrending, and differencing. The relationship between variables can be described by persistence, which records how closely a variable is related to its own past history, and coherence, which measures how closely two variables are related to each other. The ability to measure persistence and coherence enables us to document the regularities in economic data that economists call the "business cycle."

Once we have learned about the methods used to quantify the relationships between variables, we can more carefully define the way that we measure unemployment and inflation. Keeping unemployment and inflation down is a primary goal of economic policy; understanding what we are measuring is important if we are to grasp the benefits and costs of alternative strategies for controlling them.

TRANSFORMING ECONOMIC DATA

MEASURING VARIABLES

The principal macroeconomic unit of data is a list of the values of a variable at different times—a time series.[1] A time series can measure GDP, unemployment, the interest rate, or the supply of money, for example. Time series go up or down as the economy prospers or falls into recession. Some fluctuate more than others. Some move up when others move down. By learning how time series historically relate to each other, we might be able to predict how these variables will behave in the future. Government directly controls some variables, such as the money supply or government spending, and it may be possible to control these variables in ways that influence others. An example is macroeconomic stabilization policy, which attempts to reduce the fluctuations in unemployment by controlling government spending and interest rates.

Time series are collected by a number of government agencies. Much of the data we will study in this book has been collected by the Commerce Department, which is responsible, among other things, for measuring GDP and its components. The Federal Reserve system publishes time series of industrial production, monetary aggregates, and interest rates, and the Bureau of Labor Statistics publishes data on employment, wages, and other labor market statistics. A good summary of all this information is the *Economic Report of the President,* published by the Council of Economic Advisers every February. You can download the entire contents of the *Economic Report of the President* at **http://www.access.gpo.gov/eop/**.

SEPARATING GROWTH FROM CYCLES

Data are measured at different intervals. Some data are annual (recorded once a year), some are quarterly (recorded every three months), and some are monthly (recorded once a month). There are even some financial data series that are available by the minute, such as the prices of stocks on the New York Stock Exchange. Before economists analyze annual, quarterly, or monthly time series, we typically transform the data in some way to make it more amenable to analysis, such as removing the seasonal part of a time series or removing a trend.[2]

---

1.   We also record observations on many categories of a variable at a point in time; this data is called a "cross-section," for example, the 1999 GDP of every country in the world.

2.   The seasonal component of a time series is the part that goes up and down with the seasons. For example, the money supply goes up at Christmas when people demand more cash for Christmas shopping; GDP goes down in August when many people are on vacation. In this book, we mainly deal with data reported annually, so the issue of removing seasonal fluctuations does not arise. Each number in an annual time series represents a variable for a whole year.

The **trend** in a time series is the **low-frequency component** of the series. The deviation of the series from its trend (the part of the series that moves up and down over the business cycle) is called the **high-frequency component**. Detrending decomposes a time series into the sum of its high- and low-frequency components. The theory of economic growth focuses on what determines the low-frequency movements in economic time series, and the theory of business cycles studies the causes of their high-frequency movements.

REMOVING A TREND

The most common detrending method works by fitting a trend line to a set of points and defining the cycle as the differences between the original series and the trend. Before we fit a trend to economic data, we typically take the logarithm of the original series. The following example explains why.

Suppose that a variable, Y, is growing at a constant, compound rate. **Compound growth** (also called **"exponential growth"**) means that annual increments to the series themselves contribute to growth in subsequent years. Examples include population growth (our children grow up and have children of their own) and compound interest earned on a bank account (the interest on the account itself earns interest). To make the example concrete, think of Y as the value of a bank account that was equal to $1 in 1890 and that earned compound interest of 5% per annum. Variables that grow at a constant rate explode over time because each period the increases are themselves multiplied by the growth rate. The result is a variable that has exponential growth.[3] Figure 3.1 (panel A) illustrates an exponentially growing series and its logarithm. Note that the graph of the logarithm of Y is a straight line.

Many variables in economics have an underlying growth rate that is constant, but they fluctuate randomly around this underlying rate from one year to the next. Suppose, for example, that money is added to the bank account in some years, and in other years money is withdrawn. If deposits and withdrawals are random and equal to zero on average, then the value of the bank account will fluctuate around a trend. Panel B of Figure 3.1 illustrates this idea.

The red line in the bottom panel is the value of the account in dollars, and the blue line is its logarithm. Notice that although Y itself moves up and down around a curve, the logarithm of Y fluctuates around a straight line. Many time series fluctuate in this way. The goal of detrending is to separate the movements in these variables that occur because of an underlying trend growth rate from the movements that occur because of random fluctuations around this trend. Linear detrending accomplishes this task by fitting the best straight line through the graph of the logarithm. The fitted line is called the **linear trend** and the deviations of the log series from the fitted line are called the **linear cycle**. The linear trend is the low-frequency component of the series and the linear cycle is the high-frequency component.

---

3.   Mathematical Note: If a bank account that earns compound interest i was worth Y_t in year t, it would be worth Y_{t+1} in year $t+1$, where $Y_{t+1} = Y_t(1+i)$. Variables like this are said to be growing exponentially because, as the length of a period becomes small, the formula that describes the value of the account is given by Y_t $\exp(it)Y_0$, where Y_0 is the initial amount invested and Y_t is the value of the account at date t.

FIGURE 3.1

How to Construct a Linear Trend

The logarithm of a growing variable is a straight line when plotted against time. The red curve, measured on the left axis, shows the value of a bank account each year from 1890 to 2000 if $1 were invested at 5% interest compounded annually. The blue line shows the **logarithm** of the value of this account.

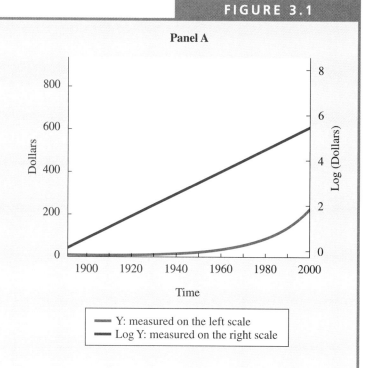

Panel A

Many economic variables have a constant average growth rate, but annual observations fluctuate randomly around this average rate. The red curve is the value of a bank account that pays 5% per year when the owner of the account adds to or subtracts some random amount from the account each year. The blue line shows the value of the logarithm of this account. The green line is the linear trend.

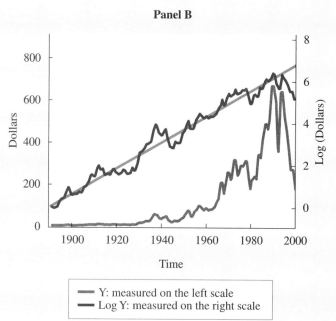

Panel B

DETRENDING METHODS

Although the linear trend is relatively simple to construct, it has the disadvantage that the trend itself is assumed constant. Many economists believe that the trend reflects an underlying growth rate that changes slowly from one decade to the next. These economists prefer to fit a **flexible trend**. Instead of fitting a straight line through the logarithm of a variable, flexible detrending fits a curve.[4] If a series is detrended using the linear method, the series itself may deviate from its underlying growth rate for long periods of time. Linear detrending does not allow these protracted deviations from trend to alter our view of the underlying growth rate. In contrast, flexible detrending interprets protracted deviations from the linear trend as swings in the underlying growth rate.

A third method of revealing the high-frequency relationship between time series is to look at growth rates of data rather than at the raw data itself. This method, called **differencing**, defines the cycle in a variable as the percentage change in the original series. For example, the differenced value for GDP in 1987 is given by the formula

$$DGDP_{1987} = \frac{GDP_{1987} - GDP_{1986}}{GDP_{1986}}$$

where DGDP is the differenced data and the subscript 1987 refers to the year.

THE IMPORTANCE OF DETRENDING

Detrending reveals relationships between time series that exist at one frequency but not at another. Figure 3.2 illustrates this idea by comparing the raw data on unemployment and real GDP with the detrended series. Panel A of this figure plots the raw data series on unemployment and GDP; panel B plots the high-frequency component of GDP against unemployment using linear detrending to detrend the series. The raw series do not appear connected, because at low frequencies unemployment fluctuates around a constant level, whereas GDP has an upward trend. A graph of unemployment against GDP would reveal no particularly striking relationship between them.

Although unemployment and GDP are unrelated at low frequencies, they are quite strongly related at high frequencies. The high-frequency relationship is revealed in panel B of Figure 3.2, which reveals that unemployment and the cycle in real GDP move quite closely together in opposite directions. Only by detrending real GDP could we have uncovered this important economic fact. For this reason, detrending is an important component of the macroeconomist's toolkit.

QUANTIFYING BUSINESS CYCLES

The business cycle is an irregular, persistent fluctuation of real GDP around its trend growth rate that is accompanied by highly coherent co-movements in many other economic

---

4.   One popular flexible detrending method, called the Hodrick-Prescott filter, is commonly used by a group of economists from the real business cycle school. We will learn more about their ideas in Chapter 4.

FIGURE 3.2

High and Low Frequencies Compared

Detrending can uncover relationships between time series that are not apparent in the original series.

Panel A: GDP and Unemployment at Low Frequency

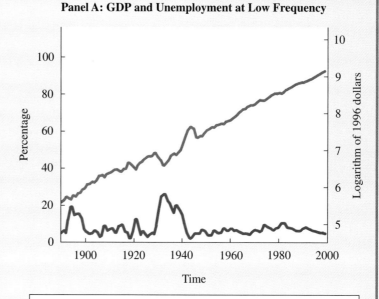

Percentage of the labor force unemployed (left scale)
Logarithm of real GDP in billions of 1996 dollars (right scale)

Panel B: GDP and Unemployment at High Frequency

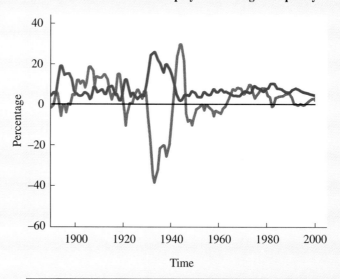

Percentage deviation of real GDP from a linear trend
Percentage of the labor force unemployed (common scale)

FIGURE 3.3

A Stylized Business Cycle

The maximum value of the deviation of GDP from trend over a cycle is called a business cycle peak, and the minimum value is a business cycle trough. The period from peak to trough is called a recession, and the period from trough to peak is an expansion.

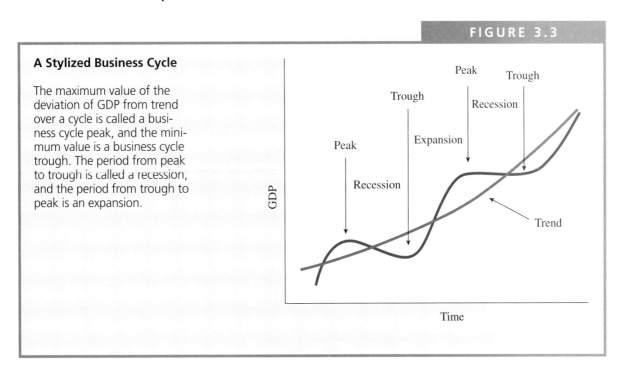

variables. One tool used to describe business cycles is the **correlation coefficient**, which measures the strength of a statistical relationship. The correlation coefficient is used in two ways: to measure the strength of a relationship between two variables and to measure the strength of the relationship between a single variable and its own history. We call the strength of a relationship between two variables their degree of **coherence**. We call the strength of the relationship between a single variable and its history its degree of **persistence**.

PEAKS AND TROUGHS

The common features of business cycles are peaks, troughs, expansions, and recessions. GDP displays a tendency to cycle around a growing trend. A business cycle **peak** is the point at which the growth rate of GDP begins to decline, and a business cycle **trough** is when it starts to increase again. The period between a trough and its subsequent peak is called a business cycle **expansion**, and the period from the peak to the subsequent trough is a **recession**. Figure 3.3 illustrates each of these concepts on a stylized picture of a business cycle.

Real data do not display the kinds of regularities suggested by Figure 3.3. The regularities in economic data are statistical rather than deterministic. No two business cycles are exactly alike, so their regularities must be uncovered by looking at the average behavior of data over many different expansions and contractions. By applying one of the three methods of removing a trend, we can study the average relationships between the high-frequency components of economic time series. Economic theory aims to explain the regularities in these average relationships.

FIGURE 3.4

Positively and Negatively Correlated Variables

Panel A plots the cycle in real GDP against the cycle in total consumption. These points tend to follow a positively sloped line. The correlation coefficient between consumption and GDP is 0.95.

Panel B plots plots the cycle in real GDP against unemployment. These points tend to follow a negatively sloped line. The correlation coefficient is −0.87.

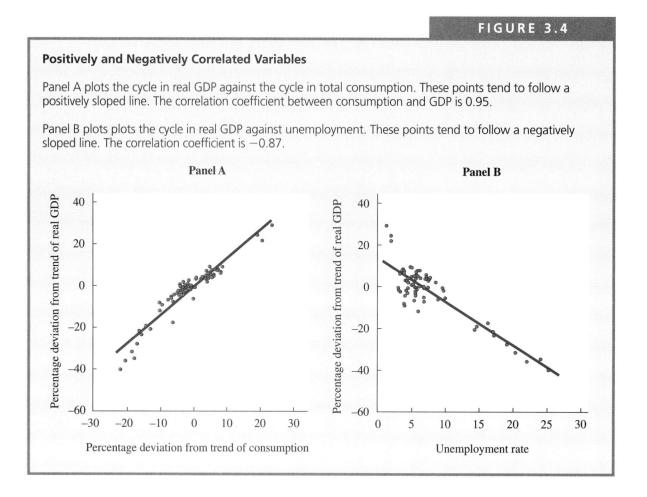

THE CORRELATION COEFFICIENT

Economic data are not perfectly regular, and we can model this by employing equations that contain random elements. These random elements might be caused by our inability to properly measure the variables studied, or they might reflect our inability to capture the world's true complexity.

In either case, an equation that links two variables will contain a random term that will be positive in some years and negative in others. When we plot one variable against another on a graph, the random elements that we are unable to account for will show up as discrepancies between the observations plotted and the true relationship measured. When these random elements are strong, two time series that are theoretically linked may in practice seem to be unrelated to each other. When these random elements are weak, the relationship between the two time series will show up clearly in a graph. One way of measuring the strength of the linear relationship between two variables is to plot a graph on which each point represents a particular year, and to see how closely the points on the graph follow a straight line.[5] A graph in which each point represents an observation from two different variables at a given time is called a **scatter plot**.

Statisticians have developed a way of quantifying the relationship between two variables in a scatter plot with a single number, called the "correlation coefficient."[6] It measures how closely a scatter plot lies to a straight line. The symbol used to represent the correlation coefficient is ρ_{xy}. Figure 3.4 illustrates the use of the correlation coefficient to measure the strength of the relationship between two sets of variables—consumption and real GDP, and unemployment and real GDP. The deviations from trend of consumption and real GDP are positively correlated, whereas the deviations from trend in unemployment and real GDP are negatively correlated. Notice that the cycles in consumption and GDP follow a positively sloped straight line. Not every point is exactly on the line, but the line itself represents a good approximation of the relationship between the two variables. Unemployment and GDP, on the other hand, follow a negatively sloped straight line.

PERSISTENCE

You frequently read in the newspapers that GDP is forecast to increase by 1.3% next month, or that unemployment is going to go down by 3 points. You may wonder where these numbers come from and if you should have any faith in them. Persistence means that if we plot the value of the deviation of GDP from trend in one year against its own value in the previous year, these deviations from trend follow a straight line. Figure 3.5 constructs this plot for real GDP. If the data tends to closely follow a straight line, this means that if we know the value of GDP at date t (where t is a number that indexes the year), then we will be able to accurately predict what it will be equal to at date $t + 1$ (a number that indexes the subsequent year). The best forecast of GDP predicts that the deviation next year of GDP from trend will be equal to the point that follows the straightest line through the scatter of past points. This forecast will not be 100% accurate, because the points do not exactly follow a straight line; but the closer the points are to a straight line, the more accurate is the forecast.

There is a simple, quantitative way of measuring how accurate our forecasts are likely to be. By looking at the correlation coefficient between a variable and its past values, we can quantify what we mean by persistence. If the correlation coefficient is close to $+1$, then a big deviation from trend will persist for a long time; if it is close to zero, the series will

---

5.   A linear relationship between two variables, x and y, can be expressed by an equation: $y = a + bx$, where b represents the slope of a graph of y against x, and a is the intercept with the y-axis. Although there is no reason to believe that all economic relationships are linear, in practice, most applied work uses a linear equation as a first approximation.

6.   The correlation coefficient is defined by the formula

$$\rho_{xy} = \frac{\sum_{i=1}^{n}\left(x_i - \bar{x}\right)\left(y_i - \bar{y}\right)}{\sqrt{\sum_{i=1}^{n}\left(x_i - \bar{x}\right)^2} \cdot \sqrt{\sum_{i=1}^{n}\left(y_i - y\right)^2}}$$

where a bar over a variable denotes its arithmetic mean.

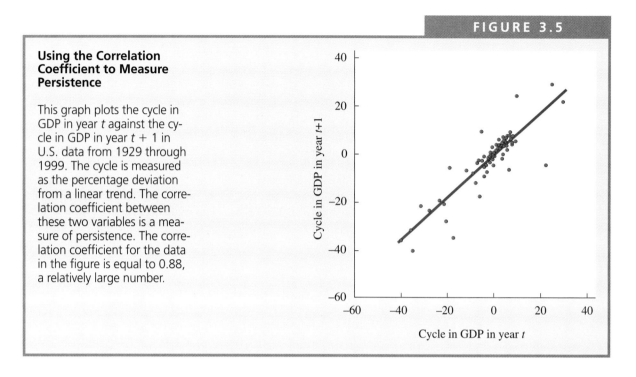

FIGURE 3.5

Using the Correlation Coefficient to Measure Persistence

This graph plots the cycle in GDP in year *t* against the cycle in GDP in year *t* + 1 in U.S. data from 1929 through 1999. The cycle is measured as the percentage deviation from a linear trend. The correlation coefficient between these two variables is a measure of persistence. The correlation coefficient for the data in the figure is equal to 0.88, a relatively large number.

quickly return to trend. The correlation coefficient for the data in Figure 3.5 is equal to 0.88, which is a relatively large number. Data that shows no persistence would have a correlation coefficient with its own past of zero.[7] Modern economic forecasting models exploit the tendency of economic data to display persistence, so the fact that many economic time series display a high degree of persistence accounts for the success of economic forecasters over relatively short forecast horizons. Box 3.1 illustrates the use of the correlation coefficient to measure the strength of the relationships between several different time series.

COHERENCE

A second important feature of economic time series is that they tend to move together; this tendency is called "coherence." Economists classify time series according to whether they move in the same direction or the opposite direction to GDP. If a time series goes up when GDP goes up (and down when it goes down), we say the series is procyclical. A series that moves in the opposite direction to GDP is countercyclical.

Consumption and investment are examples of procyclical time series variables; other time series variables are countercyclical, such as unemployment. Just as we used the cor-

---

7.   The technical term for persistence is "autocorrelation." If a time series is (strongly) correlated with its own past values, we say that it is (strongly) autocorrelated.

BOX 3.1

A CLOSER LOOK
The Sign of ρ

When a scatter of points tends to follow a positively sloped straight line, the correlation coefficient is a positive number; when they tend to follow a negatively sloped straight line, it is a negative number.

The points in Panel A tend to follow a line with a positive slope. In this example, the correlation coefficient is a positive number between 0 and +1.

The points in Panel B tend to follow a line with a negative slope. In this example, the correlation coefficient is a negative number between 0 and −1.

The points in Panel C do not seem to have any strong relationship with each other. In this example, the correlation coefficient is equal to 0.

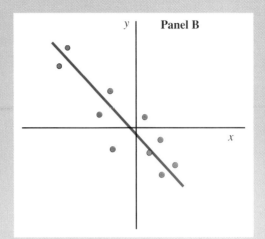

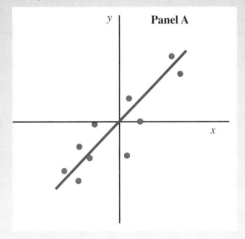

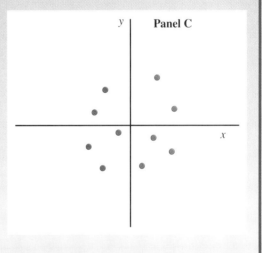

relation coefficient between GDP and its own past values to measure persistence, so can we use the correlation coefficient between two time series to measure coherence. If two time series move very closely together in the same direction, they have a correlation coefficient that is close to +1. In this case, we say that they display high positive coherence. If two time series move very similarly but in opposite directions, they have a correlation coefficient that is close to −1, and we say that they display high negative coherence.

Although coherence can be used to define the degree in which any two series are related, we use GDP as a reference series to define the ups and downs of the business cycle.

BOX 3.1 *(continued)*

A CLOSER LOOK
The Magnitude of ρ

The magnitude of the correlation coefficient measures the strength of the linear relationship among the points in a scatter diagram. The closer the points follow a line, the closer is ρ to +1.

The points in panel A lie exactly on a positively sloped straight line. In this example, the correlation coefficient is equal to +1.

The points in Panel B tend to closely follow a positively sloped straight line, but the relationship is not exact. In this case, the correlation coefficient equals +0.9.

The points in Panel C also follow a positively sloped straight line, but the relationship is not as strong as in Panels A and B. In this case, the correlation coefficient equals +0.5.

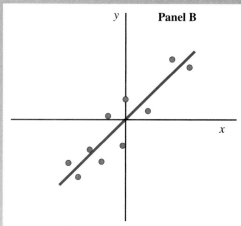

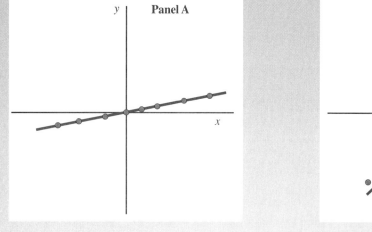

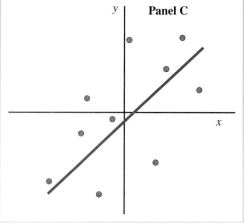

Although many of the time series studied are either highly procyclical or highly counter-cyclical, other series do not display strong co-movements in either direction. Table 3.1 summarizes the ways that the correlation coefficient is used to catalog the behavior of time series over business cycles.

    To summarize, (any) two time series are coherent if their scatter plots follow a straight line. The degree of coherence is measured by the absolute value of a single number—the correlation coefficient.[8] If the points in the diagram cluster very closely to a straight line

---

8.   Mathematical Note: The absolute value of a number is its magnitude, regardless of its sign. For example, +7 has the same absolute value as −7.

TABLE 3.1

Coherence and Business Cycles

The absolute value of the correlation coefficient between two arbitrary time series measures their degree of coherence.		Correlation Coefficient	Degree of Coherence is Measured by	Scatter Plot
	$\rho_{XY} > 0$ X and Y are two arbitrary time series.	$+\rho_{XY}$	If X and Y are positively correlated	Slope is positive
	$\rho_{XY} < 0$	$-\rho_{XY}$	If X and Y are negatively correlated	Slope is negative

When a time series has a positive correlation coefficient with the cycle in GDP it is *procyclical.* When it has a negative correlation coefficient with the cycle in GDP it is *countercyclical.*	Correlation Coefficient	Meaning	Scatter Plot
	X is GDP and Y is some other time series. $\rho_{XY} > 0$	Y is procyclical	Slope is positive
	$\rho_{XY} < 0$	Y is countercyclical	Slope is negative

with a positive slope, the correlation coefficient is very close to $+1$; if they very closely follow a line with a negative slope, the correlation coefficient is very close to -1. When a series has a high correlation coefficient with its history, we say that it is persistent. A time series with a positive GDP correlation coefficient is procyclical; one with a negative GDP correlation coefficient is countercyclical.

MEASURING UNEMPLOYMENT

The unemployment rate, as an indicator of economic activity, is highly correlated with the high-frequency movements in GDP. To understand how unemployment is measured, we will introduce two new concepts: the labor force and the labor force participation rate.

PARTICIPATION AND THE LABOR FORCE

The Bureau of Labor Statistics, the agency responsible for collecting employment data, recognizes one of three situations: A person is either employed, unemployed, or out of the labor force. People who are working or looking for work are part of the **labor force**. People who are not employed or who are not looking for a job are out of the labor force. They may be

WEBWATCH

You Can Find the Economic Report of the President at http://www.access.gpo.gov/eop/

The Economic Report of the President is produced by the Council of Economic Advisors and is transmitted to Congress every February. It contains the assessment of the Council on the state of the U.S. economy. You can order a copy from the Government Printing Office in Washington D.C., or you can access the entire document electronically.

This was the homepage for the Council of Economic Advisors on September 1, 2000. From this site you can download an enormous number of historical time series on macroeconomic variables both in Adobe Acrobat Reader (.pdf) form and in spreadsheet form.

EXERCISE

Use your browser to download, in spreadsheet form, data for table B-42 in the *Economic Report of the President,* 2000. Print out the table. How many people were unemployed in December of 1999? How many of these people left their jobs voluntarily? (These are called job leavers.) What percentage of the unemployed had been unemployed for 27 weeks or more? What percentage had been unemployed for less than five weeks?

The Executive Office of the President

Council of Economic Advisers

ECONOMIC REPORT OF THE PRESIDENT

Transmitted to the Congress | February 2000

∑ Economic Report of the President (PDF, size: 5 MB)

You can **download** the entire report from **previous years** in PDF format (1995-forward) as well as access the statistical tables from Appendix B as spreadsheet files (1997-forward) by clicking here.

To download **current year** statistical tables in spreadsheet format click here.

∑ Changing America -- Indicators of Social and Economic Well-Being by Race and Hispanic Origin

TABLE B–42.—*Unemployment by duration and reason, 1950–99*
[Thousands of persons, except as noted; monthly data seasonally adjusted[1]]

Year or month	Unemployment	Duration of unemployment						Reason for unemployment					
		Less than 5 weeks	5–14 weeks	15–26 weeks	27 weeks and over	Average (mean) duration (weeks)	Median duration (weeks)	Job losers[3]			Job leavers	Re-entrants	New entrants
								Total	On layoff	Other			
1988	6,701	3,084	2,007	801	809	13.5	5.9	3,092	851	2,241	983	1,809	816
1989	6,528	3,174	1,978	730	646	11.9	4.8	2,983	850	2,133	1,024	1,843	677
1990	7,047	3,265	2,257	822	703	12.0	5.3	3,387	1,028	2,359	1,041	1,930	688
1991	8,628	3,480	2,791	1,246	1,111	13.7	6.8	4,694	1,292	3,402	1,004	2,139	792
1992	9,613	3,376	2,830	1,453	1,954	17.7	8.7	5,389	1,260	4,129	1,002	2,285	937
1993	8,940	3,262	2,584	1,297	1,798	18.0	8.3	4,848	1,115	3,733	976	2,198	919
1994	7,996	2,728	2,408	1,237	1,623	18.8	9.2	3,815	977	2,838	791	2,786	60
1995	7,404	2,700	2,342	1,085	1,278	16.6	8.3	3,476	1,030	2,446	824	2,525	579
1996	7,236	2,633	2,287	1,053	1,262	16.7	8.3	3,370	1,021	2,349	774	2,512	580
1997	6,739	2,538	2,138	995	1,067	15.8	8.0	3,037	931	2,106	795	2,338	569
1998	6,210	2,622	1,950	763	875	14.5	6.7	2,822	866	1,957	734	2,132	520
1999	5,880	2,568	1,832	755	725	13.4	6.4	2,622	848	1,774	783	2,005	469

BOX 3.2

FOCUS ON THE FACTS
Labor Force Participation Since 1950

Panel A shows an upward trend in the unemployment rate from 1950 to 1980. Since 1980, the trend in the unemployment rate has been downward.

Panel B shows that the employment rate has been rising since 1950. Its rate of growth has been higher since 1980 than before 1980.

Panel C shows that the participation rate has been increasing at a constant rate since 1950.

There is an active debate in the macroeconomics community about whether the unemployment rate, as opposed to the employment rate, is the more interesting variable to try to understand. The difference between the employment rate and the unemployment rate would not matter very much if the two measures of activity in the labor market always moved in opposite directions. But as A through C show, unemployment and employment can move independently of each other. The reason why these two series can both move in the same direction, as they did before 1980, is that the unemployment rate is defined as the percentage of the labor force who are looking for work but are not currently employed, whereas the employment rate is the percentage of the population who are employed. Since 1945, the labor force has increased substantially, mainly as a result of an increase in participation by women.

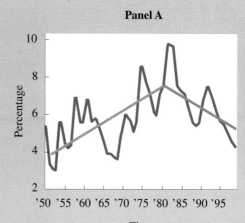

Panel A

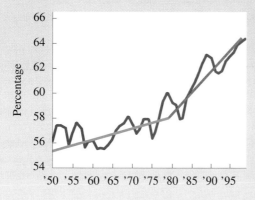

Panel B

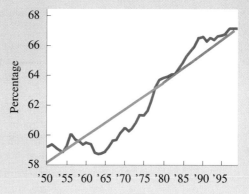

Panel C

retired; they may be performing unpaid work in the home, such as housekeeping or child rearing; or they may be wealthy enough that they do not need to work to support themselves.

The labor force expressed as a percentage of the civilian population over the age of 16 is called the **labor force participation rate**. In 1999, the labor force consisted of approximately 139 million people out of a civilian adult population of roughly 208 million people. The participation rate for 1999 was equal to 139/208, or 67.1%. The participation rate is an important economic variable, because one of the major ways in which families vary the number of hours they supply to the market is by deciding how many members of the household will participate. As an exercise, point your browser to http://www.access.gpo.gov/eop, where you will find the *Economic Report of the President*. Find the table where the data on labor force participation is reported. What was the unemployment rate in 1998? What was the participation rate?

EMPLOYMENT AND UNEMPLOYMENT

There are two important measures of labor market activity: the **employment rate** and the **unemployment rate**. The employment rate is the fraction of the population employed. The unemployment rate is the fraction of the labor force looking for a job. Box 3.2 shows that the employment rate trended up since 1950. And since 1980, the growth of employment trend rate has been greater than before 1980. From 1950 to 1980, the unemployment rate also drifted upward, but since 1980 the trend has been down. The employment rate and the unemployment rate can move independently of each other because employment is the ratio of employed people to the population, whereas unemployment is the ratio of the unemployed to the labor force. The labor force changes over time as a result of changes in participation; there are more people in the labor force now than in the 1950s, mainly as a result of increasing numbers of women finding paid employment outside the home.

Of the 139 million people in the labor force in 1999, 4.2% were unemployed (see Table 3.2). Unemployed people are, by definition, searching for a job. Some may be temporarily between jobs, but some have been unemployed for very long periods of time. This is particularly true in Europe, where unemployment insurance programs are more generous than in the United States. In 1989, only 13% of unemployed Americans had been searching for a job for 12 months or longer. In Germany the comparable figure was 40%, in the United Kingdom 47%, and in Italy 58%.[9] In other words, over half of the unemployed in Italy had been looking for a job for more than a year!

Some economists focus on the unemployment rate in their models of economic activity; others focus on the employment rate. The main difference between these two measures of labor market activity is that employment varies when the participation rate changes but the unemployment rate need not.

MEASURING GDP GROWTH

Traditionally, real GDP was measured by the base-year method. This values all of the goods and services produced in a year at the prices that prevailed in a fixed base year. Re-

---

9.   Data is from Employment Outlook, Organisation for Economic Cooperation and Development (OECD), 1991.

TABLE 3.2

Employment Statistics

	Definition	Number of People (in thousands)	% of Population	% of Labor Force
Civilian Adult Population	Everyone in the United States over 16 and not institutionalized or in the armed forces.	207,753	100.0%	149.1%
Employed	Everyone who worked full-time during the past week or was on sick leave or vacation.	133,492	64.2% (employment rate)	95.8%
Unemployed	Everyone who did not work in the previous week but looked for work during the past four weeks.	5,876	2.8%	4.2% (unemployment rate)
Civilian Labor Force	Employed plus unemployed.	139,368	67.1% (participation rate)	100.0%
Out of the Labor Force	Everyone who did not work during the previous week and did not look for work during the previous four weeks.	68,385	32.9%	49.1%

From *Economic Report of the President,* Government Printing Office. All figures are monthly averages for 1999.

cently, however, the Commerce Department has switched to the chain weighted method as an alternative. To see why, consider Table 3.3, which records the total output of the fictitious Econoland for the four years from 1999 through 2002.

Econoland produces two commodities, potato chips and computers. As in the U.S. economy, Econoland has been producing more computers at lower prices. To arrive at nominal GDP in a given year, recall that we add up the values of all goods and services produced. Real and nominal GDP figures for Econoland, using base-year prices for 1999, 2000, 2001, and 2002 are given in Table 3.3, panel B.

The following example shows how to compute real GDP using the fixed base-year method. This method, which was used in the United States until 1996, works by choosing a set of base-year prices at which to value all goods and services.[10] In the base year, real and

---

10. In practice, the base was occasionally switched, and when this occurred the Commerce Department would publish new sets of estimates. The last time that GDP was constructed using the fixed base method, the weights were from 1987, although the method was in place until 1996 when the current chain weighting method was adopted.

W E B W A T C H

Visit the Bureau of Labor Statistics at http://www.stats.bls.gov

This is the home page for the Bureau of Labor Statistics (BLS). Here you will find both national and regional data on all aspects of the labor market. There are articles and reviews, news and information, as well as historical and contemporary statistics.

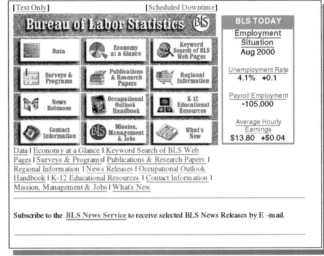

The Bureau of Labor Statistics is an agency within the U.S. Department of Labor.

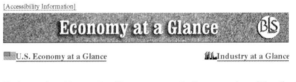

This is an example of the regional data available at The BLS site. By clicking on any state, you will be able to obtain employment data by region.

EXERCISE

Point your browser to http://www.stats.bls.gov/eag/eag.map.htm. What was the unemployment rate in the most recent month available for the state in which you live? How does this compare with the regional average? How does it compare with the national average? Which state has the highest unemployment rate?

TABLE 3.3

GDP and Growth in Econoland

Panel A: Production and Prices

	Potato Chips (by bag)		Computers (by unit)	
Year	Number Produced	Price	Number Produced	Price
1999	10,000	$2.00	1	$10,000.00
2000	11,000	2.50	2	5,000.00
2001	12,000	3.00	4	2,500.00
2002	13,000	3.50	8	1,250.00

Panel B: Real GDP Measured by Base-Year Method

Real GDP in Thousands of Dollars	1999 Prices	2000 Prices	2001 Prices	2002 Prices
1999	30.00	30.00	32.50	36.25
2000	42.00	37.50	38.00	41.00
2001	64.00	50.00	46.00	47.00
2002	106.00	72.50	59.00	55.50

Panel C: Different Measures of Real GDP Growth (Percentage Change)

Period	1999 Prices	2000 Prices	2001 Prices	2002 Prices	Chain weighted measure
1999-2000	**40.00**	**25.00**	16.90	13.10	32.50
2000-2001	52.40	**33.30**	**21.10**	14.60	27.20
2001-2002	65.60	45.00	**28.30**	**18.10**	23.20
Three-year average	52.70	34.40	22.10	15.30	27.60

nominal GDP are always equal, since they value the final commodities produced in that year using the same prices. This implies that we can read nominal GDP from the diagonal entries of panel B. In 1999, nominal GDP was equal to $30,000, since the Econoland economy produced 10,000 bags of potato chips at $2.00 per bag (worth $20,000.00) and one computer (worth $10,000.00). Nominal GDP is the sum of these two numbers.

Using 2002 as a base year, we can compute real GDP for 1999. This is found by adding up the values of the goods produced in 1999 valued at 2002 prices. In 2002, Econoland produced 10,000 bags of potato chips worth $3.50 per bag (a total value of $35,000.00) and one computer worth $1,250.00. Real GDP in 1999 valued at 2002 prices was equal to $36,250.00

Panel C gives estimates of real GDP growth obtained for each of the four possible sets of weights and an alternative chain weighted estimate. To compute the growth in real GDP between 1999 and 2000 using 2002 as the base year, we calculate the percentage increase in real GDP between 1999 and 2000. Real GDP increased from $36,250 to $41,000. Using the formula for percentage increase, the growth rate was equal to:

$$\text{Growth from 1999 to 2000} = \left(\frac{41{,}000 - 36{,}250}{36{,}250} \right) \times 100 = 13.1\%$$

Notice from the final row of panel C that the average three-year growth rate of real GDP was 52.7% using 1999 prices but only 15.3% using 2002 prices. This tremendous divergence arises because the relative prices and quantities of potato chips and computers have been changing dramatically during this period in Econoland, just as the relative importance of computers and noncomputer goods has been changing in the United States. Econoland growth is enormous if 1999 prices are used, since in 1999 computers were very expensive. But in 2002, computers are relatively cheap, and even though computer production increased eightfold in four years, growth did not increase as dramatically when using 2002 as the base year; it is the relative price of a commodity that determines its weight in the GDP index.

As a compromise solution to the differences in growth rates that occur when using different base years, in 1996 the Commerce Department adopted a chain weighting method to compute GDP growth. Using this method, the growth rate of GDP between years 2001 and 2002 must be calculated twice. First, the year 2001 is taken as the base year and real GDP for 2001 and 2002 is computed. Using this calculation, real GDP grew by 28.3% between 2001 and 2002. Next, take 2002 as the base year and recompute real GDP growth between 2001 and 2002. This calculation yields real GDP growth of 18.1%. Now, take the average of the two growth rates to come up with a chain weighted GDP growth rate of 23.2%. In Table 3.3, panel C, the bold figures in each row are averaged to give the chain weighted growth rates in the final column of the table.[11]

FROM GDP GROWTH TO GDP

We have learned how the chain weighting method is used to construct an index of growth. How about GDP itself? To construct an index of real GDP, the Commerce Department picks an arbitrary year as the base, currently 1996, and they let real GDP in 1996 be 100.

---

11. This section draws on the article, "Chain-weighting: The New Approach to Measuring GDP" by Charles Steindel of the Federal Reserve Bank of New York. Steindel's very readable article was published in *Current Issues in Economics and Finance,* Vol. 1, no. 9, published by the Federal Reserve Bank of New York in December 1995. It is available at **http://www.ny.frb.org**, search for "Steindel." We have also reproduced Table 3.3 from Steindel's article, although the years have been altered.

Real GDP in 1997 is equal to 100 plus the percentage real GDP growth from 1996 to 1997 using the chain weighted method to compute real GDP growth. Similarly, real GDP in 1998 is equal to real GDP in 1997 multiplied by 1 plus the real GDP growth rate from 1997 to 1998.

Although the chain weighting method still uses a base year, this choice is irrelevant since the ratio of real GDP in one year to real GDP in any other year is independent of the choice of the base. This is very different from the old method of GDP accounting in which a change of base year could change the Commerce Department estimates of the real GDP growth rate because it altered the prices that were used to weight quantities in the construction of the index.

Measuring Inflation

Inflation is the average rate of change of the price level, and since there are several different ways of measuring a price index, there are also several corresponding ways to measure inflation. In Chapter 1, we mentioned five measures of the price level: the consumer price index, the producer price index, the GDP deflator, the GDP price index, and the PCE price index. There are different measures of the price level because the economy produces a variety of goods, and the relative prices of different goods change from one year to the next. A price index is an attempt to capture the average value of a large number of commodities measured in units of money. By attaching more or less importance to one commodity or another in the averaging process, we arrive at different measures of the average price.

The importance of a commodity in the construction of a price index is measured by its weight. A price index is a weighted average of the prices of many different commodities, where weights are constants that are multiplied by each price and that sum to one. For example, if an economy produces apples, oranges, and bananas, a price index could be constructed by taking one-third the price of apples plus one-third the price of oranges plus one-third the price of bananas. In this case, the weight attached to each commodity would be one-third. Alternatively, we might have noticed that consumers eat more apples than oranges, and therefore give more weight to apples in our construction of an index; in this case we could set the weight on apples equal to one-half and the weight on bananas and oranges equal to one-quarter. Different price indices are constructed by averaging the values of different bundles of commodities and by using different weights.

Different Kinds of Price Indices

There are three alternative kinds of price indices: Laspeyres, Paasche, and Superlative (see Box 3.3), and recently there was a major debate over which index to use when measuring changes in the average household's cost of living. The CPI, the PPI, and the GDP deflator are all Laspeyres indices; of these, the CPI has been the benchmark measure of inflation since World War I. The GDP price index and the personal consumer expenditure (PCE) price index are Superlative indices. Because a Laspeyres index uses historical weights, it tends to overstate the importance of inflation. Overstatement of inflation occurs because

A CLOSER LOOK
Which Price Index Should We Use To Measure Inflation?

For many purposes, it is important to properly measure increases in a representative household's cost of living. For example, the government indexes pensions to inflation, and many wage contracts are also index-linked. What is a good way to measure inflation?

Laspeyres, Paasche or Superlative?

Economic theory offers three alternative types of price indices; Laspeyres indices, Paasche indices and Superlative indices. A Laspeyres index measures the current cost, relative to the past cost, of a given bundle of goods consumed at some time in the past. A Paasche index measures the current cost relative to the past cost of the currently consumed bundle of goods and services. These two indices differ according to whether the prices of different goods are weighted according to their importance in the household budget before the price changes occurred or after they occurred.

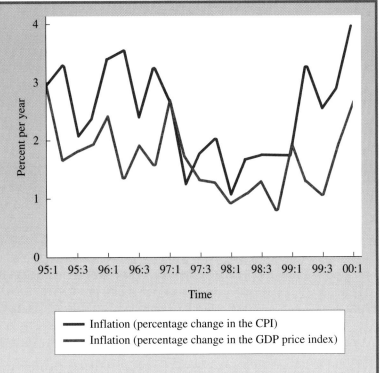

A Laspeyres index tends to overstate inflation because when prices increase, consumers are able to substitute cheaper for more expensive items. For the same reason, a Paasche index tends to understate inflation. A superlative index solves this problem by taking the geometric average of the corresponding Laspeyres and Paasche indices for two adjacent years. The GDP price index and the PCE price index are superlative indices.

The CPI, a Laspeyres price index, is widely used to adjust contracts for cost-of-living increases. The GDP price index, a superlative price index, is an alternative. Notice that in most years, inflation as measured by the CPI has exceeded inflation as measured by the GDP price index, often by as much as a percentage point.

Point your browser to the article "Are there Good Alternatives to the CPI" by Charles Steindel, Senior Vice President of the Federal Reserve Bank of New York. You will find it at **http://www.ny.frb.org/**, search for Steindel. Download and read the article. Using the information in the article, write a short essay to answer the question: Should we replace the CPI with the PCE? If not, why?

consumers adjust their spending habits more rapidly than the CPI updates the basket of goods that it uses to measure inflation. Consumer habits change from month to month, but the CPI updates its basket of commodities every 10 years. In the past two decades, the mix of goods purchased by the average household has dramatically changed as new technology rendered old practices obsolete. Microwave ovens and personal computers were unheard of 30 years ago, but now they are common items in the budgets of most middle-class Americans.

WHY IS IT IMPORTANT TO ACCURATELY MEASURE INFLATION?

When inflation began to occur on a regular basis in the 1970s, people started to index their financial contracts to the Consumer Price Index. Many wage agreements, for example, include automatic pay increases if the CPI goes up, and almost a third of federal spending, mainly in the form of retirement programs, is directly indexed to the CPI. Changes in the CPI also affect federal revenues because income tax brackets are indexed. The indexing of inflation critically demands accurate figures because a 1% point increase in the CPI can change the budget deficit by as much as $6.5 billion.

To assess the importance of the problem, the Senate Finance Committee commissioned five economists, led by Michael Boskin of Stanford University, to study the issue. They concluded in their report that the CPI has recently overstated the true increase in the cost of living by 1.5%.[12] They also projected that bias forward and concluded that the CPI could overstate inflation by as much as 2% in coming years. Even using the more conservative estimate of a 1% bias, correcting this would reduce projected inflation from 3% per year to 2% per year. Because the CPI is used to decide how much to pay in pensions and how much to alter tax brackets from one year to the next, the effect of this correction could have a substantial impact on our lives.

THE CPI AND THE PPI

The CPI, compiled by the Bureau of Labor Statistics, is the index most commonly used to measure inflation. It is a monthly measure released three weeks after the referring month. The procedures used to collect individual prices that make up the CPI are very sophisticated, but there are still problems with the index. For example, it fails to properly account for quality changes in individual items, and it does not properly account for the recent increase in sales by volume retailers. Its greatest shortcoming, however, is that the CPI overstates inflation because it uses a historical set of weights that is infrequently updated.

The PPI, like the CPI, is compiled monthly. It differs from the CPI in the bundle of goods that is used to compute the index. Whereas the CPI tries to measure the average cost of living of a representative household, the PPI measures the average cost of the inputs of a representative producer. Many economists watch the PPI closely, since price increases that occur in the PPI often eventually end up in the CPI. Time series that have this property are said to be **leading indicators**, and the PPI is a leading indicator of inflation.

THE GDP DEFLATOR AND THE GDP PRICE INDEX

Corresponding to the Commerce Department's switch from a base-year to a chain weighted measure of growth, there has been a switch from the GDP deflator to the GDP price index as a general index of prices. This index is computed like the chain weighted estimate of GDP. When relative prices are changing, like the relative prices of computers

---

12. Advisory Commission to Study the Consumer Price Index. "Towards a More Accurate Measure of the Cost of Living," Washington, DC GPO, September 1997. The full report is available at **http://www.ssa.gov/history/reports/boskinrpt.html**.

and potato chips in Table 3.3, changing the base year by which real GDP is computed can have a big impact on the inflation figures that are generated by the GDP deflator. For example, computing the GDP deflator for Table 3.3 yields a value of roughly 10% inflation from 1999 to 2000 using 2002 as the base year, but it yields a deflation of about the same magnitude using 1999 as the base year. The reason for this big difference is that the price of potato chips has been increasing but computer prices have been falling. The 1999 index puts a heavy weight on computers because in 1999 they were very expensive items. The 2002 index puts a much lower weight on computers because by 2002 their average price had come down. This artificial example is stark, but something very similar has been happening in the U.S. economy over the past 40 years.

To resolve the issue of different inflation measures from different base years, the Commerce Department now publishes the GDP price index, which measures inflation in the same way that the chain weighted GDP method measures growth. For any given pair of years, inflation is measured as the average of the percentage change in the price indices obtained from using adjacent years as the base.

THE PCE PRICE INDEX

An alternative to the CPI is the PCE (personal consumer expenditure) price index. Like the GDP price index, the PCE is a Superlative index. Like the CPI, the goods included in the PCE are household consumption items. Whereas the GDP price index includes items like steel mills and automobile plants, the PCE includes only those commodities that represent personal consumption expenditures by households. The PCE has some advantages over the CPI, but it also has its own problems. One disadvantage is that as a Superlative index, the PCE price index is computed by taking the weighted average of indices that use base years on either side of the period for which one would like to compute inflation. This means that it can only be computed after data has been compiled for future periods. Since a contemporaneous index of inflation is required in order to adjust nominal contracts, the PCE would have to be estimated if it were to be used as a replacement to the CPI.

INFLATION AND THE BUSINESS CYCLE

Recall that a variable is procyclical if it is positively correlated with GDP and countercyclical if it is negatively correlated. Many time series are strongly procyclical (e.g., consumption) or strongly countercyclical (e.g., unemployment). Inflation is an exception to this rule. Figure 3.6 presents the data on inflation and GDP growth for the years 1890 through 2000. Notice that inflation over the century is neither procyclical nor countercyclical; its coherence with GDP is only 0.03, a number that is not significantly different from zero.[13]

---

13. Significance is a well-defined statistical concept. To say that the correlation coefficient is not significantly different from zero means that there is so much variation in the recorded observations that we can have no confidence in the statement either that ρ_{XY} is positive or that it is negative.

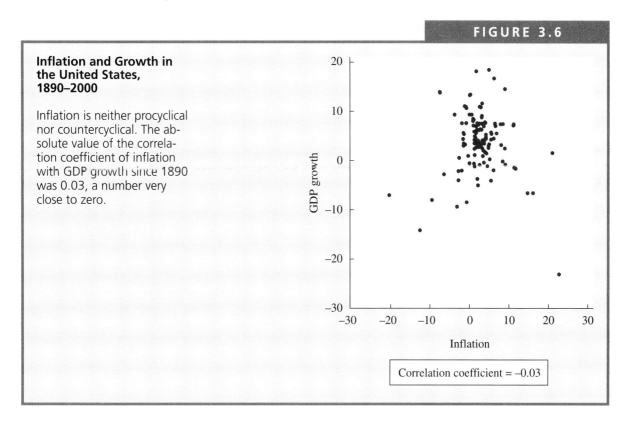

FIGURE 3.6

Inflation and Growth in the United States, 1890–2000

Inflation is neither procyclical nor countercyclical. The absolute value of the correlation coefficient of inflation with GDP growth since 1890 was 0.03, a number very close to zero.

Correlation coefficient = –0.03

Although inflation has been weakly correlated with GDP over the century, there have been periods in history when the price level has been either strongly procyclical or strongly countercyclical. Figure 3.7 illustrates this point by isolating two historical episodes. The left-hand side of the figure shows how inflation was associated with growth during the period from 1920 through 1940. This period included the Great Depression, and the behavior of prices during the Depression led John Maynard Keynes to predict that inflation would be procyclical.

However, procyclical movements in prices have not been characteristic of more recent experience. Real business cycle theory sees the Depression as an unusual event, remarkable for its differences rather than its similarities with other, more typical episodes of business cycles. Real business cycle theorists assert that most business fluctuations occur as a result of changes in productivity, and their theories predict that inflation should be countercyclical, as reflected by postwar data. They point to the two largest postwar recessions, which were triggered by increases in the world price of oil in 1973 and again in 1979.[14] If inflation moves sometimes procyclically and sometimes countercyclically,

14.   Thomas F. Cooley and Lee Ohanian. "The Cyclical Behavior of Prices," *Journal of Monetary Economics,* Vol. 3, no. 105, pp 439–472.

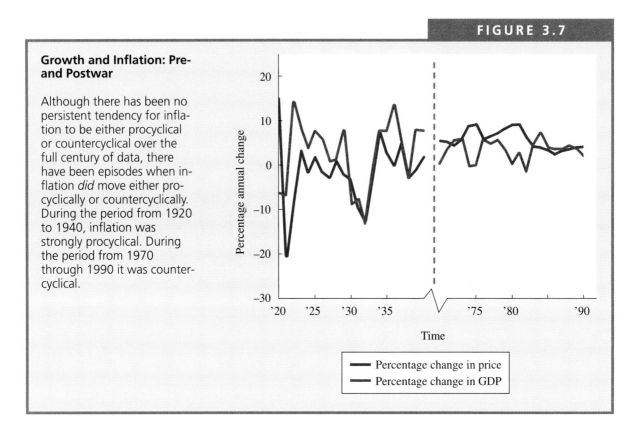

FIGURE 3.7

Growth and Inflation: Pre- and Postwar

Although there has been no persistent tendency for inflation to be either procyclical or countercyclical over the full century of data, there have been episodes when inflation *did* move either procyclically or countercyclically. During the period from 1920 to 1940, inflation was strongly procyclical. During the period from 1970 through 1990 it was countercyclical.

perhaps some recessions are caused by the factors isolated by Keynes and some are caused by supply shocks.

CONCLUSION

Economic data are recorded using time series. To analyze time series, we split them into a low-frequency component (the trend) and a high-frequency component (the cycle). The three principal ways of decomposing a time series are linear detrending, flexible detrending, and differencing.

The business cycle is an irregular, persistent fluctuation of real GDP around its trend growth rate that is accompanied by highly coherent co-movements in many other economic variables. To measure business cycles, we first need to separate the high- and low-frequency components of economic time series by detrending the raw series. The low-frequency component is the trend, and the high-frequency component is the cycle. Detrending allows us to uncover relationships between time series that hold at one frequency but not at another.

We measure the strength of the statistical relationship between two series with the correlation coefficient. A time series that has a high correlation coefficient with its history is persistent; two series that have a high correlation coefficient with each other are coherent. Coherence can be positive (both series go up and down together) or negative (one series moves up as the other moves down). If a series is positively correlated with GDP, it is procyclical; if it is negatively correlated with GDP, it is countercyclical.

Unemployment and employment are two different measures of economic activity. The employment rate is the percentage of the population that are employed; the unemployment rate is the percentage of the labor force that are unemployed. Because the labor force increased in the United States after World War II, the employment rate and the unemployment rate both increased at the same time. The unemployment rate is countercyclical and highly coherent with GDP.

Output is measured by real GDP. Until recently, real GDP was measured by computing the values of all goods and services produced in a given year, valued using prices from a single base year. More recently, GDP has been measured by the chain weighted method.

Inflation is the rate of change of a price index. There are five principal price indices. Recently, there has been a controversy over the best way to measure inflation because some prices are increasing faster than others. Inflation was procyclical before World War II but has been countercyclical since then.

KEY TERMS

Coherence	Leading Indicators
Compound growth (exponential growth)	Linear cycle
Correlation coefficient	Linear trend
Differencing	Low-frequency component
Employment rate	Peak
Expansion	Recession
Flexible trend	Scatter plot
High-frequency component	Trend
Labor force	Trough
Labor force participation rate	Unemployment rate

QUESTIONS FOR CHAPTER 3

1. List three methods for detrending a time series, and briefly explain how these methods differ. Why is detrending used in macroeconomics?

2. Explain what each of the following terms means:

   a. a recession

   b. an expansion

   c. a business cycle peak

   d. a business cycle trough

3. Explain how to statistically determine if a variable is procyclical or countercyclical.

4. Consider the following time series:

   a. unemployment

   b. total consumption

   c. exports

   d. imports

   e. total investment

   f. the inflation rate

   Which of these series are procyclical? Which are countercyclical?

5. Consider the following time series data (measured as deviations from trend):

	1995	1996	1997	1998	1999	2000
X	0.4	0.1	0.0	0.2	−0.6	0.1
Y	0.9	0.5	−0.1	−0.1	−0.8	0.2

   a. Explain what the correlation coefficient measures.

   b. Are the two series X and Y positively or negatively correlated?

   c. Explain what the terms *procyclical* and *countercyclical* mean. If X represents GDP, is Y procyclical or countercyclical?

6. Consider the following small economy's data:

Year	GDP	Consumption	Unemployment
1997	15	5	4
1998	25	22	3
1999	35	13	2
2000	40	27	1
2001	35	33	2

a. Plot a graph with consumption on the vertical axis and GDP on the horizontal axis, and another graph with unemployment on the vertical axis and GDP on the horizontal axis. Are consumption and unemployment procyclical or countercyclical?

b. The average (arithmetic mean) of a variable is obtained by adding up all the values and dividing by the number of values summed. Calculate average GDP, average consumption, and average unemployment for this economy.

c. The correlation coefficient is defined by the formula

$$\rho_{xy} = \frac{\sum\limits_{i=1}^{n}(x_i - \bar{x})(y_i - \bar{y})}{\sqrt{\sum\limits_{i=1}^{n}(x_i - \bar{x})^2} \cdot \sqrt{\sum\limits_{i=1}^{n}(y_i - \bar{y})^2}}$$

where $\bar{x}, \bar{y}$ is the average, or arithmetic mean.

Using this formula, calculate the correlation coefficients of consumption with GDP, and calculate the correlation coefficients of unemployment with GDP. Which series is more strongly correlated with GDP?

d. Construct a measure of the degree of persistence of GDP. How persistent is GDP?

7. In 1992, a small economy had 25,000 citizens, of whom 20,000 were in the labor force. The unemployment rate was 10%. In 2002, the economy had 30,000 citizens, of whom 25,000 were in the labor force. The unemployment rate was 12%. For each of the two years,

a. How many people were unemployed?

b. What was the labor force participation rate?

c. What was employment per person?

Show that the unemployment rate and employment per person both increased between 1992 and 2002. Explain how this happened.

8. What has happened to the labor participation rate in the U.S. since the 1950s? Why? How do you think that this has affected U.S. GDP during this period?

9. Is it always true that when the employment rate rises, the unemployment rate falls? Explain why or why not.

10. Do you think that the way the Bureau of Labor Statistics calculates the unemployment rate considers every worker who is unemployed? Explain. What biases might this create in our unemployment statistics?

11. What is meant by *chain weighted GDP?* How is it different from the traditional *base-year method* of calculating real GDP? Why has the U.S. Commerce Department adopted this procedure?

12. The following prices and quantities existed in an economy between 1997 and 1999:

	Prices			Quantity		
	'97	'98	'99	'97	'98	'99
Beer	$2	$3	$3	100	120	140
Cake	$10	$11	$13	20	30	35
Gum	$1	$2	$2	200	250	300

a. Calculate nominal and real GDP for 1997, 1998, and 1999, using 1997 as the base year.

b. Calculate the growth rate in real GDP between 1997 and 1998, and between 1998 and1999.

c. Repeat part (a) and part (b), only now use 1998 as the base year. Do you get the same growth rates as in part (b)? Why or why not?

d. Compute the chain weighted growth rate of real GDP between 1997 and 1998. Explain your results.

13. Use the same data in question 12 to answer the following questions.

a. Calculate the GDP deflator for each year, using 1997 as the base year.

b. Calculate the inflation rate between 1997 and 1998, and between 1998 and 1999.

c. Repeat part (a) and part (b), only now use 1998 as the base year. Do you get the same inflation rates as in part (b)? Why or why not?

d. Compute the GDP price index (or the chain weighted GDP deflator) for the period between 1997 and 1998. Explain your results.

14. Briefly describe the three types of price indices. What are the problems with each?

15. Briefly discuss the differences between the GDP deflator and the CPI. Which one is likely to measure inflation at a higher rate? Why?

16. Are there any potential problems with relying solely on the CPI to measure inflation? What are they? How might any potential measurement errors in inflation affect other aspects of the economy, such as the public sector?

The Classical Approach to Aggregate Demand and Supply

In Chapters 4, 5, and 6, we move from a description of data to an explanation of it. We study the *classical* model of the economy, which was developed over the course of 150 years, beginning in the late eighteenth century and ending in the early twentieth century.

Chapter 4 deals with the labor market and the theory of aggregate supply. Chapter 5 covers the classical theory of inflation, and in Chapter 6, we study the classical model of the capital markets.

Overall, Part B looks at aspects of the equilibrium method—the idea that demand equals supply. This method can be applied to understand real world economic problems.

The Theory of
Aggregate Supply

Introduction

In this chapter and Chapters 5 and 6, we build a model of the entire economy based on the ideas of the classical economists. Classical economists developed their theories over an approximately 70-year span, beginning with Adam Smith in 1776 and ending with John Stuart Mill in 1848. Following Mill, a group of neoclassical economists, including Stanley Jevons in England and Leon Walras in France, developed the marginal utility theory. The combined ideas of the classical and the neoclassical economists constitute the classical theory of aggregate demand and supply. Box 4.1 gives short biographies of some of the most important classical and neoclassical economists.

The Theory of Production

Let us imagine for a moment an economy in which all output is produced from labor and capital, and in which everyone has the same preferences. An economy of this kind is called a **representative agent economy**, and economists often refer to the representative agent as Robinson Crusoe, after the hero in Daniel Defoe's novel of the same name. By looking

BOX 4.1

A CLOSER LOOK
Six Influential Economists

Adam Smith 1723–1790

Adam Smith is regarded as the founder of economics. His best-known idea is that of the 'invisible hand' a doctrine which asserts that we are all better off in a society in which individuals are allowed to pursue their own self-interests. His most famous book is *An Inquiry into the Nature and Causes of the Wealth of Nations,* which is the 'Old-Testament' for economists.

Smith was born in Scotland and studied moral philosophy at Glasgow University. It was in his mid-twenties that he first expounded the economic philosophy of the "obvious and simple system of natural liberty."

Smith stressed that the wealth of a country comes from physical attributes, such as land and the abilities of its citizens, rather than from ownership of precious metals. He was a strong proponent of the idea of 'laissez faire'—that an economy prospers when there is minimal intervention from the state.

David Ricardo 1772–1823

Ricardo was born in London. He amassed a fortune on the stock market at an early age and then turned his mind to economics (very much influenced by his reading of Adam Smith). His major work, *The Principal of Political Economy and Taxation*, contained his influential theories of the determination of wages and value.

In Ricardo's theory, the interests of landowners directly oppose those of general society, and in this aspect he preempted Karl Marx in describing adversarial class relations. Marx, in fact, based a great deal of his economic theory on Ricardo's writings, although Marx identified capitalists, not landlords, as the source of social problems. Ricardo developed the labor theory of value, and he thought that wages tended to stabilize around a subsistence level.

Ricardo was also important for his work on the theory of international trade and for his ideas on the determinants of rent based on relative land productivity.

Jean-Baptiste Say: 1776–1832

Say was born in Lyons, France, to middle-class parents and spent most of his early years in Geneva and London. He regarded his own major work, *A Treatise on Political Economy*, as an elaboration and popularization of the ideas of Adam Smith. But it was much more than that.

Say is best known for his "law of markets," according to which "supply creates its own demand." He argued that a general oversupply of any commodity could not exist because the supply of one commodity is necessarily the demand for another: "It is because the production of some commodities has declined that all other commodities are superabundant." This is a situation that Say saw as temporary, and he believed that, left to its own devices, the market would correct such imbalances. Since labor is a commodity, Say's theory implies that unemployment cannot persist. In the 1930s, Keynes attacked this idea in his book, *The General Theory of Employment Interest and Money*.

BOX 4-1 *continued*

John Stuart Mill: 1806–1873

Mill was a philosopher, political scientist and an economist. In his political writings he stressed the freedom of the individual and responsible democratic participation, and he was an ardent supporter of the rights of women.

Mill contributed to many ideas in philosophy. His politics were guided by the doctrine of "utilitarianism," according to which society should pursue the "greatest happiness for the greatest number."

In economics, he wrote *Political Economy,* which has been regarded by some as an improved Adam Smith and by others as a popularized Ricardo. He believed in the doctrine of laissez faire, but he also recognized the possibility of modifying the economic system through politics. His best-known philosophical work is his essay *On Liberty,* which is a passionate defense of the rights of the individual.

William Stanley Jevons: 1835–1882

Jevons was born in Liverpool and schooled in London. He is best known in economics for his development of marginal utility, and his best-known work is contained in his *Theory of Political Economy*. Marginal utility (an idea that was developed independently by Walras) was a breakthrough that enabled economists to explain how demand as well as supply could influence the price of a commodity. Before Jevons, value was explained by the labor "embodied in it." After the marginal revolution, economists recognized that subjective preferences could also be important.

The labor theory of value was a purely supply-based concept. The marginal utility theory recognizes that demand also matters. The word "marginal" is important since it explains why commodities, such as water, that have enormously high usefulness are nevertheless relatively cheap. According to marginal utility theory, it is the marginal unit that determines value. The first cup of water drunk by a thirsty man is very valuable. The twentieth is not.

Leon Walras (1834–1910) was a Frenchman of Dutch ancestry, and hence his name is pronounced "Valrasse" rather than "Valra." He was a socialist in his political leanings, and he subscribed to socialist ideas on land reform and taxation. He believed that mathematical ideas held the key to the advancement of economics.

Walras' major work, *Elements of Pure Economics,* was written while he taught at Lausanne, Switzerland. He correspondenced with Stanley Jevons, and both were sympathetic to the use of mathematics in economics and to subjective ideas in the theory of value.

Walras is particularly known for his development of general equilibrium theory, a mathematical theory that explains how the prices of all commodities are simultaneously determined by the interaction of demand and supply.

at simple economic models with a representative agent, we find many issues that we will be unable to address. For example, unemployment might be higher (or lower) in a society with a very unequal distribution of resources than in a society with a more egalitarian income distribution. By studying an economy with a single agent, we are taking a stand on this issue. Our position will be that for most macroeconomic issues (e.g., the determination of the inflation rate, the unemployment rate, or the growth rate), differences in wealth across the population are of secondary importance.

THE PRODUCTION FUNCTION

Production is the activity of transforming resources, such as labor and raw materials, into finished goods. A method for transforming resources into finished goods is called a **technology**. Figure 4.1 illustrates a technology from which a single commodity, Y, is produced using the services of labor, L. Reading from left to right, the horizontal axis measures the amount of time that Robinson Crusoe spends working; reading from right to left, beginning at point B, it measures the amount of time he spends at leisure.

The distance 0B is the total time available (24 hours a day). The longer Robinson Crusoe spends working, the more commodities he is able to produce. For example, he may decide to spend $0–L_1$ hours at work and L_1–B hours at leisure. The distance $0–Y_1$ measures his output.

Robinson Crusoe's feasible choices, given the state of his technology, are called his **production possibilities set**, and the boundary of this set is the **production function**. In Figure 4.1, the production possibilities set is the blue-shaded area 0–A–B. The points on the production function (boundary of this set) are clearly better than the points inside the set because these points deliver the maximum number of produced commodities for any given input of labor time. The production function slopes upward, reflecting the fact that Robinson Crusoe can produce more goods by working harder. The slope flattens out as he puts in more effort, reflecting the assumption of diminishing returns.

Diminishing returns means that the extra output produced when we input an extra unit of labor is smaller as we add more and more labor to a fixed stock of land or capital. It occurs because labor time is combined with other fixed resources. If we think of Robinson Crusoe literally as the hero in Daniel Defoe's novel, the resources at his disposal might be fixed by the quantity of animals on Crusoe's desert island. The more time Robinson Crusoe spends working, the less is his work's marginal return because eventually he will deplete the island's stock of animals; he will have to work longer and harder to catch the remaining ones. In a modern industrial economy, there is an analogous reason why the production function gets flatter as we work harder. As the labor time of more workers is combined with a fixed stock of capital and land, the additional labor becomes relatively less productive.

MARKETS AND FIRMS

Robinson Crusoe's island may seem a long way from a modern market economy, but we can add a simple element of trade to illustrate the classical theory of markets. First, imagine a number of identical agents or families. Each family operates a firm, which buys labor services and combines them with capital to produce output. Labor services and output

FIGURE 4.1

The Production Function

The more time Robinson spends working, the more commodities he produces. As Robinson works more hours, he produces proportionately less output because his labor is combined with a fixed stock of capital. This is illustrated by the fact that the slope of the production function diminishes as L increases from point **0** to point **B**.

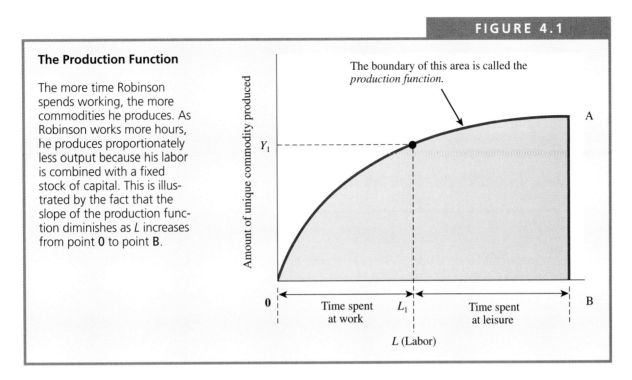

The boundary of this area is called the *production function.*

Amount of unique commodity produced

Y_1

A

0 — Time spent at work — L_1 — Time spent at leisure — B

L (Labor)

are traded with other families and firms in a **market**, a network of traders who buy and sell from each other. To distinguish this economy from the Robinson Crusoe economy, no family can use its own labor in the family firm, nor can it consume the goods that it produces. In the real world, these are realistic assumptions simply because we do not typically produce the same commodities that we consume.

COMPETITION AND THE DETERMINATION OF WAGES AND PRICES

In a market economy, firms buy labor, households sell labor, and each household and firm has the opportunity to trade with thousands of other agents. Classical theory assumes that no one individual can influence prices. In our example there are only two commodities, labor and the produced good, so this assumption means that no one household or firm is able to influence the wage or the price level.

In the real world, wages are set by firms, but the extent to which firms are able to vary their wage rates is strictly limited by competition. For example, if a large corporation offers a wage of $3 an hour when every other firm is paying $5 an hour for identical work, the corporation is unlikely to find many people willing to work. The more alternative options there are available to workers, the less influence any one firm will have in setting wages. When the market consists of many buyers and sellers, each of whom is trading a small fraction of total market sales, the power of any single buyer or seller to influence prices will become arbitrarily small. In this case, economists say that the market is perfectly competitive, or simply a **competitive market**.

THE NOMINAL WAGE AND THE REAL WAGE

In this chapter we do not try to explain why money is used or how money prices are set; that subject is covered in Chapter 5. Instead, we assume that all trade takes place through bartering labor for commodities, and we measure wages in units of commodities. The money paid to the worker for each hour of work is called the **nominal wage**. The amount of the final commodity that a firm must give up in order to purchase an hour of labor time is called the **real wage**.

If the average price of bread is $2 and an hour of labor costs $6, then a bakery worker will receive enough money to buy three loaves of bread for each hour of work. In this example, the nominal wage is $6 per hour and the real wage is three loaves of bread.

THE DEMAND FOR LABOR

We now explain the classical theory of labor demand, which can be summarized by a graph called the "labor demand curve" that plots the real wage against the quantity of labor demanded. According to the classical theory, as the real wage falls, the quantity of labor demanded increases.

Classical theory assumes that markets are competitive. Firms choose how much labor to hire, taking the wage, w, and the price, P, as given, in order to try to make as much profit as possible. The competitive assumption implies that the firm has no control over how much to pay its workers in real terms. If it tries to pay less than w/P, no one will want to work for the firm. There is no point in paying more than w/P because the firm can hire as many hours of labor as it requires, providing it is willing to pay these workers the market wage.

4.1

π	$=$	Y^S	$-$	$(w/P)L^D$
Profit of the family firm		**Commodities supplied**		**Cost of labor demanded**

Equation 4.1 uses symbols to define the profit of the firm, which is equal to the quantity of the commodities supplied minus the cost of hiring labor to produce these commodities.

THE LABOR DEMAND CURVE

The classical theory of production states that firms will try to maximize profits. According to the assumption of perfect competition, they will pay the same wage for labor input and charge the same price for output supplied as all other firms in the market. These assumptions let us derive a relationship between the real wage and the quantity of labor demanded. If the real wage is plotted on the vertical axis of a graph and if the quantity of labor demanded is plotted on the horizontal axis, this relationship, called the "labor demand curve," slopes downward.

Figure 4.2 shows how the labor demand curve and the production function are related. Panel A depicts the production function. Recall that the slope of the production function

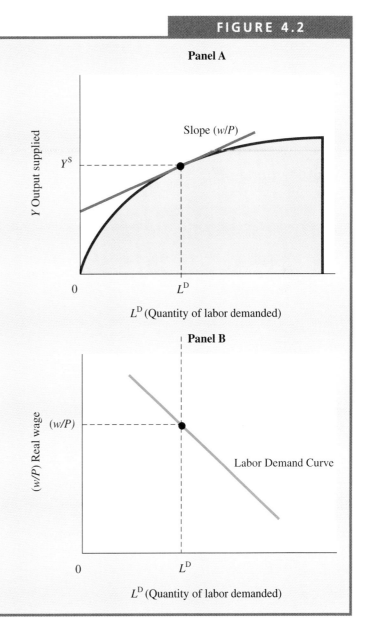

FIGURE 4.2

Labor Demand and the Production Function

Panel A shows the production function—the amount of output produced for any given input of labor.

As the firm employs more workers, the extra output produced by the last worker hired decreases: This extra output is called the *marginal product.*

The firm chooses to hire workers up until the point at which the marginal product equals the real wage.

On Panel A, the slope of the production function represents the marginal product. At the point at which the firm decides to produce, this slope is equal to the real wage. At this point the firm's profit is at a maximum.

Panel B shows the labor demand function. This is a graph of the real wage against the quantity of labor demanded. If the wage increases, the firm will choose to employ fewer workers.

The labor demand curve slopes down.

gets flatter at higher levels of output. This important assumption is called diminishing returns. Recall that diminishing returns occurs because as the firm adds more workers to a fixed quantity of land and capital, the output of each additional worker is smaller than the worker before him. The fixed quantity of capital and land must be shared among an increasing number of workers.

BOX 4.2

A CLOSER LOOK
Deriving the Labor Demand Curve
A Mathematical Example

This box presents a mathematical example of how to derive a labor demand curve from profit maximization by firms. The example uses calculus, and you can safely skip it without losing the thread of the chapter. If you are comfortable with mathematics, you may find that the example makes the economics of labor demand a little easier to understand. This is certainly the position that was taken by Jevons and Walras, two of the founders of the marginal revolution in economics, both of whom believed strongly in the use of mathematics to clarify their ideas.

Remember that the firm tries to maximize profit by choosing combinations of labor demanded and output supplied that lie within the production possibilities set. We will assume that the boundary of the production possibilities set (the production function) is given by the following expression:

4.2.1 Y^S $=$ $L^D - (1/2)(L^D)^2$ $L \leq 1.$

Equation **4.2.1** is a simple example of a production function called a **quadratic** function. Notice that the firm must choose labor less than or equal to one unit. This reflects the assumption that there is a maximum capacity to production, perhaps dictated by the size of the factory. Since we have not specified the units in which we are measuring labor, there is nothing special about the number 1; it is simply a normalization.

The firm will choose how much labor to employ by trying to maximize profit. If we combine the expression for the production function (Equation **4.2.1**) with the definition of profit, we can write down the problem that the firm will try to solve:

4.2.2   max π $=$ $L^D - (1/2)(L^D)^2$ $-$ $(w/P)L^D.$

The firm tries to make this as big as possible.	This is the output produced by L^D labor hours. We call it the total product.	This is the total cost of L^D labor hours measured in units of output.

The solution to this problem is found by setting the derivative of profits, with respect to labor input, equal to zero.

4.2.3 $1 - L^D$ $=$ (w/P)

This is the derivative of the total product. It is called the marginal product of labor.	This is the derivative of the total cost. It is called the marginal cost.

Equation 4.2.3 is the mathematical expression for the labor demand curve and is found by equating the marginal product to the real wage. For the case of a quadratic production function, it is a straight line with a negative slope that tells the firm how much labor to demand (this is the term L^D) for any given real wage (this is the term w/P).

As the firm employs more workers, the extra output produced by the last worker hired decreases: This extra output is called the **marginal product**. As long as the marginal product is greater than the real wage, the firm should keep adding more workers, since each additional worker adds more to revenue than to cost. The firm will maximize its profit by continuing to hire more workers as long as the marginal product of an extra worker is greater than the real wage. The firm should stop hiring workers at the point where the marginal product is just equal to the real wage. On panel A of Figure 4.2, this point occurs when the purple line (with a slope equal to the real wage) is tangent to the production function (with a slope equal to the marginal product). The firm produces the quantity of output, Y^S, and it demands the quantity of labor, L^D.

Panel B shows how the real wage is related to the quantity of labor demanded. As the real wage increases the firm will hire fewer workers, hence the labor supply curve slopes downward. Box 4.2 provides a closer look at the mathematics behind the result.

THE SUPPLY OF LABOR

The classical economists, from Smith to Mill, did not have a well-developed theory of household choice. This came with the work of Jevons, Walras, and other neoclassical economists who developed the theory of marginal utility. They used this theory to explain the labor supply curve.

In marginal utility theory, neoclassical economists assumed that households make choices that are subject to constraints. Their choices make the family as happy as possible, where happiness is measured by a mathematical function called **utility**. Since time spent working takes away from leisure time, we can think of work as bad; more work makes us less happy. But by working harder and longer hours, we earn income that can be used to purchase commodities. These commodities make us happy. According to neoclassical economic theory, families balance the benefits and costs of working harder by maximizing utility.

HOUSEHOLD DECISIONS

Consider a family that both owns a firm and sends family members out to work for other firms in the economy. Perhaps the parents own and operate a small business, but their daughter works in a factory down the street. The family as a whole must decide how many commodities to demand and how much labor to supply to the market. We'll use Y^D to represent the household's demand for commodities and L^S to represent the quantity of labor supplied. In Chapter 6 we will delve deeper into the question of whether the commodities demanded by households are consumed or invested, but for now we will suppose that consumption and investment affect preferences in the same way, and we will refer to them collectively as "commodities demanded."

Families purchase commodities with income from two sources. First, households own firms, and the ownership of firms yields profits. Second, households supply labor and earn income by sending one or more of their members out to work in the market. To express the tradeoff between more commodities demanded and more labor supplied to the market, the household must examine its budget constraint, represented by Inequality 4.2.

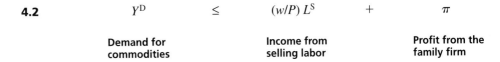

4.2 Y^D $\leq$ $(w/P)\,L^S$ $+$ π

Demand for   **Income from**   **Profit from the**
commodities   **selling labor**   **family firm**

The family must choose how much labor to supply and how many commodities to demand subject to this constraint: the value of the goods that the family demands cannot be greater than the value of its income. According to the neoclassical economists, this choice is made to maximize a subjective utility function that represents the preferences of the household.

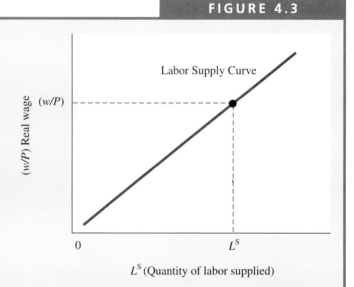

FIGURE 4.3

Labor Supply and the Real Wage

The household chooses how many hours to work. As the real wage increases, it becomes more attractive to work longer hours because leisure is more expensive relative to produced commodities. This is called the substitution effect because the family is substituting produced commodities for leisure as the relative price of leisure (the real wage) goes up.[1]

The labor supply curve slopes up.

[1] As the real wage goes up, families become richer, and they will try to consume more of all commodities, including leisure. This is called the wealth effect. It works in the opposite direction from the substitution effect, and, if the wealth effect were very strong, it is possible that the labor supply curve could slope downward. The neoclassical economic theorists assumed that the substitution effect is more important, hence the labor supply curve slopes upward.

THE LABOR SUPPLY CURVE

The assumption that households maximize utility leads to a relationship between the real wage and the quantity of labor that households choose to supply. This relationship, called the "labor supply curve," is plotted in Figure 4.3.

When the real wage increases, the household will be pulled in two conflicting directions. The real wage is the relative price of leisure to produced commodities. As the real wage goes up, leisure becomes relatively more expensive, and this effect (called the **substitution effect**) tends to make the household want to substitute consumption goods for leisure; that is, the household will work more hours. But an increase in the real wage makes the household wealthier, and this effect (called the **wealth effect**) tends to make the household consume more of all commodities, including leisure.[1] This effect makes the household work fewer hours. If the substitution effect is bigger than the wealth effect, the labor supply curve will slope upward. If the wealth effect is bigger, it will slope downward. The neoclassical theorists assumed that the substitution effect is bigger and that the labor supply curve slopes upward. Box 4.3 provides a closer look at a mathematical example of a utility function and it uses this example to derive a labor supply curve.

---

1.   Some authors refer to the wealth effect as an "income effect," although wealth effect is better terminology when considering problems in which resources can be transferred through time by borrowing and lending.

BOX 4.3

A CLOSER LOOK
Deriving the Labor Supply Curve
A Mathematical Example

In this box, we provide an example of a utility function and show how to derive the labor supply curve. As with the mathematical example of a production function, you can safely skip it without losing track of the main argument of the chapter. The most important idea to remember is that the labor supply curve slopes upward. This example shows how Jevons and the other neoclassical economists arrived at this proposition from a subjective theory of utility.

To capture the idea of subjective utility, the neoclassical economists wrote down a mathematical expression, a utility function, that tells us the number of **utils** obtained for any given combination of consumption commodities and labor supplied. Equation 4.3.1 is an example of a utility function.

4.3.1
$$U \qquad = \qquad Y^D \qquad - \qquad (1/2)(L^S)^2$$

| This is the utility of the household. | This is the utility derived from commodities. | This is the disutility derived from working. |

Households try to make utility as big as possible, but they cannot spend more than their available income. This is controlled by their budget constraint. Putting together the budget constraint and the utility function, we arrive at the problem faced by the household.

4.3.2
$$\max U \qquad = \qquad (w/P)L^S + \pi \qquad - \qquad (1/2)(L^S)^2.$$

| The household tries to make this as big as possible. | These are the commodities that can be purchased if the household works for L^S hours to supplement its profit income. | This is the disutility of working L^S hours. |

The solution to this problem is found by setting the derivative of utility to zero.

4.3.3
$$(w/P) \qquad = \qquad L^S$$

Maximizing utility gives an expression for the labor supply curve.

Equation 4.3.3 is the mathematical expression for the labor supply curve. For our example, it is a straight line with a positive slope that tells the household how much labor to supply (this is the term L^S) for any given real wage (this is the term w/P).

FACTORS THAT SHIFT LABOR SUPPLY

Neoclassical theory not only predicts that the labor supply curve will slope upward, it also predicts that income taxes and wealth are two factors that will shift the relationship.

Taxes reduce the supply of labor by lowering the wage received by households. For example, when a household is in the 30% tax bracket, it receives only $7 of every $10 earned. The remaining $3 is paid to the government in taxes. Although many of us feel overtaxed, Americans actually pay a much lower fraction of their wages in income taxes than the residents of many other countries. The top tax bracket in the United States was cut to 28% in 1988. New legislation in 1993 increased the top tax rate to 39.6%, but this top rate only applies to incomes above $250,000 per year, a tiny fraction of U.S. taxpayers. Even this top rate is low compared with European rates, which can be as high as 70% or 80%.

BOX 4.4

FOCUS ON THE FACTS
Supply Side Economics
(Taxes and Labor Supply)

In the 1980s, an influential group of political commentators, supporters of Ronald Reagan, argued for supply-side economics. The central proposition of this doctrine is that tax cuts cause economic growth by increasing the rewards for effort and stimulating people to work harder and save more. Although supply-side economics was popular politically, it is not a theory that is supported by most economists. In the 1980s, the nonpartisan American Economics Association recorded only 12 of approximately 18,000 members who called themselves supply-side economists.[1]

A central proposition behind supply-side economics is the Laffer Curve, an idea developed in a series of dinner conversations in a New York restaurant between the economist Arthur Laffer and Robert Bartley, a journalist with the *Wall Street Journal*.

In Laffer's curve, tax revenue is graphed against the tax rate. If the tax rate is zero, the government clearly collects no revenue. On the other hand, if the tax rate were 100%, no one would work, nothing would be produced, and, once again, the government would collect no revenue. Since the curve that relates revenue to tax rate must begin and end at zero, there must be some tax rate between zero and 100% at which revenue is maximized. This implies that there are always two tax rates that will collect the same revenue.

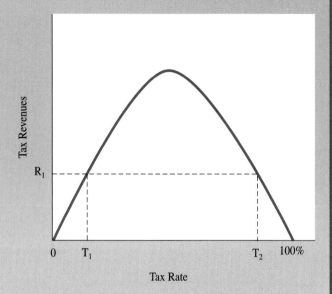

The Laffer Curve
On this graph, the government can collect revenue R_1 with a low tax rate (T_1) or with a high tax rate (T_2). The supply-siders believe that taxes are so high that we are at a point like T_2, and hence, lowering taxes will increase revenue.

The Laffer curve is not a controversial proposition since all economists would recognize that people may work less if taxes rise. What *is* controversial is the belief of supply-siders that in practice we are on the "wrong side of the Laffer curve" (a point like T_2 rather than T_1). The supply-siders argued successfully that Reagan should cut taxes without increasing spending. Most conservative economists wanted instead to cut taxes *and* to cut spending. In practice, the effect of the Reagan tax cuts in 1981 was to cause an increase in the deficit. It went from 2.7% of GDP in 1980 to 5.2% of GDP in 1986. This does not in itself say that the tax cut was a bad thing or that it did not stimulate people to work harder, but it does throw doubt on the idea of the supply-siders that the economy was on the wrong side of the Laffer curve.

[1] James Carville, *We're Right, They're Wrong: A Handbook for Spirited Progressives* (New York: Random House,1996), p.12.

There is a good critique of supply-side economics in *Slate* at http://www.slate.com (search: "Paul Krugman" AND "supply-side economics") by Paul Krugman, an economics professor at Massachusetts Institute of Technology. For a systematic overview of supply-side economics, visit http://www.polyconomics.com/, the Web site of Jude Wanniski, one of the major proponents of supply-side economics.

A second important variable that influences labor supply is wealth. Independently wealthy families are less likely to work long hours. Similarly, as society gets richer, we all tend to consume more commodities, including leisure commodities. Thus, increased

BOX 4.5

FOCUS ON THE FACTS
The Wealth Effect

Wages have grown by a factor of five in the past 100 years, but the employment rate has remained roughly constant. The reason is that we are wealthier today than we were in 1890, and households choose to consume more leisure as a result. The effect of raising wealth tends to reduce labor supply, but the effect of rising wages tends to increase it. The two effects offset each other in the data.[1]

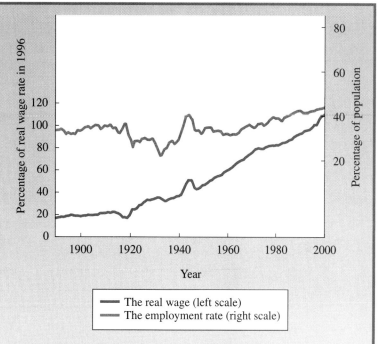

The real wage (left scale)
The employment rate (right scale)

[1] Data on the employment rate for 1929 on is based on civilian employment over 16 deflated by total population. For data before 1929, the employment series is from R.J. Gordon, *The American Business Cycle,* published by the National Bureau of Economic Research. Data on the real wage is constructed by dividing a nominal wage series by the GDP deflator. For pre-1929 data, the nominal wage is from Gordon. Post 1929, it is compensation to employees divided by nominal GDP and divided by employment.

wealth shifts the labor supply curve to the left. As households get richer, if all other things remain equal, they work fewer hours. Of course, this does not mean that all wealthy people do not work; many of the richest families in America acquired their wealth precisely because of the long hours they put into building up their businesses. For the most part, however, we expect to see that those with large, inherited fortunes are less likely to be working long hours in paid employment. Box 4.4 takes a closer look at the effects of taxes on labor supply.

If greater wealth shifts the labor supply curve to the left, perhaps this means that hours worked will drop over time. In fact, this is not true: The employment rate has been roughly constant over a century's worth of data. In fact, the effect of increasing wealth on labor supply is offset by the rise in the real wage. The effect of wealth on labor supply is called a "wealth effect." The effect of a higher real wage on labor supply is called a "substitution effect." The employment rate has been roughly constant because the wealth and substitution effects balance each other out over long periods of time. Box 4.5 illustrates the data on the real wage and employment in the United States since 1890.

THE CLASSICAL THEORY OF AGGREGATE SUPPLY

Now let us put together the theories of labor demand and supply to show how the classical economists believed that output, employment, and wages are determined. The classical theory of aggregate supply explains these variables.

PUTTING TOGETHER DEMAND AND SUPPLY

The labor demand and supply curves in Figure 4.4 illustrate the choices of the household and the firm. In the classical model, the labor market is assumed to be in equilibrium.

The real wage and the level of employment are determined by the point of intersection of the labor demand and supply curves, denoted by $(w/P)^E$ and L^E, where the superscript E stands for equilibrium. In practice, the equilibrium values L^E and $(w/P)^E$ depend on the economy's technology and the households' preferences; these features of the economy determine the positions and slopes of the labor demand and supply curves.

For any value of the real wage, households and firms make plans that express the amount of labor and commodities they would like to buy and sell. For some values of the wage, firms plan to buy more labor than households plan to sell; for other values, the opposite occurs. For most values of the real wage, the plans of households and firms are mutually inconsistent.

For example, Figure 4.4 depicts a relatively high value of the wage measured in terms of commodities, $(w/P)_1$. Given this relatively high value of the real wage, the firm will choose to demand a low amount of labor, L^D_1, and households will supply a large amount, L^S_1; in this case, supply will exceed demand. Alternatively, if the wage is low at $(w/P)_2$, the firm's demand for labor will exceed household supply. Only at the equilibrium real wage, $(w/P)^E$, are the quantities demanded and supplied equal to each other. The value of labor and commodities at which the quantities of labor and commodities demanded equal the quantities of those supplied is called a "competitive equilibrium allocation." Box 4.6 (page 100), takes a closer look by deriving a mathematical example of an equilibrium.

WHAT IS SPECIAL ABOUT THE EQUILIBRIUM?

It seems reasonable to ask: Why do classical economists focus on the equilibrium point rather than some other real wage at which demand is not equal to supply? The answer is that the equilibrium wage is the only one at which there are no mutually beneficial gains from trade.

Suppose, for example, that every firm in the economy offered to pay a wage of $(w/P)_1$, which is greater than the equilibrium real wage $(w/P)^E$. In this situation, there would be some workers who would be unable to find a job at the market wage because when (w/P) is above its equilibrium level, more hours of labor will be offered for sale than are demanded by firms. The classical theorists assumed that in this situation, an unemployed worker would work for less than the going wage. Since a firm could profitably hire such a worker, both parties would willingly make trades. Similarly, firms that are already employing workers would be in a strong bargaining position. They would be able to force

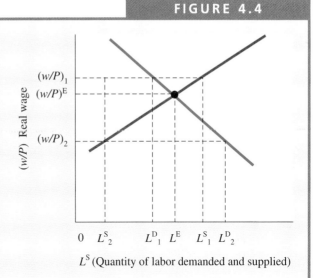

FIGURE 4.4

Labor Market Equilibrium

At wage $(w/P)_1$, households supply L^S_1 hours of labor and firms demand L^D_1 hours; the quantity supplied exceeds the quantity demanded.

At wage $(w/P)_2$, households supply L^S_2 hours of labor and firms demand L^D_2 hours; the quantity demanded exceeds the quantity supplied.

Only when $(w/P) = (w/P)^E$ does the quantity demanded equal the quantity supplied. Then the labor market is in equilibrium and employment equals L^E.

their workers to accept lower wages by firing those who refuse, and replacing them with unemployed workers who agree.

Suppose, on the other hand, that the real wage is at some level, $(w/P)_2$, which is less than the equilibrium real wage, $(w/P)^E$. In this case, firms would try to hire more hours of labor than were being supplied by households. A firm that was unable to find enough labor would try to lure workers away from other firms by offering higher wages. Workers that already had jobs at lower wages would be in a strong bargaining position and would be able to threaten to leave in favor of a more lucrative employer. The only wage at which there is no pressure to either raise or lower the rate is the real wage, $(w/P)^E$, at which the quantity of labor demanded is exactly equal to the quantity supplied.

WALRAS LAW

The classical theory of aggregate supply helps us determine the quantity of goods produced as well as the quantity of labor employed; but so far we have focused exclusively on the market for labor. How do we know that when the demand is equal to the supply of labor it will simultaneously be true that the demand is equal to the supply of commodities? The answer, in our simple example, is that there are only two things being traded: produced commodities and labor. Every offer to buy labor is simultaneously an offer to sell commodities because the firm uses commodities to pay wages. The same argument holds for households. An offer to supply labor to the firm is simultaneously an offer to buy commodities. If a household is happy with the amount of labor that it is supplying, it must

BOX 4.6

A CLOSER LOOK
Deriving the Aggregate Supply Curve
A Mathematical Example

In this section, we put together the example of a labor demand curve from Box 4.2 with that of the labor supply curve from Box 4.3. Each of these curves has a mathematical representation as an equation relating the real wage to the quantity of labor demand or supplied. By solving these two equations simultaneously, we can find the equilibrium value of the real wage and the equilibrium value of the quantity of labor employed. Let's begin with the labor demand curve that has the representation:

4.6.1 $1 - L^D \quad = \quad (w/P)$

   This is the equation of the labor demand curve.

From the theory of marginal utility we were able to derive the labor supply curve:

4.6.2 $(w/P) \quad = \quad L^S$

   This is the equation of the labor supply curve

If we solve these equations simultaneously, we find that when $L^S = L^D = L^E$,

4.6.3 $1 - L^E = L^E,$ or $L^E = 1/2.$

Substituting this solution for L^E back into either the labor demand or the labor supply curve gives the expression for the equilibrium real wage:

4.6.4 $(w/P)^E = L^E = 1/2$

To find the quantity of output supplied, we must use the equation of the production function:

4.6.5 $Y^S \quad = \quad L^D - (1/2)(L^D)^2$

In equilibrium, the quantity of labor demanded is equal to 1/2; so the quantity of output supplied must be:

4.6.6 $Y^E \quad = \quad L^E - (1/2)(L^E)^2 \quad = \quad (1/2) - (1/2)(1/2)^2 = 3/8.$

simultaneously be happy with the amount of goods that it is purchasing. Similarly, if a firm is happy with the amount of labor it is demanding, it must simultaneously be satisfied with the amount of goods that it is selling.

This idea can be extended to more complicated examples of economic models in which there are many goods being bought and sold. This extension is called Walras Law, after the French economist Leon Walras. In economies where firms produce many different types of commodities, equilibrium is defined in much the same way as in the one-commodity world. Firms choose how much labor to demand and how much of each commodity to produce in order to maximize profits. Households maximize utility by choosing how much labor to supply and how much of each commodity to demand. The competitive assumption is that households and firms take all prices as given. For arbitrary prices, supply will not equal demand for any commodity or for labor. In this multicommodity world, Walras Law says that if demand equals supply for all but one of the commodities and for labor, then supply must also equal demand for the last commodity.

W E B W A T C H

Edward C. Prescott and James Tobin: What Two Leading Economists Think About Real Business Cycles

The Region

The Region is a magazine published by the Federal Reserve Bank of Minneapolis. The Minneapolis Fed is closely linked with the economics department at the University of Minnesota, and the research department at the Fed has a group of macroeconomists who are strongly supportive of real business cycle ideas. You can find selected articles from *The Region* at http://www.minneapolisfed.org.

 The Region is an excellent source of articles on modern research topics in macroeconomics that are written for the nonspecialist. It also publishes a series of interviews with leading economists.

 In September of 1996, *The Region* published an interview with Edward C. Prescott, a leading proponent of real business cycle theory. You will find the entire interview on the Web at http://www.minneapolisfed.org; search "Edward Prescott" AND "real business cycle".

 In Prescott's words, "If you take a coin and flip it repeatedly, assign a 1 to heads and a –1 to tails, and sum up the values of the last 15 flips, the resulting time series will display cyclical fluctuations—that is, fluctuations that look a lot like cycles. This is Eugene Slutsky's (Russian economist and econometrician) observation in his famous 1927 paper: that cycles can be the sums of random causes—a translation of which appears in the 1937 *Econometrica*. With real business cycle models, a given shock's effect declines only 5 percent per quarter. This implies after three and a half years, the shock still has half its effect. The current state of the business cycle depends upon things that have happened over the last four years."

 In December of 1996, *The Region* published an interview with James Tobin, a leading Keynesian economist and winner of the Nobel Prize for Economics in 1981. Tobin's interview is available at http://www.minneapolisfed.org; search "James Tobin". According to Tobin, the difference between he and Prescott is ". . . about what's going on in the real economy during business cycles: He [Prescott] thinks fluctuations are moving equilibrium in which supply and demand are equal to each other all the time, and he attributes most of the cycle to productivity fluctuations; whereas I believe that in business cycles we don't have market clearing. Instead, we do have, for example, involuntary unemployment and other situations of excess supply, predominantly. We're losing output that would be valuable to the economy, to society. It's not a moving equilibrium."

The Region
September 2000

Edward C. Prescott

James Tobin

WHO HOLDS THE MONEY?

You have probably noticed that the economy we have described is quite different from the world in which we live. Some of the simplifications made are probably not very important, but others are critical.

The firms and households in our model do not use money; instead they barter labor directly for commodities. In more complicated examples of the classical theory, there may be many different commodities and many different types of people, but the theory still does not integrate money into the theory in a satisfactory way. It is possible to define the price of output in terms of money and call it P. Similarly, it is possible to define the price of labor in the model and call it w. This doesn't change the fact that nobody in the classical model cares about w or P directly; they care only about the rate at which they can trade labor for commodities. The answer to the question "Who holds money?" in the classical theory of aggregate supply is "Nobody does."

If no one holds money, you may wonder how the classical theory of competition can be extended to discuss prices in terms of money. We address this in Chapter 5.

USING CLASSICAL THEORY

Economists explain data with models—sets of mathematical equations that explain how variables are related to each other. Some variables, called "endogenous variables," are explained within the model; others, called "exogenous variables," are explained outside the model. The solution to a model is a set of equations, one for each endogenous variable, that expresses the endogenous variables as functions of the exogenous variables.

By matching up the predictions of our models with observations from the world, we evaluate our theories. When models make false predictions, we change or refine them in ways that improve our understanding of the world. We now evaluate the classical model by examining its answers to one of the fundamental questions of macroeconomics: What drives business cycles?

BUSINESS FLUCTUATIONS

According to the classical theory of employment and GDP, the explanation of business fluctuations lies with the factors that determine equilibrium in the labor market. There are three of these factors: preferences, endowments, and technology.

PREFERENCES, ENDOWMENTS, AND TECHNOLOGY

The employment level is determined by equality of demand and supply in the labor market. It follows that the factors that cause fluctuations in the level of output are those that cause shifts in the demand curve or the supply curve of labor. Two factors that shift labor demand are improvements in the productivity of technology and increases in the endowment of resources. A factor that shifts labor supply is a change in preferences.

Consider the effect of a productivity improvement that arises from the discovery of a new technology. Improvements of this kind occur continuously and may have different effects on the labor market depending on their relative impact on the marginal products of capital and labor. Suppose, as an illustration, that a new technique is discovered that makes labor more productive, such as mass production in the automobile industry at the turn of the century. After the advent of mass production, firms were willing to pay a higher real wage for any given quantity of labor because, by using the new techniques, they were able to produce more commodities from each hour of labor employed.

The effect of a productivity improvement is depicted in Figure 4.5. Before the improvement, the economy produces output from labor with production function 1. After the improvement, it produces output more efficiently with production function 2. The introduction of the new technology causes the labor demand curve to shift from labor demand 1 to labor demand 2 as firms compete more vigorously to hire the existing supply of labor. As the labor demand curve shifts to the right, the intersection of labor demand and supply curves moves upward and to the right along the labor supply curve. As firms try to attract additional workers into the labor force, they must pay a higher wage to persuade households to supply additional hours of labor. The amount that the real wage rises depends on the slope of the labor supply curve. Thus, the productivity improvement increases employment to L^{E2} and the real wage to $(w/P)^{E2}$.

The top panel of Figure 4.5 illustrates the impact of a new technology on the supply of commodities. Aggregate supply goes up for two reasons. First, more workers are drawn into the labor force, causing GDP to increase as labor hours increase. Second, the production function shifts upward, causing the quantity of output produced to increase even if labor remains unchanged. These two effects combined raise aggregate supply from Y^{E1} to Y^{E2}.

A second possible cause for an increase in equilibrium GDP would be the discovery of new deposits of natural resources. A natural gas discovery, for example, would increase the productivity of labor and create new jobs as firms seek to mine the deposit. The economy's stocks of natural resources, including the time of its people, are called its "endowment." The fact that these resources are in fixed supply is responsible for the production function displaying diminishing returns to scale. The discovery of a new natural resource shifts the production function the same way a new invention does, and it has similar effects on the real wage, employment, and aggregate supply.

The final factor that shifts aggregate supply is a change in household preferences. Figure 4.6 shows what would happen if households spontaneously decided to supply more labor for any given value of the real wage. This increase in labor supply, represented as a shift to the right of the labor supply curve, lowers the equilibrium value of the real wage and increases equilibrium employment and GDP. An example of an increase in the supply of labor due to mainly noneconomic factors is the increase in participation rates for women since the end of World War II. In 1948, the female participation rate was 32.7%; by 1993 this figure had increased to 57.9%.

THE REAL BUSINESS CYCLE SCHOOL

Recently, the classical model was revived by a group of economists led by Edward C. Prescott at the University of Minnesota. The classical revival is called the real business cycle (RBC) school because these economists believe that 70% of post–World War II

FIGURE 4.5

The Effect of a New Invention on the Labor Market

The effect of a new invention is to shift the production function from production function 1 to production function 2. Innovations like this occur all the time. For example, the miniaturization of electronics stimulated the development of the computer industry and generated a whole new wave of productivity increase. Productivity increases affect the labor market by allowing firms to pay higher wages. The immediate effect is to shift out the labor demand curve and to increase the real wage and the quantity of employment.

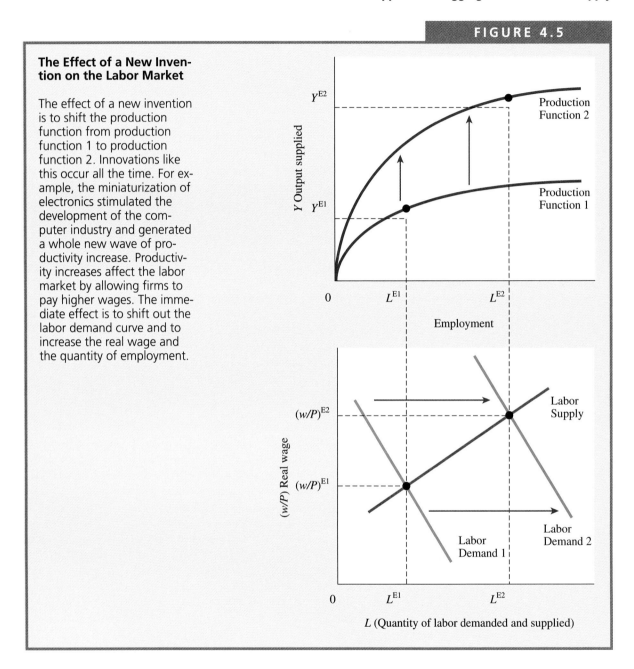

business cycles can be explained by random shocks to technology (see Figure 4.7). This claim, if accepted, has important implications for the design of economic policy. The predominant belief in the immediate postwar period was that business cycles were inefficient, and it was government's role to try and prevent these fluctuations. The implied RBC

FIGURE 4.6

The Effect of a Change in Tastes on Employment and Output

In the 1960s and 1970s, women began to enter the labor force in much greater numbers than they had in previous decades. The effect was to increase employment and allow the U.S. economy to produce much greater output.

The graph shows the theoretical impact of an increase in labor supply. A shift in household preferences causes the labor supply curve to shift from labor supply 1 to labor supply 2. The immediate impact is to increase employment and lower the real wage below what it would otherwise have been.

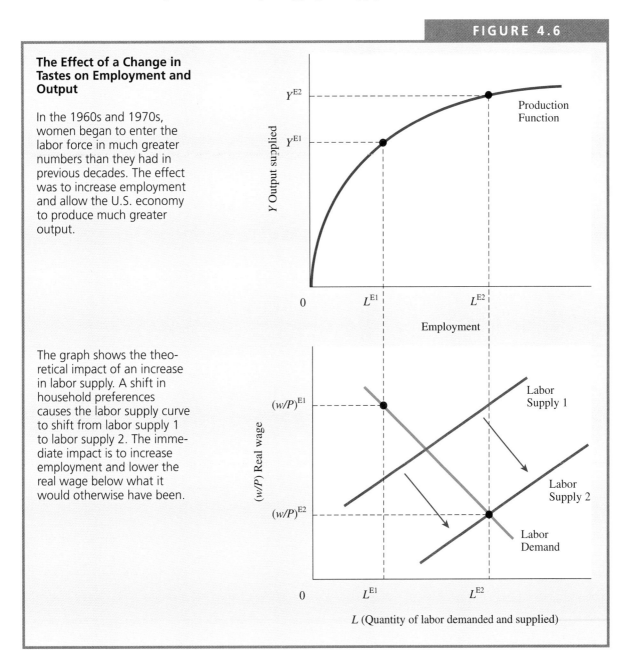

view is different because, in the RBC economy, economic fluctuations are the unavoidable responses of optimizing agents to changing productive opportunities. In the RBC economy there is no role for policy because the agents themselves cope with economic fluctuations in the most efficient way possible.

FIGURE 4.7

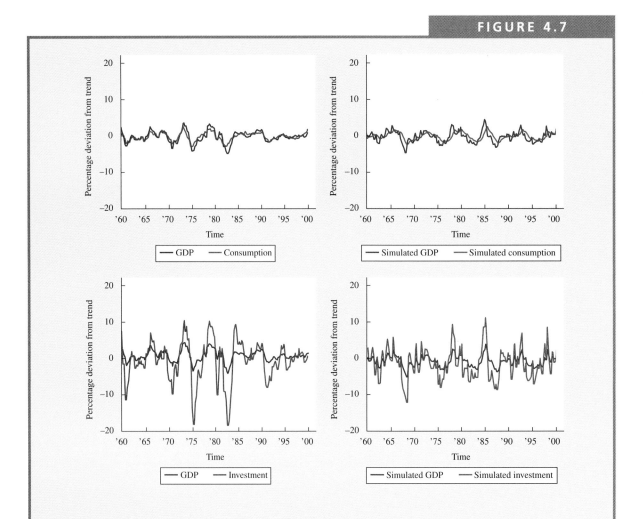

Real Business Cycles

The real business cycle economists, led by Edward C. Prescott of the University of Minnesota, believe that random shocks to technology account for 70% of post–World War II business cycle fluctuations. They back up their claims by simulating business cycles in model economies and showing that the fluctuations in the simulated models mimic the features of the actual data.

In the graphs above, the left panels are actual data and the right panels are a simulated time series from a business cycle model in which all fluctuations are due to shocks to technology. In each case, the blue line is GDP and the red line is consumption (in the top graphs), investment (in the middle graphs), and employment (in the bottom graphs).

The RBC model does a fairly good job of mimicking the statistical properties of the actual data.

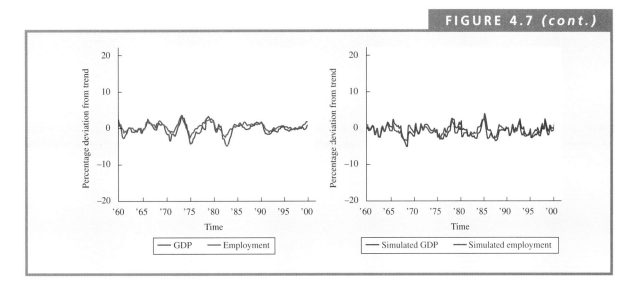

FIGURE 4.7 *(cont.)*

The initial reaction to the RBC model was mixed. Many macroeconomists were overtly hostile to the revival of the classical model. In the past 15 years, however, the methodology advocated by RBC economists has become more widely accepted. This does not mean that today every macroeconomist believes that all business cycles are efficient responses to fluctuations in productivity. But the idea that demand equals supply is now widely used by modern researchers in macroeconomics.

Although the impact of the RBC school has been important, their ideas have not overtaken the mainstream of the economics profession, partly because, although the RBC model provides a partial explanation of economic fluctuations, it is not the whole story. The principal causes of business fluctuations in classical models are changes in technology, endowments, and preferences. Although it is likely that some of the fluctuations we observe from one year to the next are due to these factors, it is unlikely that all of them can be explained in this way.

A second reason that many economists are skeptical of the RBC model is that it pays little or no attention to unemployment. In RBC models, as in the classical model, all fluctuations in employment arise as the result of voluntary household decisions to vary the quantity of hours they supply to the market. There is no room in these models for workers who are unable to find a job. Although unemployment has not been as important in postwar America as it was during the Great Depression, hopefully a theory of macroeconomics can explain both prewar and postwar data with a single model.

CONCLUSION

The idea of equilibrium explains how employment, output, and the real wage are determined. The real wage is the wage measured in units of commodities. Firms maximize profits and demand more labor when the real wage falls. The labor demand curve is the relationship between the real wage and the quantity of labor demanded. Households maximize utility and supply more labor when the real wage rises. The relationship between the real wage and the quantity of labor supplied is the labor supply curve. Classical economists believed that the point at which the labor demand curve and labor supply curve intersect determines employment.

Recently, an influential group of economists from the real business cycle school argued that we should not dismiss the classical model too quickly. These economists maintained that the Great Depression was an unusual event; most of the time the classical model does a good job of explaining economics.

KEY TERMS

Competitive market   Real wage
Diminishing returns   Representative agent economy
Marginal product   Substitution effect
Market   Technology
Nominal wage   Utility
Production   Walras Law
Production function   Wealth effect
Production possibilities set

QUESTIONS FOR CHAPTER 4

1. What is meant by a *representative agent?* Why do you think that the classical economic theorists assumed representative agents? What types of issues do you think are precluded from being investigated in a model with representative agents?

2. Explain the difference between the *real* and the *nominal wage*. Which one matters when firms and households make their decisions in the labor market? Why?

3. What is meant by the term *diminishing returns?* Explain the role that diminishing returns plays in determining the slope of the labor demand curve.

4. a. Explain the difference between the *substitution effect* and the *wealth effect*. According to neoclassical economic theorists, which of these effects dominates? What does this assumption imply about the slope of the classical labor supply curve?

b. Looking at the data presented in Box 4.5, does the substitution effect or the wealth effect dominate? What does this data imply about the slope of the historical labor supply curve in the U.S. economy?

5. Using the classical model of aggregate supply, briefly discuss the impact of a *tax on labor income*. Make sure to discuss its effects on labor, wages, the marginal product of labor, and aggregate output.

6. Using the classical model of aggregate supply, briefly discuss the impact of a *tax on capital investment*. Make sure to discuss its effects on labor, wages, the marginal product of labor, and aggregate output.

7. Using the classical model of aggregate supply, briefly discuss the impact of a *stock market crash that reduces household wealth*. Make sure to discuss its effects on labor, wages, the marginal product of labor, and aggregate output.

8. Consider the following labor supply function, $L^S = (w/P)(1 - t)$, where t is the tax rate on nominal wages.

a. Calculate what happens to labor supplied if the tax rate is reduced from its current rate of 30% (i.e., $t = 0.3$) to 20%.

b. If $L^d = 4/(w/P)$, calculate how the equilibrium real wage rate changes when the tax rate is reduced from 30% to 20%.

c. Provide a graph of the labor market to illustrate the effects of the tax reduction in part (b). Is your graph consistent with your calculations in (b)?

d. Calculate what happens to the government's tax revenues as a result of the tax cut described in part (b).

e. What is the *Laffer curve?* Are your calculations in part (d) consistent with the predictions of the Laffer curve? Why or why not?

9. Consider an economy with the following aggregate production function: $Y = L^{1/2}$.

a. Find the marginal product of labor. (Hint: If a production function takes the form of $Y = AL^\alpha$, then the marginal product of labor equals $\alpha AL^{\alpha-1}$.)

b. Show that the aggregate production function in this economy exhibits diminishing returns by choosing different values for labor and calculating what happens to its marginal product.

c. If w/P is the real wage, derive the labor demand curve by equating the real wage with the marginal product of labor you derived in part (a).

d. If the labor supply curve is $L^S = 2(w/P)$, calculate the equilibrium values of labor and the real wage.

e. Calculate aggregate output, Y.

10. Discuss what makes real business cycle (RBC) models distinctive from other models in economics. What do RBC theorists think are the sources of business cycles in the United States? What is attractive about their hypotheses? What do you think are their shortcomings?

11. Read the interviews with James Tobin and Edward C. Prescott in *The Region* magazine. Briefly summarize the views of these two economists on the causes of business cycles. Do they agree with one another? If not, explain their main points of disagreement.

CHAPTER 5

Aggregate Demand and the Classical Theory of the Price Level

INTRODUCTION

The classical theory of the price level is sometimes called the quantity theory of money or the classical theory of aggregate demand. It was developed in the latter part of the nineteenth century and the early part of the twentieth century, although early versions of the theory can be found in the work of David Hume, an eighteenth-century Scottish economist.

Why be interested in a theory that is now almost 200 years old? First of all, there are some questions to which the classical theory still provides very good answers. The most important of these is the classical explanation for the cause of inflation, particularly where the rate of inflation is, or has been very high, such as in Brazil, Bolivia, Argentina, or Israel. Classical theory works well in high-inflation countries for the same reason that Newton's theory of gravity works well at velocities that are well below the velocity of light. Both theories are wrong in some dimensions, but sometimes those dimensions are not important.

The second important reason for studying the classical theory is that it can help you understand how modern intertemporal equilibrium theories work. These theories build on the classical theory by being explicit about the factors that lead households and firms to vary their demands and supplies for labor through time. The classical theory makes some unrealistic simplifications, but it is a good idea to start with simple concepts and learn about the complicated ones later.

Last but not least, learning the classical theory of aggregate demand and supply is worthwhile because the classical theory has been incorporated into the **neoclassical synthesis**, the theory used by almost all economic journalists and policymakers to understand today's economy. The neoclassical synthesis developed as economists tried to merge two alternative lines of research. One line was initiated by John Maynard Keynes, who proposed an alternative to the classical theory to explain how output and employment fluctuate during booms and recessions. A second line of analysis, called neoclassical growth theory, developed the classical theory of aggregate demand and supply, and it was used to determine the economy's long-run trend level of output. According to the neoclassical synthesis, Keynesian economics should be used to describe year-to-year fluctuations in employment, output, and inflation, but neoclassical growth theory applies in the long run.

THE THEORY OF THE DEMAND FOR MONEY

The **classical theory of the price level**, or **classical theory of aggregate demand**, is a hybrid that adds a theory of money to the classical theory of aggregate supply, which we studied in Chapter 4. To integrate money into this theory, we begin with the budget constraint of a family in a static, one-period economy, and we show how this constraint is altered when a family engages in repeated trade through time, using money as a medium of exchange.

THE HISTORICAL DEVELOPMENT OF THE THEORY

The classical theory of aggregate demand is a modern name for the **quantity theory of money**. The quantity theory of money was an attempt to explain how the general level of prices is determined. It has a long history, dating back at least as far as David Hume (1711–1776), whose delightful essay, *Of Money,* is still relevant to modern economics. Later economists who worked on the quantity theory include the American Irving Fisher (1867–1947) and the English economist Alfred Marshall (1842–1924). The approach taken in this chapter is based on Marshall's work because it was Marshall who first argued for an explicit treatment of money using the framework of demand and supply.

THE THEORY OF THE DEMAND FOR MONEY

To understand why people use money, the classical theorists extended their static theory of the demand and supply of commodities by constructing a **theory of the demand for money**. Just as a household demands goods up to the point where the marginal benefit of an additional purchase of a commodity equals its marginal cost, so the classical theory of the demand for money argues; people 'demand money' up to the point where its marginal benefit equals its marginal cost. Money is a durable good that is not consumed the way butter or cheese is consumed. Money is more like a television set or a refrigerator; it yields a flow of services over time. A television set yields a flow of entertainment services, and

WEBWATCH 5.1

An Interview with Milton Friedman

The most influential modern figure in monetary economics is Milton Friedman, formerly a professor at the University of Chicago and now a fellow of the Hoover Institution at Stanford University. In the period immediately following World War II, the dominant paradigm was Keynesian economics. Many of Keynes' followers argued that money was relatively unimportant as a determinant of inflation and that, instead, inflation was caused by strong trade unions. Friedman was largely responsible for reviving the classical idea that inflation is caused by increases in the quantity of money. His ideas on money and inflation appear in "The Quantity Theory of Money—a Restatement," in *Studies in the Quantity Theory of Money* (University of Chicago Press, 1956).

You can find an interview with Milton Friedman, in which he discusses contemporary economic issues ranging from the role of government in society to monetary union in Europe, in *The Region*, the magazine of the Federal Reserve Bank of Minneapolis. The interview is available at http://www.federalreserve.gov; search: "Milton Friedman."

money yields a flow of **exchange services** that increase the convenience of buying and selling goods. The cost of holding money is the opportunity cost of forgoing consumption of some other commodity; the marginal benefit is the additional usefulness gained by having cash on hand to facilitate the process of exchange.

Let us examine both the costs and benefits of holding money, beginning with the costs. Our first task is to show how holding money can reduce the household's ability to buy other commodities; we will examine the household's budget constraint in a monetary economy. If households continue to use money when holding money is costly, they must be gaining some benefit. The classical theorists assumed this benefit to be proportional to the volume of trade.

BUDGET CONSTRAINTS AND OPPORTUNITY COST

Money imposes an **opportunity cost** because the decision to use money reduces the resources available for other goods. In Chapter 9, we discuss the opportunities for borrowing and lending, and modify our analysis of the opportunity cost of holding money. But for the moment, we assume that money is the only asset available to households as a store of wealth. In our simple model, the opportunity cost of holding money arises from the fact

BOX 5.1

A CLOSER LOOK
Three Influential Economists Who Worked on Monetary Theory

David Hume

David Hume was the son of a Scottish landowner. He was a friend and contemporary of Adam Smith, and both were active in the Scottish Enlightenment, a remarkable resurgence of intellectual activity centered around Edinburgh in the eighteenth century. Hume's most important philosophical ideas are contained in *A Treatise of Human Nature,* in which he sought to "introduce the experimental method of reasoning into moral subjects"—or, more simply, to bring the scientific methods of the Enlightenment, of Newton and Bacon, to bear on five human subjects. These subjects were laid out in five volumes in the Treatise—I (Of the Understanding), II (Of the Passions), III (Of Morals), IV (Of Politics), and V (Of Criticism).

Hume's contributions to economics are contained in a series of essays of which his essay *Of Money,* written in 1752, is a beautiful and elegant statement of the quantity theory of money.

Alfred Marshall

Marshall was born in London and studied mathematics at Cambridge where he became a professor of political economy. Along with Jevons and Walras, he was one of the founders of the neoclassical school. Marshall studied economics because he hoped to improve the lot of mankind. He thought that for the bulk of the population, mired in poor living and working conditions, little progress in habits, aspirations, and self-esteem could be expected without prior improvement in economic conditions.

Marshall's *Principles of Economics* (1890) became a standard reference book for future students of economics, including John Maynard Keynes, who studied under Marshall at Cambridge. In monetary economics, Marshall helped to develop the "Cambridge Approach to Monetary Theory" that viewed the real value of cash balances as a commodity that yields a flow of services. It is Marshall's approach that we develop in this chapter.

Irving Fisher

Fisher was born in New York and was a professor of economics at Yale. He made a fortune by inventing a card-filing system known as the Rolodex — although his fortune was lost and his reputation was severely marred by the 1929 Wall Street crash. Just days before the crash, he was reassuring investors that stock prices were not overinflated but, rather, had achieved a new, permanent plateau.

Fisher made numerous important contributions to neoclassical economics, among which was his work on the quantity theory of money contained in his 1911 book, *The Purchasing Power of Money.* Fisher stressed a transactions approach to the demand for money in which a given stock of money is required to finance a flow of transactions. He suggested that the rate at which money flows around the economy is a constant that he called the *velocity of circulation*.

that if the household chooses not to hold money, it will be able to purchase additional commodities. We will illustrate this idea by contrasting the budget constraint in a static model (in which all exchange takes place at a single point in time) with the budget constraint in a dynamic model (in which exchanges take place at different points in time). The purpose of this examination is to show how the use of money imposes a cost on consumers by reducing the resources available for purchasing other commodities.

Budget Constraints in a Static Barter Economy

The type of economy we studied in Chapter 4 is called a **static barter economy**. The word "barter" means that commodities are directly exchanged for one another without the use of money. The word "static" means that the economy lasts for only one period of time: agents exchange labor for commodities they produce and consume, then the world ends.

We can rewrite the budget constraint faced by families in the static barter economy by measuring everything in terms of dollars instead of real commodities. Recall that P refers to the money price of commodities, and the symbol w is the money wage.

5.1

$$PY^D \quad = \quad P\pi \quad + \quad wL^S$$

Demand for   Profit   Labor income
commodities

Equation 5.1 represents the household budget constraint in a static barter economy. In this economy, no money changes hands and no family uses money for trade, but money can be used as an accounting unit. To illustrate how this accounting device works, suppose that you offered your labor services to a farmer who owns an orchard. The farmer offers to pay you $5.00 per hour, and he sells his apples for $0.20 each. Rather than accept $5 an hour, you could well agree to accept 25 apples per hour. The real wage (w/P) in this economy is 25 apples per hour; the money wage (w) is $5.00 per hour; and the price of commodities (P) is $0.20 per apple. The budget constraint in the barter economy, given in Equation 5.1, expresses relative prices by quoting labor and commodities in terms of money, even though money is never used in exchange.

Budget Constraints in a Dynamic Monetary Economy

How would this budget constraint be altered in a world in which money *must* be used in exchange? The classical theorists argued that since the typical household does not buy commodities at the same time that it sells its labor, during an average week the household has a reserve of cash on hand to facilitate the uneven timing of purchases and sales.

Consider a household that starts the week with some cash on hand. We call this the household's supply of money. The household earns income each week and makes routine purchases, such as groceries, movie tickets, or restaurant meals. Perhaps the household is also saving a little money each week to pay for a vacation in July. Because of the coming vacation, the household ends the week holding more cash than it began with. We call the cash held at the end of the week the household's "demand for money." If we measured the cash held by this particular household, we would see that it increases steadily from August through June as the household saves for its vacation and then decreases again in July as the household spends its savings.

The economy as a whole consists of many households just like the one we described. Some of these households accumulate cash to buy cars, some pay for Christmas gifts, and others finance weddings. Because these households all plan to spend their accumulated cash at different points in time, on average we see that the cash held across the whole economy at the end of the week is equal to the cash held at the beginning.

By separating purchases and sales at points in time, the classical theory explicitly models production and exchange as an ongoing dynamic process rather than as static episodes. To formally model this idea, we need to make a change to the household's budget constraint.

5.2

$$M^{\text{D}} + PY^{\text{D}} = P\pi + wL^{\text{S}} + M^{\text{S}}$$

| Demand for money | Demand for commodities | Profit | Labor income | Supply of money |

Equation 5.2 adds two additional terms to the budget constraint of a barter economy. M^{S} represents the money that the household owns at the beginning of the week; we call this the household's *supply of money* because it will be supplied by the household during the week to other households in the economy in exchange for commodities. M^{D} is the money that the household owns at the end of the week. We call this the household's *demand for money* because it represents cash that the household chooses to keep on hand at the end of the week—money that will be used to buy and sell commodities in the future. The supply of money owned by the household at the beginning of the week is like additional income that is available to be spent on commodities. The demand for money at the end of the week is like a demand for any other commodity because the decision to keep cash on hand from one week to the next reduces the funds that the household has available to spend on produced goods. Because the household's supply of money could be used to purchase additional commodities, the decision to hold money imposes an opportunity cost on the household. The lost opportunity that arises from holding money is the additional utility that could have been gained by purchasing additional commodities.

THE BENEFIT OF HOLDING MONEY

If households continue to hold money, and if that money imposes a cost, then money must also yield a benefit. To classical theorists, this benefit was the advantage that comes from being more easily able to exchange commodities with other households in the economy; in other words, money is a generally acceptable medium of exchange.

Consider the process of exchange in a barter economy. Suppose that an individual is a seller of good X and a buyer of good Y; we will call him Mr. Jones. For example, good X might be an economics lecture and good Y might be a haircut. In the barter economy, Mr. Jones must find a second individual, Mr. Smith, who wants both to sell good Y and to buy good X. This problem is called the **double coincidence of wants**; it implies that in a barter economy, it would be necessary for Mr. Jones, if he wants a haircut, to find a barber who wants to hear an economics lecture. Exchange is greatly simplified if everyone agrees on a commodity that they will accept in exchange, not for its own sake, but because by convention others will also accept this commodity. This is the purpose of money.

Classical theorists argued that the stock of money that the average household needs at any point in time is proportional to the dollar value of its demand for commodities. Households that purchase a higher value of commodities each week will on average need to keep more cash on hand. The constant of proportionality between the average stock of cash held by the household during the week and the value of its flow demand for commodities is called the **propensity to hold money**, and it is represented in the demand for money equation by the symbol k.

5.3

$$M^D \qquad - \qquad k \qquad \times \qquad PY^D$$

Demand for money		Propensity to hold money		Nominal value of commodities demanded

Notice that the demand for money in the classical theory is the relationship between a stock (money on hand) and a flow (weekly purchases of commodities). The theory predicts that a person who earns $200 per week will on average carry half as much cash and keep half the checking account balances as a person who earns $400 dollars per week. Because the theory describes the relationship between a stock and a flow, the constant k has units of time: the number of weeks of income that the average family carries in the form of money. Using a measure of money called $M1$ (mainly cash and checking accounts), the propensity to hold money in the postwar United States has been equal to 10 weeks (of income) on average, although k has been falling since the end of World War II.

AGGREGATE DEMAND AND THE DEMAND AND SUPPLY OF MONEY

The classical theorists used the classical theory of the demand for money to explain more than the use of cash in exchange. By putting a theory of the demand for money together with the assumption that the quantity of money demanded is equal to the quantity of money supplied, they explained the quantity of commodities demanded by households at a given price level. This relationship between the aggregate demand for commodities and the price level is called the "classical theory of aggregate demand."

FROM MONEY DEMAND TO A THEORY OF THE PRICE LEVEL

A critical step in the development of the classical theory of aggregate demand is the assumption that the quantity of money demanded is always equal to the quantity of money supplied. To understand the logic behind this assumption, suppose instead that, on average, households hold more cash each week than they need to buy and sell commodities. When a household finds that it has more money on hand than it needs, it can plan to buy more commodities than it would purchase during a normal week. But although a single household can reduce its money holdings by planning to buy more commodities, the community as a whole *cannot* reduce its money holdings in this way. Every attempt to buy a commodity by one household must necessarily lead to an accumulation in the cash held

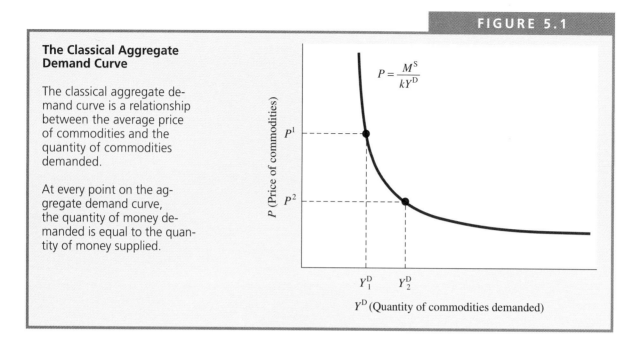

FIGURE 5.1

The Classical Aggregate Demand Curve

The classical aggregate demand curve is a relationship between the average price of commodities and the quantity of commodities demanded.

At every point on the aggregate demand curve, the quantity of money demanded is equal to the quantity of money supplied.

by another. For the community as a whole, the demand for money must always be equal to its supply. The fact that the demand for money must equal its supply can be used to develop a theory of how the aggregate demand for commodities varies with the nominal price. This relationship between price and the flow of GDP demanded is called the **classical aggregate demand curve**.

$$\textbf{5.4} \qquad P \quad = \quad \frac{M^S}{k\,Y^D}$$

Price level   = $\dfrac{\textbf{Supply of money}}{\textbf{Propensity to} \times \textbf{Aggregate demand}}$
$\qquad\qquad\qquad\quad$ **hold money** $\;$ **for commodities**

Equation 5.4 illustrates the classical aggregate demand curve. It is derived from Equation 5.3 by making the assumption that the demand for money is equal to the supply of money and rearranging terms to write the price level on one side of the equation. Figure 5.1 graphs this equation, plotting the price of commodities on the vertical axis and the quantity of commodities demanded on the horizontal axis. Although the graph in Figure 5.1 is called an aggregate demand curve, it is not a demand curve in the sense the term is used in microeconomic theory. It is an equation that shows how the price level would have to be related to the level of GDP if the quantity of money demanded and the quantity of money supplied were equal. As we move along the aggregate demand curve from left to right, the nominal value of GDP is constant. Since the quantity of money demanded is proportional to nominal GDP, each point along the aggregate demand curve is associated with the same demand for money. The position of the curve is determined by the quantity of money demanded at each point on the curve being exactly equal to the nominal money supply. At every point on the classical aggregate demand curve, the quantity of money demanded and the quantity of money supplied are equal.

To understand why the aggregate demand curve slopes downward, suppose that the price is at P_1 and the quantity of commodities demanded is at Y_1^D. If the price were to fall to P_2, the average family in the economy would have more cash on hand than it needed to buy commodities during the week because excess dollars would now be able to finance a greater flow of transactions. Each family would try to eliminate its excess cash by planning to purchase additional commodities. Thus, the economy experiences an increase in the aggregate quantity of commodities demanded, and the aggregate demand curve slopes downward.

IRVING FISHER AND THE VELOCITY OF CIRCULATION

The theory of aggregate demand, as we have described it so far, was developed in Cambridge, England, by Alfred Marshall. At about the same time, Irving Fisher of Yale University worked on a parallel development that led to similar conclusions. A key component of Fisher's version is a concept called the **velocity of circulation**. This measures the average number of times that the stock of money circulates in the economy, and it is defined as the ratio of the average value of transactions per unit of time to the nominal stock of money. In the following formula, V is the velocity of circulation, P is the price level, T is the number of transactions per unit of time, and M^S is the stock of money.

5.5
$$V = \frac{PT}{M^S}$$

$$\text{Velocity of circulation} = \frac{\text{Average value of transactions}}{\text{Nominal money supply}}$$

As it stands, Equation 5.5 is a definition of V. To make this into an operational theory, quantity theorists make two extra assumptions. The first is that T, the average number of transactions per unit of time, can be approximated by real aggregate demand for goods and services, Y^D. The second is that V is a constant. Using these additional assumptions, we can write Fisher's version of the quantity theory as follows:

5.6
$$P = \frac{VM^S}{Y^D}$$

$$\text{Price level} = \frac{\text{Velocity of circulation} \times \text{Supply of money}}{\text{Aggregate demand for commodities}}$$

If you compare Equation 5.6, which comes from Fisher's version of the quantity theory, with the Cambridge version of the theory from Equation 5.4, you will see that if we let $V = 1/k$, the two theories lead to the same equation for aggregate demand. We will now explore this equation and see how it can be used to explain the classical theory of the price level.

THE CLASSICAL THEORY OF THE PRICE LEVEL

THE ROLE OF THE PRICE LEVEL IN THE THEORY OF AGGREGATE SUPPLY

The classical theory of aggregate demand and supply is a complete explanation of the factors that determine the level of employment, the level of GDP, the relative price of labor and commodities (the real wage), and the prices of labor and commodities in terms of money (the nominal wage, w, and the price level, P). In this section, we fill in the remaining part by explaining how the classical theory of aggregate supply can be amended to accommodate the fact that trades take place using money as a medium of exchange. We explain the role of the price level in the theory of aggregate supply using three diagrams: the labor demand and supply diagram, the production function diagram, and the aggregate supply diagram.

THE PRICE LEVEL AND THE LABOR DEMAND AND SUPPLY DIAGRAM

Assume that the labor demand and supply decisions of households in a dynamic monetary economy are the same as the decisions that would be made in a static barter economy. This assumption, used by classical economists to simplify the theory of aggregate supply, is valid if the way that people make choices is greatly simplified. These simplifications are modified in the modern theory of dynamic equilibrium, which is discussed in Chapter 17.

In Figure 5.2, the labor demand and supply curves plot the choices of the household and the firm. In the classical model, the labor market is assumed to be in equilibrium. The real wage and the level of employment are determined by the intersection point of the labor demand and supply curves, denoted by $(w/P)^E$ and L^E, where E stands for equilibrium. The important feature of the classical analysis is that households and firms care only about the real wage because the ratio of w to P indicates how many commodities the household will receive for a given labor effort. The equilibrium values of L^E and $(w/P)^E$ depend in practice on the nature of the technology and the preferences of the households, since these features of the economy determine the positions and the slopes of the labor demand and supply curves.

THE PRODUCTION FUNCTION DIAGRAM

The second step in the classical theory of aggregate supply is to determine the supply of output. For a given level of employment, the supply of output is determined by the production function. The higher the level of employment, the greater the supply of output. Figure 5.3 reproduces the production function. The equilibrium supply of output, Y^E, is the amount of output that would be produced when the demand is equal to the supply of labor; that is, when the labor input is equal to L^E. The characteristics of the production function and the preferences of the households determine this particular output value.

FIGURE 5.2

The Labor Demand and Supply Diagram

In the classical theory of aggregate supply, aggregate employment is found by equating the quantity of labor demanded to the quantity of labor supplied.

The theory determines the wage in equilibrium. For any given price level there is a nominal wage such that the real wage is equal to its equilibrium level.

For example, suppose that (w^E/P) = 2. If $P = 2$ then $w^E = 4$; if $P = 5$ then $w^E = 10$. Only the ratio of w to P is determined by the theory.

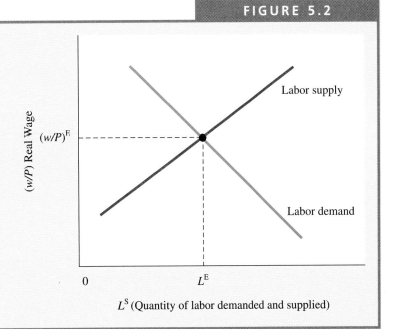

FIGURE 5.3

The Production Function Diagram

Once the real wage and the level of employment have been determined by the labor demand diagram, the supply of output is determined from the production function.

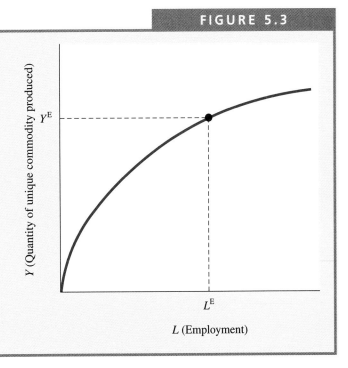

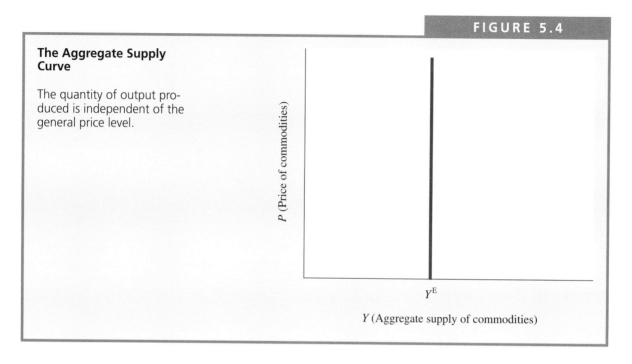

FIGURE 5.4

The Aggregate Supply Curve

The quantity of output produced is independent of the general price level.

THE AGGREGATE SUPPLY DIAGRAM

The final step is to determine how the supply of output is related to the money price of commodities. Since the quantities of labor demanded and supplied are both determined by the real wage, there is no relationship between the price of commodities and the supply of output. In other words, a classical economy will supply exactly Y^E units of commodities per week, regardless of the dollar price of commodities. When the price increases the nominal wage increases proportionately, leaving the real wage, the quantity of employment, and the supply of commodities unchanged.

The diagram in Figure 5.4 illustrates the classical theory of aggregate supply by plotting the price of commodities on the vertical axis and the aggregate supply of commodities on the horizontal axis. Because there is no relationship between the price of output and the aggregate supply of commodities, this graph is a vertical line at the level of output Y^E. At every point on this vertical line, the quantity of labor demanded is equal to the quantity of labor supplied.

THE COMPLETE CLASSICAL THEORY OF AGGREGATE DEMAND AND SUPPLY

We have used three diagrams to show how the classical theory of aggregate supply determines the real wage, the level of employment, and the aggregate supply of output. Figure 5.5 puts these three diagrams together to illustrate how the price level, output, and

FIGURE 5.5

Equilibrium in the Complete Classical System

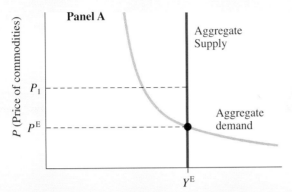

Panel A

P (Price of commodities)

Aggregate Supply

P_1

P^E

Aggregate demand

Y^E

Y (Quantity of commodities demanded and supplied)

Panel A is the aggregate demand and supply diagram. The downward-sloping curve is the classical aggregate demand curve. The vertical line is the classical aggregate supply curve.

Panel B has a 45° line that is used to translate the quantity Y^E from the vertical axis of panel C to the horizontal axis of panel A.

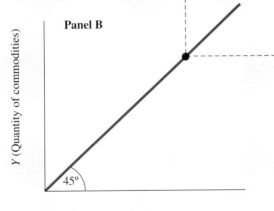

Panel B

Y (Quantity of commodities)

45°

Y (Quantity of commodities)

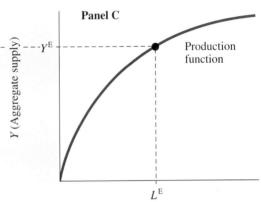

Panel C

Y (Aggregate supply)

Y^E

Production function

L^E

L (Employment)

Panel C is a production function; given the level of employment, L^E, the production function determines the quantity of commodities supplied, Y^E.

Panel D is the labor demand and supply diagram. This is used to determine equilibrium employment, L^E, and the equilibrium real wage, $(w/P)^E$.

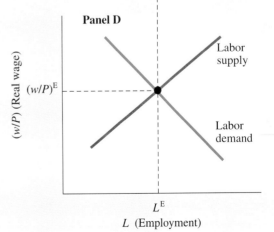

Panel D

(w/P) (Real wage)

$(w/P)^E$

Labor supply

Labor demand

L^E

L (Employment)

employment are determined in the complete classical system. Panel A plots the aggregate demand and supply curves on a single diagram; panel D is the labor demand and supply diagram; panel C is the production function; and panel B has a line at 45° to the axis that is used to take vertical distances from panel C and plot them as horizontal distances on panel A. We use this panel to translate the supply of output, determined by panels C and D, to the aggregate demand and supply diagram in panel A.

The following analysis explains why the aggregate supply curve is a vertical line. Beginning with panel A, pick an arbitrary value for the price of commodities. Call this arbitrary value P_1. To find a point on the aggregate supply curve, we must find the quantity of output produced when the price level equals P_1. We turn to panel D, the labor demand and supply diagram, to establish a value for the quantity of output supplied.

From panel D we find that at any commodity price, the equality of the quantity of labor demanded with the quantity of labor supplied will result in L^E hours of labor being traded at a real wage of $(w/P)^E$. To find the equilibrium supply of output, we may read off the quantity of GDP produced when L^E hours of labor are employed from the production function on panel C. The final step is to use the 45° line in panel B to translate the distance Y^E from the vertical axis of panel C to the horizontal axis of panel A. This step establishes that the point $\{P_1, Y^E\}$ is on the aggregate supply curve.

To find a second point on the aggregate supply curve, we could begin with a price value that is either lower or higher than P_1. Once again, we find that the equality of the quantity of labor demanded with the quantity of labor supplied will require the household to supply exactly L^E hours of labor. The crucial point in this argument is the fact that the quantities of labor demanded and supplied depend on the real wage and not on the nominal wage or the price level. If the price level doubles, a labor market equilibrium will exist in which the nominal wage is twice as high. This equilibrium will have the same employment level and the same quantity of output supplied as the labor market equilibrium at the price level P_1. Because the equilibrium quantity of employment depends only on the real wage and not on the price level, the assumption of labor market equilibrium generates the same supply of output for every possible value of the price level.

CLASSICAL THEORY AND THE DISTINCTION BETWEEN REAL AND NOMINAL VARIABLES

It is possible to classify all economic variables as either **real variables** or **nominal variables**. A real variable is measured in units of commodities. A nominal variable is measured in monetary units (like U.S. dollars). Table 5.1 presents an example of how to classify some of the variables we have seen so far.

An important proposition logically follows from the classical assumption that all markets are in equilibrium. In the classical model, the aggregate supply curve is vertical. A vertical aggregate supply curve implies that a fall in aggregate demand will cause a fall in the price level and leave all real variables unaffected. Since the demand for money is proportional to the demand for commodities, a 10% fall in the supply of money is predicted to lead to a 10% fall in all nominal variables, including the price level and the nominal wage. The proposition that nominal variables will move in proportion to changes in the quantity of money and that real variables will be invariant to these changes is referred to as the **neutrality of money**.

TABLE 5.1

Real and Nominal Variables

	Variable	Type	Units
M	The nominal money supply	Nominal	Dollars
P	The price level	Nominal	Dollars per commodity
w	The wage	Nominal	Dollars per hour
(w/P)	The real wage	Real	Commodities per hour
Y	Real GDP	Real	Commodities per year
PY	Nominal GDP	Nominal	Dollars per year
L	Employment	Real	Hours per year
(M/P)	Real money balances	Real	Commodities

THE NEUTRALITY OF MONEY

Figure 5.6 illustrates the response of output, employment, the real wage, and the price level to a reduction in the quantity of money, as predicted by the classical model. Suppose that the average household begins each week with $500 cash. During the week it receives labor income and profits, and it purchases commodities from other households equal to the value of its income. In a typical week, the stock of cash held at the beginning of the week will equal the stock of cash on hand at the end of the week. Consider how this economy would respond to an exogenous event that reduced the stock of cash in circulation. In practice, there are several ways this might happen. Suppose that the government removes $100 from the average household.[1] The week the money supply contracts, the outlays of the household will be higher than usual because it must both finance its purchases and pay $100 to the government. If it were to maintain its normal spending pattern, the household would end the week holding only $400 in cash. This would not be consistent with the equality of the demand and supply of money because the household requires $500 in cash at the end of the week to meet its future need for money as a medium of exchange. In the classical economy, the household tries to return its cash holdings to normal by spending less on goods and services, but although a single household can choose to hold $500 in cash, the economy as a whole cannot.

---

1.   In practice, most changes in the stock of money are accomplished by actions of the central bank, called *open market operations*. An open market operation involves the sale of interest-bearing bonds to the public. In return for bonds, the public surrenders some of its money to the central bank. The public ends up holding more bonds and less money.

FIGURE 5.6

The Response to a Reduction in the Money Supply Predicted by the Classical Model

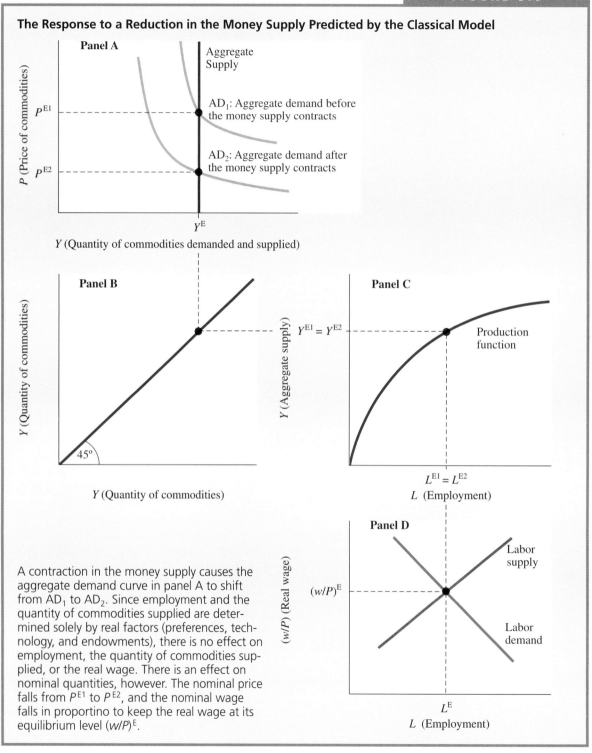

A contraction in the money supply causes the aggregate demand curve in panel A to shift from AD$_1$ to AD$_2$. Since employment and the quantity of commodities supplied are determined solely by real factors (preferences, technology, and endowments), there is no effect on employment, the quantity of commodities supplied, or the real wage. There is an effect on nominal quantities, however. The nominal price falls from P^{E1} to P^{E2}, and the nominal wage falls in proportino to keep the real wage at its equilibrium level $(w/P)^E$.

Figure 5.6 shows the household's reduction in spending as a leftward shift in the aggregate demand curve in panel A. Before the reduction in the stock of money, the aggregate demand curve is AD_1 and the equilibrium price of commodities is P^{E1}. After the fall in the stock of money, the aggregate demand curve is AD_2 and the equilibrium price is P^{E2}. To restore equality between the quantity of commodities demanded and the quantity of commodities supplied, the price level must fall by the same proportion as the stock of money, since the demand for money is proportional to GDP. Once the price level has fallen, the household is content to hold the lower quantity of nominal balances. A drop in the nominal supply of money does not affect the real wage, the quantity of employment, or the quantity of commodities supplied because they are each determined by technology, endowments, and preferences. Real variables are not altered by a drop in the money supply, but nominal variables fall in proportion. This proposition is called the neutrality of money.

USING THE CLASSICAL THEORY TO UNDERSTAND DATA

In Chapter 4, we evaluated the predictions of the classical model for the theory of business cycles. Now we turn our attention to the predictions of the classical theory of the price level. How well does the theory enable us to understand the problem of inflation? Box 5.2 presents a numerical example of how to determine the price level.

THE CLASSICAL EXPLANATION OF INFLATION

Classical theory determines the price level as the point of intersection of the aggregate demand curve with a vertical aggregate supply curve. Because inflation is the percentage rate of change of the price level from one year to the next, this theory also explains inflation. An important component of classical theory is the assumption that output is determined by equilibrium in the labor market. This assumption allows us to draw a vertical aggregate supply curve on panel A of Figure 5.6.

Table 5.2 describes the dependence of the price level on the propensity to hold money, the aggregate supply of commodities, and the quantity of money supplied. The first equation in this table takes the aggregate demand curve, Equation 5.4, and replaces the quantity of commodities demanded by Y^E, the equilibrium quantity of commodities supplied. The equation, expressed in this way, is called the **quantity equation of money**. Table 5.2 lists the factors that, according to the quantity equation, possibly cause increases in the price level: the propensity to hold money, the equilibrium quantity of commodities supplied, or the supply of money.

The first factor that could be responsible for changes in the price level is k. Because classical theory assumes k is constant, this explanation can be ruled out. The second factor that could cause changes in the price level is the level of aggregate supply. But in order for changes in aggregate supply to be responsible for inflation, output would have to fall continuously over time. This would be equivalent to a continuous leftward shift of the aggregate supply curve. In fact, most countries' economies have been growing over time, which tends to cause the price level to fall. The only remaining possible explanation of inflation

BOX 5.2

A CLOSER LOOK
A Mathematical Example of Aggregate Demand and Supply

In this box, we use the example from Box 4.5 to show how the price level is determined. In that example, the production function of a typical firm was given by

5.1.1 $$Y^S = L^D - (1/2)(L^D)^2,$$

and the labor demand curve was given by the formula

5.1.2 $$1 - L^D = (w/P)$$

where (w/P) is the real wage. The labor supply curve was given by

5.1.3 $$(w/P) = L^S;$$

and in equilibrium we established that

5.1.4 $$(w/P)^E = 1/2, \qquad L^E = 1/2, \qquad \text{and } Y^E = 3/8.$$

Notice that neither P nor w is determined individually; it is only their ratio that is set in the labor market.

To complete the classical model, suppose that the propensity to hold money, k, is equal to 2, and the stock of money, M^S, equals 100. The classical aggregate demand curve is given by the equation:

5.1.5 $$P = \frac{M^S}{k\,Y^E}$$

Plugging in the numbers for M^S, k, and Y^E, the equilibrium price level in this economy can be found to be

5.1.6 $$P = \frac{100}{2 \times (3/8)} = 133.33.$$

Finally, since

5.1.7 $$(w/P)^E = 1/2,$$

the equilibrium money wage in this economy is given by

5.1.8 $$w^E = P^E \times (1/2) = 133.33 \times 1/2 = 66.66.$$

is an increase in the stock of money, which would cause the aggregate demand curve to keep shifting rightward over time.

Equation 5.7 depicts the quantity equation in the form of proportional changes.[2] Assuming that k is constant, the classical theory predicts that the rate of inflation, $\Delta P/P$,

---

2. Mathematical Note: The notation ΔX, where X is any economic variable, means the change in X from one year to the next. The notation $\Delta X/X$ means the change in X divided by the level of X; that is, $\Delta X/X$ is the proportional change in the variable X. The exact relation between growth rates and levels is:

$$\text{if } m = \frac{M}{P} \text{ then } \frac{\Delta m}{m} \cong \frac{\Delta M}{M} - \frac{\Delta P}{P}$$

where $\cong$ means "is approximately equal to." As the period gets very small (i.e., as Δ tends toward zero) the approximation becomes exact. This is true for instantaneous growth rates.

TABLE 5.2

The Factors That Determine the Price Level

<table>
<tr><td colspan="3" align="center">The Quantity Equation of Money: $P = \dfrac{M^S}{kY^E}$</td></tr>
<tr><td>k</td><td>Propensity to hold money</td><td>This is assumed to be constant by the classical theory.</td></tr>
<tr><td>Y^E</td><td>Aggregate supply</td><td>This grows at a rate determined by preferences, technology, and endowments.</td></tr>
<tr><td>M^S</td><td>The money supply</td><td>This grows at a rate determined by the government.</td></tr>
</table>

should be equal to the rate of money growth, $\Delta M^S/M^S$, minus the rate of growth of output, $\Delta Y^S/Y^S$.

$$5.7 \qquad \frac{\Delta P}{P} \quad = \quad \frac{\Delta M^S}{M^S} \quad - \quad \frac{\Delta Y^S}{Y^S}$$

**Rate of
Inflation**   **Rate of money
supply growth**   **Rate of output
growth**

Before the middle of the twentieth century, money was backed by precious metals, usually gold or silver. During this period, no government could issue money unless it had enough gold or silver in the treasury to meet the public's demands to convert their paper currencies back into gold. In the sixteenth century, with the discovery of gold in the New World, European economists recognized that there was a connection between increases in the stock of money and increases in prices. These early empirical observations gave an impetus to the development of the quantity theory of money.

Since the 1930s, the world monetary system has been uncoupled from precious metals; nothing backs the currency in any country other than the promises of national central banks. In some countries, such as the United States, the United Kingdom, and Japan, the nation's central bank has maintained a relatively tight control over the supply of money, and these countries have experienced relatively low inflations. In other countries, such as Israel, Argentina, and Brazil, the central bank has printed money to finance government expenditure programs instead of raising government revenues by taxation. These countries have experienced very rapid inflations. The different experiences of three low-inflation countries and three high-inflation countries are illustrated in Figures 5.7 and 5.8.

Figure 5.7 plots money growth and inflation for the period from 1960 through 1999 for Japan, the United Kingdom, and the United States. None of these countries experienced

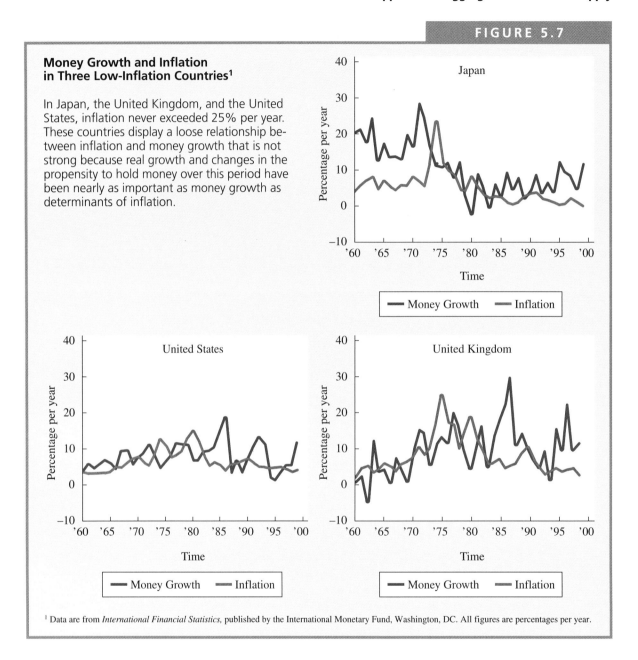

FIGURE 5.7

Money Growth and Inflation in Three Low-Inflation Countries[1]

In Japan, the United Kingdom, and the United States, inflation never exceeded 25% per year. These countries display a loose relationship between inflation and money growth that is not strong because real growth and changes in the propensity to hold money over this period have been nearly as important as money growth as determinants of inflation.

[1] Data are from *International Financial Statistics,* published by the International Monetary Fund, Washington, DC. All figures are percentages per year.

inflation exceeding 25% over this period. The figure illustrates that even in low-inflation countries, there is a connection between money growth and inflation. This connection is not particularly strong, because real GDP growth and changes in the propensity to hold money have been almost as important as the rate of money creation in determining the rate of inflation.

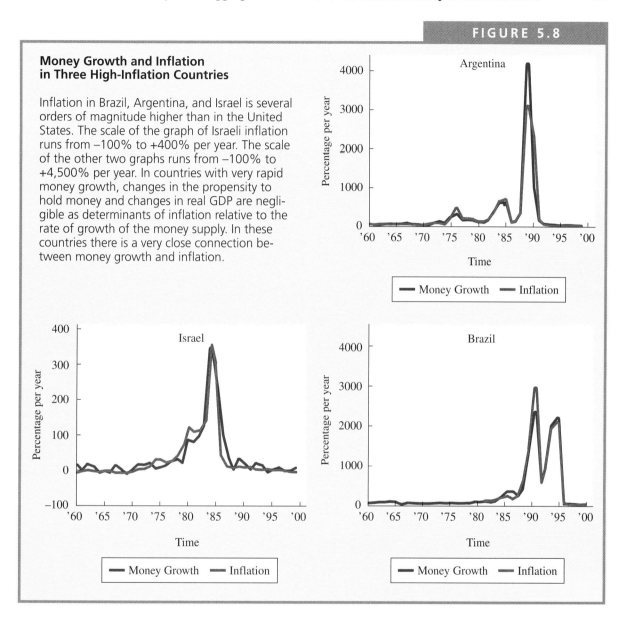

FIGURE 5.8

**Money Growth and Inflation
in Three High-Inflation Countries**

Inflation in Brazil, Argentina, and Israel is several orders of magnitude higher than in the United States. The scale of the graph of Israeli inflation runs from −100% to +400% per year. The scale of the other two graphs runs from −100% to +4,500% per year. In countries with very rapid money growth, changes in the propensity to hold money and changes in real GDP are negligible as determinants of inflation relative to the rate of growth of the money supply. In these countries there is a very close connection between money growth and inflation.

Figure 5.8 plots money growth and inflation in Argentina, Israel, and Brazil over the same period. Here, the scale of the vertical axis runs from −100% to +400% per year in the case of Israel and −100% per year to +4,500% per year in the cases of Argentina and Brazil. These countries have experienced very high inflation. Notice that in the high-inflation countries, there is a very close connection between the rate of money creation and the rate of inflation. The connection between money growth and inflation is strong in countries with very high inflation because movements in the propensity to hold money and movements in real GDP growth are very small relative to huge movements in the stock of money. Control of the money supply by the central bank is essential if a country is to avoid the very high inflations like those of Brazil and Argentina in 1990. These periods of very high inflation are extremely disruptive to the average household.

SEIGNORAGE AND THE INFLATION TAX

Since inflation is caused by excessive money creation, why do some governments engage in this behavior? One reason is that the government can generate revenue, called **seignorage**, by issuing money. Households and firms that hold money can choose instead to hold their wealth as interest-bearing securities by lending to corporations or to the government. If they choose to hold money, they will be able to buy fewer commodities in a year than they would otherwise. Inflation erodes the value of money.

In an economy in which there is no inflation, the value of money is worth as much at the end of the year as it is at the beginning of the year. If the government chose to increase the stock of money at the same rate as the underlying rate of real economic growth, there would be no inflation. If, instead, the government creates money at a faster rate than the rate of growth, then the purchasing power of the existing bills in the economy will be eroded. This erosion of purchasing power on the part of private agents is matched by an increase in purchasing power on the part of government. As the new money enters general circulation, it is exchanged for goods and services. In effect, the government is able to increase its purchase of real goods and services without raising income or sales taxes. Instead, it raises revenue from seignorage, also referred to as the "inflation tax."

In economies like the United States, the United Kingdom, and Japan, the government is well developed, and there are institutions in place that make it efficient and easy to raise revenue from income taxes or sales taxes. But even in Western democracies, there can be situations when the normal channels of revenue creation break down. One example was in Germany after World War I. The Allies forced Germany to pay war reparations that were so large that it was not possible to raise the revenue by standard channels. Instead, the government resorted to money creation, and the result was a hyperinflation of enormous proportions. Brazil, Argentina, and Israel have all resorted to money creation as a means of raising revenue. The results are apparent in Figure 5.8.

ASSESSING THE CLASSICAL EXPLANATION OF INFLATION

The main feature of the classical explanation of inflation is the concept of a demand function for money that is stable over time; the stability of the equation is represented by the classical assumption that the propensity to hold money, k, is a constant. There have been two principal challenges to the classical explanation. The first claims that k is not, in fact, a constant, and that inflation is just as frequently due to changes in k as to increases in the supply of money. According to this challenge, an increase in the supply of money is just one of the possible causes of inflation, and there is no reason to single out changes in the money supply over and above other causes of inflation. Figure 5.9 illustrates that k has indeed fluctuated considerably over the past century. We will return to this fact in chapter 9.

A second challenge to the classical explanation of inflation recognizes that there is indeed a connection between inflation and money growth, but it asserts that classical econo-

FIGURE 5.9

The Propensity to Hold Money in the United States

The propensity to hold money has fluctuated considerably since 1890. In the early part of the century it was relatively stable. During the 1930s and 1940s it increased dramatically, reaching a peak of nearly 25 weeks of income in 1946. Since the end of World War II it has been falling.

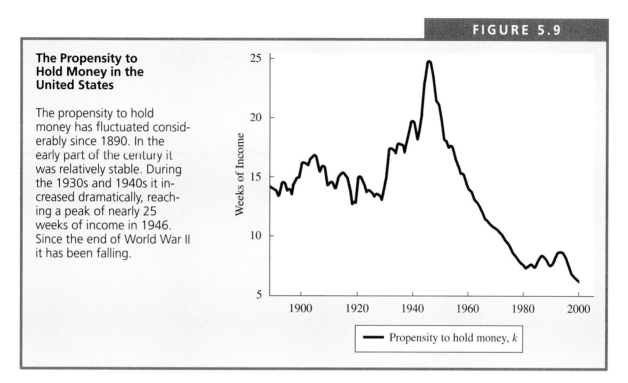

Propensity to hold money, k

mists have the direction of causation wrong. In other words, inflation causes money growth and not the other way around. This criticism is most often stated as a political or sociological explanation of inflation that denies the economic assumption that the rate of money growth can legitimately be considered an exogenous variable.[3] Critics of the economic explanation of inflation argue that the growth of trade unions is responsible for the spread of inflation. As unions push for higher wages, wage gains are in turn fed into price hikes. The increases in the stock of money that are often observed to accompany inflation are explained as the accommodating response of a central bank that raises the rate of money growth in order to avoid a recession. The main problem with this criticism is that there is no strong correlation between the growth of trade union power and inflation.

Perhaps the most troubling aspect of the classical theory of aggregate demand is its failure to explain the Great Depression; output fell 20% below trend and prices were strongly procyclical. In the classical model the aggregate supply curve is vertical and the aggregate demand curve is shifted only by changes in the stock of money. A leftward shift of the aggregate demand curve would lower prices, but it would not cause a drop in output because of the vertical aggregate supply curve. A leftward shift of the aggregate supply

---

3.   Political theories of inflation based on union pressure are called *cost push* theories. Cost push theories were influential in the 1960s, although more recently they have become less popular. A good example of the cost push view can be found in P.J. Wiles: "Cost inflation and the state of economic theory," *Economic Journal,* 83, pp 377–398, 1973.

curve would lower output, but it would be expected to *raise* prices. The failure of the classical model to easily account for procyclical prices during the Great Depression led to the development of Keynesian economics, a topic that we take up in Chapter 8.

CONCLUSION

The quantity theory of money, the classical theory of the price level, and the classical theory of aggregate demand are different names for the same theory. The theory assumes that the use of money in exchange has costs and benefits. The cost is in resources that are tied up in cash—resources that could be used to purchase additional commodities. The benefit is in the utility yielded by the use of money to bridge the uneven timing of purchases and sales. The theory assumes that the quantity of money demanded is proportional to GDP with a constant k: the propensity to hold money.

To move from a theory of the demand and supply of money to a theory of aggregate demand, we assume that for the community as a whole, the quantity of money demanded must always equal the quantity supplied. If the price level falls, the real value of the existing stock of money will increase and individual households will experience an excess supply of cash. As they attempt to spend this excess cash, the aggregate quantity of commodities demanded will increase.

The classical theory of aggregate demand can be combined with the classical theory of aggregate supply to explain how output, employment, the real wage, the nominal wage, and the price level are determined. The classical theory implies that if the nominal quantity of money is doubled; all nominal variables will also double; but all real variables will remain unchanged. This is the neutrality of money.

The classical theory of the price level works well for countries that are experiencing very rapid inflations, such as Argentina, Israel, and Brazil. It does not work as well in low-inflation countries, such as the United States, the United Kingdom, and Japan, because the propensity to hold money is, in reality, not a constant. In high-inflation countries, movements in k are swamped by movements in the money supply; in low-inflation countries, this is not the case. The biggest problem with the classical theory is that it cannot explain why prices were procyclical during the Great Depression.

KEY TERMS

Classical aggregate demand curve

Classical theory of aggregate demand

Classical theory of the price level

Double coincidence of wants

Exchange services

Neoclassical synthesis

Neutrality of money

Nominal variable

Opportunity cost

Propensity to hold money

Quantity equation of money

Quantity theory of money

Real variables

Seignorage

Static barter economy

Theory of the demand for money

Velocity of circulation

QUESTIONS FOR CHAPTER 5

1. The following data are from the U.S. economy. GDP is measured in trillions of dollars per year and M1 is a measure of the money stock, also in trillions of dollars.

Year	GDP	M1
1980	2.7	0.41
1981	3.0	0.44
1982	3.1	0.47
1983	3.4	0.52
1984	3.8	0.55
1985	4.0	0.62

a. Calculate the value of the propensity to hold money, k, for each year.

b. In what units is k measured?

c. Draw a graph of k against time, measured by the year. Was k approximately constant over this period? (Hint: find the average value of k. Calculate the maximum percentage that k deviates, in any given year, from its average).

d. What is the relationship between k and velocity, V?

2. Describe the quantity theory of money. Why is it a theory of aggregate demand? Intuitively, why does the aggregate demand curve, according to the quantity theory, slope downward?

3. According to the quantity theory, what is the relationship between the money supply and the inflation rate? Is this relationship a perfect one? Explain in detail.

4. Explain the distinction between *real* and *nominal* variables. What role does this distinction play in the concept of money neutrality?

5. Two important assumptions in the classical model are that markets are perfectly competitive and that prices are perfectly flexible. Would money neutrality necessarily hold if prices were not perfectly flexible? Why or why not?

6. If high rates of inflation are caused by governments printing too much money, why, then, do governments print too much money?

7. In the classical model, is the price level procyclical or countercyclical? Use an aggregate demand and aggregate supply graph to illustrate why. Is this prediction consistent with U.S. historical data? Explain.

8. Explain how each of the following occurrences would affect the equilibrium values of the real wage, the nominal wage, the quantity of labor, aggregate output, and the price level. Use graphs to illustrate.

   a. the discovery of a large natural resource deposit (such as oil)

   b. a 20% reduction in the money supply

   c. the discovery of a new technology that increases productivity

9. Using the classical model, examine the effects of the large increase in the labor force participation rate among women in the U.S. since the 1950s. Make sure to discuss any effects on the price level, the real wage, the nominal wage, and employment. Provide the appropriate graphs to illustrate.

10. Give examples of changes in preferences, endowments, and technology that would raise the price level. Have any events of this kind been important in the United States in recent years?

11. The economist Jean-Baptiste Say posited a theory that has become known as *Say's Law*, according to which "supply creates its own demand." In what sense is the classical model that is developed in Chapters 4 and 5 consistent with Say's Law? Explain.

12. Consider an economy with the following aggregate production function: $Y = 6L^{1/2}$.

   a. Derive the labor demand curve. (Hint: If a production function takes the form $Y = AL^\alpha$ then the marginal product of labor equals $\alpha AL^{\alpha-1}$.

   b. Assume that $M^S = 96$ and $k = 8$. Use the quantity theory to derive the aggregate demand curve.

   c. If the labor supply curve is $L^S = 2(w/P)$, what is the equilibrium level of labor and the real wage in this economy?

   d. What is the equilibrium level of aggregate output, Y?

   e. What is the equilibrium price level?

13. Consider an economy with the following aggregate production function, $Y = 3L^{1/3}$.

   a. Derive the labor demand curve. (Remember: If a production function takes the form $Y = AL^\alpha$, then the marginal product of labor equals $\alpha AL^{\alpha-1}$.

   b. Assume that $A = 1$. If the labor supply curve is $L^S = (w/P)$, calculate the equilibrium levels of the real wage, labor, and aggregate output.

   c. Assume that $M^S = 45$ and $k = 3$. What is the equation of the aggregate demand curve for this example and what is the equilibrium price level?

   d. Now assume that because of a new innovation, the productivity of labor rises, and A increases from 1 to 4. Calculate what happens to the real wage, labor, the price level, and aggregate output. Provide graphs of the labor and output markets to illustrate your results.

14. Consider the following classical economy with these characteristics:

$$Y = 8L^{1/2} \qquad\qquad k = 3$$
$$L^S = 2(w/P) \qquad\qquad M^S = 96$$

a. Calculate equilibrium in this classical model by solving for the equilibrium values of the real wage, nominal wage, labor, aggregate output, and the price level.

b. Suppose that the money supply increases by 25%. Calculate what happens to the equilibrium values of the real wage, nominal wage, labor, aggregate output, and the price level.

c. Explain how your answers to part a and part b are consistent with the concept of money neutrality.

15. An economy produces output using the technology

$$Y = L$$

And the representative agent has a utility function given by

$$U = \log(Y) + \log(1 - L)$$

a. How much output would be produced in equilibrium?

b. How much labor would be employed in equilibrium?

c. If the price level were equal to $6 per unit of output, what would the nominal wage be in equilibrium?

d. If the stock of money equals $20 and the propensity to hold money equals 1, what would the price level be in equilibrium?

16. This question is based on Milton Friedman's views, as expressed in his interview in *The Region.*

a. Does Friedman think that the Federal Reserve System should be made more powerful? If not, why not?

b. Why, according to Friedman, is federal deposit insurance no longer useful?

c. Why does Friedman think that the European monetary union will be unsuccessful?

d. Does Friedman agree with real business cycle theorists?

e. Why does Friedman think that more episodes of high inflation and hyperinflation are likely in the world during the next decade?

CHAPTER 6

SAVING AND INVESTMENT

INTRODUCTION

In this chapter, we will apply the classical model of demand and supply to the capital market. Theory argues that the rate of interest is a price that equates the demand for investment to the supply of saving, and this theory is widely accepted by economists of all persuasions, even those who do not believe that the classical model should be applied to the labor market.

The starting point for classical economics is the representative household. In the classical model, consumption, investment, GDP, and employment can be viewed as chosen by a household that decides how hard to work and how much to save, based on its rational assessment of the costs and benefits of reallocating resources. The decision to reallocate time between work and leisure results in employment fluctuations that are highly correlated with GDP. The decision to reallocate production between consumption goods and investment goods provides a way of redistributing commodities over time. Classical economists believe that business fluctuations are caused by a series of shocks to technology that alter the productivity of labor in a random way from one year to the next. These shocks are transmitted to the capital market through changes in investment, and they cause saving, investment, and the interest rate to go up and down during the business cycle in an apparently random way.

Keynesian economists do not accept that changes in investment are caused by fundamental shocks to the productivity of technology, but they do accept the classical view that explains how these shocks are transmitted to the rate of interest. A Keynesian would take the view that investment moves up and down over the business cycle because of the irrational beliefs of individual investors. But although Keynesians do not agree with classical economists on the cause of investment shocks, they do accept much of the analysis of how investment shocks feed into saving and the rate of interest.

SAVING, INVESTMENT, AND THE CAPITAL MARKET

Saving occurs when households choose not to spend part of their income. Investment occurs when firms purchase new capital equipment. Because the decision to invest is made by firms and the decision to save is made by households, there must be a mechanism for channeling funds from savers to investors. This mechanism is the capital market.

SAVING AND INVESTMENT

What are the facts about consumption, saving, and investment? Figure 6.1 illustrates the annual detrended observations on U.S. GDP, consumption, and investment per person since 1960. In each panel, the solid blue line is GDP, measured as percentage deviations from a flexible trend. The solid red lines measure consumption and investment per person, also as deviations from trend. Notice that consumption and investment are strongly procyclical, but they differ considerably in how much they move up and down over the business cycle.

Table 6.1 measures the smoothness of these time series using a statistical measure called the "standard deviation."[1] Roughly speaking, the standard deviation is the average difference from the average. A series that is constant has a standard deviation of zero; a series that moves around a lot has a high standard deviation. Table 6.1 shows that GDP has a standard deviation of 1.59, consumption has a standard deviation of 1.09, and investment has a standard deviation of 5.56. This gives us a convenient way of quantifying what it means for a series to be more volatile than another; a more volatile series has a higher standard deviation. Consumption is roughly two-thirds as volatile as GDP. Investment is nearly three times as volatile as GDP.

---

1. Mathematical Note: The standard deviation is given by the formula $\sigma_x = \left(\dfrac{\sum_{i=1}^{n} (x_i - \bar{x})^2}{n - 1} \right)^{\frac{1}{2}}$ where $\bar{x} = \dfrac{\sum_{i=1}^{n} x_i}{n}$ is the arithmetic mean.

FIGURE 6.1

Consumption, Investment, and GDP in the United States

These graphs illustrate the consumption, investment, and GDP business cycle history in the United States since 1960. In each case, the blue line is the deviation of GDP from a flexible trend.

Panel A plots the deviation of consumption from trend as the red line; notice that consumption does not fluctuate as much as GDP.

Panel B plots the deviation of investment from a flexible trend as the red line; notice that investment fluctuates much more than GDP.

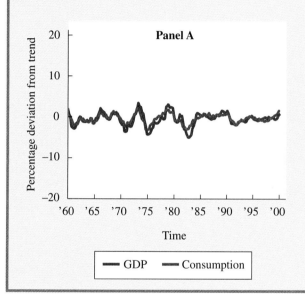

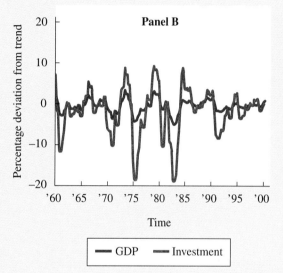

TABLE 6.1

How Smooth Is Consumption?

	GDP	Consumption	Investment
Standard deviation	1.59	1.09	5.56
Standard deviation relative to GDP	1.00	0.68	3.50

ANIMAL SPIRITS OR FUNDAMENTALS?

Why is investment so volatile? There are two possible answers. According to the classical economists, investment fluctuates because firms respond to changes in technology; this is called a **fundamental explanation** because in classical theory, output and employment are determined by the fundamentals: preferences, endowments, and technologies. An example of a fundamental explanation for an investment boom would be an invention that requires an investment in new kinds of machines in order to exploit the invention. Some economists believe that fundamentals, particularly the invention of new technologies, are the most important source of business fluctuations. This is the basis for the real business cycle school and one of the leading modern explanations for the causes of business cycles.

A second possibility, one suggested by John Maynard Keynes, is that highly volatile investment does not reflect changes in preferences, endowments, or technology. Instead, it represents changes in the mass psychology of investors. Keynes called the mass psychology of investors **animal spirits**. Followers of Keynes believe that animal spirits lead to variations in output and employment that could be avoided if investment were more efficiently coordinated. Therefore, they favor the implementation of government policies to stabilize the business cycle. This Keynesian view, which favors government intervention, is in contrast to the policy prescription of the new classical economists, who believe that business cycles are a necessary and unavoidable feature of the market economy.

The idea that investment is driven by animal spirits is an old one that goes by many different names. The sociologist Robert K. Merton coined the term **self-fulfilling prophecy**, which maintains that if enough people believe in some aspect of the social world, then it will be so.[2] This term is now widely used in economics to refer to the same idea that Keynes called "animal spirits." David Cass of the University of Pennsylvania and Karl Shell of Cornell University use the term **sunspots** to refer to a closely related idea.[3] Yet another related concept is that markets may sometimes be driven by **irrational exuberance**, a term used by Alan Greenspan, the chairman of the Federal Reserve Board, when referring to the recent stock market experience in which the market's value seems to some to be far greater than is justified by economic fundamentals. In this book we will use the terms animal spirits, sunspots, self-fulfilling prophecies, and irrational exuberance interchangeably when referring to situations in which markets are driven by elements other than market fundamentals.

CONSUMPTION SMOOTHING

Why is consumption so smooth? Although Keynesian and classical economists differ on the cause of volatile investment spending, they agree on the reason why consumption is

---

2.   Robert K. Merton. "The Self-Fulfilling Prophecy," *The Antioch Review*, pp 193–211, 1948.
3.   David Cass and Karl Shell. "Do Sunspots Matter?" *Journal of Political Economy*, 91, pp 193–227, 1983. When Cass and Shell refer to sunspots, they mean a nonfundamental cause of business cycles. This is in contrast to Stanley Jevons' original usage; he believed that sunspot activity causes business cycles as a result of the effect of solar flares on the weather.

smooth. Consumption is smooth because households borrow and lend in the capital market in an effort to redistribute their income more evenly over time.

We can illustrate consumption smoothing with an example. Suppose that you are faced with two possible consumption plans over a two-year horizon. In plan A you get to eat five meals a day in the first year and only one meal a day in the second year. In plan B you get to eat three meals a day for two years. **Consumption smoothing** means that most people would prefer plan B to plan A, even though they get to consume the same quantity of food in both plans.

To understand how consumption smoothing works in a classical model, consider how Robinson Crusoe would respond to changing productive opportunities. Suppose that he grows grain each year, but his productivity fluctuates with the weather. In some years the weather is favorable and he grows a relatively large amount of grain. In other years the harvest is bad and he grows relatively little. If we associate the harvest in this economy with GDP, we would observe fluctuations in Crusoe's GDP from year to year in response to changes in productivity.

Suppose that in one year Crusoe gets a particularly good harvest. If he prefers a smooth consumption plan, his best response to a good harvest is to store the excess grain, over and above a normal year's consumption, in order to distribute it more evenly over future years. Because there are many more years in the future than in the present, this storage plan implies that Crusoe's consumption will rise by less than the increase in GDP. The grain he stores would be recorded as investment, so an economist observing the Robinson Crusoe economy would see investment fluctuate much more, in relative terms, than GDP. This underlies the classical explanation of the relative volatilities of consumption, investment, and GDP over the business cycle.

BORROWING CONSTRAINTS

Keynesian economists agree on the basic logic that the capital market is used by households to smooth income, but they do not agree that the market works as well as it could. Some economists point out that although aggregate consumption is smoother than income, it is not as smooth as it could be, and the real business cycle model predicts that consumption should be much less volatile than it actually is. A possible reason for this is that although it is relatively easy to lend money to firms, it is extremely difficult to borrow money without security. Many people have low incomes early in life and high incomes later in life, once they have an education and work experience. We often attempt to borrow more money than we are able to when we are young. The reason it is sometimes difficult to borrow money is that it is hard for banks to enforce repayment later on.

How does the presence of borrowing constraints alter the classical theory? Suppose that some households prefer to consume more than their income and opt to repay their loans later in life. If the credit markets are imperfect, these households will be constrained; their optimal decision will be to consume all of their income. The presence of credit-constrained individuals implies that aggregate consumption will fluctuate more than would otherwise be the case since some households in the population will be consuming all of their income. For these households, consumption will fluctuate just as much as real GDP.

THE THEORY OF INVESTMENT

We now explore the theory of investment and saving by developing a demand and supply diagram. The demand curve, called the **demand for investment**, plots the quantity of investment demanded on the horizontal axis and the rate of interest on the vertical axis. The supply curve, called the **supply of saving**, plots the quantity of saving supplied on the horizontal axis and the rate of interest on the vertical axis. We explain the determination of the rate of interest and the quantity of resources saved and invested by arguing that the capital market is typically in equilibrium at the point where these two curves intersect. By developing an explanation of the factors that shift the demand curve for investment and the supply curve of saving, we can explain the co-movements of investment, saving, and the rate of interest observed in the data.

THE PRODUCTION POSSIBILITIES SET

We begin by asking: How would Robinson Crusoe make decisions if he were both a producer and a consumer? We illustrate the options available to Robinson Crusoe with a production possibilities set in which inputs and outputs occur at different points in time.

Once we introduce time explicitly into Robinson Crusoe's decision problem, he must decide not only how much to produce but also how to allocate his produced commodities between consumption goods and investment goods. For example, a few hours spent producing a fishing net will reduce the current production of fish, but it will greatly augment Robinson Crusoe's ability to catch additional fish in the future. The same kinds of decisions must be made in an advanced industrial economy when resources are allocated between the production of factories, roads, and houses, and the production of food, entertainment, and other nondurable consumer goods.

We represent the opportunities for investment as Robinson Crusoe's **intertemporal production possibilities set**. This set is the shaded blue region in the graph on Figure 6.2. The distance **OA** represents the resources available to Robinson Crusoe, resources to be divided between consumption and investment. The horizontal axis of the diagram measures two things. Reading from left to right, beginning at point **O**, it measures the quantity of commodities that Robinson Crusoe invests. Reading from right to left, beginning at point **A**, it measures the quantity of commodities he consumes. For example, suppose that Crusoe chooses to invest the resources **OB** and to consume the resources **BA**. In this case, he leaves himself the resources **OE** to be divided between consumption and investment in the future.

The production possibilities set has an upward-sloping frontier because the more Crusoe invests in the present, the greater his income will be in the future. Moving from left to right, beginning at point **O**, the slope of this frontier gets flatter, reflecting the assumption of diminishing returns. Diminishing returns means that as Crusoe spends more time building tools, each additional tool is marginally less productive than the one before. For example, building one spear may be very useful to him because it will increase his ability to hunt. But building a second spear will be less useful because the second spear is only useful if the first spear becomes broken. And, after all, Crusoe can only throw one spear at a time. In a modern industrial society, diminishing returns to investment applies because so-

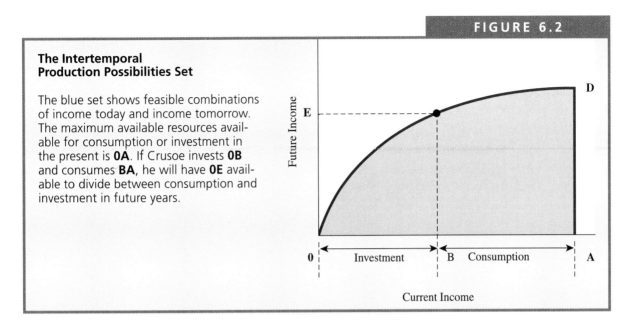

FIGURE 6.2

**The Intertemporal
Production Possibilities Set**

The blue set shows feasible combinations of income today and income tomorrow. The maximum available resources available for consumption or investment in the present is **0A**. If Crusoe invests **0B** and consumes **BA**, he will have **0E** available to divide between consumption and investment in future years.

ciety as a whole has a fixed stock of people. Building extra factories and machines increases the productive capacity of the economy, but only to the extent that there are enough people to operate them.

THE REAL RATE AND THE NOMINAL RATE OF INTEREST

In modern economies, most borrowing and lending contracts are denominated in dollars. But it has not always been this way; in medieval times, for example, it was common to borrow and lend commodities. A farmer might lend 10 sacks of flour to his neighbor. If the farmer's contract with his neighbor was to repay 11 sacks one year later, we would say that the **real interest rate** was 10% per year.

If the farmer in this example had been living in a currency-based economy, instead of lending 10 sacks of flour he might have lent dollars. Let us suppose that one sack of flour costs $5. Instead of borrowing 10 sacks of flour, an equivalent way of financing would be to borrow $50 and repay $55 in one year. In this case, we say that the **nominal interest rate** was 10%.

As long as the price of flour is the same next year as it is this year, a loan denominated in units of flour is equivalent to a loan denominated in dollars. But when the price of commodities changes from one year to the next, the real rate of interest is calculated from the nominal rate of interest by subtracting the rate of inflation. The relationship between the real interest rate, the nominal interest rate, and the rate of inflation is given in Equation 6.1, where we use the symbol r to represent the real interest rate, i to represent the nominal interest rate, and $\Delta P/P$ to represent the rate of inflation.[4]

---

4.   The symbol Δ means "the change in." $\Delta P/P$ is the proportional change in the price level, which is the definition of inflation.

6.1 r $=$ i $-$ $\Delta P/P$

Real interest rate   Nominal interest rate   Inflation rate

The rest of this chapter will deal exclusively with the real interest rate and loans that are denominated in units of commodities.

MAXIMIZING PROFITS

The classical theory of production assumes that markets are competitive. Firms borrow current resources in the capital markets and invest those resources in factories and machines. Classical theory assumes that firms choose how much labor to demand in order to maximize profits, so the classical economists applied the same logic to the decision about how much to invest. In the future, the factories and machines are used to produce commodities that are sold in the market. A firm's profit is the value of its produced output minus the accrued principal and interest on loans needed to purchase current investment goods. Firms invest up to the point at which the output produced by an extra unit of investment is equal to its cost.

The theories of the demand for labor and the demand for investment goods are very similar. In the theory of the demand for labor, the firm equates the marginal product of labor to the real wage. In the theory of the demand for investment, the firm equates the marginal product of investment to the real interest rate. Because the return from investment occurs in the future, there is an element of uncertainty associated with future profitability, which injects an element of risk into the investment decision. In this chapter, we will ignore this risk and analyze the firm's decisions as if the future were certain.

BORROWING AND THE INVESTMENT SCHEDULE

The classical theory of saving and investment assumes that firms and households can borrow and lend freely at a single rate of interest, called the **market rate**. Borrowing and lending take place in the capital market. Let's suppose that the market rate is r and that a firm can produce output tomorrow of value Y from an investment of I resources today. In this case, the profit of the firm is given by the formula in Equation 6.2.

6.2 π $=$ Y $-$ $(1+r)I$

Profit   Value of future sales   Cost of borrowing

The classical theory of production maintains that firms try to maximize expected profits. According to the assumption of perfect competition, all firms will pay the same interest rate when they borrow funds and use these funds to make new investments. This assumption lets us derive a relationship between the real interest rate and investment. If the real interest rate is plotted on the vertical axis of a graph and if the quantity of investment goods demanded is plotted on the horizontal axis, this relationship, called the "investment demand curve," slopes downward.

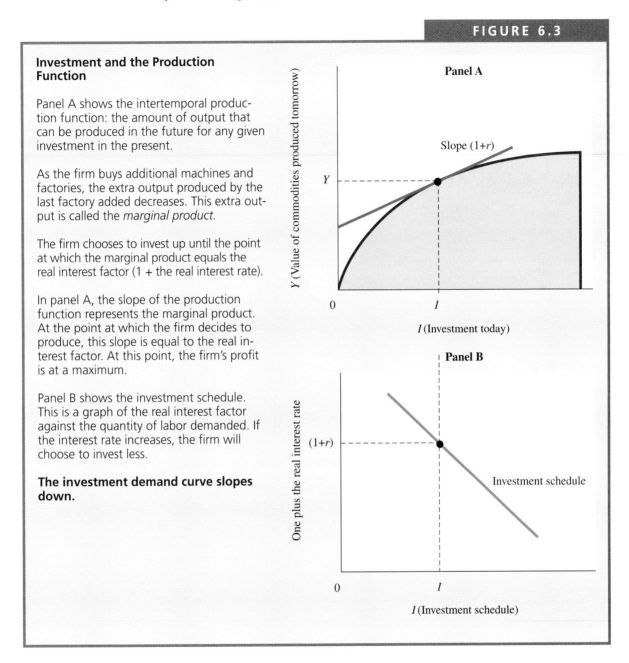

FIGURE 6.3

Investment and the Production Function

Panel A shows the intertemporal production function: the amount of output that can be produced in the future for any given investment in the present.

As the firm buys additional machines and factories, the extra output produced by the last factory added decreases. This extra output is called the *marginal product.*

The firm chooses to invest up until the point at which the marginal product equals the real interest factor (1 + the real interest rate).

In panel A, the slope of the production function represents the marginal product. At the point at which the firm decides to produce, this slope is equal to the real interest factor. At this point, the firm's profit is at a maximum.

Panel B shows the investment schedule. This is a graph of the real interest factor against the quantity of labor demanded. If the interest rate increases, the firm will choose to invest less.

The investment demand curve slopes down.

Figure 6.3 shows how the investment schedule and the production function are related to each other. Panel A depicts the production function. Recall that the slope of the production function gets flatter at higher levels of output. This assumption is called diminishing returns to a factor. Diminishing returns occurs because as the firm adds more machines and factories to a fixed quantity of land and labor, the output of each additional machine is

BOX 6.1

A CLOSER LOOK
Deriving the Investment Schedule: A Mathematical Example

This box presents a mathematical example of how to derive the investment schedule from profit maximization by firms. The example is very closely related to the problem that we solved in Box 4.1, where we derived a labor demand curve. This is because both topics use the idea that firms maximize profits.

The firm tries to maximize profit by choosing combinations of investment demanded and output supplied that lie within the intertemporal production possibilities set. We will assume that the boundary of the intertemporal production possibilities set (the production function) is given by the following expression:

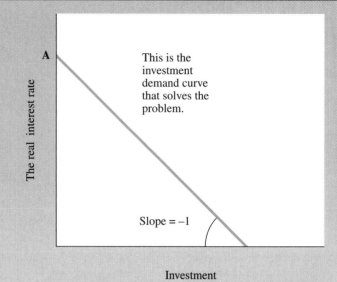

A

The real interest rate

This is the investment demand curve that solves the problem.

Slope $= -1$

Investment

6.1.1 $$Y^s = AI - (1/2)(I)^2$$

As in Chapter 4, we have chosen a quadratic function to represent the production function. This is mainly a matter of convenience since the quadratic function gives rise to a linear investment schedule. The term A is important. We use it to represent shifts in the productivity of investment by improvements in technology. If A increases, then investment will become more productive.

The firm will choose how much to invest by trying to maximize profit. If we combine the expression for the production function (Equation **6.1.1**) with the definition of profit, we can write down the problem that the firm will try to solve:

6.1.2 $$\max \pi = AI - (1/2)(I)^2 - (1 + r)I$$

The firm tries to make this as big as possible.	**This is the total product, the output produced tomorrow by an investment (I) today.**	**This is the total cost of borrowing to invest I units.**

The solution to this problem is found by setting the derivative of profits, with respect to investment equal to zero.

6.1.3 $$A - I = (1 + r)$$

This is the derivative of the total product. It is called the marginal product of Investment.	**This is the derivative of the total cost. It is called the marginal cost.**

6.1.3 is the mathematical expression for the investment schedule and is found by equating the marginal product to the real interest factor. For the case of a quadratic production function, it is a straight line with a negative slope and an intercept equal to A. If A increases, the investment schedule will shift up and to the right.

less than the previous machine's output. The fixed quantity of labor and land must be shared with more capital.

As long as the marginal product of investment is greater than the real interest factor, the firm should keep adding more machines, since each additional machine adds more to total product than to total cost. The firm will maximize its profit by continuing to invest as long as the expected marginal product of an extra unit of capital is greater than the real interest factor. The firm will stop investing at the point where the marginal product is just equal to one plus the real interest rate. On panel A of Figure 6.3, this point occurs when the purple line (with a slope equal to one plus the real interest rate) is tangent to the production function (with a slope equal to the marginal product). The firm produces the quantity of output Y, and it demands the quantity of investment goods I. Box 6.1 takes a closer look at the algebra of the investment schedule.

HOUSEHOLDS AND THE SAVING SUPPLY CURVE

The application of the theory of marginal utility to the problem of saving is called the **intertemporal utility theory**, and it forms the basis for most modern explanations of how income is divided between consumption and saving. Intertemporal utility theory argues that, given the choice, families would prefer that consumption be evenly distributed over time. Just as preferences between leisure and consumption are represented by a mathematical expression called utility, so are preferences for consumption at different points in time.

THE INTERTEMPORAL BUDGET CONSTRAINT

Just as we use a budget constraint to illustrate the opportunities available to a household when trading leisure for consumption, so we can also use a budget constraint to represent the trades available to the household at different points in time. Suppose that instead of consuming its income, the household puts it into the capital market by lending to another household or to a firm. In return, the household receives future resources with interest. Because we receive interest on our saving, income that is saved for the future may purchase more future consumption goods than present ones. The amount of additional goods that we can buy in the future grows with the rate of interest. In this sense, the rate of interest is the price at which consumption in the present can be exchanged for consumption in the future.

PRESENT VALUE

Just as the capital market can be used to transfer resources from the present to the future, it can also be used to transfer resources from the future to the present. When you borrow against future income, the amount you can borrow is its **present value**.

For example, suppose John Smith, an economics student, will inherit $10,000 next year when he turns 21 years old. John would like to spend his inheritance on a used car, but he is impatient and unable to wait until next year. If he buys the car right away, the bank manager will lend him

$$\frac{1}{(1 + r)}Y = \frac{1}{1 + 0.1}\,\$10,000 = \$9,901,$$

which is the sum that can be exactly repaid with $10,000 in one year if the interest rate is 10%.

When the rate of interest is positive, future commodities are cheaper than current commodities in real terms because the household can increase its purchasing power by waiting. For example, if you have $20,000 to buy a car, you will be able to buy a mid-class sedan like a Toyota Camry or a Ford Taurus. If instead you were willing to wait five years, you could invest your money with interest, and in 10 years' time (if the interest rate was 7%, compounded annually), you would have $40,000, which would buy an entry-level luxury sedan like a BMW or an Audi. Alternatively, you could buy two Toyota Camrys. In this example, the relative price of a Camry today for a Camry 10 years from now is equal to 2.

BORROWING AND LENDING TO SMOOTH CONSUMPTION

A household can use the capital market to redistribute its resources over time. Let's use Y_1 to represent present income and Y_2 for future income. You might like to think of "the present" as the working years of two adults and "the future" as their retirement years. If the household does not save, it will be forced to reduce its consumption upon retirement. But by using the capital market, the household can buy financial assets that will pay off with interest in old age. Inequality 6.3 shows the constraint on lifetime choices that comes from the use of the capital market to smooth consumption. This inequality, called the **intertemporal budget constraint,** places a bound on the amount of consumption that is available over a household's lifetime.

6.3
$$C_1 \quad + \quad \frac{1}{(1+r)}C_2 \quad \leq \quad Y_1 \quad + \quad \frac{1}{(1+r)}Y_2$$

| Present consumption | Present value of future consumption | Current resources | Present value of future resources |

The left side of the constraint adds the values of present and future consumption; it represents the value of the goods that a person consumes at every point in life, valued in terms of current consumption goods. The right side adds the values of present and future income; it is the value of the income that a person earns at every point in life, valued in terms of current consumption goods. The price of future consumption is $1/(1+r)$, where r is the interest rate.

THE SAVING SUPPLY CURVE

The assumption that households maximize utility can be shown to lead to a relationship between the real interest rate and the quantity of saving that households choose to supply to the capital market. This relationship, called the "saving supply curve" is plotted in Figure 6.4.

When the real interest rate increases, there are two effects that influence saving. As the real interest rate goes up, current consumption becomes relatively more expensive, and this effect, the substitution effect, tends to make the household want to substitute consumption today for consumption tomorrow; that is, the household will tend to save

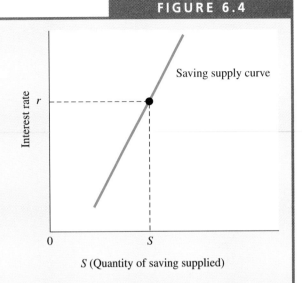

FIGURE 6.4

**Saving and the
Real Interest Rate**

The household chooses how much to save. As the real interest rate increases, it becomes more attractive to save because by giving up current consumption the household will increase its future purchasing power by more than one for one. In this sense, future commodities are cheap relative to current commodities. This is the substitution effect. A higher interest rate reduces the net present value of wealth. This may lead the household to save more or less, depending on how its income is spread over its life cycle. In practice, the sum of the two effects causes the saving supply curve to slope upward, although the slope is very steep.

The saving supply curve slopes upward.

more. But an increase in the real interest rate makes the household wealthier, and this effect (the **wealth effect**) has an ambiguous effect on saving. Neoclassical theory assumes that the supply of saving slopes upward. This is based in part on an assumption that the substitution effect dominates. The ultimate test, however, must be an empirical one: What happens in the data? Here the evidence suggests that the supply of saving does slope upward, but the curve is very steep. In other words, in practice, the effect of the interest rate on saving is very small. Box 6.2 on pages 152 and 153 takes a closer look at the algebra of the saving supply curve.

EQUATING DEMAND AND SUPPLY

By putting the theories of investment and saving together, we can explain how the capital market allocates resources between different points in time. We begin by looking at how the rate of interest adjusts to equate saving and investment in a closed economy. Then we modify this theory to account for trade in the international capital markets in an open economy.

SAVING AND INVESTMENT IN A CLOSED ECONOMY

Figure 6.5 on page 153 shows how the interest rate, saving, and investment are simultaneously determined. The saving supply curve represents the funds that are flowing into

BOX 6.2

A CLOSER LOOK
Deriving the Saving Supply Curve:
A Mathematical Example

In this box, we provide an example of an intertemporal utility function and show how to derive the saving supply curve.

To capture the idea of intertemporal utility, we will write down a mathematical expression for utility. Equation 6.2.1 is an example of a quadratic utility function.

6.2.1
$$U \quad = \quad -\frac{(2 - C_1)^2}{2} \quad + \quad C_2$$

| This is the utility of the household. | This is the utility derived from current commodities. | This is the utility derived from future commodities. |

Households try to make utility as big as possible, but they cannot spend more than their available wealth. This is given by their budget constraint, which we will break into two parts. In the current period, the household saves S from its income Y and consumes C_1:

6.2.2
$$S \quad = \quad Y \quad - \quad C_1$$

| Saving | Income | Current consumption |

In the second period (think of this as old age), the household consumes the principal and interest on its saving $(1+r)S$. To keep the algebra simple, we assume that the household has no income in old age.

6.2.3
$$C_2 \quad = \quad (1 + r)S$$

| Future consumption | Interest plus principal on saving |

S will be positive in this problem, although in general (if there were second-period income) there would be nothing in the theory to prevent young households from borrowing. In this case, S would be negative and the old households would have to pay back in old age what they borrowed in youth.

We can put the constraints **6.2.2** and **6.2.3** directly into the utility function. This leads to the following expression that involves only the choice variable S. (We have used **6.2.2** and **6.2.3** to eliminate C_1 and C_2.)

6.2.4
$$\max U \quad = \quad -\frac{(2 - Y + S)^2}{2} \quad + \quad (1 + r)S$$

| The household tries to make this as big as possible by choosing S. | This is the household's utility in the present if it chooses to save S. | This is the household's utility in the future if it chooses to save S. |

The solution to this problem is found by setting the derivative of utility with respect to saving equal to zero.

6.2.5
$$-(2 - Y + S) \quad + \quad (1 + r) \quad = \quad 0$$

| This is the utility lost today by saving one more unit. | This is the utility gained tomorrow by saving one more unit. |

Equation **6.2.5** tells the household how to weigh up the loss of saving an extra dollar today against the benefit of spending it tomorrow. The solution to this equation is the saving function.

6.2.6
$$S \quad = \quad Y - 1 + r$$

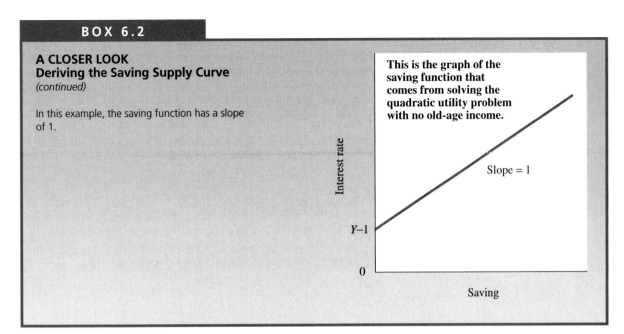

BOX 6.2

A CLOSER LOOK
Deriving the Saving Supply Curve
(continued)

In this example, the saving function has a slope
of 1.

This is the graph of the
saving function that
comes from solving the
quadratic utility problem
with no old-age income.

Slope = 1

Interest rate

$Y-1$

0

Saving

FIGURE 6.5

Capital Market Equilibrium

At interest rate r_1, households supply S_1 in saving to
the capital market and firms
want to borrow I_1 to finance
investment projects; investment exceeds saving.

At interest rate r_2, households supply S_2 in saving to
the capital market and firms
want to borrow I_2. Saving exceeds investment.

Only when $r = r^E$ does saving
equal investment. Then the
capital market is in equilibrium and investment equals
saving which equals I^E.

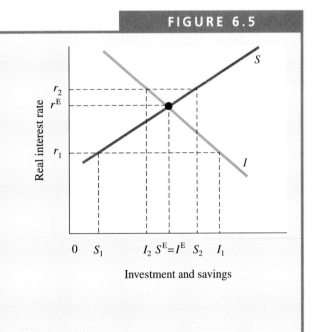

r_2
r^E

Real interest rate

r_1

S

I

0   S_1 I_2 $S^E = I^E$ S_2 I_1

Investment and savings

the capital market from households. This flow of saving is channeled through banks, savings and loan institutions, pension funds, and direct ownership of shares by individual investors. When the interest rate rises, households are more willing to save. This increased willingness to defer consumption is translated into an increase in funds available for corporations to borrow. The investment demand curve represents the funds flowing out of the capital market to firms that borrow the money to build new factories and machines. This curve slopes downward because when the interest rate falls it is cheaper to borrow money, and investment becomes more profitable. The model predicts that the interest rate will be equal to r^E and that saving and investment will be equated at $S^E = I^E$.

What would happen if the interest rate were different from r^E? Suppose it were equal to r_1, a value that is lower than r^E. At r_1, the quantity of investment demanded is equal to I_1, but the quantity of saving supplied is equal to S_1. At this interest rate, investment exceeds saving; some firms will be unable to borrow all of the funds that they need. They will offer to pay a higher rate of interest and, as the interest rate increases, additional funds will be channeled into the market from savers. If the interest rate were higher than r^E, the reverse situation would occur: Saving would be higher than investment, and some savers would be forced to accept a lower rate of interest. Only at r^E is the capital market in equilibrium.

PRODUCTIVITY AND THE INVESTMENT DEMAND CURVE

Two leading contenders for the causes of business cycles are the classical view, made popular in recent years by Edward Prescott, and the animal spirits theory of John Maynard Keynes. Both of these theories have the same implications for the movements of investment and the interest rate.[5]

To illustrate the classical view of business cycles, suppose that a new invention makes investment more productive. A good example would be the invention of the personal computer in the 1970s, which spurred a rash of new developments in the consumer electronics industry. Box 6.5 illustrates the effect of the computer on the economy and Figure 6.6 (on page 156) shows that a productivity increase causes the firm to demand more investment for any given rate of interest.

Panel A of Figure 6.6 illustrates the production function. Panel B shows the investment demand curve and the saving supply curve. The interest rate begins at r_1; this is an equilibrium interest rate for which saving equals investment. After the increase in productivity, the firm demands more investment for every possible interest rate. On the graph in panel A, the productivity improvement causes the production function to shift upward from production function 1 to production function 2. On the graph in panel B, it causes the investment demand curve to shift to the right. If the interest rate were to remain at r_1,

---

5.   Although the animal spirits theory and the real business cycle theory have similar implications for investment and saving, they have very different implications for the role of economic policy. Because of this policy difference, it is important to find ways of separating them. Much current research effort is being directed to this question.

BOX 6.3

FOCUS ON THE FACTS
The New Economy

The most obvious example of the effect of productivity improvements on the economy is the tremendous recent advance in communications technologies spurred by a revolution in microelectronics.

Panel A illustrates Moore's law, an observation by the computer scientist Gordon Moore that each new generation of computer chips contains roughly twice as much capacity as its predecessor, and successive generations of chips are spaced 18–24 months apart. If this trend continues, he reasoned, computing power would rise exponentially over relatively brief periods of time.

In 26 years, the number of transistors on a chip has increased more than 3,200 times, from 2,300 on the 4004 in 1971 to 7.5 million on the Pentium II processor.

The increase in computing power was initially perceived to have very little effect on the economy, but in the past decade this situation has changed dramatically. Panel B shows that personal computer purchases alone now account for almost 3% of GDP. This excludes the tremendous increase in purchases of digital phones, new communications infrastructure (such as laser cables and satellite networks), and computer-guided assembly lines recently introduced into a wide range of manufacturing processes. When one includes all sources of computer-aided products, it has been estimated that the new technology accounts for half of all new business fixed investment. And this share is growing!

Panel C shows that national investment (government plus private) has grown in the 1990s from 16% of GDP in 1991 to 22% in 1999. The so-called "new economy" has set in motion changes in all our lives that some commentators see as potentially significant as the invention of the printing press.

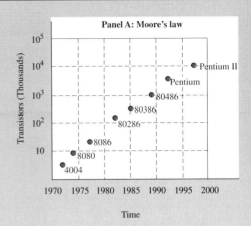

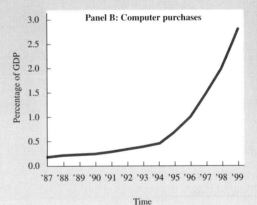

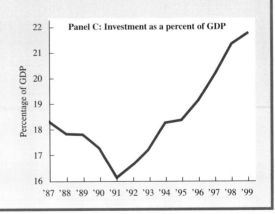

FIGURE 6.6

Productivity and the Investment Demand Curve

Panel A shows that an increase in productivity shifts up the production function. Before the technology improvement, the interest rate is r_1. The firm uses production function 1 and invests $I_1(r_1)$. After the productivity improvement, if the interest rate stayed at r_1, the firm would use production function 2 and invest $I_2(r_1)$.

Panel B shows that the interest rate does not stay at r_1 because it is no longer at equilibrium. The effect of the productivity improvement is to shift investment demand from curve 1 to curve 2. In equilibrium, the increase in productivity will raise the interest rate to r_2.

An increase in productivity will shift the investment demand curve to the right.

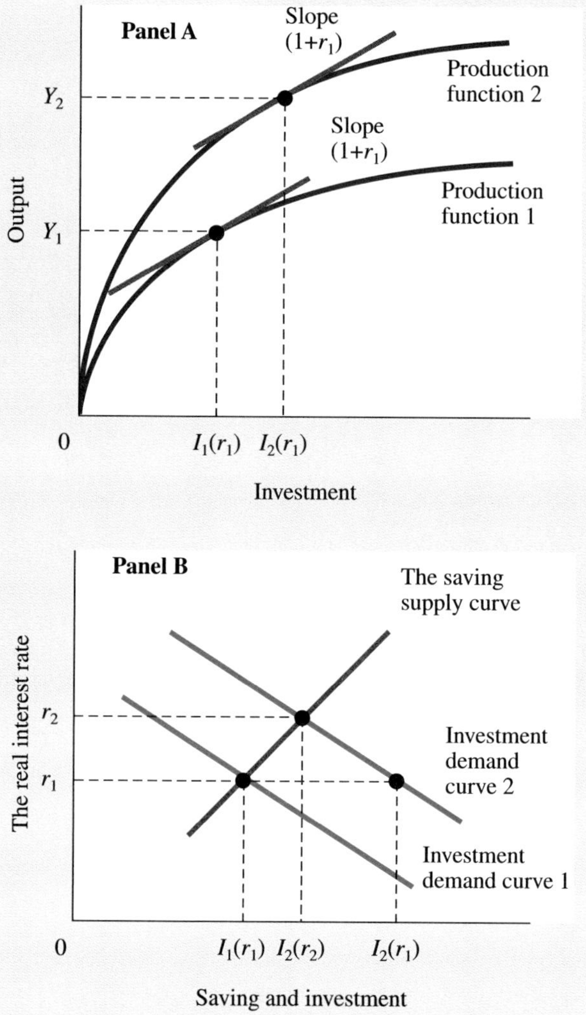

panel B shows that investment would go upward to $I_2(r_1)$; but at this interest rate, saving is no longer equal to investment. Instead, the shift of the demand curve causes the equilibrium interest rate to increase to r_2, and this increase causes households to save more. The new equilibrium is at $\{r_2, I_2(r_2)\}$, for which investment is higher than before the productivity increase, and the interest rate has also gone up.

Box 6.3 shows the history of investment and the interest rate over two different historical periods, and Box 6.5 on page 158 takes a closer look at the algebra behind equilibrium in the capital market.

BOX 6.4

FOCUS ON THE FACTS
Is It the Investment Function or
the Saving Function?

The investment function slopes downward; the saving function slopes upward. By studying how the interest rate is correlated with investment, we can figure out whether fluctuations in the interest rate are caused by shifts in the demand curve for investment or shifts in the supply curve for saving.

Panels A and B show the relationship between investment growth and the interest rate in the United States during the 1970s. Panel A is a time series and panel B is a scatter plot. During the period from 1970 to 1980, the investment demand curve was relatively stable, and most movements in investment were caused by movements of the supply curve of saving. This is apparent from the fact that most of the points in panel B follow a downward-sloping line.

There were two major recessions during this period that were caused by sharp increases in the price of oil in 1973–1974 and again in 1978–1979. These recessions caused the supply curve of saving to shift to the left and triggered movements *along* the investment demand curve.

Panels C and D show the relationship between investment growth and the interest rate in the United States during the 1980s. During this period, the investment demand curve was very unstable, and swings in investment caused movements up and down the supply of saving curve.

The situation depicted in panel B has been the rule over most of recent U.S. history. Investment has been by far the most volatile component of GDP, and consequently the interest rate and investment have been positively correlated.

In modern business cycle theories, shifts in the investment demand curve are the most important source of business-cycle fluctuations. Keynesian economists believe that these swings arise from animal spirits. Real business-cycle economists believe that they arise from productivity shocks.

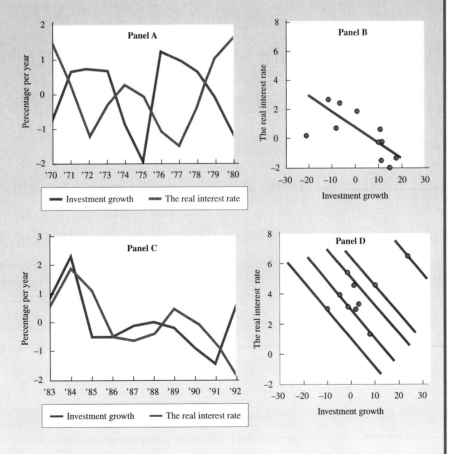

BOX 6.5

A CLOSER LOOK
Equilibrium in the Capital Market:
A Mathematical Example*

In this box, we derive the equilibrium interest rate when the saving and investment curves are those that we derived in Boxes 6.1 and 6.2. Recall that the investment demand curve is given by the expression

6.5.1 $A - I$ $=$ $(1 + r)$

and the saving supply curve is

6.5.2 S $=$ $Y - 1 + r.$

In a capital market equilibrium, $I = S$. This implies that the interest rate is

6.5.3 r $=$ $\left(\dfrac{A - Y}{2} \right)$

and saving and investment are equal to

6.5.4 $S = I = \dfrac{(Y + A)}{2} - 1.$

ANIMAL SPIRITS AND THE INVESTMENT DEMAND CURVE

Because investment and production do not take place at the same time, investors may make mistakes. Keynes believed that it is not possible to make rational calculations about the probability of the future success of an investment, and he thought that irrational swings of optimism and pessimism might be more important driving forces in the stock market than fundamentals. From the point of view of an investor, a new technology (such as the personal computer) is unproven, and investments that are made on the basis of mistaken beliefs about future productivity have the same effect on the capital market as investments that later turn out to be profitable. History is littered with examples of investments that failed.[6] In 1996 when Alan Greenspan, the chairman of the Federal Reserve system, used the term "irrational exuberance" to describe the stock market, Greenspan was worried that the value of the market seemed to be too high by standard measures. Since a stock is a claim to a stream of future earnings, its fundamental value should be related to the under-lying company's potential to earn profits. A standard measure of the value of a stock is the price divided by a 10-year historical average of earnings, a period long enough to average out business cycle fluctuations.

---

6.   The swings in animal spirits that Keynes talked about were not rational in the sense that economics cur-rently defines "rational." (We cover rational expectations in Chapter 18.) Recently, researchers have studied the idea that swings in optimism and pessimism may be fully rational. Rational animal spirits occur when the beliefs of investors are self-fulfilling because they cause changes in prices that justify the original belief. Self-fulfilling beliefs are one of the exciting new research topics that economists are researching today.

BOX 6.6

FOCUS ON THE FACTS
Irrational Exuberance

This graph is the price/earnings ratio for the Standard and Poors stock market index. Historically, this ratio has averaged around 15. By 2000, it was above 40.

When the price is very high, there is concern that future earnings may not be large enough to sustain the price, and the result could be a large and sudden fall in the market.

Data is from Robert Shiller at http://www.aida.econ.yale.edu/~shiller/.

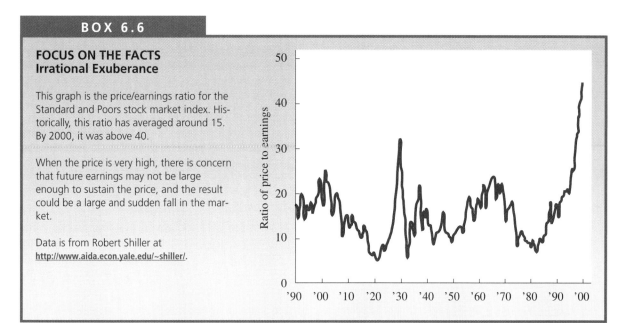

The idea behind using a 10-year historical average is that a 10-year period is long enough to smooth out temporary fluctuations in earnings in the stock market. By taking the average over a long period one hopes to get a good measure of the long-run earnings that investors will be able to expect in the future. Box 6.6 shows the price earnings ratio for the Standard and Poors (S&P) index, a commonly used indicator of the value of the market.

Historically, the price earnings ratio for the S&P index has been about 15. This means that the average value of a stock has been about 15 times as great as the income that would be earned by that stock averaged over a 10-year period. There have been two previous examples of markets in which price earnings ratios were much higher than this. One was in 1901 and the other in 1929, and in both cases, well-known economists argued that history could safely be ignored because the economy had entered new territory. In 1929, the American economist Irving Fisher claimed that the market had reached a new plateau. The following week the market crashed, heralding the Great Depression and an unprecedented drop in economic activity.

Is the market overvalued today? Two arguments suggest not. The first is that we are entering a new era in which the economy will witness unprecedented growth. In other words, future earnings will be much higher than past earnings; hence, the price earnings ratio is using the wrong deflator. The second argument is that the information age has made markets more efficient, narrowing the gap between debt and equity as more households begin to invest in the market on a daily basis. Historically, the stock market has paid an average of three to four percentage points more than debt. If this spread disappears, then the present value of future earnings will increase because the present value of the market is equal to future earnings divided by the rate of interest. As the rate of interest falls, the present value increases. Therefore, stocks should be worth more.

Although these arguments sound enticing (we would all like to believe that we can get rich by putting our money into the market), history suggests caution. In a recent book, *Irrational Exuberance*, Yale economist Robert Shiller argues that the high value of the current market represents a "bubble" that is not justified by fundamentals.[7] He cautions that an overvalued market is, by historical standards, inherently precarious. Among his prescriptions is an end to what he argues are perilous schemes to privatize Social Security rather than reforming it, and he calls on our savings and investment institutions to take more sensible account of emerging risk-management principles.

THE BABY BOOM, PENSIONS, AND SAVING

An important reason to save is to provide income for retirement. In the period immediately following World War II, the United States experienced an increase in the birth rate because many couples had deferred marriage and having children until the end of the war. The postwar spurt of births caused a bulge in the population called the Baby Boom. As the Baby Boom generation ages, it causes changes in the demand and supply of all kinds of commodities, from schools and universities to fast food, music, and clothes. One of the most important effects of Baby Boom demographics is on saving and investment.

Along with the Baby Boom came a windfall for the postwar economy as a flood of productive, tax-paying workers entered the labor market. Governments throughout the world took advantage of the increased tax revenues and instituted new entitlement programs. One of the most important of these new spending programs was the establishment of government-funded pensions.

Table 6.2 shows the ratio of the average pension to the average wage for 1939 and 1980. We see from this table that in the United States, pensions increased from 21% of the average wage in 1939 to 44% of the average wage in 1980. Pensions in 1980 were more than twice as generous as in 1939. In Italy, they were more than four times as generous. Generous pensions would not be a problem if governments had wisely saved the taxes of the young and invested them in the stock market. Instead, the pension contributions of the young were used to pay the pensions of the currently old. This was politically very popular in the postwar period because it seemed as if everyone was a winner. Now the Baby Boom generation is aging, and there are not enough young people to pay the pensions that the Baby Boomers think they are owed.

Pension systems do not have to be run the same way as the U.S. system, in which the taxes of the young are used in part to pay the pensions of the old. An alternative system is one that is fully funded. Alan Greenspan, the chairman of the Federal Reserve system, nicely summarized the issue of funding of a Social Security scheme in a testimony before Congress on March 3, 1999:[8]

---

7.   Robert Shiller. *Irrational Exuberance*, Princeton University Press, 2000.
8.   Testimony of Chairman Alan Greenspan before the Subcommittee on Finance and Hazardous Materials, Committee on Commerce, U.S. House of Representatives, March 3, 1999. See: http://www.federalreserve.gov; search: Greenspan AND "March 3, 1999."

TABLE 6.2

Pensions as a Percentage of Wages in Selected Countries

	1939	1980
Canada	17	34
Germany	19	49
Italy	15	69
United Kingdom	13	31
United States	21	44

Source: *Essays on Pension Reform*, by Max Alier, Ph.D. (thesis, University of California, Los Angeles, 1997).

This issue of funding . . . focuses on the core of any retirement system, private or public. Simply put, enough resources must be set aside over a lifetime of work to fund retirement consumption. At the most rudimentary level, one could envision households saving by actually storing goods purchased during their working years for consumption during retirement. Even better, the resources that would have otherwise gone into the stored goods could be diverted to the production of new capital assets, which would, cumulatively, over a working lifetime, produce an even greater quantity of goods and services to be consumed in retirement.

In practice, most systems (including the U.S.) do not store enough resources to fund their liabilities. This is not a problem as long as the population is growing because there are always enough young people coming into the system and paying taxes to cover the state's liabilities to the existing old. But in recent years, the birth rate has fallen and life expectancy has increased. This has led to a problem that is worldwide, but which is particularly serious in countries with generous pension systems. Pension commitments to the old represent an implicit source of government debt, and in most countries this debt is even larger than conventional government liabilities. Table 6.3 on page 162 compares conventional government debt with implicit pension debt for five countries.

In the United States, conventional debt was 35% of GDP in 1990, but implicit pension debt was nearly three times that size. Although the U.S. situation is bad, it is by no means the worst case; in Italy, for example, net pension liabilities are 259% of GDP. Many governments are beginning to recognize this big problem and are taking steps to rectify it. In Chile, for example, after a pension reform in 1981, the Chilean government began to invest the savings of its young workers in the capital market, just as Alan Greenspan discussed in his testimony before Congress. This way of paying pensions is called "fully funded." When today's Chilean workers retire, the government will be able to pay their pensions from the interest income it makes on the money that it has invested for them.

TABLE 6.3

**Government Debt and Pension Liabilities
as Percent of GDP in 1990**

	Net Conventional Debt	Net Pension Liabilities
Canada	52	121
Germany	22	157
Italy	100	259
United Kingdom	27	156
United States	35	90

Source: *Essays on Pension Reform*, by Max Alier, Ph.D. (thesis, University of California, Los Angeles, 1997).

THE SOCIAL SECURITY TRUST FUND AND THE BUDGET SURPLUS

In the United States, Social Security is partially funded by the **Social Security Trust Fund**, an asset that has been accumulating steadily since 1936 as part of tax payments of the young that are set aside to offset their own future pensions. But unlike a fully funded system, the Social Security Trust Fund is not large enough to cover pension obligations. There is a substantial unfunded liability.

In the federal budget transmitted to Congress in February 2000, the Clinton administration proposed that 62% of the surplus for the next 15 years should be used to help pay Social Security obligations. This position is strongly supported by Alan Greenspan, who has noted that national saving (private plus government) must increase substantially if the current Baby Boom generation is to receive the same level of pension funding as their parents. The following assessment of the situation, written by the President's Council of Economic Advisors, is taken from the February 2000 *Economic Report of the President.*

For many years, annual tax revenues going into the combined trust[9] have exceeded benefit outlays, a situation projected to continue through 2012. The excess revenues are invested in special interest-bearing Treasury securities. These securities, like regular Treasury securities, are backed by the full faith and credit of the U.S. Government. The trust funds are credited with the amount of principal as well as the interest paid on the securities. However, with no changes to current law, beginning in 2013, the program will use interest income from these trust fund reserves to help pay benefits. Starting in 2021, payroll tax and interest income will no longer be sufficient. The program will need to spend the principal held in reserve in order to meet benefit obligations. The Trustees forecast that the reserves will run out in 2032. At that point, annual payroll tax revenue will be sufficient to pay

---

9.   The combined trust referred to in the quote is the Social Security Trust Fund and a parallel fund that is designed to fund disability payments.

W E B W A T C H

Read About Pension Reform in *The Economist*

An excellent source of articles on current issues in macroeconomics is *The Economist* magazine. You can subscribe to *The Economist* print edition, or you can find an electronic version at http://www.economist.com.

A subscription will give you the ability to access *The Economist* online library, which contains articles on a wide range of economic and political topics taken from past issues of the magazine. I searched for "pension reform" in the online library and found 33 articles, several of which were very useful in helping me to write this chapter.

about 72 percent of benefits promised under current law. . . .

. . . The long-range fiscal health of the trust fund is determined by economic as well as demographic factors. Such things as productivity improvements contribute to economic growth, which in turn bolsters revenues coming into the trust funds as workers enjoy low unemployment rates and higher real wages. However, even under optimistic assumptions about future productivity improvements and real wage growth, the demographic forecasts indicate that there simply will not be enough workers in the labor force to cover the expected retirement costs of the baby boom and subsequent generations.

The situation described by the presidential advisors is projected to occur because life expectancy has increased and birthrates have declined. The implication is that there will be fewer people of working age in the future to support a larger population of old people. Notice that according to current projections, the Social Security Trust Fund will be bankrupt by the year 2032. At this point, one of two things will happen: The elderly will receive much lower pensions than they currently expect or young people will pay much higher taxes. Neither alternative is particularly attractive. Instead, the Council proposes that we act now.

Luckily (see Box 6.7 on page 164), an increase in productivity, spurred in part by the Internet revolution, has led to a turnaround in the budget situation. In 1991, the federal government was running a 4% deficit of GDP, whereas in 1998 and 1999, we had budget surpluses that optimists are predicting will continue into the indefinite future. Both presidential candidates in the 2000 election were proposing that substantial portions of the surpluses, should they continue, be used to shore up the large, unfunded Social Security obligation. Alan Greenspan summed up his advice in a 1999 testimony to Congress:

In this light, increasing our national saving is essential to any social security reform. Privatization proposals that begin to address social security's existing unfunded liability would significantly enhance domestic saving; so would fuller funding of the current social security program. But the size of the unified budget surplus implied by such funding, many

BOX 6.7

FOCUS ON THE FACTS
Private and Government Saving

Panel A shows that private saving has been falling since 1985, from 9% to less than 4% of disposable income. This is a much lower private saving rate than in many other countries.

But national saving has been increasing from 15% to 19% of GDP. The difference is due to an increase in government saving (see panel B).

Panel B shows the government budget deficit (the negative of government saving). This panel explains why national saving increased when private saving fell. The reason is a huge increase in government saving. Since 1991, the deficit has been falling (government saving has been increasing), and since 1998, the budget has moved into surplus. The existence of growing federal surpluses has sparked a fierce political debate about what to do with the money that is now rolling into the Treasury.

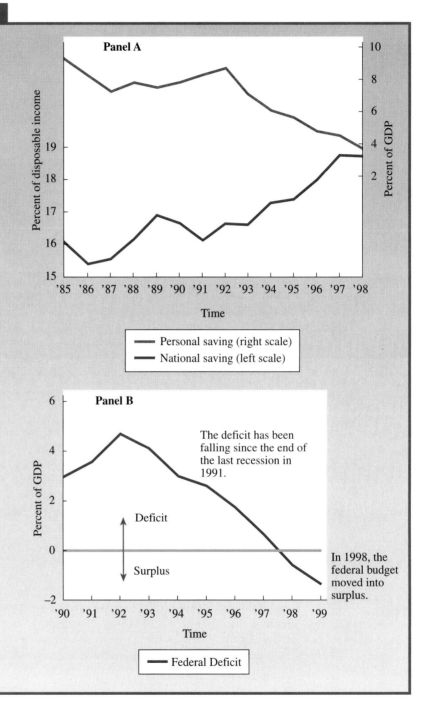

have argued, would be politically unsustainable. The President, recognizing this political risk, has proposed changing the budgetary framework so as to support a large unified budget surplus. This is a major step in the right direction that, if effective, would ensure that the current rise in government's positive contribution to national saving is sustained. The large surpluses projected over the next 15 years, if they actually materialize, would significantly reduce the fiscal pressures created by our changing demographics. Whichever direction the Congress chooses to go, whether toward privatization or fuller funding of social security, augmenting our national saving rate has to be the main objective.

SAVING AND INVESTMENT IN AN OPEN ECONOMY

We can now modify the theory of saving and investment to explain borrowing and lending in the world capital market of an open economy. The difference between the open economy and the closed economy models is that, in the open economy, domestic saving does not equal domestic investment; the deficit is made up by net borrowing from abroad.

EQUILIBRIUM IN THE WORLD CAPITAL MARKET

Figure 6.7 on page 166 illustrates how equilibrium in the world capital market is determined. Panel A reproduces the domestic saving and investment diagram from Figure 6.5. We will use this diagram to show how much money the domestic economy will borrow from abroad for different world rates of interest.

For example, suppose that the United States can borrow and lend to the rest of the world at a rate of interest equal to r_1. Panel A shows that when the interest rate is equal to r_1, the United States will demand investment of I_1^{NAT}, and U.S. savers will supply savings of S_1^{NAT}. The superscript "NAT" reminds us that we are dealing with *national* investment and *national* saving (private plus government investment and saving). Because I_1^{NAT} is greater than S_1^{NAT}, at this rate of interest the United States will be a net borrower from the rest of the world. The amount borrowed is denoted as NB_1. Suppose instead that the world interest rate is r_2. Panel A shows that for an interest rate of r_2, U.S. investors will demand I_2^{NAT} and U.S. savers will supply S_2^{NAT} to the world capital market. Because I_2^{NAT} is less than S_2^{NAT}, panel A shows that for this interest rate the United States will be a net lender to the rest of the world. This is represented by the fact that net borrowing (NB_2) is less than zero.

Panel B plots a downward-sloping line for the U.S. demand for capital from the world. This is the difference between national domestic investment and national domestic saving for different values of the world interest rate. For example, when the interest rate is r_1, domestic investment is greater than domestic saving. This information is plotted on graph B as point **A**. The vertical axis of the graph represents the interest rate in the world capital market. The horizontal axis measures the quantity of capital demanded and supplied on the world market. When the interest rate is equal to r_1, the domestic demand for capital (the difference between domestic investment and domestic saving) is equal to NB_1. When the interest rate is r_2, the domestic demand for capital is equal to r_2, and the United States will be a net saver because domestic investment, I_2^{NAT}, is less than domestic saving, S_2^{NAT}.

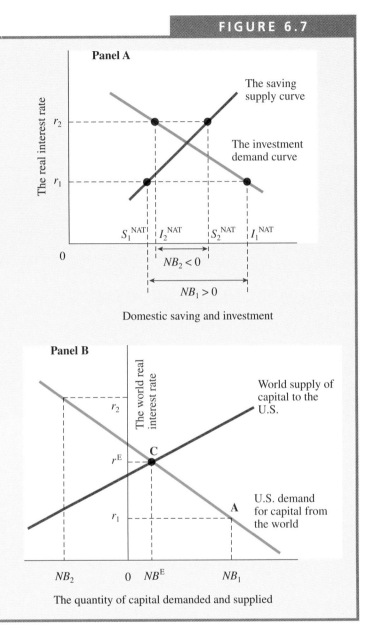

FIGURE 6.7

Saving and Investment in an Open Economy

This graph shows how the rate of interest is determined in the world economy.

Panel A shows saving and investment in the domestic economy. At interest rate r_1, national domestic investment (private plus government) is greater than national domestic saving. The difference in domestic investment over domestic saving is paid for by borrowing the amount NB_1 (NB stands for net borrowing) in the world capital market.

Panel A also shows that if the world interest rate were to increase to r_2, national domestic saving would be greater than national domestic investment. In this case, net borrowing would be negative as funds flow *from* the United States to the world capital market.

Panel B plots the U.S. demand for capital and the world supply of capital on the horizontal axis and the world interest rate on the vertical axis. In equilibrium, U.S. investment exceeds U.S. saving. The difference is made up by net borrowing from abroad—NB^E.

What determines the world rate of interest? We can find an investment and saving curve for every country in the world. If we put together all of the other countries' saving and investment curves, we can find out how much the rest of the world is prepared to lend to the United States for different values of the world interest rate. The result, called the

world supply of capital curve, slopes upward because when the interest rate is higher, other countries are more willing to lend to us. Equilibrium in the world capital market occurs at the point where the world supply of capital equals the domestic demand for capital. On panel B this occurs at point **C** when the world interest rate is equal to r^E and U.S. demand for capital is equal to NB^E. We have drawn this graph so that at r^E, the domestic demand for capital, is positive, reflecting the fact that the United States is a net borrower from the rest of the world.

CONCLUSION

We can use the tools of demand and supply to study the allocation of commodities over time. Investing is a way of transferring goods from the present to the future, and firms invest to maximize profit. Saving is a way of deferring consumption, and households save to maximize utility. The interest rate is the relative price of current and future commodities and, in the capital market, is determined at the point where the quantity of investment demanded equals the quantity of saving supplied.

Over the business cycle, investment is very volatile and consumption is relatively smooth. New classical economists of the real business cycle school believe that investment fluctuates in response to changes in productivity caused by new inventions. Keynesian economists believe that many of the changes in investment are due to changes in the beliefs of investors, called animal spirits. Both groups believe that the model of the demand and supply of capital can be used to explain the determination of the rate of interest.

The apparatus of the demand and supply of capital helps us to understand the effect of changes in productivity and changes in population demographics on the capital market. We can also use it to study the effect of U.S. government borrowing on the international capital market.

KEY TERMS

Animal spirits

Consumption smoothing

Demand for investment

Fundamental explanation

Intertemporal budget constraint

Intertemporal production possibilities set

Intertemporal utility theory

Irrational exuberance

Market rate

Nominal interest rate

Present value

Real interest rate

Self-fulfilling prophecy

Social Security Trust Fund

Sunspots

Supply of saving

Wealth effect

World supply of capital curve

QUESTIONS FOR CHAPTER 6

---

1. Define the terms *saving* and *investment*. Carefully describe some activities that can accurately be described as saving or investment. Is putting money in the stock market saving or investment?

2. Why does the saving supply curve slope upward? What does this imply about the relative strength of the substitution effect versus the wealth effect when the real interest rate changes?

3. Why does the investment demand curve slope downward? What role does the concept of diminishing returns play in determining the slope of the investment demand curve?

4. How do classical and Keynesian economists differ in their explanations of the fluctuations in investment that we see over the business cycle? Do Keynesians and classical economists also disagree about the way that changes in investment are translated into changes in the interest rate?

5. Suppose that the interest rate is 5% per year. Calculate the year-2002 'present value' of the following:

   a. a $1,000 inheritance to be received in 2003

   b. a $1,000 inheritance to be received in 2004

   c. a lottery winning that pays $1,000 each year in 2003, 2004, and 2005

   d. a lottery winning that pays $1,000 each year, forever

6. Suppose that the nominal interest rate remains constant, but firms expect that there will be a higher inflation rate in the future. How would this expectation of future inflation affect investment? Explain your reasoning.

7. Consider an economy with the following aggregate production function: $Y = 4I^{\frac{1}{2}}$, where I is the level of investment.

   a. Find the marginal product of investment. (Hint: If a production function takes the form $Y = AI^{\alpha}$, then the marginal product of labor equals $\alpha AI^{\alpha - 1}$.)

   b. Show that the aggregate production function in this economy exhibits diminishing returns by choosing different values for investment and calculating what happens to its marginal product.

   c. If r is the real interest rate, derive the investment demand curve by equating the marginal cost of investment, $(1 + r)$, with the marginal product of investment you derived in part (a).

    d. If the saving supply curve is $S = 2(1 + r)$, calculate the equilibrium values of investment and the real interest rate.

    e. Calculate aggregate output, Y.

8. During the 1980s, investment and real interest rates were strongly and positively related in the United States. How can this fact be reconciled with the fact that the investment demand curve slopes downward? Explain.

9. How do you think that changes in stock market valuations affect investment demand and the supply of saving? If changes in the stock market are heavily based on expectations of future economic conditions, how might these expectations be self-fulfilling? Explain.

10. The current U.S. Social Security system is often referred to as a "pay-as-you-go" system, as opposed to being fully funded. What do you think the difference is between these systems? How might investment demand, the supply of saving, and interest rates be different in countries with retirement systems that are pay-as-you-go as opposed to being fully funded?

11. Do you think that government budget deficits tend to be procyclical or countercyclical? Explain. Does this imply that national saving is procyclical or countercyclical? Explain.

12. a. Suppose that a government in a small open economy raises taxes without changing government spending. What will happen to this country's domestic investment and trade balance? Illustrate using a graph of the domestic capital market. HINT: Assume that the world supply of capital is horizontal at the world interest rate.

    b. Now, suppose that a large group of foreign countries raise taxes without changing their government spending. What will happen to the investment and trade balance in the small open economy from part (a)? Illustrate using a graph of the domestic capital market.

13. a. Many economists have recently argued for a drastic change in the U.S. tax code. They would like to see our current federal income tax replaced with a national sales tax on consumption goods in an effort to increase national saving. Analyze the effects of such a policy using the classical model, and be sure to discuss its effects on real and nominal wages, the labor market, output, the price level, the real interest rate, investment, and saving. Provide appropriate graphs to illustrate.

    b. If the policy described in part (a) were adopted within a small open economy, what would happen to that country's level of net exports? How about their net foreign borrowing and lending? Use a graph of the country's capital market to illustrate.

The Modern Approach to Aggregate Demand and Supply

Part C contains seven chapters that go beyond the classical model to develop a more modern understanding of the theory of aggregate demand and supply. We begin, in Chapter 7, with the new-Keynesian theory of unemployment and in Chapter 8, we develop the Keynesian theory of aggregate supply.

In Chapters 9 through 12, we study a modern approach to the theory of aggregate demand. This approach is based on ideas from Keynes's book, *The General Theory of Employment Interest and Money*. Chapter 13, the last chapter in Part C, explains how the idea of demand management must be modified in an open economy.

CHAPTER 7

UNEMPLOYMENT

INTRODUCTION

This chapter is about unemployment. Economists first began a systematic study of unemployment during the Great Depression when Keynes challenged the orthodox view that the economic system tends to return quickly to full-employment equilibrium. Before the Great Depression, the most pressing macroeconomic problem was how to maintain a stable currency. Keynes himself wrote extensively on this subject, in part stimulated by the deep social problems that were caused by hyperinflation in Germany, Austria, Poland, and Hungary at the end of World War I. But in the late 1920s, unemployment in England climbed to unprecedented levels. In 1929, the stock market crashed in the United States, heralding the transmission of the Great Depression from the United Kingdom to North America, and for the next decade the Western World experienced an economic catastrophe that caused theorists to completely rethink the classical model.

We now deal with the question: What is unemployment? We will study a model that incorporates elements from each of several modern theories of unemployment into a framework similar to that of the classical theory. We will also compare unemployment in the United States with unemployment in Europe and look at structural theories of the labor market that try to account for the differences between these two regions.

BOX 7.1

A CLOSER LOOK
The Beginning of Modern Macroeconomics

John Maynard Keynes,
1883–1946

Keynes was born in Cambridge, England, the same year that Karl Marx died. He studied under Alfred Marshall at Cambridge University where he later became an economics lecturer. Keynes' most influential book was *The General Theory of Employment Interest and Money* in which he introduced the idea of involuntary unemployment. In this book, Keynes put forward the then radical idea that government can and should be responsible for maintaining a low unemployment rate.

Keynes thought that the classical equilibrium in which the demand always equals the supply of labor was a special case of the more general situation in which the economy could be in equilibrium with any level of unemployment. Keynes' theorization was based on the level of the community as a whole, rather than the level of the individual firm or household. His work heralded the beginning of a modern discipline of macroeconomics that has only recently begun to be reunited with microeconomic principles.

As well as being an academic, Keynes was an influential and popular writer, an influential statesman (he had an important role in setting up the International Monetary Fund), and a member of the Bloomsbury group, an English literary circle that included Lytton Strachey and Virginia Wolf.

In Chapter 8 we will discuss a related question: Why does unemployment vary systematically over the business cycle? To address this, we will learn how Keynesian theory connects changes in unemployment with changes in the price level.

THE HISTORY OF UNEMPLOYMENT

The idea that government can and should try to control the unemployment rate is a relatively modern idea that was introduced into economics by John Maynard Keynes in the 1930s (see Box 7.1). During the late nineteenth century, the U.S. economy experienced a series of severe recessions that were associated with banking panics, sharp drops in investment spending, and increases in the unemployment rate. One of the worst of these was in the 1890s when unemployment reached 18% of the labor force.

One important feature of eighteenth-century recessions was a series of recurrent episodes during which the public lost confidence in the banking system. These episodes are called "banking panics." During banking panics, many savers try to withdraw their money from the banking system at the same time. Since banks typically invest their depositors' assets in long-term projects, these panics cause banks to fail. During bank failures, savers lose money, and the economy experiences a loss of output and an increase in unemployment. The Federal Reserve system (Fed) was created in 1913 to help to prevent banking panics by insuring the savings of depositors and providing liquidity to the system during a crisis.

Box 7.2 illustrates the history of unemployment in the United States since 1890. Notice the big recession in the 1890s in which unemployment increased to 18% of the labor force. Shortly after this recession the Fed was created, and the United States began to sys-

BOX 7.2

FOCUS ON THE FACTS
The History of Unemployment in the United States

Panel A shows the annual unemployment rate in U.S. data, 1890–2000. For most of the past century, the unemployment rate has averaged about 7%. There are two notable exceptions. In the 1890s, there was a major recession where the unemployment rate reached 18%, and in the 1930s, during the Great Depression, the unemployment rate reached 25%.

Panel B shows monthly data on the unemployment rate and on the average duration of unemployment, 1968–2000. The pale-blue shaded areas are NBER recessions.

During recessions, unemployment rises sharply. For example, in the recessions following the oil shock in 1973, the unemployment rate rose by 4 percentage points from 5% to 9% over 30 months. Declines in unemployment are much gentler, reflecting the fact that expansions last longer than recessions.

Notice also from panel B that unemployment duration moves very closely with the unemployment rate. This reflects the fact that when a lot of people are looking for a job it takes much longer to find one.

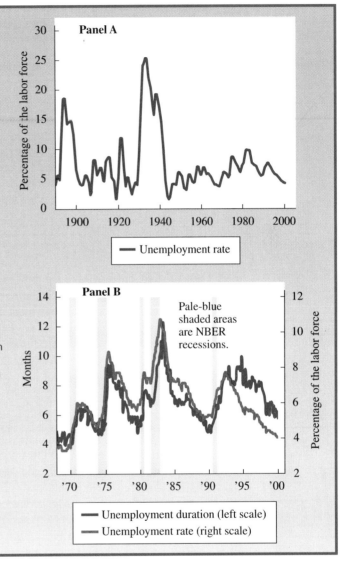

tematically conduct monetary policy. The creation of the Fed was the beginning of a series of political changes that gradually increased the role of government over the course of the twentieth century. But it was not until the Great Depression in the 1930s that governments began to consciously attempt economic control by raising and lowering government expenditure and taxation.

Panel A of Box 7.2 illustrates that in the 1930s unemployment climbed to 25% of the labor force. The social effects of large-scale unemployment were catastrophic, and the political fallout was wide-reaching as governments throughout the world adopted the role of economic managers in an attempt to prevent the recurrence of unemployment. John Maynard Keynes provided the intellectual rationale for government intervention in the economy. He argued that in a recession, the government should spend more rather than less. This was a radical departure from the orthodox view that when times are hard, government should tighten its belt. Instead, Keynes argued that government should spend more in a recession and less in a boom. This policy, called **countercyclical fiscal policy,** was an implication of his theory of deficient demand. In Chapter 12, we will study this theory and investigate his argument further.

Box 7.2 also illustrates the more recent history of unemployment in the United States. Notice that unemployment increases rapidly during recessions, but it falls more gently during expansions. Unemployment is correlated with a number of other economic and social variables, including the duration of unemployment (panel B) and many social statistics, such as crime rates and poverty (see the discussion in Chapter 1).

EXPLAINING UNEMPLOYMENT

There are two dimensions to the problem of explaining unemployment. First, there is the problem of explaining why anyone is unemployed at all. This chapter addresses that question. Second: Why does unemployment move in a systematic way with other business cycle variables and, in particular, why did unemployment and the price level move in sharply opposite directions over the period from 1929 through 1940? We will delve into this issue in Chapter 12 and construct a theory that can account for the history of the price level during the Great Depression.

FRICTIONAL UNEMPLOYMENT

Explaining why there is *any* unemployment does not require particularly deep insight. The classical economists recognized that equality of demand and supply in the labor market does not imply the absence of unemployment, since unemployment may result from labor turnover. Unemployment of this kind is called **frictional unemployment**.

Figure 7.1 presents a dynamic view of unemployment as a process with flows into and out of the labor market. Because it takes time to find a job, there is always a pool of unemployed people. The demand and supply curves of labor are flows, like the water flowing into and out of a tank. But unemployment is a stock, like the water sitting in a bathtub. If we turn up the faucet but leave the plug out of the bath, the level of water in the tub will rise until the extra pressure causes the outflow to once more equal the inflow. The new-Keynesian model of unemployment says something similar about the labor market.

CYCLICAL UNEMPLOYMENT

The existence of frictional unemployment is not a cause for concern, since it is a feature of any smoothly operating economy as workers take time to move from one occupation to

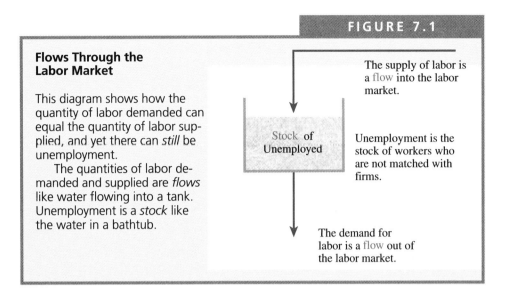

FIGURE 7.1

Flows Through the Labor Market

This diagram shows how the quantity of labor demanded can equal the quantity of labor supplied, and yet there can *still* be unemployment.

The quantities of labor demanded and supplied are *flows* like water flowing into a tank. Unemployment is a *stock* like the water in a bathtub.

Stock of Unemployed

The supply of labor is a flow into the labor market.

Unemployment is the stock of workers who are not matched with firms.

The demand for labor is a flow out of the labor market.

another. But when unemployment reaches 25%, such as occurred during the Great Depression, it is unlikely that these workers are all unemployed as a result of job turnover. Since recessions are cyclical in nature and since unemployment moves systematically over the business cycle, the increased unemployment that occurs during a recession is called **cyclical unemployment**. Cyclical unemployment *does* concern politicians because it is associated with widespread hardship and increased social problems.

Keynesian economists believe that cyclical unemployment occurs because the economy does not respond to shocks as efficiently as it should. During the Great Depression, the price level fell but unemployment rose. They explain this with a model in which the nominal price index does not quickly adjust to its equilibrium level. We will amend the classical model by allowing firms to choose the wages they pay. This will allow us to describe unemployment as an equilibrium phenomenon, and it will provide us with a framework for Chapter 8's discussion of fluctuations in unemployment over the business cycle.

THEORIES OF UNEMPLOYMENT

Ever since Keynes wrote *The General Theory*, economists have been trying to interpret his ideas. Keynes was above all a practical man, and the policies he advocated for alleviating the Great Depression worked. But the microeconomics of his theory were never spelled out; his followers spent vast amounts of time attempting to make sense of Keynesian economics in terms of the theory of rational behavior. The attempt to explain the microeconomic foundations of Keynesian economics is called the **new-Keynesian research program.**

One question asked by new-Keynesian economists is: How can a pool of unemployed workers exist when the labor market is in equilibrium? To answer this question, we will develop the **efficiency wage theory**. It argues that firms choose to pay a higher wage than the classical equilibrium wage because it is in their best interests to keep their workers happy. Because the real wage paid by firms is higher than the wage at which the stock of workers employed is equal to the labor force, the model predicts there will be unemployment in equilibrium.

EFFICIENCY WAGE THEORY

According to the theory of efficiency wages, the real wage is chosen to minimize the turnover costs of the firm.[1] The economists who developed this theory believed that unemployment is typically "too high." "Too high" means that the government can and should try to keep the unemployment rate down through an active policy of managing aggregate demand. They argue that firms pay a higher wage than one would observe in a classical economy because high wages are beneficial to the firm. High wages ensure workers' best efforts as well as their loyalty, thereby the firm can avoid costly recruiting efforts.

There are three main strands to efficiency wage theory. According to the first, a firm that has a happy, conscientious workforce will make more profits because happy workers will likely be more productive. Thus, the firm has an incentive to pay a high wage to ensure the productivity of its workers. A second approach to efficiency wages argues that firms that offer higher wages will attract high-quality applicants. This idea relies on the assumption that the quality of a worker is not directly observable. The third and final strand argues that firms use the wage as a device to minimize turnover costs. If fewer workers quit, recruiting costs incurred to replace workers will be minimized. A common element of all three approaches is the proposition that the real wage will be higher than the classical market-clearing wage. This proposition implies the existence of a stock of unemployed workers in equilibrium.

SEARCH THEORY

Search theory is a natural companion to efficiency wage theory, although it is not exclusively a new-Keynesian approach. It studies the costly and time-consuming process of matching workers with firms. For our purposes, the main idea is that the pool of workers employed at a firm is a stock, but the quantities of labor entering and leaving its labor force are flows.

Much of the work in search theory and efficiency wage theory is highly abstract. However, some of it can easily be incorporated into a model similar to the one we have studied so far in this book. By adding these ideas to the classical model of the labor market, we will be able to develop a model in which unemployment arises as a natural consequence of frictions inherent in the process of matching workers with jobs.

---

1.   There is a huge amount of literature on efficiency wage theory. One of the earliest pieces is by Carl Shapiro and Joseph Stiglitz, "Equilibrium Unemployment as a Worker Discipline Device," in the *American Economic Review*, 74, pp 443–444, June 1984. You can learn more about this topic in the book by George Akerlof and Janet Yellen, *Efficiency Wage Models of the Labor Market*, published by Cambridge University Press, 1987.

FIGURE 7.2

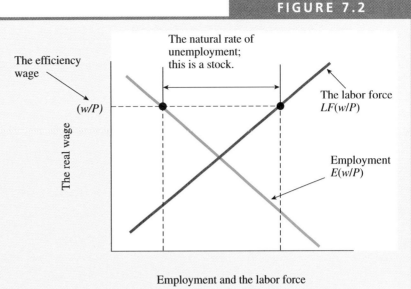

The New-Keynesian Model of the Labor Market

In this graph, the labor force is an increasing function of the real wage, and employment is a decreasing function of the real wage. The wage that prevails in equilibrium is called the *efficiency wage*. Note that equilibrium is not the point where the curves cross; instead it is a wage that is chosen to minimize costs. When the real wage is equal to the efficiency wage, unemployment is at its *natural rate*.

THE NEW-KEYNESIAN THEORY OF UNEMPLOYMENT

We now develop the new-Keynesian theory of unemployment. Figure 7.2 describes the main features of this theory. In the classical model of the labor market, firms can instantly adjust the quantities of labor that they employ and do so without cost. Similarly, households can instantly adjust the number of household members that work in paid employment without incurring costs. In this environment where adjustment is costless, it is not necessary to distinguish between stocks and flows of labor.

In contrast to the classical model, the new Keynesians assume that the firm explicitly recognizes its pool of workers as a stock. Any given stock of workers can be associated with fast or slow labor turnover. At one extreme, the firm may keep the same workers for 20 years. This firm would rarely pay the costs of searching for new workers. At the other extreme, the firm may hire new workers every week. This firm would face very high recruiting costs. The firm minimizes the costs of maintaining a stock of employed workers by adjusting the real wage.[2]

The stock of workers sent to the labor market by households is called the "labor force." Since households may decide to supply more workers to the market when the real wage rises, the labor force is an increasing function of the real wage. The stock of workers

---

2.   It is beyond the scope of this book to provide a fully articulated model of a dynamic labor market in which stocks differ from flows. Instead, our approach assumes that the firm can adjust employment quickly. Chapter 8, introduces the idea that the nominal wage adjusts slowly. The important point is that in new-Keynesian theory, quantities adjust much more quickly than money wages.

employed by the firm is called "employment." Since the firm will demand fewer workers as the real wage rises, employment is a decreasing function of the real wage. In the classical model, the real wage is determined by the point of intersection of the upward-sloping supply curve (the labor force) and the downward-sloping demand curve (the employment curve). The new-Keynesian theory differs from the classical model in that the wage is not chosen to equate employment to the labor force. Instead, the wage is chosen at a point where there is a pool of unemployed workers. The real wage chosen by firms is called the **efficiency wage**, and the level of unemployment associated with the efficiency wage is called the **natural rate of unemployment**.

TURNOVER COST AND THE EFFICIENCY WAGE

In the new-Keynesian model, the firm must devote resources to the search process. Firms must actively seek workers and they may vary the intensity of their search for workers by sending recruiters to colleges and universities or by posting advertisements in newspapers and magazines. The firm chooses its wage to minimize its wage bill. One element of the wage bill is the wage paid to each worker. A second component is the cost of recruiting new workers. We will use the expression $C(w/P, L)$ to represent the turnover cost where the terms w/P and L remind us that the firm can influence C by offering a different real wage and by changing the number of workers it employs. We say that C is a function of the real wage and employment.

For the purpose of illustrating the efficiency wage we will study a special case of a turnover cost function:

$$C(w/P, L) = c(w/P)L,$$

and we refer to $c(w/P)$ as the per-worker turnover cost. This special case has the property that turnover costs are proportional to the number of workers. It's easy to study because when the firm chooses the efficiency wage its problem can be broken into two parts. First, the firm minimizes costs per worker by choosing the efficiency wage. This problem, illustrated in Box 7.3 with a mathematical example, amounts to choosing the efficiency wage to make $w/P + c(w/P)$ as small as possible. Second, given the efficiency wage, the firm chooses L to maximize profit. This problem is illustrated with a mathematical example in Box 7.4.

Why might C depend on the real wage? Because better-paid workers are more likely to remain loyal and less likely to quit the firm thereby lowering the firm's turnover cost. More precisely, we will assume that that as w/P gets bigger, C gets smaller. We say that the turnover cost is a decreasing function of the real wage. In addition to this assumption, we need to assume something stronger. Define the *marginal benefit* of an increase in the real wage to be equal to the reduction in the turnover cost for a given increase in the real wage. In efficiency wage theory we assume that the marginal benefit gets smaller as the real wage increases.

CHOOSING THE EFFICIENCY WAGE

In classical theory the firm must pay no less than other firms pay and, in equilibrium, the real wage is determined at the point where the employment demand of firms equals the

> ### BOX 7.3
>
> **A CLOSER LOOK**
> **Deriving the Efficiency Wage:**
> **A Mathematical Example***
>
> In this box, we provide an example of turnover cost function and show how to derive the efficiency wage. As with the mathematical examples in earlier chapters, you can safely skip it without losing track of the main points of the chapter.
>
> Equation **7.3.1** is a special example of a turnover cost function. It is special because the turnover cost can be broken into parts. $c(W/P)$ depends on the real wage and L is the number of workers. When $C(W/P,L) = c(W/P)L$, as in the example, the firm can solve for the efficiency wage independently of its choice of how many workers to employ. We assume that the function $c(W/P)$ is defined for $(w/P) < 1$, and that if $(w/P) > 1$ then $c = 0$.
>
> **7.3.1** $$c \quad = \quad 1 - 2(w/P) + (w/P)^2$$
>
> **This expression describes how the turnover cost depends on the real wage.**
>
> Our example illustrates two important properties of the turnover cost function. First, as the real wage increases, the turnover cost falls, and this is a benefit to the firm since it tends to increase profit. Second, the marginal benefit falls as the real wage increases.
>
> The marginal benefit for this turnover cost function is given by the following expression (the negative of the derivative of **7.1.1**). We take the negative because the negative of a cost is a benefit.
>
> **7.3.2** $$\textit{Marginal benefit} \quad = \quad -(-2 + 2(w/P))$$
>
> **This expression describes the positive contribution to profit from raising the real wage.**
>
> If the firm pays a real wage of (w/P), its costs for each worker will be given by the real wage. The wage bill is increased one for one by an increase in the wage. Hence, the marginal cost of raising the real wage is equal to 1.
>
> **7.3.3** $$\textit{Marginal cost} \quad = \quad 1$$
>
> Profit is maximized when the marginal benefit equals the marginal cost. This condition is given in equation **7.3.4**:
>
> **7.3.4** $$1 \quad = \quad 2 - 2(w/P)$$
>
> **Marginal cost**   **Marginal benefit**
>
> Setting the marginal cost equal to the marginal benefit gives the efficiency wage for this example:
>
> **7.3.5** $$(w/P)^* \quad = \quad 1/2$$
>
> **This is the efficiency wage.**

supply of workers to the market by households. In new-Keynesian theory, the firm chooses its wage rate to minimize the cost of maintaining a pool of employed workers. Let's look at the special case in which the turnover cost function is proportional to the number of workers to see how the efficiency wage theory works.

Equation 7.1 is a new-Keynesian expression for profit. It differs from the profit equation of the classical economy because the firm must pay a cost $c(w/P)L$ to maintain a workforce of L members. The nominal wage w is not given by the market; it is chosen by the firm. By offering a higher wage, the firm will increase its wage bill, and this adds to costs. But by increasing the wage it will increase worker loyalty, and this will lower costs because it will reduce the bill to recruit new workers.

$$\textbf{7.1} \qquad \underset{\text{Profit}}{\pi} \quad = \quad \underset{\substack{\text{Commodities}\\\text{supplied}}}{Y} \quad - \quad \underset{\substack{\text{Cost of}\\\text{labor demanded}}}{\frac{w}{P}L} \quad - \quad \underset{\substack{\text{Turnover}\\\text{cost}}}{c\left(\frac{w}{P}\right)L}$$

Panel A of Figure 7.3 illustrates the firm's choice of the real wage. Increasing the wage affects profit in two ways. If the wage goes up by one dollar, the firm's wage bill increases by one dollar per worker. This is called the marginal cost of a change in the wage. A second effect of increasing the wage is to reduce the firm's turnover cost per worker $c(w/P)$. This is called the marginal benefit of a change in the wage. In efficiency wage theory the firm chooses the wage that minimizes its costs and maximizes its profit. This wage, called the efficiency wage, is found by equating the marginal cost of raising the wage to its marginal benefit.

CHOOSING A STOCK OF WORKERS

In the classical theory the firm chooses employment to maximize profit, taking the real wage as given. In the new-Keynesian theory, the firm also chooses employment to maximize profit. But instead of taking the real wage as given, it *chooses* the real wage to minimize the per-worker wage bill. Since the efficiency wage exceeds the classical market-clearing wage, there will be a stock of unemployed workers in equilibrium.

How large a workforce will the new-Keynesian firm choose to employ compared to the firm in the classical model? We illustrate the employment decisions of both classical and Keynesian firms in panel B of Figure 7.3. The classical firm equates the real wage to the marginal product of labor. This leads to the downward-sloping purple curve that represents the labor demand curve of the classical firm for any given real wage. The key assumption used to derive the classical employment curve is that there are no hiring or firing costs.

Figure 7.3 illustrates a special case of the problem solved by a new-Keynesian firm. In this special case, turnover costs are given by

$$C(w/P, L) = c(w/P)L.$$

When turnover costs are separable in this way, the firm first minimizes turnover costs per worker, equal to

$$\frac{w}{P} + c\left(w/P\right)$$

by choosing the efficiency wage. It then chooses employment. More generally, the choice of the efficiency wage and the choice of employment are interdependent problems.

In the new-Keynesian model, hiring and firing costs play a central role. In addition to the real wage (w/P) the new-Keynesian firm pays the cost $c(w/P)$ per worker leading to the downward-sloping green curve that represents the new-Keynesian employment curve. This curve is consistently below the employment curve (also called the labor de-

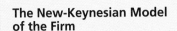

FIGURE 7.3

The New-Keynesian Model of the Firm

A: The Efficiency Wage
The blue curve represents the marginal turnover cost. As the real wage is increased, the extra benefit in terms of lower turnover costs falls.

The purple line is the cost per worker of paying a higher real wage. This is equal to 1 because a $1 increase in the wage costs the firm $1 per worker.

The efficiency wage equates the marginal benefit of increasing the wage to its marginal cost.

B: Employment
The purple curve represents the stock of workers that would be chosen by the classical firm. It equates the real wage to the marginal product of labor.

The green curve represents the stock of workers that would be the new-Keynesian firm. It equates the real wage to the marginal product of labor **minus** the turnover cost $c(w/P)$.

The gap between the curves is smaller when the real wage is higher because for a high real wage, the turnover cost is lower.

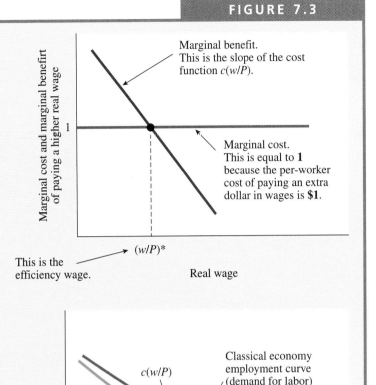

mand curve) in the classical economy because the firm must pay a turnover cost in addition to the real wage.

The example covered in Figure 7.3 is the same special case as the mathematical example in Boxes 7.3 and 7.4. For this special case the turnover cost is proportional to the number of workers. It is easy to solve because the efficiency wage is chosen independently of the number of workers. In more general examples the firm chooses the number of workers and the efficiency wage simultaneously.

BOX 7.4

A CLOSER LOOK
Deriving the Labor Demand Curve:
A Mathematical Example*

In this box, we show how labor demand is determined in the efficiency wage economy. Equation **7.4.1** is the expression for profit of a firm that uses the same technology as the firm we used as an example in Chapter 4, **Box 4.2.**

7.4.1
$$\pi \quad = \quad L^D - (1/2)(L^D)^2 \quad - \quad (w/P)L^D \quad - \quad c(w/P)L^D$$

Profit   This is the production   This is the   This is the
                          function.   wage bill.   turnover cost.

The firm first chooses the efficiency wage to minimize the per-worker cost, $(w/P)+c(w/P)$. When the turnover cost is equal to $(1-2(w/P)+(w/P)^2)$, this problem leads the firm to choose the efficiency wage $(w/P)^*=1/2$. This is the problem we solved in **Box 7.3**. When the efficiency wage is equal to 1/2, the turnover cost is equal to:

7.4.1
$$c \quad = \quad 1 - 2(w/P) + (w/P)^2 \quad = \quad 1/4$$

Turnover cost   This is how to evaluate   This is the value of the
                             the turnover cost for   turnover cost when the
                             any real wage.   real wage equals 1/2.

Given this choice of the efficiency wage, the firm chooses L^D to maximize profit. This causes it to set the marginal product equal to the real wage plus the turnover cost.

7.4.2
$$1 - L^D \quad = \quad (w/P)^* + c(w/P)^* \quad = \quad 1/2 + 1/4 = 3/4$$

This is the   This is the efficiency wage   This is the value of the real
marginal product.   plus the turnover cost.   wage plus the turnover cost.

This problem has the following solution:

7.4.5
$$L^D \quad = \quad 1/4$$

This is the amount of labor demanded in the economy with efficiency wages.

In general it will not be possible to write the turnover cost as the product of the per-worker cost $c(w/P)$ and the number of workers, L. For the more general problem, the firm will maximize profit with respect to the wage and with respect to employment. The first-order conditions for this more general problem lead to two equations that are solved *simultaneously* for the efficiency wage and the stock of workers.

THE AGGREGATE LABOR MARKET AND THE NATURAL RATE OF UNEMPLOYMENT

In classical theory, the real wage and the quantity of labor employed are determined by finding the point where the quantity of labor demanded is equal to the quantity of labor supplied. Since there are no frictions in this model, it is not necessary to distinguish stocks from flows: The firm can adjust the number of workers it employs without incurring a cost. In contrast, in new-Keynesian theory, the real wage is chosen to maximize profit. Since the cost of maintaining a given stock of workers may fall as the real wage increases, the new-Keynesian firm will choose to employ fewer workers than the classical firm, resulting in equilibrium unemployment.

Figure 7.4 illustrates this idea. The upward-sloping red line represents the labor force. It slopes upward because when the real wage increases, households choose to increase the

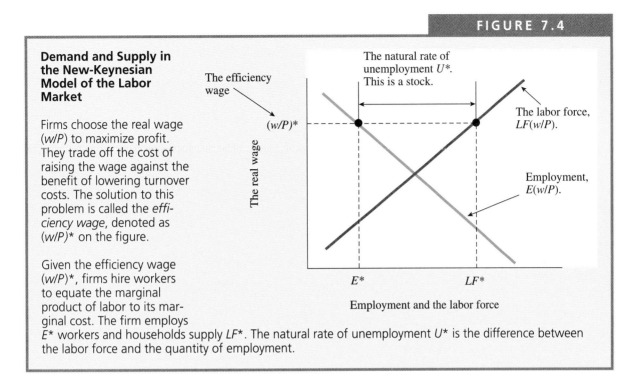

FIGURE 7.4

Demand and Supply in the New-Keynesian Model of the Labor Market

Firms choose the real wage (*w*/*P*) to maximize profit. They trade off the cost of raising the wage against the benefit of lowering turnover costs. The solution to this problem is called the *efficiency wage*, denoted as (*w*/*P*)* on the figure.

Given the efficiency wage (*w*/*P*)*, firms hire workers to equate the marginal product of labor to its marginal cost. The firm employs *E** workers and households supply *LF**. The natural rate of unemployment *U** is the difference between the labor force and the quantity of employment.

number of family members that seek paid employment. The downward-sloping green line represents the employment curve. It slopes downward because firms choose to hire fewer workers as the real wage increases. Since firms choose to employ fewer workers in the new-Keynesian model than in the classical model, there exists a stock of unemployed workers in equilibrium. When the real wage is equal to the efficiency wage, the number of unemployed workers as a percentage of the labor force is the natural rate of unemployment.

One final aspect of the new-Keynesian theory is the question: How do we know that there will be unemployment in equilibrium? The answer is that, in our development of the theory, we took the cost function as given. In practice there is an interaction between the turnover cost of any given firm and aggregate unemployment. Workers are less likely to leave the firm when unemployment is high, and they are more likely to quit when unemployment is low. Hence, the turnover cost will itself depend on the state of the labor market. It is this feature of the theory that guarantees that there will be unemployment in equilibrium.

UNEMPLOYMENT AND ECONOMIC POLICY

There are two approaches to the design of economic policies that are designed to alleviate unemployment. First, many economists believe that the natural rate of unemployment is too high. Policies designed to control the natural rate are called **structural policies**, and the unemployment that results from poorly designed labor-market institutions is called

BOX 7.5

A CLOSER LOOK
Deriving the Natural Rate of Unemployment:
A Mathematical Example*

In this box, we write down the equations that determine the demand and supply for a stock of workers and we use these equations to determine the natural rate of unemployment. In **Boxes 7.3** and **7.4**, we established that the efficiency wage is equal to 1/2 and that at this wage the firm would choose to keep a labor stock of 1/4. We will assume that labor supply is given by the same equation as in the example that we studied in Chapter 4 (4.2.3).

7.5.1 L^S = (w/P) =   1/2

            This is the labor   This is the quantity of labor supplied
            supply curve.   when the wage is equal to the efficiency wage.

The natural rate of unemployment is given by the difference between the demand and the supply.

7.5.1 U^* = $1/2 - 1/4$ =   1/4

                    This is the natural rate of unemployment for this example.

structural unemployment. A second approach deals with the control of cyclical unemployment as it fluctuates over the business cycle (see Chapter 8).

STRUCTURAL UNEMPLOYMENT

A comparative study of unemployment across countries suggests that policy matters. We review the evidence and ask the question: What kinds of labor market policies can be implemented to reduce the natural rate of unemployment?

Evidence that policy matters comes from studying the history of unemployment in North America and Europe. During the 1970s and 1980s, unemployment in North America fluctuated in the range of 6% to 7%. In the countries that now make up the European Union, unemployment has historically been much higher. For example, in 1988, the European average rate of unemployment was 9.7%; in some countries, Spain for example, it was as high as 19%. More recently, unemployment rates have been falling both in the United States and Europe, although European unemployment has a long way to go before reaching U.S. levels. Data for a selection of European countries and for the United States is presented in Table 7.1.

Table 7.1 illustrates that U.S. unemployment is extremely low when compared with France, Germany, and Spain. Unemployment in France and Germany has been around 10% for a decade, and it rose between 1988 and 1998; U.S. unemployment fell over this same period. Further, there are aspects of European unemployment that make it a more troubling social problem than it might be in the United States. For example in 1998, over 50% of the unemployed in Europe had been out of work for more than a year, whereas only 8% had been unemployed in the United States for a year or more. Unemployment in Spain has been around 18% to 19% percent, and youth unemployment is even higher.

TABLE 7.1

Ten-year Trends in Unemployment Rates in a Selection of Countries[1]

	(% of total labor force)	
	1988	1998
France	10.0	11.8
Germany	7.6	9.3
Italy	11.8	12.2
Spain	19.1	18.6
United Kingdom	8.3	6.3
United States	5.4	4.5
EU-15	9.7	10.0

[1] Source: OECD at http://www.oecd.org.

UNEMPLOYMENT AND SKILL

A second dimension that differentiates the United States and Europe is that European unemployment is particularly high among those without skills. This is not true to the same extent in North America, where the unskilled find low-paying jobs. Over the past two decades in North America, the gap between wages earned by high- and low-skilled workers has widened, but aggregate unemployment has remained roughly constant. Edward Leamer of the University of California, Los Angeles, points out that the gap between garment workers (a low-skill occupation) and those in machinery, metals, or electronics professions has increased by a factor of 20% since 1960.[3] In Europe, the gap between high- and low-paid workers has not changed as much, but unemployment, particularly among the low-skilled, has risen dramatically. What might account for these disparate changes in Europe and North America? One explanation is that there has been a change in the composition of the demand for labor over the past 30 years in the industrialized countries that has favored the skilled over the unskilled. Because of differences in the structure of the European and North American labor markets, this change has caused different effects in the two regions. Some of the key differences are discussed in Box 7.6 on page 188.

The change in labor markets in industrialized countries has taken the form of an increase in the demand for the services of skilled workers as opposed to unskilled workers. Education

---

3. Edward Leamer. "U.S. wages, technological change, and globalization," *Jobs and Capital,* Milken Institute for Jobs and Capital Formation, Summer 1995.

BOX 7.6

FOCUS ON THE FACTS
Unemployment and
Labor Market Rigidities

This table illustrates four measures of rigidities in the labor market that might account for high European unemployment. The employment protection and labor standards indexes are measures of the legal protection afforded to workers in matters of hiring and firing, and in other aspects, such as union representation and minimum wage laws. The replacement rate shows the share of income paid in unemployment benefits, and the benefit duration is the number of years for which benefits are received.

TABLE A

	Employment Protection	Labor Standards	Benefit (Replacement Rate %)	Benefit Duration (Years)
France	14	6	57	3.0
Germany	15	6	63	4.0
Italy	20	7	20	0.5
Spain	19	7	70	3.5
U.K.	7	0	38	4.0
U.S.	1	0	50	0.5

In a recent article in the *Journal of Economic Perspectives,* Stephen Nickel of Oxford University analyzes the effect of the labor market rigidities reported in Table A on the unemployment rate. His main conclusions (based on this and other data) are that some labor market rigidities are more important in causing high unemployment than others.[1]

"High unemployment is associated with . . . 1) generous unemployment benefits that are allowed to run on indefinitely, combined with little or no pressure on the unemployed to obtain work . . . 2) high unionization with wages bargained collectively and no coordination between either unions or employers in wage bargaining 3) high overall taxes impinging on labor . . . and 4) poor educational standards.

Labor market rigidities that do not. . . . [raise unemployment] . . . are 1) strict employment protection legislation. . . . 2) generous levels of unemployment benefits . . . accompanied by pressure to take jobs and 3) high levels of unionization with a high degree of coordination in wage bargaining particularly among employers."

[1] Stephen Nickel. "Unemployment and Labor Market Rigidities," *The Journal of Economic Perspectives,* Vol. 11, no. 3, pp 55–74, September 1997.

is much more valuable in today's labor market than it was 20 years ago. There are two competing explanations for this. The first is that changes in technology favor highly skilled workers over unskilled workers. For example, the level of education required to work in the modern computer industry as a software engineer is higher than the level of education required to operate a sewing machine. The second explanation is that because industrialized countries have lowered trade barriers, there is now a much greater degree of competition between low-skilled workers in the United States and low-skilled workers in developing countries. Because the average worker in the apparel industry in China makes just one-twentieth as much as the average worker in the apparel industry in the United States (even though they are sewing the very same garments), it seems possible that increased competition with low-skilled foreign labor has increased the wage dispersion in the United States.

But why has the wage gap between skilled and unskilled workers increased more in the United States than in Europe? One explanation is that the European labor market is considerably more rigid than the U.S. market. In the United States, workers have relatively

W E B W A T C H

Check Out the OECD on the Web at http://www.oecd.org

The Organization for Economic Cooperation and Development based in Paris, France, is a unique forum permitting governments of the industrialized democracies to study and formulate the best policies possible in all economic and social spheres. The OECD differs from other governmental organizations in three respects:

As it has neither supranational legal powers nor financial resources for loans or subsidies, its sole function is direct cooperation among the governments of its member countries.

At the OECD, international cooperation means cooperation among nations essentially on domestic policies where these interact with those of other countries, in particular through trade and investment. Cooperation usually means that member countries seek to adapt their domestic policies to minimize conflict with other countries. Governments frequently seek to learn from each others' experiences with specific domestic policies before they adopt their own courses of action, whether legislative or administrative.

By focusing the expertise of various OECD directorates and those of various member government departments on specific issues, the OECD approach particularly benefits from a multidisciplinary dimension. The organization deals both with general macroeconomic and with more specific or sectoral issues.

The OECD is also an excellent source of data. The following page is available at http://www.oecd.org/eco/surv/www.htm. It contains links to country data and reports on the 29 countries listed below.

Macroeconomic reports and data

The OECD does not necessarily endorse these sources and cannot vouch for their accuracy.

Australia	Finland	Ireland	Netherlands	Sweden
Austria	France	Italy	New Zealand	Switzerland
Belgium	Germany	Japan	Norway	Turkey
Canada	Greece	Korea	Poland	United Kingdom
Czech Republic	Hungary	Luxembourg	Portugal	United States
Denmark	Iceland	Mexico	Spain	

EXERCISE

Go to the OECD Web site and find the most recent data on unemployment rates in five OECD countries of your choice.

little legal protection from losing their jobs, and unemployment benefits are less generous and last for a shorter period of time than in many European countries. In the United States, for example, an unemployed worker can expect to receive only 50% of his or her working wage in the form of unemployment benefits and, more importantly, can go on collecting for only six months. An unemployed worker in Spain receives 70% of his or her working wage and can collect benefits for three and a half years. Correspondingly, approximately 19% of the labor force in Spain is unemployed, a level that hasn't been seen in the United States since the Great Depression. It is likely that rigidities in the European labor market prevented the fall in the demand for unskilled labor from causing their wage to drop, and the result has been increased European unemployment.[4]

POLICIES TO ALLEVIATE STRUCTURAL UNEMPLOYMENT

The issue of what to do about structural unemployment is the subject of a great deal of discussion in policy circles. The answer must surely depend on its causes, but there is no consensus here. No one argues that unemployment should be eliminated entirely; some level of frictional unemployment is necessary in a dynamic labor market in which workers frequently change occupations to keep up with new technologies. Several European countries have much higher unemployment rates than that of North America, and solving long-term structural unemployment is a central concern in these countries. Some economists have argued that one of the major causes of high European unemployment is the fact that these countries have legislation to protect jobs, legislation that makes it difficult for firms to hire and fire workers. Other economists point to minimum wage legislation, which is thought by some to raise unemployment. But although economic theory clearly predicts that a high minimum wage will cause additional unemployment, the evidence on this issue is less clear, and economists are divided.

Europeans envy the U.S. labor market for its efficiency and low levels of unemployment, but U.S. policy is also frequently criticized in the European press for its low level of concern for the welfare of the unemployed. But even if European labor market policies could be proven responsible for higher unemployment, it is by no means clear that these policies should be eliminated. Many people argue that unemployment insurance benefits are an important component of a civilized society, and that the working members of society must be prepared to pay for these benefits with higher taxes and higher levels of unemployment because they too may face unemployment at some time in their lives.

CONCLUSION

Unemployment has typically averaged 6% to 7% in the United States. But there have been some major recessions, such as in the 1890s when unemployment reached 18% and the Great Depression during the 1930s when it reached 25%. Unemployment has been falling

---

4.   For a very readable summary of the European unemployment problem, see "Europe hits a brick wall." *The Economist,* April 5, 1997.

recently, and U.S. unemployment in 2000 was equal to 4.9%. European unemployment is much higher, averaging 10% in 1998 across the 15 countries of the European Union.

Modern theories on the causes of unemployment began with John Maynard Keynes, who argued that the system does not typically return quickly to the classical equilibrium. Instead, Keynes thought that the economy could experience prolonged periods of high cyclical unemployment, periods that he thought were inefficient. Keynes was responsible for the modern view, according to which governments should be held responsible for maintaining a low and stable unemployment rate throughout the operation of governmental policy.

Unemployment rates differ across countries for institutional reasons. Some of these differences can be influenced by government policies that regulate microeconomic aspects of labor markets. These include minimum wage laws, levels of unemployment insurance benefits, and the duration for which unemployment benefits are paid. Currently, there is an active debate over the best way to deal with high levels of unemployment in Europe, and some economists have advocated reforms to make labor markets more flexible.

KEY TERMS

Countercyclical fiscal policy
Cyclical unemployment
Efficiency wage
Efficiency wage theory
Frictional unemployment

Natural rate of unemployment
New Keynesian
Search theory
Structural policies
Structural unemployment

QUESTIONS FOR CHAPTER 7

1. Explain the difference between *frictional* and *cyclical* unemployment. Why is this distinction important in order to understand the causes of unemployment?

2. Suppose that economists focused on the duration of unemployment as opposed to the unemployment rate. Would they come to different conclusions regarding the behavior of unemployment over the business cycle? Explain.

3. Looking at Box 7.2, what has happened to the standard deviation of the unemployment rate over the past 100 years? Do you have a hypothesis as to why this might be?

4. In this chapter, the efficiency wage theory of unemployment was justified by the fact that firms incur search costs whenever they have labor turnover. As a result, firms are willing to pay real wages above market-clearing wages in order to reduce labor turnover and search costs. Can you think of other benefits that a firm might also enjoy when paying real wages above the market-clearing wage? Explain.

5. What is "natural" about the natural rate of unemployment in a model with efficiency wages? Why doesn't the real wage simply fall to clear the labor market and eliminate unemployment?

6. Unemployment in the classical labor market is often referred to as *voluntary unemployment*, while unemployment in Keynesian models is often referred to as *involuntary unemployment*. What do you think economists are referring to when they make such a distinction?

7. In a model with efficiency wages, is the labor market perfectly competitive? Explain. What effect does this have on the slope of the labor demand curve?

8. Suppose that a one-time tax is imposed on a firm every time it *hires* a new worker. What would happen to the efficiency wage as a result of this tax? What happens to employment and unemployment? Provide a graph of the labor market to illustrate.

9. Suppose that a one-time tax is imposed on a firm every time it *fires* a worker. What would happen to the efficiency wage as a result of this tax? What happens to employment and unemployment? Provide a graph of the labor market to illustrate.

10. With the invention of the Internet, many firms are finding it easier and less costly to advertise job openings and find better-qualified applicants at a lower cost. What would happen to the efficiency wage as a result of this technology? What would happen to employment and unemployment? Provide a graph of the labor market to illustrate.

11. Suppose that a typical firm faces the following turnover cost function:

$$c = 4(1/(w/P))$$

a. What happens to c as the real wage, w/P, increases? Is this consistent with efficiency wage theory?

b. What is the marginal benefit to a firm of an increase in w/P?

c. What is the marginal cost to a firm of in increase in w/P?

d. Calculate the equilibrium efficiency wage.

e. If $L^D = 2(1/(w/P))$, calculate the amount of labor demanded at the efficiency wage.

f. If $L^S = (w/P)$, calculate the natural rate of unemployment.

g. Calculate the market-clearing real wage. Is the efficiency wage greater or less than the market-clearing real wage? Explain.

12. Discuss how the behavior of unemployment has differed between the United States and Europe. Describe in detail the four reasons offered by Professor Nickel to explain these differences in the behavior of unemployment.

13. Provide three explanations for the growing wage gap between low-skilled and high-skilled workers in the United States What policies might you recommend to correct for this growing wage gap? Might your recommendations, if enacted, have an effect on the unemployment rate as well?

CHAPTER 8

THE NEW-KEYNESIAN THEORY OF AGGREGATE SUPPLY

INTRODUCTION

This chapter explains the new-Keynesian theory of aggregate supply. This theory was developed because the classical theory of aggregate supply has difficulty accounting for certain features of the Great Depression. According to the classical theory, if the money supply falls, all nominal variables will fall in proportion and all real variables will remain unchanged. This proposition, the neutrality of money, in the classical theory is depicted in the graph of aggregate supply as vertical. Keynesians do not disagree with the predictions of the classical theory as a description of the long-run effects of a fall in the money supply. But they argue that the process by which the economy gets from one long-run equilibrium to another takes time.

In the new-Keynesian theory of aggregate supply, the quantity of output supplied slopes upward as a function of the price level because the nominal wage is assumed to be **sticky**. This means that it is slow to adjust when there is a shock to the economy, such as a change in the money supply that shifts the aggregate demand curve or a new invention that shifts the aggregate supply curve. In the new-Keynesian model, after a shock, the nominal wage and the nominal price level do not adjust instantly to their new long-run equilibrium levels. As a consequence, output falls after a negative shock and unemployment increases. Following a positive shock, output increases and unemployment falls.

BOX 8.1

A CLOSER LOOK
Interpreting Keynes

Don Patinkin (1922–1995) was trained at the University of Chicago where he wrote his doctoral dissertation, *Money Interest and Prices* (1956). This book became a classic in the field of macroeconomics. In it, Patinkin integrates Keynes' *General Theory* with Walrasian general equilibrium theory by including the real value of money as if it were a good that gives utility. Patinkin was one of the first economists to try to make sense of Keynes' theory using the methods of neoclassical microeconomics.

Patinkin was instrumental in the "nominal rigidity" interpretation of Keynesian theory that will be covered in this chapter. According to this interpretation, Keynesian unemployment occurs because the nominal level of prices is very slow to adjust to its classical equilibrium level.

After leaving the University of Chicago, Patinkin moved to the Hebrew University in Jerusalem, although he maintained close ties with colleagues in the United States where he frequently spent extended visits. In his later years, Patinkin worked mainly on the history of thought, specializing in interpretations of Keynes.

Our first task is to explain why a sticky nominal wage leads to an upward-sloping aggregate supply curve. We will then examine the adjustment process by which the economy moves from one long-run equilibrium to another. In the new-Keynesian theory, the nominal wage rises if unemployment is too low, and the nominal wage falls if unemployment is too high. In the long run, the response of the new-Keynesian economy to a change in aggregate demand is the same as the response of the classical economy. But in the short run, the new-Keynesian model allows quantities to adjust in response to a change in the price level. The fact that quantities adjust, rather than prices, is a direct consequence of the assumption that the nominal wage is sticky.

Ever since Keynes wrote *The General Theory*, economists have been trying to interpret his ideas. Keynes was above all a practical man, and the policies he advocated to alleviate the Great Depression worked. But the microeconomics of his theory were never spelled out, and his followers have spent vast amounts of time attempting to make sense of Keynesian economics in terms of the theory of rational behavior.

One of the first systematic attempts to study the microfoundations of Keynes' *General Theory* was by an Israeli economist, Don Patinkin, who wrote an influential book entitled *Money Interest and Prices*. In it, Patinkin pointed out that we must assume that there is a nominal rigidity in the economy in order to develop an interpretation of Keynes' *General Theory* that is consistent with the microeconomic general equilibrium theory of Leon Walras.[1]

---

1.   For this reason, I think of Patinkin as the first new Keynesian, although he most probably would have been uncomfortable with this label. Keynes himself resisted the idea that his theory rested on nominal rigidity, but Patinkin pointed out that nominal rigidity was the only way to make the theory internally consistent. Modern macroeconomics has followed the path laid down by Patinkin, and almost all modern approaches to the subject use the framework that he laid out in his graduate thesis at the University of Chicago, which was later published as *Money Interest and Prices*.

THE THEORY OF NOMINAL RIGIDITY

We will now explain what new-Keynesian economists mean by a "theory of nominal rigidity." There are two different approaches to this theory. The first, the **menu cost** approach, leads to models with slow nominal price adjustment. The second, the **contract theory** of wages, leads to models with slow nominal wage adjustment. In practice, researchers have combined both approaches to develop a theory of aggregate supply in which the quantity of output supplied is an increasing function of the price level. In this chapter, we will develop a theory with rigid nominal wages since it leads to a theory of aggregate supply that is easy to explain.[2]

A PREVIEW: THE CLASSICAL AND NEW-KEYNESIAN THEORIES COMPARED

Figure 8.1 on page 196 illustrates why it is important for the new-Keynesian approach to develop a theory of nominal rigidity. In the classical model, the aggregate supply of output depends on economic fundamentals: preferences, endowments, and technology. According to this theory, the aggregate supply curve (the quantity of output supplied as a function of the price level) is vertical. Panel A shows what would happen in the classical theory in response to a fall in aggregate demand. Suppose, for example, that there is a fall in the money supply that causes the aggregate demand curve to fall from AD_1 to AD_2. In the classical model, this fall in demand causes a fall in the nominal price level from P_1 to P_2, but there is no change in the quantity of output supplied. Therefore, this theory cannot account for the Great Depression as a response to a fall in aggregate demand.

Suppose instead that we explain the Great Depression as a fall in aggregate supply. Using the classical model, this explanation would also fail, because a leftward shift of the aggregate supply curve would cause the price level to rise, not fall. In practice, during the Great Depression, the price level and output both fell and unemployment rose. This combination of events is difficult to explain within the classical theory.

Panel B illustrates how a theory of nominal rigidity can explain all of the facts of the Great Depression. In the new-Keynesian theory, the aggregate supply curve slopes upward as a function of the price level. According to this theory, when the price level falls, there is an increase in the real wage because some firms cannot quickly adjust nominal wages. As the real wage rises, firms lower employment, and unemployment increases above the natural rate. This is illustrated in panel B as a fall in aggregate demand that causes the equilibrium of the economy to move from point **A** to point **B**. In the new-Keynesian model, there is a fall in the price level from P_1 to P_2 and a simultaneous fall in output from Y_1 to Y_2. The rest of this chapter develops the theory that underlies this graph.

A THEORY OF STICKY WAGES

The new-Keynesian theory of aggregate supply is based on the theory of efficiency wages. According to this theory, firms choose their wages in order to minimize the wage

---

2.   The conclusions of both approaches are similar, although they have different implications for whether wages are procyclical or countercyclical over the business cycle.

FIGURE 8.1

The Classical and New-Keynesian Theories of Aggregate Supply Compared

Panel A shows what happens in the classical theory if there is a fall in aggregate demand from AD_1 to AD_2.

The equilibrium moves from point **A** to point **B**.

Since output is determined by fundamentals (preferences, endowments, and technology), the fall in demand causes a fall in the price level from P_1 to P_2.

Panel B shows what happens in the new-Keynesian theory if there is a fall in aggregate demand from AD_1 to AD_2.

The equilibrium moves from point **A** to point **B**.

Since the new-Keynesian aggregate supply curve slopes upward, the fall in demand causes a fall in the price level from P_1 to P_2 and a simultaneous drop in output supplied from Y_1 to Y_2.

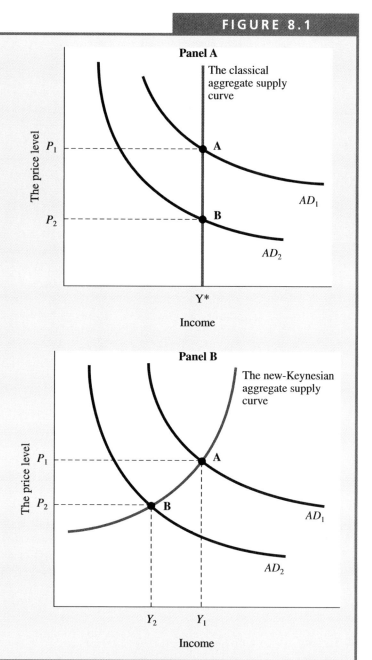

bill and they choose employment in order to maximize profit. If these decisions were taken simultaneously, the new-Keynesian theory would not be able to explain why the aggregate supply curve slopes upward. To see why this is so, suppose that the nominal quantity of money were to fall. Since efficiency wage theory determines the *real* efficiency wage, a drop in the money supply would be consistent with both a fall in the nominal wage and a fall in the price level that left all real variables the same. Efficiency wage theory is still an improvement over the classical theory because it can account for the existence of unemployment in equilibrium. But it cannot explain why the aggregate supply curve slopes upward.

The new-Keynesian theory of aggregate supply begins with the efficiency wage model and adds to it, assuming that the nominal wage is chosen less frequently than employment. The nominal wage in this model is said to be sticky. This is a realistic assumption because many workers sign employment contracts that specify the nominal wage for a period of one to four years; the average duration of labor contracts in the United States is two years. Since not all labor contracts are revised at the same time, one group of firms is writing new contracts while another group of firms is paying according to contracts written in the past. As a consequence of overlapping contracts, the aggregate real wage may differ from the efficiency wage over long periods of time.

UNEMPLOYMENT AND THE PRICE LEVEL WHEN THE NOMINAL WAGE IS STICKY

This section illustrates the decisions made by a firm that sets its wage rate less frequently than it hires or fires workers. We will study an example of an economy that begins in equilibrium with unemployment at its natural rate, and we will subject this economy to a thought experiment: What happens to the price level, the real wage, employment, and output in response to an increase in aggregate demand if the nominal wage cannot adjust quickly to a change in the money supply?

Let the initial real wage equal $(w/P)^*$. Suppose further that the nominal wage paid by firms is equal to some number, say w_1, and the price level is equal to some other number, say P_1, so that $(w/P)^* = (w_1/P_1)$. This situation is illustrated in Figure 8.2 on page 198, which also shows that when unemployment is at the natural rate, U^* people are unemployed. Now, suppose that the price level increases from P_1 to some higher level, P_2. Later we will ask why the price level might increase, but for now we will take it as given and ask how firms and workers react to the situation. In the classical model, we saw that an increase in the price level would immediately be met by an increase in the nominal wage in order to restore equilibrium between the quantity of labor demanded and the quantity supplied. But new Keynesians argue that because of nominal rigidity, this process of nominal wage adjustment takes time. In the short run, the wage will remain at its nominal level, w_1.

Because the price level has risen, the nominal wage of w_1 is now lower in real terms than the real efficiency wage $(w/P)^*$. Firms will respond by recruiting more workers and creating more jobs. As the real wage falls, households will send fewer workers to the labor market. The net effect will be a reduction in unemployment from U^* to U_2. The effect of an increase in the price level from P_1 to P_2 on unemployment is illustrated in panel A of Figure 8.2.

FIGURE 8.2

How Changes in the Price Level Affect Employment

Panel A shows what happens in the new Keynesian model if the price level increases to P_2. Because the nominal wage is slow to adjust, the increased price level causes the *real wage* to fall. Employment rises to L_2 and unemployment falls to U_2, below the natural rate.

Panel B illustrates what happens if the price level falls to P_3. Because the nominal wage is slow to adjust, the lower price level causes the *real wage* to rise. Employment falls to L_3 and unemployment rises to U_3, above the natural rate.

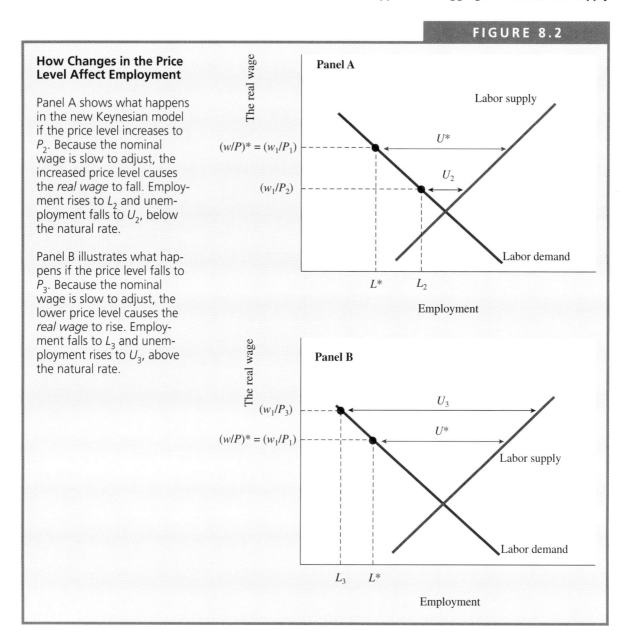

Panel B illustrates what happens, beginning from full employment, if the price level falls from P_1 to some lower level, P_3. Once again, because of nominal rigidity, the nominal wage remains at w_1; and in this case the fall in the price level causes the real wage to increase. Firms now expect to make fewer profits and they employ fewer workers. Employment falls from L^* to L_3, and unemployment increases above the natural rate.

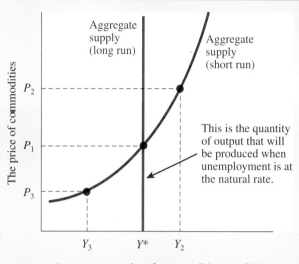

FIGURE 8.3

The New-Keynesian Theory of Aggregate Supply

This graph shows how aggregate supply responds to changes in the price level. In the short run, the nominal wage is slow to adjust, and a change in the price level causes the *real wage* to change.

If the nominal price rises, the real wage falls and unemployment drops below the natural rate.

If the nominal price falls, the real wage increases and unemployment increases above the natural rate.

In the long run, the nominal wage is fully flexible and unemployment is *at* the natural rate.

Within the figure:
- Aggregate supply (long run)
- Aggregate supply (short run)
- The price of commodities
- P_2, P_1, P_3
- This is the quantity of output that will be produced when unemployment is at the natural rate.
- Y_3 Y^* Y_2
- Aggregate quantity of commodities supplied

AGGREGATE SUPPLY AND THE PRICE LEVEL WHEN THE NOMINAL WAGE IS STICKY

According to the Keynesian theory of unemployment, the quantity of output supplied is an increasing function of the nominal price level because, in the short run, the nominal wage is slow to adjust to changes in aggregate demand. We will now explain the connection between aggregate supply and the price level.

Figure 8.3 shows why changes in the price level cause changes in the aggregate quantity of commodities supplied. Let the price level begin at P_1, a level where output is equal to its long-run level and unemployment is equal to the natural rate. Now, suppose that the price level increases above P_1. Because the nominal wage is sticky, this increase in the price level causes a reduction in the real wage. As the real wage falls, firms hire more workers, and the level of unemployment falls below U^*. Figure 8.3 illustrates that in this case the quantity of output supplied would increase from Y^* to Y_2. Y_2 is greater than Y^* because at P_2 the real wage is lower than at P_1, and firms are willing to employ more workers.

A similar process applies when the nominal price level falls below P_1. In this case, because the nominal wage is fixed in the short run, the reduction in the price level causes the real wage to increase and firms hire fewer workers. The unemployment rate increases above the natural rate because fewer workers are employed. When the price level is P_3,

[handwritten margin note:] So, lower unemployment, but $\frac{w}{p}\downarrow$ — would this lead to a increase in y?

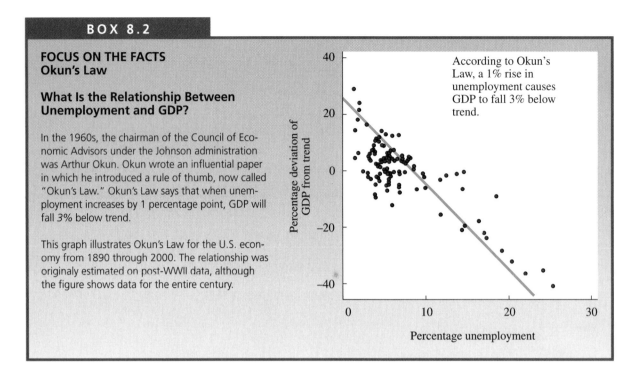

BOX 8.2

FOCUS ON THE FACTS
Okun's Law

What Is the Relationship Between Unemployment and GDP?

In the 1960s, the chairman of the Council of Economic Advisors under the Johnson administration was Arthur Okun. Okun wrote an influential paper in which he introduced a rule of thumb, now called "Okun's Law." Okun's Law says that when unemployment increases by 1 percentage point, GDP will fall 3% below trend.

This graph illustrates Okun's Law for the U.S. economy from 1890 through 2000. The relationship was originaly estimated on post-WWII data, although the figure shows data for the entire century.

According to Okun's Law, a 1% rise in unemployment causes GDP to fall 3% below trend.

firms supply the quantity of output Y_3. Y_3 is less than Y^* because at P_3 the real wage is higher than at P_1, and firms are less willing to employ workers.

The link between unemployment and output at business cycle frequencies is called **Okun's Law** after Arthur Okun, chairman of the President's Council of Economic Advisors in the 1960s. Okun's Law is illustrated in Box 8.2 using data from 1890 through 2000.

GETTING FROM THE SHORT RUN TO THE LONG RUN

According to the new-Keynesian theory, there are forces that cause the nominal wage to move toward a level where the real wage equals the efficiency wage. When the real wage equals the efficiency wage, we say that unemployment is equal to its natural rate, and we refer to the quantity of output produced as the "natural rate of output." The natural rate of unemployment and the natural rate of output depend only on the fundamentals of the economy: preferences, endowments, and technology. They do not depend on the money supply or on any of the other factors that shift the aggregate demand curve. This feature of the model implies that the new-Keynesian theory has the same predictions, in the long run, as the classical theory. An increase in the quantity of money will cause a proportional increase in all nominal variables and leave all real variables unchanged.

In the short run, the new-Keynesian model makes different predictions. Because the nominal wage is slow to adjust, changes in the price level cause changes in the real wage.

FIGURE 8.4

Getting from the Short Run to the Long Run

This figure illustrates how the economy gets from the short run to the long run.

When the price equals P_2, the real wage is too low and unemployment is below the natural rate. In this situation, firms begin to offer higher nominal wages and employment falls until the unemployment rate returns to the natural rate, U^*.

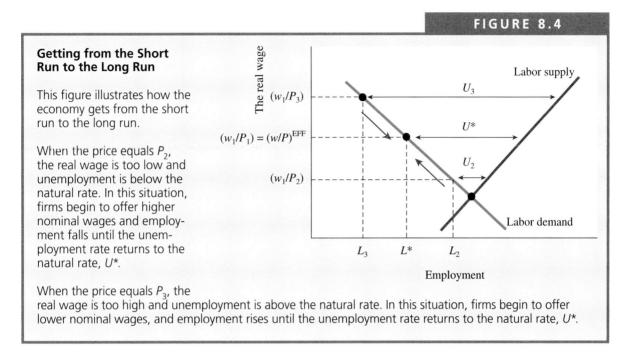

When the price equals P_3, the real wage is too high and unemployment is above the natural rate. In this situation, firms begin to offer lower nominal wages, and employment rises until the unemployment rate returns to the natural rate, U^*.

As real wages go up or down, firms adjust their volume of employment, and unemployment rises above or falls below its natural rate. Let's examine how the economy gets from the short run to the long run.

HOW THE ECONOMY GETS FROM THE SHORT RUN TO THE LONG RUN

Figure 8.4 illustrates the adjustment path of the economy from a short-run equilibrium to a long-run equilibrium. When the price level is equal to P_2, unemployment is below the natural rate, and when the price level is equal to P_3, it is above the natural rate. The red arrows illustrate how unemployment adjusts as the nominal wage changes.

In the most common theory of dynamic adjustment, it is assumed that some fraction of firms adjust their wages over any given period of time. Those firms that adjust their wages will also adjust their employment levels. But not all firms will adjust right away, since the nominal wage is revised only when labor contracts come up for renegotiation. As time passes after a nominal shock, more firms will adjust their nominal wages, and eventually the economywide average wage will move back to equilibrium.

The sequences of events following both positive and negative demand shocks are illustrated in Figure 8.4. The economy begins with unemployment equal to the natural rate U^*, and the wage (w_1/P_1) is equal to the efficiency wage $(w/P)^{EFF}$. In response to a positive demand shock, the price level increases from P_1 to P_2, the real wage falls from (w_1/P_1) to (w_1/P_2), and unemployment falls to U_2. As each firm renegotiates its labor contract, it also resets its nominal wage. But not all firms do this at once. Instead, as each firm renegotiates its labor contract the average nominal wage increases, and the economywide average real wage slowly increases back to $(w/P)^{EFF}$.

In response to a negative demand shock, the price level falls from P_1 to P_3, the real wage increases from (w_1/P_1) to (w_1/P_3), and unemployment increases to U_3. Over time, the average nominal wage decreases until the real wage returns to the efficiency wage $(w/P)^{EFF}$. In the case of both a positive and a negative shock, the real wage returns to the efficiency wage in the long run, and the level of unemployment returns to its natural rate.

New-Keynesian Theory and Economic Policy

Unemployment and the Neutrality of Money

According to the new-Keynesian theory, the price level and the nominal wage may not always be at the "right" level. This has important consequences for one of the central propositions of classical economic theory, the proposition that money is neutral.

The neutrality of money is a statement to describe events resulting from a change in the supply of money. In the classical model, a 10% fall in the supply of money will immediately result in a new equilibrium in which all nominal variables are also 10% lower and all real variables are unaltered. Keynes did not disagree with the proposition that the neutrality of money would hold in the long run. Instead, he argued that the establishment of a new equilibrium might take a very long time.

The insight that the labor market might not always be in equilibrium in the classical sense was one of the most important ideas that Keynes introduced to macroeconomics. But it was not his only contribution. A second, very important contribution was Keynes' theory of aggregate demand, which explains how factors other than the money supply can shift the aggregate demand curve. The Keynesian theory of aggregate demand is covered in Chapters 9 through 12. But in order to understand how just one of these factors, the supply of money, can affect unemployment, we need only part of the Keynesian aggregate demand apparatus.

The New-Keynesian Model and the Non-Neutrality of Money

Figure 8.5 illustrates how the new-Keynesian model responds to a reduction in the quantity of money. Let's conduct a thought experiment in which the government demands that every household must pay an extra $100 in taxes. Let the economy begin from an equilibrium in which unemployment is equal to the natural rate. Let w_1 be the nominal wage, P_1 is the price level, L^* is employment, and Y^* represents GDP. Further suppose that the average household begins the week with $500 and that during a normal week it plans to spend its income on commodities, ending the week with the same stock of cash that it started with.

When the reduction in the money supply takes effect, the household must plan to spend less during the week than it would normally spend on commodities in order to meet its tax obligation. We can represent the reduction in the money supply as a leftward shift in the aggregate demand curve, shown in Figure 8.5 as the shift from demand curve

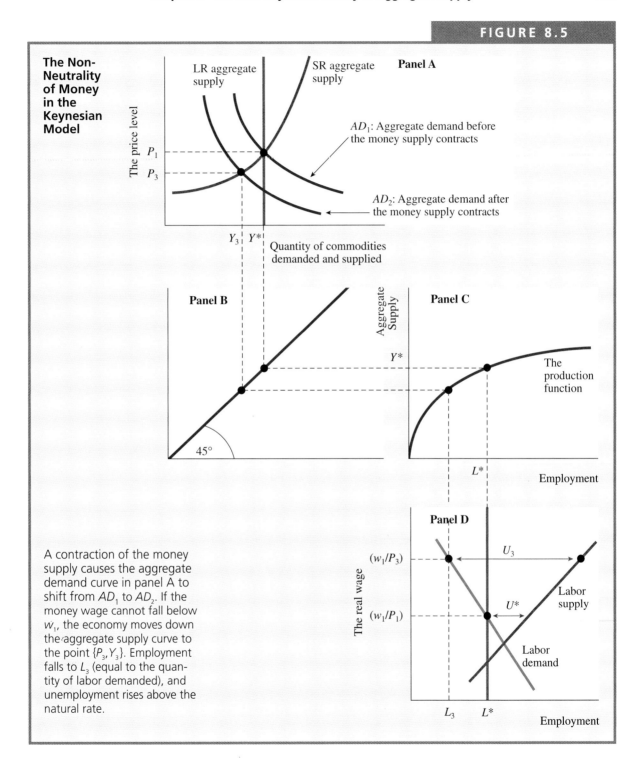

FIGURE 8.5

The Non-Neutrality of Money in the Keynesian Model

A contraction of the money supply causes the aggregate demand curve in panel A to shift from AD_1 to AD_2. If the money wage cannot fall below w_1, the economy moves down the aggregate supply curve to the point $\{P_3, Y_3\}$. Employment falls to L_3 (equal to the quantity of labor demanded), and unemployment rises above the natural rate.

AD_1 to AD_2 in panel A. This shift in the aggregate demand curve is the same as would be observed in the classical theory. But unlike the classical model, the fall in the supply of money does not cause all nominal variables to fall in proportion, since the nominal wage is slow to adjust. Instead, the reduction in aggregate demand causes a fall in employment and production as the economy moves down the aggregate supply curve. The fall in employment is represented in panel D of the figure as a shift from $L*$ to L_3 caused by an increase in the real wage (w_1/P_1) to (w_1/P_3). At the same time, unemployment increases from $U*$ to U_3.

How is the short-run price level P_3 determined? This is indicated in panel A of Figure 8.5 as the point at which the new aggregate demand curve AD_2 intersects the short-run aggregate supply curve. If wages were to adjust immediately downward, the fall in demand would cause the nominal wage and the price level to fall in proportion, and unemployment would remain at the natural rate. But in the Keynesian model, the nominal wage stays temporarily at w_1 and the real wage is driven up to (w_1/P_3).

CONFRONTING THE THEORY WITH THE FACTS

How does the Keynesian theory of unemployment fare as an explanation of the data? To address this question, in Box 8.3, we examine what happened to the U.S. labor market during the Great Depression. During this period, the price level fell by 30% and unemployment increased by 25%. Keynes argued that the combination of these events was inconsistent with the classical notion of equilibrium, and he constructed an alternative explanation that showed that the level of unemployment can be very high over long periods of time.

Because the Keynesian theory of the Great Depression assumes that the nominal wage does not fall fast enough to restore full equilibrium in the labor market, one test of the theory is to ask how much wages moved during the 1930s. Box 8.3 shows that wages fell almost as much as prices during the Depression. But although the nominal wage fell, it did not fall as fast as the price level. Keynesian economists argue that although the nominal wage fell, it did not fall fast enough to restore unemployment to its natural rate.

SHOULD WE STABILIZE THE BUSINESS CYCLE?

There are two possible answers to the question of what the government should do about cyclical unemployment. Economists from the real business cycle school believe that most recessions are generated by fluctuations in the natural rate and that the mechanism that restores equilibrium is very fast. If this is true, then there is not much need to stabilize unemployment over the business cycle since most recessions are caused by the economy adapting to a new technology. One would think, in this case, that some increase in the unemployment rate during recessions is a healthy sign because workers change jobs and learn new skills.

But although some increase in the unemployment rate during recessions should probably be tolerated, Keynesians argue that some business cycles are not caused by changes in technology. The Great Depression is one example of a recession in which the balancing

BOX 8.3

FOCUS ON THE FACTS
Wages and Prices in the United States During the Great Depression[1]

Panel A illustrates the behavior of the nominal wage and the price level during the Great Depression. It is clear that the strict version of the Keynesian theory of aggregate supply is not consistent with the evidence since although the price level fell, the nominal wage fell by almost as much.

But although the nominal wage fell, this evidence does not lead us to reject the Keynesian theory since it is possible that the nominal wage did not fall *enough*. The critical Keynesian assumption is that in response to a drop in aggregate demand, the real wage rises above its equilibrium level. This can occur if the nominal wage is completely inflexible, but it might also occur if the nominal wage falls less than proportionately to the drop in the supply of money.

[1] The nominal price level is a price index—the GDP deflator. The nominal wage is constructed by dividing the total wage bill from the GDP accounts by an index of employment (the number of full-time equivalent employees). The wage index has then been normalized (multiplied by 10) to fit it onto the same scale as the price index.

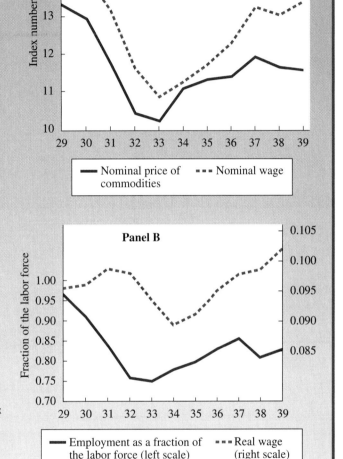

mechanisms of the market system seem to have gone very wrong. If most recessions are like the Great Depression, perhaps the government should actively intervene to speed the process that restores unemployment to its natural rate. But in order to better understand the arguments for and against government intervention, we first need to understand how the complete economy functions.

CONCLUSION

To understand cyclical unemployment, the new Keynesians begin with the efficiency wage model. They modify this model by adding the assumption that the nominal wage is sticky, and this modification leads to a theory in which the aggregate supply of output slopes upward as a function of the real wage. According to the new-Keynesian theory of recessions, shifts in aggregate demand cause employment to fluctuate over the business cycle because the nominal wage adjusts slowly to shocks. The new Keynesians use this theory to explain why unemployment increased and the price level fell during the Great Depression.

Economists disagree over whether government policy should seek to stabilize cyclical unemployment. Real business cycle economists think that most business cycles are caused by fluctuations in the natural rate that are induced by supply shifts. New Keynesians think that some recessions are induced by changes in aggregate demand. They argue that government has a role in stabilizing the business cycle.

KEY TERMS

Contract theory   Okun's Law
Menu cost   Sticky

QUESTIONS FOR CHAPTER 8

1. Compare and contrast the classical and new-Keynesian aggregate supply curves, making sure to focus on how their assumptions regarding the labor market differ.

2. Discuss two reasons why nominal wages are sticky. In the real world, do you think that nominal wages are more likely to be upwardly sticky or downwardly sticky? Explain your answer.

3. Do you think that the speed at which nominal wages adjust differs across countries? What factors might affect this speed of adjustment? How does the aggregate supply curve of a country with slow wage adjustment compare to the aggregate supply curve of a country with fast adjustment? Explain.

4. Discuss what is meant by the *neutrality of money*. Is money neutral in the new-Keynesian model? Explain.

5. Suppose that all wages in the economy were automatically linked to a price index through a cost-of-living adjustment. How would this institutional change alter the Keynesian theory of aggregate supply?

6. What is meant by Okun's Law? If the unemployment rate were to increase from 3% to 4%, how much would you predict that output would fall below trend?

7. Discuss the effects of a 10% increase in the money supply in the new-Keynesian model, using aggregate demand and aggregate supply. Examine both the short-run and long-run effects of this increase, making sure to explain how the economy makes the transition from the short run to the long run.

8. Examine the effects a 10% increase in the money supply in the classical model using the aggregate demand and aggregate supply model. Discuss in detail how your answer differs from your answer to question 7, which used the new-Keynesian model.

9. Reconsider question 11 from Chapter 5. Do you think that Say's Law necessarily holds in the new-Keynesian model? Why or why not?

10. Are real wages procyclical or countercyclical in the new-Keynesian model? What about the classical model? Are either of these models consistent with the U.S. experience during the Great Depression? Explain.

CHAPTER 9

THE DEMAND FOR MONEY AND THE LM CURVE

INTRODUCTION

In the classical theory of aggregate demand, the only variable that shifts the aggregate demand curve is the quantity of money. But if we want to understand all of the reasons why unemployment might fluctuate over the business cycle, we need to expand on the classical theory. Some recessions may be caused by contractions in the quantity of money, but others may have different causes. Therefore, the first reason we study the Keynesian theory of aggregate demand is to aid in our understanding of the causes of business cycles.

The Keynesian theory of aggregate demand is essential to Keynes' idea of **demand management**. Demand management is the active intervention by government through fiscal policy (e.g., changing taxes and/or government spending) or monetary policy (e.g., changing the interest rate) in an attempt to maintain the economy's steady growth rate without deep recessions or bouts of high inflation.

How does the Keynesian theory of aggregate demand differ from the classical theory? The classical theory of aggregate demand is based on the quantity theory of money and assumes that the quantity of money demanded by households is a constant fraction of their income. This assumption implies that the propensity to hold money, k, is constant. In practice, the propensity to hold money is a variable that depends on the interest rate. Once we

209

allow for the influence of the interest rate on the propensity to hold money, we must examine how the interest rate is itself determined. The determination of the interest rate and the determination of aggregate demand are two separate pieces of a puzzle. When we put the pieces together in Chapter 12, we can show all of the forces that determine business cycles, and we will have an apparatus for proposing how the government can influence aggregate demand through fiscal and monetary policy.

THE OPPORTUNITY COST OF HOLDING MONEY

To understand the modern theory of the demand for money, we construct an idealized economy in which the interest rate influences money demand by altering the allocation of saving between money and bonds.

LIQUIDITY PREFERENCE

Some assets pay higher rates of interest than others, even when the two assets are equally risky. Assume that all of the assets in our ideal economy can be divided into two types: those that pay interest (bonds) and those that are held even though they do not pay interest (money). The theory of why private agents hold money when they could earn interest by holding bonds is called the theory of **liquidity preference.**

The theory of liquidity preference asserts that households hold money because it is commonly accepted in exchange for services or commodities. Assets that are useful because other agents will accept them in exchange are called **liquid assets.** Although our theory divides assets into just two categories, in the real world there is a spectrum of assets with differing degrees of liquidity. Assets that are more liquid pay a lower rate of return. An example of two similar assets that are both held even though one pays a higher rate of interest than the other are dollar bills and bank accounts. All of us carry dollar bills even though we could put our cash into a bank account that pays a positive rate of interest. We carry cash because it is convenient. Dollar bills are more liquid than a bank account because sometimes, when we wish to purchase a commodity, the vendor will accept cash but not a check.

In the real world, there is a second reason why some assets pay a higher rate of return than others: They are riskier. Other things being equal, most individuals prefer a steady income to an income that fluctuates; economists call this **risk aversion.** As a consequence of risk aversion, securities with a less-certain payment must on average pay a higher return. Risk aversion is secondary to our investigation, so we assume that all assets are equally risky.

BALANCE SHEETS OF FIRMS AND HOUSEHOLDS

We begin with a simplified description of the assets and liabilities held by households and firms.[1] One kind of asset held by households is the bonds issued by firms. We refer

---

1.   In our example, households own no real assets. In reality, households own houses and durable goods, and corporate liabilities include equity, stock options, and futures contracts.

TABLE 9.1

The Balance Sheets of Households and Firms

Households

Assets		Liabilities	
Corporate bonds	$P^B B$		
Money	M	Net Worth	W
	W		W

The household owns two types of financial assets: money and corporate bonds.

Firms

Assets		Liabilities	
Capital stock	PK		
		Corporate bonds	$P^B B$
	PK		$P^B B$

The firms own a real asset: the capital stock that is offset by financial liabilities in the form of corporate bonds.

to these bonds as B and call them **corporate bonds** to distinguish them from government bonds. A corporate bond is a promise to make a fixed payment, called the **coupon**, on the bond every year forever. This kind of bond is called a **perpetuity**, and its price is denoted by P^B. Another asset held by households is money, M. The sum of the value of bonds and money held by households is the household's net worth, also referred to as household **wealth**; we use W to represent wealth (not to be confused with w, the nominal wage).

In our model, we assume that the only asset owned by firms is the **capital stock**. The value of this capital stock is equal to the price of commodities, P, multiplied by K, the physical quantity of capital goods.[2] On the liability side of their balance sheet, firms owe the value of corporate debt, $P^B B$, to households. The value of this corporate debt is equal to the number of bonds outstanding multiplied by the price of bonds, P^B. The balance sheets of households and firms are described in Table 9.1.

WEALTH AND INCOME

The assets and liabilities of households and firms change over time as a consequence of changes in production, consumption, and exchange. At the beginning of a typical week,

---

2.   In the real world, firms hold money for the same reason households do: to smooth the timing of their purchases and their sales. To keep our presentation simple, we assume that all of the cash in the economy is in the household sector and that the only asset held by firms is the capital stock.

households own stocks of money and bonds. The composition of their wealth is illustrated in Equation 9.1. The composition of household wealth affects household income because bonds earn a flow of interest payments but money does not.

9.1 $$W = M + P^B B$$ | Wealth must be held as either money or bonds. |

During the week, households sell labor to firms, purchase consumption commodities, and receive income from ownership of firms in the form of interest on corporate bonds. Households accumulate wealth by adding to their stocks of money and bonds. The accumulation of wealth by deciding not to consume is called **saving**. The relationship between saving, income, consumption, and wealth is illustrated in Equation 9.2. Additions to wealth, $\Delta W/P$, are equal to saving.

9.2 $$\frac{\Delta W}{P} = S = Y - C$$ | Saving by households is used to accumulate wealth (delta, Δ, means "the change in"). Saving is equal to income, Y, minus consumption, C. |

Households choose how much of their income to save. In addition, they decide how to allocate their existing wealth between alternative assets; this is called **portfolio allocation.** Since the households in our model only hold money or bonds, their portfolio allocation decision is relatively simple. Household wealth, W, must be divided between assets that bear interest (bonds) and assets that do not bear interest (money).

To show how the household perceives the tradeoff between income and liquidity, we can develop the household's budget constraint. Equation 9.3 divides household income into two parts: the interest rate, i, multiplied by the real value of corporate bonds (the income from wealth) and the real wage multiplied by labor hours supplied (labor income).

9.3 $$Y = i\frac{P^B B}{P} + \frac{w}{P}L$$ | Income has two parts: income from owning bonds and labor income. |

If the household were to transfer its entire portfolio to interest-bearing bonds, it would maximize its income. Equation 9.4 defines this maximum possible income, Y^{MAX}. In general, the household does not want to earn Y^{MAX} because it would have to give up the convenience of using money in transactions.

9.4 $$Y^{MAX} = i\frac{W}{P} + \frac{w}{P}L$$ | If all wealth were held as bonds (and none as money), the household could earn the maximum possible income, Y^{MAX}. |

Equation 9.5 is an expression for the income earned by a household that decides to allocate some portion of its wealth to money. By holding money, it chooses to earn income Y, which is less than the maximum.

9.5 $$Y = Y^{\text{MAX}} - i\frac{M}{P}$$

> When the household chooses to hold some of its wealth as money, it loses income it could otherwise have earned. The lost income is equal to the interest rate multiplied by the value of the household's average money holding.

The modern theory of the demand for money views Equation 9.5 as a constraint on household actions. According to this theory, households choose how much income to earn (in the form of held bonds) and how much money to hold. As individuals transfer their wealth from money to bonds, they increase their income but simultaneously decrease their liquidity.

THE UTILITY THEORY OF MONEY

The utility theory of money explains how the representative household chooses a point on its budget constraint. To describe the reason for holding money, we assume that money yields utility, which we model with a utility function. The utility function describes the utility attained by the household for alternative combinations of money and income. Income yields utility because it can be used to purchase commodities. Money yields utility because of its liquidity, which facilitates exchange. Mathematically, economists represent utility with a function that describes how utility is gained by the interaction of the income received by households and the real balances held to facilitate transactions.

MONEY DEMAND AND THE PRICE LEVEL

Since the utility gained by holding money is indirect, this suggests that it is different from the utility yielded by other commodities. What units should we use to measure the way that money influences utility? One possible answer is to measure money by the number of dollars that we hold, just as we would measure an orchard by the number of apples or oranges it contains. This answer, however, fails to capture the idea that money is not useful for its own sake; it is useful only because we can exchange it for other commodities.

If a person carries twice as much money around one week as the week before, he will be able to buy and sell twice as many commodities. Similarly, if a person carries exactly the same quantity of cash, but the prices of all of the goods are cut in half, he will once again be able to buy and sell twice as many commodities. Money is useful because we use it to trade commodities, which suggests that we should measure money in units of commodities. The value of money measured in units of commodities is called **real money balances**. To measure real balances, we divide the nominal quantity of money by an index of the general level of prices, and we represent the demand for real balances by the symbol (M^D/P).

MONEY DEMAND AND THE INTEREST RATE

According to the utility theory of money, households are better off if they hold more real balances. But the utility gained from holding an extra unit of money decreases as the household holds a larger portion of its wealth in the form of cash. This assumption is similar to diminishing returns-to-scale in production, and it holds for a similar reason. The household needs to hold cash to exchange for commodities. For a given flow of income, the benefit from having a little cash on hand is very large, since by holding money the household can engage in monetary exchange instead of barter. But as the household converts more of its portfolio from bonds into money, the additional benefit in terms of added convenience gets smaller. We frequently make small purchases that require cash. But most of us do not need to keep enough cash on hand to make large purchases, such as for automobiles or houses.

According to the utility theory of money, the household allocates its portfolio between money and bonds to maximize its utility. Starting with a portfolio of 100% interest-bearing bonds, the marginal utility of holding cash is very large—greater than the interest rate. As the household allocates more of its portfolio to cash, the marginal utility of moving an extra dollar falls, and if this process continues, eventually the marginal utility of real balances would be less than the interest rate. At this point the household could increase utility by moving wealth back into bonds. The household transfers wealth up to the point where the marginal utility of transferring an extra dollar from bonds into money is exactly equal to its cost—the interest rate.

In Figure 9.1, the marginal utility of money is graphed, and the interest rate (i) is represented on the vertical axis. The household equates the marginal utility of money to the nominal interest rate to determine how much cash to hold in its portfolio. For example, if the interest rate equals i_1, the household chooses to hold real balances $(M^D/P)_1$. If the interest falls to i_2, the quantity of real balances demanded increases to $(M^D/P)_2$. The quantity of real balances expressed as a function of the nominal interest rate is called the **demand for money.**

MONEY DEMAND AND INCOME

Money alone does not yield utility. Instead, money is held because it helps the household make transactions. The household will receive higher utility if it receives a higher income because income can be used to purchase consumption commodities and make investments that bring the household higher future income. Liquidity increases the utility of any given flow of income. But as income increases, the household must hold more cash to yield the same utility. For this reason, the demand for money, as a function of the interest rate, increases as income increases.

This proposition is illustrated in Figure 9.2. The downward-sloping green line labeled $L(Y_1)$ represents the money demand of the household as a function of the interest rate when the household has income Y_1. We use the symbol L to stand for liquidity preference. The downward-sloping green line labeled $L(Y_2)$ is the household's money demand (or liquidity preference) function when the household receives income Y_2. Since we assume Y_2 is greater than Y_1, $L(Y_2)$ is consistently to the right of $L(Y_1)$.

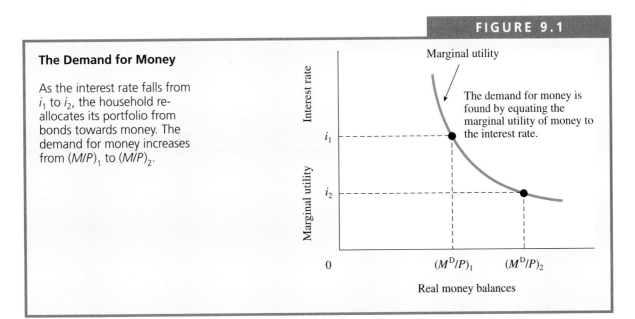

FIGURE 9.1

The Demand for Money

As the interest rate falls from i_1 to i_2, the household re-allocates its portfolio from bonds towards money. The demand for money increases from $(M/P)_1$ to $(M/P)_2$.

Marginal utility

The demand for money is found by equating the marginal utility of money to the interest rate.

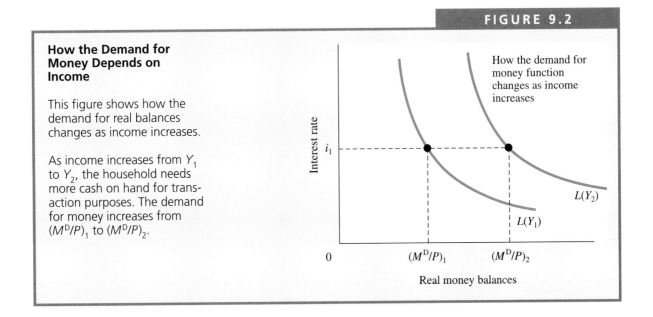

FIGURE 9.2

How the Demand for Money Depends on Income

This figure shows how the demand for real balances changes as income increases.

As income increases from Y_1 to Y_2, the household needs more cash on hand for trans-action purposes. The demand for money increases from $(M^D/P)_1$ to $(M^D/P)_2$.

How the demand for money function changes as income increases

A MATHEMATICAL REPRESENTATION OF THE THEORY

Equation 9.6 represents the utility theory of money.

9.6 $$U = U\left(Y, \frac{M}{P}\right)$$

The function U symbolically represents the utility theory.

Recall that the utility theory assumes that money will be measured in units of goods. This is represented in Equation 9.6 by the fact that M/P enters the function U as a ratio, rather than M and P separately. The other properties that we discussed restrict the kinds of functions that we are allowed to choose to represent the utility U. For example, since more income yields more utility, this means that U must be *increasing* in Y. In other words, U must become greater when Y becomes greater. Similarly, we must choose a function for which U increases when M/P increases. This reflects the assumption that real balances give utility. The fact that marginal utility decreases as real balances increase means that if we draw the graph of U against M/P, the slope of this graph gets flatter as M/P increases.[3]

The properties discussed restrict the possible functions that can represent utility. But which function is the true one? To answer this, we need to compare the predictions of different examples of utility functions with real-world data. In practice, economists choose the simplest example of a utility function that yields predictions consistent with the facts.

HOW MONEY MARKET EQUILIBRIUM IS ESTABLISHED IN THE KEYNESIAN MODEL

From the viewpoint of individual households, the interest rate, price level, and household income are taken as given, and households choose how much money to hold. But from the viewpoint of the economy as a whole, the quantity of money demanded must equal the quantity of money supplied. Income, the price level, and the interest rate must adjust to ensure that this equality holds.

The quantity of liquidity in the system is determined, in part, by the Federal Reserve Bank (Fed). Suppose, for example, that the Fed chose to alter its portfolio and buy government bonds from the public. This is called an **open market** operation because the central bank is buying securities in the open market. As the Fed buys bonds, the quantity of bonds available to the public will decrease. Since the Fed pays for its purchases with cash, the quantity of money in the hands of the public will increase. The Fed, in this example, has increased liquidity without a corresponding change in taxation or expenditure by the Treasury. Assume that before the open market purchase households were willingly holding the existing quantity of money in circulation. But now the Fed has increased the quantity of circulating money. We have already established three main variables on which the demand for (nominal) money depends: income, Y; the interest rate, i; and the price level, P. To restore equilibrium, any one of these variables could adjust.

In the classical model, the price level adjusts immediately to restore the equality of money demanded versus money supplied. We learned in Chapter 8 that in the Keynesian

---

3.   The mathematical name for this assumption is that U is a **concave function** of M/P.

W E B W A T C H

WEBWATCH 9.1

New Forms of Money

The Federal Reserve Bank of Chicago maintains a Web site at http://www.frbchi.org/. One of the features of this site is a section on economic education where you can find a range of articles on all aspects of monetary economics.

Economists have found that the relationship between the velocity of circulation and the interest rate has been shifting in recent years. Velocity is higher today than one would have predicted based purely on the historical relationship between money, income, and the interest rate. Some economists have speculated that the demand for money function is shifting as technological changes make new forms of money more attractive and there is less need for paper money.

What are these new forms of money? They include ATM machines, smart cards, and electronic funds transfers—all of which are growing rapidly as Internet and other electronic communications grow in importance.

For excellent articles on these new technologies and an assessment of their likely impact on our lives, check out:

http://www.chicagofed.org; search: "electronic money."

theory, the price level is slow to adjust because there are nominal rigidities in the system. Income is also slow to adjust because it takes time for firms to hire and fire workers. In the Keynesian theory, the immediate effect of a change in the money supply, caused by an open market operation, is a change in the interest rate.

USING THE THEORY OF MONEY DEMAND

The classical theory assumes that the propensity to hold money is a constant, but in the real world, the propensity to hold money has fluctuated in a systematic way over 100 years' worth of data. The modern theory is able to explain why these fluctuations have occurred.

THE MATHEMATICS OF THE UTILITY THEORY OF MONEY

In general, the solution to the household's money demand problem depends on the nature of its utility function. One function that fits the data well is given by the following equation:

9.7
$$U = Y \times \left(\frac{M}{P}\right)^{h}$$

BOX 9.1

A CLOSER LOOK
Deriving the Demand for Money:
A Mathematical Example

This box presents a mathematical example that shows how to derive a money demand curve from the utility theory of money. As with all the mathematical examples in this book, you can safely skip this box without losing the flow of the chapter.

We start from a particular representation of utility.

9.1.1 U $=$ Y $\times$ $\left(\dfrac{M}{P}\right)^{h}$

Utility   **Income**   **Real balances raised to the hth power**

The budget constraint is given by:

9.1.2 Y $=$ Y^{MAX} $-$ $i\left(\dfrac{M}{P}\right)$

Income   **Maximum income**   **Income lost from holding money**

We substitute the budget constraint into the utility function to give:

9.1.3 U $=$ $\left(Y^{MAX} - i\left(\dfrac{M}{P}\right)\right)\left(\dfrac{M}{P}\right)^{h}$

To find the maximum utility, we set the derivative of U with respect to (M/P) equal to zero:

9.1.4 $\dfrac{\partial U}{\partial(M/P)} = 0$ $\Rightarrow$ $-\dfrac{iU}{Y^{MAX} - i\dfrac{M}{P}} + \dfrac{hU}{\dfrac{M}{P}} = 0$

Rearranging these terms (using the budget constraint, Equation **9.1.2**) gives:

9.1.5 $\dfrac{i}{Y} = \dfrac{h}{\dfrac{M}{P}}$

or

9.1.6 $\dfrac{M}{P} = \dfrac{h}{i}Y,$

which is the money demand equation for this utility function.

The parameter h measures the relative importance of liquidity to the household. This function leads to a formula for the demand for money that is easy to compare with the classical model. We can show that a household with this utility function will choose to hold a fraction, h/i, of its income as cash in every period. (The proof of this statement uses calculus and is covered in Box 9.1.) Unlike the classical demand for money, in the modern theory, the propensity to hold money is equal to a parameter, h, divided by the interest rate, i:

9.8

$$\frac{M^{\text{D}}}{P} \quad = \quad \overset{k}{\overbrace{\left(\frac{h}{i}\right)}} \quad \times \quad Y$$

| Demand for real balances | Propensity to hold money | GDP |

    Equation 9.8 can be used to compare the classical theory of the demand for money with the modern theory of the demand for money as formulated in the utility theory of money. Like the classical theory, the modern theory predicts that the quantity of money demanded, measured in units of commodities, is equal to the propensity to hold money, k, multiplied by GDP. Unlike the classical theory, k is not a constant in modern theory; it is equal to the parameter, h, divided by the interest rate, i.

EVIDENCE FOR THE MODERN THEORY

    To compare the classical and modern theories, we introduce time series observations from the period 1890 to 2000 of the rate of interest, i, and the velocity of circulation, v. The velocity of circulation is the number of times per year that the average dollar bill circulates in the economy, measured in units of 1/years. The propensity to hold money is the fraction of a year's income that is held on average as a stock of money. It is the inverse of the propensity to hold money, k. In 1993, for example, k was equal to 1/6 years, reflecting that the stock of money was equal to two months (one-sixth of a year) of income. The velocity of circulation in the same year was equal to 6, meaning that the average dollar circulated the economy six times during the year.

9.9
$$V \quad \equiv \quad \frac{1}{k}$$

| The velocity of circulation measured in units of 1/years | The propensity to hold money measured in units of years |

    We choose to present evidence of the movement of V rather than k because the connection between i and V (two variables that move in the same direction) is more apparent in a graph than is the relationship between i and k (two variables that move in opposite directions).

    There are many concepts of money. In panel A of Box 9.2, the red line represents the velocity of circulation for the most frequently used concept ($M1$), which includes cash, checking accounts, and a few smaller items. The velocity of circulation is plotted on the right-hand scale of panel A. Notice that it is far from a constant, which contradicts the classical theory of money demand. In 1942, the velocity of circulation fell to 2, and in 2000 it exceeded 8. But although the velocity of circulation is not a constant, it has closely paralleled the interest rate for most of the historical record, as predicted by the modern theory of the demand for money. The blue line represents the rate of interest on Treasury bills, measured on the left-hand scale in percent per year. Notice that although the velocity of circulation has moved substantially over the century, its movements have always been accompanied by movements in the interest rate.

During the Great Depression (beginning in 1930), the velocity of circulation fell from 4 to 3 in the space of a few months. This drop was accompanied by a steep drop in the interest rate from 5.0% to 2.5%. At the end of World War II, the interest rate began to climb—and so did the velocity of circulation. According to the modern theory of the demand for money, these changes in velocity were caused by the associated increase in the interest rate. As the opportunity cost of holding money increased after the war, people reduced the amount of cash that they kept on hand by passing it from one person to another more quickly; that is, the velocity of circulation increased. This increasing velocity continued right up until 1981, when the interest rate peaked at 14%. After 1981, interest rates began to drop again, and once more this drop was accompanied by a decrease in velocity, just as it had been in the 1930s.

THE LM CURVE

The rate of interest can be influenced by the Federal Reserve Bank via changes in the supply of money. Manipulation of the money supply in order to influence endogenous variables, such as the interest rate or the income level, is called **monetary policy.** To illustrate the effects of monetary policy on the interest rate, we develop an equation that explains the relationship between the interest rate and GDP when the quantities of money demanded and supplied are equal. The graph of this equation is called the **LM curve.**[4]

THE SUPPLY OF MONEY

In developing the LM curve, we assume that the entire money supply is an exogenous variable directly under the control of the Federal Reserve Board. The assumption that money is exogenous is represented by Equation 9.10, in which we place a bar over the symbol M to represent a fixed number that is picked each period as an instrument of policy.

9.10 $$M^S \qquad\qquad = \qquad\qquad \overline{M}$$

Supply of money   **Exogenous money supply**

The assumption that the money supply is exogenous is an oversimplification, since the Federal Reserve Board can directly control only a small part of the stock of money. Since the rest of the money supply moves in tandem with the part that the Federal Reserve Board

---

4.   The name "LM" comes from Liquidity preference equals the supply of Money (L = M).

BOX 9.2

FOCUS ON THE FACTS
Comparing the Quantity Theory of Money and the Modern Theory of the Demand for Money

According to the quantity theory of money, the propensity to hold money, k, is a constant. The modern theory of the demand for money predicts instead that k depends on the nominal interest rate. To see this, we study the behavior of the velocity of circulation (the inverse of k) and the interest rate since 1934. Notice that velocity has not been constant. However, the low-frequency movements in velocity mirror the low-frequency movements in the interest rate.

Panel B presents the same information on a scatter plot. The red line is the best straight line through the points. The correlation coefficient between the velocity of circulation and the interest rate is 0.84.

We can infer from these graphs that the modern theory of the demand for money is a better description of the data than the quantity theory of money.

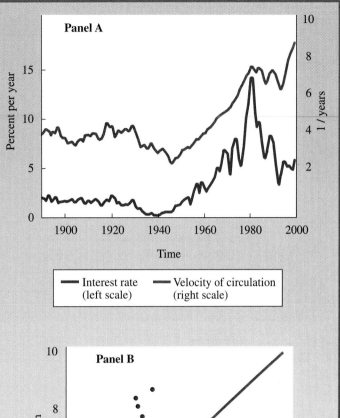

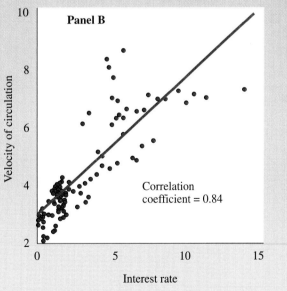

controls, it can be assumed that the Federal Reserve Board controls the entire money supply. This assumption will greatly simplify exposition of the theory.

THE PRICE LEVEL

The theory of the demand for money deals with how the real value of money depends on
income and the interest rate, but the theory of the money supply is a theory of how the
nominal quantity of money is controlled by the Federal Reserve Board. The real supply of
money depends not only on the behavior of the Federal Reserve Board; it also depends on
the price level. To complete our development of the LM curve, we assume that the price
level is exogenous, or fixed.

9.11 P $=$ $\overline{P}$

          Price level   **Exogenous price level**

To derive a relationship between the interest rate and GDP (the LM curve), we suppose
that the price is equal to some specific value, for example, 100. If the price level changes
to some other value, say 200, we must draw a new LM curve that has a different position.
(We will return to this idea in Chapter 12 when we develop the Keynesian theory of aggregate demand.)

DERIVING THE LM CURVE

Figure 9.3 shows how to derive the LM curve. Both panels plot the nominal interest rate
on the vertical axis; the horizontal axes measure different variables. Panel A plots the
nominal interest rate against income, and panel B plots the nominal interest rate against
the quantity of money demanded and the quantity of money supplied.

   We know that the quantity of money demanded, measured in commodity units, is a
function of the nominal interest rate. Because there is a different demand for money function for every level of income, we use the symbol $L(Y)$ to represent the demand for money
schedule that would apply if the level of income were equal to Y. Panel B draws two such
schedules, $L(Y_1)$ and $L(Y_2)$, one for each of two levels of income. $L(Y_2)$ is to the right of
$L(Y_1)$ because Y_2 is greater than Y_1. For every value of the rate of interest, the demand for
money will be greater, and with it the value of income will also be greater. The vertical
line in panel B depicts the supply of money, measured in commodity units. Notice that the
curves $L(Y_1)$ and $L(Y_2)$ intersect the line M^S/P at different points.

   The LM curve is derived by moving back and forth between the two panels. Begin in
panel A and pick a particular value for GDP, say Y_1. Now move to panel B and draw the
demand for money as a function of the interest rate, given that income is equal to Y_1. For
this demand for money schedule, the equilibrium interest rate (i.e., the interest rate at
which the quantity of money supplied equals the quantity of money demanded) is equal to
the interest rate i_1. Translate i_1 back to panel A to find point **A** on the LM curve. By re-
peating this process for the level of income Y_2, you can find a second point on the LM

FIGURE 9.3

Deriving the LM Curve

This figure shows how to derive the LM curve. Panel B shows that there is a different demand for money curve for different values of income. Panel A plots the graph of the LM curve. At every point on the LM curve, the quantity of money demanded is equal to the quantity supplied.

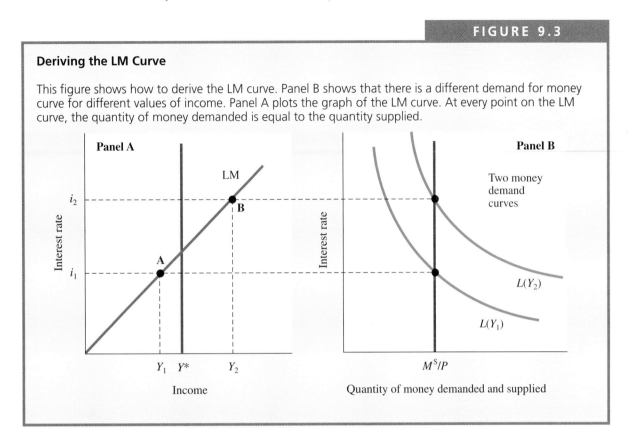

curve, point **B**. At a higher level of income, the equilibrium interest rate must also be higher, so point **B** is above and to the right of point **A**. In other words, the LM curve slopes upward.

In Figure 9.3, the natural rate of output is Y^*. It is tempting to think that the nominal interest rate will be determined at the point where Y^* intersects the LM curve, but there is no reason why this should be so, since in the short run income can differ from its natural rate. There must be a relationship between the nominal interest rate and income such that the quantity of money demanded is equal to the quantity supplied, but we cannot say which combination of income and the interest rate will be determined in equilibrium. We examine this issue in Chapter 12.

THE IMPORTANCE OF THE LM CURVE

Why are combinations of income and the nominal interest rate that lie on the LM curve any different from those that do not? The answer is that the combinations of Y and i that lie on the LM curve are the only Y and i combinations for which the quantity of money in circulation is willingly held. Another way of saying this is that on the LM curve, the quantity of money demanded is equal to the quantity supplied.

What would happen if, at a given level of income, the interest rate were too high or too low? Suppose first that the interest rate is above the LM curve. In this case, households will find that they are holding too much money, and they will try to convert some of their cash into bonds. But because there is a finite supply of bonds on the market, the sellers of bonds (firms that are borrowing money) will be able to offer lower interest rates and still find lenders. This process of converting money to bonds ends at the point when the interest rate returns to the LM curve, since the stock of money is only willingly held at this point. Now suppose that the opposite situation occurs, and the interest rate drops below the LM curve. In this case, households find that they do not have enough liquidity, and they will sell some of their bonds in an attempt to hold more cash to meet their daily transaction needs. But as households sell bonds, some firms will not be able to borrow all of the money that they need for investment purposes, and they will bid up the interest rate to attract funds back into the capital market. This process of bidding up the interest rate only stops when the nominal interest rate returns to the LM curve. To summarize, the LM curve represents points for which the existing stock of money in circulation is willingly held.

The LM curve balances two opposing forces. Consider a point on this curve. When income increases, holding interest at a fixed rate, the quantity of money demanded will increase because households need more liquidity to finance extra transactions. But the money supply is regulated by the Federal Reserve Board. If income remains higher, the quantity of money demanded will exceed the quantity supplied. Equality can be restored by increasing the interest rate and making bonds more attractive, thereby tempting households to switch back to buying bonds. Higher levels of income are compensated by a higher rate of interest because these variables pull the quantity of money demanded in different directions, and this is why the LM curve slopes upward.

THE ALGEBRA OF THE LM CURVE

In Equations 9.12 through 9.15, we make a special assumption about the utility function in order to derive an algebraic equation for the LM curve. This assumption is the same one made in Box 9.1 (see page 218). Different assumptions about the slope of the utility function will lead to different predictions about the exact function that describes the demand for money.

DERIVING THE LM CURVE

9.12 $$M^S = M^D$$ | Step 1: Quantity of money demanded equals quantity supplied.

9.13 $$MS = \overline{M}$$ | Step 2: Replace quantity of money supplied by exogenous quantity (determined by the Federal Reserve Board).

9.14
$$\frac{M^D}{P} = \frac{h}{i}Y$$

> Step 3: Replace quantity of money demanded in step 1 by money demand function from the modern theory of the demand for money.

9.15
$$i = \frac{hP}{M}Y$$

> Step 4: Rearrange the terms to find the equation of the LM curve.

As shown above, the LM curve is derived in four steps. Step 1 sets the quantity of money demanded equal to the quantity of money supplied. If households are holding too much money, they can choose to spend more income either on goods and services or on bonds. Similarly, if households are holding too little money, they can choose to spend less income by either cutting back on expenditures or by selling some of their bonds in the financial markets. Step 2 assumes that the quantity of money supplied is chosen by the Federal Reserve Board. Step 3 is the formula for the quantity of money demanded as a function of income and the interest rate. Finally, Step 4 puts together demand and supply to generate an equation that characterizes the values of the interest rate and the GDP level for which the demand equals the supply of money. This equation is the LM curve.

MONETARY POLICY AND THE LM CURVE

To understand how changes in the money supply affect the economy, we must first understand how the position of the LM curve changes in response to changes in monetary policy.[5]

The slope and position of the LM curve are determined by the real value of the supply of money because money is held for its ability to buy goods and not for its own sake. It follows that changes in the real value of the money supply can come about either as a result of an increase in the nominal quantity of money, M, or as a result of a fall in the price of commodities, P. In either case, the real value of the supply of money rises. Let's trace the effect on households of an increase in the real value of the supply of money.

As the real money supply increases, households find that they are holding more money than they require for their daily transactions. Some households try to eliminate the excess cash by lending it to firms. But that results in more lenders than borrowers at the current interest rate, and firms find themselves able to attract funds at a lower nominal interest rate. Therefore, the net effect of an increase in the quantity of money is a drop in the nominal interest rate. This is reflected in Figure 9.4 as a rightward shift in the LM curve—a lower equilibrium interest rate for every value of income.

The graphs in Figure 9.4 show why an increase in the quantity of money supplied causes a shift of the LM curve. The two LM curves in panel A are drawn for two values of the supply of money. Point **A** is on the LM curve associated with a money supply of M_1, and point **B** is on the LM curve associated with the supply of money M_2. Notice that when the quantity of money supplied is greater, the equilibrium interest rate that causes the quantity of money demanded to equal the quantity supplied is lower at every level of

---

5.   In Chapter 12, we will add a second equilibrium relationship, the IS curve, to the LM curve and show how the two curves are used to analyze the effects of monetary and fiscal policy on the equilibrium of the whole economy.

FIGURE 9.4

How an Increase in the Money Supply Shifts the LM Curve

This figure shows how changes in the money supply shift the LM curve. Panel B shows how the rate of interest changes when the stock of money increases. Panel A shows how the LM curve shifts in response.

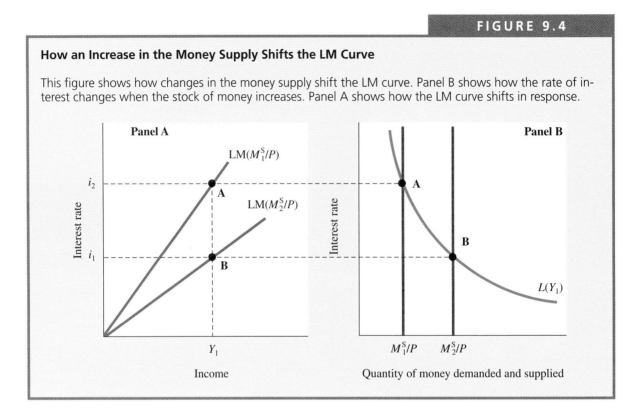

income. This is illustrated in panel B by the point at which the demand for money curve $L(Y_1)$ that applies when the level of income is Y_1 crosses the money supply curve for each of two values of the money supply, M_1 and M_2.

CONCLUSION

Assets have different degrees of liquidity depending on how useful they are in exchange. Less-liquid assets pay a higher interest rate to induce us to hold them. We model this by assuming that there are two kinds of assets: bonds that pay interest and money that does not.

In order to explain why households use money, we assume that the real value of money yields utility. Holding money is costly because more income can be earned by holding bonds; this income can be used to purchase commodities. Households balance the marginal utility of real money against the interest lost by holding money. The resulting money demand function generalizes the quantity theory of money by allowing the velocity of circulation (the inverse of the propensity to hold money) to depend on the interest rate. The data support the utility theory of money over the quantity theory of money that sets the velocity of circulation as constant. We consider a century's worth of data and find that the velocity of circulation has not been constant; it varies directly with the interest rate.

In equilibrium, the quantity of money demanded equals the quantity supplied. Higher income causes the quantity of money demanded to increase; households hold additional cash to finance additional transactions. A higher interest rate causes the quantity of money demanded to fall because holding cash becomes more costly in terms of income forgone. There is an upward-sloping locus of points on a graph of income against the interest rate; this graph, the LM curve, describes combinations of income and the interest rate for which the quantity of money demanded equals the quantity supplied.

KEY TERMS

Capital stock	Monetary policy
Corporate bonds	Open market
Coupon	Perpetuity
Demand management	Portfolio allocation
Demand for money	Real money balances
Liquid assets	Risk aversion
Liquidity preference	Saving
LM curve	Wealth

QUESTIONS FOR CHAPTER 9

1. Does the marginal utility of money balances increase or decrease as real balances rise? Explain why the answer to this question is critical in order to understand what the money demand curve looks like in the utility theory of money demand.

2. How does the variable Y^{MAX} change when the price of bonds increases? Why? How does this change shift the budget constraint of the household?

3. What is meant by the *velocity of circulation* and the *propensity to hold money?* Explain the relationship between these two variables. In what units is each variable measured?

4. How well does the utility theory of money explain U.S. movements in velocity over the past 100 years? Compare and contrast this with the ability of the quantity theory of money to explain these fluctuations.

5. In the utility theory of money, is it the nominal or real interest rate that matters? Explain your answer.

6. Compare and contrast how interest rates, both nominal and real, are determined in the classical quantity theory and in the new-Keynesian utility theory of money.

7. What does the utility theory of money predict will happen to *nominal interest rates* when the central bank increases the money supply? Do you think that this is consistent with what happens in the real world? Explain.

8. What does the classical quantity theory predict will happen to *nominal interest rates* when the central bank increases the money supply? Do you think that this is consistent with what happens in the real world? Explain.

9. What do you think usually happens to money demand as Christmas approaches? What happens to the LM curve? How should the Fed respond if its objective is to keep interest rates constant?

10. Why does the LM curve slope upward? Use a graph of the money market to illustrate.

11. What does the LM curve look like, assuming the classical quantity theory of money? How does it differ from the LM curve derived using the utility theory of money demand?

12. Analyze the effects of a decrease in the price level using the utility theory of money demand. What happens to interest rates? What happens to the LM curve? Explain.

13. Suppose that the supply of money and the price level both increase by 25%. What effect will these changes have on the money market and the LM curve?

14. The following equations describe the money market of an economy:

$$\frac{M^D}{P} = Y - 200i$$

$$M^S = 1,000$$

$$P = 5$$

Derive the LM curve for this economy.

15. Find the equation of the LM curve when the utility of money is given by the expression

$$U = \frac{\left(\dfrac{M}{P}\right)^{1-\lambda} + \theta Y^{1-\lambda}}{1 - \lambda}$$

CHAPTER 10

THE SUPPLY OF MONEY

INTRODUCTION

In modern societies, the supply of money comes in different forms. Some societies use gold or silver as money, others use paper or even electronic currency. In modern capitalist societies, money predominantly takes the form of bank money that is supplied by the commercial banking system. Commercial banks have evolved over the past 500 years by developing various forms of money, like bank accounts and credit cards, which did not exist in precapitalist societies.

How is the money supply controlled in a modern society? At the head of the commercial banking system is the nation's central bank. In the United States this is the Federal Reserve System. The central bank cannot directly control the money supply since it is in part controlled by commercial banks that have the power to create money. But by setting the stock of notes and coins in circulation, and by restricting private bank deposits with the central bank, the Federal Reserve Board can indirectly control the money supply. This chapter explains how this process works.

BOX 10.1

FOCUS ON THE FACTS
What Is Money?

Barter is uncommon today, but has it ever been the dominant mode of exchange? How did the use of money come about? What kinds of monies have existed historically, and what kinds are likely to exist in the future?[1]

In much of the world, the use of money in exchange is so commonplace that we cannot conceive of exchanging commodities in any other way. But it has not always been this way, and even today in certain countries in Africa, 60% to 70% of transactions are carried out without the use of money. Barter remained the rule over very large areas between the fifteenth and eighteenth centuries, and at the time of the American Revolution barter was common. The following quote comes from Clavier and Brissot, two well-known figures in the French revolution:[2]

> Instead of money incessantly going backwards and forwards into the same hands, it is the practice here [in America] for country people to satisfy their needs by direct reciprocal exchanges. The tailor and the bootmaker go and do the work of their calling at the home of the farmer who requires it and who, most frequently, provides the raw material for it and pays for the work in goods.

Monetary exchange developed throughout the world as three metals, gold, silver and copper, gradually began to be used regularly in the process of exchange. The use of copper was generally restricted to low-value transactions within a country, and gold and silver were used primarily in international trade.

---

[1] An excellent discussion of the historical development of money can be found in *The Structures of Everyday Life* by Fernand Braudel (Siân Reynolds, Trans. Harper and Row, 1981). The book was first published in France under the title *Les Structures du quotidien: le possible et l'impossible* (Paris: Librairie Armand Colin, 1979).
[2] Braudel, op cit., p 447.

WHAT IS MONEY?

Money has three important functions. It serves as a store of value, a medium of exchange, and a unit of account. The **store of value** function means that an object used as money must retain its value because the object is used in separate exchanges over time. Precious metals are good objects to use as money because they are durable: Ice cream would make a poor money because it is not durable; it melts.

The **medium of exchange** function of money is nicely described by the following quote by the Subcommittee on Banking and Currency:

Money is anything that people will accept in exchange for goods and services in the belief that they may, in turn, exchange it, now or later, for other goods or services. Any number of different materials—including paper IOUs—may serve as money. In the United States today, the American people use coins, currency (paper money), and bank deposits (checkbook money) as money.[1]

---

[1]   *169 Questions and Answers on Money.* Supplement to *A Primer on Money,* Report of the Subcommittee on Banking and Currency transmitted to the House of Representatives of the 88th Congress 2nd Session on September 21, 1964.

A **unit of account** is a standard that is used to measure value. Usually, but not always, this is also the medium of exchange. In hyperinflations, it is common to use one currency as a medium of exchange and another as a store of value. For example, during the Israeli hyperinflation in 1984, prices were often quoted in U.S. dollars, although the shekel was the Israeli medium of exchange, at least for small transactions.

A Short History of Money

In Chapter 9, we distinguished two kinds of financial assets: money and bonds. If an asset is more acceptable than another in exchange, we say that this asset is more liquid. Money is more liquid than bonds because it is generally more acceptable in exchange than bonds. A supermarket will accept U.S. bank notes (cash or checks) in exchange for groceries, but it will not accept U.S. government bonds. Similarly, cash is more liquid than a check because there are more kinds of exchanges in which cash is accepted but a check is not. In reality, there are many kinds of financial assets, all with differing degrees of liquidity.

One of the roles of the banking system is to convert assets that are relatively nonliquid into assets that are more readily accepted in exchange. Banks create liquidity by substituting their own liabilities for the liabilities of other agents in the economy. An example of creating liquidity is the process in which a bank makes a loan to a firm. The firm takes the loan and buys capital. The bank creates a liability in the form of a deposit that the firm may write checks on. Through this process, the banking system substitutes liabilities that are acceptable in exchange (bank accounts with checking privileges) for liabilities that are not (loans to corporations).

Early Forms of Money

All societies engage in trade, and all use money of one form or another. The earliest forms of money were commodities that were easily transported, and that were divisible and durable. In many societies, these commodities (monies) took the form of precious metals. Gold and silver have been used in Europe as a means of exchange since Roman times, although the relative importance of these two metals has varied from one century to the next. As trade developed in the Middle Ages, merchants began to store their wealth with goldsmiths for safekeeping. It became possible to buy or sell a commodity without ever physically moving the gold itself; instead, buyers wrote notes to the goldsmiths, who in turn transferred ownership of the gold to the sellers. This practice eventually developed into the modern institution of banking.

How Banks Create Money

Today in a good part of the world, the money stock is in the form of accounts at banks, rather than in the form of notes and coins. The practice of writing a check on an account is the modern equivalent of the medieval practice of writing a note to the goldsmith.

Banks keep some of their customers' funds in their vaults. These are called **reserves**. Historically, bankers found that they needed to keep only a small fraction of their deposits in the form of reserves, and they took advantage of this fact by lending out their customers' money, at interest, thereby realizing a profit. When a commercial bank lends money, this results in the creation of new money because it creates an asset (the loan to a new customer) and a liability (a new deposit). Since this new deposit is a medium of exchange (the customer can write checks on the new account), the bank has created money.

Consider the example described in Table 10.1. A new bank begins with customer deposits of $2 million in currency (coins and paper money). This bank now has reserves of $2 million in currency and deposits of $2 million in the form of customer accounts (panel A). Since a bank's depositors do not require access to their funds on a daily basis, it is not necessary for the bank to keep reserves on hand equal to 100% of its deposits. The fact that customers do not continually withdraw funds is due, in part, to the service offered by the banking system. Instead of withdrawing currency and physically transferring it to another location, the bank transfers money from one account to another on paper. If the account to which the funds are paid is at the same bank, this process does not require any action other than a bookkeeping entry to the two customer accounts. If the account is at another bank, the bank notes and coins can be transferred from the vaults of one bank to the other without the money ever leaving the banking system as a whole.

Suppose the bank finds that, on average, it needs to keep an amount equal to 20% of its deposits on hand in the form of cash reserves. It can create new deposits by lending money to businesses in the form of new accounts, up to the point at which the total deposits of the bank are equal to five times (the inverse of 20%) its reserves. In our example, this would imply that the bank can create new deposits of $8 million—giving the bank total liabilities of $10 million, total deposits of $10 million, and reserves of $2 million. This is the situation depicted in panel B. The feature that prevents the bank from making more than $8 million in loans is that, if it were to continue, its reserves would fall to less than 20% of its deposits, and the bank would have insufficient reserves to meet the day-to-day requirements of its customers.

Banking seems profitable because banks can create money at will, but this is an illusion; competition keeps banks from generating excess profits. If individual banks make large profits, new banks will enter the industry and try to attract customers by offering to pay interest on deposits. Competition for customers bids up the interest rate on deposits and bids down the interest rate on loans. The equilibrium of the competitive process keeps the banking system as a whole earning enough interest on its loans to pay interest on its customers' deposits.[2]

In most countries, the government regulates the amount of reserves held by the private banking system. In the United States, the regulatory role is carried out by the Federal Reserve System, which requires commercial banks to keep a minimum ratio of reserves to deposits. This ratio is adjusted periodically as part of Federal Reserve policy.

---

2.   Putting aside the bank's operating expenses, the relationship between the loan rate, deposit rate, and reserves is simple. If the bank holds reserves of 20% of its deposits, for example, it must charge an interest rate on its loans 20% higher than the interest rate that it receives on its deposits, just to stay in business. If the bank must also cover operating expenses, this spread must be even greater.

TABLE 10.1

The Creation of Money by a Commercial Bank

Panel A: Commercial bank balance sheet before making a loan				**Panel B:** Commercial bank balance sheet after making a loan			
Assets		Liabilities		Assets		Liabilities	
Reserves	2			Reserves	2		
Loans	0	Deposits	2	Loans	8	Deposits	10
	2		2		10		10

All figures are in millions of dollars.

THE DEVELOPMENT OF FIAT MONEY

Although monetary systems were originally based on commodities, there has been a steady, worldwide move away from commodity money toward a system of **fiat money**. Fiat money does not represent a claim to any physical commodity; instead it is backed by laws that require money to be accepted in all legal transactions. Even during the period of commodity money, there were typically more claims to gold circulating, in the form of bank notes, than there was gold in existence. In effect, these bank notes were fiat money because if all of the note-holders had demanded repayment at once, the world stock of gold would not have been great enough to meet the demand. The system of notes that were partially backed by gold was the origin of our modern system of payments in which money is 100% fiat.

The medieval practice of entrusting gold to goldsmiths was also the origin of paper money, which originally represented a claim to gold that was held on deposit at the goldsmith's place of business. A **bank note** is like a check, except that it is transferable from one person to another. There is no reason why commercial banks should not issue bank notes, and there have been periods in history when private notes *did* circulate. In most societies however, the power to issue bank notes has been claimed as a monopoly right by the government. Issuing money is a revenue-generating activity. In some societies, money creation is almost the only source of revenue because the government's power to tax is severely limited by the absence of an organized and efficient system of tax collection.[3]

Until the 1930s, money was universally at least partially backed by commodities. And beginning in the nineteenth century, gold remained the dominant commodity for a

---

3. In Argentina, the revenue from money creation was an important component of government finance and was responsible for the recurrent hyperinflations in the 1970s, 1980s, and early 1990s (see Figure 5.8 in Chapter 5, page 131).

considerable period of time. The money that circulated was partly in the form of gold coins, but most of it consisted of paper money that represented a claim to gold. A national currency that is convertible to gold is said to operate on a **gold standard**. During the time when the gold standard prevailed, most nations guaranteed to convert their currencies to gold at a fixed price. At the end of World War II, most nations agreed to maintain a fixed exchange rate against gold, but there was some flexibility built into the system that allowed countries to change their exchange rates periodically in response to domestic shortages of foreign exchange. In 1973, the world moved to a system of **flexible exchange rates**, and since then nothing has backed the value of the U.S. dollar other than the credibility of the U.S. government.

As long as governments maintained convertibility of paper money to gold they were limited in their ability to create more money. Central banks had to keep a certain reserve of gold to meet the public demand, just as private banks today are limited in their ability to create deposits by the need to keep reserves of cash. During the 1930s, the gold standard collapsed irrevocably, and one by one, all the countries in the world lost their ability to convert their currencies, thereby removing the limit that the gold standard had placed on their ability to create money. For the past 60 years, the world monetary system has moved steadily closer to a purely fiat money system. With the 1973 move to a flexible exchange rate system, there is now no limit on the quantity of each currency in circulation, other than the choices of national governments.

THE ROLE OF THE CENTRAL BANK

The stock of money in circulation at any point in time is fixed. Because trade involves passing money from one person to another, it is not possible for all individuals to reduce their holding of money at the same time. Therefore, the demand for money must be identically equal to its supply. But although the stock of money at a point in time is fixed, this stock can vary from one week to the next. We will now examine how this happens.

THE FEDERAL RESERVE SYSTEM

Most countries in the world have a **central bank**, which is a branch of their government. In the United States, the central bank consists of not one, but a system of 12 districts, each with its own **Federal Reserve Bank** (see Figure 10.1). The **Federal Reserve System** was created in 1913 to regulate the nation's money supply and to operate as a banker to the commercial banks. At that time, there was a general concern over fluctuations in interest rates, which moved not only with the business cycle but also with the seasons. One of the original intentions of the politicians who created the Federal Reserve System was that it would act to stabilize these interest rate fluctuations by actively borrowing and lending in the credit markets. The nineteenth century also witnessed a number of banking panics, in which depositors withdrew their money all at once from commercial banks, resulting in their collapse. By acting in a timely fashion to provide reserves to the system in times of crisis, the Federal Reserve System would, it was thought, be able to prevent such events from reoccurring.

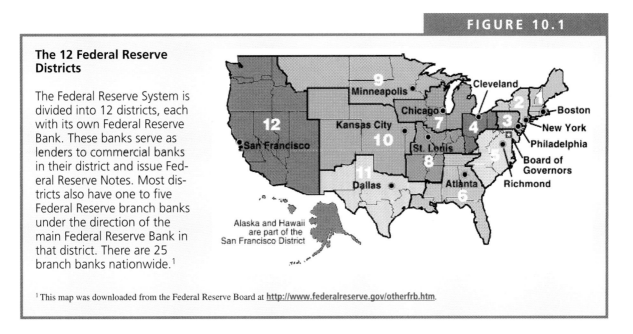

FIGURE 10.1

The 12 Federal Reserve Districts

The Federal Reserve System is divided into 12 districts, each with its own Federal Reserve Bank. These banks serve as lenders to commercial banks in their district and issue Federal Reserve Notes. Most districts also have one to five Federal Reserve branch banks under the direction of the main Federal Reserve Bank in that district. There are 25 branch banks nationwide.[1]

Alaska and Hawaii are part of the San Francisco District

[1] This map was downloaded from the Federal Reserve Board at http://www.federalreserve.gov/otherfrb.htm.

In some countries, elected officials decide monetary policy, and the central bank has little independence from the government. For example, until very recently in the United Kingdom, the central bank had little independence. In the United States, monetary policy is conducted by a committee, the **Federal Open Market Committee (FOMC)** of the Federal Reserve System. The Federal Reserve System itself is run by the **Board of Governors of the Federal Reserve System**. The Board of Governors has seven members that are appointed by the president and confirmed by the Senate, and each governor serves a nonrenewable 14-year term. The chairman is chosen from the seven board members and serves a four-year term.

The FOMC meets eight times a year and is responsible for the day-to-day running of monetary policy. The voting members of the committee consist of the seven members of the Board of Governors, the president of the Federal Reserve Bank of New York, and presidents of four other Federal Reserve Banks. These four voting members rotate among the other 11 Federal Reserve Banks. Although only five of the Federal Reserve presidents vote at any one time, all of them are present at FOMC meetings and can, therefore, influence policy. The American system, in contrast to most countries' single central bank, was designed to spread the power to regulate the money supply, both regionally and among diverse interest groups. In 1913, Americans were deeply distrustful of the power of East Coast financial interests, and two earlier attempts to set up a central bank had already failed.[4]

---

4.   The First Bank of the United States was disbanded in 1811, and the Second Bank of the United States was abolished in 1836.

How the Federal Reserve System Operates

The money supply in the United States consists of currency and coins in the hands of the public, plus items such as checking accounts at commercial banks. As commercial banks go about their day-to-day operations of borrowing and lending, they expand and contract the volume of bank deposits. For example, when a commercial bank makes a loan to a customer, it simultaneously creates a deposit. The key to understanding the operation of a central bank is in recognizing that the creation of deposits by private banks is not unlimited. Private banks can only create deposits to the extent that they have reserves of cash and currency. By expanding and contracting the availability of reserves, the FOMC can effectively control the money supply of the entire country.

The definition of money can include only checking accounts, or it can encompass all kinds of deposits with financial institutions. In the United States, the different definitions of money are ordered in terms of increasing broadness. The most commonly used definition, called M1, consists of cash and currency in the hands of the public, checkable deposits at commercial banks, and a few smaller items. Another definition, M2, includes savings deposits, and M3 still is a broader definition. All of the items included in M1 are also in M2, and all of the items in M2 are in M3. All of these concepts regarding the money supply can be controlled to a greater or lesser extent by manipulating the reserves of the banking system.

There are three ways that the Federal Reserve System controls the reserves of the banking system. First, the FOMC mandates that commercial banks must keep a minimum percentage of their deposits on hand in the form of liquid reserves of cash and currency.[5] This minimum percentage of deposits is called the **required reserve ratio**. By changing the required reserve ratio from time to time, the FOMC controls the ability of commercial banks to create money. Second, the Federal Reserve System acts as a **lender of last resort**. This means that if a commercial bank is short on reserves, the Federal Reserve will lend money to bail them out. The rate at which the Federal Reserve System lends to the commercial banks is called the **discount rate**.[6] The third way that the Federal Reserve System controls reserves is through open market operations. This has been the principal mode of Reserve System Control in recent years.

Open Market Operations

Whenever the Federal Reserve System buys an asset, that asset is turned into money. This ability of the FOMC to create or destroy money by selling or buying financial assets on the open market explains how the Federal Reserve System is able to expand or contract the nation's money supply.

---

5.   These reserves may also be in the form of accounts held by private banks with the Federal Reserve System.
6.   From the inception of the Fed in 1913 to the onset of the Great Depression in 1929, private banks were allowed to borrow at the discount rate as a matter of course. The consequence of this policy was that the Fed lost its power to manipulate the monetary base with open market operations since, whenever the Fed tried to reduce the nonborrowed reserves of private banks (by selling bonds on the open market), private banks responded by replacing the lost funds with funds borrowed from the Fed. Since World War II, the Federal Reserve Board has actively discouraged banks from using this facility.

WEBWATCH

Check out the Board of Governors on the Internet

The Federal Reserve Board building is in Washington, DC. The following information is from the Board of Governors' home page at **http://www. federalreserve.gov/otherfrb.htm**.

The Federal Reserve System is the central bank of the United States. It was founded by Congress in 1913 to provide the nation with a safer, more flexible, and more stable monetary and financial system; over the years, its role in banking and the economy has expanded.

Today, the Federal Reserve's duties fall into four general areas:

1. Conducting the nation's monetary policy by influencing the money and credit conditions in the economy in pursuit of full employment and stable prices;
2. Supervising and regulating banking institutions to ensure the safety and soundness of the nation's banking and financial system, and to protect the credit rights of consumers (Federal Reserve Regulations);
3. Maintaining the stability of the financial system and containing systemic risk that may arise in financial markets; and
4. Providing certain financial services to the U.S. government, to the public, to financial institutions, and to foreign official institutions, including playing a major role in operating the nation's payments system.

The daily financial operations of the government are conducted by the Treasury Department, which collects tax revenues and finances government expenditures and transfer payments. At any time, the Treasury may make expenditures that are either greater or less than its revenues from taxation. An expenditure plan that exceeds revenues results in a **deficit**; an expenditure plan that is less than revenues results in a **surplus**. In order to finance a deficit or a surplus, the Treasury will sell or buy bonds in the capital markets. At any point in time, a given quantity of government debt will exist, B^T, which is owned in part by private agents, B^P, and in part by the central bank, B^F. We use the symbol B to stand for bonds. Equation 10.1 breaks the government debt into the part held by the Fed and the part held by the public.

10.1
$$B^T \quad = \quad B^F \quad + \quad B^P$$

| Total government debt | Government debt held by the Federal Reserve System | Government debt held by the public |

When the Federal Reserve buys an asset, any asset, an equal quantity of money is created and placed in the hands of the public. The assets of the Federal Reserve System consist mainly of government debt, although there are also other items, such as gold reserves and holdings of foreign currencies. The liabilities of the Federal Reserve System consist of Federal Reserve notes and the deposits of commercial banks. If we lay aside the complications that arise from the existence of the commercial banking system, we can envisage a world in which the *only* form of money is bank notes. In this simple world, the central bank prints notes and gives them to the Treasury in return for its debt. The Treasury then uses these bank notes to purchase commodities from the public.

10.2 $$B^{\text{F}} = M$$

Loans to the Treasury	**Monetary base**

> The assets of the Federal Reserve System consist of loans made to the Treasury. These loans consist of Federal Reserve holdings of government debt. In a world without commercial banks, the liabilities of the Federal Reserve would equal the supply of money. In the real world, these liabilities are equal to the monetary base on which broader concepts of money are built.

Equation 10.2 illustrates the relationship between government debt and money in a world without commercial banking systems. In this world, there would be a single concept of money that is equal to the liabilities of the Federal Reserve System. These liabilities would consist solely of bank notes circulating among the public.

In the real world, the liabilities of the Federal Reserve System are called the **monetary base**. Firms and households hold a fraction of the Federal Reserve notes in circulation; the remainder of these notes make up the reserves of the commercial banking system. Private banks create new deposits by making loans to firms and households based on their holdings of reserves. To the extent that private agents can write checks on their deposits, the commercial banking system creates additional money. Because the ratio of deposits to the monetary base is stable, in practice the central bank can control the money supply (including commercial bank deposits) by manipulating the monetary base.

THE MONETARY BASE AND THE MONEY MULTIPLIER

The liabilities of the Federal Reserve System create a base for the entire commercial banking system by providing reserves on which commercial banks build additional liquid assets. We have already described a world in which the liabilities of the Federal Reserve System consist entirely of bank notes. In the real world there is an additional important component of the Federal Reserve's liabilities: reserves of the commercial banks held as accounts by the Federal Reserve System. These accounts are assets to the commercial banking system and liabilities to the Federal Reserve System in the same way that a private bank account is an asset to its owner and a liability to the bank at which it is held. We use the symbol R (for reserves) to refer to these deposits. It makes no difference whether these reserves exist as bookkeeping entries at Federal Reserve Banks or in the form of bank notes held in the vaults of the commercial banks. In either case, the commercial banks can access them at short notice to provide bank notes to their customers.

WHO HOLDS THE MONETARY BASE?

Equation 10.3 asserts the equality between the assets and liabilities of the Federal Reserve System in a model that allows for commercial banks. We again assume that the Federal Reserve System holds only government bonds, B^F, in its asset portfolio. The liabilities side

10.3 $\quad MB \quad = \quad B^F$

> The Federal Reserve System's liabilities are called the monetary base, MB. The assets consist of the Treasury's liabilities, B^F (that part of the government debt that is held by the Federal Reserve System).

10.4 $\quad MB \quad = \quad R + CU$

> The monetary base is held partly as the reserves, R, of the banking system and partly as currency, CU, in the hands of the public.

10.5 $\quad M \quad = \quad D + CU$

> The money supply, M, consists of the deposits of customers with commercial banks, D, plus currency in the hands of the public, CU.

of the Federal Reserve balance sheet is, however, no longer identical to the money supply because the money supply consists not only of circulating currency but also of deposits with commercial banks that are subject to withdrawal via bank checks. In this more realistic environment, the liabilities of the Federal Reserve System are referred to as the monetary base. Equation 10.4 divides the monetary base into two components: circulating currency, CU (Federal Reserve bank notes), and the reserves of the commercial bank, R. These reserves are held partly in the vaults of commercial banks as cash and partly as accounts at the Federal Reserve System. Equation 10.5 defines the money supply, M, as the sum of currency in the hands of the public, CU, and checking accounts (deposits) with the commercial bank, D.

THE MONEY SUPPLY AND THE MONETARY BASE

The money supply can be described as a multiple of the monetary base, called the **money supply multiplier**. The idea behind the money supply multiplier is that the ratio of currency to deposits and the ratio of reserves to deposits are relatively stable. If we view these ratios as constants, the money supply multiplier is a constant, and the Federal Reserve System exogenously controls the money supply.

To derive the money supply multiplier, we begin with two definitions. Let cu be the ratio of currency to deposits, and let rd be the ratio of reserves to deposits.

TABLE 10.2

Deriving the Money Multiplier

10.6	$\dfrac{MB}{D} = \dfrac{R}{D} + \dfrac{CU}{D} = rd + cu$	*Step 1:* Divide the definition of the monetary base by deposits.
10.7	$\dfrac{M}{D} = \dfrac{D}{D} + \dfrac{CU}{D} = 1 + cu$	*Step 2:* Divide the definition of the money supply by deposits.
10.8	$M = \left(\dfrac{1 + cu}{rd + cu}\right) MB$	*Step 3:* Take the ratio of step 2 to step 1 and substitute the definitions of *cu* and *rd*.
10.9	$m = \left(\dfrac{1 + cu}{rd + cu}\right)$	*Step 4:* This leads to *m*, the definition of the money supply multiplier.

$$cu = \frac{CV}{D}, \qquad rd = \frac{R}{D}$$

From the definition of the money supply (Equation 10.5) and the definition of the division of the monetary base (Equation 10.4), it follows that the money supply is a fixed multiple of the monetary base. Table 10.2 shows how the money supply is related to the monetary base. In step 1 (Equation 10.6) we divide through the definition of the monetary base by D. In step 2 (Equation 10.7) we divide the definition of the money supply by D. In step 3 (Equation 10.8) we take the ratio of steps 1 and 2 and substitute the definitions of *rd* and *cu* for the ratios R/D and CU/D. The final step, Equation 10.9, defines the money supply—currency held by the public plus checking accounts at commercial banks—as a multiple m of the monetary base. Because the Federal Reserve System can control the monetary base through open market operations, it can also control the entire money supply as long as the money multiplier remains stable.

THE IMPORTANCE OF THE MONEY SUPPLY MULTIPLIER

At several points in this chapter we have stressed the fact that part of the money supply is controlled by the private banking system. When banks lend more funds than they have in reserve, this process creates new checking accounts that serve as money. This process is limited by the need of private banks to hold reserves. Because the ability of private banks to create money is limited, the money supply is ultimately controlled by the Fed.

We showed in Table 10.2 that the total money supply (deposits plus currency in circulation) is a multiple *m* of the monetary base, and this multiple *m* bears a stable relationship to the ratio of reserves to deposits and the ratio of currency to deposits. If these ratios remain constant, whenever the Fed changes the monetary base, the money supply will increase by a multiple *m* of the increase in the base. In practice, the reserve deposit ratio and the currency deposit ratio are not constant; however, they move in predictable ways. In fact, the reserve deposit ratio and the currency deposit ratio are functions of the interest rate. In practice, the Fed allows for the changes in the money multiplier that are implied by this dependence on the interest rate when it adjusts the monetary base.

CONCLUSION

Commercial banking began with the practice of depositing gold and silver coins with goldsmiths for safekeeping. Since their customers did not typically demand access to their coins at the same time, the goldsmiths could lend them at interest to other traders, creating deposits that themselves began to circulate in the form of promissory notes. Our modern banking system mirrors this medieval system, with the difference that coins and paper money have replaced gold as the ultimate means of payment.

The Federal Reserve System controls the money supply by setting the discount rate and choosing reserve requirements; but its major tool is open market operations, the purchase and sale of government bonds on the open market. Open market operations result in changes in the outstanding liabilities of the Federal Reserve System. The Federal Reserve System's own liabilities, called the monetary base, are partly held by commercial banks and partly held by the public in the form of circulating bank notes. The money supply consists of circulating currency in the hands of the public plus the deposits of households and firms with commercial banks. Although the Federal Reserve Board cannot control the money supply directly, it *can* control the monetary base, and, because the money supply is a multiple of the monetary base, the Federal Reserve can indirectly control M1.

KEY TERMS

Bank note

Board of Governors of the Federal
    Reserve System

Central bank

Deficit

Discount rate

Federal Open Market Committee (FOMC)

Federal Reserve Bank

Federal Reserve System

Fiat money

Flexible exchange rates

Gold standard

Lender of last resort

Medium of exchange

Monetary base   Store of value
Money supply multiplier   Surplus
Required reserve ratio   Unit of account
Reserves

QUESTIONS FOR CHAPTER 10

1. Why do you think that the U.S. banking system is often referred to as a *fractional reserve banking system*?

2. What were *goldsmiths?* What relation do they bear to modern banks?

3. What is a *barter economy?* Provide three reasons why barter economies are less efficient than economies with money.

4. Consider the balance sheet of a financial institution that issues a credit card with a limit of $5,000. Analyze the asset and liability side of the institution's balance sheet as the household uses its credit card to make a $4,000 purchase. Is the credit card money? Is the unused portion of the credit limit ($1,000) money?

5. Look at the following balance sheet for a bank:

Assets		Liabilities	
Total reserves	$100,000	Deposits	$180,000
Loans	$40,000		
Government bonds	$40,000		

a. If the reserve ratio is 10%, what is the maximum amount of *new loans* that this bank could make in the future?

b. If $10,000 is withdrawn from this bank, what is the maximum amount of *new loans* that this bank could then make in the future?

c. If $20,000 is deposited into this bank, what is the maximum amount of *new loans* that this bank could make in the future?

6. Use the same balance sheet from Question 4. Suppose the Federal Reserve conducts an open market purchase of $20,000 with this bank. What is the maximum amount of new loans that this bank can now make?

7. What is meant by the "gold standard"? What are the potential advantages of this sytem? What are the potential disadvantages?

8. Average inflation before World War II was significantly lower (approximately 0% per year) than average inflation after World War II (approximately 3% per year). How would you explain this?

9. Define the terms *monetary base* and *money supply*. Does a central bank have perfect control over these variables? Why or why not?

10. Suppose that the Federal Reserve Board sells Japanese yen on the open market. Explain how this transaction would affect the position of the LM curve.

11. What is the FOMC? Who votes on the FOMC? How often does it meet?

12. a. List three methods the Federal Reserve can use to increase the money supply.

   b. Why is it that a small change in the monetary base leads to a larger increase in the money supply? What would happen to the money multiplier if the Federal Reserve increased the required reserve ratio?

13. a. Suppose that the required reserve ratio is equal to 10%. If the currency-to-deposit ratio is fixed at 20%, what is the money multiplier? If the monetary base is $100 million, what is the money supply?

   b. Suppose the currency-to-deposit ratio is 15%, the required reserve ratio is 5%, and total deposits in the banking system are $10,000. What are the monetary base, the money supply, and the money multiplier?

   c. Use the same information from part (b). Now suppose that an increase in consumer pessimism regarding the safety of the banking system leads the population to increase their currency-to-deposit ratio to 25%. How should the central bank respond to keep the money supply from changing? By how much?

14. Suppose that the money supply multiplier, *m(i)*, is a function that increases when the interest rate increases. Suppose that the Federal Reserve System controls the monetary base. (*Hint*: In this specification the money supply is endogenous.)

   a. How would this modification affect the slope of the LM curve? Would it become flatter or steeper? Why?

   b. In the real world the money supply is positively correlated with the interest rate. Can you explain why this is so?

15. Read the article "The Economic Organization of a P.O.W. Camp" by R.A. Radford in *Economica*, Vol. 12, November 1945, pp 194–198. Answer the following questions.

   a. What served as money in this prisoner of war (P.O.W.) camp?

   b. What functions did money serve in this camp's economy?

   c. What is Gresham's Law? How did Gresham's Law work in this economy?

   d. Describe how changes in the money supply and money demand affected the price level in this camp's economy.

   e. Describe the process by which this economy moved to paper money.

CHAPTER 11

THE IS CURVE

INTRODUCTION

The classical economists made assumptions that allowed them to put the economy's puzzle pieces together in a sequence of independent steps. Their two most important assumptions were that employment is always equal to its natural rate and the quantity of money demanded is independent of the interest rate. In the real world both of these assumptions are false. Employment fluctuates around its natural rate, and the interest rate is not determined independently of the equilibrium that prevails in the labor market. Once we drop the classical assumptions, we need to go back and reformulate the theory of aggregate demand. This chapter takes a first step in this process.

We are going to return to the theory of the capital market that we studied in Chapter 6, and we will amend this theory to incorporate the new-Keynesian theory of unemployment. According to the new Keynesians, output is not always equal to its natural rate. An implication of this is that the interest rate is no longer pinned down by the assumption that saving equals investment. Instead, we will show that there is a relationship between the interest rate and output, called the **IS curve**. At every point on this curve, the capital market is in equilibrium. In Chapter 12 we will put together the theory of the IS curve with the theory of the LM curve (Chapter 9). By combining them, we will be able to develop the Keynesian theory of aggregate demand.

THE THEORY OF THE CAPITAL MARKET

According to the classical theory of the capital market, the real interest rate equates investment and saving. To determine the interest rate, classical theory does not consider output, which is fixed at its natural rate. But in the Keynesian model, output can fluctuate, and we must account for this possibility when developing a theory of what determines the interest rate. The classical theory of the capital market must be modified to account for these facts, and now we find out how.

TWO DEFINITIONS OF THE REAL INTEREST RATE

We begin by revisiting a topic that we studied in Chapter 6; we learned to distinguish the *real interest rate* from the *nominal interest rate*. Recall that the real rate is the nominal rate adjusted for a change in the purchasing power of money, and it is the real rate that influences saving and investment decisions. But although equilibrium in the capital market determines the real interest rate, it is the nominal interest rate that we observe directly. If the nominal interest rate remains fixed, then inflation will lower the real interest rate. In practice this happens if inflation is unanticipated. We will learn about two ways of defining the real interest rate in order to distinguish between the effects of anticipated and unanticipated inflation.

The real interest rate that agents expect is called the **ex ante** real rate. The real interest rate that actually occurs is the **ex post** real rate. We have met the ex post real rate already. It is defined as:

11.1
$$r = i - \frac{\Delta P}{P}$$

> This equation defines the ex post real interest rate.

where i is the nominal interest rate and $\Delta P/P$ is the inflation rate that will hold over the life of a loan. The ex post real rate is found by subtracting the actual inflation rate from the nominal interest rate. "Ex post" means "after the fact," and represents the idea that the ex post real interest rate will not be known until the loan is repaid.

Because the inflation rate is unknown at the time that borrowers and lenders enter into commitments in the capital markets, households and firms must form an expectation of the future inflation rate. This observation leads to a second definition of the real interest rate, the ex ante real rate, which is defined as the difference between the nominal interest rate and the expected inflation rate.

11.2
$$r^E = i - \frac{\Delta P^E}{P}$$

> This equation defines the ex ante real interest rate r^E. The superscript "E" stands for "expected."

BOX 11.1

A CLOSER LOOK
How to Buy a House: A Case Study of Interest Rates and Inflation

Expected inflation is reflected in interest rates because if lenders expect inflation, they will demand a higher nominal interest rate as compensation for their loss in purchasing power of the money with which the loan is repaid. It is possible to gauge how much inflation market participants expect over different horizons by looking at the differences between long-term interest rates and short-term interest rates. One decision that you may face at some point in your life is how to finance the purchase of a house. Typically, you will have two options: to borrow money over a long-term horizon, or to borrow money over a series of short-time horizons. This graph shows how much you would have paid for these loans each month, beginning in May of 1971.

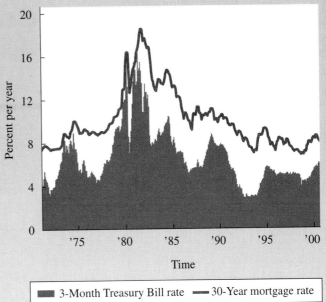

3-Month Treasury Bill rate ──── 30-Year mortgage rate

Short-term mortgages are typically indexed at 2 or 3 percentage points above a short-term rate, such as the rate paid on 3-month Treasury Bills by the government. The 3-month T-bill rate is graphed in this figure, along with the rate on 30-year loans. If you had taken out a 30-year loan in October of 1993, you would have locked in a rate of 6.8% for the life of the loan.

In September of 1981, the interest rate was very high. A family that bought a house faced two options. They could take out a 30-year fixed-rate mortgage at 18.4%, or they could take out a series of 1-year mortgages. Over a five-year horizon, the sequence of short mortgages would have resulted in substantial saving because interest rates fell substantially from 1981 through 1986.

In January of 1979, the situation was very different. Thirty-year mortgages were available at 10.39%, but over a five-year horizon the short rate climbed as high as 15.02%. On a $100,000 mortgage, a 5–percentage-point interest rate rise would result in increased monthly payments of $416, a substantial increase for a young family on a tight budget. A fixed-rate mortgage was a better bet.

Unfortunately, there is no hard-and-fast rule as to when it is a good idea to borrow long term and when it is better to borrow short term. It all depends on whether you are better at guessing the future inflation rate than other players in the market.

The ex ante real interest rate would be the same as the ex post real interest rate if households and firms could predict the future price level with absolute certainty, but this is rarely the case. In times of rapid, unexpected inflation, the ex post real interest rate and the ex ante real interest rate may be very different from each other. For example, during the period immediately following the oil price shocks in 1973 and 1979, inflation rose very rapidly in a way that no one had expected, and both lenders and borrowers were surprised. Lenders were hurt because the value of the interest that they received was lower

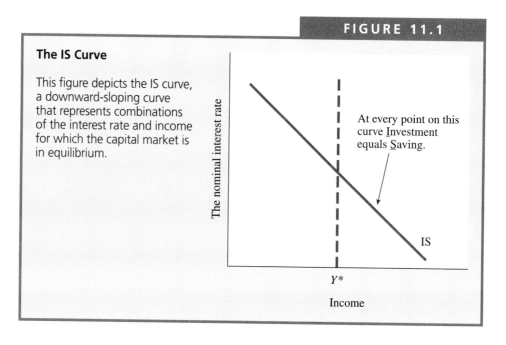

FIGURE 11.1

The IS Curve

This figure depicts the IS curve, a downward-sloping curve that represents combinations of the interest rate and income for which the capital market is in equilibrium.

At every point on this curve Investment equals Saving.

IS

$Y*$

Income

The nominal interest rate

(in terms of the commodities that it could purchase) than they had anticipated when they lent their money, but many borrowers were very pleasantly surprised. For example, a household might have borrowed money to buy a home by taking out a 30-year fixed-rate mortgage. In 1970 the mortgage interest rate was less than 8%, but by 1980 it had climbed close to 15%. Families with fixed-rate mortgages found that inflation increased the value of their homes, whereas the cost of their debts was fixed in nominal terms, and many borrowers became quite rich in a relatively short period of time.

WHAT IS THE IS CURVE?

In the classical theory, income is determined by the assumption that there is no unemployment. Given this assumption, saving is represented by an upward-sloping line on a graph that represents saving supplied as a function of the interest rate, given that output is at its natural rate. According to classical theory, the equilibrium real interest rate equates saving and investment.

In the Keynesian model there is no unique level of income. Instead, income may be at the natural rate, above the natural rate, or below the natural rate. The fact that income can fluctuate over the business cycle affects the interest rate because households are more willing to save if they are rich rather than if they are poor. When income is high (unemployment is low), there will be a relatively large supply of saving to the capital market. Firms will not need to offer high interest rates to attract lenders, so high income will be associated with a low equilibrium interest rate. If instead income is low (unemployment is high), investors will compete with each other to borrow into a small pool of savings, and they

Economic Charts on Command

Do you need a graph of economic data to fill out a report or to help you with a term project? Check out Economagic, a site developed by Ted Bos at the University of Alabama School of Business: http://www.economagic.com.

This graph of the daily interest rate on Federal Funds (an important indicator of the stance of monetary policy) is one of thousands of graphs that are available at this site. You can choose one of many ready-made graphs, or you can use the page to custom-make your own charts.

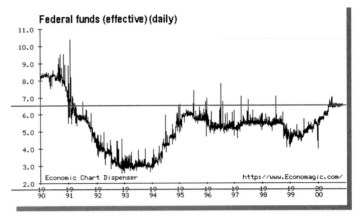

Federal funds (effective) (daily)

will bid up the interest rate. Low income will be associated with a high equilibrium interest rate. In the Keynesian model, we summarize this idea by deriving a schedule, the IS curve depicted in Figure 11.1, which plots the nominal interest rate on the vertical axis and the level of income on the horizontal axis. At every point on the IS curve, the capital market is in equilibrium.[1]

HOW EXPECTED INFLATION AFFECTS THE CAPITAL MARKET

The IS curve plots values of the nominal interest rate against income for which the capital market is in equilibrium. But the saving and investment schedules that we derived in Chapter 6 depend on the real interest rate, not the nominal rate. To derive the IS curve, we need to recognize that saving may depend not only on the real interest rate, but also on income. Second, we must recognize that the real interest rate is equal to the nominal interest rate minus expected inflation. The saving function, accounting for these amendments, can be written as $S(Y, i - \Delta P^E/P)$, and the investment function can be written as $I(i - \Delta P^E/P)$, where the terms Y and $i - \Delta P^E/P$ remind us that saving and investment depend on these two variables. We use the ex ante real interest rate, not the ex post rate,

---

1.   The term "IS curve" comes from the fact that, in a closed economy model with no government, investment (I) equals saving (S) at every point on this curve.

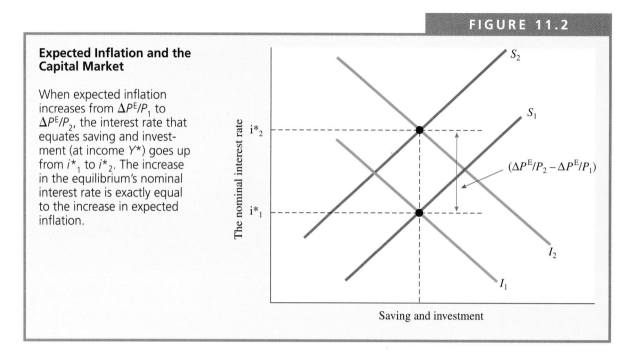

FIGURE 11.2

Expected Inflation and the Capital Market

When expected inflation increases from $\Delta P^E/P_1$ to $\Delta P^E/P_2$, the interest rate that equates saving and investment (at income Y^*) goes up from i^*_1 to i^*_2. The increase in the equilibrium's nominal interest rate is exactly equal to the increase in expected inflation.

because at the time that saving and investment decisions are made, the future price level is unknown.

To show how the nominal interest rate is determined, we can develop a diagram (see Figure 11.2) that plots the nominal interest rate against the quantity of investment demanded and the quantity of saving supplied. We have drawn two saving schedules and two investment schedules. Consider first the schedule labeled S_1, which plots the quantity of saving supplied on the horizontal axis against the nominal interest rate on the vertical axis, given that the household earns income Y^* and expects inflation of $\Delta P^E/P_1$. Now consider the investment schedule labeled I_1. This schedule plots the quantity of investment demanded on the horizontal axis against the nominal interest rate on the vertical axis, given that the firm expects that the inflation rate equals $\Delta P^E/P_1$. For this common level of expected inflation, the nominal interest rate that equates the quantity of saving supplied to the quantity of investment demanded equals i^*_1.

What happens in the capital market when both firms and workers revise their expectation of inflation from $\Delta P^E/P_1$ to some higher level, $\Delta P^E/P_2$? [2] In this case, we draw a new saving schedule, S_2, and a new investment schedule, I_2. Notice that the saving schedule S_2 is shifted upward from the saving schedule S_1 by exactly the increase in expected inflation $(\Delta P^E/P_2 - \Delta P^E/P_1)$. Similarly, the new investment schedule translates upward from the old one by the same distance. This happens because investment and saving depend on the

---

FIGURE 11.3

Investment, Saving, and the IS curve

Panel A represents equilibrium in the capital market for three different levels of income. When income is equal to Y_1, households are willing to save an amount represented by S_1. Similarly, when income is Y^* and when it equals Y_2, the corresponding saving schedules are S^* and S_2. Panel B shows the IS curve. At every point on this curve, the quantity of investment demanded equals the quantity of saving supplied. For higher levels of income, the equilibrium interest rate is lower because households are willing to save more at every value of the interest rate. At every point on the IS curve, investment equals saving.

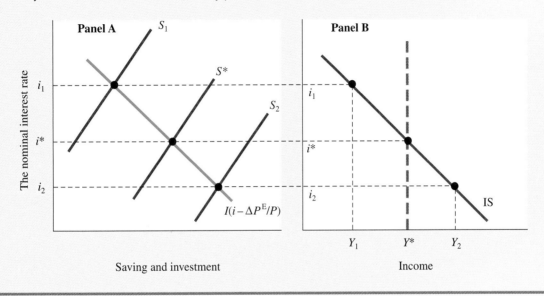

real interest rate, and when the nominal interest rate goes up by the amount of the additional expected inflation, households supply the same saving and demand the same investment as before the increase. Because i^*_1 was at equilibrium before inflation increased, $i^*_2 = i^*_1 + (\Delta P^E/P_2 - \Delta P^E/P_1)$ must be an equilibrium afterwards.

DERIVING THE IS CURVE

We will now use the theory of the capital market to derive a relationship between income and the interest rate—the IS curve.

THE IS CURVE IN A GRAPH

In Figure 11.3 we derive the IS curve. On panel A, we plot the nominal interest rate on the vertical axis. We plot the quantity of saving supplied and the quantity of investment demanded on the horizontal axis. On panel B, we plot the nominal interest rate on the vertical axis and the level of income on the horizontal axis. Both schedules are drawn for a given expectation of inflation.

Unlike the classical model, the Keynesian model admits the possibility that saving may depend not only on the interest rate but also on income. When households have high income they save more than when they have low income. Beginning with panel B, suppose that income is at the natural rate Y^*. To represent the way that saving depends on income, we must draw a different saving schedule for each value of income. Given the saving schedule S^*, we see from panel A that when income equals Y^*, i^* is the interest rate that equates the supply of saving to the demand for investment. We can translate this interest rate across to panel B and plot a point on the IS curve at $\{Y^*, i^*\}$.

What about different values of income? Suppose that instead of $Y = Y^*$, we ask: What interest rate will clear the capital market when Y is lower or higher than Y^*? In Figure 11.3, we have derived two other points on the IS curve, one when output is at Y_1, a level that is lower than the natural rate Y^*, and one at Y_2, a level that is higher than the natural rate Y^*. When $Y = Y_1$, the quantity of saving supplied is lower for every interest rate than when $Y = Y^*$. We represent this by the saving schedule S_1, a saving schedule that is consistently to the left of the schedule S^*. At Y_1, households have lower income than at Y^* and are less willing to supply saving to the capital market. Because the investment schedule slopes downward, the interest rate, i_1, that equates saving and investment when $Y = Y_1$ is *higher* than i^*. We can translate this equilibrium interest rate across to panel B to plot a second point on the IS curve at $\{Y_1, i_1\}$. Finally, we repeat the argument when income is equal to Y_2, a level that is higher than the natural rate Y^*. A similar argument shows that in this case the equilibrium interest rate i_2 is *lower* than i^*, and we may translate this rate across to panel B to find a third point on the IS curve at $\{Y_2, i_2\}$.

The dashed vertical line on panel B represents the natural rate of income (equal to the natural rate of output). In the classical model, the economy is always at full employment, but in the Keynesian approach output may be above, at, or below Y^*. What are the factors that would cause the economy to operate at a point other than Y^*? The demand and supply of money can be combined with the analysis of the IS curve to determine a level of demand other than Y^*. But before we study the interaction of money with the real economy, we need to explore the factors that are responsible for shifts in the IS curve. These factors can help us understand how government policies that change taxes and government expenditure interact with the private economy to influence employment and GDP.

VARIABLES THAT SHIFT THE IS CURVE

Various exogenous variables influence the economy through their effect on the IS curve. These variables include government spending, taxes, and factors that affect the beliefs of investors about future productivity. We will now study the effects of changes in these variables on the capital market.[3]

Suppose that the government plans to run a budget deficit. Government deficits influence the equilibrium interest rate because the government competes with investors for pri-

---

3.   In Chapter 13, we amend this analysis to allow for the fact that countries may borrow from abroad.

vate saving. Deficits also influence the capital market equilibrium by shifting the saving schedule—households have less **disposable income** when the government takes away part of their private income in taxes net of transfers. We can take into account the impact of the government on the capital market by amending the capital market equilibrium equation in the following way:

11.3
$$I(i - \Delta P^E/P) + D = S(Y, T - TR, i - \Delta P^E/P)$$

The left side of Equation 11.3 is the total demand for borrowing by firms and government. This consists of the demand for investment, $I(i - \Delta P^E/P)$, which firms finance by borrowing in the capital market, plus D, the government budget deficit, which the government must finance by borrowing in the capital market. The notation $S(Y, T - TR, i - \Delta P^E/P)$ indicates that saving depends on income, Y, net taxes, $(T - TR)$, and the expected real interest rate, $i - \Delta P^E/P$.

GOVERNMENT PURCHASES AND THE IS CURVE

What happens if the deficit goes up? This depends in part on whether government purchases of goods and services go up or net taxes go down. Let's take the case in which government purchases go up and assume that government goods and services cannot easily be substituted for private consumption goods. This is often, although not always, a reasonable assumption. Some government purchases *are* good substitutes for private purchases, such as education. If the government increases expenditure on education, private saving is likely to increase because some households will choose to send their children to public schools instead of to private schools, and they will save part of the income they would have spent on tuition. But for now we assume that the private saving schedule is unaffected by an increase in government purchases. The effect of an increase in government purchases is illustrated on Figure 11.4.

On panel A of Figure 11.4, we have drawn the demand for investment plus the demand for funds by the government for two different values of government purchases. This combined demand for funds in the capital market is the locus $I + D_1$, which assumes that government purchases equal G_1, and again when government purchases are at the higher level G_2. The notation D_1 refers to the government budget deficit when government expenditure equals G_1. Similarly, D_2 refers to the government budget deficit when government expenditure equals G_2. To find out what happens to the IS curve at different values of government purchases, we must first pick a level of income so that we can draw the appropriate saving schedule. Let's choose the natural rate Y^*. Because we are not explicitly considering changes in taxes or transfers in this diagram, we have suppressed saving's dependency on net taxes. We have written the saving schedule "when $Y = Y^*$" as "S^*."

When income is equal to Y^*, what nominal interest rate is consistent with equilibrium in the capital market? If government purchases equal G_1, the equilibrium interest rate when $Y = Y^*$ is i^*_1 because this is the interest rate for which the quantity of funds demanded by government plus the quantity of investment demanded by firms equals the quantity of saving supplied by households. But if government purchases increase to G_2, the equilibrium interest rate when $Y = Y^*$ increases to i^*_2. This second interest rate is

FIGURE 11.4

Government Purchases and the IS Curve

The green arrows indicate the shifts in the $I + D$ curve and the IS curve that occur when government purchases increase from G_1 to G_2. Panel A illustrates equilibrium in the capital market for two different values of the government budget deficit, D_1 and D_2. The supply of saving is drawn for the case in which $Y = Y^*$. By assumption, D_2 is bigger than D_1. The deficit increases in this picture because government spending has increased from G_1 to G_2. As the government deficit increases, the government competes with firms for private saving and drives up the interest rate from i^*_1 to i^*_2. This is illustrated as a shift in the curve $I + D$. Panel B shows that the effect of this increase in government expenditure is to shift the IS curve to the right.

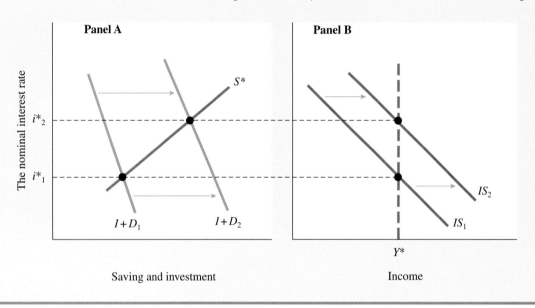

higher than the first because the government competes with private firms for the savers' funds and drives up the interest rate in a capital market equilibrium.

TAXES, TRANSFERS, AND THE IS CURVE

To analyze the effect of a change in net taxes on the IS curve, assume that taxes are levied as a lump sum on households and firms, and ignore the fact that tax revenues rise when income increases. This is the simplest case to analyze because it allows us to disregard the effects of changes in tax rates on labor supply. Assume as well that net taxes affect saving only through their effect on disposable income. Figure 11.5 illustrates the way that the IS curve shifts when net taxes go up under these two assumptions.

Figure 11.5 plots the same two graphs that we used to analyze how government purchases shift the IS curve (see Figure 11.4). For the case of a change in net taxes, we need to consider two effects of an increase in taxes on the capital market. First, a direct effect

FIGURE 11.5

Taxes and the IS Curve

The green arrows indicate the shifts in the $I + D$ curve and the IS curve that occur when tax revenues increase from T_1 to T_2. Panel A illustrates equilibrium in the capital market for two different values of the government budget deficit, D_1 and D_2. By assumption, D_2 is smaller than D_1. The deficit falls in this picture because tax revenues have increased from T_1 to T_2. As the government deficit falls, competition with firms for private saving decreases, and this effect tends to lower the real interest rate. The effect on the demand for funds by borrowers (both private firms and government) is illustrated as a leftward shift in the curve $I + D$. There is another offsetting effect, since as taxes increase, households will be less willing to supply saving to the capital market; they have a smaller disposable income. This effect is illustrated as a leftward shift of the supply of saving schedule from S^*_1 to S^*_2. The net effect is to lower the equilibrium interest rate from i^*_1 to i^*_2, but not by as much as if the fall in the deficit had occurred because of a drop in government purchases. The supply of saving schedule in panel A is drawn for the case in which $Y = Y^*$. When tax revenues increase, the equilibrium interest rate (for the level of income Y^*) goes down from i^*_1 to i^*_2. Panel B shows that the effect of this increase in tax revenues is to shift the IS curve to the left.

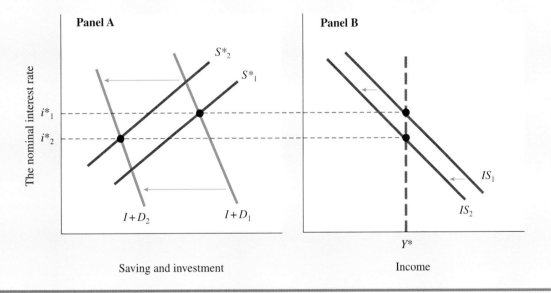

follows because when net taxes increase, the government demands less funds in the capital market. This direct effect shifts the $I + D$ schedule to the left. Second, an indirect effect follows because when net taxes increase, households have less disposable income and their supply of saving falls. Let's consider these two effects and how they influence capital market equilibrium.

Beginning with panel B, we ask the question, what is the interest rate for which the capital market is in equilibrium when income is at the natural rate Y^*? We analyze the direct effect of a tax increase first. From panel A, we see that when taxes are equal to T_1, the demand for funds by firms and government is given by the curve $I + D_1$, where the notation D_1 means the deficit when tax revenues equal T_1. When taxes increase to T_2, the government borrows less money in the capital market, and this reduced demand is represented by a leftward shift of the $I + D$ schedule from $I + D_1$ to $I + D_2$. D_2 is smaller than D_1 for every value of the interest rate because the government borrows less when tax revenues are higher.

Now consider the indirect effect of an increase in net taxes. Consider first the supply of saving schedule when taxes equal T_1 as S^*_1. Now let taxes increase to T_2. The effect of this increase shifts the supply of saving schedule to the left, back to S^*_2, because households have less disposable income available for saving. Which of these effects is greater, the direct effect or the indirect effect? Because households typically save only a fraction of their disposable income, it seems reasonable to assume that the direct effect will dominate the indirect effect, and the $I + D$ schedule will shift to the left by more than the saving schedule.[4] Because the $I + D$ schedule shifts by more than the saving schedule, the net effect of an increase in net taxes is to shift the IS curve to the left. The leftward shift of the IS curve when taxes increase is smaller than the rightward shift when government purchases increase because, in the case of taxes, the saving curve shifts to partially offset the change in the government's demand for funds.

SHIFTS IN THE INVESTMENT SCHEDULE AND THE IS CURVE

A third variable that can shift the IS curve has nothing to do with government. Shifts may occur as a result of private behavior. In Chapter 6, we identified two factors that might shift the investment schedule: a change in productivity due to a new invention or a change in beliefs about future rates of return. Both of these events cause shifts in the IS curve.

Figure 11.6 illustrates the effect of a shift in the investment schedule on the IS curve. The investment schedule can shift to the right for one of two reasons. If firms encounter a new technology that will increase profitability, they may have to build new kinds of capital equipment in order to exploit this technology. The growths of the computer industry in the 1980s and the biotechnology industry in the 1990s are examples of investment demand shocks that shift the IS curve to the right in this way. These kinds of shocks shift the IS curve because they increase investors' beliefs about the future profitability of the technology. The IS curve can also shift if firms and households expect increased inflation, and if the current nominal rate seems low in terms of the commodities that will be produced in the future. An increase in expected inflation shifts the IS curve to the right because it lowers the expected real cost of borrowing.

ANIMAL SPIRITS VERSUS PRODUCTIVITY SHIFTS

Investment is the most variable component of GDP, and the investment shifts depicted in Figure 11.6 are the single most important cause of movements in the IS curve. The cause of these movements is hotly debated. Some economists think that shifts in investment are rationally anticipated fluctuations that arise from the forecasts of future productivity

---

4.   Robert Barro of Harvard University has argued that the shift in the saving schedule in this case equals the shift in the $I + D$ schedule, and the IS curve does not move at all. Barro's argument is called Ricardian equivalence and is discussed in Chapter 14.

FIGURE 11.6

Shifts in Investment and the IS Curve

The green arrows indicate the shifts in the $I + D$ curve and the IS curve that occur when investors forecast that productivity will increase or that there will be higher future inflation. Panel A illustrates equilibrium in the capital market for two different values of the investment schedule, I_1 and I_2. The supply of saving is drawn for the case in which $Y = Y^*$. By assumption, I_2 is bigger than I_1. As investment increases, firms compete harder for private saving and drive up the interest rate from i^*_1 to i^*_2. This is illustrated as a shift in the curve $I + D$. Panel B shows that the effect of this increase in investment is to shift the IS curve to the right.

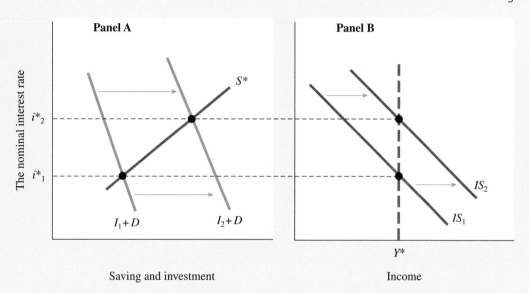

Panel C shows how investment, as a share of GDP, has fluctuated since 1970. Notice how investment has increased in the 1990s. If investment crashes again, as it did in 1974 and 1979, then the economy will probably fall into another recession.

Some economists argue that the investment boom of the 1990s represents investment in new technology that will result in large future increases in GDP. These increases are in anticipation of the fruits of new technologies, such as the Internet. Other economists think that this investment boom may be partly a result of mistaken beliefs and that some investors are over-optimistic about the likely payoff of the new technologies.

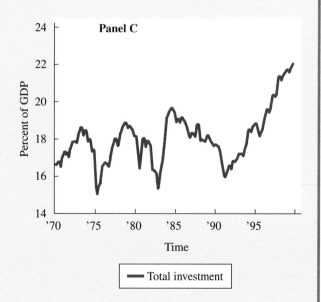

changes by businesses. Others believe that the expectations of businesspersons are often wrong and driven by mass psychology.

From panel C of Figure 11.6, we see that in the 1990s, the share of investment in GDP had increased dramatically. This increase in investment was largely responsible for the current business cycle expansion. But is it sustainable?

According to the real business cycle view, the investment boom results from rational, forward-looking investors who are exploiting the new opportunities afforded by the Internet and related technologies. It is possible that the boom will come to end, but if this happens, it will be because the opportunities have dried up. There is no guarantee that prosperity will last forever. Previous recessions in 1974 and 1979 were accompanied by falls in investment spending that were triggered by sharp increases in the price of oil. These recessions were classical in nature since they arose as a result of changes in productive opportunities. In the 1970s and 1980s, oil was extremely important to the smooth running of the economy. This is probably less true in the current economy because alternatives to oil have been developed in some industries. But even if oil shocks are less important today, other kinds of fundamental shocks could easily bring the investment boom to an end and trigger a recession.

The Keynesian view of investment fluctuations is different. Keynesians do not deny that fundamental shocks are important, but they believe that they are not the only source of fluctuations in investment spending. According to the Keynesian position, much of the increase in investment spending that occurred in the 1990s may well be unsustainable. Many firms have rushed into the marketplace to exploit the new technologies, but not all of them will be successful. The Keynesians believe that many of these new firms will fail; and as this happens, investment will decline. At this point, there will likely be a recession, probably accompanied by a drop in value of the stock market.

CONCLUSION

In this chapter, we learned two different definitions of the real interest rate: ex ante and ex post. We used two facts—that investment depends on the real interest rate and that saving depends on the real interest rate and income—to derive a downward-sloping graph called the IS curve. At every point on the IS curve, investment equals saving. We showed that government spending, taxes, and the expectations of investors are three different factors that cause the IS curve to shift.

Deriving the IS curve is a lot of work without an obvious, immediate payoff. But now that we understand how it works, we will be able to use the ideas that we have developed to explain the Keynesian theory of aggregate demand (Chapter 12). This theory has rich implications for the causes of business cycles and for the kinds of policies that might be used to stabilize them.

KEY TERMS

Disposable income	Ex post
Ex ante	IS curve

QUESTIONS FOR CHAPTER 11

1. Explain the difference between the *ex ante* and *ex poste* real interest rate. Which one matters when firms and households make their investment and saving decisions?

2. Explain how unexpectedly high inflation affects real interest rates and how this in turn affects debtors and lenders. Who gains and who loses?

3. Why does the IS curve slope downward? Use a graph of the capital market to illustrate.

4. If investment demand becomes more responsive to changes in the interest rate, how would this affect the slope of the investment demand curve? How would this affect the slope of the IS curve?

5. If saving becomes less responsive to changes in the interest rate, how would this affect the slope of the saving supply curve? How would this affect the slope of the IS curve?

6. Explain how the IS curve would respond to the following events:

a. a tax increase in which the proceeds are used to reduce the government budget deficit

b. a reduction in government spending in which the proceeds are used to reduce the government budget deficit

c. a wave of pessimism that sweeps the country and changes many firms' current investment plans

7. How will a 1% decrease in the expected inflation rate impact the capital market? How much will nominal interest rates change as a result? What happens to the IS curve when the expected price level falls?

8. If firms expect higher inflation, but households do not, will the IS curve shift to the right or the left? Explain your answer.

9. Why did investment demand boom during the 1990s? Was it a temporary or a permanent change? Discuss both the Keynesian and classical (or real business cycle) perspectives on these questions.

10. The following equations describe the capital market of an economy:

$$C = 100 + .75(Y - T)$$
$$I = 50 - 25i$$
$$T = G = 50$$

where C is aggregate consumption, I is aggregate investment, T is taxes, G is government purchases, and i is the interest rate. Derive the IS curve for this economy.

11. Point your browser to **http://www.economagic.com/**. Using the chart-maker at this site, construct graphs of five different interest rate series for the 1990s. You may choose any five series you like. Write down any differences you see between the series. Can you rank them? Is one always higher than the others? Is one more volatile than the others? Try to explain the differences you see.

IS-LM AND AGGREGATE DEMAND

INTRODUCTION

In Chapter 12, we will explain the Keynesian theory of aggregate demand. According to this theory, aggregate demand depends not only on the money supply, as in classical theory, but also on fiscal policy and on the expectations of households and firms.

We develop the theory in two steps. First, we hold the price level fixed, and we put together the IS curve with the LM curve to develop an apparatus called the IS-LM model, which shows us how to simultaneously determine the interest rate and the level of income. Then we relax the assumption of a fixed price level and show how to use the IS-LM model to determine aggregate demand. The Keynesian aggregate demand curve, when combined with the new-Keynesian aggregate supply curve, can be used to explain the effects of different kinds of shocks on output, unemployment, and the price level. It can also be used as a tool in the formulation of government policies for managing aggregate demand and/or stabilizing business cycles.

THE IS-LM MODEL

We are now ready to put together the two parts of the Keynesian theory of aggregate demand: the IS and LM curves. At every point on the LM curve, the quantity of money demanded equals the quantity supplied. At every point on the IS curve, the capital market is in equilibrium. We will show that the aggregate demand for commodities is determined at the point where the IS and LM curves intersect.

Constructing the IS-LM model is similar to deriving the aggregate demand curve in the classical model. In order to draw the LM curve (Chapter 9), we assumed that the price level was fixed at the level *P*. To construct the IS-LM model, we make the same assumption. When we put together the IS and LM curves, we can describe the simultaneous determination of the nominal interest rate and income in an **IS-LM equilibrium**. We can also go beyond the IS-LM analysis by showing that there is a different IS-LM equilibrium for every value of the price level. The relationship between the price level and the equilibrium value of income in the IS-LM model is called the **Keynesian aggregate demand curve.**

RATIONAL EXPECTATIONS: WHICH VARIABLES ARE EXOGENOUS?

Before we explain the determination of aggregate demand in the Keynesian model, let's be precise about what in our analysis is fixed and what is not fixed. Recall that variables determined outside the model are called exogenous and those determined inside the model are called endogenous. This is an important distinction in modern policy analysis because of a concept called **rational expectations,** the idea that households' and firms' beliefs of future prices and the future value of their incomes must be modeled endogenously.

In this chapter we do not model expectations endogenously. Instead, the predictions of the model must be taken as conditional, based on the assumption that expectations will not be altered in response to specific policy changes. For example, we assume that an increase in the money supply is not expected to alter the future course of inflation.

We will assume that the Federal Reserve Board fixes the supply of money, *M*. For every possible value of *M* there will be a different LM curve. We will show how changes in monetary policy alter the position of the LM curve and demonstrate that changes in *M* can be used to influence the interest rate, income, and employment. We will also assume that the government fixes government purchases, *G*, transfer payments, *TR,* and taxes, *T*. We will show that there is a different IS curve for every value of *T*, *TR,* or *G,* and we will use our knowledge of how fiscal policy shifts the IS curve to predict the effects of different policies on the interest rate, income, and employment.

The price level will be dealt with in two steps. When we build the IS-LM model, we will take *P* as fixed; later, when we combine aggregate demand and supply, we will show how *P* is determined in the complete model. To fully describe an IS-LM equilibrium in a rational expectations model, policies must be described as rules that enable households to forecast their future impact. We will take up this idea in Chapter 18, after we deal more carefully with dynamic economics.

FIGURE 12.1

The Complete IS-LM Model

The equilibrium of the IS-LM model is determined at the intersection point of the IS and LM curves. At every point on the LM curve, the quantity of money demanded is equal to the quantity of money supplied. At every point on the IS curve, the capital market is in equilibrium. Only at the point of intersection of IS and LM are both markets simultaneously in equilibrium. Notice that IS-LM equilibrium does *not necessarily occur at the natural rate of output, Y*.*

The red arrows indicate one possible adjustment path back to equilibrium.

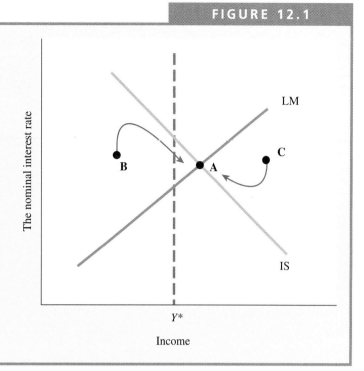

IS-LM Equilibrium

In Figure 12.1, we combine the LM curve from Chapter 9 with the IS curve from Chapter 11. Recall that the LM curve is special because it denotes values of the interest rate and income for which the quantity of money is willingly held. Alternatively, we can say that the quantity of money demanded is equal to the quantity supplied. Similarly, the IS curve is special because it represents values of the interest rate and income for which the capital market is in equilibrium.

The equilibrium of the IS-LM model occurs at point **A,** where the IS and LM curves intersect. This is the only point at which the capital market is in equilibrium and, simultaneously, the quantity of money in circulation is willingly held. Could the economy be at equilibrium at a point *other* than point **A**? There are two forces pulling the economy back to the point of intersection of the IS and LM curves. First, suppose that the economy is at a point below the IS curve: Pick a point on the IS curve and lower the interest rate, but hold income as fixed. As the interest rate falls, investment increases and saving falls; hence, points below the IS curve are points for which investment exceeds saving. Investors bid up the interest rate in an attempt to secure funds, and the interest rate rises. A similar argument establishes that points above the IS curve are points for which saving exceeds investment. Investors can offer lower interest rates because there is an excess of savers in the market.

What about points that are off the LM curve? At any point to the left of the LM curve, income is lower but with the same interest rate. Because income is lower, the quantity of money demanded must also be lower. It follows that points to the left of the LM curve are points for which there is an excess supply of money. Households are holding more money than they need to finance their daily transactions and will try to spend this money by demanding more commodities; thus, the aggregate demand for goods and services will increase. As demand increases, firms hire more workers, and employment and income rise until the economy is back on the LM curve. A similar reasoning establishes that if the economy is to the right of the LM curve, there is an excess demand for money. Households buy fewer commodities, and aggregate demand falls. As demand falls, firms lay off workers, and employment and income fall until the economy is back on the LM curve. Point **A** is special because of the forces that move the economy toward the IS-LM equilibrium.

THE KEYNESIAN AGGREGATE DEMAND CURVE

We are now ready to put together the complete Keynesian theory of aggregate demand by dropping the assumption that the price level is fixed and asking how equilibrium income in the IS-LM model differs for different values of the price level. We derive a graph, the aggregate demand curve that links the price level to the aggregate quantity of commodities demanded.

Figure 12.2 illustrates the aggregate demand curve in two panels. On panel A, we plot the price level against income. Notice that panel A has a downward-sloping curve. This curve resembles the aggregate demand curve from the classical model that was presented in Chapter 5. Our new curve is different from that model because in the Keynesian theory, the position of the aggregate demand curve depends not only on the money supply but also on fiscal policy and on expectations. We can show how this curve is derived by relating it to the IS-LM model, which is plotted in panel B of Figure 12.2.

Begin with panel A and choose a price level, P_1. At the price level P_1, what level of aggregate demand for goods and services is consistent with IS-LM equilibrium? To answer this question we turn to the IS-LM diagram. We must know the price level to construct this diagram since the real value of the supply of money depends on it. Given the price level P_1, the LM curve is $LM(M/P_1)$, and the IS-LM equilibrium is at **C** on panel B. Tracing equilibrium income up to panel A gives a point, **A**, on the Keynesian aggregate demand curve. At point **A**, it is simultaneously true that the quantity of money demanded equals the quantity supplied, and the capital market is in equilibrium.

To find a second point on the AD curve, let the price level drop from P_1 to P_2. As the price level falls, the LM curve shifts to $LM(M/P_2)$, and the equilibrium income level increases to Y_2. The new IS-LM equilibrium is at **D**. Tracing equilibrium income back to panel A, we can plot a second point, **B**, on the aggregate demand curve. Because a fall in the price level shifts the LM curve to the right, the aggregate demand curve slopes downward.

FISCAL POLICY AND THE AGGREGATE DEMAND CURVE

The Keynesian theory of aggregate demand provides a more complete account than the classical theory of the causes of business fluctuations. Keynesian theory can be put into

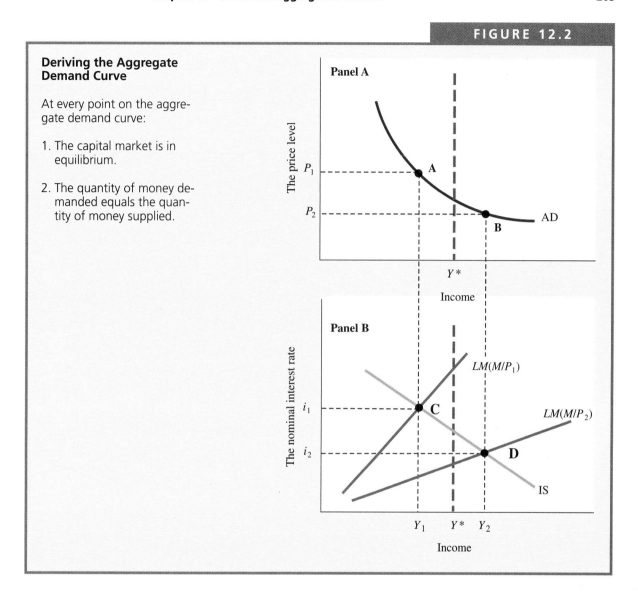

FIGURE 12.2

Deriving the Aggregate Demand Curve

At every point on the aggregate demand curve:

1. The capital market is in equilibrium.

2. The quantity of money demanded equals the quantity of money supplied.

Panel A

The price level

P_1 ⚫ A

P_2 ⚫ B

AD

$Y*$

Income

Panel B

The nominal interest rate

$LM(M/P_1)$

i_1 ⚫ C

$LM(M/P_2)$

i_2 ⚫ D

IS

Y_1 $Y*$ Y_2

Income

practice by studying changes in the aggregate demand curve that occur in response to changes in monetary and fiscal policy. We begin by looking at changes in fiscal policy and how they alter aggregate demand.

Suppose that government purchases of goods and services increase from some level G_1 to a higher level G_2. Figure 12.3 graphs the effect of this increase. On panel B of the figure, we have drawn two IS curves and one LM curve. The LM curve is drawn with the assumption that the price level is equal to P_1. We can show that the IS-LM equilibrium

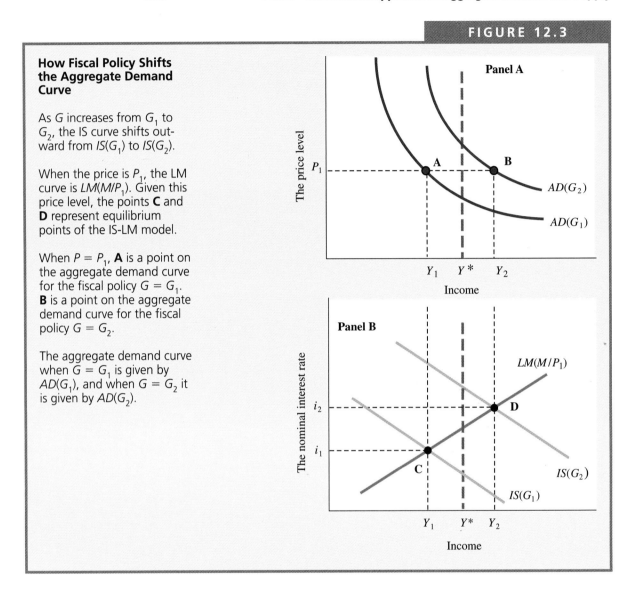

FIGURE 12.3

How Fiscal Policy Shifts the Aggregate Demand Curve

As G increases from G_1 to G_2, the IS curve shifts outward from $IS(G_1)$ to $IS(G_2)$.

When the price is P_1, the LM curve is $LM(M/P_1)$. Given this price level, the points **C** and **D** represent equilibrium points of the IS-LM model.

When $P = P_1$, **A** is a point on the aggregate demand curve for the fiscal policy $G = G_1$. **B** is a point on the aggregate demand curve for the fiscal policy $G = G_2$.

The aggregate demand curve when $G = G_1$ is given by $AD(G_1)$, and when $G = G_2$ it is given by $AD(G_2)$.

occurs at a higher level of income when government purchases equal G_2 than when they equal G_1 by drawing two IS curves, one for each level of government expenditure. The effect of increasing government expenditure at a given price level is an increase in equilibrium income from point **C** to point **D**. By tracing the old and new equilibrium levels of income onto panel A, we can plot points on two aggregate demand curves, both at the same price level, P_1. Point **A** is associated with the level of spending G_1 and point **B** is associated with the level of spending G_2.

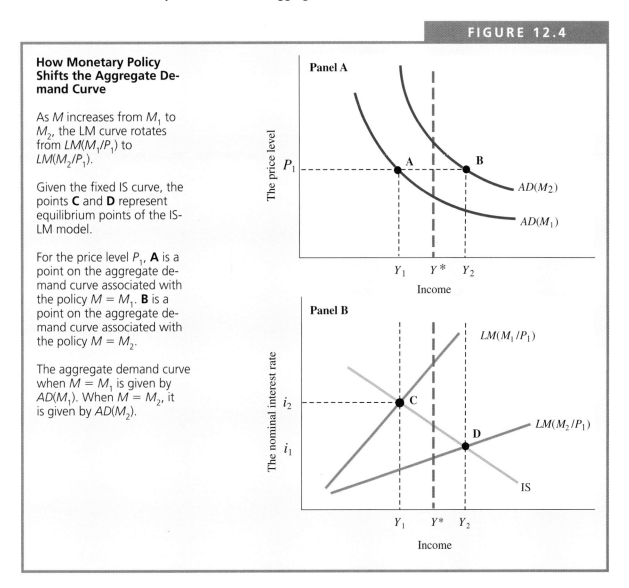

FIGURE 12.4

How Monetary Policy Shifts the Aggregate Demand Curve

As M increases from M_1 to M_2, the LM curve rotates from $LM(M_1/P_1)$ to $LM(M_2/P_1)$.

Given the fixed IS curve, the points **C** and **D** represent equilibrium points of the IS-LM model.

For the price level P_1, **A** is a point on the aggregate demand curve associated with the policy $M = M_1$. **B** is a point on the aggregate demand curve associated with the policy $M = M_2$.

The aggregate demand curve when $M = M_1$ is given by $AD(M_1)$. When $M = M_2$, it is given by $AD(M_2)$.

MONETARY POLICY AND THE AGGREGATE DEMAND CURVE

Figure 12.4 analyzes monetary expansion. Panel B depicts one IS curve and two LM curves. Both LM curves are drawn with the assumption that the price level is equal to P_1; for one LM curve the nominal money supply is M_1, and for the other it is at the higher level of M_2.

First suppose that the money supply is equal to M_1. When the price level equals P_1, at what level of income will the capital markets be in equilibrium and, simultaneously, the

TABLE 12.1

Factors That Shift the Aggregate Demand Curve

	Variables	Direction of Shift
$\Delta P^E / P$	Expected inflation	Right
G	Government expenditure	Right
I	Investment	Right
TR	Transfers	Right
T	Taxes	Left
M	Money supply	Right

quantity of money demanded equal the quantity supplied? To answer this question, we must draw the LM curve on panel B that corresponds to the nominal money supply M_1 and the price level P_1: $LM(M_1/P_1)$. The LM curve $LM(M_1/P_1)$ crosses the IS curve at point **C** and results in an IS-LM equilibrium with income Y_1. Now trace this level of income up to panel A to find a point on the aggregate demand curve, $AD(M_1)$. To find additional points on the same aggregate demand curve, we repeat the exercise for different price levels using the same nominal money supply, M_1.

At a greater quantity of money, M_2, there is a different aggregate demand curve, $AD(M_2)$, which is consistently to the right of the curve $AD(M_1)$. We must conduct a similar exercise to find a point on this curve. Once again we begin on panel A with the price level P_1; but when the money supply equals M_2, the LM curve on panel B is now given by $LM(M_2/P_1)$. This LM curve is farther to the right of the LM curve $LM(M_1/P_1)$ because the nominal quantity of money is greater. It follows that the IS-LM equilibrium, when the money supply is M_2, is at point **D** with income Y_2, a higher level of income than the equilibrium when the money supply is M_1. Tracing Y_2 up onto panel A, we can find point **B** on the curve $AD(M_2)$. We can analyze the effects of any of the other variables that shift the IS or LM curves in a similar way. For example, if taxes fall, the effect would once again be a shift of the aggregate demand curve to the right, since for any given price level the equilibrium value of income on the IS-LM diagram will be greater.

Table 12.1 summarizes the effect of changes in the exogenous variables in the IS-LM model on aggregate demand. With the exception of the price of commodities, the variables that shift the aggregate demand curve are the same variables that shift the IS and LM curves. If government purchases increase, if taxes fall, or if expectations of inflation increase, the IS curve will shift to the right. Because a rightward shift of the IS curve causes the level of income to go up, for every possible value of the price of commodities, the variables that shift the IS curve to the right will also shift the aggregate demand curve to the right. A similar argument applies to an increase in the quantity of money. If the Federal Reserve increases the money supply, the LM curve will shift to the right. Because the quantity of commodities demanded will be higher for any price level, it follows once again that the aggregate demand curve will also shift to the right.

There is one exception to the premise that the variables that shift the IS and LM curves will also shift the aggregate demand curve; that exception is the price level itself. Because the aggregate demand diagram has the price level on the vertical axis, the effect of a change in the price level on aggregate demand is captured by a movement *along* the curve, not by a shift of the aggregate demand curve to the left or right.

AGGREGATE DEMAND AND SUPPLY

We are now ready for a more complete theory of business cycles, one which improves on the theory developed by the classical economists.

WHAT CAUSES BUSINESS CYCLES?

In Figure 12.5, the aggregate demand curve is combined with the short-run and long-run aggregate supply curves from Chapter 8. This figure examines the predictions of the Keynesian model and compares those predictions with data from three historical episodes. Most economists agree that the first epoisode, 1921 through 1939, was a period when business cycles were caused by fluctuations in aggregate demand (panel B). The second episode, from 1970 through 1989 (panel D), was a period when business cycles were caused by fluctuations in aggregate supply. Third, as shown in panel E, business cycles were also caused by aggregate supply fluctuation.

KEYNESIANS, MONETARISTS, AND THE GREAT DEPRESSION

Panel A of Figure 12.5 plots two aggregate demand curves and a short- and long-run aggregate supply curve. Panel A shows the predicted effects of a leftward shift in the aggregate demand curve from AD_1 to AD_2. Many economists believe that this is what happened during the Great Depression, although they disagree about what caused the movement in aggregate demand. Keynes thought that the causal factor was a collapse in the confidence of investors, which reduced demand for investment goods. But Milton Friedman, a leading monetarist, has argued that the Federal Reserve Board was responsible for the drop in demand. Both Keynesians and monetarists agree that the problem was a drop in demand, but they differ as to its cause.

According to the monetarist interpretation of events in the 1920s and 1930s, the Federal Reserve Board is at fault for failing to increase the money supply during the period immediately preceding the Great Depression. Between 1921 and 1929, there was a big increase in investment and a surge in GDP growth, which led to an increase in the demand for liquidity. The effect of failing to increase the money supply in a fast-growing economy is the same as lowering the money supply in an economy that is stagnant. For example, suppose that (beginning at a point like **A** on panel A of Figure 12.5)

FIGURE 12.5

Demand and Supply Shocks

Panel A illustrates the effect of demand shocks in the complete Keynesian model. If most shocks were due to shifts in demand, we would expect the data to show most observations following an upward-sloping supply

Panel A: Effect of Demand Shock

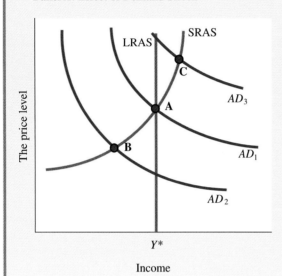

**Panel B: Pre–World War II
Inflation and Growth,
1921–1939**

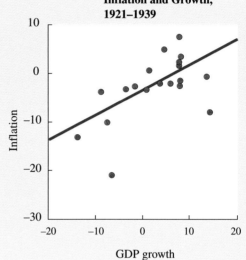

Panel C: Effect of Supply Shock

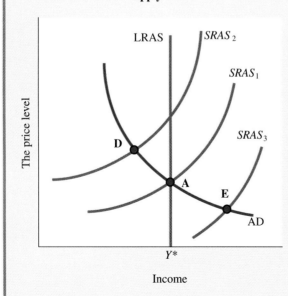

**Panel D: Inflation and Growth
1970–1989**

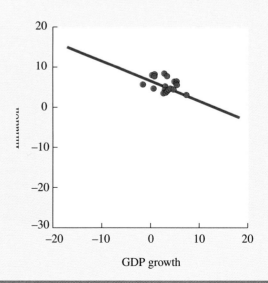

FIGURE 12.5 *(cont.)*

curve. Panel B illustrates that this is indeed what we observed in the period from 1921 through 1939. Panel C shows that temporary supply shocks also cause fluctuations in output. If most shocks in a given period are due to shifts in aggregate supply, we would expect to see most observations in the data following a downward-sloping aggregate demand curve.

Panel D illustrates this observation for the period from 1970 to 1989. An example of a supply shock was the 1973 increase in the price of oil. Since oil is highly complementary with other factors, the aggregate production function shifted downward as oil became scarce and it became more difficult to produce a given quantity of output from U.S. labor and capital.

Panel E illustrates that in the period from 1990 to 2000, supply shocks have again been more important than demand shocks. As in the 1970s and 1980s, the predominant source of shocks over this period caused inflation and growth to move together.

If business cycles are caused by demand shocks, prices should be procyclical; if they are caused by supply shocks, prices should be countercyclical. This analysis suggests that before WWII, most shocks were demand shocks. After the war, most shocks were supply shocks.

Panel F illustrates the monthly price of crude oil since January of 1970. In December of 1973, the price of West Texas Intermediate oil jumped from $4.30 to $12.10 per barrel as producers in OPEC (the Organization of Petroleum Exporting Countries) colluded and began to restrict the quantity that they supply to the market in order to increase their profits. The result was a major recession in Western economies. The price jumped again from $14.85 per barrel in January of 1979 to $39.50 per barrel in April of 1980, and another recession followed.

At the end of 1999, oil prices again began to rise, but so far there has been no recession. It is likely that this episode is induced by an increase in demand for oil rather than by a reduction in supply and, if this is the case, the increase in the oil price will not trigger a recession this time around.

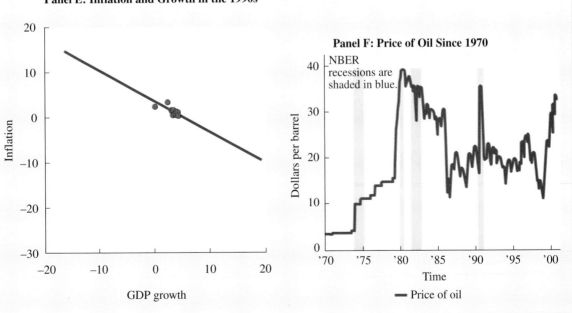

Panel E: Inflation and Growth in the 1990s

Panel F: Price of Oil Since 1970

Y^* shifts to the right. Now the short-run equilibrium is at a point at which short-run aggregate supply intersects aggregate demand, but it is to the left of long-run aggregate supply.

Keynes was aware of the arguments for the monetary causes of the Great Depression, but he rejected these arguments based on the belief that increasing liquidity in 1929 was unlikely to have solved the problem. In the early 1930s, the nominal interest rate on short-term assets was less than a half of a percentage point, and Keynesians argue that the Fed could not have had much effect on aggregate demand by lowering the interest rate further.

PROCYCLICAL AND COUNTERCYCLICAL PRICES

By studying the relation between inflation and growth, and comparing the data with simple models, we can gain insight into the causes of business cycles. Consider first the history of prices and output during the Great Depression. This history, depicted in panel B of Figure 12.5, is explained by a demand shift of the kind shown in panel A of that figure.

According to the demand-shift interpretation, the Great Depression occurred because the aggregate demand curve shifted from AD_1 to AD_2. Because the nominal wage was slow to adjust downward, the economy moved down the short-run aggregate supply curve to point **B**. At **B**, the real wage has risen, firms hire fewer workers, the price level has fallen, and unemployment is above the natural rate. When the United States entered World War II, aggregate demand picked up rapidly, and the aggregate demand curve shifted to the right to AD_3. The new equilibrium was at point **C**. At **C**, the real wage has fallen, firms hire more workers, the price level has increased, and unemployment is below the natural rate. The largest business cycle of this century is well explained by a large downward shift in aggregate demand that reversed when the United States entered World War II; a large demand movement of this kind can explain why prices and output moved in the same direction.

The history of business cycles in the postwar period has been very different, and many economists believe that business cycles over this period have been induced by temporary shocks to aggregate supply. The archetypal example of a supply shock is an increase in the price of oil. Shocks of this nature occurred in 1973, 1979, and again in 1990, and in each case these price increases were accompanied by NBER recessions. Oil-price increases cause domestic technology to produce less output for a given input of labor and capital because many of these technologies rely heavily on oil products, either as a direct input in manufacturing or as an indirect input for transportation.

The theoretical effect of supply shocks on prices and output are depicted in panel C of Figure 12.5. As shown, when the short-run supply curve SRAS shifts from $SRAS_1$ to $SRAS_2$, this movement causes a recession. Similarly, when the supply curve shifts to $SRAS_3$, the result is a boom. Notice that if business cycles are mainly caused by supply shocks, the price level should be *countercyclical,* because the economy is swinging back and forth along a downward-sloping aggregate supply curve. But from panel A, we saw that if most shocks are caused by shifts in aggregate demand then prices should be procyclical.

Panels B, D, and E of Figure 12.5 illustrate U.S. data in the pre– and post–World War II eras. Notice that from 1921 to 1939, most business cycles were due to demand swings, but in the postwar period supply moved more than demand. In the two periods 1970–1989 and 1990–2000, three out of four recessions have been associated with large increases in the price of oil. The oil price is graphed in panel F, along with the NBER recessions since 1970.

Could the price of oil once again trigger a recession? In December of 1999, the oil price jumped substantially from $12 per barrel in February of 1999 to $33 per barrel in October of 2000, and it is quite possible that this increase will again cause a sharp slowdown in the U.S. economy. It is also possible that the economy has learned to adapt to oil shocks; many industries have turned to technologies that are less dependent on oil. If this is the case, then the effect of fossil fuels on our economy may be different now than in previous episodes.

COULD THE GREAT DEPRESSION HAPPEN AGAIN?

If we accept the Keynesian view of business cycles, it seems apparent that government can intervene to reduce the magnitude of economic fluctuations. Indeed, a major theme of Keynes' book, *The General Theory of Employment, Interest and Money,* was that government can and should manage aggregate demand to prevent major recessions. The idea that government is responsible for maintaining a high and stable level of employment is directly attributable to Keynes, and it became the dominant theme of postwar economic policy. How successful was this idea?

A close comparison of panel B with panels D and E in Figure 12.5 reveals an interesting fact: The magnitude of business cycles has been much lower in the postwar period than in the period between the wars. One optimistic explanation for this is that we are doing a better job of managing the economy in the postwar period as a direct result of the influence of Keynesian demand management. The Federal Reserve learned important lessons from the Great Depression, and it is unlikely to allow the banking system to collapse as it did in the early 1930s. Box 12.1 contains a summary of this viewpoint with comments from Gary Stern, president of the Federal Reserve Bank of Minnesota.[1]

THE GOVERNMENT'S ROLE IN STABILIZING BUSINESS CYCLES

It seems clear that the government can intervene in the economy by changing fiscal and monetary policies. Whether interventions reduce or exacerbate economic fluctuations is a much more contentious issue. How would economic stabilization work? First, the government must recognize that the economy is in recession. Because economic statistics are collected and compiled over a relatively long period of time, this in itself is no easy task. Preliminary estimates of GDP in a given quarter are, at best, guesses, and they are often still being revised as much as three or four years after the date for which they were made. Once it has been supposed that the economy really is in recession, the government must then act to stimulate aggregate demand. Changing expenditures or taxes could take a year or more

---

1.   A second, less-optimistic view of the stability of the postwar period has been put forth by Christina Romer of the University of California at Berkeley. By reconstructing the postwar data using the prewar methods, Romer produced a comparable data series for the entire period. Using these data, she argues that part of the "apparent" improvement in stability is an illusion created by more accurate data-measuring methods.

BOX 12.1

A CLOSER LOOK
Could the Great Depression Happen Again?

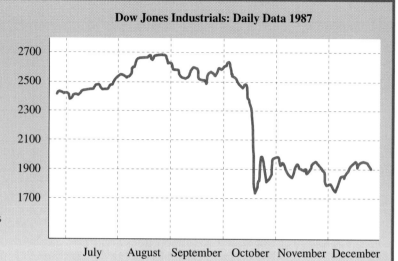

Dow Jones Industrials: Daily Data 1987

In October of 1987, the Dow Jones Index, a leading measure of stock market values, fell by 20% in a single day. This drop in value was comparable to the stock market crash in 1929 that preceded the Great Depression, and it left many analysts wondering: Could the Great Depression happen again?

In 1987, the answer was "No." Although there was a major drop in the value of the stock market, this was *not* followed by a major recession. What was the difference between 1987 and 1929?

Gary H. Stern, president of the Federal Reserve Bank of Minneapolis, identifies four lessons for policy management that we learned from the 1929 experience, lessons which may have contributed to our successful management of the 1987 episode. These include:

1. maintaining the stability of the banking system;
2. supporting normal credit extension practices and smoothly functioning financial markets;
3. ensuring adequate growth of the money supply; and
4. sustaining and enhancing international trade.

You can read Gary Stern's article, "Achieving Economic Stability: Lessons From the Crash of 1929" at **http://www.woodrow. mpls.frb.fed.us/** see: about the Minneapolis Fed, speeches by Gary H. Stern, Annual Report essays. As president of one of the 12 regional Feds, Gary Stern actively participates in the creation of U.S. monetary policy, and his views on the role of demand management are guided by practical experience.

---

to get through the Legislature. If the Federal Reserve System stimulates demand by increasing the money supply and lowering the interest rate, there may again be a long and unpredictable lag before the private sector responds. Advocates of stabilization policy argue that these lags are unimportant, and that the government can and should act to maintain a high and stable level of aggregate demand. Critics argue that trying to stabilize the economy is a hopeless task, and the best thing the government can do is refrain from adding additional noise to the economic system by constantly changing policy.

A second, more subtle argument against active economic stabilization is based on the idea that expectations are not exogenous, as was assumed in this chapter. In modern equilibrium theories, expectations are determined rationally as part of the behavior of households and firms in an economic equilibrium. Whereas the models studied so far have been static, rational-expectation theories are explicitly dynamic; that is, they explicitly account for the passing of time. Rational-expectation theories lead to conclusions that are different from the classical or Keynesian models because households and firms can take actions today that depend on beliefs about the future. The fact that beliefs enter into economic decisions in nontrivial ways has many implications that we are only now beginning to understand. In Chapter 18, we study the theory of rational expectations and how intertemporal equilibrium theory has influenced the debates over government's role in managing the economy.

CONCLUSION

The real interest rate is equal to the nominal interest rate minus expected inflation. Investment depends on the real interest rate; saving depends on the real interest rate and on income. The interest rate that equates saving and investment is different for different levels of income, and the schedule of values of income and the interest rate for which saving equals investment is called the IS curve. The IS curve slopes downward because when the interest rate falls, firms want to invest more. To restore equilibrium in the capital market, income must also be increased so that saving and investment are once again equal. The position of the IS curve is shifted by expected inflation, government purchases, taxes, and transfer payments. If government purchases or transfers increase, if taxes fall, or if expected inflation increases, the IS curve shifts to the right.

An IS-LM equilibrium is a level of income and an interest rate for which the capital market is in equilibrium and the quantity of money demanded equals the quantity supplied. It occurs at the point at which the IS and LM curves intersect. Because the position of the LM curve depends on the price level, there is a different IS-LM equilibrium for every value of P. As the price level falls, the LM curve shifts to the right and equilibrium income increases. The schedule of all pairs of price levels and equilibrium income levels is the Keynesian aggregate demand curve. The position of the Keynesian aggregate demand curve depends on government purchases, transfers, taxes, expected inflation, and the nominal money supply.

The complete Keynesian theory explains changes in income and the price level by shifts in aggregate demand and supply. If aggregate demand movements cause most business cycles, then the price level should be procyclical. This is what happened in the prewar period. If supply shocks cause most business cycles, then the price level should be countercyclical. This is what happened in the postwar period. Economists disagree over whether business cycles can or should be stabilized through active government intervention.

KEY TERMS

IS-LM equilibrium   Rational expectations
Keynesian aggregate demand curve

MATHEMATICAL APPENDIX: THE ALGEBRA OF THE KEYNESIAN THEORY OF AGGREGATE DEMAND

This appendix is optional and is intended for those readers who are more comfortable with algebra than with graphs. We derive the equation of the IS curve and the aggregate demand curve under some simple assumptions about saving and investment. Assume that the saving function can be represented by the equation:

12.1
$$S = s(Y + TR - T)$$

The notation $s(Y + TR - T)$ means s (a number between zero and one) multiplied by disposable income. This way of writing the saving schedule assumes that saving is a constant fraction of disposable income, $(Y + TR - T)$, and that it does not depend on the interest rate. The way that saving depends on disposable income is captured by the single parameter s. We call this parameter the *marginal propensity to save*. The assumption that saving does not depend on the interest rate means that the graph of the saving function, in this case, would be a vertical line.

The saving function represents the money that households are willing to lend to borrowers when the real interest rate is $i - \Delta P^E/P$. The other side of the capital market is represented by the investment schedule plus the demand for funds by government; an amount that is equal to the budget deficit. We refer to the net demand for funds by firms and government as the $I + D$ schedule, and we model the $I + D$ schedule with the equation:

12.2
$$I + D = \left[\overline{I} - e\left(i - \frac{\Delta P^E}{P} \right) \right] + (G + TR - T)$$

Here we assume that the investment function $I(i - \Delta P^E/P)$ depends on two parameters, $\overline{I}$ and e. The parameter $\overline{I}$ is the amount of investment that is independent of the interest rate, and the parameter e is the slope of the investment function.

To derive the equation of the IS curve, we must find the interest rate for which the capital market is in equilibrium for each value of income. The algebra of the IS curve comes from solving the equation

12.3
$$s(Y + TR - T) = \left[\overline{I} - e\left(i - \frac{\Delta P^E}{P} \right) \right] + (G + TR - T)$$

to find i in terms of Y. The left side of Equation 12.3 is saving and the right side is investment plus government borrowing. The expression we seek is then:

12.4
$$i = \frac{\Delta P^E}{P} + \frac{1}{e}[\overline{I} + G + (TR - T)(1 - s)] - \frac{s}{e}Y$$

The slope of the IS curve is represented by the ratio of the parameters $-(s/e)$. This slope will be flat if e is high or if s is small. The intercept of the IS curve with the vertical axis is given by the parameters

$$\frac{\Delta P^E}{P} + \frac{1}{e}[\bar{I} + G + (TR - T)(1 - s)],$$

and the curve will shift if any of these variables (or parameters) changes.

Now let's turn to the aggregate demand curve. Recall that in Chapter 8 we found the equation of the LM curve:

12.5
$$i = \frac{hP}{M}Y$$

Putting together Equations 12.4 and 12.5 and arranging terms, we can find an expression for the aggregate demand curve:

12.6
$$P = \frac{M}{h}\left\{\frac{\dfrac{\Delta P^E}{P} + \dfrac{1}{e}[\bar{I} + G + (TR - T)(1 - s)]}{Y} - \frac{s}{e}\right\}$$

The graph of this equation is a downward-sloping line that approaches $P = \infty$ when $Y = 0$, and that cuts the horizontal axis at

$$Y = \frac{e}{s}\left\{\frac{\Delta P^E}{P} + \frac{1}{e}[\bar{I} + G + (TR - T)(1 - s)]\right\}.$$

QUESTIONS FOR CHAPTER 12

1. Examine the effects of an increase in the expected inflation rate using the IS-LM model. What happens to the aggregate demand curve as a result of this increase in expected inflation?

2. Show that in the IS-LM model, fiscal policy cannot affect output if the LM curve is vertical. Explain how this fact affects the way that fiscal policy alters aggregate demand in the complete Keynesian model. How is your answer related to the classical theory of aggregate demand?

3. Explain, in words, why the AD curve slopes downward. Why does an increase in the money supply shift the AD curve? Trace out the economic mechanism that causes this shift.

4. How are the factors that shift the aggregate demand curve in the Keynesian model different from the factors that shift the aggregate demand in the classical quantity theory? Explain in detail.

5. What factors affect the slope of the aggregate demand curve? Explain in particular how the slope of the aggregate demand curve would change if investment became more sensitive to the interest rate. Contrast two cases, one in which a 1% increase in the interest rate leads to a 1% drop in investment (all other things held constant), and a second case in which a 1% increase in the interest rate leads to a 2% drop.

6. What did Keynes mean by *animal spirits?* Using IS-LM and AD-AS graphs, illustrate how animal spirits can be the cause of business cycles.

7. If business cycles are created by changes in aggregate demand, are prices procyclical or countercyclical? How did prices behave in the United States during the Great Depression? Does your answer provide an indication as to the cause of the Great Depression?

8. Were prices procyclical or countercyclical during the 1970s? During the 1990s? What does this suggest about the source of business cycles during these periods of time?

9. Between the spring of 1990 and the spring 1991, interest rates in the United States dropped by nearly 2 percentage points, but output rose at the same time. How would you explain this? Use a graph of the IS-LM model to illustrate.

10. Compare and contrast the Keynesian explanation of the Great Depression with the monetarist explanation. What policy solution did each propose to get the economy out of the depression?

11. Explain *Keynesian aggregate demand management.* Under what circumstances should the government attempt to stimulate the economy? How?

12. What is the argument for government intervention in order to stabilize business cycles? What is the argument against government intervention?

13. How do you think a central bank should respond to a negative supply shock within an economy if the central bank is concerned about stabilizing output? Use an AD-AS graph to illustrate the effects of your proposed policy. Do you see any potential negative side-effects to the policy that you recommend?

14. The following table provides data on GDP, the price level, and nominal interest rates for an economy. In your opinion, what is the likely source of the changes in GDP? Justify your answer, being as specific as possible. If you were to recommend a fiscal or monetary policy, what would it be? Why?

Year	GDP	Price level	Nominal interest rate
1996	150	100	6.5%
1997	142	80	5.6%
1998	140	75	6.0%
1999	128	72	4.7%
2000	111	61	3.1%

15. Consider the following economy.

$C = 100 + 0.8(Y - T)$
$I = 50 - 25i$
$G = T = 50$
$M^S = 400$
$M^d = Y - 100i$
$P = 2$

a. Calculate the IS and LM curves. Briefly explain the intuition as to why they are upward or downward sloping.

b. Calculate the equilibrium levels of output and the interest rate, Y and i.

c. Suppose that the central bank increases the money supply from 400 to 500. Calculate what happens to the equilibrium values of Y and i. Provide a graph to support your answer.

16. Consider the following economy.

$C = 400 + 0.75(Y - T)$
$I = 400 - 20i$
$G = 300$
$T = 400$
$M^S = 1,000$
$$\frac{M^d}{P} = 0.25Y - 10i$$
$P = 2$

a. Calculate the IS and LM curves. Briefly explain the intuition as to why they are upward or downward sloping.

b. Calculate the equilibrium levels of output and the interest rate, Y and i.

c. Suppose the government decides to eliminate the budget surplus by either: i. a tax cut of 100; or (ii). an increase in government spending of 100. What happens to output in each case? Which alternative will result in the greater change in output? Provide some reasoning to justify your calculations.

17. Read the article by Gary Stern at **http://woodrow.mpls.frb.fed.us/pubs/ar/ar1987.html** and write a short essay summarizing his main arguments.

CHAPTER 13

THE OPEN ECONOMY

INTRODUCTION

Monetary policy in the world economy has operated under two systems: fixed exchange rates and floating exchange rates. Under a fixed-rate system, the rate at which the currency of each country can be exchanged with every other currency is fixed. From 1948 through 1973, the world operated under a fixed exchange rate system; subsequently the world switched to a floating exchange rate regime. Under floating exchange rates (our current system), the relative price of one country's money fluctuates with the relative price of another country's money on a daily basis.

FIXED AND FLEXIBLE EXCHANGE RATES

EXCHANGE RATE REGIMES

Money is a commodity that is widely accepted in exchange; if there were a single world money, the topic of international trade would be relatively easy. However, every country in the world uses different currency, and the relative prices of international currencies change from one day to the next. The rate at which one currency trades for another is called an **exchange rate.**

TABLE 13.1

Exchange Rates on December 1, 2000, in Currency Units per Dollar

Country	Currency	Exchange Rate
Canada	Dollar	1.545800
Germany	Deutsche mark	2.226580
France	Franc	7.467630
Italy	Lira	2,204.310000
European Monetary Union	Euro	1.138430
Japan	Yen	111.220000
United Kingdom	Pound	0.693866

Table 13.1 lists the exchange rates for eight currencies on December 1, 2000. On that day, one dollar would buy 2,204.31 Italian lira, but it would only buy 2.22658 deutsche marks.

Before World War II, most currencies were convertible to gold; therefore, currency value was set at a fixed rate. At an important international conference held at Bretton Woods, New Hampshire, in 1944, representatives from the leading countries of the world met to discuss the postwar international economic order. The **Bretton Woods conference** set up a new system in which the United States fixed the price of the dollar in terms of gold and guaranteed to buy or sell dollars at this fixed rate. All of the other countries in the world fixed their exchange rates to the U.S. dollar. Under the Bretton Woods system, the rates at which world currencies are exchanged for dollars could be altered periodically. Called the "gold exchange standard," this resulted in a 20-year period of relatively stable exchange rates. At the same conference, the **International Monetary Fund** (IMF) was created to monitor the arrangement and to act as a kind of world central bank. The period from 1948 to 1973 was a period of **fixed exchange rates** because it was possible, during this period, to trade international currencies with a fair degree of predictability of their future value.

The fixed exchange rate system works via the active intervention of the participating nations' central banks. Each central bank guarantees to buy or sell its own domestic currency at a fixed rate. In order to intervene in the markets this way, the central banks hold reserves of foreign exchange, and they sell these reserves if there is an excess supply of the domestic currency in the private markets. If there is an excess demand for the domestic currency, the central bank buys foreign currency, thereby increasing its reserves. For this system to operate effectively, the demands and supplies of the private market have to average out to zero over time. In practice, however, some countries found that their reserves of foreign currency became seriously depleted, and they no longer had enough for-

WEBWATCH

Exchange Rates on the Web

How many Canadian dollars can you exchange today for $100 U.S.? How many Saudi Arabian riyals? On Saturday January 1, 2000, $100 would buy 375.080 Saudi Arabian riyals. You can check out the current exchange rates yourself at the Universal Currency Converter on the Web at http://www.xe.net.

eign currency to maintain the official exchange rate. These countries engaged in **devaluation** of their currencies; that is, they increased the domestic currency price of foreign exchange (lowering the foreign price of the currency), thereby making it cheaper for foreigners to buy domestic goods and increasing the demand for the domestic currency.

The fixed exchange rate system became increasingly unworkable as different countries pursued different monetary policies. Some countries, (e.g., France and the United Kingdom) expanded their domestic money supplies relatively rapidly, and other countries (e.g., Germany and Japan) kept strict control over monetary growth. Because the exchange rate is the rate at which one money exchanges for another, all other things being equal, a large increase in the quantity of one country's currency over another's makes that currency relatively less scarce, and its market price falls. This is what happened to the currencies of France and the United Kingdom; both countries were forced to devalue their currencies (France in 1956 and the United Kingdom in 1965). Eventually, the attempts of different countries to follow different monetary policies led to the collapse of the system. In 1973, the fixed exchange rate system was finally abandoned in favor of **floating exchange rates,** a system in which the demands and supplies of each currency in the free market determine the rate at which one currency trades for another.

Because the U.S. dollar is widely used as an international medium of exchange, it is common to quote prices in terms of the dollar. In the United States, we quote exchange rates in terms of the number of foreign currency units that can be bought for a dollar. Using e to represent the number of foreign currency units per dollar, we can discuss exchange-rate movements four ways. In a fixed exchange rate system, movements in the exchange rate were relatively infrequent. If e increased in this system, the movement was called a devaluation of the foreign currency (devaluation because the dollar would buy more foreign currency, so the currency was relatively less expensive). Similarly, if a country were to reduce e under the fixed-rate system, this was called a **revaluation** because Americans would be able to buy less of the foreign currency for a dollar, implying that the foreign currency had become more expensive. Under a floating exchange rate regime, currency movements occur on a daily basis. In this case, if e increases it is called a **depreciation** of the currency, and if e decreases it is called an **appreciation** of the currency. These terms are summarized in Table 13.2 on page 284.

Figure 13.1 on page 284 illustrates the effect of the move from fixed to flexible exchange rates. It plots the exchange rates of the **Group of Seven** (G7) industrialized nations.

TABLE 13.2

Terms Used To Discuss Exchange Rates

Concept		Fixed-Rate Regime	Flexible-Rate Regime
Definition: e is the number of foreign currency units per dollar.	e increases	Foreign currency devalued	Foreign currency depreciates
	e falls	Foreign currency revalued	Foreign currency appreciates

FIGURE 13.1

Exchange Rates of the G7 Industrialized Countries

Before 1973, there were occasional changes in the relative purchasing power of different currencies; but for the most part, exchange rates were relatively stable. Since 1973, exchange rates have been completely determined by market forces. 1950 is normalized to 1.

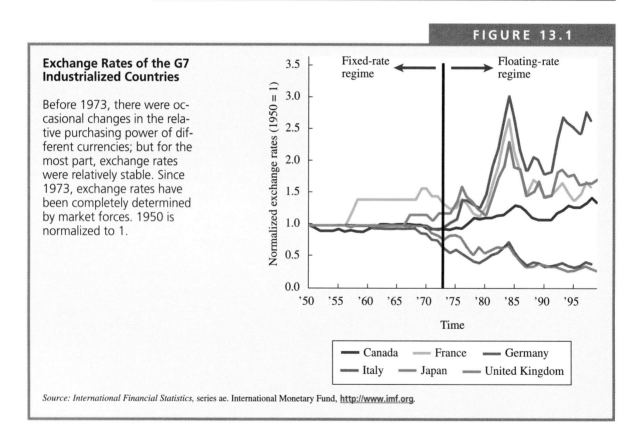

Source: International Financial Statistics, series ae. International Monetary Fund, http://www.imf.org.

The G7 nations are Canada, France, Germany, Italy, Japan, the United Kingdom, and the United States. In Figure 13.1, the exchange rates have been normalized to 1 in 1950. Notice how much more variability there has been in the period of floating rates since 1973 than in the period of fixed rates from 1950 to 1973.

REAL EXCHANGE RATES AND PURCHASING POWER PARITY

One way of enriching the theory of demand and supply so that it takes international trade into account is to think of the goods produced in the world as location specific. For example, a German automobile in New York is a different good from a German automobile in Munich. A simple extension of a model with a single commodity would treat the output of each country as a distinct commodity with its own price.

According to this way of analyzing trade, Americans do not just produce and consume one commodity, they consume American commodities, Japanese commodities, Mexican commodities, and so forth. When the relative price of a foreign commodity changes, the amount of the commodity that Americans purchase also changes. The relative price of a basket of foreign goods, valued in terms of a basket of American goods, is called the **real exchange rate.** Changes in the real exchange rate shift the demand for domestic commodities as Americans substitute into or out of imported goods. When foreign goods are substituted for American goods, a decrease in the price of foreign goods leads to an increase in the percentage of GDP going to imports. If, on the other hand, they complement American goods, a fall in the price of the foreign good could lead to a drop in the share of domestic spending devoted to imports.

Figure 13.2 on page 286 shows what happened to real exchange rates for the G7 countries over the postwar period. Each graph shows the cost of a basket of foreign goods relative to the cost of a basket of American goods. The particular basket of goods in each case is the one that makes up the consumer price index in each country. Because these goods may be different, it doesn't make much sense to compare the values of the real exchange rate in an absolute sense; however, it does make sense to see how these bundles of goods have become relatively more or less expensive over time. The most dramatic feature of the graphs in Figure 13.2 is the big swing in the relative costs of the goods available in different countries. An American tourist in Tokyo, for example, could buy three times as much of the average Japanese consumer basket in 1975 than in 1990; Japan is a lot more expensive for an American tourist than it used to be. Italy, on the other hand, is much cheaper.

The definition of the real exchange rate is given in Equation 13.1. The units of the domestic price index are in dollars per basket of U.S. goods, where the basket of U.S. goods is the bundle that goes into the formation of the consumer price index. The units of P^f, the foreign price index, are foreign currency units per basket of foreign goods. Finally, the nominal exchange rate is measured in foreign currency units per U.S. dollar. Putting all of this together gives us a real exchange rate that measures the number of units of the basket of foreign goods per basket of U.S. goods.

13.1
$$re = e \times \frac{P}{P^f}$$

| **Real exchange rate** | **Nominal exchange rate** | **Ratio of the domestic price index to the foreign price index** |

FIGURE 13.2

Real Exchange Rates for the G7 Countries

This graph compares the relative purchasing power of a given bundle of commodities with an equivalent bundle of commodities in the United States for each of six different countries. The figure shows that relative prices across countries change dramatically over long periods of time. For example, the average American will find that Italian goods were relatively much less expensive in 1999 than they were in 1950; but goods in Japan were much more expensive. When real exchange rates change like this over long periods of time, economists say there is a *failure* of *purchasing power parity*.

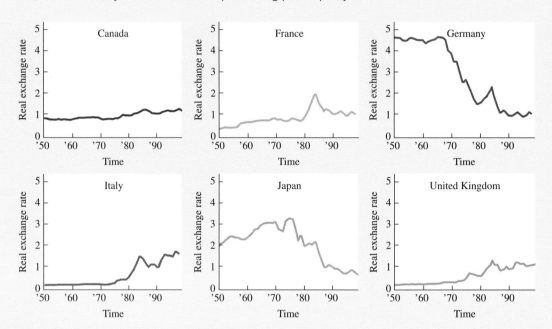

Source: International Financial Statistics, series ae for nominal exchange rates and series 64 for consumer prices. The International Monetary Fund, http://www.imf.org.

Purchasing power parity is the idea that the real exchange rate should be equal to 1 because, so the argument goes, free trade should lead to real prices being equalized everywhere. In its weaker form, people sometimes refer to **relative purchasing power parity,** which means that the relative value of the GDP deflator between different countries should not change systematically over time. Relative purchasing power parity means that the real exchange rate of each country should show no systematic tendency to rise or fall. It is clear from Figure 13.2 that in the real world, real exchange rates move considerably over time. This does not contradict economic theory because there is no reason why different goods should sell at the same price; commodities in different locations are simply different commodities. The fact that a haircut in Lima, Peru, is cheaper than a haircut in New York City, U.S., is of little consolation to a New Yorker, since the haircut in Lima cannot be transported to New York. Even relatively homogenous goods that are easily transported may acquire trademarks that depend on the country of origin. For example, a German automobile may become a prestige item even if a comparable American car is just as good. There is also no reason to expect that the relative prices of different countries' goods should remain stationary over time. In short, used mainly as a benchmark, purchasing power parity is a useful theoretical concept.

NOMINAL EXCHANGE RATES AND INTEREST RATE PARITY

Although the theory of purchasing power parity does not support the data, there is a second relationship called **uncovered interest rate parity** that fares somewhat better.[1] Uncovered interest rate parity means that the rates of return on comparable assets should be equalized throughout the world. If the interest rate in Germany is twice as high as the interest rate in the United States, then Americans can be expected to move their money abroad in search of the higher rate of return.

Looking at Figure 13.3 on page 288, you may think that you should invest your money abroad. The graphs show the differences between the average monthly interest rates on overnight loans in each of the six G7 countries and interest rates in the United States. Italy, for example, looks like a relatively good place to invest money: An investment in Italy has paid on average 6% more than a comparable investment in the United States since 1973. If you had invested in Italy, however, you might have been disappointed, because this analysis misses one significant factor—the possibility that the exchange rate might change. Consider the following two strategies for investing assets:

1. Take $1,000, buy U.S. government bonds on January 1, 1990, and cash them in, with interest, on January 1, 1991. The return from this strategy is equal to the U.S. interest rate, i.
2. Take $1,000 and buy Italian lira on January 1, 1990. Use lira to buy Italian government bonds. Cash the bonds in on January 1, 1991. Convert the lira, with interest, back into U.S. dollars. The return from this strategy is equal to $i^f - \Delta e/e$, where i^f is the Italian interest rate and $\Delta e/e$ is the change in the exchange rate between 1990 and 1991.

In order to assess which strategy is better, we must predict whether the Italian lira will increase or decrease in value. It should be generally true that the interest rate in the domestic country equals the interest rate in the foreign country minus the expected

---

1.   It is possible to conduct statistical tests of the proposition of uncovered interest rate parity; the strict test of the proposition, in fact, fails these formal tests. Economists are not too concerned about these failures because the strict form of the proposition does not allow for the fact that most investors are *risk averse*. In other words, the foreign interest rate can be a little higher than the domestic interest rate when the investment is very risky. An excellent summary of the empirical work on interest rate parity is contained in the article by Kenneth Froot and Richard Thaler, found in *Journal of Economic Perspectives,* Summer 1990.

FIGURE 13.3

Interest Rate Differentials and the U.S. Economy

This figure shows the difference between the foreign interest rate and the U.S. interest rate for each of six different countries from 1960 through 1999. In some years this difference has been greater than 10%. Why do people buy U.S. bonds when they could earn a higher rate of interest in a foreign country? The answer is related to changes in the exchange rate.

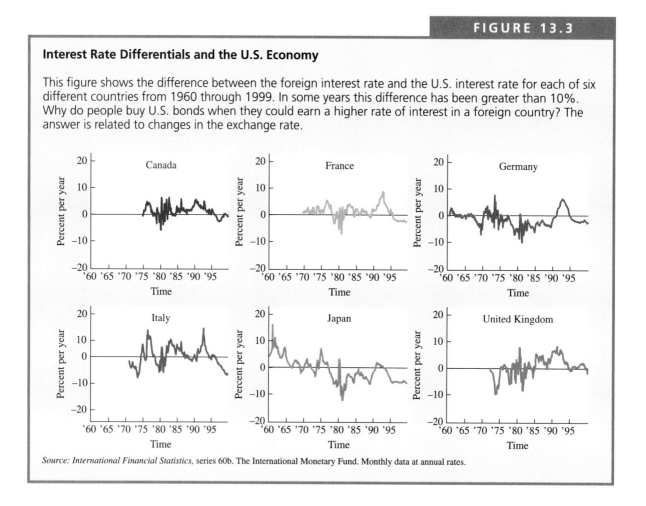

Source: International Financial Statistics, series 60b. The International Monetary Fund. Monthly data at annual rates.

proportional change in the exchange rate; this statement is called uncovered interest rate parity.[2] Equation 13.2 defines uncovered interest rate parity for two countries.

$$\textbf{13.2} \qquad i \quad = \quad i^{\text{f}} \quad - \quad \frac{\Delta e}{e}$$

	Domestic interest rate		Foreign interest rate		Proportional change in the exchange rate

2.   It is possible to earn interest in Italy without *any* exposure to exchange rate risk by arranging the sale of foreign exchange at a future date at a guaranteed price. The market for the sale of foreign currencies at future dates is very well developed, and international companies trade in this market frequently as a way of removing the risk of currency fluctuations. Not surprisingly, there are no differences in international interest rates when currencies are converted using the futures market, and this fact is called **covered interest rate parity.** The proposition stated in Equation 13.2 is called uncovered interest rate parity, to distinguish it from the covered case.

The premise behind uncovered interest rate parity is a powerful concept called the **absence of arbitrage.** Absence of arbitrage means that economists don't expect to see big opportunities available in the real world for individuals; we don't get something for nothing. If such an opportunity existed, people would rush in and exploit the opportunity, thus causing it to disappear. In the case of international currency trades, if the rate of interest is much higher in another country, and if exchange rates are stable, investors will invest their money overseas, thereby bidding up the domestic interest rate and bidding down the foreign interest rate until the two rates are equalized.

Uncovered interest rate parity implies that the difference between interest rates on comparable assets, adjusted for exchange rate changes, should average zero. Figure 13.4 illustrates these adjusted differentials for the same six G7 countries. Notice that there is no obvious tendency for the adjusted interest rate differentials to be either positive or negative over time; the scale of interest rate differentials between countries, adjusted for exchange rate changes, runs from $+200\%$ to -200%. Interest rate differentials are only of the order of 5% to 10% after 1973 because the raw interest rate differentials are dwarfed by exchange rate fluctuations. For example, although Italy paid on average 6% more interest than the United States, currency risk for holding Italian assets can amount to plus or minus 180% to 200%.

The data for Figure 13.4, page 290, is only really meaningful for the floating-rate period, which began in 1973.[3] For example, Japan looks like a good investment over the fixed-rate period because it paid a higher interest rate than the United States and the dollar-yen exchange rate did not change. However, the market for the Japanese yen was not free during this period, and the Japanese government restricted the amount of yen that could be purchased by foreigners and prevented investors from repatriating profits from their Japanese investments. In other words, although there was a potential arbitrage opportunity in the yen, trade restrictions prevented anyone from exploiting this opportunity.

Managing an Open Economy

In 1973, the world economy moved to a flexible exchange rate system. But before 1973, most countries in the world pegged their exchange rates to the U.S. dollar. Because different countries tried to follow conflicting policy objectives, this system proved to be unworkable. We will now look at the economic theory that will allow us to understand why this change occurred.

The Capital Market in a Closed Economy Contrasted with a Small Open Economy

The capital market is the conduit through which the savings of households are channeled to private firms and to government. In a closed economy, borrowing by domestic firms

---

3.   The interest rates used to compute these graphs are for overnight funds in the money market. In the United States, this interest rate is called the *federal funds rate,* and the major borrowers and lenders in this market are commercial banks, some of which need to borrow to meet their reserve requirements. Prior to 1973, the international money market was not as well developed, and in some countries no such market existed.

FIGURE 13.4

Interest Rate Differentials Adjusted for Exchange Rate Changes

This figure shows the differences in returns that are adjusted for changes in the exchange rates. Compare the difference in the scale used on the vertical axis of Figure 13.4 with that of Figure 13.3. The magnitude of the potential gain (or loss) from speculation in foreign currencies is 10 times greater than the differences between foreign and domestic interest rates. Investing in foreign bonds can be *very* risky.

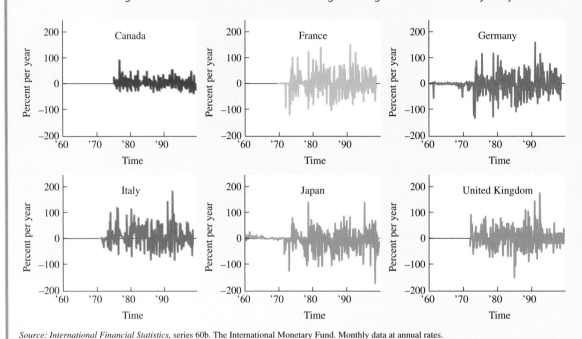

Source: International Financial Statistics, series 60b. The International Monetary Fund. Monthly data at annual rates.

plus borrowing by the domestic government is equal to the saving of domestic households. In an open economy this is no longer true. Instead, the international capital market supplies the excess borrowing by domestic firms plus government over and above the saving of domestic households.

A few economies, like the United States or Japan, are relatively large players in the international financial markets. When the U.S. government borrows on the world markets, the effect may be large enough to alter the world interest rate. But most economies are not that large, and the amount that the residents of these economies borrow or lend is not large enough to influence the interest rate at which other players in the market can trade with each other. When we analyze these small economies, assuming that the real interest rate is determined exogenously in the rest of the world, we say that we are studying a **small open economy.**

How are output, the nominal interest rate, the exchange rate, and the price level determined? To help in our analysis, we will make some assumptions about the beliefs of individuals, about the policy regime that prevails in the present, and about the values of exchange rates and of inflation rates that are expected to prevail in the future. These assumptions are as follows:

1. **Zero expected inflation.** We assume that the inflation rate is zero, and that it is expected to remain equal to zero in the future. This analysis is easily extended to allow for constant expected inflation, but the extension would make our explanation more complicated without adding much to our understanding.

2. **Static exchange rate expectations.** Market participants do not expect the exchange rate to move systematically either up or down. Remember that in free capital markets the domestic interest rate is determined by uncovered interest rate parity. For example, if market participants expect the exchange rate to depreciate, they will demand a higher interest rate in compensation.

Figure 13.5, page 292, contrasts the capital market in a closed economy (panel A) with that of a small open economy (panel B). The downward-sloping line on panels A and B, labeled X^{*D}, is the net domestic demand for capital in the world market. This net demand is denominated in domestic currency units, and it can be either positive or negative. It equals the demand to finance investment capital by firms, I, plus the demand for borrowing by government to finance the deficit, D, minus the supply of capital by domestic households S^*. Since the net demand for capital depends on domestic income, the asterisks on the terms, S^* and X^{*D} are used to remind us that S^* is full-employment saving and X^{*D} is the full-employment demand for capital.

Panel A represents a closed economy. In this case, the supply of capital on the world market is equal to zero and is represented by a vertical line. Panel B represents a small open economy for which domestic residents can borrow any amount at the world interest rate i^f. In this case, the supply of capital on the world market is represented by a horizontal line. Panel B depicts a case in which, at an interest rate of i^f, domestic residents will be net suppliers of capital to the world markets. This is reflected in the fact that the demand for capital is negative and equal to $-X^f$.

IS-LM in an Open Economy

In Chapter 12, we combined the capital market equilibrium condition with asset market equilibrium to determine income and the interest rate in an IS-LM equilibrium. We then allowed for flexible prices and showed how the price level would be determined in the short run and the long run. Now we develop a similar analysis in a small open economy.

To determine the IS curve in a closed economy, we showed that for different values of income there would be a different interest rate for which the capital market is in equilibrium. When income increases, households save more. The increase in saving causes the equilibrium interest rate to fall, and the IS curve slopes downward. In an open economy, it is still true that saving will be higher as income increases. But the interest rate is determined on the world market. For higher values of income, households save more, but these funds flow out of the country and are lent to foreign borrowers on the world capital market. In an open economy, the IS curve is horizontal at the world interest rate of i^f.

FIGURE 13.5

The Capital Market in a Closed Economy and in a Small Open Economy

The following two graphs depict the capital market in a closed economy and an open economy.

Panel A represents the world capital market in a closed economy model. The curve X^{*D} is the domestic economy's net demand for capital from the rest of the world when income equals full-employment income, Y^*. This is equal to domestic demand for investment plus government borrowing minus full-employment domestic saving, S^*.

If domestic borrowers were able to borrow on the world market at the interest rate i_1, the country as a whole (private plus government sector) would choose to supply capital X_1 to the world market. Net demand would be negative.

In a closed economy, borrowing from the rest of the world is impossible. This assumption is represented by the vertical supply of capital $X^S = 0$. A domestic equilibrium occurs when the interest rate equals i^*.

Panel B amends the capital market to consider the case where the country can borrow or lend capital at the world interest rate i^f. This is called a "small open economy" because the world supply of capital is horizontal. This means that the country is not large enough for its demand for capital from the world market to influence the world interest rate.

When the world interest rate is i^f, the domestic economy is a net supplier of capital to the world market. It supplies capital X^f (net demand is equal to $-X^f$).

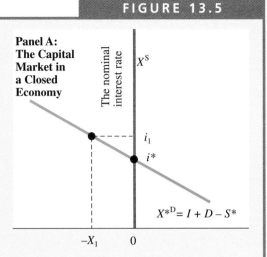

Panel A: **The Capital Market in a Closed Economy**

Capital demanded from and supplied by the world market in domestic currency units

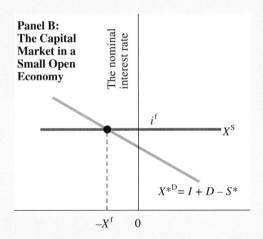

Panel B: **The Capital Market in a Small Open Economy**

Capital demanded from and supplied by the world market in domestic currency units

To determine the LM curve in a small open economy, we must equate the quantity of money demanded to the quantity supplied. This analysis is the same in an open economy as in a closed economy. However, the factors that shift the LM curve need to be expanded to allow for competition in the goods market with foreign producers.

Recall that the position of the LM curve depends on the stock of money and on the price level. In a closed economy, the price level is determined domestically. In an open

WEBWATCH

Robert Mundell Initiates Open Economy Analysis

The 1999 Nobel Prize in economics was awarded to Canadian economist Robert Mundell "for his analysis of monetary and fiscal policy under different exchange rate regimes and his analysis of optimum currency areas."

Mundell was the initiator of the open economy analysis of fiscal and monetary policy. The Nobel committee described his achievements as follows:

> Robert Mundell has established the foundation for the theory, which dominates practical policy considerations of monetary and fiscal policy in open economies. His work on monetary dynamics and optimum currency areas has inspired generations of researchers. Although dating back several decades, Mundell's contributions remain outstanding and constitute the core of teaching in international macroeconomics.
>
> Mundell's research has had such a far-reaching and lasting impact because it combines formal—but still accessible—analysis, intuitive interpretation, and results with immediate policy applications. Above all, Mundell chose his problems with uncommon—almost prophetic—accuracy in terms of predicting the future development of international monetary arrangements and capital markets. Mundell's contributions serve as a superb reminder of the significance of basic research. At a given point in time, academic achievements might appear rather esoteric; not long afterwards, however, they may take on great practical importance.

You can read Mundell's Nobel lecture at http://www.columbia.edu/%7Eram15/nobelLecture.html.

economy, competition implies that movements in the real exchange rate are limited by competition. In our analysis, we will make the extreme assumption that purchasing power parity holds; that is, $P = P^f/e$, so the real exchange rate is 1. We saw in Figure 13.2 that in the real world, the exchange rate for the G7 countries has changed substantially over the past 50 years. For some countries the real exchange rate has appreciated, and for others it has depreciated. The factors that cause the real exchange rate to appreciate or depreciate over long periods of time are the same factors that cause productivity shifts in an individual country. These include the adoption of new technologies, discoveries of natural resources, and other factors that systematically alter the worth of the national output on world markets.

Our assumption of purchasing power parity is important in helping to simplify our analysis because it implies that domestic demand for liquidity is determined by foreign prices and by the exchange rate.

FIGURE 13.6

Restoring Full-Employment Equilibrium in an Open Economy

This figure shows how full-employment equilibrium is restored in an open economy. Beginning at income Y_1, the economy is at over full employment. The domestic price level is equal to the foreign price level divided by the exchange rate. That is, $P = P^f/e$. As the domestic price level rises, one of two things happens. Either:

1. the exchange rate falls, or
2. the money supply falls.

In a flexible exchange rate economy, equilibrium is restored by a depreciation of the domestic exchange rate (e falls).

In a fixed exchange rate economy, equilibrium is achieved by a fall in the money supply (M falls).

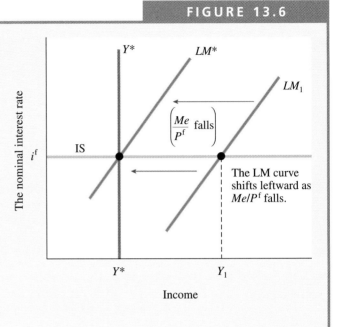

HOW FULL-EMPLOYMENT EQUILIBRIUM IS RESTORED IN AN OPEN ECONOMY

Figure 13.6 illustrates the IS-LM diagram in an open economy. The initial money supply is M, the foreign price level is exogenous and equal to P^f, and the exchange rate is equal to e. In the short run, the economy operates at above full employment. This initial short-run equilibrium is represented by the intersection of LM curve LM_1 with the horizontal IS curve. In this initial short-run situation, the position of the LM curve depends on Me/P^f, since competition with foreign suppliers ensures that the domestic price level is equal to $P = P^f/e_1$.

In the situation depicted in Figure 13.6, the initial price level is too low because when $P = P_1$, the LM curve intersects the IS curve at Y_1, which is to the right of full-employment output Y^*. At Y_1, employment exceeds the natural rate. Competition for workers will cause the wage to be bid up. This will put upward pressure on domestic prices. As the domestic price level begins to rise, net exports fall because domestic goods become more expensive relative to foreign goods. The decrease in the demand for net exports is associated with a decrease in demand for the domestic currency. This occurs because exporters no longer need to convert foreign currency into domestic currency as their export sales decline. There are two possible mechanisms that could restore equilibrium. One is associated with a flexible exchange rate regime, the other with a fixed-rate regime.

RESTORING FULL-EMPLOYMENT EQUILIBRIUM IN A FLEXIBLE EXCHANGE RATE REGIME

First let's study the case of a flexible exchange rate regime. Here, the domestic money supply is fixed at M by the central bank. At the initial equilibrium, Y_1, there is overemployment. This puts upward pressure on the nominal wage and on the price level. As the domestic price level starts to rise, there is a temporary reduction in demand for the domestic currency as exports start to decrease and imports increase. This reduced demand for the domestic currency causes a depreciation of the domestic exchange rate (the relative price of the domestic currency) that restores equilibrium in the market for foreign exchange. A decrease in domestic real balances is achieved through an increase in the price level and a depreciation of the exchange rate.

RESTORING FULL-EMPLOYMENT EQUILIBRIUM IN A FIXED EXCHANGE RATE REGIME

In a fixed exchange rate regime, the central bank gives up control of the money supply. Instead, it stands ready to buy or sell foreign exchange at a fixed price. When the central bank buys an asset, it increases the asset side of its balance sheet. But to pay for the asset, it prints money. For this reason, a central-bank purchase of foreign exchange results in an increase in the money supply. When the central bank sells an asset, the reverse effect is achieved. As the bank sells foreign exchange, it receives domestic currency in exchange. There is now less domestic currency in circulation and the money supply has decreased.

In Figure 13.6, there is overemployment at Y_1 and upward pressure on domestic prices. This causes downward pressure on the exchange rate as exporters find less demand for their more-expensive products in overseas markets. But the central bank does not permit the exchange rate to fall. Instead, it must use its reserves of foreign exchange to buy back domestic currency and support the exchange rate. This action results in a fall in the domestic money supply and a leftward shift in the LM curve. In the case of a fixed exchange rate regime, a fall in real balances is achieved through a reduction in the money supply.

STERILIZATION AND BALANCE OF PAYMENTS CRISES

The nominal exchange rate, like the domestic money supply, is a nominal variable. When a country maintains its exchange rate fixed, we say that it **pegs** its exchange rate. Suppose that a small open economy tries to peg its exchange rate and simultaneously fix the domestic money supply. To see how this might work, suppose that the economy is at full-employment equilibrium with income Y^* and interest rate i^f. This is the long-run situation depicted in Figure 13.6. Now, let the central bank engage in an open-market operation by buying domestic government bonds. This may be possible for a short period of time, even though the central bank is pegging the exchange rate, since the bank holds both domestic government bonds and foreign exchange in its portfolio. The act of selling foreign exchange while buying government bonds is called **sterilization** because it prevents the act of pegging the exchange rate from influencing the domestic money supply.

TABLE 13.3

IS-LM in Closed and Small Open Economies

	Closed Economy	Small Open Economy
IS curve	IS slopes downward	IS is horizontal
LM curve	Position depends on M/P	Position depends on Me/P^f
Effect of output greater than Y^*	The LM shifts left and the price level rises.	The LM shifts left and the domestic exchange rate depreciates (e falls). This also causes the price level to rise.

It seems as if the domestic money supply can be controlled independently of the exchange rate. But this cannot work for long; as the central bank expands the money supply, the LM curve will shift out and to the right. This causes the economy to move to over full employment, and there is upward pressure on prices. As we saw previously, this leads to downward pressure on the exchange rate. To maintain the exchange rate, the central bank must sell its reserves of foreign exchange and buy domestic currency. But now the problem with this strategy is apparent: The central bank has a finite stock of foreign exchange reserves, and when these reserves are exhausted, it loses control of either the domestic money supply or the exchange rate.

When the central bank intervenes in the foreign exchange market to peg the exchange rate, it must either buy or sell assets in the foreign exchange market. If, at the pegged exchange rate, the central bank is a net demander of the domestic currency, we say there is a **balance of payments deficit.** If the central bank is a net supplier of the domestic currency, we say there is a **balance of payments surplus.**

IS-LM COMPARED IN CLOSED AND OPEN ECONOMIES

Table 13.3 compares IS-LM analysis in an open economy with that of a closed economy. In the closed economy, the IS curve slopes downward; in the small open economy, it is horizontal. In the both economies, the position of the LM curve depends on real balances, and if output exceeds full-employment output, the LM curve shifts to the left. In the closed economy, this happens as excess demand for labor causes the wage and the price level to increase. This also happens in the small open economy with flexible exchange rates, and in this case, the increase in the domestic price level is accompanied by a depreciation of the domestic currency. In the open economy with fixed exchange rates, the leftward shift of the LM curve is caused by a reduction in the domestic money supply as the central bank sells foreign exchange reserves.

In sum, the exchange rate or the money supply in an open economy adjusts until the LM curve intersects the horizontal IS curve at full-employment output. The interest rate is given by the world rate i^f, and at full-employment equilibrium the country can be either a borrower or a lender in the world capital market.

THE COLLAPSE OF BRETTON WOODS

We can use the analysis of borrowing and lending in an open economy to understand the history of the world financial system since 1948. When the Bretton Woods system was put in place at the end of World War II, each country in the world agreed to peg its exchange rate to the U.S. dollar at a fixed rate. The system allowed for occasional devaluation or revaluation to correct long-term imbalance, but this possibility was envisaged as rare. At the time of the system's inception, the International Monetary Fund was created to monitor the international monetary system and to provide emergency credit to countries experiencing balance-of-payment problems.

In a fixed exchange rate system with free capital markets, domestic borrowers and lenders can trade in world markets without fear of exchange-rate risk. If the central bank tries to peg an interest rate that is lower than the world rate, domestic lenders will put all of their money in foreign bonds. If the bank tries to raise the rate above the world rate, borrowers will turn to the world capital markets. The central bank can intervene in the market by pegging the exchange rate, but it cannot simultaneously pick the interest rate.

There is one exception to the central banks' freedom to choose the interest rate, and it is an important one. Under the Bretton Woods agreement, exchange rates were pegged not to gold, but to the U.S. dollar. This arrangement gave the United States the ability to pursue an independent monetary policy, since it could rely on other countries to maintain the exchange-rate agreement. In a fixed exchange rate system, one country can pursue an independent interest rate policy, and in the postwar era from 1944 through 1973, that country was the United States.

The balance of payments in a fixed exchange rate world is the change in the central bank's reserves as a consequence of its interventions in the foreign exchange markets in order to maintain the value of its currency. Under the Bretton Woods system, domestic monetary policies conflicted with the balance of payments of many countries in the world. This conflict arose because countries agreed to peg their exchange rates under Bretton Woods, but they did not agree to coordinate their monetary policies. Some countries, such as Japan and Germany, expanded their money supplies relatively slowly. Other countries, such as Italy and France, chose rapid monetary expansion in an effort to stimulate domestic employment. In the long run, forces that move the economy toward the natural rate of unemployment work by causing the rate of inflation to be equated with the rate of monetary expansion. It follows that countries with rapid money growth were effectively choosing high inflation rates; countries with slow money growth were choosing low inflation rates.

The fact that countries choose different inflation rates is not a problem in a flexible exchange rate world. But in a fixed exchange rate world, changes in the purchasing power of different currencies are directly translated into changes in the exchange rate. In practice, countries like Germany and Japan that ran nonexpansionary monetary policies managed to amass large foreign exchange reserves, and there was pressure on their currencies to revalue. Countries like France and the United Kingdom that ran expansionary monetary policies were forced to borrow repeatedly to replenish their exchange reserves, and eventually they were forced to devalue their currencies. The culmination of this process was the collapse of the Bretton Woods agreement in 1973 and the move to a system of flexible exchange rates.

Long-Run Equilibrium in a Flexible Exchange Rate System

In a flexible exchange rate regime, it becomes possible for each central bank to pursue an independent monetary policy without generating a crisis in balance of payments. If a central bank chooses to give up control over the exchange rate, it *can* set the interest rate. However, this possibility in itself creates uncertainty in those businesses involved in international trade because they are aware that the monetary policy of each central bank will ultimately determine the exchange rate. For example, if the central bank of Italy decides to set a higher rate of interest than the central bank of the United Kingdom, the lira must depreciate relative to the pound over time. If this were not the case, world investors would invest in Italy. In the real world, currency movements in pursuit of perceived arbitrage opportunities are substantial, and international investors are responsible for moving roughly $430 billion *per day* from one country to another, about 20 times the daily value of the U.S. GDP![4]

Uncovered interest rate parity suggests that exchange rates should be determined by expected future policy changes. For example, suppose that you lived in a world with absolutely no uncertainty whatsoever, and you knew that the interest rate in Italy would forever be 6% higher than the interest rate in the United States. This world would have an equilibrium in which the lira depreciated by 6% per year to compensate investors for the differences in international rates of interest. But what if you were unsure about future policy actions by the Italian central bank? If the Italian interest rate were to change, the exchange rate would have to change to reflect the new future path of depreciation. This uncertainty about the value of the currency is responsible for the wild swings in exchange rates that have occurred since the move to a flexible-rate system. The Asian financial crisis was the most recent example of the problems that can occur in a flexible exchange rate system (see Box 13.1).

In a flexible exchange rate system, domestic governments never experience balance of payments difficulties because the exchange rate is determined by the equality of demand and supply in the capital markets. Instead, the system may lead to wildly fluctuating exchange rates as private agents try to guess the future monetary policies of central banks.

Fixed Versus Flexible Rates

Open-Economy Macroeconomics

Our experiment with a flexible-rate regime is relatively new, and although we have some ideas about how a flexible-rate system works, in many ways we are still learning. Economists,

---

4.   These figures, which are for 1989, are from "Foreign exchange," by Kenneth Froot and Richard Thaler. *Journal of Economic Perspectives,* Summer 1990.

BOX 13.1

FOCUS ON THE FACTS
The Asian Crisis

During the 1980s and the first half of the 1990s, many Asian countries grew at an astonishing rate. These countries included Hong Kong, South Korea, Singapore, Indonesia, and Thailand. Rapid growth in these countries was associated with a very high level of foreign investment. But in 1997, the Asian economies suffered a severe financial crisis.

The crisis began in January of 1997 when Hanbo Steel, a large Korean conglomerate, collapsed under $6 billion in debts. This was the first bankruptcy of a leading Korean conglomerate in a decade. In February of 1997, a leading Thai corporation defaulted on its debts, and panic soon spread throughout the Asian markets. Investors sought to withdraw their funds from Thailand, The Philippines, Korea, and Malaysia, causing huge depreciations of the currencies and financial failures of enormous magnitude.

The magnitude of the recessions in the Asian countries affected by the crisis was similar to that of the Great Depression in Europe and the United States in the 1930s. There is no clear consensus on what caused the Asian crisis, but part of the reason is an opening of the world financial system in recent decades that permits the free movement of capital.

The following perspective on the crisis is drawn from an article by Paul Krugman of Massachusetts Institute of Technology (MIT), **http://web.mit.edu** Search for Krugman.

	Average Growth Rates[1]	
	1980–1996	1997–2000
Hong Kong	6.360588	0.4950
Indonesia	6.433529	−2.6375
Korea	7.800588	1.6500
Malaysia	7.041176	0.9650
The Philippines	2.340588	2.4225
Singapore	7.877647	3.5475
Thailand	7.823529	−1.1075

The problem began with financial intermediaries—institutions whose liabilities were perceived as having an implicit government guarantee, but were essentially unregulated and therefore subject to severe moral hazard problems. The excessive risky lending of these institutions created inflation—not of goods but of asset prices. The overpricing of assets was sustained in part by a sort of circular process, in which the proliferation of risky lending drove up the prices of risky assets, making the financial condition of the intermediaries seem sounder than it was.

This table shows growth rates of GDP in a selection of Asian countries before and after 1997. With the exception of The Philippines, all of these countries experienced very rapid growth in the 1980s and 1990s. In 1997 with the advent of the Asian financial crisis, growth rates fell dramatically.

[1]Data is from the IMF World Economic Outlook, available in spreadsheet form at **http://www.imf.org/external/pubs/ft/weo/1999/02/data/index.htm**.

And then the bubble burst. The mechanism of crisis, I suggest, involved that same circular process in reverse: falling asset prices made the insolvency of intermediaries visible, forcing them to cease operations, leading to further asset deflation. This circularity, in turn, can explain both the remarkable severity of the crisis and the apparent vulnerability of the Asian economies to self-fulfilling crisis—which in turn helps us understand the phenomenon of contagion between economies with few visible economic links.

For a chronology of the crisis and links to a wide range of articles and data sources, see Nouriel Roubini's Web site at the Stern School of Business, **http://www.stern.nyu.edu/globalmacro/**.

though, are fairly certain about the constraints on domestic policies that are implied by a fixed exchange rate system.

LESSON NUMBER 1: THE CENTRAL BANK CANNOT CONTROL THE DOMESTIC INTEREST RATE IF IT WISHES TO MAINTAIN A FIXED EXCHANGE RATE.

In an open economy with fixed exchange rates, the interest rate must be the same in all countries. Since we assume that households and firms are free to invest abroad, and we also assume that the exchange rate is effectively controlled by the central bank, the interest rate available in one country must equal the rate in every other country. If this were not the case, investors would shift their money to the country paying the highest rate of interest, thereby bidding down the high interest rate and bidding up the low one.

There is an important qualification to this lesson. Although it is true that arbitrage will equalize interest rates across countries in a world of perfectly free international capital markets, during the Bretton Woods period, from 1948 through 1973, many governments tried to prevent this kind of arbitrage. Many national governments imposed strict **exchange controls,** that is, limits on the amount of currency that any one individual or firm could exchange at any one point in time.

Figure 13.7 graphs long-term interest rates, the yields on long-term bonds issued by national governments. These bonds represent similar kinds of assets, and in a fixed exchange rate world with open capital markets, we would expect to see their yields equalize. It is clear from the figure that although bond yields were not exactly equalized over the fixed exchange rate period, they did move much closer together than they did after 1973 in the period of flexible exchange rates. The discrepancies between interest rates across countries in the fixed exchange rate period persisted mainly due to the imposition of exchange controls. The fact that these rates did tend to move together in this period, however, suggests that the effectiveness of exchange controls was limited.

LESSON NUMBER 2: THE CENTRAL BANK CANNOT CONTROL THE MONEY SUPPLY IN A FIXED EXCHANGE RATE SYSTEM.

The idea that the interest rate is determined by world economic conditions has important implications for the ability of the central bank to influence its own stock of money.

The collapse of Bretton Woods was not inevitable. It followed from the attempts by each country to follow an independent monetary policy. Instead of borrowing to maintain the exchange rate, countries like France and the United Kingdom could instead have accepted lower rates of monetary expansion and hence lower inflation rates. These countries chose not to pursue these policies (see Chapter 18). Economists draw a distinction between the short run (the period over which prices are fixed and output is determined by the intersection of the IS and LM curves) and the long run (the period over which prices are flexible and output is determined by the vertical aggregate supply curve). The basic problem with a lower monetary growth rate is that, although it will result in less inflation in the long run, in the short run, slowing the rate of monetary growth leads to a recession.

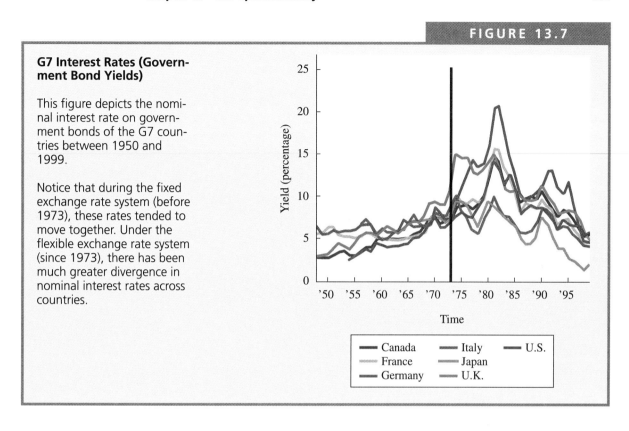

FIGURE 13.7

G7 Interest Rates (Government Bond Yields)

This figure depicts the nominal interest rate on government bonds of the G7 countries between 1950 and 1999.

Notice that during the fixed exchange rate system (before 1973), these rates tended to move together. Under the flexible exchange rate system (since 1973), there has been much greater divergence in nominal interest rates across countries.

Legend:
— Canada   — Italy   — U.S.
— France   — Japan
— Germany — U.K.

LESSON NUMBER 3: THE CENTRAL BANK CANNOT, IN THE LONG RUN, CONTROL INFLATION IN A FIXED EXCHANGE RATE SYSTEM.

A third implication of a fixed-rate system is that, in the long run, a country in a fixed exchange rate system will not be able to control its own rate of inflation. This implication follows from the fact that in the long run, the inflation rate must equal the money growth rate. Since money growth rates are equalized in an open economy with fixed exchange rates, in the long run, inflation rates must also be equalized. In a fixed-rate system, the monetary policies of the countries are very closely tied together. Because any currency can be converted to any other currency at a fixed rate, there is essentially one world money. In a flexible exchange rate system, on the other hand, each country's monetary policies are totally independent.

Figure 13.8 on page 302 graphs the effects of this difference on inflation rates across the G7 countries. In the fixed exchange rate era, inflation rates moved quite closely, with the exception of France in 1956, which coincides with the devaluation of the franc. In the post-1973 world there was a much greater divergence of inflation rates as domestic monetary policies became decoupled from each other and exchange-rate movements absorbed the differences in policy.

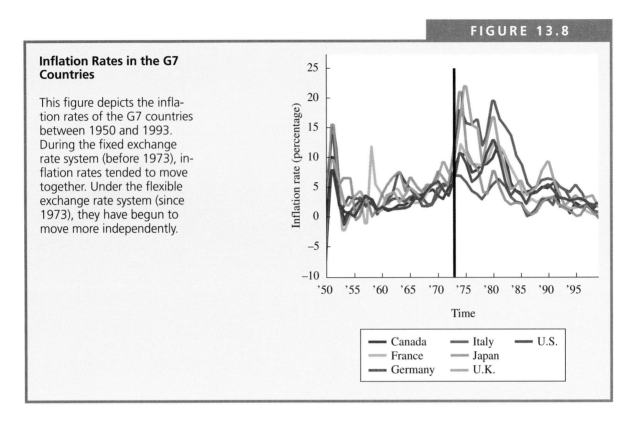

FIGURE 13.8

Inflation Rates in the G7 Countries

This figure depicts the inflation rates of the G7 countries between 1950 and 1993. During the fixed exchange rate system (before 1973), inflation rates tended to move together. Under the flexible exchange rate system (since 1973), they have begun to move more independently.

INFLATION AND THE VIETNAM WAR

The three lessons from international economics are relatively simple, yet they have some important implications. For example, in the late 1970s and early 1980s, most countries experienced a period of high inflation and high interest rates, which was very disruptive to financial markets. High inflation tends to be associated not only with increases in all prices, but also with increases in the volatility of relative prices; nominal prices for different commodities tend to rise in jumps, and these jumps do not all occur together. Economists do not fully understand why this relative price volatility occurs, but they do know that it disrupts the functioning of the price system. The price system serves to coordinate the flow of money from savers to investors. In a time of high inflation, savers are less willing to lend because the increased volatility of prices makes them uncertain about the real rate of return that they can expect.

Because the 1970s' inflation rate increase was almost universal, it is natural to look for a common cause. The most likely cause of the world inflation was that the U.S. government began to dramatically expand borrowing in the late 1960s in order to pay for the Vietnam War. At the time, U.S. monetary policy was directed toward maintaining a low rate of interest. As the quantity of government debt expanded (to pay for the war), a good part of this debt was bought by the Federal Reserve. In other words, the increased government debt was converted into increases in the money supply. This expansion in the U.S. money supply was exported to the rest of the world through the fixed exchange rate system. But foreign central banks were unwilling to accept the continued monetary expansion implied by the fixed-rate system; and this eventually led to the collapse of the fixed exchange rate system in 1973. As is evident from Figure 13.8, the collapse of the fixed exchange rate system came too late to prevent a burst of worldwide inflation that lasted for a decade or more.

MONETARY UNION IN EUROPE

The 15 countries of the European Economic Community (EEC) are currently debating the pros and cons of fixed versus flexible exchange rates. The existing countries of the EEC are Austria, Belgium, Denmark, Finland, France, Germany, Greece, Ireland, Italy, Luxembourg, The Netherlands, Sweden, Portugal, Spain, and the United Kingdom. This list is likely to expand in the next few years with the addition of 12 more countries, mainly from the former soviet bloc. Some politicians within the EEC foresee Europe developing into a single federalist state, much along the lines of the United States, while other politicians would prefer a much looser federation with more powers held by the sovereign member states.

As part of the integration process, a European Parliament has limited (but growing) powers to make laws for the community and to enforce common regulations. In January of 1999, 11 of the 15 EEC countries adopted a common currency, the euro, and at that time they irrevocably fixed their exchange rates. Of the 15 European Union (EU) countries, the United Kingdom, Denmark, and Sweden have not yet entered monetary union, and they retain their own currencies. Greece became a member in January of 2001, bringing the number of monetary member countries to 12.

Prior to the initiation of a common currency, the European Union embarked on a system of fixed exchange rates within the Europe. This system, called the "European Monetary System" (EMS), predated the creation of the euro, and it mimicked Bretton Woods, but on a smaller scale. In the Bretton Woods system, one country (the United States) had the ability to conduct an independent monetary policy. In the EMS, Germany took on this role, and all of the other member countries accepted the monetary policies of the German central bank, the Bundesbank. The collapse of the Berlin wall in 1989 and the subsequent reunification of Germany placed unique demands on German fiscal policy as the government borrowed heavily to pay for reconstruction in the former East Germany. Unlike the U.S. experience of the 1970s, the Bundesbank was not prepared to finance reunification with monetary expansion; in other words, the Bundesbank did not monetize the growth in German government debt. Rising German interest rates resulted as the private sector was forced to absorb the increased German borrowing. These rising interest rates were then transmitted to the rest of Europe through the EMS.

Just as the Bretton Woods system collapsed under increased U.S. borrowing, triggered by the Vietnam war, so too did the EMS in 1991 when Italy and the United Kingdom devalued their currencies and withdrew from the system. The experiences of the EMS and Bretton Woods system suggest one important lesson for the future of Europe: For a system of fixed exchange rates (*a fortiori* for a common currency) to be effective, the member states must run consistent fiscal policies.

INTERNATIONAL ECONOMICS: EUROPE VERSUS NORTH AMERICA

Open-economy macroeconomics has traditionally received much less attention in the United States than in Europe. The reason is simple: In the postwar world order, the United States was much less constrained by international considerations than were other countries. Historically, there are two reasons why. First, the United States is a relatively closed economy. Exports still account for only 15% of GDP, and in the past this figure was much smaller. Second, the United States was the lead country in the postwar monetary order, and the Federal Reserve was free to pursue an independent monetary policy without concern for the exchange rate. But both of these factors are eroding. We live in a world that is becoming increasingly integrated, and trade will inevitably grow as a proportion of GDP worldwide. Increasing trade allows increasing specialization. We are already seeing the effects of this as manufacturing is increasingly shifted to low-wage countries and high-wage countries, such as the United States, specialize in the service, information, and communications industries. As a consequence of increasing trade, we need to develop a trading system that ensures that businesses can buy and sell commodities overseas at prices that are not subject to huge fluctuations. Currently, the world is experimenting with a system of flexible exchange rates, but it is likely that the number of world currencies will fall as blocks of countries that trade frequently with each other, such as the EEC, experiment with single currencies.

CONCLUSION

The exchange rate is defined as the number of foreign currency units that can be bought for a dollar. Given this definition, we can then define appreciation, depreciation, revaluation, and devaluation. When the exchange rate goes up, this movement is called a depreciation of the foreign currency; when the exchange rate goes down, it is called an appreciation of the foreign currency. The same movements in exchange rates in a fixed exchange rate regime are called devaluation and revaluation, respectively.

We also examined the meaning of the terms "real exchange rate" and "absolute" and "relative" purchasing power parity. In absolute purchasing power parity, the real exchange rate is assumed to be the same across different countries. In relative purchasing power parity, real exchange rates are assumed to move in step. In the real world, neither of these assumptions characterizes the data because different countries produce different bundles of commodities, and there have been big differences in relative prices over the past 25 years. Finally, we examined uncovered interest rate parity, which maintains that the rate of interest, adjusted for expected exchange-rate changes, should be the same across different countries.

The world economy behaves very differently under fixed and flexible exchange rate regimes. The main modification that must be made to the domestic IS-LM model in the case of fixed exchange rates is that the interest rate is no longer under the control of the central bank because central-bank policy must be directed toward supporting the exchange rate. If the exchange rate is set at the wrong level, there can be a conflict in the fixed exchange rate world between domestic monetary policies and exchange-rate targets. This tension between conflicting goals led to the collapse of the fixed exchange rate system in 1973. In the case of a flexible exchange rate system, countries can follow independent monetary policies, and world interest rates no longer need to move in step.

Along with introducing and defining some concepts that are important in international economics, this chapter contains one important lesson. For all countries but one, the functioning of domestic macroeconomic policy is very different in a world of fixed exchange rates than it is in a world of flexible exchange rates. The main benefit of a fixed exchange rate system is that it reduces the risk of investing abroad and thereby encourages trade. The main cost is that it removes the ability of a country to pursue independent monetary and fiscal policies. As long as we live in a world of nation states, the tension between the costs and benefits will remain, and, in the absence of a coordinated system of world government, we will likely continue to see many world currencies.

KEY TERMS

Absence of arbitrage	Floating exchange rates
Appreciation	Group of Seven (G7)
Balance of payments deficit	International Money Fund
Bretton Woods conference	Pegs
Balance of payments surplus	Purchasing power parity
Covered interest rate parity	Real exchange rate
Depreciation	Relative purchasing power parity
Devaluation	Revaluation
Exchange controls	Small open economy
Exchange rate	Sterilization
Fixed exchange rates	Uncovered interest rate parity

QUESTIONS FOR CHAPTER 13

1. Explain the difference between the *nominal* and *real exchange rates*. Which one matters when determining the long-run levels of exports and imports within an economy?

2. Briefly explain the difference between depreciation and devaluation. If the lira were to depreciate, would you get more lira for your dollar or less?

3. Define *purchasing power parity*. What does it imply about the long-run level of real exchange rates? Looking at Figure 13.2, does purchasing power parity accurately describe the real world? Why or why not?

4. Define *uncovered interest rate parity*. What does it imply about the relationship between domestic and foreign nominal interest rates? Looking at Figure 13.4, does uncovered interest rate parity accurately describe the real world? Why or why not?

5. Suppose that you find out that the yen has been steadily appreciating against the dollar over the past year and is anticipated to do so in the foreseeable future.

 a. How would this affect you as a tourist visiting Japan?

 b. What would you expect to be true about nominal interest rates in the United States relative to those in Japan? Why?

 c. What should be true about the real exchange rate between the two countries in the long run if purchasing power parity holds?

6. Suppose that the price of a typical bundle of consumer goods is $100 in the United States, and the price of an equivalent bundle of goods in Japan is worth 8,000 yen. If the current exchange rate is 100 yen to the dollar, then what should happen to the dollar under purchasing power parity? Calculate the exchange rate under which purchasing power parity will hold.

7. The following table gives some artificial data for the United States and an imaginary country called Lubania, which has a currency called the lotty. Suppose that in 1951, Lubania had left the Bretton Woods system and decided to pursue a separate, floating exchange rate.

Year	United States		Lubania		(Lotties per $)
	P dollars per U.S. basket	*i*	*P* Lotties per Lubanian basket*	*i**	*e*
1950	100	3	100	3	25
1951	102	3.5	51	3.5	25
1952	104	4	78	7	30
1953	108	4.5	108	9	60

 a. Calculate the real exchange rate for Lubania for each year from 1950 through 1953. What units is it measured in?

 b. Identify years in which depreciations, appreciations, devaluations, or revaluations of the lotty occurred.

 c. Calculate, for each year from 1950 through 1952, the interest differential between Lubanian and U.S. bonds.

 d. Calculate, for each year from 1950 through 1952, the interest differential adjusted for exchange-rate changes. Are there years in which you would have been better off investing in Lubania rather than in the Uniter States?

 e. Would an American tourist be better off in Lubania in 1951 or 1952?

 f. Does purchasing power parity hold between the United States and Lubania?

8. Define *sterilization*. What role do foreign exchange reserves play when a country attempts to sterilize its domestic money supply? Can a central bank perpetually sterilize its money supply in all situations? Explain.

9. Suppose that the United States and Great Britain adopt a fixed nominal exchange rate between their currencies. Inflation in the United States is 1%, and in Britain it is 5%.

   a. What will happen to the real exchange rate between these countries as long as they maintain their fixed exchange rate? Can these countries maintain this fixed exchange rate forever? Explain.

   b. Suppose that these countries give up fixing their exchange rate and allow it to float. What will happen to the nominal and real exchange rates? What should happen to nominal interest rates in these two countries?

10. How is the adjustment process back to the natural rate of unemployment different in a small open economy than it is in a closed economy? Explain for the cases in which:

   a. the economy is above full employment, and

   b. the economy is below full employment.

11. Consider a small open economy that has a zero trade balance. Analyze the effects on output, the trade balance, and the exchange rate of the following events. Provide IS-LM graphs to illustrate.

   a. An increase in the domestic money supply

   b. An increase in the world interest rate

   c. An increase in the foreign price level

12. Consider a small open economy that has a zero trade balance. Suppose that each of the G-7 countries adopts a large tax increase in order to reduce its budget deficit.

   a. What should happen to the real exchange rate and the trade balance over time within this small open economy? Use an IS-LM graph to illustrate.

   b. If this small open economy's goal is to keep its exchange rate fixed, what monetary policy would you recommend? Explain using an IS-LM graph.

13. What are the costs of a fixed exchange rate system? What are its benefits? Do these costs and benefits apply to a monetary union as well?

14. Describe how the Bretton Woods agreement operated. Discuss in detail why this agreement eventually collapsed.

Dynamic Macroeconomics

Part D contains five chapters that are united by their concern with economic dynamics, an explicit theory of how the economy moves from one period to the next. Chapter 14 introduces the idea of a difference equation, the tool that we use to study the movement of economies through time. Chapters 15 and 16 use difference equations to explain economic growth.

In Chapters 17 and 18, you will learn how to extend the neoclassical model to a dynamic setting. Chapter 17 begins by introducing dynamics into the neoclassical model, and in Chapter 18, we will study the theory of *rational expectations*, a theory that underlies modern analyses of the role of monetary policy.

The sixth chapter in Part D, Chapter 19, provides a brief synopsis of what we know and economic challenges of the future.

CHAPTER 14

THE GOVERNMENT BUDGET

INTRODUCTION

In previous chapters, we analyzed how the economy behaves at a given point in time; this is called **static analysis.** Now, **dynamic analysis** is introduced—the study of how the economy behaves at different points in time. Although static analysis can go a long way toward answering questions that interest economists and policymakers, some issues in macroeconomics are explicitly dynamic. In this chapter, we analyze one such issue—the economics of debt and deficits.

Following the publication of *The General Theory*, Keynesian economists advocated a policy of stabilization. They suggested that the government should raise government expenditure when unemployment is high and lower expenditure when unemployment is low. Following World War II, the pursuit of these policies made deficits grow as the government found it politically more expedient to increase spending than to raise taxes. Difference equations enable us to understand how these deficits accumulated and led to a crisis in the early 1990s that caused the government to raise taxes to balance the budget.

DEBT AND DEFICITS

THE RELATIONSHIP OF THE DEBT TO THE DEFICIT

The government's budget equation is an example of a **difference equation,** an equation that shows how a variable changes from one period to the next. We can use this equation to study the connection between the national debt and the government budget deficit.

14.1 B_t = B_{t-1} × $(1 + i)$ + D_t

| Nominal value of new government debt | Nominal value of outstanding government debt | One (1) plus the nominal interest rate | Primary government budget deficit |

Equation 14.1 assumes that government debt is all of one-year maturity.[1] This means that the government issues bonds each year that it repays the following year at the nominal interest rate i. Variables dated in the current year are denoted by the subscript t, and variables from the previous year are denoted by the subscript $t-1$. For example, B_{t-1} represents the nominal value of existing government debt carried over from year $t-1$, and B_t is the new debt issued in year t. For simplicity, we assume that the interest rate is the same every year.

The variable D_t is the **primary deficit.** This is equal to the value of government expenditures plus transfer payments, minus the value of government revenues. It is *not* the same as the deficit reported in the newspapers; the primary deficit excludes the value of interest payments on outstanding debt. Table 14.1 uses data from 1993 and 1999 to illustrate the relationship between the primary and reported deficits. Over this period, the budget went from a $75 billion deficit to a $354 billion surplus.

Table 14.1 lists the values of the components of federal government expenditures and receipts in billions of dollars. The first column shows data from 1993, and the second column shows 1999's data. The primary deficit, D_t, was equal to $75.5 billion in 1993 and –$354.0 billion in 1999. This negative amount for 1999 means that receipts exceeded outlays; the primary budget was in surplus. The **reported deficit** was equal to $274.1 billion in 1993 and –$124.4 billion in 1999. The reported deficit includes interest payments on the outstanding debt: In 1993, these interest payments amounted to $198.7 billion, and in 1999 they were $229.7 billion. Adding interest payments on the debt to the primary deficit leads to the reported deficit. *This* is the deficit that you see reported in the newspapers, but the primary deficit is more useful when studying how the debt accumulates over time.

Figure 14.1 illustrates why policymakers in the mid-1990s were concerned with the debt and the deficit. One obvious feature is that the national debt, represented by the solid

---

1.   The maturity of a bond is the length of time before the principal must be repaid. The government issues debt of many different maturities. Because the complications introduced by allowing for different maturities do not add anything of substance to the problem, we treat the case in this chapter as though all bonds had one-year maturity.

TABLE 14.1

Federal Receipts and Expenditures ($ Billions)

	1993	1999
Receipts	1,197.3	1,874.6
Expenditures including interest on the debt	1,471.5	1,750.2
Expenditures excluding interest on the debt	1,272.8	1,520.5
Interest on the debt	198.7	229.7
Reported deficit (Surplus)	274.1	−124.4
Primary deficit (Surplus)	**75.5**	**−354.1**

FIGURE 14.1

The Debt and the Deficit

The government debt has grown in the postwar period. The blue line is debt, the purple line is the deficit, and the orange line is the deficit excluding interest on the debt. This is called the *primary deficit*.

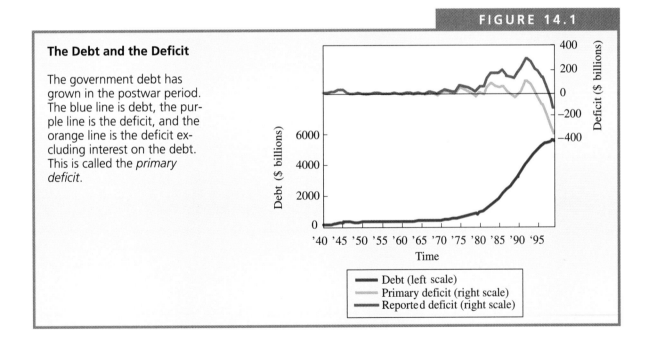

— Debt (left scale)
— Primary deficit (right scale)
— Reported deficit (right scale)

blue line, grew dramatically in the 1980s. A related problem was that from 1940 through 1970, the government's budget was on average approximately balanced; but in the 1980s, the deficit grew significantly. There was a reported deficit (the purple line) every year from 1970 through 1997.

FIGURE 14.2

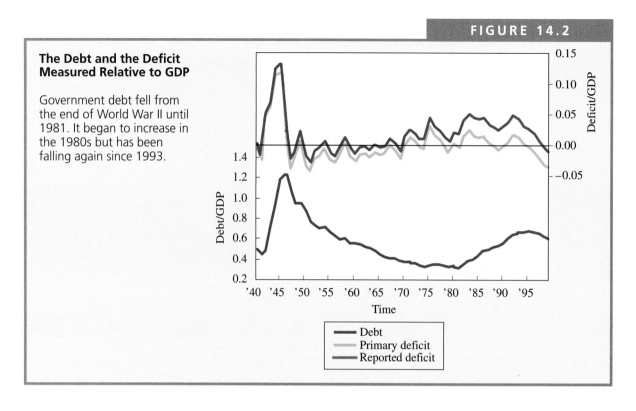

The Debt and the Deficit Measured Relative to GDP

Government debt fell from the end of World War II until 1981. It began to increase in the 1980s but has been falling again since 1993.

Although the growth of the debt in the 1980s was a problem, Figure 14.1 overstates how important this problem really was. Figure 14.2 puts the budget figures in a more appropriate light by presenting the same data measured as a percentage of GDP. To understand why it is appropriate to measure debt and deficits relative to GDP, consider an analogy in which a student leaves college with a credit card bill of $100. Suppose the student allows his credit card bill to grow by 2% per year. Whether or not growing debt of this kind is a problem depends on whether the student's income increases at a sufficient rate to be able to pay the interest on the debt and eventually to repay the debt itself. As long as the student's income grows by more than 2% per year, the ratio of debt to income will actually be shrinking. Just as the student's credit card debt should be measured relative to his ability to repay it, so the national debt should be measured relative to the government's ability to repay. Because the ultimate source of the government's ability to repay is its ability to tax GDP, the appropriate measures of debt and the deficit of the United States are relative to GDP. Although government debt has grown nominally every year, Figure 14.2 shows that it peaked relative to GDP in 1946 at a little over 1.2 GDPs. In 1946, the debt-to-GDP ratio was much higher than it is now, but for a good reason. The government had borrowed heavily to pay for World War II. Because the benefit of paying for a war accrues to future taxpayers as well as to contemporary taxpayers, the use of deficit financing in wartime makes good sense. The situation in the 1980s was different because in this instance the government deficit increased in peacetime.

MODELING THE GROWTH OF GOVERNMENT DEBT

Now we are ready to write a mathematical model based on Equation 14.1 that shows how the national debt is related to the budget deficit. The government budget equation is a difference equation. The feature that distinguishes it from an ordinary algebraic equation is the variable B and its time subscript, t; that is, there is a different value of B for every value of t. The government budget equation tells us how the debt in any given year is related to that year's deficit, the interest rate, and the debt in the previous year. Once we know the deficit, the interest rate, and the initial level of debt, Equation 14.1 allows us to compute the stock of debt in every subsequent year. Finding the values of debt for each subsequent year, given an initial value of debt, involves solving the difference equation.

USING THE GDP AS A UNIT OF MEASUREMENT

Government debt, measured in dollars, has been growing almost every year since the United States began borrowing. But so have all of the other dollar-denominated variables in the U.S. economy. For this reason, Equation 14.1 is not a very useful tool: It cannot tell us whether debt is growing too fast relative to the government's ability to repay. A more useful method is to transform the government budget equation by measuring debt and deficits relative to GDP.

To make our task simpler, we assume that the growth rate of nominal GDP (n), the nominal interest rate (i), and the ratio of the primary deficit to GDP (d) are all constants. Nominal GDP grows because of real growth and inflation, both of which are included in the term n. The assumption that the deficit-to-GDP ratio is constant means that the government fixes the size of its primary deficit as a fraction of GDP. This fixed value equals d. Finally, we assume that the Federal Reserve Board fixes the interest rate at i by buying or selling debt in the open market.

14.2 $$ b_t \quad = \quad d \quad + \quad \frac{(1+i)}{(1+n)} \quad \times \quad b_{t-1} $$

New debt as a fraction of GDP	Deficit as a fraction of GDP	Interest relative to the growth rate	Existing debt as a fraction of GDP

Equation 14.2 rewrites the budget constraint of the government using the GDP as a unit of measurement.[2] The variable b_t is the value of the debt this year as a fraction of this year's GDP, and b_{t-1} is the value of the debt last year relative to last year's GDP. The debt-to-GDP ratio grows for two reasons. First, the government must issue debt to cover a

---

2. Mathematical Note: Equation 14.2 is derived from Equation 14.1 by dividing both sides by nominal GDP at date t. Letting Y_t^N represent nominal GDP, we get the expression

$$ \frac{B_t}{Y_t^N} = \frac{D_t}{Y_t^N} + (1+i)\frac{B_{t-1}}{Y_{t-1}^N}\frac{Y_{t-1}^N}{Y_t^N} $$

We have multiplied and divided the second term on the right-hand side by Y_{t-1}^N because b_{t-1} is defined as B_{t-1}/Y_{t-1}^N. We get Equation 14.2 by recognizing that Y_t^N/Y_{t-1}^N is defined to be $(1+n)$ and D_t/Y_t^N is defined as d.

primary deficit; this is the term d, which measures the ratio of the deficit to GDP. Second, the government must pay interest on existing debt. This is captured by the coefficient $(1 + i)/(1 + n)$.

Suppose that the primary deficit is equal to zero; that is, the government raises exactly enough taxes to cover its expenditure, excluding interest. What will happen to the ratio of debt to GDP? The government must increase debt by a factor of $(1 + i)$ to pay the interest on existing debt. This factor makes the debt-to-GDP ratio increase. But nominal GDP is itself increasing at the rate of $(1 + n)$, thereby expanding the capacity of the government to generate revenue through taxes. This factor makes the debt-to-GDP ratio decrease. The net effect of these two factors is captured by the ratio $(1 + i)/(1 + n)$. If i is greater than n, the debt-to-GDP ratio will grow. If it is smaller than n, the ratio will shrink.

USING GRAPHS TO ANALYZE DIFFERENCE EQUATIONS

A difference equation describes how a variable that changes over time (a **state variable**) depends on its own past value and on a number of parameters. The state variable in Equation 14.2 is the debt-to-GDP ratio, b, and the parameters are d, i, and n. The parameter d represents the intercept, and the compound parameter $(1 + i)/(1 + n)$ is the slope of a graph that plots the value of the debt-to-GDP ratio in year t against the debt-to-GDP ratio in year $t - 1$.

The solution to a difference equation is a list of values for the state variable, one for each date in the future. To compute the solution, we need to know the initial value of the debt-to-GDP ratio. We then iterate Equation 14.2 to generate successive future values of this variable. The solution tells us how big the government's debt-to-GDP ratio will be in every future year. By examining how the solution to the equation changes as we change the deficit or as the interest rate goes up or down, we can predict what policy changes are necessary to bring the debt down to any particular level within a specified number of years. These are exactly the kinds of questions that currently absorb politicians, and in order to answer these questions, it is essential to solve difference equations.

The solution to a difference equation can display very rich behavior. For example, the value of b_t could increase without bound. Alternatively, it could grow for a while and then settle down to a fixed value. Both kinds of behavior are possible, depending on the values of the parameters. A simple way of discovering how a difference equation behaves is to use a diagram that plots state variable values in successive periods on the two axes of a graph. This kind of diagram for the government budget equation is given in Figure 14.3. The blue, upward-sloping line is the graph of the difference equation

$$b_t = d + \frac{(1 + i)}{(1 + n)}b_{t-1}$$

this is the government budget equation. The purple line at $45°$ to the axis is the steady-state condition $b_t = b_{t-1}$, and the bold black line that zigzags back and forth is the solution to the budget equation if the initial debt equals b_0.

The point where the blue and purple lines intersect is called a **steady-state solution.** A steady-state solution is a value of the state variable that satisfies the government budget Equation 14.2 and that is independent of time. These two requirements are summarized in Equation 14.3, which reproduces Equation 14.2 without the subscript t on the variable b.

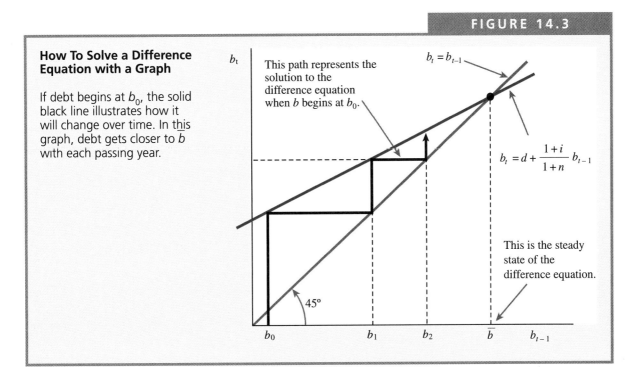

FIGURE 14.3

How To Solve a Difference Equation with a Graph

If debt begins at b_0, the solid black line illustrates how it will change over time. In this graph, debt gets closer to b with each passing year.

This path represents the solution to the difference equation when b begins at b_0.

$b_t = b_{t-1}$

$b_t = d + \dfrac{1+i}{1+n} b_{t-1}$

This is the steady state of the difference equation.

45°

b_0　　　b_1　　b_2　　$\overline{b}$　　b_{t-1}

Rearranging Equation 14.3 leads to an expression for the steady-state solution in terms of the parameters d, i, and n; we refer to the steady state with the symbol $\overline{b}$ and solve for this steady state in Equation 14.4. The steady-state solution is very special because if b ever equals $\overline{b}$, it will never change.

14.3　　　$b = d + \dfrac{(1 + i)}{(1 + n)} b$

> The steady state of the difference equation solves this equation.

14.4　　　$\overline{b} = \dfrac{(1 + n)}{(n - i)} d$

> Collecting terms in b on one side of the equation leads to the formula for the steady state.

The stationary solution in which b begins at $\overline{b}$ and stays there is one possible solution to the difference equation. But what if the variable begins at a value less than b, such as b_0? What will happen to subsequent values of b? The graph in Figure 14.3 can be used to answer this question.

For any given period, let the variable t stand for a specific number. Suppose, for example, that we let t equal 1. We can then plot b_0 on the horizontal axis of the graph and read off the value of b_1 as the point on line $b_1 = d + (1 + i)/(1 + n)b_0$, which is directly above b_0. This process can be repeated for $t = 2$, and we can plot the distance b_1 along the horizontal axis and read the value of b_2 from the line $b_2 = d + (1 + i)/(1 + n)b_1$ in the same way. The first step of the solution gives us b_1 as a point on the vertical axis of the graph. To plot this same distance along the horizontal axis, we use the line $b_t = b_{t-1}$ (the 45° line) to translate the point b_1 from the vertical to the horizontal axis. Zigzagging between the blue line, $b_t = d + (1 + i)/(1 + n)b_{t-1}$, and the purple 45° line, we can trace the complete solution to the difference equation. This solution is represented on the figure as the zigzag black arrow.

STABLE AND UNSTABLE STEADY STATES

One property of steady states is called **stability.** If the steady state of the government budget equation is stable, the deficit is a much less pressing problem than if it is unstable.

Panels A and B of Figure 14.4 graph the solutions to two difference equations. Both are special cases of Equation 14.2. The slope of the difference equation in panel A is a positive number between zero and one: in panel B, it is a positive number greater than one. For both figures, the intercept of the difference equation is the same number, d.

The different values of the slopes of the equations cause the behavior of their solutions to differ. The steady state in panel A is stable, and in panel B it is unstable. To understand why, look at the path of the variable b_t that begins at some positive value b_0. This is represented in panel A as the zigzag arrow that gets increasingly closer to the steady state. Contrast this to the situation in panel B, in which the zigzag arrow moves consistently farther away from the steady state as time progresses: b grows without bound. In panel B, the steady state is unstable.

The fact that d is the same number in panels A and B of Figure 14.4 means that the government is running the same deficit-to-GDP ratio in both cases. The slope of the difference equation is the ratio of one plus the interest rate $(1 + i)$ to one plus the growth rate of nominal GDP $(1 + n)$. In panel A this slope is less than 1.0, which corresponds to a situation in which the interest rate is less than the growth rate. In panel B it is greater than 1.0, which corresponds to a situation in which the interest rate is greater than the growth rate. Later, we will return to these observations as we analyze some economic consequences of stable versus unstable steady states.

SUMMARIZING THE MATHEMATICS OF DIFFERENCE EQUATIONS

Let's recap. We have examined an equation of the form $b_t = d + (1 + i)/(1 + n) b_{t-1}$, where b is the state variable and d, i, and n are parameters. The solution is a list of values for b_t, one for each value of t that satisfies the difference equation. To solve the equation, we need to provide the values of b_t at all future dates for some given value of b at an initial date.

A special kind of solution to the difference equation, the steady-state solution, solves the equation; and that solution is the same at every point in time. This solution is expressed algebraically by the formula

$$\overline{b} = \frac{(1 + n)}{(n - i)}d.$$

FIGURE 14.4

Stable and Unstable Steady States

In a stable steady state, n is greater than i, and the difference equation cuts the 45° line from above. Solutions to the difference equation get closer to the steady state through time.

In an unstable steady state, i is greater than n, and the difference equation cuts the 45° line from below. Solutions to the difference equation get farther from the steady state through time.

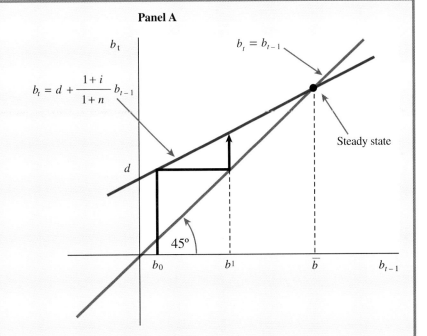

Panel A

$$b_t = d + \frac{1+i}{1+n} b_{t-1}$$

$b_t = b_{t-1}$

Steady state

b_t

d

45°

b_0 b^1 $\bar{b}$ b_{t-1}

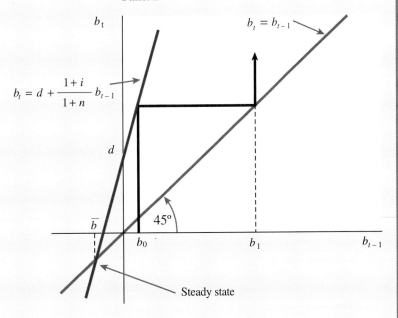

Panel B

b_t

$b_t = b_{t-1}$

$$b_t = d + \frac{1+i}{1+n} b_{t-1}$$

d

$\bar{b}$

45°

b_0 b_1 b_{t-1}

Steady state

If the state variable starts at a steady state, then it will stay there forever. Steady states can be either stable or unstable. If a steady state is stable, the state variable moves closer toward the steady state over time, regardless of where it starts from. If a steady state is unstable, the state variable moves farther away from the steady state for any starting point other than the steady state itself. The difference equation that we use has a stable steady state if the interest rate is less than the growth rate of nominal GDP, and it has an unstable steady state if the interest rate is greater.

THE SUSTAINABILITY OF THE BUDGET DEFICIT

Suppose that we live in an economy in which the nominal interest rate is less than the growth rate of nominal GDP, as opposed to an economy in which the interest rate exceeds the growth rate. The behavior of the debt and the deficit are very different in the two situations.

Figure 14.5 presents data from the postwar-U.S. economy. Notice that in the period from 1940 through 1979, the government was able to borrow at an interest rate that was less than the rate of nominal GDP growth. Although government debt increased every year, the government's income from tax revenues increased at an even faster rate, so the debt relative to GDP decreased. In the 1980s, prior to the 1993 deficit reduction act, the interest rate on short-term Treasury bills often exceeded the growth rate of nominal GDP. During this period, government debt grew at the rate of interest as the government borrowed to pay the principal and interest on existing debt. But its income did not grow as quickly because tax revenues are proportional to GDP and, from 1980 through 1993, the rate of nominal GDP growth was lower than the interest rate.

Figure 14.5 is divided into three time periods that are separated by two key policy events. In October of 1979, there was a change in the stewardship of the nation's central bank as Paul Volcker took over from Arthur Burns. Volcker raised interest rates in an effort to fight inflation, but his action also had dramatic consequences for the fiscal health of the nation. For the first time in decades, the interest rate was higher than the growth rate of nominal GDP. Government debt began to climb as a percentage of GDP until Congress passed the Omnibus Budget Reconciliation Act in 1993, resulting in an increase in the tax rate for high-income individuals and corporations. Following the 1993 legislative changes, the deficit fell substantially as a percentage of GDP. It is also true that since 1993, the interest rate has once more been on average lower than the growth rate of nominal GDP.

Table 14.2 summarizes data on the deficit-to-GDP ratio, the interest rate, and the nominal growth rate for three separate subperiods. In the first period, 1950 to 1979, tax revenues were, on average, slightly higher than primary expenditures, and there was a small primary surplus of 1.2% of GDP (the deficit was negative). The average growth rate of nominal GDP was 7.5%, and the average interest rate on short-term government debt was 4.1%. The average growth rate of nominal GDP exceeded the average rate of interest at which the government could borrow by 3.4 percentage points.

Contrast the situation in the pre-1979 period with the period from 1980 through 1993, after the change in Fed policy but before the Budget Reconciliation Act. In 1981, the Reagan administration began a defense buildup that was associated with a tax cut; this led to

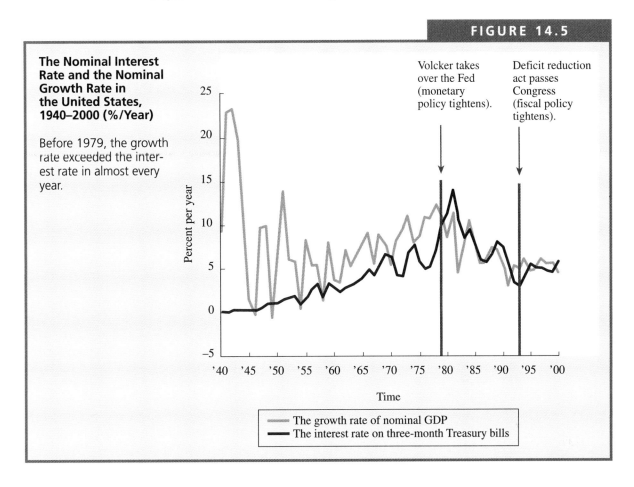

FIGURE 14.5

The Nominal Interest Rate and the Nominal Growth Rate in the United States, 1940–2000 (%/Year)

Before 1979, the growth rate exceeded the interest rate in almost every year.

Volcker takes over the Fed (monetary policy tightens).

Deficit reduction act passes Congress (fiscal policy tightens).

The growth rate of nominal GDP
The interest rate on three-month Treasury bills

an increase in the primary deficit to nearly 2.5% of GDP by 1983. Notice that over this period a primary surplus of 1.2% turned into a primary deficit of 0.7% of GDP. At the same time that the deficit increased, the interest rate on government debt rose from a pre-1979 average of 4.1% to a post-Volcker average of 7.5%. Since Congress passed a tax increase in 1993, the situation looks more like the pre-1979 period. Over this more recent period, the federal government again ran a primary surplus, and once more the growth rate of nominal GDP has exceeded the nominal interest rate.

The figures for d, n, and i are given in the first three rows of Table 14.2. The last row of the table calculates the slope of the difference equation in the periods before and after 1979.

THE BUDGET EQUATION FROM 1946 THROUGH 1979

At the end of World War II, debt was equal to 120% of GDP. For 30 years thereafter, the debt-to-GDP ratio fell steadily. The reduction occurred because the interest rate was lower

TABLE 14.2

U.S. Fiscal Data Since 1950

	Average Value 1950–1979	Average Value 1980–1993	Average Value 1994–1999
d	−1.2%	0.7%	−1.9%
n	7.5%	6.8%	5.5%
i	4.1%	7.5%	4.9%
$(1 + i)/(1 + n)$	0.97	1.01	0.99

than the growth rate. Using Equation 14.4, we can calculate that, if the interest rate and the growth rate had remained unchanged, the economy would eventually have settled into a steady state.

Between 1946 and 1979, the slope of the government budget equation was 0.97, implying that the steady state of the budget equation was stable. During this period, debt declined slowly, and by 1979 it had fallen to 31% of GDP. Figure 14.6 illustrates how a difference equation can be used to describe the decline in debt that occurred during this period. In reality, the primary deficit fluctuated. Sometimes it was positive and sometimes it was negative, but it never exceeded 3% of GDP. The figure shows what would have happened to the debt if the interest rate had continued to remain less than the nominal GDP growth rate and if the government had continued to run a small surplus of 1.2% of GDP. Under this scenario, the government would eventually have repaid its debt and accumulated a stock of positive assets equal to 38% of GDP.[3] In the pre-1979 situation, it would also have been possible for the government to sustain a permanent deficit. In this case, in the steady state, the government would have ended up with a permanent stock of debt that was a consistent fraction of GDP. When the growth rate exceeds the interest rate, the government need not balance the budget because income growth always outstrips the growth of its debt.

If the growth rate of nominal GDP in the 1990s had continued to exceed the interest rate by 3.4 percentage points, and if the deficit-to-GDP ratio had remained constant, politicians would not have been concerned with balancing the budget. However, the nominal GDP growth slowed considerably in the 1980s, in part as a result of a slowdown in productivity growth, and in part as a result of reduced inflation. At the same time, there was a big increase in the average interest rate. This led to a serious situation.

---

3.   The exact relationship of the steady-state debt ratio to the deficit is given by Equation 14.4. For the period from 1946 through 1979 (excluding the immediate postwar years), $(1 + n)/(n − i)$ is equal to $(1.075)/(0.075 − 0.041)$, which is approximately equal to 32. If d equals –0.012 (1.2%), then b equals –0.012 × 32 = –0.38.

FIGURE 14.6

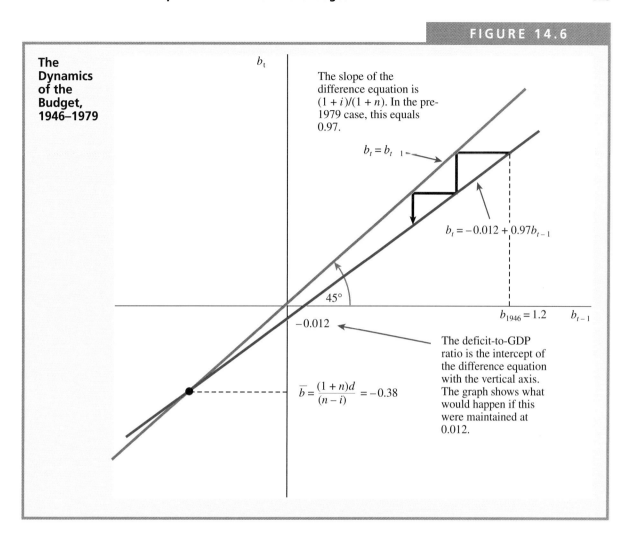

The Dynamics of the Budget, 1946–1979

The slope of the difference equation is $(1 + i)/(1 + n)$. In the pre-1979 case, this equals 0.97.

$b_t = b_{t-1}$

$b_t = -0.012 + 0.97b_{t-1}$

45°

-0.012

$b_{1946} = 1.2$ b_{t-1}

The deficit-to-GDP ratio is the intercept of the difference equation with the vertical axis. The graph shows what would happen if this were maintained at 0.012.

$\bar{b} = \dfrac{(1 + n)d}{(n - i)} = -0.38$

The Budget Crisis of the 1980s

When the interest rate exceeds the growth of nominal GDP, the steady state of the budget equation must involve either a negative primary deficit or a negative debt.[4] This has important economic implications.

---

4.   Mathematical Note: Remember that the steady state is given by the expression

$$\bar{b} = \frac{(1 + n)}{(n - i)}d.$$

We know that $(1 + n)$ is positive. If i is greater than n, the denominator of this expression is negative. If d is positive, then $\bar{b}$ must be negative. If d is negative, then $\bar{b}$ is positive.

FIGURE 14.7

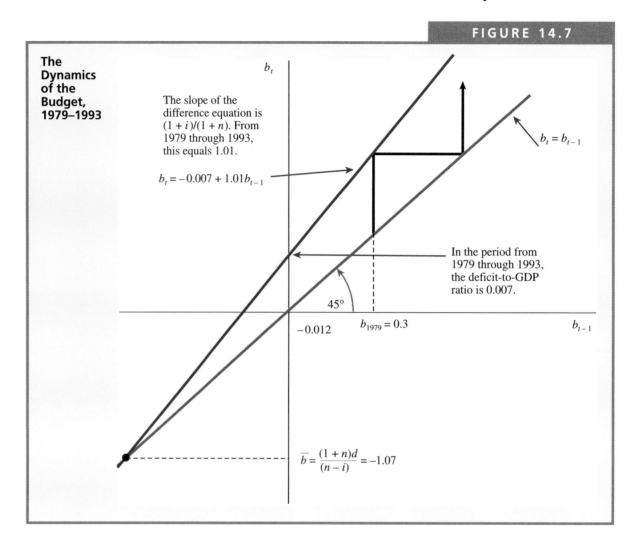

The Dynamics of the Budget, 1979–1993

The slope of the difference equation is $(1 + i)/(1 + n)$. From 1979 through 1993, this equals 1.01.

$b_t = -0.007 + 1.01 b_{t-1}$

$b_t = b_{t-1}$

In the period from 1979 through 1993, the deficit-to-GDP ratio is 0.007.

45°

-0.012 $b_{1979} = 0.3$ b_{t-1}

$\bar{b} = \dfrac{(1 + n)d}{(n - i)} = -1.07$

Figure 14.7 illustrates the situation in the period from 1979, when the Fed raised the interest rate to control inflation, through 1993, when Congress passed a bill to raise taxes. The debt-to-GDP ratio in 1979 was approximately 30.0%, but the interest rate was 0.7% *higher* than the growth rate of nominal GDP. The slope of the difference equation (the blue line) is equal to 1.01, which is *steeper* than the purple 45° line. Because nominal GDP was growing at a slower rate than the interest rate, a positive primary deficit was not sustainable. The figure illustrates that if the government were to try to maintain a positive primary deficit of 0.7% of GDP under these conditions, the debt-to-GDP ratio would explode, and eventually the U.S. government would become bankrupt. This, indeed, did begin to happen in the 1980s. The bold zigzag line represents the path of the debt-to-GDP ratio during this period. Because the government's income cannot be bigger than GDP, bankruptcy will occur when the debt becomes so large that the entire U.S. GDP is unable to pay the interest. In practice, since the government's tax revenues are substantially less than GDP, bankruptcy would have occurred well before this point.

Figure 14.7 also illustrates that when the interest rate exceeds the growth rate and the deficit is positive, the steady-state debt is again negative. A negative debt means that the government must lend to the private sector instead of borrowing from it. A policy of this kind is feasible and could be accomplished by increasing taxes above expenditures, using the revenues to first pay off the existing government debt and then to purchase financial assets from the private sector. Under the 1979 1993 configuration of interest rates and growth rates, the government would need to accumulate private-sector assets equal to 107% of GDP in order to sustain a permanent budget deficit of 0.7% of GDP.

To accumulate enough assets to sustain a positive deficit, the government would need to run a large primary surplus for many years. An alternative policy, one which is easier to attain, is to live with the existing level of debt and raise enough revenue to service the interest on it. This policy is referred to as **balancing the budget.** There was a lot of talk in the 1980s about passing an amendment to the Constitution that would require the government to balance its budget. Under a balanced-budget policy, the government would try to set its reported deficit equal to zero. This policy prevents the debt-to-GDP ratio from exploding by raising enough revenue from taxation each period to pay the interest on outstanding debt. Because interest payments on the debt are positive, a reported deficit of zero implies that the government needs to run a primary surplus, as it did in the period from 1946 through 1979.

THE BUDGET SURPLUS SINCE 1993

In 1993, Congress passed the Omnibus Budget Reconciliation Act in an attempt to get the deficit under control. As a consequence, an average deficit of 0.7% of GDP was turned into a surplus of 1.9%. At the same time that the fiscal situation improved, the Fed also began to lower the interest rate and, in the period since 1993, the average growth rate has once more exceeded the average interest rate. This most recent period looks a lot like the immediate postwar era. Figure 14.8 illustrates the changes in the debt-to-GDP ratio that have occurred since 1993. Over this period, the growth rate of nominal GDP has exceeded the interest rate by 0.6%, on average, and the average budget surplus has been 1.9% of GDP. Assuming these conditions continue, the debt-to-GDP ratio will stabilize at –33%; that is, the government will pay off its debt and begin to accumulate positive net assets equal to 33% of GDP.

DIFFERENT PERSPECTIVES ON DEBT AND DEFICITS

RICARDIAN EQUIVALENCE

We have maintained throughout this chapter that the increase in debt that occurred in the 1980s was a problem that needed to be addressed. One group of economists argues that this assumption is false and that high debt is not in itself a problem. The leading proponent of

FIGURE 14.8

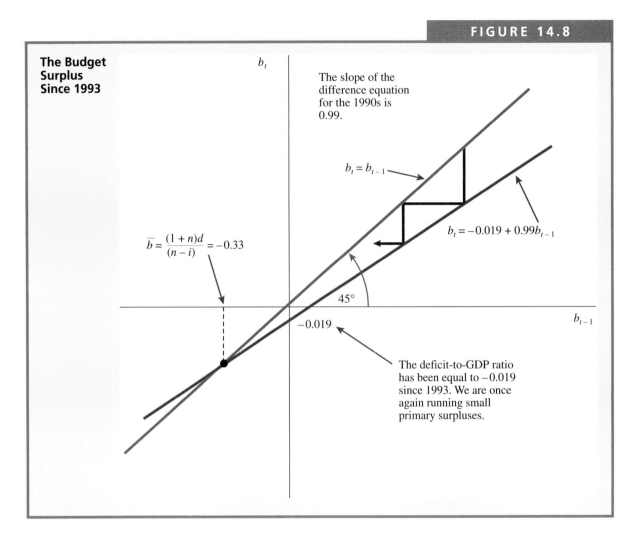

The Budget Surplus Since 1993

The slope of the difference equation for the 1990s is 0.99.

$b_t = b_{t-1}$

$b_t = -0.019 + 0.99b_{t-1}$

$\bar{b} = \dfrac{(1+n)d}{(n-i)} = -0.33$

45°

-0.019

b_t

b_{t-1}

The deficit-to-GDP ratio has been equal to -0.019 since 1993. We are once again running small primary surpluses.

this view is Robert Barro of Harvard University; Barro's position is called **Ricardian equivalence,** after the English economist David Ricardo, and to whom Barro traces his ideas.[5] Barro believes that the problems of the 1980s were caused by increased government spending. To a first approximation, according to Barro, it doesn't matter whether government spending is financed by debt or taxes. If government spending is financed by debt, households will choose to hold all of this increased debt without reducing the amount of saving that they devote to investments. The reason that households are willing to increase

5.   A very readable source on these issues is the exchange between advocates and critics of Ricardian Equivalence in the *Journal of Economic Perspectives,* Spring 1989. See in particular: the article by Robert J. Barro, "The Ricardian Approach to Budget Deficits," pp 37–54; and the replies by B. Douglas Bernheim, "A Neoclassical Approach to Budget Deficits," pp 55–72; and Robert Eisner, "Budget Deficits and Reality," pp 73–94.

WEBWATCH

How To Balance the Budget

An Internet site provided by University of California (UC) at Berkeley's Center for Community Economic Research allows you to choose your own cuts in expenditure or increases in revenues in an effort to balance the budget. You can find the budget simulator at http://www.berkeley.edu; search: "budget simulator".

The following information is quoted from their budget simulator page:

Welcome to the National Budget Simulation!
This simple simulation should give you a better feel of the trade-offs which citizens and policymakers must make to balance the budget.

The National Budget Simulation is a project of UC-Berkeley's Center for Community Economic Research and was created by Anders Schneiderman and Nathan Newman.

This simulation asks you to cut the fiscal deficit in order to achieve a balanced budget. In order to make the choices we face in the budget clearer, we assume that you make the cuts all in one year. You may also want to increase spending in areas that you think are being shortchanged under present budget priorities.

their saving in this way is that they anticipate that they will need extra wealth in the future to pay increased taxes. These households recognize that the government will eventually need to raise taxes in order to pay the principal and interest on its debt. Although the Ricardian view is not widely held by policymakers, the theory has been very popular among academics.

THE RELATIONSHIP BETWEEN THE BUDGET AND THE RATE OF INTEREST

The period after 1979 was qualitatively different from the period before 1979 for two reasons. First, the budget deficit increased gradually as a fraction of GDP. Second, and more important, the interest rate began to systematically exceed the growth rate of nominal GDP. To keep our analysis simple, we have treated these two changes as independent of each other. In fact, this may not be the case. There are good reasons to think that the increase in the budget deficit in the United States may have *caused* the increase in the interest rate. However, before rushing to this conclusion, that one must have caused the other because the two events occurred together, we should consider some international evidence.

Why should an increase in U.S. government borrowing drive up the U.S. interest rate? There are plausible reasons why. A simple economic model of borrowing and lending, such as we discussed in Chapter 6, suggests an effect of this kind. However, at the same

FIGURE 14.9

The Interest Rate and the Growth Rate in the G7 Countries (Excluding the U.S.)

Why has the situation in the United States been so different since 1979? We have already pointed to a change in federal policy. It has also been suggested that productivity growth slowed down in 1979 due to a change in our pace of discovering new technologies.

Whichever explanation is correct, these graphs illustrate that the phenomenon of slow growth and high interest rates is worldwide. Every country in the G7 group of industrialized nations has experienced similar difficulties. This could be due to the fact that the underlying rate of productivity growth is common worldwide. It could also be due to the fact that world capital markets are linked, and a high deficit in the United States influenced the interest rate throughout the world economy.

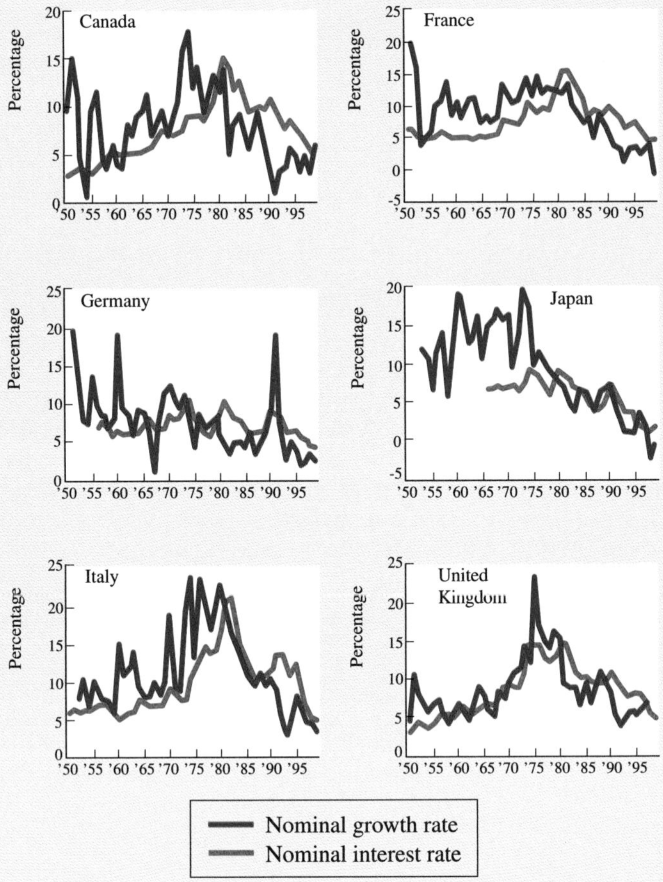

— Nominal growth rate
— Nominal interest rate

time that the interest rate began to exceed the growth rate in the United States, a similar phenomenon occurred in all of the G7 nations. Figure 14.9 presents evidence from Canada, France, Japan, Italy, Germany, and the United Kingdom—the other six members of the Group of Seven. Notice that the pattern in these countries is comparable with the experience of the United States. In all cases, the interest rate before 1979 was less than the growth rate of nominal GDP in almost every year. After 1979, the situation was reversed.

All of this suggests that there was a common cause at work. Perhaps the increase in the U.S. budget deficit is responsible for the increase in the domestic interest rate. This is a possible explanation for the change in events—even in light of the international evidence—because the United States occupies a unique place in the international financial markets, and many currencies are in practice tied to the U.S. dollar even though in principle, in the era of floating exchange rates, there is no explicit link. The central banks of the G7 countries (other than the United States) often act to prevent dramatic changes in their exchange rates with the dollar. This international linkage implies that U.S. interest-rate increases put pressure on nominal interest rates to increase throughout the world.

CONCLUSION

To sum up, the deficit experienced by the United States in the 1980s was a worldwide problem because the interest rate and the growth rate displayed similar patterns in many countries. It is possible that the problem originated with the United States government's increase in its primary deficit in the 1970s. This policy might have put pressure on the U.S. interest rate, which was in turn transmitted to other countries. But this is not the only possible explanation, and to date there has been insufficient research on the issue to reach a definite conclusion.

Difference equations are used to describe how a state variable changes over time. The solution to a difference equation is a list of numbers that describes the values of the state variable in successive periods. A steady-state solution to a difference equation is special in that the state variable is the same in every period. Steady states can be stable or unstable. If a steady state is stable, the state variable converges towards it for any initial value; if it is unstable, the state variable diverges away from it.

The relationship of the government debt to the government budget deficit is described by a difference equation in which the debt-to-GDP ratio is the state variable. The behavior of this equation depends on the ratio of the interest rate to the growth rate. If the interest rate exceeds the growth rate, the steady state is unstable; if the interest rate is less than the growth rate, it is stable.

The U.S. debt-to-GDP ratio was described by a stable difference before 1979; from 1979 through 1993 it was unstable. In 1993, the United States raised taxes, and since then the budget situation has reverted to the pre-1979 scenario. Before 1979, the government ran small budget surpluses. After 1979, the interest rate exceeded the growth rate, and politicians were forced to reduce the deficit in order to balance the budget. The same phenomenon occurred throughout the world, and it may have had a common cause; a likely candidate is the increase in the U.S. deficit, which caused an increase in the interest rate. This increase in the interest rate was transmitted to the rest of the world through the international capital market.

KEY TERMS

Balancing the budget   Ricardian equivalence
Difference equation   Stability
Dynamic analysis   State variable
Primary deficit   Static analysis
Reported deficit   Steady-state solution

QUESTIONS FOR CHAPTER **14**

---

1. Explain in words the difference between the government debt and the government budget deficit.

2. Explain in words the difference between the primary deficit and the reported deficit. Is one always bigger than the other? If so why? If not, why not?

3. Why are the debt-GDP and deficit-GDP ratios more appropriate measures of a country's indebtedness than the levels of the debt and the deficit alone?

4. Many developed countries, including the United States, are experiencing a significant increase in the average age of their population. How is this likely to affect future budget deficits or surpluses? Explain.

5. For each of the following equations

    i. $x_t = 1.5 + (2/3)x_{t-1}$ iv. $x_t = 2 + 0.5x_{t-1}$

    ii. $x_t = 1.5\,x_{t-1}$ v. $x_t = 1 + x_{t-1}$

    iii. $x_t = 3 + 2\,x_{t-1}$

    a. Draw a graph of x_t against x_{t-1}.

    b. Find the value of the steady state.

    c. Say whether this steady state is stable or unstable.

6. Define a *stable steady state*. In the deficit difference equation in the text (Equation 14.2), what condition must exist in order to create a stable steady state? Can you explain the reasoning behind this condition?

7. Using the budget difference equation, consider the case where $d = 0.1$, $i = 3\%$, and $n = 4\%$.

    a. Calculate the steady state level of the debt-GDP ratio, b.

    b. Suppose that the current debt-GDP ratio is 1. What will be the government's debt obligations next year?

    c. Now suppose that i increases to 5%. Calculate the new steady state. Is this new steady state stable? Why or why not?

8. Discuss how the 1980–1993 period differs from the 1994–1999 period in terms of the stability of the budget deficit. Provide appropriate graphs of the budget difference equation to illustrate. What three changes occurred around 1993 to change the stability of the budget situation?

9. In Italy the government ran a budget deficit equal to 8% of GDP in 1995.

a. If the Italian interest rate is 5% and the growth rate of nominal GDP is 6%, calculate the steady-state ratio of debt to GDP.

b. Suppose that the maximum the government can possibly raise in taxes is equal to 50% of GDP. Assuming that the interest rate equals 5% and the nominal growth rate of GDP equals 6%, at what value of the deficit will the interest payments on the steady-state debt exceed the government's ability to finance these payments through taxes?

10. Suppose that the budget difference equation has an unstable steady state. If the government cannot change either the interest rate or the growth rate, can you think of a solution that might avoid the problem of exploding debt? Provide a graph of the budget difference equation to illustrate your solution.

11. Define *Ricardian equivalence*. Suppose a $1 billion deficit-financed tax cut is adopted within an economy. According to rational expectations, what should happen to interest rates and national saving as a result? By how much?

12. What is the relationship between interest rates and the budget deficit? Discuss this question both within the classical model using a graph of the capital market and within the Keynesian model using an IS-LM graph.

13. Using the GDP accounting identity ($Y = C + I + G + NX$), derive the relationship between investment, private saving, government budget deficit, and the trade balance in an open economy. Based on this relationship, and all else being equal, what is the correlation between the budget deficit and the trade deficit? Explain.

14. Using the national budget simulator at http://garnet.berkeley.edu:3333/budget/budget.html, create your own budget for the United States.

CHAPTER 15

Neoclassical Growth Theory

Introduction

Growth theory is a tremendously active area of economic research. Until recently, growth theorists concentrated on documenting the sources of growth. We know that per capita income in the United States has grown at 1.89% on average over the past century. How much of this 1.89% was due to increases in population, how much to increases in the capital stock, and how much to new discoveries and innovations? The major work on these issues was carried out in the 1950s, and the leading contributors were Robert Solow and T.W. Swan. Solow and Swan showed that investment in new capital and the growth of population cannot, in themselves, lead to continued growth in per capita income. Instead, they attributed growth to the invention of new technologies that made labor more productive. Since the source of these innovations was unexplained in the models of Solow and Swan,[1] their theory became known as the **exogenous growth theory**.

From the 1950s until the late 1980s, the theory of economic growth was a stagnant area for economic research. All of this changed for two reasons. First, a group of economists

---

1.   T.W. Swan. "Economic Growth and Capital Accumulation," *Economic Record,* No. 32, pp 334–361, November 1956. Robert M. Solow. "A Contribution to the Theory of Economic Growth," *Quarterly Journal of Economics,* No. 70, pp 65–94, February 1953.

working at the University of Pennsylvania completed a project called the **Penn World Table**.[2] This comprehensive set of national income and product data accounts for every country in the world, beginning in 1950 or 1960 (depending on the country). Originally the data ended in 1988, but it is now revised on a regular basis. The Penn World Table was innovative because it reported data that was comparable across countries and allowed for the fact that the GDP basket of goods differed from country to country. The Penn World Table records national income in every country using the 1985 U.S. dollar as a common unit of measurement. The data shows that the world is changing in an unprecedented way. In the early 1800s, several countries began to experience sustained growth in per capita income. In the twentieth century, economic growth became increasingly common, and the new data set enables us to compare growth rates for different countries and regions.

A second reason for the resurgence of growth theory in the 1980s is that a comprehensive source of data stimulated a whole new generation of research; theorists now had a way to check their conjectures about sources of growth. Two theoretical papers were instrumental in the resurgence of growth theory, one by Paul Romer of Stanford University and one by Robert E. Lucas, Jr., of the University of Chicago.[3] Lucas and Romer were not satisfied with the exogenous explanations of growth put forward by Swan and Solow. Instead, they searched for an explanation of the sources of technological progress. One of the main ideas pursued by the new growth theory is that innovations are accompanied by learning on the job, and this learning leads to the accumulation of knowledge. Economists refer to accumulated knowledge as **human capital**. Because the new growth theory accounts for the reasons that per capita income grows, rather than taking this growth as exogenous, it is referred to as the **endogenous growth theory**.

The Sources of Economic Growth

Growth theory begins with the assumption that GDP is related to aggregate capital and labor through a production function. To keep things manageable, suppose that all of the output in the economy is produced from a single input.[4] Figure 15.1 on page 336 presents data on input and output per person for the U.S. economy from 1929 through 1995. Output per person is GDP measured in thousands of 1987 dollars per capita. Input per person is an aggregate measure that is constructed by combining capital and labor in a way that will be described in this chapter.

The data is unambiguous—more input leads to more output. The issue that separates exogenous growth theory from newer endogenous theories is how to interpret this data. Both theories agree that at a given point in time and with a given state of technology, output should

---

2.   Robert Summers and Alan Heston. "The Penn World Table," *Quarterly Journal of Economics,* pp 327–368, May 1991.

3.   Paul M. Romer. "Increasing Returns and Long-Run Growth," *Journal of Political Economy,* No. 94, pp 1002–1037, October 1986. Robert E. Lucas, Jr. "On the mechanics of economic development," *Journal of Monetary Economics,* No. 22, pp 3–42, July 1988.

4.   In reality, there are many inputs. Even in macroeconomics, which is highly aggregated, we usually think of there being at least two inputs: capital and labor. Introducing additional inputs complicates matters, but it does not change the main message: Exogenous and endogenous growth theorists disagree about the shape of the production function.

WEBWATCH

Penn World Tables Online

The Penn World Tables are available on the Internet at several different sites. One of the most accessible is provided by the University of Toronto at http://www.utoronto.ca; search: "Penn World Tables." The University of Toronto site provides a graphing option that lets you plot graphs of any of the data series. These currently include data on 29 different variables for 152 countries.

Penn World Tables 5.6
by Alan Heston and Robert Summers of the University of Pennsylvania

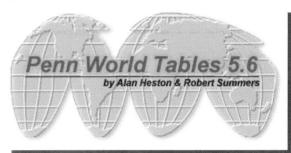

The graph in this panel was downloaded from the University of Toronto site. It represents investment as a share of GDP for the People's Republic of China for the period from 1960 through 1993.

CHN/I investment share of GDP % (1985 international prices)

be related to input through a production function. Exogenous growth theory insists, however, that the state of technology does not remain constant over time. The implication of this view is that each of the points in Figure 15.1 comes from a different production function.

Exogenous growth theory assumes that the production function satisfies a property called **constant returns to scale (CRS).** In the case of a production function with a single input, constant returns to scale means that the production function must be a straight line through the graph's origin. Because the points in Figure 15.1 do not lie on a straight line through the origin, the slope of the production function must have changed from one year to the next. The figure presents two production functions, one for 1929 and one for 1999. Notice that the production function is steeper in 1999 than in 1929. According to exogenous growth theory, this slope is a measure of productivity. Increases in productivity are

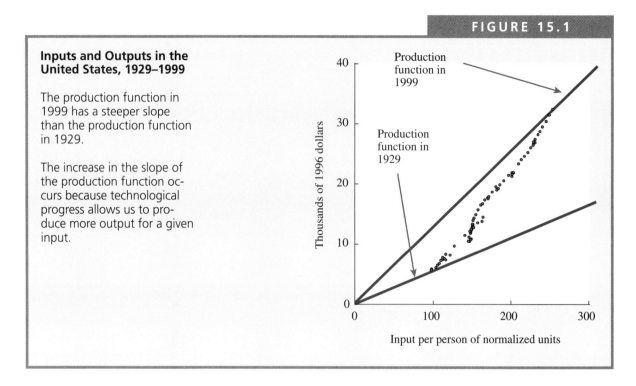

FIGURE 15.1

Inputs and Outputs in the United States, 1929–1999

The production function in 1999 has a steeper slope than the production function in 1929.

The increase in the slope of the production function occurs because technological progress allows us to produce more output for a given input.

due to the discovery of new technologies and inventions. Because early work in growth theory did not try to explain the influence of invention and innovation, productivity was left exogenous. In contrast, endogenous growth theory rejects the assumption of constant returns to scale and allows for the possibility that the points in Figure 15.1 may all come from the same production function.

PRODUCTION FUNCTIONS AND RETURNS TO SCALE

In applied work, we usually specify a particular functional form for the production function. One function that is frequently used because it can successfully account for a number of features of the data is the **Cobb-Douglas function**, which is represented by Equation 15.1.

15.1

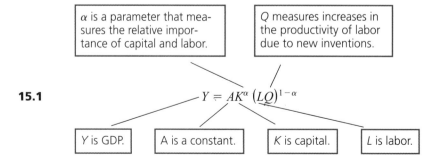

α is a parameter that measures the relative importance of capital and labor.

Q measures increases in the productivity of labor due to new inventions.

$$Y = AK^{\alpha}(LQ)^{1-\alpha}$$

Y is GDP. A is a constant. K is capital. L is labor.

The symbols Y, K, and L stand for GDP, aggregate capital, and aggregate employment, respectively. Q is the efficiency of labor. Notice that there are two inputs in the production function, capital, K, and labor, L, multiplied by its efficiency, Q.

The Cobb-Douglas production function contains two parameters that affect its shape. The constant A is a scale parameter that keeps the units of measurement consistent with each other. The parameter α (alpha) measures the relative importance of capital and labor in producing a unit of output. If the production function contains a complete description of all of the relevant inputs to the production process, this process should be reproducible at any scale. In other words, if all of the inputs to the production function are increased by a fixed multiple, then output should increase by the same multiple. This is the property of constant returns to scale. In the Cobb-Douglas production function, constant returns to scale means that the exponents on capital and labor add up to 1.[5]

THE NEOCLASSICAL THEORY OF DISTRIBUTION

The **neoclassical theory of distribution** explains how the output of a society is distributed to the owners of the factors of production, labor, and capital. It helps us account for the importance of labor and capital as productive inputs. The theory asserts that factors are paid their marginal products (see Chapter 4). The marginal product of a factor is the amount of extra output that would be produced if the firm were to employ an extra unit of the factor. In other words, every hour of labor used by the firm earns the output that would be produced if an *extra* hour of labor were used to produce output. Similarly, every hour of capital earns the output that would be produced if an extra hour of capital were used in production. If factors of production are paid their marginal products, we can measure how much labor and capital contribute to growth by observing how much they are paid.

THE THEORY OF DISTRIBUTION AND THE COBB-DOUGLAS FUNCTION

Neoclassical distribution theory assumes that output is produced by a large number of competitive firms, each of which uses the same production function. If we assume that this production function is Cobb-Douglas, we can derive expressions for the firm's profit-maximizing rules. Using these expressions, we can infer the magnitude of one of the key parameters of the production function by observing the share of national income that is paid to workers.

Because we assume that all firms use the same production function, the marginal product formula holds between aggregate variables. The profit-maximizing firm sets the

---

5.   Mathematical Note: To check that the Cobb-Douglas function exhibits constant returns to scale, we need to multiply both capital and labor by a fixed number and see whether GDP is multiplied by the same number:

$$A\left(nK\right)^{\alpha}\left(nLQ\right)^{1-\alpha} = AK^{\alpha}\left(LQ\right)^{1-\alpha}n^{1-\alpha+\alpha} = nY$$

Multiplying capital by n causes the GDP to be multiplied by n raised to the power α; multiplying labor by n multiplies the GDP by n raised to the power $(1 - \alpha)$. The total effect is the sum of these two effects: GDP multiplied by n raised to the power $\alpha + (1 - \alpha)$, or simply by n.

marginal product of labor (*MPL*) equal to the real wage (*w/P*). If this is the case, *MPL* multiplied by employment and divided by income should equal labor's share of income:

15.2 $MPL\dfrac{L}{Y} = 1 - \alpha = \dfrac{wL}{PY}$

> For the Cobb-Douglas function, labor's share of income is a constant equal to $1 - \alpha$.

For most production functions, the expression *MPL* is a complicated function of capital and labor; but for the Cobb-Douglas function, the marginal product of labor has a simple form.[6] For this function, the marginal product of labor multiplied by labor and divided by output is equal to $1 - \alpha$. This expression measures the percentage increase in output that will be gained by a given percentage increase in labor input; we call this the **labor elasticity** of the production function.[7]

We can also find an expression that describes the **capital elasticity** of the production function. The capital elasticity measures the percentage increase in output that will be produced by a given percentage increase in capital; for the Cobb-Douglas function, this is α. It is important to know the labor and capital elasticities of the production function because they determine the relationship between the growth rate of output and the growth rates of factor inputs. Equation 15.2 is key because we can use it to estimate $1 - \alpha$. Once we know $1 - \alpha$, then we also know α, and we can calculate how much of the growth in GDP per person is due to growth in labor and capital per person.

The right side of Equation 15.2 is the share of wages in income. The left side is the labor elasticity of production. In general, there is no reason why this expression should be constant. For the Cobb-Douglas function, however, this quantity is constant and is given by the expression $1 - \alpha$. This means that we can directly measure the share of wages in income and use our measurement to estimate $1 - \alpha$, the labor elasticity of production.

As shown in Figure 15.2, labor's share of national income from 1929 through 1999 has been approximately constant and equal to 2/3. We can therefore set α equal to 1/3 and $1 - \alpha$, to 2/3 when we calculate the relationship of growth in capital and labor to the GDP growth per person.

GROWTH ACCOUNTING

In Figure 15.1, we observed a graph of input per person against GDP per person. To construct a measure of input per person, we divided capital, employment, and real GDP by the population, N_t, to arrive at data in per capita terms. Now we explain this construction.

---

6.   Mathematical Note: The marginal product of labor is found by taking the derivative of the production function with respect to labor. For the Cobb-Douglas function, this is given by $MPL = (1 - \alpha)Y/L$.

7.   Mathematical Note: Another way of expressing the marginal product is $\Delta Y/\Delta L$ where Δ (delta) means "the change in." The labor elasticity, e_L, of the production function is the proportional change in Y for a given proportional change in L; that is,

$$e_L = \frac{\Delta/Y}{\Delta L/L},$$

which can also be written as $MPL \times (L/Y)$.

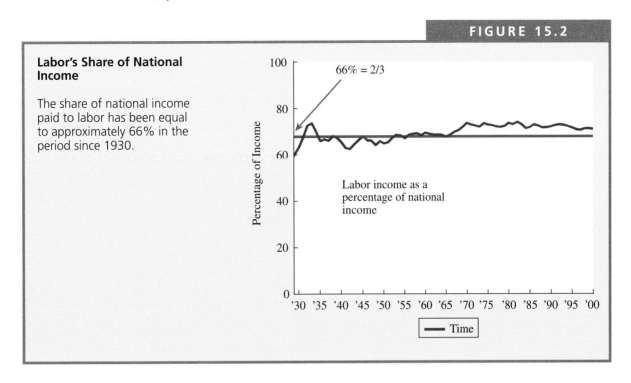

FIGURE 15.2

Labor's Share of National Income

The share of national income paid to labor has been equal to approximately 66% in the period since 1930.

Equation 15.3 presents the Cobb-Douglas production function in per capita terms. Because we can infer (from national income accounts) that the exponent on capital is 1/3 and the exponent on labor is 2/3, we can combine labor and capital in a single measure of input per person. To construct this measure, we raise capital per person to the 1/3rd power and employment per person to the 2/3rd power, and then multiply them. This construction links output per person to input per person.

15.3
$$\left(\frac{Y_t}{N_t}\right) \quad = \quad \left(\frac{K_t}{N_t}\right)^{1/3}\left(\frac{L_t}{N_t}\right)^{2/3} \quad \left(Q_t^{2/3}A\right)$$

Output per person   **Input per person**   **Total factor productivity (slope of the production function)**

Output per person equals input per person multiplied by a term called **total factor productivity**.[8] If we construct the aggregate input as described by this equation, the graph of the production function is a straight line through the origin. On this graph, GDP per person is plotted against input per person, and total factor productivity corresponds to the slope of the production function. In Figure 15.1, we found that if we plot points on the production function for different years, these points do not follow the same straight line

8.   Total factor productivity differs from labor productivity, which is the ratio of GDP to labor hours employed.

FIGURE 15.3

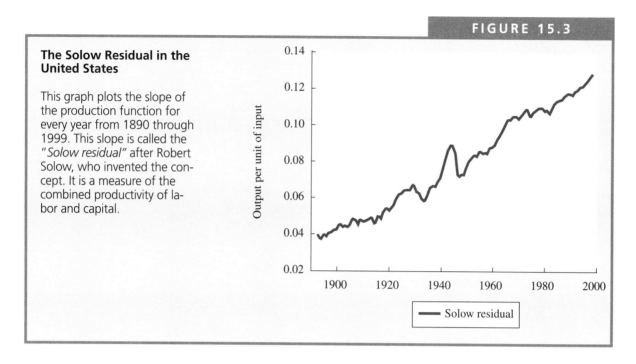

The Solow Residual in the United States

This graph plots the slope of the production function for every year from 1890 through 1999. This slope is called the *"Solow residual"* after Robert Solow, who invented the concept. It is a measure of the combined productivity of labor and capital.

through the origin. Solow took this as evidence of the fact that productivity has increased; that is, the slope of the production function has been increasing over time.

    The fact that the slope of the production function has increased over time means that growth in labor and capital cannot on their own account for all economic growth. Growth in labor and capital would be represented as a movement along the production function when the aggregate measure of input increases. In addition to this movement along the production function, part of GDP growth per person must be due to changes in total factor productivity as measured by increases in the slope of the production function. Economists call total factor productivity the **Solow residual**.[9] The graph of the Solow residual, plotted against time, is presented in Figure 15.3.

    The theory underlying the construction of the Solow residual is called **growth accounting** because it allows us to account for the sources of growth by dividing the growth rate of GDP per person into its component parts. Figure 15.4 presents a pie chart of this division for the United States, 1890 through 1999. On average, GDP per person grew by 1.89% per year, of which 0.63% was accounted for by growth in capital per person, and

---

9.   Robert Solow won the Nobel Prize in economics in 1987 for his work on the theory of economic growth. His work was originally introduced in "A Contribution to the Theory of Economic Growth" in the *Quarterly Journal of Economics,* pp 65–94, February 1956. The formula used to construct the Solow residual is

$$SR_t = \frac{Y_t}{(K_t)^{1/3}(L_t)^{2/3}}$$

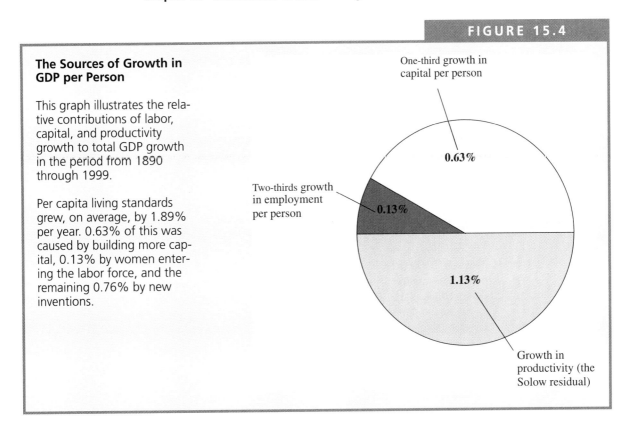

FIGURE 15.4

The Sources of Growth in GDP per Person

This graph illustrates the relative contributions of labor, capital, and productivity growth to total GDP growth in the period from 1890 through 1999.

Per capita living standards grew, on average, by 1.89% per year. 0.63% of this was caused by building more capital, 0.13% by women entering the labor force, and the remaining 0.76% by new inventions.

One-third growth in capital per person

0.63%

Two-thirds growth in employment per person

0.13%

1.13%

Growth in productivity (the Solow residual)

0.13% was accounted for by growth in employment per person. Because capital and employment growth only add up to 0.76%, the remaining 1.13% must be accounted for by increases in productivity.

Figure 15.4 reports averages spanning a century's worth of data. Although century averages are useful, they can mask a considerable amount of year-to-year variation. For example, most of the growth in employment per person after World War II was a consequence of many more women entering the labor force. Figure 15.4's point, though, is that although the economy has used greater quantities of the factors of production over the century, this is not the major source of increases in GDP per person. The largest contribution to growth in GDP per person came from increases in productivity.

THE NEOCLASSICAL GROWTH MODEL

We have described the factors that account for growth in GDP per person and have measured the relative contributions of each factor to a century's worth of data. One of these factors is the growth in capital per person, a variable that can be increased by increasing investment. This raises an obvious question: Can we increase growth by investing more as a nation? To answer this question, we need to construct a model that spells out the link between investment and growth. This model, based on neoclassical assumptions about the theory of distribution, is called the **neoclassical growth model**.

Increases in productivity are necessary if a nation is to experience sustained growth in its standard of living. You may think that we can continue growing simply by building more factories and machines; but capital, on its own, cannot produce more output. Capital must be combined with labor. If an economy increases its investment rate, for a short period of time it will experience higher growth. But as more capital is added to a fixed quantity of labor, the incremental gains in output decrease. The neoclassical growth model shows that an economy with a fixed production function that is subject to constant returns to scale cannot grow forever.

THREE STYLIZED FACTS

The neoclassical growth model begins with three "stylized facts" that characterize the U.S. data to a first approximation. The first is that GDP per person has grown at an average rate of 1.89% over the past century. The slope of the line in panel A of Figure 15.5 captures the growth rate of GDP per person. The second and third stylized facts, the share of consumption in GDP (panel B) and labor's share of income (panel C), have each remained approximately constant. The neoclassical growth model builds these constants into an economic model based on a competitive theory of production and distribution, and it uses this model to explain the per capita GDP growth rate.

ASSUMPTIONS OF THE NEOCLASSICAL GROWTH MODEL

The growth model is described by a difference equation similar to the one we used in Chapter 14's examination of the government budget. This difference equation is derived from Equations 15.4, 15.5, 15.6, and 15.7. Equations 15.4 and 15.5 are accounting identities and are true by definition. Equations 15.6 and 15.7 are more substantive. Equation 15.7 is the Cobb-Douglas production function. Equation 15.6 reflects an assumption about behavior.

15.4 $S_t = I_t$

15.5 $K_{t+1} = K_t(1 - \delta) + I_t$

> These two equations are accounting identities. They are true by definition.

15.6 $\dfrac{S_t}{Y_t} = s$

> This equation assumes that the saving rate is constant and is based on one of the three stylized facts.

15.7 $Y_t = A(K_t)^{1/3}(Q_t L_t)^{2/3}$

> This is the equation of the Cobb-Douglas production function. It combines the neoclassical theory of distribution and the stylized fact that labor's share of income is constant.

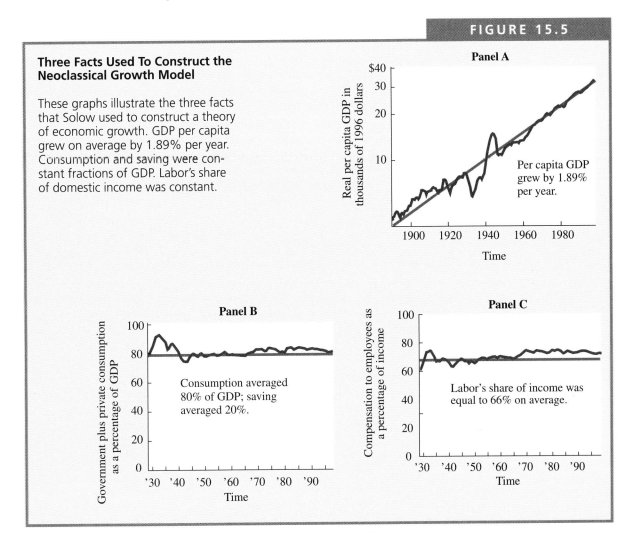

FIGURE 15.5

Three Facts Used To Construct the Neoclassical Growth Model

These graphs illustrate the three facts that Solow used to construct a theory of economic growth. GDP per capita grew on average by 1.89% per year. Consumption and saving were constant fractions of GDP. Labor's share of domestic income was constant.

Panel A

Per capita GDP grew by 1.89% per year.

Panel B

Consumption averaged 80% of GDP; saving averaged 20%.

Panel C

Labor's share of income was equal to 66% on average.

Equation 15.4 says that saving, S_t, equals investment, I_t. In the real world, U.S. saving can be used either for investment at home or for investment abroad. It is not strictly true that domestic saving equals domestic investment; the difference is made up by net exports. In practice, net exports are a relatively small fraction of GDP, and the assumption that they are zero is not too far from the truth.

Equation 15.5 defines the relationship between gross investment, I, and the stock of capital, K, at different points in time (t). It means that next year's capital stock is equal to the fraction of this year's capital stock that is left over after depreciation plus any new investment in capital measured by gross investment, I. The δ (delta) represents the rate of depreciation, which we assume is 6%.

Equation 15.6 represents an important assumption about economic behavior. It asserts that the fraction of GDP that is saved, and therefore the fraction that is invested, is a constant denoted by s. This assumption fits one of the three stylized facts. For the U.S. economy, s is equal to 0.2 (80% of GDP is consumed by government or by private households and firms, and 20% is saved).

Equation 15.7 is the Cobb-Douglas production function parameterized with a value of α equal to 1/3. This value of the output elasticity of capital is taken from the fact that labor's share of national income is equal to 2/3. There are many assumptions involved in writing down this function, and some are controversial (see Chapter 16). However, given the neoclassical theory of distribution, the fact that the production function is Cobb-Douglas is implied by the fact that labor's share of income is constant.

SIMPLIFYING THE MODEL

Equations 15.4 through 15.7 are all important components of the neoclassical growth model. Now we make three assumptions that are not strictly necessary, but that will help simplify the exposition.

Assumption one is that each person in the economy supplies exactly one unit of labor to the market. Using L to represent aggregate employment and N to represent the population of the economy, we represent this assumption with the formula $L/N = 1$. U.S. data shows some growth in employment per person over the century. However, the contribution of increases in employment per person to economic growth has been relatively small, and we lose little by neglecting it in our model.[10]

Assumption two is that population is constant: We represent the size of the population with the symbol N. Population growth is an obvious source of GDP growth, although it cannot explain growth in GDP per person. Because we are interested in explaining growth in GDP per person (the variable that accounts for advances in our standard of living), we will ignore population growth for the time being.

Assumption three is that there are no changes in the efficiency of labor. We represent the constant efficiency of labor with the symbol Q. The case of fixed Q is easier to understand than the case in which technological change causes Q to grow, and using a fixed Q helps us to understand why technological change is so important to neoclassical theory.

DIMINISHING MARGINAL PRODUCT

Armed with our simplifying assumptions, we can show what happens to output per person if capital is increased and labor is fixed. To derive Equation 15.8, we divide both sides of the production function by population in order to arrive at the per capita production func-

---

10.   It is now much more typical than it was 20 years ago for women to work in the marketplace rather than in the home. This shift in economic organization has resulted in an expansion of measured employment hours per person. In practice, the contribution of expanded hours per person has had a relatively minor effect on growth in GDP per person. Figure 15.4 shows that this effect accounted for 0.13% of the 1.89% per capita GDP growth over the century.

tion, which is the relationship between output per person and capital per person.[11] We use lowercase letters to represent per capita variables: y for output per person and k for capital per person. The production function in per capita terms describes the technology that would be faced by a firm planning to add more capital to a fixed supply of labor.

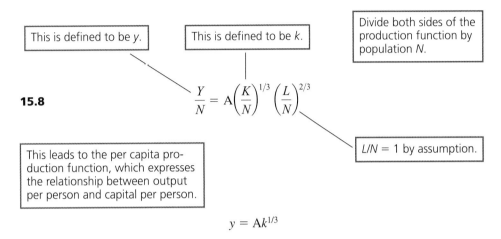

15.8

$$\frac{Y}{N} = A\left(\frac{K}{N}\right)^{1/3}\left(\frac{L}{N}\right)^{2/3}$$

This is defined to be y.

This is defined to be k.

Divide both sides of the production function by population N.

$L/N = 1$ by assumption.

This leads to the per capita production function, which expresses the relationship between output per person and capital per person.

$$y = Ak^{1/3}$$

The per capita production function is graphed in Figure 15.6 on page 346. Notice that the curve gets flatter as k grows. This reflects the fact that the marginal product of capital gets smaller as more capital is added to the economy. Although the production function satisfies constant returns to scale, it displays a diminishing marginal product of capital. Do not confuse these concepts. Constant returns to scale implies that if capital and labor both change by a fixed percentage, output will change by the same percentage. Diminishing marginal product of capital means that if capital changes by a fixed percentage, holding the input of labor constant, then output will change by a smaller percentage.

THREE STEPS TO THE NEOCLASSICAL GROWTH EQUATION

The neoclassical growth equation, a difference equation, describes the relationship between per-person capital in any two successive years. In Chapter 14 we saw that difference equations can behave in different ways. For example, a variable that is modeled by a difference equation can either grow without bound or it can converge to a steady state. The neoclassical growth equation has a stable steady state that the economy will converge to for any initial positive stock of capital per person. GDP per person depends only on capital per person, so per capita GDP must also converge to a steady state. But because GDP per person converges to a steady state, the neoclassical growth model cannot, in the long run, explain growth. The following equations derive the neoclassical growth equation in three steps.

---

11. The constant returns to scale (CRS) assumption lets us do this. Recall that if we multiply capital and labor by a fixed number, CRS means that we multiply GDP by the same number. We choose the number $1/N$.

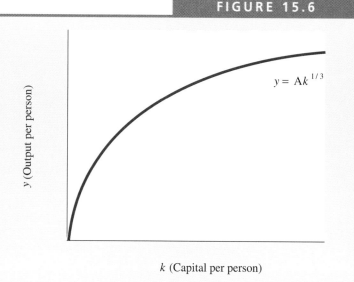

FIGURE 15.6

The Per Capita Production Function

This is a graph of *the per capita production function*. It plots output per person (on the vertical axis) against capital per person (on the horizontal axis).

Notice that the slope of the per capita production function gets flatter as the economy adds more capital to a fixed amount of labor (as k increases).

$y = Ak^{1/3}$

y (Output per person)

k (Capital per person)

Step 1	$k_{t+1} = k_t(1 - \delta) + i_t$	This is the investment identity. It defines how capital accumulates.
Step 2	$k_{t+1} = k_t(1 - \delta) + sy_t$	This step assumes that investment (equal to saving) is proportional to output.
Step 3 **15.9**	$k_{t+1} = k_t(1 - \delta) + sAk_t^{1/3}$	This step replaces output with the production function to generate the neoclassical growth equation.

The first step in deriving the neoclassical growth equation is to restate the capital identity in per capita form. In step 1, capital per person next year, k_{t+1}, equals the capital per person that is left this year after subtracting depreciation, $k_t(1 - \delta)$, and adding new investment per person, i_t. Step 2 replaces investment per person by a constant fraction, s, of GDP per person, y_t. This uses the assumptions that investment and saving are equal, and that saving is a constant fraction of GDP. Step 3 replaces GDP per person, y_t, with the per capita production function. The result is a difference equation for the single-state variable, k, that is very similar to the equations we studied in Chapter 14. We can use Equation 15.9 to describe how capital and GDP per person change over time.

GRAPHING THE NEOCLASSICAL GROWTH EQUATION

In Figure 15.7, the blue curve is the graph of the neoclassical growth equation. The line that is 45° to the horizontal axis represents the steady state condition for the difference

FIGURE 15.7

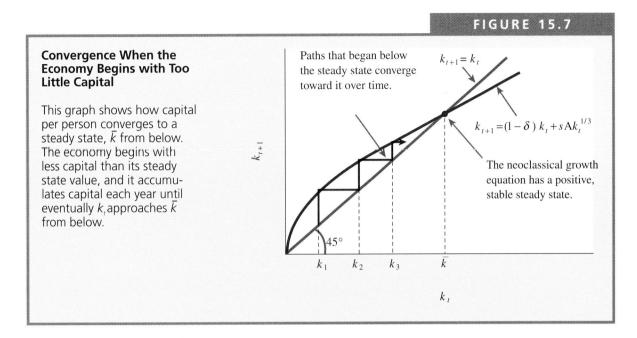

Convergence When the Economy Begins with Too Little Capital

This graph shows how capital per person converges to a steady state, $\bar{k}$ from below. The economy begins with less capital than its steady state value, and it accumulates capital each year until eventually k_t approaches $\bar{k}$ from below.

Paths that began below the steady state converge toward it over time.

$k_{t+1} = k_t$

$k_{t+1} = (1 - \delta)\,k_t + s A k_t^{1/3}$

The neoclassical growth equation has a positive, stable steady state.

$45°$

k_1 k_2 k_3 $\bar{k}$

k_t

k_{t+1}

equation; at every point on this line, the capital stock per person in year $t + 1$ is equal to the capital stock per person in year t. The points where the neoclassical growth equation intersects the purple 45° line are the steady states of the model: the steady state in which the economy has zero capital and a positive steady state labeled $\bar{k}$.

We can use this graph to study changes in the economy over time. Figure 15.7 illustrates what would happen to per-person capital if the economy began with an initial stock of capital, k_1, less than the steady state stock $\bar{k}$. In the first period, as the economy begins with capital stock k_1, it produces output per person equal to $A k_1^{1/3}$. If we save a fraction of this output and add it to the undepreciated capital, we increase the subsequent periods' capital stock to a higher value, k_2. In this way, the economy will grow. But although the economy grows each period, the amount by which it grows gets consistently smaller. This is because the economy is adding more capital to a fixed stock of labor. The additional GDP that can be produced in this way declines as diminishing returns to capital sets in. The steady state to which the economy converges is a state in which the new investment each period is only just sufficient to replace the capital that is worn out due to depreciation. This steady state occurs at $\bar{k}$.

Figure 15.8 shows what will happen if the initial stock of capital, k_1, is greater than the steady state stock, $\bar{k}$. In this case, the level of capital is so high that the new investment is not sufficient to replace the capital that wears out from depreciation; and in the subsequent period, the level of capital declines. Eventually, the economy shrinks to the point where the constant fraction of GDP per person that is saved is just large enough to replace the depreciated capital; this is the steady state capital stock per person, $\bar{k}$.

FIGURE 15.8

Convergence When the Economy Begins with Too Much Capital

This graph shows how capital per person converges to a steady state, $\bar{k}$, from above. The economy begins with more capital than its steady state value, and it deaccumulates capital each year until eventually k_t approaches $\bar{k}$ from above.

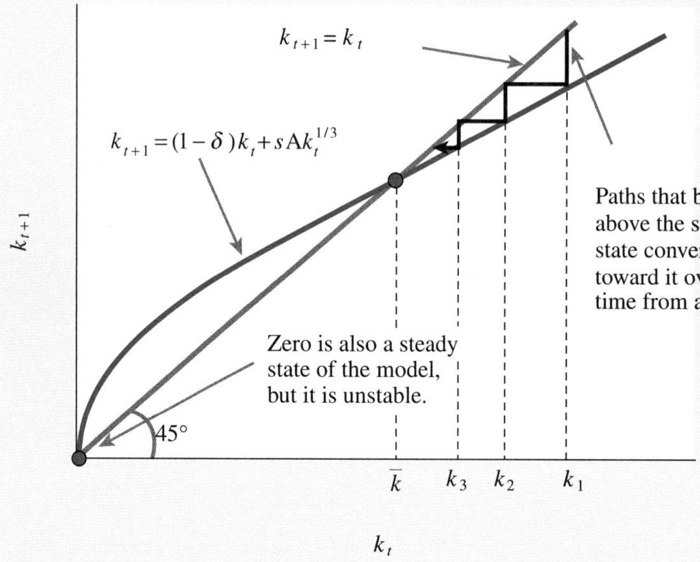

$$k_{t+1} = k_t$$

$$k_{t+1} = (1-\delta)k_t + sAk_t^{1/3}$$

Paths that began above the steady state converge toward it over time from above.

Zero is also a steady state of the model, but it is unstable.

$45°$

$\bar{k} \quad k_3 \quad k_2 \quad k_1$

k_t

k_{t+1}

The steady state is interesting from an economic point of view because it is stable. If the economy has been operating for a long time, we would expect it to have reached the steady state. Which of the economy's features will tell us where the steady state is located? Equation 15.10 gives the formula for this steady state and identifies two parameters that influence the size of capital per person (and therefore GDP per person) in the steady state.

15.10 $\quad \bar{k} = \bar{k}(1-\delta) + As\bar{k}^\alpha$

> The steady state is found by solving the neoclassical growth equation (when $k_{t+1} = k_t = \bar{k}$) in terms of the model's parameters.

> The steady state value of k will be greater if the saving rate is higher.

$$\bar{k} = \left(\frac{sA}{\delta}\right)^{\frac{1}{1-a}}$$

> The steady state value of k will be less if the depreciation rate is higher.

An economy with a very high saving rate should also have very high levels of capital and GDP per person. Increased investment does not cause increased growth. Instead, the model predicts that an increase in investment raises the level of GDP per person but does not influence the growth rate in the steady state. This is because the economy always grows to the point at which new investment is just sufficient to replace worn-out capital. If there is any investment left over after replacing depreciated capital, the economy will grow further. But as it grows, the economy will need to devote a greater amount of investment to replacing worn-out capital, and there will be less left over for further growth. In the steady state, investment is just sufficient to replace depreciated capital, and at this point growth comes to a halt.

The fact that the flow of saving in the steady state is just sufficient to replace depreciated capital implies a second feature of the neoclassical model. An economy with a higher depreciation rate needs to devote more of its saving to replacing worn-out capital; therefore, less remains for growth. For a given saving rate, higher depreciation will tend to lower the steady state stock of capital because more saving will be needed to maintain any given stock. An economy with a very high depreciation rate will tend to have a low level of per capita GDP.

THE EFFECTS OF PRODUCTIVITY GROWTH

We have seen how the neoclassical growth model behaves for a given initial stock of capital. We have also learned that per capita output cannot grow forever. The key to understanding growth is in being able to explain how the input of labor per person can grow, even when the number of hours per person remains fixed. The neoclassical growth model explains how labor can grow by distinguishing labor supply that is measured in hours from labor supply that is measured in efficiency units.

MEASURING LABOR IN EFFICIENCY UNITS

Not all workers are alike. An hour of work supplied by a brain surgeon, for example, contributes more to the GDP than an hour of work supplied by a laborer. The brain surgeon has a considerable investment in training. A laborer, on the other hand, performs unskilled tasks that are relatively easy for anyone to carry out. One way to capture the concept that the brain surgeon produces goods with a higher market value is to argue that an hour of the surgeon's labor provides a greater input value to the production function than an hour's work by a laborer. Surgeons supply the same amount of labor measured in units of time, but they supply more labor when measured in efficiency units.

Recognizing that some types of labor are more productive than others at a point in time leads to the observation that the average productivity of labor is different at different points in time. The average U.S. worker in the twenty-first century, for example, is highly skilled relative to their nineteenth-century counterpart. Most workers today are literate, are able to operate complicated machinery, and possess a range of skills that were unknown even a few decades ago. For this reason, labor hours may not be a good measure of the true input to the production function. A better measure would be labor measured in efficiency units—that is, labor hours multiplied by labor efficiency.

15.11 $$E = N \times Q$$ | *E* is total labor supplied, measured in efficiency units. |

Equation 15.11 defines labor supply in efficiency units. This measure of labor supply, E, is equal to the number of people, N, each of whom supplies one unit of time multiplied by their efficiency, Q. Although we have assumed that the population is constant and that each person supplies a fixed number of hours, it will still be possible for the labor supplied by each person to increase as long as we measure labor in efficiency units. This observation

TABLE 15.1

The Labels Used To Measure Growth Rates

Variable	Formula	Definition
k_t $=$	$\dfrac{K_t}{Q_t N_t}$	Capital per efficiency unit of labor
y_t $=$	$\dfrac{Y_t}{Q_t N_t}$	Output per efficiency unit of labor
$(1 + g_Q)$ $=$	$\dfrac{Q_{t+1}}{Q_t}$	gQ is the growth rate of labor efficiency.
$(1 + g_N)$ $=$	$\dfrac{N_{t+1}}{N_t}$	gN is the growth rate of population.
$(1 + g_E)$ $=$	$\dfrac{E_{t+1}}{E_t} = \dfrac{Q_{t+1}}{Q_t} \dfrac{N_{t+1}}{N_t}$	"gE" is the growth rate of labor measured in efficiency units.

is very important because increases in labor efficiency, according to the neoclassical theory, are ultimately responsible for economic growth.

MEASURING VARIABLES RELATIVE TO LABOR

Previously, we derived the neoclassical growth equation in per capita terms. A similar equation can be used to describe growth in an economy where population and productivity are both increasing from one year to the next. The idea is to redefine the state variable of the growth model. Instead of letting k represent capital relative to population, we let it represent capital relative to the labor supply of the population, measured in efficiency units.

Table 15.1 lays out the definitions of the variables used to describe the growth model. We reinterpret the variables y and k in the first two rows of the table and add some new terms

---

12. Mathematical Note: Productivity can be derived from labor efficiency and population because the growth factor of labor $(1 + g_E)$ is the product of their growth factors. It is approximately true that the growth rate of labor is equal to the sum of the growth rates of population and productivity. The exact formula that defines the relationship between the three rates is given by

$$(1 + g_E) = (1 + g_Q)(1 + g_N),$$

which can be expanded to give the expression $g_E = g_Q + g_N + g_E g_Q$. Because g_Q and g_N are small numbers, the product $g_Q g_N$ is an order of magnitude less than g_N and g_Q, and it is approximately true that $g_E = g_Q + g_N$.

to define the rate at which labor efficiency, population, and productivity[12] are growing.

The derivation of the growth equation has a couple more steps in the case of growth in population and labor efficiency; these steps are laid out in the Appendix at the end of this chapter. The equation that describes growth is very similar to the simpler case that we have already studied.

> The neoclassical growth equation

15.12 $$k_{t+1} = k_t \frac{(1 - \delta)}{(1 + g_E)} + \frac{sA}{(1 + g_E)} k_t^{1/3}$$

Equation 15.12 is a difference equation that behaves in the same way as Equation 15.9. The state variable k, however, is now interpreted as the ratio of capital to labor measured in efficiency units. Beginning with a low level of k, the economy invests in additional capital until k converges to a steady state. If k starts out above the steady state, the economy will not be able to invest enough each period to maintain the high initial stock, and capital per efficiency unit of labor will decline. In either case, the economy will converge to a steady state value of k. Unlike the model with no growth, a steady state value of k does not mean that GDP per person will be constant. Rather, it means that GDP per person will grow at a rate fast enough to exactly keep up with the exogenous improvements in productivity.

We have shown that the neoclassical growth equation converges to a steady state, and we used this fact to argue that the model cannot explain sustained growth in GDP per person. Now we redefine the state variable of this equation and argue that even though this new variable converges to a steady state, the model can explain growth. Equations 15.13 and 15.14 show how this apparent paradox is resolved.

> The variable k_t converges to a constant in the steady state.

> This is the variable defined as y_t. It also converges to a constant in the steady state.

15.13 $$\left(\frac{K_t}{N_t}\right)\frac{1}{Q_t} = \bar{k} \qquad \left(\frac{Y_t}{N_t}\right)\frac{1}{Q_t} = \bar{y}$$

> If k_t and y_t are constant, then K_t/N_t and Y_t/N_t must be growing at the same rate as Q_t.

15.14 $$\left(\frac{K_t}{N_t}\right) = Q_t\bar{k} \qquad \left(\frac{Y_t}{N_t}\right) = Q_t\bar{y}$$

Equations 15.13 and 15.14 use the symbols $\bar{k}$ and $\bar{y}$ to represent the steady state values of capital and GDP per efficiency unit of labor, respectively. The logic of the model forces each of these variables to settle down to a steady state. But the fact that output per unit of labor converges to a steady state says nothing about output per person when there is positive productivity growth. Output per person and output per unit of labor are not the same. In the steady state, capital per person must grow because labor, measured in efficiency units, is growing. As exogenous technological progress causes improvements in the efficiency of labor, households accumulate capital to keep the relative proportions of capital and labor constant.

CONCLUSION

The neoclassical theories of production and distribution can be used to measure the sources of growth in GDP per person. Growth in capital and labor cannot in themselves account for growth in GDP per person. Instead, a good deal of the cause must be due to improvements in the efficiency of labor. But although not all of growth is accounted for by increases in capital and labor, some of it is. It might still be possible to grow faster by investing in more new capital. To see whether this is possible, we constructed a model of economic growth that links the components of growth and explains how they are related to each other.

The neoclassical growth model begins with three facts. First, GDP per capita has grown at an average rate of 1.89% over the past century. Second, the share of wages in GDP has been constant. Third, consumption has been a constant fraction of GDP. We assume the latter two facts, and then the logic of the model allows us to explain the first fact.

To explain economic growth, we use a difference equation in which the state variable is the ratio of capital to labor, measured in efficiency units. This state variable converges to a steady state. Whether or not the model predicts that output per person will grow depends on our allowing for exogenous growth in productivity. Using the distinction between these two cases, we can show that the ultimate source of growth of GDP per person is in exogenous increases in the efficiency of labor.

Productivity growth is central to the neoclassical model because constant returns to scale means that proportional increases in output require proportional increases in both capital and labor. An economy that applies increasing capital to a fixed stock of labor will eventually suffer from a diminishing marginal product of capital, and its output will increase less than proportionately. Investment is a fixed fraction of output, but in each successive period there will be less increase in output than in the previous period. Growth must eventually come to a halt as the stock of capital approaches a steady state. The neoclassical model circumvents the fact that labor hours per person are in fixed supply by assuming that labor measured in efficiency units increases as a result of exogenous improvements in productivity.

KEY TERMS

Capital elasticity   Labor elasticity
Cobb-Douglas function   Neoclassical growth model
Constant returns to scale (CRS)   Neoclassical theory of distribution
Endogenous growth theory   Penn World Table
Exogenous growth theory   Solow residual
Growth accounting   Total factor productivity
Human capital

APPENDIX: THE GROWTH EQUATION WITH PRODUCTIVITY GROWTH

The following equations show the steps used to derive Equation 15.12.

$$\left(\frac{K_{t+1}}{N_{t+1}Q_{t+1}}\right)\left(\frac{Q_{t+1}N_{t+1}}{Q_tN_t}\right) = \left(\frac{K_t}{Q_tN_t}\right)(1-\delta) + \left(\frac{I_t}{Q_tN_t}\right)$$

> This is the investment identity that defines how capital accumulates. Variables are measured relative to labor in efficiency units (rather than relative to population).

$$k_{t+1}(1 + g_E) + k_t(1-\delta) + sAy_t$$

> When efficiency units are growing over time, there is an additional term on the left-hand side of the equation that accounts for growth.

$$k_{t+1} = k_t\frac{(1-\delta)}{(1+g_E)} + \frac{sA}{(1+g_E)}k_t^{1/3}$$

> The neoclassical growth equation with productivity and population growth has two differences from the model without growth.
> 1. The variable k measures capital relative to efficiency units of labor, not capital per capita.
> 2. The term $(1 + g_E)$ appears on the denominator of the right-hand side.

QUESTIONS FOR CHAPTER 15

1. What three facts was the neoclassical growth theory designed to explain?

2. Define the terms *constant returns to scale* and *diminishing marginal product*. Can a production function exhibit both of these properties? If yes, give an example of a production function that does. If no, explain why.

3. Consider the production function

$Y = KL^{1/2}$

Does this function display constant returns to scale? Does it display diminishing returns to capital? Calculate the share of GDP that would go to capital and the share that would go to labor if the real wage and the real rental rate were equal to the marginal products of labor and capital.

4. Show how a Cobb-Douglas production function can be rewritten in per capita terms. Based on this per capita production function, what are the three sources of per capita growth in the neoclassical growth model? Which factor is the most important? How has the contribution of each of these factors changed over time?

5. Define *total factor productivity*. What does it attempt to measure? How is it calculated? How accurate is it?

6. Draw a graph of x_{t+1} against x_t for the difference equation

$$x_{t+1} = 2x_t - 3x_t^{1/2} + 2$$

How many steady states does this equation have? Find the value of each steady state and determine whether it is stable.

7. This question refers to the neoclassical growth equation

$$K_{t+1} = (1 - \delta)K_t + sK_t^\alpha N^{1-\alpha}$$

Suppose that $\alpha = 1$ and $N = 1$. Draw a graph of K_{t+1} against K_t. Does this equation have a stable steady state? Does it have an unstable steady state? Suppose that $\delta = 0.1$ and s = 0.2. Can this economy grow? If so, can you explain, in words, why this example is different from the model in the chapter? What would be labor's share of GDP in this economy?

8. Two economies are exactly identical except for the fact that country A has a higher depreciation rate than country B. Will country A or country B have a higher steady state level of per capita GDP? Which country will have a higher growth rate? Provide a graph to illustrate.

9. Consider an economy with a saving rate of 0.16, a depreciation rate of 0.1, a population growth rate of zero, A = 1, and a share of labor in GDP of 50%. Assuming that this economy has zero productivity growth, what is the steady state value of k?

10. A neoclassical growth economy can be described with the following information: s = 0.45, $\delta = 0.1$, $n = 0.05$, and $\alpha = 0.5$. Assuming that this economy has zero productivity growth, what is the steady state level of k? If $k_0 = 7$, calculate the value of per capita capital for the next period, k_1. Is this economy growing faster or slower than its long-run growth rate?

11. Consider two economies that are both experiencing exogenous growth in labor productivity of 2% per year. Also assume that both countries were previously in their steady states. Both countries are identical, except that the saving rate in country A has just fallen to a rate below that of country B.

    a. Which country will be richer in the short run? What about in the long run? Use a graph to illustrate.

   b. Which country will grow faster in the short run? What about in the long run? Use a graph to illustrate.

   c. Draw a graph with the growth rates of country A and country B on the vertical axis, and time on the horizontal axis. What happens to the growth rates of these two countries over time?

12. In the neoclassical growth model, use a graph to illustrate the effects of an increase in population growth.

   a. What happens to per capita GDP in the short run and in the long run?

   b. What happens to aggregate GDP in the short run and in the long run?

   c. What happens to the growth rate of per capita GDP in the short run and in the long run?

13. According to the neoclassical growth model, what should be the correlation between a country's saving/investment rate and its steady state per capita growth rate? Do you think that this prediction is consistent with the real world? Why or why not?

14. Some economists say that the neoclassical growth model predicts "conditional convergence." What do you think is meant by convergence? What do you think is conditional about this convergence? Explain.

CHAPTER 16

ENDOGENOUS GROWTH THEORY

INTRODUCTION

The neoclassical growth model was constructed in the 1950s to accommodate some stylized facts about the U.S. economy. At that time, relatively few countries collected economic data in a systematic way. Recently this situation has begun to change, and we now have data on most countries that extends back to 1960. To check the robustness of neoclassical growth theory, researchers have begun to compare this data with the model's predictions. They have investigated the behavior of growth rates and GDP per person across countries and have looked at the relationships between saving rates, growth rates, and relative standards of living. They have found that a number of predictions of the simplest version of the neoclassical model are inconsistent with the evidence.

Both the neoclassical and endogenous growth models make the simplifying assumption that each country in the world produces the same homogenous commodity. For this reason, they do not allow for international trade in commodities. But the models do allow for trade in capital as countries borrow from and lend to each other.

Endogenous and exogenous growth theories explain growth as increases in the efficiency of labor, Q. Because the neoclassical model assumes that Q is exogenous, endogenous growth theory explains why Q increases from one year to the next. The main idea is that Q measures the knowledge and skills of the workforce that are acquired in the process of producing goods. As the economy builds more complicated machines and workers learn to operate new machines, they acquire knowledge. This knowledge accumulates over time and contributes to the growth process.

THE NEOCLASSICAL MODEL AND THE INTERNATIONAL ECONOMY

The neoclassical growth model features a single commodity, but in the real world there are many kinds of goods and services. One of the major motives for international trade is the diversity in the abilities of different countries to produce these goods and services.[1] For example, the Japanese export cars to the United States and import beef. Trade in commodities is excluded from the neoclassical growth model because the model deals with a world in which there is only one good.

A second kind of trade is **intertemporal trade**—trade between different points in time. Intertemporal trade occurs when one country's consumption plus investment is greater than its gross domestic product. It pays for the excess by borrowing from abroad. There are three possible reasons for intertemporal trade. First, people in one country might be more patient than those in another. In the neoclassical growth model, this implies that one country has a higher saving rate than the other. The citizens of the more-patient country lends to those of the less-patient countries by trading in the international capital market. A second reason for intertemporal trade is that one country may have a higher rate of population growth than another. The high-population-growth country needs to invest at a faster rate in order to maintain a fixed capital-labor ratio. That country can expect to attract foreign investors as world saving flows in to meet the demand for new capital goods. A third reason for intertemporal trade arises when one country is richer than the others. The citizens of the rich country lend to the poorer countries by investing capital in these countries.

There is a fourth possible reason for intertemporal trade, which we will exclude by assumption: Different countries may use different production functions. If one country has access to a superior technology, savers from other countries will try to invest there in order to take advantage of the higher-potential profit opportunities. But although differences in technology can account for short-run international lending opportunities, they cannot account for long-run patterns of borrowing and lending because technologies are relatively easy to mimic. For this reason, we assume that all countries use the same production function.

In this chapter, we model the world as a collection of countries, each of which produces the same homogenous commodity using the same production function. Countries differ for only three reasons: They have different saving rates, different rates of population growth, or different initial stocks of capital.

---

1.   In international economics, this idea is called *comparative advantage.* Comparative advantage means that each country exports those commodities that it is relatively efficient at producing.

MODELING WORLD TRADE

We can model trade in the international capital markets in two ways. The first way is by assuming that world capital markets are open, meaning that a citizen can borrow or lend freely in any country in the world. The opposite assumption is that world capital markets are closed, meaning that the citizen can borrow and lend only within the geographical borders of their own country. Reality is somewhere in between the two extremes; the international capital market is not completely open, but it is not completely closed, either. Because the two extremes are easy to model, we look at the implications of the neoclassical model for the behavior of data in these two extremes.

THE NEOCLASSICAL GROWTH MODEL WITH OPEN CAPITAL MARKETS

The assumption that the world capital market is open is referred to as **perfect capital mobility.** When there is perfect capital mobility, GDP per person should be the same in every country. The Penn World Table (see Chapter 15, Webwatch 15.1) shows that the model with perfect capital mobility makes a number of predictions that are contradicted by the data. We can infer that perfect capital mobility is not a good description of the facts. Clearly, the neoclassical model must be amended.

Our first task in amending the neoclassical model is to allow for the fact that countries can borrow and lend internationally. In an open economy, domestic saving need not equal domestic investment because one country's saving can be directed to the accumulation of domestic capital *or* the accumulation of foreign capital. Instead, we should observe that world saving equals world investment.

This idea is expressed in Equation 16.1. S and I represent domestic saving and investment, and S^f and I^f represent foreign saving and investment. When individuals in each country are free to invest at home or abroad, there should be no tendency for saving in one country to equal investment in that same country. But the evidence suggests that in practice, domestic saving is very closely linked with domestic investment.

16.1 $\qquad S + S^f = I + I^f \qquad\qquad$ | World saving equals world investment. |

Figure 16.1 presents data from nine countries, year by year. In each year, domestic saving in each of these countries is very close to domestic investment. There is nothing special about the countries we have selected—all countries exhibit this same pattern, worldwide. Because the neoclassical model cannot explain why domestic saving in an open capital market should be so closely linked to domestic investment, this evidence gives us cause to question the assumptions of the theory.

A second implication of the neoclassical model is that investment in a perfect capital market should flow freely between countries to equalize the interest rate. If one country has a higher interest rate than another, capital should flow to the high-rate country as investors try to take advantage of the high rate by building factories and machines there. But, as capital flows into a country, the marginal product of capital will fall. Firms equate the rental rate to the marginal product of capital; as the marginal product of capital falls,

FIGURE 16.1

Investment and Saving as a Percentage of GDP for Nine Countries, 1960–1992

Investment rates and saving rates move very closely together.

Martin Feldstein and Charles Horioka pointed out the anomalous relationship between domestic saving and investment in the *Economic Journal,* June 1980. The data that we have used to illustrate this relationship is from the Penn World Table 5.6, which was the most up-to-date version available at the time this book was written.

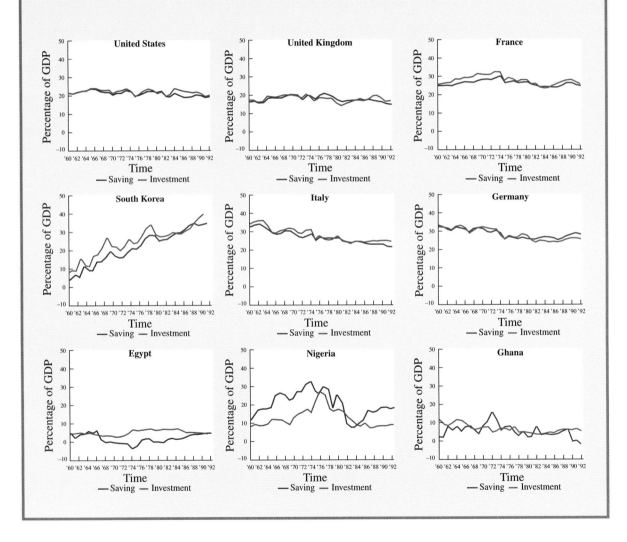

the rental rate that investors can charge for capital also falls. A free flow of capital between countries should equalize rates of return around the world.

For the neoclassical production function, the rate of return depends only on the ratio of capital to labor.[2] It follows that if the rate of return is equal in different countries, the capital-labor ratio must also be equal. In Equation 16.2, K and N represent capital and population in the home country, respectively, and K^f and N^f are the corresponding variables in the foreign country. The efficiency of labor, Q, and the capital elasticity of the production function, α, are assumed to be the same in both countries. We have also assumed that employment per person is equal to 1.[3]

16.2 $$MPK = \alpha\left(\frac{K}{NQ}\right)^{\alpha-1} = MPK^f = \left(\frac{K^f}{QN^f}\right)^{\alpha-1}$$

If capital markets are perfect, marginal products should be equalized across countries. This implies that capital per person should also be equalized.

This is the formula for the marginal product of capital using the Cobb-Douglas production function.

How can we test whether the marginal product of capital is equalized across countries? As shown in Equation 16.3, one indirect test acknowledges that equalization of capital-labor ratios implies equalization of GDP per person across countries because per capita GDP depends only on capital per person.

16.3 $$\left(\frac{Y}{QN}\right) = A\left(\frac{K}{QN}\right)^{\alpha}\left(\frac{QN}{QN}\right)^{1-\alpha} = A\left(\frac{K}{QN}\right)^{\alpha}$$

Output per efficiency unit of labor…

…depends on capital per efficiency unit of labor.

Figure 16.2 presents evidence from five countries: the United States, the United Kingdom, Mexico, Turkey, and India. The vertical axis records the GDP per person in each country relative to per capita GDP in the United States. If the neoclassical model with perfect capital markets were correct, we would see GDP per person equalized across all of these countries as capital flows to find its highest return. In reality, we see that poor countries, like India, tend to stay poor, and rich countries, like the United States, tend to stay rich.

---

2.   Mathematical Note: This property assumes constant returns to scale. We get the formula for the marginal product of capital from the production function by finding the partial derivative with respect to capital. For the Cobb-Douglas function, given by the formula $AK^{\alpha}L^{1-\alpha}$, the marginal product of capital is represented by the expression $\alpha A(K/L)^{\alpha-1}$, the formula used in the text.

3.   This argument will work as long as employment is proportional to population and the constant of proportionality is the same in the two countries. This constant can always be set equal to 1 by choosing the units of measurement appropriately.

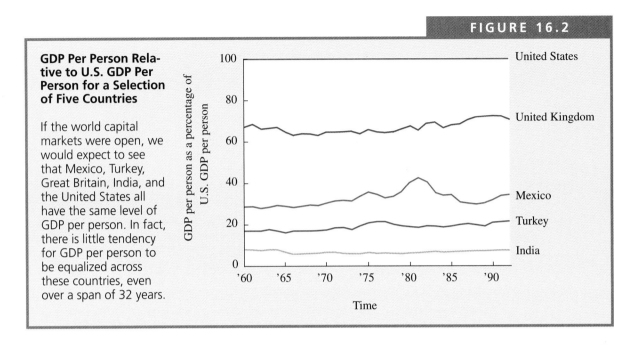

FIGURE 16.2

GDP Per Person Relative to U.S. GDP Per Person for a Selection of Five Countries

If the world capital markets were open, we would expect to see that Mexico, Turkey, Great Britain, India, and the United States all have the same level of GDP per person. In fact, there is little tendency for GDP per person to be equalized across these countries, even over a span of 32 years.

THE NEOCLASSICAL MODEL WITH CLOSED CAPITAL MARKETS

Although evidence suggests that capital does not flow freely between countries, a different version of the neoclassical model can still explain the facts. We look at the case of **zero capital mobility,** the assumption that capital markets are closed, as we develop this variation of the neoclassical model. In a world of zero capital mobility, there is no possibility of borrowing or lending abroad, and therefore domestic saving must equal domestic investment in each country.[4] As with the assumption of open capital markets, we confront the assumption of closed capital markets with the international evidence.

To begin with, we look at the predicted relationship between capital and GDP per person in two countries that are different in only one respect—one country saves more than the other. To compare these two economies, we need to recall how the neoclassical model explains the level of capital in the steady state. We can use Equation 16.4, the neoclassical equation, to obtain an expression for the steady state capital stock.

16.4
$$sY_t = sAK_t^{\alpha}(Q_tN_t)^{1-\alpha} = K_{t+1} - (1-\delta)K_t$$

Saving   Investment

4.   How can world economies be closed when some countries export as much as 60% of their GDP? The answer is that the major motives for trade involve comparative advantage in the production of different commodities. We are not capturing this motive in our model because we are making the very strong, simplifying assumption that there is a single commodity. The fact that domestic saving equals domestic investment implies that exports equal imports; it does not imply that exports or imports constitute a small percentage of GDP.

If we let g_E represent the growth rate of labor in efficiency units, we can use an algebraic expression to determine the value of capital per efficiency unit of labor in the steady state.[5] We want to establish which factors are responsible for determining the amount of capital in a country, relative to the amount of labor.

The algebraic expression for the capital-labor ratio in the steady state uncovers four factors that determine this value. These are: the saving rate, the depreciation rate, the growth rate of labor in efficiency units, and the capital elasticity of output. Equation 16.5 shows how these factors influence the capital labor ratio.

16.5
$$\frac{K}{QN} = \left(\frac{sA}{g_E + \delta}\right)^{\frac{1}{1-\alpha}}$$

| This term measures capital per efficiency unit of labor in the steady state. | This term is a constant that depends on the saving rate, s, and the growth rate of labor, g_E. |

Because we have assumed that every country uses the same production function, the depreciation rate, δ, and the capital elasticity, α, are ruled out as possible factors that differ across countries. Two factors are left—the saving rate and the growth rate of labor, measured in efficiency units.

Equation 16.5 predicts that countries that save more will accumulate more capital per unit of labor in the steady state. But how can we turn this into an observable prediction about living standards? Equation 16.6 gives the relationship between GDP per unit of labor and capital per unit of labor. This equation shows that GDP per person depends positively on the saving rate. In other words, if the saving rate goes up, steady-state GDP per person should also go up.

16.6
$$\frac{Y}{QN} = A\left(\frac{sA}{g_E + \delta}\right)^{\frac{\alpha}{1-\alpha}}$$

| Output per unit of labor depends (in part) on the saving rate. |

In the case of open capital markets, output per person should be equalized in every country in the world. When capital markets are closed, output per person should not be equalized, because output per person depends on the relative amounts of capital used in different countries, and capital per person may differ if countries have different saving rates. If country A has a higher saving rate than country B,

$$\frac{Y^A}{N^A} > \frac{Y^B}{N^B}$$

**GDP per person   GDP per person
in country A   in country B**

---

5.   This is the algebra that we used in Chapter 15 to derive the steady state of the neoclassical growth equation.

BOX 16.1

FOCUS ON THE FACTS
Investment and GDP Per Person

The neoclassical growth model predicts that countries with a high saving and investment rate should have a high steady state level of GDP per person. Panel A shows that this prediction is not borne out in the data. There is no tendency for countries with high investment ratios to have a higher standard of living.

Panel B adjusts investment ratios to allow for population growth in a way that is predicted by the steady state formula from the model.[1] This figure shows that the lack of a correlation between investment ratios and per capita GDP cannot be explained by differences in population growth rates.

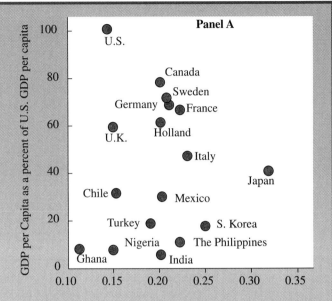

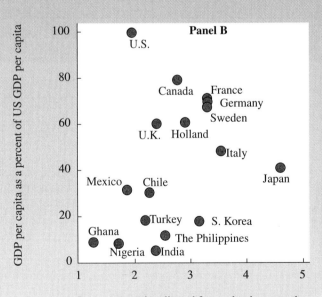

[1] Investment adjusted for population growth is defined as $s/(g_N + \delta)$, where s is the investment-GDP ratio, g_N is the population growth rate, and δ is set to 0.06.

As a test of this prediction, panel A of Box 16.1 plots average GDP per person from 1960 to 1988 against the average investment-GDP ratio for 17 countries. If the neoclassical model were correct, we would see a positive correlation between these numbers; in fact, there is little or no correlation between them.

Perhaps panel A is missing the fact that countries differ not only in their saving rates but in other factors. They also differ in their population growth rates. To check whether population growth rates are hiding the true relationship, panel B corrects the data for population growth. Once again, this figure shows that there is no strong tendency for countries to display the relationship suggested by the steady state of the neoclassical model.

The neoclassical model predicts that GDP per person should be correlated with saving rates, but the data does not support this. The model also falls short in its predictions about growth rates of GDP per person. Although the neoclassical model allows the level of GDP per person to be higher in countries with higher saving rates, it maintains that the growth rates of GDP per person should be the same. Why? Because the model states that all growth is ultimately due to exogenous technical progress.

Suppose that two countries, A and B, have different saving rates and different rates of population growth. Equation 16.7 illustrates that these two countries will converge to different levels of GDP per unit of labor in the steady state. We label these different steady states $\bar{y}_A$ and $\bar{y}_B$.

16.7

$$\frac{Y}{N_A Q} = \bar{y}_A$$

> Output per unit of labor in country A will converge to a constant.

$$\frac{Y}{N_B Q} = \bar{y}_B$$

> Output per unit of labor in country B will converge to a different constant.

Although the steady-state levels are different, they are both constant. How will the growth rate of GDP per person differ in the two countries? Because both countries use the same production function, they must both experience the same growth rate of labor efficiency as measured by changes in Q. These changes in Q are ultimately responsible for growth. Equation 16.8 illustrates that in the steady state, output per person will grow at the same rate in each country because countries that have the same production function should experience the same increases in the efficiency of labor.

16.8

$$\frac{\Delta(Y_A/N_A)}{(Y_A/N_A)} = \frac{\Delta Q}{Q} \quad \frac{\Delta(Y_B/N_B)}{(Y_B/N_B)} = \frac{\Delta Q}{Q}$$

> Countries A and B have different levels of GDP per person. But in each case, the rate of growth of GDP per person is equal to the rate of growth of labor efficiency.

How does this prediction square with the facts? Figure 16.3 on page 366 presents the frequency distribution of per capita GDP growth rates (relative to the growth in GDP per person in the United States) for our 17-country sample. Two countries, Japan and South Korea, experienced average growth rates from 1960 through 1988 that were 4% to 5% greater than the U.S. rate. Ghana grew 2% slower. The data shows that annual growth rates

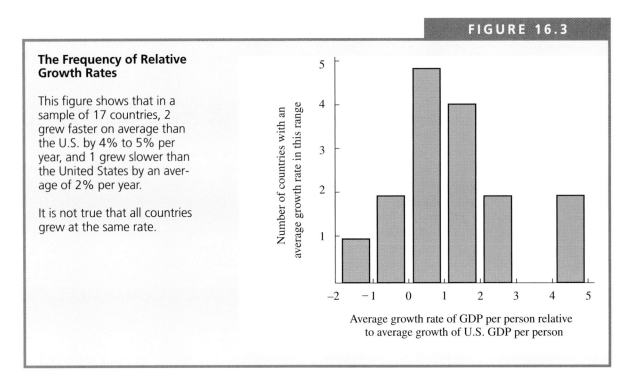

FIGURE 16.3

The Frequency of Relative Growth Rates

This figure shows that in a sample of 17 countries, 2 grew faster on average than the U.S. by 4% to 5% per year, and 1 grew slower than the United States by an average of 2% per year.

It is not true that all countries grew at the same rate.

Average growth rate of GDP per person relative to average growth of U.S. GDP per person

of GDP per person in the world economy have differed by as much as 7% over a span of 30 years. The prediction of the simple neoclassical model does not do a good job of explaining these findings because it assumes that all countries use the same production function and will therefore grow at the same rate in the steady state.

One implication of the neoclassical model is that countries with high saving rates should have high levels of GDP per person. A second implication is that all countries should grow at the same rate. The facts, however, suggest otherwise and leave the neoclassical model lacking in its explanation of the data, even under the extreme assumption that capital markets are closed.

CONVERGENCE

The neoclassical model predicts that countries will grow at the same rate. Some economists note that this prediction only holds if all the countries in the world have attained their steady states. Economies may differ in GDP per person if they are in the process of converging to this steady state. If this is the case, and when we control for factors that determine what steady state a country is converging to, such as saving and population growth, we should see that countries beginning with a low initial stock of capital grow faster than countries beginning with a high stock of capital.

Japan, Germany, and Italy—three countries that grew rapidly in the postwar period—provide one example of the possibility that the initial stock of capital may matter. All three countries experienced considerable destruction of capital equipment during World War II. It is possible that these countries grew faster than the United States in the postwar period because they were catching up by rebuilding capital. This idea is called the **reconstruction hypothesis.** But although the reconstruction hypothesis sounds plausible, two recent studies by Fumio Hayashi of the University of Pennsylvania and Lawrence Christiano of Northwestern University have shown that, at least for Japan, it doesn't explain the facts. Christiano shows that the standard model predicts that GDP per person should converge much more quickly to the steady state than was the case in the postwar Japanese experience.[6]

A second way of testing whether initial conditions matter is to look for evidence that levels of GDP per person move closer together in larger groups of countries. The neoclassical model predicts that countries beginning with low levels of GDP per person should grow faster than countries beginning with high levels of GDP per person. This idea is called the **convergence hypothesis**. A number of economists have tested the convergence hypothesis by looking at the statistical relationship between growth rates of GDP per person and initial levels of GDP per person. Most who have studied this relationship conclude that the convergence hypothesis does not hold across all of the countries in the world. However, there is some evidence of **conditional convergence.** This means that if we include variables as additional factors, such as years of schooling, political stability, and type of government, we can explain some of the differences in growth rates. A major finding reveals that even when growth rates converge, as predicted by the theory, this convergence occurs at a much slower rate than the simple neoclassical model predicts.[7]

THE MODEL OF LEARNING BY DOING

The neoclassical theory attributes growth to increases in labor efficiency, but several new theories have been put forward to explain the anomalies in the neoclassical model. Because increases in labor efficiency are not explained by other economic variables, the neoclassical theory of growth is an exogenous theory. More recently, economists have begun to study an alternative approach that assumes workers acquire skills as they learn a new technology. The skills that they acquire in this way are called human capital, and, according to endogenous growth theory, the accumulation of human capital is responsible for growth in GDP per person.

ENDOGENOUS AND EXOGENOUS THEORIES OF GROWTH

The acquisition of human capital allows a worker to operate complicated machinery or join a team of other skilled workers. A doctor, for example, has more human capital than a garbage collector, and the output that a doctor produces is correspondingly more valuable.

---

6.   Fumio Hayashi. "Is Japan's Savings Rate High?" *Federal Reserve Bank of Minneapolis: Quarterly Review,* pp 3–9, Spring 1989. Lawrence J. Christiano. "Understanding Japan's Savings Rate: The Reconstruction Hypothesis," *Federal Reserve Bank of Minneapolis: Quarterly Review,* pp 10–25, Spring 1989. Both of these articles are easy to read and are recommended supplements to this chapter.
7.   See, for example, N. Gregory Mankiw, David Romer, and David N. Weil. "A contribution to the empirics of growth," *Quarterly Journal of Economics,* No. 100, pp 225–251, February 1992; and Robert J. Barro and Xavier Sala-i-Martin. "Convergence," *Journal of Political Economy,* No. 100, pp 223–251, April 1995.

Human capital can be accumulated in the same way that physical capital is accumulated by devoting resources to the act of investment. In the case of physical capital, investment means building factories and machines. In the case of human capital, investment means acquiring knowledge (skills).

Although human capital is similar to physical capital, there is an important difference: Human capital is acquired not only through the active pursuit of learning, but also through the act of production itself. This way of acquiring knowledge is called **learning by doing.** When new products are invented or new techniques are introduced, the cost of production declines as companies learn the best way to produce these items. Workers acquire this knowledge through their experiences in the workplace.

THE TECHNOLOGY OF ENDOGENOUS GROWTH

Endogenous growth theory makes a relatively minor change to the neoclassical production function. It assumes that the aggregate production function is described by a Cobb-Douglas technology in which the capital elasticity of GDP is equal to 1. The technology of endogenous growth is given in Equation 16.9:

16.9 $Y = K^1 L^{1-\alpha}$

> According to the theory of endogenous growth, the coefficient on capital in the production function is equal to 1.

If the capital elasticity of output is equal to 1 (rather than 1/3), this means that the economy is no longer subject to a diminishing marginal product of capital. Proportional increases in capital are associated with proportional increases in GDP. As a consequence of this modification, per capita GDP can grow forever without the additional units of capital becoming relatively less productive. Growth can occur even when there is no exogenous technical progress to continually increase the efficiency of labor.

Why wasn't this theory proposed sooner? The answer lies in the foundation of exogenous growth theory. Recall that the neoclassical model uses the equation

$$Y = AK^{\alpha}(QL)^{1-\alpha}$$

where the parameter α is equal to 1/3. The 1/3 comes from the neoclassical theory of distribution, which implies that α must equal capital's share of income. If endogenous growth theory proposes a different value for this important parameter, it must explain how this alternative value can be made consistent with the fact that capital's share of income is only 1/3. This is the role of the theory of learning by doing.

SOCIAL AND PRIVATE TECHNOLOGY

The theory of learning by doing reconciles the assumption of constant returns to capital with the theory of distribution. It does so by drawing a distinction between the production function available to society as a whole—the **social technology**—and each individual firm's production function—the **private technology**. Labor becomes more productive, not because of exogenous improvements in technology, but because of the accumulation of knowledge. As a society builds new factories and machines, individuals learn new techniques, and their knowledge becomes embodied in human capital. The acquisition of human capital is a social process whose effects go beyond the individual's own productivity. One firm produces an idea, another firm copies it. As one individual learns a quick and easy way of solving a problem, another individual can duplicate it. The theory of learning by doing captures this idea by arguing that technological progress, Q, is a function of the level of industrialization of the society.

Let's suppose that an economy consists of M firms. Each firm produces output using a private technology that is identical to the Cobb-Douglas production function of the neoclassical growth model. When we let Y, K, and L be aggregate GDP, capital, and labor, respectively, the private production function is given by Equation 16.10:

16.10 $$\frac{Y}{M} = A\left(\frac{K}{M}\right)^{\alpha}\left(\frac{QL}{M}\right)^{1-\alpha}$$ $\boxed{M \text{ is the number of firms.}}$

Because we can cancel out M from both sides of this equation, it follows that aggregate output, aggregate capital, and aggregate labor must be described by the equation

16.11 $$Y = AK^{\alpha}(QL)^{1-\alpha},$$ $\boxed{\begin{array}{l}\text{In the theory of learning by doing, the private} \\ \text{production function is the same function that is} \\ \text{used in the neoclassical growth model.}\end{array}}$

which is the same as the production function used by each firm in the neoclassical theory.[8]

The new element in the theory of learning by doing is an explicit model of what determines Q. The efficiency of labor is assumed to be determined by the aggregate level of industrialization. Because industrialization increases as society becomes more capital-intensive, we can assume that the value of Q is proportional to aggregate capital per worker, K/N. By appropriately choosing the units by which we measure our variables, we can set the constant of proportionality equal to 1. The resulting **knowledge function** is defined in Equation 16.12.

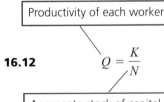

16.12 $\boxed{\text{Productivity of each worker}}$

$$Q = \frac{K}{N}$$

$\boxed{\begin{array}{l}\text{Aggregate stock of capital} \\ \text{per worker}\end{array}}$

$\boxed{\begin{array}{l}\text{The knowledge function maintains that the produc-} \\ \text{tivity of each worker is proportional to the aggre-} \\ \text{gate stock of physical capital per worker. We have} \\ \text{chosen the coefficient of proportionality to equal 1.}\end{array}}$

In other words, the efficiency of each individual worker depends on the aggregate level of capital in the economy as a whole. This relationship determines how knowledge is propagated through society as a result of increases in the stock of capital.

---

8.   Because $M^{a} \times M^{b} = M^{a+b}$

The accumulation of capital has two effects. The first is the private effect that is present in both endogenous and exogenous growth theory, and gives rise to the term K^α in the social production function. The second effect operates through the education of the workforce. As workers learn to use the new technology in one firm, they acquire skills that can be transferred to another firm. This gives rise to the term $K^{1-\alpha}$ on the right-hand side of the social production function. This second effect is an externality to the individual producer because the producer did not have to pay for the education of the workforce. The learning was acquired from the workers' exposure to ideas over the course of their work history, and the degree of exposure grows with the social acquisition of capital.

Inserting the knowledge function into the private production function, we can write the social production function as Equation 16.13:

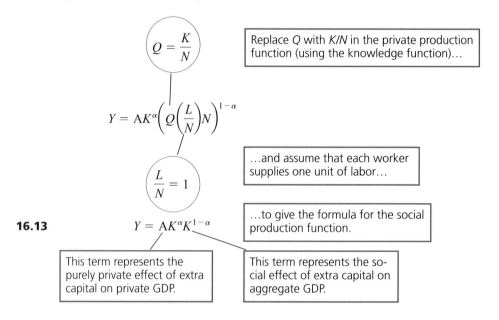

16.13

The two effects by which aggregate capital affect GDP are collected into a single term.[9] The production function that results is called the **social production function** or social technology and is given by Equation 16.14:

16.14

The difference between the social and private effects is illustrated in panels A and B of Figure 16.4. Panel A shows that as the economy adds capital to the same stock of labor, GDP increases in proportion to the increase in capital. Panel B, on the other hand, shows what happens to an individual firm if it increases its capital while every other firm's stock

---

9.   This rearrangement uses the fact that $K^\alpha \times K^{1-\alpha} = K$.

FIGURE 16.4

The Social and Private Production Functions Compared

Panel A illustrates the social production function in the model of learning by doing (holding the input of labor constant).

Panel B illustrates the private production function (holding the input of labor constant).

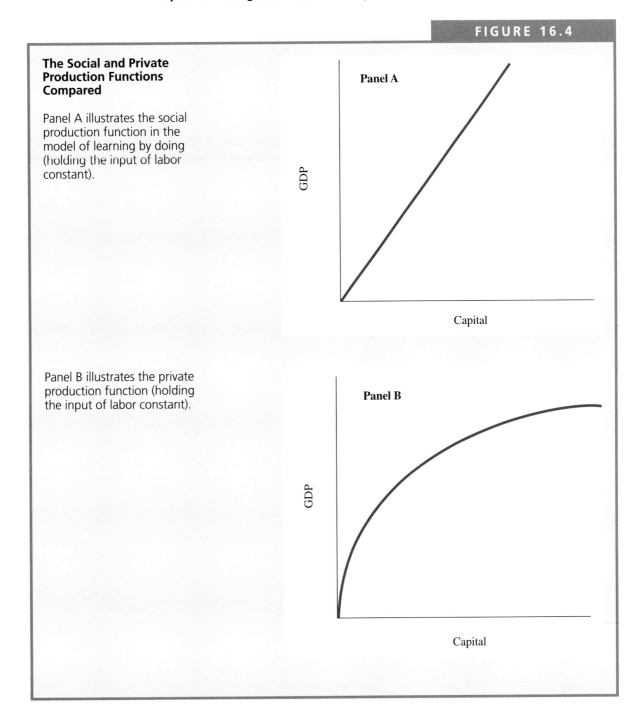

of capital is held constant. As the firm adds capital to the same stock of labor, each unit of capital becomes relatively less productive than the unit before it. This is a consequence of a diminishing marginal product of capital, the same assumption that we encountered in the neoclassical model.

What economic reasoning is responsible for the difference between the graphs in panels A and B? The answer is that when an individual firm expands its use of capital, it captures only the private impact of this additional capital. But the second effect, which is on the education of its workforce, cannot be appropriated by the individual firm. As the firm trains its workers in the use of new equipment, most of this benefit is lost when the workers leave to take new jobs. Their new skills are widely disseminated to friends and colleagues who work at other firms.

An immediate and important implication of the theory of learning by doing is that a firm will be more productive if it is part of a society with a high level of capital. Contrast this with the neoclassical model, which assumes that if a firm were transported from the United States to Ghana, it would still employ the same technology. Learning by doing argues that the firm would be less productive because the skills of the Ghanian workforce are lower than the skills of the U.S. workforce as a direct result of the lower economic degree of Ghanian industrialization.

To sum up, endogenous growth theory makes a distinction between the production function used by an individual firm and the function that applies to society as a whole. If one firm uses more capital, it gains proportionately less output than if the whole society uses more capital. The difference between the two situations can be traced to the knowledge that is acquired by workers who learn new technology. This learning-by-doing effect is spread throughout the entire society and cannot be appropriated by any individual firm. If all firms expand together, however, each benefits from the increased knowledge that is gained not only as a result of its own expansion, but also as the result of the expansion of all of the other firms.

LEARNING BY DOING AND ENDOGENOUS GROWTH

As with the neoclassical theory, endogenous growth theory must take a stand on how to model world capital markets. Because the evidence suggests that there is relatively little international borrowing and lending, we examine the extreme assumption that the world capital markets are closed. Assuming that saving is a fixed fraction of GDP and that saving equals investment, we can write an expression, Equation 16.15, that explains how capital is accumulated.

16.15 $\boxed{\text{Saving}}$ $(sY_t) = sAK_t = \left(K_{t+1} - (1 - \delta)K_t\right)$ $\boxed{\text{Investment}}$

Equation 16.15 looks similar to the expression that describes growth in the neoclassical model, but there is a big and important difference. If we plot a graph of next year's capital against this year's capital, the result is a straight line instead of a curve. If we rearrange Equation 16.15, we can find an expression for the growth equation, Equation 16.16:

FIGURE 16.5

Endogenous Growth

The difference equation that describes growth has only one steady state at a value of $K=0$; and that steady state is unstable. Suppose the economy begins at K_0. Each period, more capital will be accumulated and the economy will move along the trajectory depicted in this graph without ever reaching a new steady state.

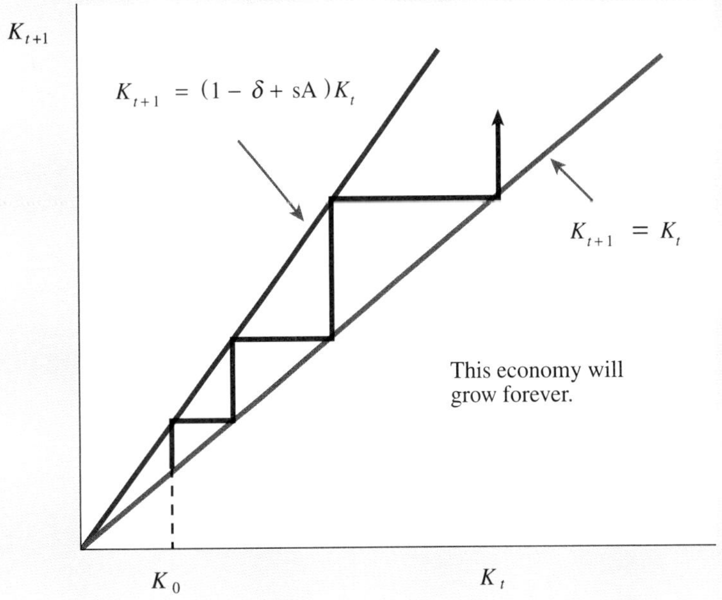

K_{t+1}

$K_{t+1} = (1 - \delta + sA)K_t$

$K_{t+1} = K_t$

This economy will grow forever.

K_0

K_t

16.16 $K_{t+1} = (1 - \delta + sA)K_t$

> In a learning-by-doing economy, the solution to the growth equation is a straight line.

The endogenous growth equation is very different from the neoclassical growth equation because its graph is a straight line. As the economy applies increasing capital to the same fixed stock of labor, the additional output produced grows in proportion. The economy does not experience diminishing returns to capital. In each period, households save a fixed fraction of GDP, and capital expands along a straight line, like the one graphed in Figure 16.5, instead of along a curve as in the neoclassical theory.

PREDICTIONS OF COMPARATIVE GROWTH RATES

This chapter began by pointing to several stylized facts that characterize the growth experiences of a number of countries. Now let's see how endogenous theory explains these facts.

We begin by examining the implication of the endogenous growth model on the behavior of two economies that have the same saving rates, country A and country B. Recall that countries with similar saving rates do not have similar levels of GDP per person. Figure 16.6 illustrates how the theory of learning by doing explains why relative standards of living do not converge over time.

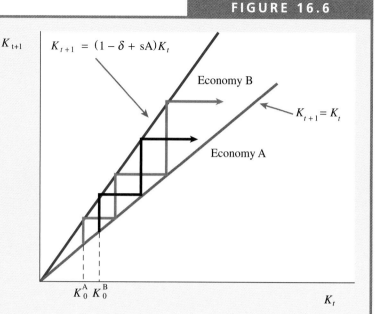

FIGURE 16.6

Two Economies with the Same Growth Rate But Different Initial Conditions

This graph illustrates the growth path of two economies that have the same growth rate, but that began with different initial stocks of capital.

Economy B began with more capital and, as a result, residents of this economy *always* have a higher standard of living than residents of economy A.

In Figure 16.6, both countries have the same saving rates and both follow the same endogenous growth equation. Suppose that country A begins with an initial level of capital, K_0^A, and country B begins with a higher level of capital, K_0^B. Notice that country B begins from a higher initial position, so it will always remain ahead of country A, but both countries' capital will grow at the same rate. This is how the endogenous growth theory explains why countries like India, the United Kingdom, Mexico, and Turkey, which have similar saving rates, grow at about the same rate.

A second piece of evidence concerns two countries with different saving rates. Once again we refer to these countries as A and B, but we suppose that country A has a higher saving rate. Figure 16.7 illustrates the predictions of the endogenous growth theory. Both countries start from the same initial condition, but country A follows a different difference equation because it saves and invests more in every period. The difference equation followed by country A is given by

$$K_{t+1} = K_t(1 - \delta + s^A A),$$

and the equation for country B is:

$$K_{t+1} = K_t(1 - \delta + s_B A).$$

Because we have assumed that the saving rate is higher in country A than in country B, the slope of the endogenous growth function for country A is also higher. But this im-

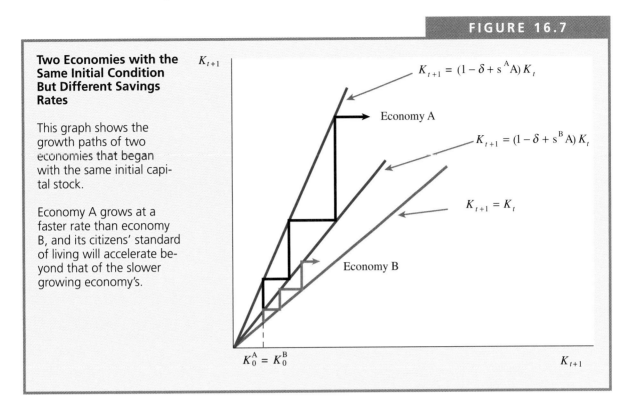

FIGURE 16.7

Two Economies with the Same Initial Condition But Different Savings Rates

This graph shows the growth paths of two economies that began with the same initial capital stock.

Economy A grows at a faster rate than economy B, and its citizens' standard of living will accelerate beyond that of the slower growing economy's.

plies that country A will grow faster than country B because it will accumulate more capital in every period. This is illustrated in Figure 16.7 as the black zigzag line. Describing economy A, it deviates more in each successive period from the gray zigzag line, which represents economy B.

As a way of comparing the predictions with the facts, Figure 16.8 shows a scatter plot of the average ratio of investment to GDP against the average growth rate from 1960 through 1988. Each point represents a country from the same sample of 17 nations that we examined earlier. Clearly, countries with high investment-to-GDP ratios tend to grow faster. Look, for example, at Mexico, Holland, India, and Canada. Although these countries have very different levels of GDP per person (see Box 16.1, page 364), they have similar growth rates. South Korea and Japan, on the other hand, have experienced very rapid growth, which has been associated with very high saving and investment rates.

ENDOGENOUS GROWTH AND ECONOMIC POLICY

One issue that concerns contemporary policymakers is the fact that GDP growth per capita was a little slower in the 1970s than it was in the immediate postwar period. If the neoclassical theory is correct, not much can be done about this. The theory of learning by

FIGURE 16.8

Investment and Growth

This scatter plot reveals that growth *is* related to investment. In our sample of 17 countries, there is a clear, positive relationship between the average investment-to-GDP ratio (over a 32–year period) and the average growth rate of GDP per person.

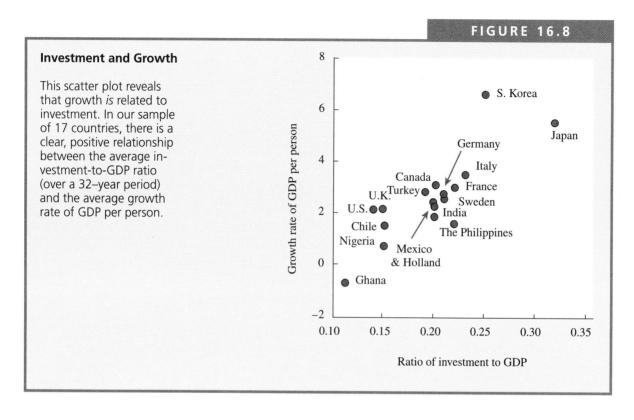

doing, on the other hand, suggests that growth is related to investment—both public and private.

Does this mean that the United States, with the highest standard of living in the world, will grow at the same rate as a country like China, which is emerging from 50 years of a centrally planned economy? The answer to this question is "No." Chinese growth reflects a large catch-up element. Under the Chinese centrally planned system, the pursuit of individual profit was actively discouraged. For example, farmers were unable to sell their produce on the open market. With the reforms of Deng Xiaoping, all of this changed. The individual accumulation of wealth is now not only permitted, it is encouraged. A large part of the very rapid growth that has occurred in the past decade has resulted from the reorganization of institutions that allows Chinese production techniques to catch up with those of the West.

The history of world growth from the eighteenth century to the present is a history of leaders and followers. From the mid-1700s through to the early 1800s, The Netherlands was the world leader in terms of GDP per person. From the 1800s through the early 1900s, the British took over. The United States currently enjoys the highest GDP per person, and has held this lead since 1920. It is likely that a country's ability to increase its standard of living may depend on whether the country is a leader or a follower. For example, a world leader like the United States can only increase GDP per person by inventing new techniques that are more efficient than existing ones. Ghana or Nigeria, on the other hand, can potentially realize big increases in the welfare of their citizens by copying the techniques that are already used in the industrialized world. The experience of Japan and South Korea suggests that the route to growth involves a high level of saving and investment as the society industrializes. But the fact that Japan, South Korea, and China are able to follow this route does not necessarily imply that the United States could achieve a similar increase in growth. In fact, the Japanese growth rate has recently slowed considerably as the Japanese level of GDP per person gets closer to that of the United States.

Where does all of this leave the current debate on public policy? The evidence suggests that investment promotes growth. However, there are reasons to believe that growth achieved through increased investment is not as great for countries that begin with a high standard of living, like the United States, as it is for countries that begin with a low standard of living, like Ghana. But even if the potential for promoting growth is not as great as the East Asian experience suggests, the possibility and benefits of social externalities to the accumulation of knowledge strongly points toward public subsidization of research and development. This is why the U.S. government is so heavily involved in subsidized education. Investment in human capital can have great public benefits. This argument drove much of Bill Clinton's 1992 presidential campaign rhetoric, and President Bush is now emphasizing education as one of his major priorities. The outcome of this policy waits to be seen.

MODIFIED THEORIES OF LEARNING BY DOING

Although economists agree that the neoclassical model does not do a good job of explaining the cross-country evidence, they don't all accept the extreme form of the learning-by-doing hypothesis. Some do not accept the assumption that a country can permanently increase its growth rate above that of other countries simply by increasing its investment rate. They believe a more likely hypothesis is that, as a country gets close to the frontier of world knowledge, part of its investment will spill over and improve growth in other world countries. A considerable international movement of human capital between advanced nations exists, which suggests that the externalities we modeled with the knowledge function can cross international boundaries.

A weaker form of the learning-by-doing hypothesis argues that the knowledge function for each country may display decreasing returns. In other words, a 1% increase in factories and machines leads to less than a 1% increase in labor efficiency as a result of the spread of knowledge. This weaker form of the learning-by-doing hypothesis leads to a model that behaves much like the neoclassical growth model. GDP per capita is predicted to converge across countries, just as in the Solow model, but the speed at which it converges is much slower. The modified learning-by-doing hypothesis can explain many of the neoclassical model's anomalies. It predicts that countries that invest more can temporarily grow faster, but eventually they will catch up with the world leaders, and at that point their growth rates will slow down.[10]

---

10. Mankiw, Romer, and Weil."A contribution to the empirics of growth," *Quarterly Journal of Economics*, No. 100, pp 225–251, February 1992.

CONCLUSION

One way in which the neoclassical growth model can be extended to allow for international trade in capital is to assume that capital markets are open (perfect capital mobility), and that Americans can borrow and lend freely in every country in the world. If this were a good characterization, we would expect to see GDP per person equalized across countries as capital flows toward high rates of return. But in the real world, we see no tendency for this equalization of living standards.

A second way to extend the model is to assume that capital markets are closed (zero capital mobility). This assumption is at least consistent with the fact that investment and saving tend to be equal within each country. However, the neoclassical growth model predicts that countries with high saving rates will tend to have high levels of GDP per person and there is no evidence of this connection in the data. The neoclassical model also predicts that the growth rate of GDP per person should be equal worldwide. In practice, we see divergence in per capita growth rates of as much as 7% for long periods of time. Because of the neoclassical model's failure to explain these facts, we turn to an alternative model of growth, the model of learning by doing.

Learning by doing builds on the neoclassical growth model, but it allows proportional increases in capital to cause proportional increases in GDP. To explain how the coefficient on capital in the production function can be different from capital's share of income, the theory distinguishes between the private and social production functions. The private production function places a weight of 1/3 on capital; the social production function places a weight of 1 on capital, and private firms do not account for their actions' effects on the social acquisition of knowledge.

The learning-by-doing theory explains growth endogenously instead of assuming an exogenous increase in technical progress. It is able to explain why GDP per person is not equalized across countries. It also explains why countries with high saving rates tend to grow faster than countries with low saving rates. A modified, weaker form of the learning-by-doing model behaves like the exogenous growth model, but this weaker model predicts much slower convergence.

KEY TERMS

Conditional convergence
Convergence hypothesis
Intertemporal trade
Knowledge function
Learning by doing
Perfect capital mobility

Private technology
Reconstruction hypothesis
Social production function
Social technology
Zero capital mobility

QUESTIONS FOR CHAPTER 16

---

1. Compare and contrast the processes that generate sustained increases in per capita GDP in the neoclassical growth model and endogenous growth model.

2. Define *perfect capital mobility*. Discuss in detail two counterfactual implications of perfect capital mobility.

3. What does the closed-economy neoclassical model predict about the relationship between saving/investment rates and the *level* of per capita GDP within a country? Is this prediction consistent with cross-country data? Why or why not?

4. What does the closed-economy neoclassical model predict about the relationship between saving/investment rates and the steady state *growth rate* of per capita GDP within a country? Is this prediction consistent with cross-country data? Why or why not?

5. Reconsider your answer to question 4. Do endogenous growth models, such as the learning-by-doing model, do a better job of explaining the relationship between a country's saving/investment rate and its per capita growth rate? Explain why or why not.

6. Explain what economists mean by an *externality*. How are externalities used to reconcile the theory of endogenous growth with the neoclassical theory of distribution?

7. What three parameters influence the growth rate in the theory of learning by doing? For each of these parameters, explain the effect of an increase in the parameter on the rate of growth of the economy.

8. Consider an economy with a savings rate s = 0.1, depreciation rate δ = 0.05, and production function $Y = AK^{1/3}(QL)^{2/3}$ where A = L = 1.

   a. Calculate the steady state levels of the capital stock and GDP if Q is exogenous. How fast will this economy grow in the steady state?

   b. Now suppose that Q is endogenous and varies directly with the level of the capital stock (i.e., $Q = K$). Can you find the steady state capital stock and GDP in this case? What is the growth rate of this economy?

   c. How do you explain the difference in the growth rate between part a and part b?

9. In a model of learning by doing, do individual firms face constant returns to scale in production? Does society as a whole face constant returns to scale in production? Explain.

10. The endogenous growth model predicts that

$$K_{t+1} = K_t(1 - \delta + sA).$$

Suppose that A = 1, that δ = 0.1, and s = 0.2. What would you predict would be the growth rate of capital?

(*Hint*: The growth rate is $\dfrac{K_{t+1}}{K_t} - 1$.)

11. The following table gives saving rates for five economies:

United States	0.16
The Philippines	0.17
Mexico	0.18
Japan	0.25
Ghana	0.09

a. Assume that in all of these countries, δ = 0.1 and A = 1. Assuming that the neo-classical growth model is true, compute the level of GDP per person in the steady state for each of these countries as a fraction of U.S. GDP per person.

b. Assume that the endogenous growth theory is correct. Compute the predicted growth rate of GDP per person in each of these countries relative to the growth rate of U.S. GDP per person.

12. Suppose that two countries are alike in all respects except that one has a higher saving rate. Suppose that the endogenous growth theory is correct. What would you predict about the relative marginal products of capital in the two countries? If you were to assume that there is perfect capital mobility, would you expect to see a flow of investment from the country with the high saving rate to the country with the low saving rate or vice versa? Would you expect to see any flow from one country to the other at all? (*Hint:* Compute the relative marginal products of capital in the two countries.)

13. Consider two countries that are identical except for the fact that country A has a lower initial per capita capital stock than country B. Now suppose that one unit of capital is added to each country. In which country will the marginal product of this additional unit of capital be the largest? Analyze this question within both the neoclassical growth model and the endogenous growth model, and make sure to compare and contrast your results.

14. Suppose that, instead of a Cobb-Douglas function, the production function takes the form

$$Y = \left(AK^\rho + (1 + a)N^\rho\right)^{1/\rho},$$

where a is a parameter between 0 and 1 and ρ is a parameter between 1 and $-\infty$.

a. Find the per capita form of this production function (find $Y/N = y$ as a function of $K/N = k$).

b. Find the marginal products of capital and labor.

c. Find an expression for labor's share of income and show that this expression is not constant. Is there a value of ρ for which it is constant?

CHAPTER 17

UNEMPLOYMENT, INFLATION, AND GROWTH

INTRODUCTION

In Chapters 4, 5, and 6, we studied a model of the complete economy based on the ideas of the classical economists. At that point we said little about economic growth, and the theories we discussed were static. Now that we have introduced difference equations, tools that describe how the economy changes from one period to the next, we are ready to study inflation and growth. Our starting point is the classical model of aggregate demand, which we combine with the new-Keynesian theory of aggregate supply.

Why study the classical theory of aggregate demand rather than the Keynesian theory? Because classical theory is simpler. But this has both advantages and disadvantages. The major disadvantage is that the classical theory makes the false assumption that the propensity to hold money is independent of the interest rate, which means the theory is unable to account for channels through which fiscal policy influences aggregate demand. The major advantage of using the classical aggregate demand curve instead of the more complex (and realistic) Keynesian approach is that we can highlight the most important advances in economic dynamics that have occurred over the past 20 years without getting bogged down in details. The Keynesian model has the same features, but it also describes the effects of the interest rate and fiscal policy on inflation, employment, and growth.

We are now going to develop a model of the whole economy and use it to explain the relationship between unemployment, inflation, and growth. Our model is built from the classical aggregate demand curve (see Chapter 5), the Keynesian aggregate supply curve (see Chapter 8), and the **new-Keynesian wage equation**, which explains how the nominal wage is adjusted from one period to the next. The new-Keynesian wage equation is part of a **dynamic theory**, unlike the static theories we have studied so far.

First we must alter the classical aggregate demand curve and the Keynesian aggregate supply curve in order to explain how variables change over time. We do this largely by allowing for productivity growth.[1] By building the classical aggregate demand curve and the Keynesian aggregate supply curve in terms of proportional changes instead of levels, we can plot a downward-sloping line (the dynamic aggregate demand curve) and an upward-sloping line (the short-run dynamic aggregate supply curve) on a graph of inflation against growth. Using these curves (with a little help from the new-Keynesian wage equation), we can show how aggregate demand and aggregate supply interact to determine all of the endogenous variables of our theory: unemployment, growth, inflation, and the nominal wage.

THE CLASSICAL APPROACH TO INFLATION AND GROWTH

We build the dynamic new-Keynesian theory of aggregate demand and supply in two stages. First, we explore how the dynamic model works if markets are extremely efficient—that is, if the nominal wage is always chosen to eliminate any possible gains from trade between firms and workers (i.e., unemployment is always at the natural rate). We call this version of our theory the **classical approach**. Beginning here gives us an idea of what must be added to a static theory in order to allow for growth.

Once we understand how the model operates when unemployment is always chosen efficiently, we study the new-Keynesian wage equation, a theory that explains how the nominal wage changes over time when unemployment fluctuates from its natural rate. The theory of wage adjustment allows us to describe an economy as Keynesian when the nominal wage moves very slowly in response to differences between the actual and natural unemployment rates. The economy is described as classical when it moves very fast.

NATURAL PATHS AND NATURAL RATES

To discuss the natural rate of unemployment in a growing economy, we need some new ideas. The most important of these is the **natural output path**, Y^*. We will see that Y is more than Y^* whenever unemployment is less than its natural rate.

We learned in Chapters 7 and 8 that there is a natural unemployment rate, a natural level of the real wage (the efficiency wage), a natural level of employment, and a natural level of output. Now we need to amend the theory of unemployment to account for technical progress. In a dynamic, growing economy, when a firm pays a turnover cost to manage its pool of workers, the natural unemployment rate and the natural level of employment remain constant each period, just as in the static economy. But the natural level of output

---

1.   We adopt the exogenous growth theory from Chapter 15. The interaction of aggregate demand and supply with endogenous theories of growth is a very new area of research.

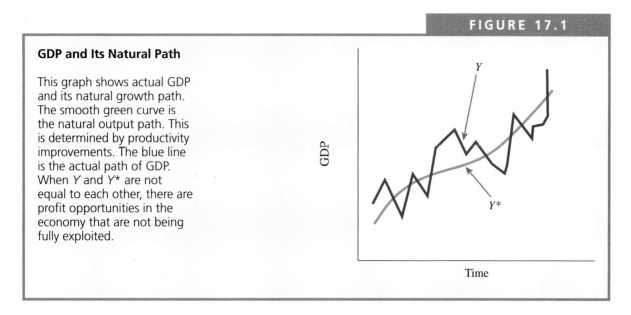

FIGURE 17.1

GDP and Its Natural Path

This graph shows actual GDP and its natural growth path. The smooth green curve is the natural output path. This is determined by productivity improvements. The blue line is the actual path of GDP. When Y and Y^* are not equal to each other, there are profit opportunities in the economy that are not being fully exploited.

and the natural real wage grow from one year to the next as technology improves. We call the list of natural levels of output, one for each year, the natural output path, and we call the list of efficiency wage levels the **natural real wage path**.

Figure 17.1 illustrates the idea that GDP may have a natural path. This is the smooth green curve labeled Y^*. The irregular blue curve is the path of actual GDP. We refer to Y^* and Y as paths because they are different from one year to the next. The natural path of GDP is determined by factors like the invention of new technology and discoveries of natural resources, factors which make technology more productive from one year to the next.[2]

THE CLASSICAL DYNAMIC AGGREGATE DEMAND CURVE

We write the classical aggregate demand curve in the form of proportional changes, as shown in Equation 17.1:

17.1
$$\frac{\Delta P}{P} = \frac{\Delta M}{M} - \frac{\Delta Y}{Y}$$

| Price inflation rate | Money growth rate | Natural GDP growth rate |

The variables $\Delta P/P$, $\Delta M/M$, and $\Delta Y/Y$ are the proportional changes in the price level, the proportional change in the money supply, and the proportional change in GDP, respectively.

---

2. Because inventions arrive randomly, the natural growth path can fluctuate up and down erratically from one year to the next. In this chapter, we ignore these fluctuations in the natural growth path in order to keep our presentation as simple as possible.

We also refer to these variables as the price inflation rate, the money growth rate, and the GDP growth rate. When the context is clear, we will refer to the rate of price inflation (as opposed to wage inflation) as the inflation rate and the rate of GDP growth as growth.

Equation 17.1 is a dynamic version of the quantity theory of money. The static version of the quantity theory (see Chapter 5) makes three assumptions: first, that the quantity of money demanded is proportional to income; second, that the quantity of money demanded is equal to the quantity supplied; and third, that the propensity to hold money is constant. When we develop the theory according to growth rates, the outcome is the **dynamic theory of aggregate demand**.

THE CLASSICAL DYNAMIC AGGREGATE SUPPLY CURVE

What are the factors that cause growth and inflation to vary over the business cycle? To answer this question, we amend the efficiency wage model of unemployment to allow for changes in productivity from one year to the next. We assume that productivity growth arises from the exogenous discovery of new technologies, which increase the quantity of output produced from any given input of labor. This assumption forms the basis of the **dynamic theory of aggregate supply** because it predicts that GDP will grow each year, even if employment does not. There are two versions of this theory. In the classical version, we assume that the real wage always grows at the natural rate of productivity growth. This assumption implies that unemployment is always at its natural rate. In the new-Keynesian version of the theory, we assume instead that real wage growth can differ from its natural rate.

Figure 17.2 shows how the classical dynamic theory of aggregate supply can be derived from a labor market diagram and a production function diagram. The figure illustrates the production function on panel A and the labor market on panel B, and the figure spans two consecutive years. Panel A shows that in year 2, a given input of labor can produce more output than in year 1. Suppose that employment is equal to its natural rate, L^{*}.[3] This would be true if the costs of finding a worker were not affected by changes in technology, and it is probably a good first approximation of the way the labor market operates. We see from panel A that even if L^{*} is the same in year 1 and year 2, the natural level of output grows from Y_1^{*} to Y_2^{*}. In the static model, the fact that employment is equal to L^{*} implies that there is a single natural level of output, Y^{*}. In the dynamic model, though, natural output follows a growing path, even when employment is fixed, because the productivity of labor increases each year as new technologies are discovered. Employment remains at its natural level, L^{*}, in every period, but output grows at the rate g.

Equation 17.2 represents the classical dynamic aggregate supply curve. The terms $\Delta Y/Y$ and $\Delta Y^{*}/Y^{*}$ represent the proportional change in GDP and the proportional change in the natural rate of output, respectively. The natural rate g is determined by exogenous factors that govern innovation and discovery.

---

3. To keep our analysis as simple as possible, we assume that there is no population growth. To illustrate this, the vertical red line representing the labor force is the same in the two consecutive years. We also impose the simplifying assumption that labor supply does not depend on the real wage. Modifying either of these assumptions would not be difficult, but it would complicate our analysis without adding further insight.

FIGURE 17.2

Growth and the Real Wage

These graphs show how the natural level of output and the natural real wage will grow as a result of exogenous productivity gains.

Panel A shows the production function in two consecutive years. The production function in year 2 is consistently higher than the production function in year 1. This reflects the fact that productivity has increased as new technologies were discovered. In the new-Keynesian model, the rate of productivity growth is exogenous.

Panel B shows how technology growth affects the natural real wage. The figure assumes that the population is constant and that households inelastically supply labor to the market (the labor force supply curve is vertical).

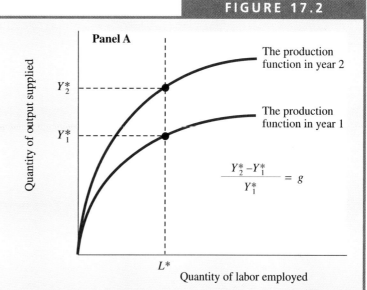

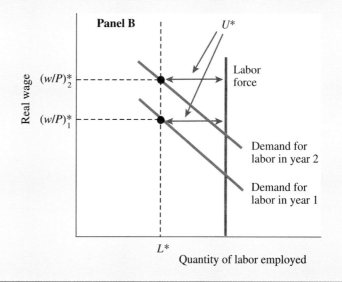

17.2	$\dfrac{\Delta Y}{Y}$	$=$	$\dfrac{\Delta Y^*}{Y^*}$	$=$	g
	GDP growth rate		Natural GDP growth rate		Productivity growth rate

FIGURE 17.3

Inflation and Growth (the Classical Case)

The vertical purple line is the classical version of the dynamic aggregate supply curve. This curve is vertical because, in the classical model, output always grows at the rate of productivity growth, g.

The downward-sloping blue line is the classical version of the dynamic aggregate demand curve.

The point at which the classical aggregate demand and supply curves intersect determines the rate of inflation. In equilibrium, this equals the difference between the money growth rate and the productivity growth rate.

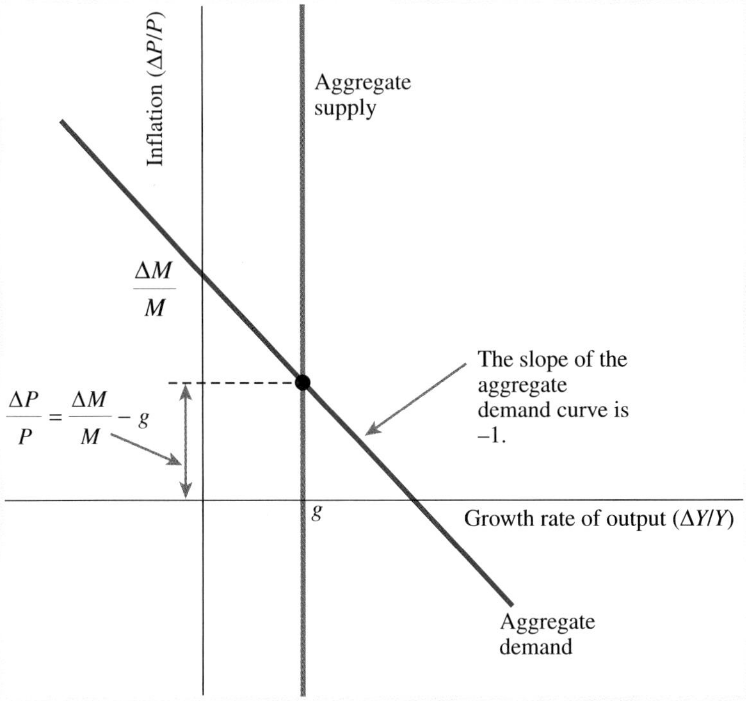

$$\frac{\Delta P}{P} = \frac{\Delta M}{M} - g$$

Inflation ($\Delta P/P$)

$\frac{\Delta M}{M}$

Aggregate supply

The slope of the aggregate demand curve is -1.

g

Growth rate of output ($\Delta Y/Y$)

Aggregate demand

Figure 17.3 combines the dynamic theories of aggregate demand and supply on a graph that plots inflation on the vertical axis and growth on the horizontal axis. The dynamic aggregate demand curve is a downward-sloping line with a slope of -1. This graph intersects the vertical axis at the rate of money growth $\Delta M/M$. The dynamic aggregate supply curve is the vertical purple line at the rate of productivity growth g. The classical dynamic aggregate supply curve is vertical because we assume that employment is always at the natural rate and that GDP grows each period at an exogenous rate determined by the rate at which society discovers new technologies.

THE WAGE EQUATION IN THE CLASSICAL MODEL

How is the real wage chosen each period in the dynamic classical theory? Panel B of Figure 17.2 graphs the labor market. We represent the constant natural level of employment by a vertical dashed line at L^*. As technological improvements make each worker more productive, the firm's labor demand curve shifts upward, firms compete with each other to hire from the existing pool of workers, and they bid up the natural real wage from $(w/P)_1^*$ in year 1 to $(w/P)_2^*$ in year 2; these are two points on the natural real wage path. Because the labor demand curve shifts at rate g and employment is constant, the real wage also grows at rate g, as shown in Equation 17.3.

17.3
$$\frac{\Delta w}{w} - \frac{\Delta P}{P} \qquad = \qquad g$$

Difference between wage inflation and price inflation   **Productivity growth rate**

Box 17.1 presents data on productivity and the real wage in the United States from 1929 to 1999. The assumption that productivity and the real wage grow at the same rate is a good one because the two variables have moved very closely over the past 70 years.

THE NEW-KEYNESIAN APPROACH TO INFLATION AND GROWTH

Now that we have developed a dynamic apparatus for analyzing aggregate demand and supply, we are ready to study the **new-Keynesian theory of aggregate supply**. This theory is more realistic than the classical theory and allows unemployment to fluctuate from its natural rate.

The new-Keynesian approach to aggregate supply has three elements. The first is a theory of wage determination, which we return to later in this chapter. The second element is a theory that explains how inflation and growth are related to each other in the short run, the period during which the real wage differs from its natural growth path. The third element explains how inflation and growth are related to each other when the real wage is on its natural growth path—the classical aggregate supply curve. In the new-Keynesian model, GDP may depart from its natural path for short periods, but it tends to return to the natural path in the long run.

AGGREGATE SUPPLY AND THE REAL WAGE

We begin by explaining the short-run new-Keynesian dynamic aggregate supply curve. Because the real wage can differ from its natural path, changes in the real wage will relate to changes in employment, and therefore to growth. If the real wage grows slower than its natural rate, firms will increase employment. If the real wage grows faster, firms will decrease employment. Expansions or contractions of employment raise or lower GDP growth above or below its natural rate, respectively. Data generated by this economy should show that output growth is inversely related to real wage growth along the aggregate supply curve.

Figure 17.4 illustrates the relationship between changes in the real wage and changes in GDP for two consecutive periods. Panel A graphs the production function, and panel B graphs the labor market. They show that if the real wage increases too quickly, GDP growth will be lower than its natural rate.

On Panel B, the real wage in year 1 is on its natural path at $(w/P)^*_1$, and employment is equal to its natural level, L^*. In year 2, the labor demand curve shifts upward in response

BOX 17.1

FOCUS ON THE FACTS
The Third Industrial Revolution?

Classical theory assumes that productivity improvements are translated into real wage growth. How realistic is this assumption? Productivity is defined as output produced per unit of labor used in production. This graph illustrates productivity and the real wage from 1929 through 2000.[1] They grew on average at the same rate over the whole period. Notice, however, that between 1974 and 1995, both productivity and real wage growth slowed down. Why is this?

One possibility is that productivity slowed as workers adapted to a new technology. If this view is correct, then we should soon see a big *increase* in productivity that will wipe out the apparent losses in wage growth of the past two decades. There is some evidence that this increase is now beginning to happen.

Economic historians have identified two major industrial revolutions in the past two centuries. The first began in 1760 and the second in 1860. Are we entering a third?

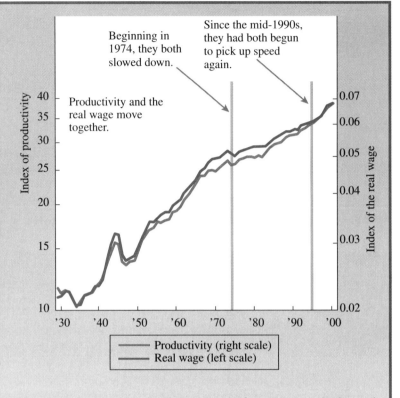

In the two decades beginning in 1760, there were several technological miracles. The introduction of new spinning technology and the invention of energy-efficient steam engines led to tremendous changes in society that generated big increases in living standards. A second jump in technological efficiency began in the 70-year period beginning in the 1860s. This era saw the introduction of electricity, the modern chemical plant, and the automobile.

In both previous industrial revolutions, the discovery of new technologies led to initial *reductions* in productivity, as well as the wages of the unskilled, reductions that were later reversed. These reductions were necessary because the introduction of a new technology requires a long period of adjustment as firms and workers learn to exploit the new ideas. Jeremy Greenwood of the University of Rochester has argued that we may now be in the throes of a third industrial revolution based on the availability of cheap computing power.[2]

Greenwood argues that the productivity slowdown that occurred in 1974 resulted from the same process that we saw in 1760 and again in 1860. We are entering a third industrial revolution, one associated with information technology. Initially, the new jobs fueled by computers are highly skill intensive, and there will be a big increase in the relative wages of those people who have the necessary skills. Low-skilled workers, those who form the major part of the labor force, will be worse off during the initial adoption phase as there are fewer routine jobs that are suited to their abilities. But as society learns to use the new information technologies, the new skills will themselves become routine, and many more people will become familiar with the operation of the new machines. As this occurs, we can expect to see that productivity will once more increase at the higher rate. Experience with the last two industrial revolutions suggests that it may take 40 years before the wage of the unskilled has caught up and overtaken the wage that they might have expected if the revolution had not occurred.

[1] The real wage is constructed by dividing compensation to employees by national income and multiplying that by an index of hours of employment supplied to the market. Productivity is defined as output per unit of labor input.

[2] Jeremy Greenwood. *The Third Industrial Revolution*, American Enterprise Institute for Public Policy Research, Washington, DC, 1997.

FIGURE 17.4

Real Wage Growth and Aggregate Supply: The New-Keynesian Model

This graph shows what will happen to GDP growth if the real wage grows faster than its natural rate.

On panel A, Y_1^* represents output in year 1; in this year output is on its natural path. In year 2, the natural path of output increases to Y_2^*, but actual output is lower at Y_2. Output between years 1 and 2 has grown at less than the natural rate, g.

Panel B shows *why* output growth has slipped below g. Growth is low between years 1 and 2 because the real wage has grown too fast, and unemployment in year 2 is above the natural rate.

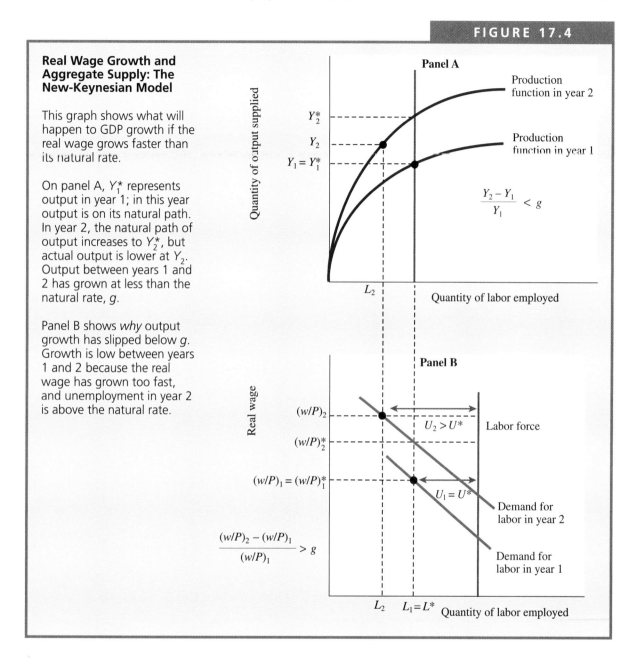

to exogenous productivity gains that are sufficient to justify an increase in the real wage to $(w/P)^*_2$. If the real wage were to increase to $(w/P)^*_2$, output would grow at its natural rate. But instead, panel B graphs the effect of the real wage increasing to $(w/P)_2$, a level that is greater than $(w/P)^*_2$. In this case, because the real wage has grown too fast, firms decrease employment and output increases by less than the natural rate.

Panel A illustrates the implications of excessive wage growth for GDP growth. In year 1, output is on its natural path at Y_1^*. Between years 1 and 2, productivity increases at rate g. If employment were to remain at its natural level, L^*, output would grow by its natural rate and GDP would increase from Y_1^* to Y_2^*. But because real wage growth between years 1 and 2 exceeds its natural rate, firms reduce employment in year 2 and output growth slows. If the real wage rate grows faster than its natural rate, the GDP growth rate will slow down.

Although Figure 17.4 illustrates the case where real wage growth exceeds the natural rate, a similar graph could be used to show that if the real wage grows by less than the natural rate, then output growth will be greater than g. Similarly, when the real wage growth rate is equal to the natural rate, output growth will follow this same rate.

THE DYNAMIC NEW-KEYNESIAN AGGREGATE SUPPLY CURVE

Because the change in the real wage is the difference between wage inflation and price inflation, a theory that explains how changes in the real wage are related to growth can also be used to show how price inflation is related to growth. Let's begin by assuming wage inflation is given, and we then examine how price inflation is related to GDP growth. Equation 17.4 shows the relationship between price inflation and growth, which is implied by the new-Keynesian theory.

17.4
$$\frac{\Delta P}{P} = \left(\frac{\Delta w}{w} - g\right) + b\left(\frac{\Delta Y}{Y} - g\right)$$

The dynamic new-Keynesian aggregate supply curve

| Rate of price inflation | Excess wage inflation (above the natural rate) | Excess GDP growth (above the natural rate) |

The left side of Equation 17.4 is the rate of price inflation. The first term on the right side is **excess wage inflation** (increases in the nominal wage over and above those that are justified by productivity gains), and the second term is **excess GDP growth** (growth in GDP over and above productivity gains). Suppose that the nominal wage grows at the rate of productivity growth, g. In this case, Equation 17.4 tells us to expect price inflation (prices rise) whenever GDP grows faster than g and price deflation (prices fall) whenever GDP grows slower than g.

When price inflation is too high, real wage growth is less than productivity growth, employment rises, and output growth exceeds the natural rate. When inflation is too low, the real wage rate grows more than productivity growth, employment falls, and output grows by less than the natural rate. How much GDP growth exceeds or falls short of natural productivity growth for a given rate of price inflation depends on preferences, endowments, and technology; and this factor is designated in Equation 17.4 by the parameter b.

Table 17.1 summarizes the channels by which inflation and growth are related to each other. In each row of the table, the nominal wage grows by the natural rate of productivity growth, but each row makes a different assumption about price inflation. The first row assumes positive price inflation. We see in the third column that price inflation causes less growth in the real wage than the rate of productivity growth; hence, employment rises (the

TABLE 17.1

**The Link Between Inflation and Growth
When Wage Inflation Equals *g***

Wage inflation	Price inflation	The real wage	Employment	Growth
$\dfrac{\Delta w}{w} = g$	$\dfrac{\Delta P}{P} > 0$	$\left(\dfrac{\Delta w}{w} - \dfrac{\Delta P}{P}\right) < g$	$\dfrac{\Delta L}{L} > 0$	$\dfrac{\Delta Y}{Y} > g$
$\dfrac{\Delta w}{w} = g$	$\dfrac{\Delta P}{P} < 0$	$\left(\dfrac{\Delta w}{w} - \dfrac{\Delta P}{P}\right) > g$	$\dfrac{\Delta L}{L} < 0$	$\dfrac{\Delta Y}{Y} < g$
$\dfrac{\Delta w}{w} = g$	$\dfrac{\Delta P}{P} = 0$	$\left(\dfrac{\Delta w}{w} - \dfrac{\Delta P}{P}\right) = g$	$\dfrac{\Delta L}{L} = 0$	$\dfrac{\Delta Y}{Y} = g$

fourth column) and output growth exceeds the natural rate (the fifth column). The second row assumes price inflation is negative. In this case, the real wage rises by more than the natural rate, employment declines, and output growth is less than the natural growth rate. The third row of the table assumes zero price inflation. Here, the real wage and GDP both grow at the natural rate.

We assume in Table 17.1 that excess wage inflation is equal to zero (wage inflation equals *g*). What would happen if excess wage inflation did not equal *g*? If excess wage inflation is positive, say 2%, the real wage will fall, but only if price inflation *exceeds* 2%. If excess wage inflation is negative, say –2%, the real wage will fall, but only if price inflation exceeds –2%. Price inflation that is greater than excess wage inflation causes output growth to exceed *g*. Price inflation that is less than excess wage inflation causes output growth to be less than *g*.

Figure 17.5 on page 392 graphs the aggregate supply curve implied by our theory. The vertical purple line is the natural rate of output growth, the long-run aggregate supply curve (LRAS). We use the label "long-run" because in the new-Keynesian theory of wage adjustment, there are forces that cause the rate of wage inflation to change whenever output differs from its natural growth path. Because of these forces, output growth cannot depart from its natural rate for long periods of time.

The upward-sloping line is the dynamic new-Keynesian short-run aggregate supply curve (SRAS). Its position depends on excess wage inflation, $(\Delta w/w) - g$. The short- and long-run curves intersect when price inflation equals excess wage inflation; in this case, the real wage and output rates both grow at the natural rate of *g*. If price inflation exceeds excess wage inflation, output must grow faster than *g*, and if price inflation is less than excess wage inflation, output growth must be less than *g*. The theory says nothing about what determines excess wage inflation; for this we must turn to the new-Keynesian wage equation.

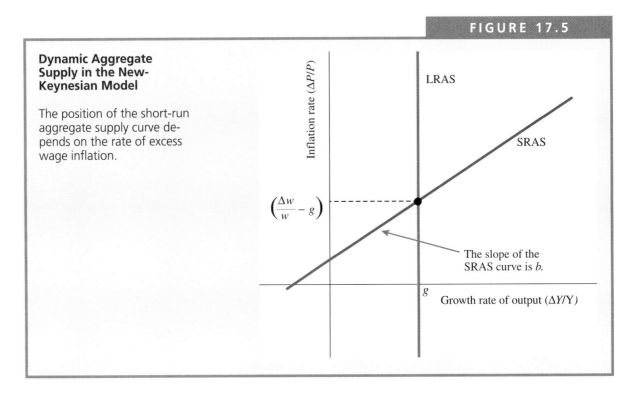

FIGURE 17.5

Dynamic Aggregate Supply in the New-Keynesian Model

The position of the short-run aggregate supply curve depends on the rate of excess wage inflation.

THE NEW-KEYNESIAN WAGE EQUATION

The new-Keynesian wage equation is best understood by comparing it with its classical counterpart. In the classical theory, the real wage follows its natural path, and there are never any opportunities for firms to make extra profits by offering to trade with workers either at a lower real wage or at a higher real wage. In the new-Keynesian version of the theory, firms can sometimes make extra profits because either the real wage is too high and unemployment is above its natural rate or the real wage is too low and unemployment is below its natural rate. The real wage is always moving toward its natural path, but in the new-Keynesian theory, adjustment takes time.

The new-Keynesian wage equation, Equation 17.5, models the idea that when there are profit opportunities (unemployment differs from its natural rate), the nominal wage moves in a direction that causes these opportunities to be eliminated.

17.5 $\left(\dfrac{\Delta w}{w} - g\right)$ $=$ $\dfrac{\Delta P^{\mathrm{E}}}{\Delta P}$ $-$ $c(U - U^*)$

The new-Keynesian wage equation

Excess wage inflation (above the natural rate)

Expected price inflation

Excess unemployment (above its natural rate)

On the left side of the new-Keynesian wage equation, the term $(\Delta w/w) - g$ represents excess wage inflation (over and above natural productivity growth). On the right side, the amount by which unemployment exceeds its natural rate is subtracted from the expected price inflation. The parameter c determines how fast the nominal wage moves to restore balance between the real wage and the real efficiency wage.

Because it takes time for firms and workers to gather information about labor market conditions, the real wage may temporarily deviate from its natural path, but strong forces should push it back. In the new-Keynesian theory, two factors influence wage inflation: expected price inflation and the difference between unemployment and its natural rate.

Expected price inflation influences wage inflation because wages are typically set for a period of time; wage contracts in the United States often last for two years or more, and firms cannot predict workers' future demand conditions. Firms must form an expectation of the rate of price inflation because this will affect the real value of the nominal wage. Unemployment influences wage inflation because if U is different from U^*, all of the possible gains from trade between workers and firms have not been exploited, leaving an opportunity for firms to profit.

The new-Keynesian model is a natural compromise between the classical model, in which the nominal wage adjusts immediately to eliminate excess unemployment, and the Keynesian model, in which the nominal wage does not adjust at all. The classical and Keynesian theories are polar cases of the new-Keynesian model that occur when the parameter c, the speed of adjustment, is either very large (infinite in the limiting case) or very small (zero in the limiting case). If firms are very quick to react to profit opportunities, the parameter c will be very large, and the model will behave like the classical model; that is, profit opportunities will quickly disappear. If firms are slow to react to profit opportunities, parameter c will be small, unemployment may deviate from its natural rate for long periods of time, and profit opportunities will be persistent.

WAGE ADJUSTMENT AND THE PHILLIPS CURVE

What evidence do we have for the new-Keynesian theory of wage adjustment? We can check the theory by searching for the existence of a relationship between wage inflation and unemployment, of the kind predicted by the new-Keynesian wage equation. One problem with this approach is that Equation 17.5 contains the variable $\Delta P^E/P$ (expected price inflation), and it is difficult to get accurate measures of expectations. Suppose, however, we examine the relationship between wage inflation and unemployment in a period when expected price inflation might reasonably be expected to have been constant. The two decades beginning in 1949 were one such period.

The graphs in Figure 17.6 depict price inflation from 1949 through 1969, and we can see that price inflation hovered at around 2% per year. Some years inflation was greater than 2%, and some years it was less. A household during this period would not have gone far wrong in forecasting that price inflation would equal 2%. After 1965, inflation began to increase at a faster rate, but it is reasonable to assume that workers and firms took some time to adjust their expectations to the changing conditions.

Suppose that expected price inflation was constant and equal to 2% from 1949 through 1969. If this assumption is correct, and if the new-Keynesian wage equation (Equation 17.5)

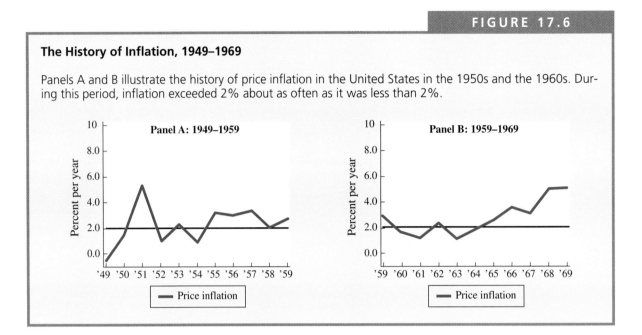

FIGURE 17.6

The History of Inflation, 1949–1969

Panels A and B illustrate the history of price inflation in the United States in the 1950s and the 1960s. During this period, inflation exceeded 2% about as often as it was less than 2%.

is correct, we should see a negative relationship between wage inflation and unemployment. Figure 17.7 presents evidence on the relationship between wage inflation and unemployment from 1949 through 1969. Notice the negative relationship predicted by the new-Keynesian theory; and furthermore, the relationship that fits the 1950s' data also fits data for the 1960s. The New Zealand economist A.W. Phillips first noticed the stability of the relationship between wage inflation and unemployment.[4] Economists in America replicated Phillips' study using U.S. data and got similar results. The relationship between the unemployment rate and wage inflation, uncovered by Phillips and known as the **Phillips curve**, provided an important stimulus to the research of theorists working on the dynamic new-Keynesian model.

THE DYNAMIC NEW-KEYNESIAN MODEL

Our theory of growth and inflation makes a number of predictions about the behavior of data. These predictions are mostly simple extensions, in a dynamic context, of the same static theory of aggregate demand and supply that we have already encountered. What is new is an explicit account of the way that wages evolve over time. We added the new-Keynesian wage equation to account for the dynamics of wage inflation.

---

4.   A.W. Phillips. "The relation between unemployment and the rate of change of money wage rates in the United Kingdom, 1861–1957," *Economica* 25, pp 283–299, November 1958.

FIGURE 17.7

Wage, Inflation, and Unemployment

A.W. Phillips argued that there is a stable relationship between unemployment and inflation. Subsequent authors called this relationship the "Phillips curve."

Panel A illustrates the relationship between unemployment and wage inflation (the annual percentage increase in the nominal wage) from 1949 to 1959.

Panel B illustrates the same relationship from 1959 through 1969. Notice that the same curve fits both sets of points.

In both cases, the slope of the Phillips curve is −2. This implies that if unemployment falls by 1%, wage inflation will increase by 2%.

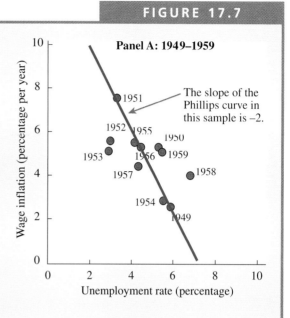

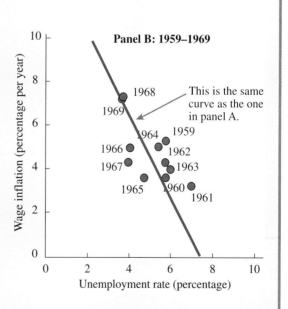

FIGURE 17.8

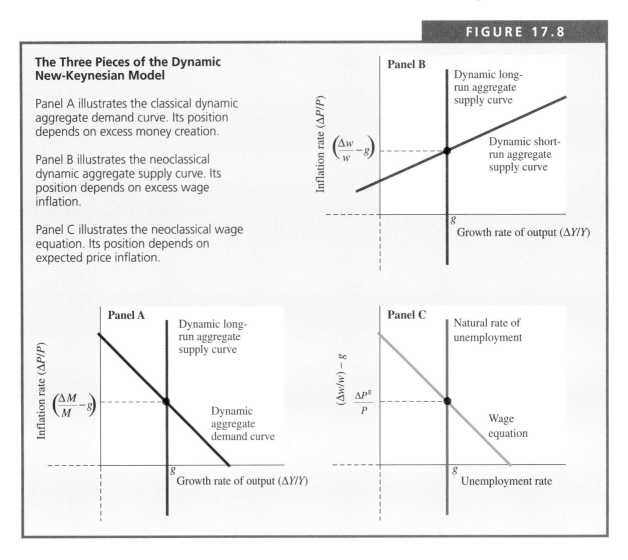

The Three Pieces of the Dynamic New-Keynesian Model

Panel A illustrates the classical dynamic aggregate demand curve. Its position depends on excess money creation.

Panel B illustrates the neoclassical dynamic aggregate supply curve. Its position depends on excess wage inflation.

Panel C illustrates the neoclassical wage equation. Its position depends on expected price inflation.

Figure 17.8 illustrates the three main pieces of the new-Keynesian model: Panel A is the dynamic theory of aggregate demand, panel B is the dynamic theory of aggregate supply, and panel C is the new-Keynesian wage equation. Now we examine how these pieces interact to determine inflation and growth over the business cycle.

INFLATION AND GROWTH WHEN EXPECTATIONS ARE FIXED

The first element of the new-Keynesian theory is the determination of wage inflation. For now, let's concentrate on a period of stable prices, like the one experienced in the United

States in the 1950s. It is reasonable to assume that in a period like this, expected price inflation is constant and equal to 2%. Under these conditions, excess wage inflation depends only on whether the unemployment rate is currently higher or lower than its natural rate. Because wages are typically set in advance, the determination of nominal wage inflation occurs *before* the determination of price inflation and growth, and excess wage inflation interacts with inflation and growth by influencing the position of the short-run aggregate supply curve. The way that current unemployment influences wage inflation is given by the new-Keynesian wage equation, which is graphed in panel C of Figure 17.8.

Once the wage inflation rate is known, we can draw the short-run aggregate supply curve (panel B). Inflation and growth are then determined at the point where the short-run aggregate supply curve (panel B) intersects the aggregate demand curve (panel A). Typically, both the demand and the supply curves fluctuate from one year to the next. If money growth is higher than average, the aggregate demand curve will shift to the right, and growth and inflation will be higher than the average. If the rate of money creation is lower than the average rate, the aggregate demand curve will shift to the left, and growth and inflation will be lower than the average. The Federal Reserve Board is aware that changes in Board policy can affect the economy in this way, so in recent years the open-market committee has deliberately tried to avoid causing unpredictable changes in demand that might either overstimulate or understimulate the economy.

It is not only aggregate demand that can shift from one year to the next. A second important source of fluctuations occurs as a result of random changes in the natural rate of productivity growth, g. If the natural rate of productivity growth is higher than the average rate, the short-run aggregate supply curve will shift to the right, and inflation and growth will again be higher than average. If the rate of productivity growth is lower than average, the short-run aggregate supply curve will shift to the left, and inflation and growth will be lower than average. Real productivity shifts of this kind were responsible for the recessions in 1973 and 1979, when supply shifted as a result of sharp increases in the price of oil.

Inflation and Growth Under Changing Expectations

The dynamic model of aggregate demand and supply implies that inflation and growth can fluctuate over the business cycle for two reasons. Shocks to aggregate demand cause growth to fluctuate around its natural rate. Demand shocks generate procyclical movements in inflation. Shocks to aggregate supply cause the natural growth rate to fluctuate, and these fluctuations result in countercyclical movements in inflation.

To derive these predictions, we assumed that inflationary expectations are constant and equal to 2%. As long as actual inflation is equal (on average) to 2%, this is a good assumption. But if realized inflation exceeds 2% for a long period of time, the assumption that expectations are fixed no longer makes sense. If price expectations start to exceed 2%, these expectations feed into actual wage inflation, and the position of the short-run aggregate supply curve will shift upward.[5]

---

5.   Until now, we have taken expectations as given and have asked how the other variables of the model behave. In Chapter 18, we will relax this assumption and examine theories of the endogenous determination of expectations.

BOX 17.2

A CLOSER LOOK
Alan Greenspan on the Economy

Several times a year, the chairman of the Board of Governors of the Fed, Alan Greenspan, testifies before Congress. His speeches are available on the Web at the Board of Governors site: http://www.federalreserve.gov; search the "Speeches" category for "Alan Greenspan."

The following excerpts are from Greenspan's testimony to Congress on February 13, 2001.

Quote	Quick Summary
The past decade has been extraordinary for the American economy and monetary policy. . . . Overall, capacity in high-tech manufacturing industries rose nearly 50% last year, well in excess of its rapid rate of increase over the previous three years. . . . Clearly, some slowing in the pace of spending was necessary and expected if the economy was to progress along a balanced and sustainable growth path.	We've done pretty well over the last 10 years, but all good things come to an end. . . .
. . . But the adjustment has occurred much faster than most businesses anticipated, with the process likely intensified by the rise in the cost of energy that has drained business and household purchasing power. . . . Inventories have risen to excessively high levels. . . . A round of inventory rebalancing appears to be in progress. As the economy slowed, equity prices fell, especially in the high-tech sector, [and] lenders turned more cautious. This tightening of financial conditions, itself, contributed to restraint on spending.	The slowdown happened faster than expected...partly because of the oil price shock.

The signs of a slowdown are increasing stocks of unsold goods (inventories), falling share prices, and tighter credit. |
| Against this background, the Federal Open Market Committee (FOMC) undertook a series of aggressive monetary policy steps. At its December meeting, the FOMC shifted its announced assessment of the balance of risks to express concern about economic weakness, which encouraged declines in market interest rates. Then on January 3, and again on January 31, the FOMC reduced its targeted federal funds rate ½ percentage point, to its current level of 5½ percent. An essential precondition for this type of response was that underlying cost and price pressures remained subdued, so that our front-loaded actions were unlikely to jeopardize the stable, low-inflation environment necessary to foster investment and advances in productivity. | Because we think that a recession is coming, the FOMC cut the interest rate that we control by a full percentage point.

We only did this because we were fairly sure that inflation was under control. |
| . . . the same forces that have been boosting growth in structural productivity seem also to have accelerated the process of cyclical adjustment. . . . As a result of information and other newer technologies, [there is] more rapid adjustment of capital goods production to shifts in demand that result from changes in firms' expectations of sales and profitability. A decade ago, extended backlogs on capital equipment meant a more stretched-out process of production adjustments. | The economy adjusts more efficiently to slowdowns in demand than it used to because of technological changes that increase the information available to firms. |

MORE-REALISTIC THEORIES OF AGGREGATE DEMAND

When we began this chapter, we justified our use of the classical theory of aggregate demand, rather than the Keynesian theory, on the grounds of simplicity. You may wonder how the conclusions of the new-Keynesian model change if we go beyond the simple the-

BOX 17.2

Alan Greenspan on the Economy *(continued)*

Quote	Quick Summary
[The] very rapidity with which the current adjustment is proceeding raises another concern of a different nature. While technology has quickened production adjustments, human nature remains unaltered. We respond to a heightened pace of change and its associated uncertainty in the same way we always have. . . . Many economic decisionmakers not only become risk-averse, but attempt to disengage from all risk. This precludes taking any initiative, because risk is inherent in every action. . . . There may not be a seamless transition from high to moderate to low confidence on the part of businesses, investors, and consumers . . . [an] unpredictable rending of confidence is one reason that recessions are so difficult to forecast. They may not be just changes in degree from a period of economic expansion, but a different process engendered by fear. Our economic models have never been particularly successful in capturing a process driven in large part by nonrational behavior.	Humans are fallible and susceptible to wild, unpredictable swings in confidence that are irrational and can make a recession worse than it would otherwise be.
. . . As the FOMC noted in its last announcement, for the period ahead, downside risks predominate. In addition to the possibility of a break in confidence, we don't know how far the adjustment of the stocks of consumer durables and business capital equipment has come. Also, foreign economies appear to be slowing, which could damp demands for exports; and, although some sectors of the financial markets have improved in recent weeks, continued lender nervousness still is in evidence in other sectors.	I would have to guess that we're in a recession, but I'm not sure because I don't have good information until its too late to do anything about it.

Economic Projections

The members of the Board of Governors and the Reserve Bank presidents foresee an implicit strengthening of activity after the current rebalancing is over, although the central tendency of their individual forecasts for real GDP still shows a substantial slowdown, on balance, for the year as a whole. The central tendency for real GDP growth over the four quarters of this year is 2 to 2½ percent. Because this average pace is below the rise in the economy's potential, they see the unemployment rate increasing to about 4½ percent by the fourth quarter of this year. The central tendency of their forecasts for inflation, as measured by the prices for personal consumption expenditures, suggests an abatement to 1¾ to 2¼ percent over this year from 2½ percent over 2000.	We at the Fed think that there will be a short, mild recession, and that the economy will grow by less than potential for the year. This implies that unemployment will be above its natural rate. Inflation will remain low.

ory. The answer is that the long-run properties of the more-complicated model are the same as the simple model. Inflation is determined by the rate of money creation, and output growth is determined by its natural rate. In the short run, variables other than the rate of money creation can shift the dynamic aggregate demand curve. These other variables can influence growth and inflation in a way that is more complicated than the model described in this chapter. In the more-complete model, changes in the interest rate interact with money creation and inflation, and these interactions add further dynamic elements to the adjustment path from the short run to the long run.

CONCLUSION

The static new-Keynesian theory explains deviations in unemployment from its natural rate, but the theory takes the nominal wage as given. In practice, the nominal wage grew at 2% to 3% per year over the past century. To account for wage inflation, we have developed an explicitly dynamic theory that has three parts: a dynamic theory of aggregate demand, a dynamic theory of aggregate supply, and a theory of wage adjustment.

During the 1950s and 1960s, expected price inflation was constant, and over this period, the new-Keynesian theory of wage adjustment is well in accord with the data. It can also account for more-recent data, but accounting requires an explicit treatment of what determines price expectations. We turn to this topic in Chapter 18.

KEY TERMS

Classical approach
Dynamic theory of aggregate demand
Dynamic theory of aggregate supply
Excess GDP growth
Excess wage inflation

Natural output path
Natural real wage path
New-Keynesian theory of aggregate supply
New-Keynesian wage equation
Phillips curve

QUESTIONS FOR CHAPTER 17

---

1. Define *productivity*. Does productivity grow at a constant rate? Explain.

2. Explain, in words, why the dynamic AD curve slopes downward. Why does an increase in the rate of money creation shift the AD curve? Trace out the economic mechanism that causes this shift.

3. At what rate do GDP and the real wage grow in the long run according to the classical aggregate supply curve? Explain the reasoning behind your answer. Do you think that the classical aggregate supply curve is a good description of reality?

4. How does the dynamic new-Keynesian aggregate supply curve differ from its classical counterpart? Explain the intuition behind each aggregate supply curve.

5. If productivity growth is 3% and the real wage increases by 4%, what must be true about unemployment? Will output growth be greater or less than 3%? Explain using graphs of the labor market, production function, and new-Keynesian aggregate demand and supply curves.

6. Assume that expected price inflation is fixed at 2%, the natural rate of unemployment is 5%, and the natural rate of productivity growth is 3%. What rate of unemployment is compatible with zero wage inflation? What rate is consistent with zero price inflation? Explain why these two rates are different. In your calculations assume that the parameter c from Equation 17.5 is equal to 2.

7. Suppose that the natural rate of productivity growth is constant and equal to 3%, and that expected inflation is constant and equal to 4%. What rate of money creation is consistent with price inflation of 4% and output growth at its natural rate? What would be the rate of wage inflation in this scenario?

8. Using the data from question 6, explain what would happen if the Federal Reserve Board were to raise the rate of money creation above the rate consistent with price inflation of 4%. Do you think that this situation would persist for long? If not, why not?

9. In the 1970s productivity growth slowed down considerably, and as a consequence real wages almost stopped growing. How would your answer to question 6 differ if productivity growth were equal to zero.

10. Consider the classical model of dynamic aggregate demand and supply. Assume that money growth is 5% and productivity growth is 3%.

   a. Calculate: (i) the inflation rate; (ii) the growth rate of GDP, (iii) the growth rate of nominal wages, and (iv) the growth rate of real wages.

   b. If productivity growth increases to 6%, what would happen to the variables calculated in part (a)?

11. Consider an economy in a short-run equilibrium. Productivity growth is 1%, the real wage is growing at 3%, the inflation rate is 1%, and the slope of the dynamic new-Keynesian aggregate supply curve is 1/2. Find the growth rate of output.

12. What is the *Phillips curve*? Which things must be assumed to be constant for the traditional Phillips curve relationship to hold?

13. According to Alan Greenspan's February 13, 2001 testimony, changes in the price of oil played an important part in the economic slowdown of late 2000.

   a. Examine the effect of this change in the price of oil within the dynamic new-Keynesian model of aggregate demand and supply.

   b. What was the Federal Reserve's response to this economic slowdown? What should be the short-run and long-run effects of this policy?

   c. How does your answer in part (b) illustrate a tradeoff that the Federal Reserve faces when conducting monetary policy? Explain.

14. Download the entire text of the Federal Reserve Chairman's most recent testimony to Congress and write a two- to three-page report for fellow students in your macroeconomics class interpreting what he said. Use as many concepts that you have learned in this and other chapters as possible. Provide graphs as necessary.

CHAPTER 18

EXPECTATIONS AND MACROECONOMICS

INTRODUCTION

We have put together a complete model of aggregate demand and supply in steps, and at each step, we have broadened the theory by explaining more of the variables of the model endogenously. For example, in Chapter 17, we introduced the new-Keynesian wage equation to explain how the nominal wage adjusts when unemployment fluctuates from its natural rate. So far, we have maintained the assumption that expectations of future inflation are exogenous. Now we relax this assumption and study the endogenous determination of expectations.

   This topic has kept some of the best economists of the postwar period thoroughly occupied. The history of the theory of expectations is one of the interaction of economic events with economic theory. Several approaches to modeling expectations were tried and rejected, and eventually one approach, rational expectations, came to dominate the way that expectations are modeled in practice.

Postwar Economic History of the United States

Immediately after the end of World War II, the United States experienced a surge in inflation that resulted from the lifting of wartime price controls. Because our theory may not apply when the government directly controls prices, as it did during World War II, we begin our model in 1949. We use new-Keynesian theory to show that a model in which expectations are fixed cannot account for the experiences of the 1970s and 1980s.

Inflation

To assume that expectations of price inflation are constant is not unreasonable when looking at the 1950s and 1960s; inflation exceeded 2% about as often as it fell short of 2%. After 1965, inflation began to climb, and by 1969 it was higher than 4%. No one who lived through this period could have anticipated what was coming next; a period of temporarily high inflation in the late 1960s might reasonably have been expected to decline in subsequent years.

The history of the 1970s and 1980s was very different from that of the two preceding decades. From 1969 through 1981, inflation climbed in almost every year. By 1981, inflation, as measured by the rate of growth of the GDP price index, reached a peak of 9%. Some measures of inflation (e.g., the CPI) indicated an even greater inflation rate.

Box 18.1 shows the history of price inflation, decade by decade. It depicts a gradual buildup and an equally gradual decline. After peaking in 1981, inflation had begun to slow down, and by 1996 it had returned to the levels of the 1950s.

The Phillips Curve

The new-Keynesian wage adjustment equation that we worked with in Chapter 17 was not an established part of economic theory in the 1960s. The role of expectations was poorly understood, and expected price inflation was typically omitted from the right side of the equation. This led to a crisis in economic theory when, as inflation took hold, the previously stable Phillips curve began to break down.

Equation 18.1 is the new-Keynesian wage adjustment equation. Recall that, according to new-Keynesian theory, wage inflation occurs for two reasons. First, households and firms can expect inflation, which is why the term $\Delta P^E/P$ appears on the right side of the equation. Second, if unemployment is currently too high, the real wage must also be too high; households and firms will negotiate for wage contracts that lower the expected real wage in order to bring unemployment down to its natural rate. This is why the term $(U - U^*)$ appears on the right side of the equation.

18.1
$$\left(\frac{\Delta w}{w} - g \right) \quad = \quad \frac{\Delta P^E}{P} \quad - \quad c(U - U^*)$$

Excess wage inflation	Expected price inflation	Excess unemployment

BOX 18.1

FOCUS ON THE FACTS
The History of Inflation in the United States Since WWII

Panels A through D illustrate the history of price inflation in the United States, decade by decade, since 1949. In each case, the green line represents a base-line case of 2% inflation.

Notice that in the first two decades (panels A and B) it would not have been unreasonable to expect that price inflation would equal 2% per year. At least through 1965, inflation exceeded 2% about as often as it was less than 2%.

In the mid-1960s, things began to change; and by the 1970s (panel C), inflation was consistently above 2%.

Anyone expecting that price inflation would equal 2% in the 1970s would have been seriously mistaken. Only recently has inflation been reduced again to the levels of the 1950s.

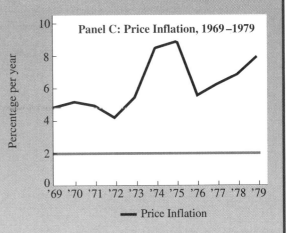

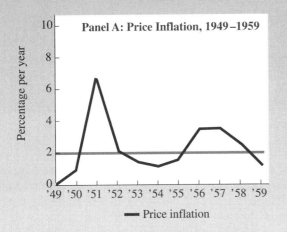

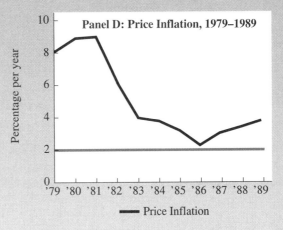

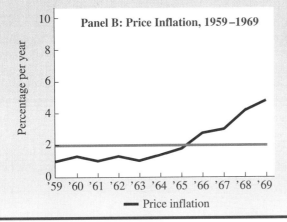

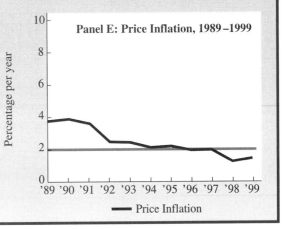

As long as expectations of inflation remain fixed at 2% per year, the new-Keynesian wage equation predicts a relationship exactly like the Phillips curve between nominal wage inflation and unemployment. But in the 1970s and 1980s, inflation did not remain at 2%, and households during this period needed to revise their expectations. Because we do not have good measures of expected inflation, one approach to testing the validity of the new-Keynesian wage equation would be to replace expected inflation by actual inflation. If we replace $\Delta P^E/P$ with $\Delta P/P$, we can write Equation 18.1 as

18.2
$$\left(\frac{\Delta w}{w} - \frac{\Delta P}{P} - g \right) \qquad = \qquad -c\left(U - U^* \right)$$

Excess wage inflation   Excess unemployment

Stated in this way, the equation predicts that unemployment above its natural rate should cause the *real* wage to grow at a slower rate than natural productivity growth, and unemployment below the natural rate should cause it to grow more quickly. Assuming that U^* and g are constant, a graph of real wage inflation against unemployment should be a downward-sloping line.

Box 18.2 shows the history of nominal wage inflation and unemployment in the left two graphs and real wage inflation and unemployment in the right two graphs. Although the Phillips curve as a graph of nominal wage inflation against unemployment is unstable, the graph of **real wage inflation** against unemployment retains its position throughout postwar history.

WHY THE PHILLIPS CURVE SHIFTED ITS POSITION

The macroeconomics journals in the 1960s discussed the idea that the Phillips curve offers a trade-off. Policymakers were able to choose a low rate of inflation and a high level of unemployment, or a high rate of inflation and a low rate of unemployment, but not both. According to this view, the goal of economic policy was to pick a point on the Phillips curve by choosing the rate of money creation. Supposedly, if the Federal Reserve Board chose rapid monetary expansion, high inflation but low unemployment would result. If it chose a low rate of money creation, low inflation but high unemployment would result.

Over the period from 1949 to 1969, real wages grew at 2.4%, on average, as new technology made labor more productive. Because real wages grew, economists argued that nominal wages could be allowed to grow at 2.4% without risking price inflation. But, according to the graph of the Phillips curve, economists surmised that if they wanted to eliminate price inflation entirely they would have to incur unemployment of at least 5.8%.

This estimate is found by reading from the Phillips curve (see Figure 18.1 on page 409)—the level of unemployment that would occur if the rate of wage inflation were equal to 2.4%, the same as productivity growth in the period from 1949 to 1969. When productivity is growing, nominal wages can increase at the productivity growth rate without generating price inflation. Some economists argued that if the government were willing to accept a positive rate of inflation, policymakers would be able to reduce unemployment below the equilibrium level of 5.8%, which is consistent with zero price inflation.

BOX 18.2

FOCUS ON THE FACTS   The Phillips Curve Since WWII

The left column shows graphs of nominal wage inflation plotted against unemployment for each decade since 1949. The right column shows graphs of real wage inflation (the proportional growth rate of the real wage) plotted against unemployment. In the 1970s, the Phillips curve relationship began to break down; notice from the left column on page 408 that during this decade the points are above and to the right of the curve as the U.S. economy experienced high wage inflation *and* high unemployment, simultaneously. This occurred because in the 1970s it was no longer reasonable to expect that price inflation would remain at 2%. We do not have good measures of *expected* price inflation. Instead, the right column shows the relationship that would hold between wage inflation and unemployment if firms and households formed accurate predictions of price inflation. These graphs show how *actual* real wage inflation was related to unemployment. The graphs show that the relationship between real wage inflation and unemployment has remained constant during the entire five decades since the end of WWII.

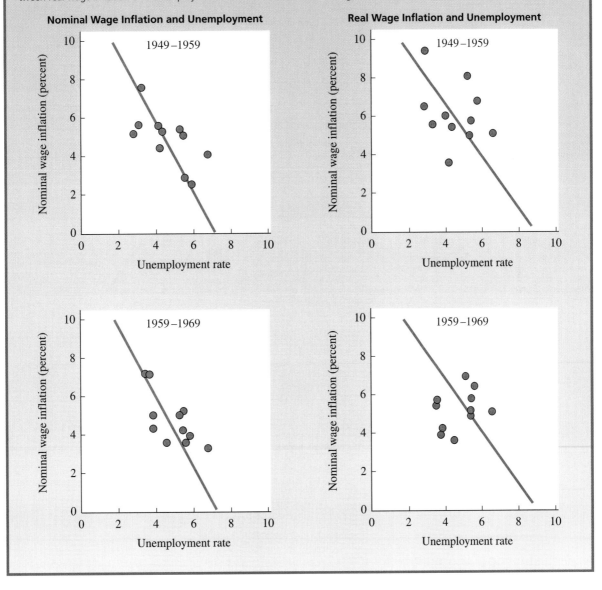

BOX 18.2

The Phillips Curve Since WWII *(continued)*

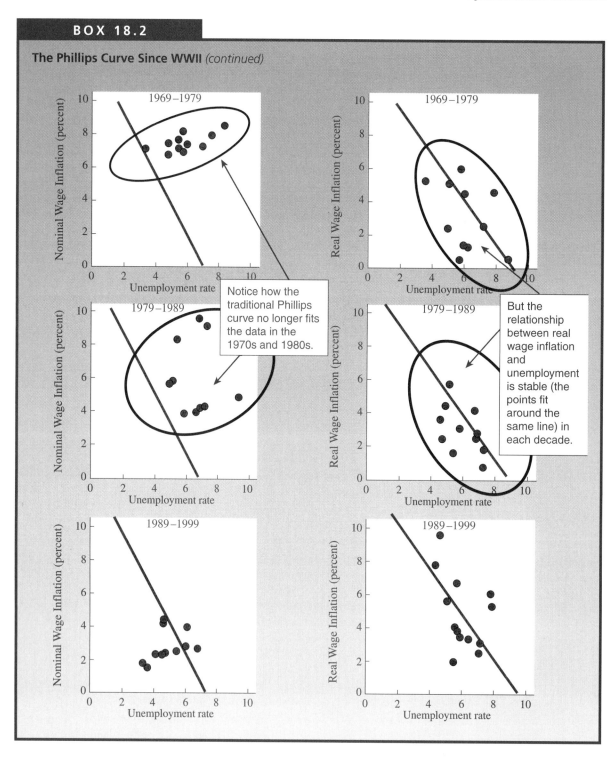

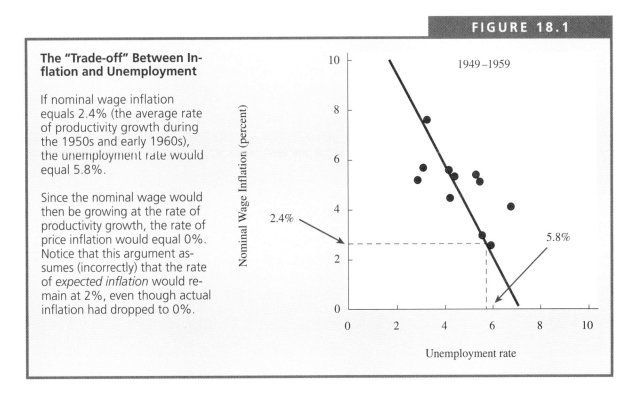

FIGURE 18.1

The "Trade-off" Between In-flation and Unemployment

If nominal wage inflation equals 2.4% (the average rate of productivity growth during the 1950s and early 1960s), the unemployment rate would equal 5.8%.

Since the nominal wage would then be growing at the rate of productivity growth, the rate of price inflation would equal 0%. Notice that this argument as-sumes (incorrectly) that the rate of *expected inflation* would re-main at 2%, even though actual inflation had dropped to 0%.

These economists suggested that the Phillips curve should be viewed as an exploitable trade-off between inflation and unemployment.

THE NATURAL RATE HYPOTHESIS (NAIRU)

The view of the Phillips curve as a trade-off led to a fierce debate in the 1960s. Two promi-nent critics of the trade-off view were Edmund Phelps of Columbia University and Milton Friedman of the University of Chicago.[1] Phelps and Friedman believed that permanently low unemployment is unsustainable in the long run because eventually workers and firms will build expectations of price inflation into their wage-setting behavior. They argued that the observed relationship between inflation and unemployment occurs as a result of mis-taken expectations on the part of households and firms. Any attempt to exploit the trade-off between inflation and unemployment will eventually be frustrated as households and firms come to expect higher levels of inflation.

Friedman and Phelps argued that the economy has a natural rate of unemployment, which is independent of the variables that shift the aggregate demand curve. Unemploy-ment can only be above or below this natural rate as a result of mistaken expectations on

---

1.   Milton Friedman's ideas on this topic appeared in his presidential address to the American Economic Asso-ciation, published in the *American Economic Review* (March, 1968). Edmund Phelps wrote "Phillips curves, ex-pectations of inflation and optimal unemployment over time." *Economica,* August 1967.

FIGURE 18.2

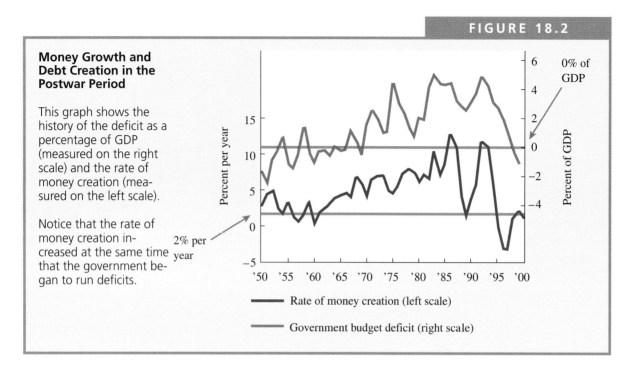

Money Growth and Debt Creation in the Postwar Period

This graph shows the history of the deficit as a percentage of GDP (measured on the right scale) and the rate of money creation (measured on the left scale).

Notice that the rate of money creation increased at the same time that the government began to run deficits.

—— Rate of money creation (left scale)

—— Government budget deficit (right scale)

the part of private decisionmakers. If policymakers try to maintain unemployment below its natural rate, Phelps and Friedman argued, the inflation rate will accelerate with each successive attempt to reduce unemployment. The result is a self-fulfilling spiral of wage and price increases. For this reason, some economists refer to the natural unemployment rate as the **nonaccelerating inflation rate of unemployment (NAIRU).**

Economists did not have to wait long for spectacular confirmation of the Phelps-Friedman hypothesis. Beginning in the mid-1960s, the Federal Reserve System began to expand the money supply at a faster rate than it had done in previous decades. During the 1950s and early 1960s, GDP grew at almost 4% per year. The Federal Reserve Board was committed to keeping interest rates low, but as the economy expanded and the demand for money increased, this policy led to an ever-increasing rate of money growth.

Figure 18.2 shows the rate of money growth from 1949 through 2000, measured on the left scale.[2] This figure also shows what was happening to the government budget deficit over this period, measured as a percentage of GDP on the right scale.

In the early 1970s, the government began to run larger deficits, partly because slower economic growth reduced taxable revenues. In addition, a number of government spending programs, such as Medicare and Social Security, began to increase government expenditure as the population aged and claimed pensions and medical benefits. A third reason

---

2.   The money supply in Figure 18.2 is M1. This is a relatively narrow measure of the money stock that includes currency in the hands of the public and various kinds of checkable deposits. Different definitions of the money supplied are explained in Chapter 10.

was the buildup of defense expenditures to finance the Vietnam War. Because the Vietnam War was domestically unpopular, it would have been difficult to satisfy the required military expenditures by raising taxes. Instead, increased expenditures were financed by new government bonds, and some of these new bond issues were bought by the Federal Reserve as it tried to keep down the nominal interest rate. As the Federal Reserve System bought government debt, it created new money to pay for it, and the rate of money creation began to climb. Increases in the money supply eventually led to higher inflation as the aggregate demand curve shifted to the right.

If the Phillips curve did indeed represent an exploitable policy trade off, then the increased inflation in the 1970s should have resulted in an upper-left movement along the Phillips curve; that is, the increase in aggregate demand should have resulted in higher inflation but lower unemployment. The facts were very different. Box 18.2 illustrates that during the 1970s and 1980s, the stable Phillips curve of the previous decades proved to be an illusion; higher money growth led to higher inflation, but the economy experienced higher unemployment at the same time. Called **stagflation** (simultaneously high unemployment and inflation), this convinced many economists that the natural rate hypothesis was correct and that the Phillips curve represents only a short-run relationship between unemployment and inflation that relies on misperceptions of future inflation.

THE NEW-KEYNESIAN MODEL

The most important lesson learned from the postwar events, when using the new-Keynesian model of aggregate demand and supply, is that expectations cannot be modeled using mechanical rules. Instead, we must use a more sophisticated approach. First we examine the implications of the new-Keynesian model in the short run, and then we will look at its implications in the long run.

DETERMINING GROWTH AND INFLATION

Figure 18.3 illustrates two equations of the new-Keynesian model on the same diagram. The downward-sloping line is the aggregate demand curve (AD) and the upward-sloping line is the short-run aggregate supply curve (SRAS). Growth and inflation are determined at the point where these two curves intersect. In Figure 18.3, growth is equal to its natural rate, g, as can be seen from the fact that SRAS and AD intersect where $\Delta Y/Y = g$. We call the line $\Delta Y/Y = g$ the long-run aggregate supply curve; if growth deviates from its natural rate, forces will push the economy back to the long-run supply curve over time.

We can use Figure 18.3 to make short-run predictions about the effects of policy on growth and inflation. First, we must be clear about how the position of the AD and SRAS curves depend on policy and expectations. Figure 18.3 shows that the aggregate demand curve crosses the LRAS curve when inflation equals $\Delta M/M - g$. We call this term **excess money growth.** If GDP grows at its natural rate, inflation will equal the difference between the money growth rate and g. If the Federal Reserve System creates money faster than the natural growth rate, the economy will experience inflation. If the Federal Reserve System creates money more slowly than the natural growth rate, it will experience deflation.

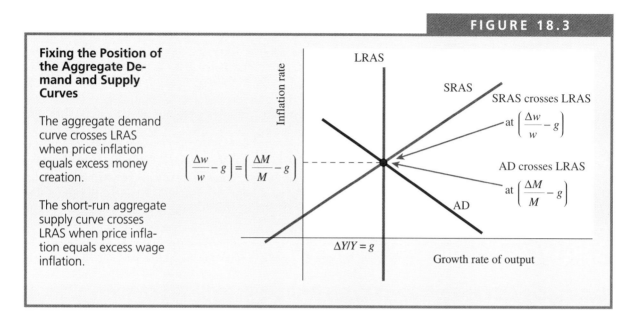

FIGURE 18.3

Fixing the Position of the Aggregate Demand and Supply Curves

The aggregate demand curve crosses LRAS when price inflation equals excess money creation.

The short-run aggregate supply curve crosses LRAS when price inflation equals excess wage inflation.

Figure 18.3 shows that the short-run aggregate supply curve crosses the line $\Delta Y/Y = g$ when inflation equals excess wage inflation, $\Delta w/w - g$. If price inflation equals excess wage inflation, the real wage will grow at its natural rate and output will grow at rate g.

Short-Run Growth and Inflation

Now that we understand how the position of the aggregate demand and supply curves are determined, we can use the AD-AS diagram to explain how changes in monetary policy influence inflation and growth in the short run.

Let's consider what happens if the rate of money growth increases. We'll begin with a baseline case in which wage inflation and money growth are equal.

18.3
$$\frac{\Delta w}{w} - g \qquad = \qquad \frac{\Delta M}{M} - g$$

Excess wage inflation   **Excess money growth**

When wage inflation equals money growth, GDP must grow at its natural rate. Remember that the aggregate demand curve intersects the $\Delta Y/Y = g$ line when price inflation equals excess money growth. The aggregate supply curve intersects the $\Delta Y/Y = g$ line when price inflation equals excess wage inflation. If nominal wage inflation equals money growth, these two curves both cross the $\Delta Y/Y = g$ line at the same point and output growth equals g.

Price inflation must equal excess money creation in order to keep the propensity to hold money constant. When GDP grows at its natural rate, the demand for real balances

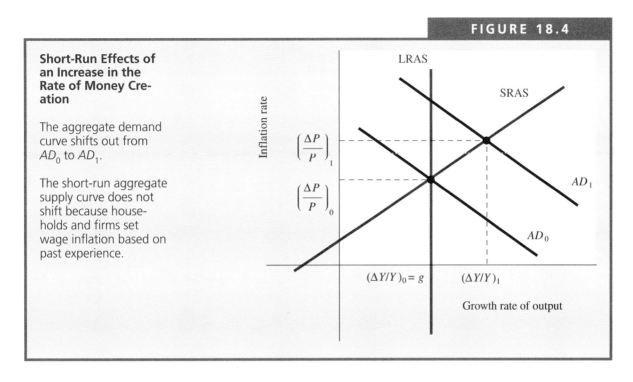

FIGURE 18.4

Short-Run Effects of an Increase in the Rate of Money Creation

The aggregate demand curve shifts out from AD_0 to AD_1.

The short-run aggregate supply curve does not shift because households and firms set wage inflation based on past experience.

also grows at the rate g because households and firms need more money each year to finance the growing demand for transaction services. When nominal money grows faster than g, price inflation keeps real balances growing at the same rate as GDP. This is the demand side of the equation. On the supply side, price inflation must equal the rate of excess wage inflation in order to keep the real wage growing at the natural growth rate. When nominal wage inflation exceeds the rate of productivity growth, price inflation keeps the real wage growing at its natural rate. Putting these two pieces together, we can see that when wage inflation (which determines the position of aggregate supply) equals money creation (which determines the position of aggregate demand), aggregate demand and short-run aggregate supply are equated at exactly the natural rate of GDP growth, g.

Figure 18.4 shows what happens when the rate of money growth increases so that $\Delta M/M$ and $\Delta w/w$ are no longer equal. The increase in the rate of money growth shifts the aggregate demand curve from AD_0 to AD_1. Because we assume that wage inflation does not change in the short run, the increase in aggregate demand causes price inflation to increase from $(\Delta P/P)_0$ to $(\Delta P/P)_1$. But now the real wage has fallen below its natural path, and firms increase employment above its natural rate, causing growth to be faster in year 1 than in year 0, and GDP growth goes up from $(\Delta Y/Y)_0$ to $(\Delta Y/Y)_1$.

We started with the assumption that the rate of wage inflation is given. The new-Keynesian wage equation assumes that wages are determined in advance by expectations of price inflation and by pressure on wages from fluctuations in the unemployment rate. Given that households and firms expect price inflation to remain at historical levels, and given that there is no excess unemployment in the initial period, wage inflation will be equal to the same historical level. This was the situation during the 1950s and the first part of the 1960s.

Suppose now that the rate of money creation increases, as it did in the second half of the 1960s. We model this in Figure 18.4 as a shift of the aggregate demand curve from AD_0 to AD_1. The new-Keynesian model predicts that the increase in the rate of money creation should initially lead to an increase in inflation, a reduction in unemployment, and GDP that grows faster than its natural rate. This is exactly what happened between 1965 and 1970; inflation increased and unemployment fell.

LONG-RUN GROWTH AND INFLATION

The Federal Reserve System can (and did) increase employment and growth in the short run. But what would be the long-run effect of a policy that increases the rate of money growth? Can a change in the rate of money growth permanently affect the rate of unemployment, or would the effect be temporary?

Figure 18.5, an aggregate demand and supply diagram, illustrates the effects of an increase in the rate of money creation in the long run as predicted by the new-Keynesian model. We assume in this figure that the aggregate demand curve remains at AD_1, and after the increase in the rate of money creation, the economy temporarily grows faster than the natural rate. The period immediately following the increase in the rate of money growth is represented as point **A** on the graph.

Now two factors cause upward pressure on the rate of wage inflation. First, at point **A**, because output is growing faster than its natural rate, unemployment is below its natural rate, and the rate of wage inflation will begin to increase. The second factor causing additional wage inflation is that firms and households are surprised by the level of price inflation and revise upward their expectations of future price inflation. Both of these factors cause the short-run aggregate supply curve to shift upward. As this happens, the rate of inflation increases, and the rate of growth begins to decrease until the economy ends up in a new long-run equilibrium, which is depicted in Figure 18.5 as point **B.**

EXPLAINING EXPECTATIONS ENDOGENOUSLY

A key element in the explanation of historical events is the idea that expectations adjust endogenously when actual inflation is higher than expected inflation. In order for our theory to be useful, we must be able to model this process and understand the factors that determine expected inflation. If expectations are left unexplained, any observed correlation between inflation, unemployment, and growth could be considered as consistent with the theory, and any discrepancy between theory and data could be attributed to the unobserved variable: expectations.

Early theories of price formation provided mechanical rules to represent the process whereby households and firms formed their beliefs. This approach proved unsatisfactory because it failed to capture the innovative ways in which thinking human beings adapt to their circumstances. Any given rule for forecasting the future may work well in a given environment, but when the environment changes, people change the way in which they

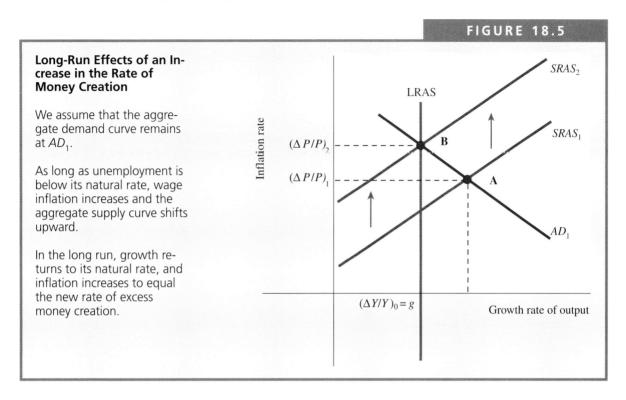

FIGURE 18.5

Long-Run Effects of an Increase in the Rate of Money Creation

We assume that the aggregate demand curve remains at AD_1.

As long as unemployment is below its natural rate, wage inflation increases and the aggregate supply curve shifts upward.

In the long run, growth returns to its natural rate, and inflation increases to equal the new rate of excess money creation.

forecast the future. The fact that human beings adapt to their environment led to the theory of rational expectations.

RATIONAL EXPECTATIONS

Rational expectations is based on the idea that the world is a lot like a casino. In reality, nothing is certain, and sometimes there are unpredictable changes in either aggregate demand or aggregate supply as a result of wars, famines, political disputes, new inventions, or a host of other uncertainties that affect our lives. Some of these events have a primary effect on aggregate demand, and some influence aggregate supply. To keep our models simple, let's focus on cases in which all uncertainty is associated with aggregate demand, such as a war that causes the Federal Reserve System to print money to help pay for defense. If the Federal Reserve System expands the money supply faster than the average, the aggregate demand curve will shift to the right. In another example, suppose the Federal Reserve open market committee is dominated by cautious men and women who are afraid that excessive monetary expansion might lead to inflation; so as a result, the money supply increases less quickly than it otherwise might, and aggregate demand shifts to the left.

The idea that aggregate demand may be random is a powerful one because it lets us handle the expectation of inflation in the same way that a casino handles risk. When you bet a dollar that a coin will come up heads on a single flip, statisticians say that the

expected value of this gamble is zero. They compute the expected value by adding the different possible outcomes and weighting them by probabilities. Half of the time you will gain a dollar ($+1.0 \times 0.5$), and half of the time you will lose a dollar (-1.0×0.5). Adding up these two possibilities yields an expected value of zero. The expected value of a variable is a statistical term for the average.

The theory of rational expectations models individuals' beliefs in the same way that a statistician calculates averages. We say that it is rational to calculate inflation using probabilities. If half of the time the money supply grows faster than $\Delta M/M$, then half of the time the aggregate demand curve will shift to the right. If half of the time the money supply grows slower than $\Delta M/M$, then half of the time the aggregate demand curve will shift to the left. The actual inflation rate is determined by the intersection of the aggregate demand curve with the short-run aggregate supply curve. When the money supply grows faster than average, inflation is higher than average. When it grows slower than average, inflation is lower than average. The rational expectation of the inflation rate is equal to the high rate multiplied by the probability that it will be high, plus the low rate multiplied by the probability that it will be low.

We can illustrate this idea by showing how the new-Keynesian theory of aggregate demand and supply explains the determination of inflation and growth in a hypothetical world in which expectations are not rational. We use two cases—one in which inflationary expectations are too low and one in which they are too high. These extreme examples naturally lead to a theory of the factors that determine whether an expectation of price inflation is rational. In our example, all of the uncertainty in the economy is associated with aggregate demand. The aggregate supply curve is fixed, but the aggregate demand curve fluctuates.

EXPECTED PRICE INFLATION IS TOO LOW

Figure 18.6 illustrates what happens when workers and firms expect the inflation rate to equal an arbitrary value that we denote as $(\Delta P/P)_1$. Expectations of price inflation affect the position of the aggregate supply curve because they influence actual wage inflation. When expected price inflation is low, the position of the aggregate supply curve is also low. In the figure, the expectation $(\Delta P/P)^E = (\Delta P/P)_1$ is too low; that is, if workers and firms believe that inflation is equal to $(\Delta P/P)_1$, they are mistaken, and their mistakes are systematically in one direction.

Consider a situation in which unemployment is equal to the natural rate. Firms and workers expect that inflation will equal $(\Delta P/P)_1$, and the money supply is, on average, growing at a rate of $\Delta M/M$. Because unemployment is equal to the natural rate, excess wage inflation equals expected price inflation. This is reflected in Figure 18.6 by the fact that the short-run aggregate supply curve crosses the long-run curve (the line $(\Delta Y/Y) = g$) at the expected rate of price inflation, $(\Delta P/P)_1$.

Given these beliefs, what will actually happen depends on the rate of money creation. In Figure 18.6, the money supply fluctuates randomly between two levels. When the money supply grows quickly, the aggregate demand curve is at AD_2, and when the money supply grows slowly, the curve is at AD_1. The actual rate of inflation is determined by the intersection of the aggregate demand curve with the short-run aggregate supply curve; half of the time the equilibrium is at **B**, and the rest of the time it is at **C**. A worker or a firm that lived in this economy would observe that sometimes inflation is equal to $(\Delta P/P)_3$, and

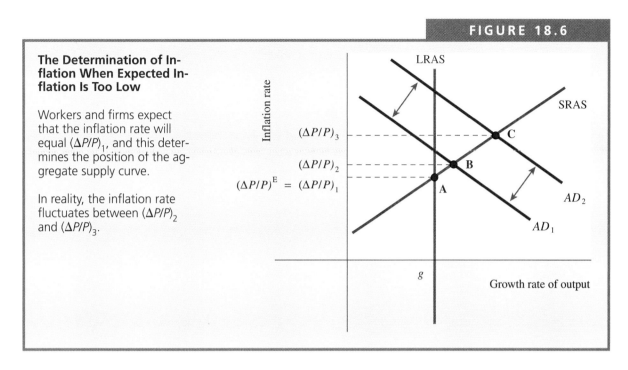

FIGURE 18.6

The Determination of Inflation When Expected Inflation Is Too Low

Workers and firms expect that the inflation rate will equal $(\Delta P/P)_1$, and this determines the position of the aggregate supply curve.

In reality, the inflation rate fluctuates between $(\Delta P/P)_2$ and $(\Delta P/P)_3$.

sometimes it is equal to $(\Delta P/P)_2$. But notice that both of these possible outcomes lead to higher inflation than they had expected.

EXPECTED PRICE INFLATION IS TOO HIGH

Figure 18.7 illustrates what would happen if workers and firms had instead expected the higher inflation rate $(\Delta P/P)_4$. In this case, the aggregate supply curve would cross the natural rate line at **D**. Once again, we assume that the only shocks are to aggregate demand. If the aggregate demand shock is equal to its highest value, equilibrium will occur at **E**, and the actual inflation rate will be $(\Delta P/P)_5$. If it is equal to its lowest value, the equilibrium will occur at **F**, and the actual inflation rate will be $(\Delta P/P)_6$. In reality, the aggregate demand curve fluctuates between these two extremes, and the observed inflation rate varies between $(\Delta P/P)_5$ and $(\Delta P/P)_6$. Notice, however, that if firms and workers expect the price level to equal $(\Delta P/P)_4$, the actual inflation rate will turn out to be lower than they expected. Clearly in this case, the expected inflation rate is too high.

RATIONAL EXPECTATIONS OF PRICE INFLATION

Rational expectations, a method of modeling expectations that accounts for the ability of human beings to adapt to their environment, was first suggested in 1961 by John Muth.[3] Muth's

---

3.   J.F. Muth. "Rational expectations and the theory of price movements," *Econometrica*, No. 29, 1961.

FIGURE 18.7

The Determination of Inflation When Expected Inflation Is Too High

Workers and firms expect that the inflation rate will equal $(\Delta P/P)_4$, and this determines the position of the aggregate supply curve.

In reality, the inflation rate fluctuates between $(\Delta P/P)_5$ and $(\Delta P/P)_6$.

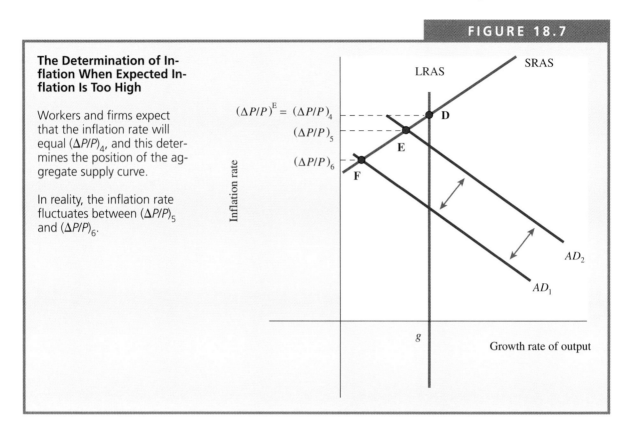

concept of rational expectations was introduced to the macroeconomics community in 1972 by Robert Lucas.[4] It has since become a standard way of treating expectations. Rational expectations assumes that the predictions of workers and firms will, on average, be correct.

Figure 18.8 illustrates rational expectations of inflation. The same two aggregate demand curves that we saw in Figures 18.6 and 18.7 are depicted. In addition, the average aggregate demand curve has been added, the one that applies if the monetary shock is equal to its average value of zero. The inflation rate at which this average aggregate demand curve crosses the aggregate supply curve is the rational expectation of inflation and is equal to $(\Delta P/P)_7$. Notice that this is also the point at which the aggregate supply curve intersects the natural rate line.

In Figures 18.6 and 18.7, the expected inflation rate was either too high or too low; the actual inflation rate would be either consistently above or consistently below the expected inflation rate. In Figure 18.8, however, the expectations of firms and households are rational. Whatever random events occur in the future, the observed inflation rate will sometimes turn out to be higher than expected and sometimes turn out to be lower.

---

4.   Robert E. Lucas, Jr. "Expectations and the neutrality of money," *Journal of Economic Theory*, 1972.

W E B W A T C H

An Interview with Robert E. Lucas, Jr.

The most influential macroeconomist of the past 25 years is Robert E. Lucas, Jr. Robert Lucas was awarded the Nobel prize in 1995 "for having developed and applied the hypothesis of rational expectations, and thereby having transformed macroeconomic analysis and deepened our understanding of economic policy." You can read his autobiography at: http://www.nobel.sdsc.edu/laureates/economy-1995-1-autobio.html and you will find an interview with Lucas in the *Region Magazine* at: http://www.woodrow.mpls.frb.fed.us/pubs/region/int936.html.

FIGURE 18.8

The Rational Expectations of Inflation

Workers and firms expect that the inflation rate will equal $(\Delta P/P)_7$, and this determines the position of the aggregate supply curve. The actual inflation rate fluctuates between $(\Delta P/P)_8$ and $(\Delta P/P)_9$.

The rational expectation depends on monetary policy.

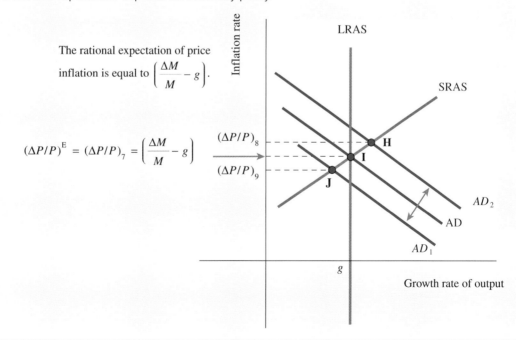

The rational expectation of price inflation is equal to $\left(\dfrac{\Delta M}{M} - g\right)$.

$$(\Delta P/P)^{\mathrm{E}} = (\Delta P/P)_7 = \left(\frac{\Delta M}{M} - g\right)$$

The rational expectation of the inflation rate is equal to its average value. In turn, this value depends on the factors that alter the set of positions of the aggregate demand curve—the factors that determine $\Delta M/M$. Therefore, rational expectations implies that beliefs depend on the policies pursued by the Federal Reserve Board.

The major insight of the rational expectations literature is that what individuals expect has consequences for the actual set of outcomes. A series of higher-than-expected inflation rates could be blamed on bad luck, like a gambler who throws a string of ones on the die. But a consistent string of outcomes that are higher than expected would cause workers and firms to revise their expectations of inflation upwards. Rational expectations means that in our economic models, we should assume expectations are chosen so that they are not systematically wrong.

RATIONAL EXPECTATIONS AND LEARNING

Most economists currently accept some version of the rational expectations hypothesis, but not all are comfortable with the strictest form of the hypothesis. Rational expectations ascribes a degree of knowledge to households and firms that many economists find implausible. In order to form a rational expectation of the future inflation rate, households and firms must be able to accurately predict the future rate of money growth. Predicting future money growth is difficult because the policies of the Federal Reserve Board are constantly changing as policymakers respond to changing circumstances. Many economists believe that rational expectations is a sensible way of modeling the equilibrium of an economy, but the assumption must be supplemented by a description of how individuals learn about their environment.

THE FEDERAL RESERVE SYSTEM AND MONETARY POLICY

The theory outlined in this chapter, supplemented by a more sophisticated version of the dynamic theory of aggregate demand, is extremely influential among policymakers in the Federal Reserve System. Rational expectations is currently accepted by most economists as a constraint on policy, and it is widely thought that the credibility of economic policy is an important determinant of its effects. But the Federal Reserve System did not arrive at this position overnight. The economy had some tough lessons to teach first.

ARTHUR BURNS AND THE BUILDUP OF INFLATION

Inflation did not become a problem in the United States until the 1970s. Prices remained relatively stable for 30 years following World War II, but by the mid-1970s, the inflation rate was following a detectable, upward trend. Figure 18.9 illustrates the history of the money growth and inflation rates over this period. Clearly, an upward trend is apparent in both rates. Because economic theory states that constraining the rate of money growth can control inflation, why would the Federal Reserve System allow this inflation to occur?

In 1970, Arthur Burns became chairman of the Federal Reserve Board. Under Burns, inflation built up from 5% in 1970 to 9% in 1980. Evidence that Arthur Burns was aware of the consequences of the Federal Reserve Board's actions can be found in a speech he made to the U.S. Congress in 1977:

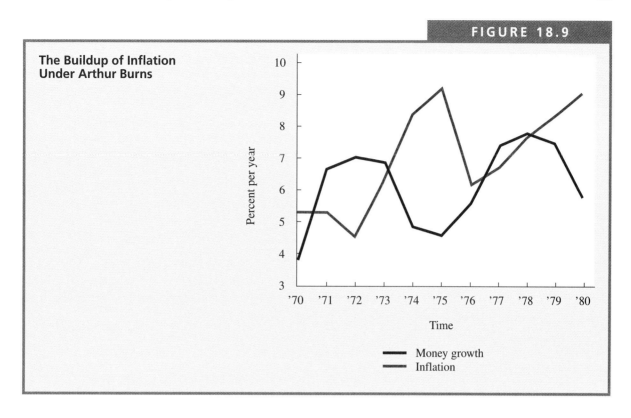

FIGURE 18.9

The Buildup of Inflation Under Arthur Burns

Neither I nor, I believe, any of my associates would quarrel with the proposition that money creation and inflation are closely linked and that serious inflation could not long proceed without monetary nourishment. We well know—as do many others—that if the Federal Reserve stopped creating new money, or if this activity were slowed drastically, inflation would soon either come to an end or be substantially checked.[5]

But Burns chose to accommodate inflationary expectations rather than accept a costly recession. Burns put it this way in testimony before the Committee on Banking and Currency of the House of Representatives on July 30, 1974:

. . . an effort to use harsh policies of monetary restraint to offset the exceptionally powerful inflationary forces in recent years would have caused serious financial disorder and economic dislocation. That would not have been a sensible course for monetary policy.[6]

In other words, Burns' policy deliberately allowed the money supply to grow in order to avoid a recession. The probable cause of the inflationary forces that Burns refers to was

---

5. Arthur F. Burns. "Reflections of an economic policy maker, speeches and congressional statements: 1969–78," American Enterprise Institute for Public Policy Research, Washington DC, p 417. These passages are cited in a recent discussion paper, "Expectation traps and discretion," by V.V. Chari, Lawrence Christiano, and Martin Eichenbaum.
6. Burns, op cit., p 171.

a large increase in the world price of oil in 1973. The oil price increase can be interpreted as a negative supply shock that shifted the aggregate supply curve to the left. In the language of macroeconomics, we say that the Federal Reserve Board reacted to the oil price increase by conducting a **discretionary monetary policy.** A discretionary policy is one that allows the rate of monetary growth to react to contemporaneous shocks. Some economists, notably Milton Friedman of the University of Chicago, have argued that the Federal Reserve System has no business trying to stabilize recessions, and that the best way to conduct monetary policy is to set a fixed target for the monetary growth rate and stick to it. Discretionary monetary policy, according to Friedman, only adds to uncertainty and creates additional sources of shocks that exacerbate business cycles.

V.V. Chari of the University of Minnesota and Lawrence Christiano and Martin Eichenbaum of Northwestern University raised a second argument against discretion. They argued that it was the Federal Reserve Board's being allowed to run a discretionary monetary policy that was responsible for the inflation of the 1970s. According to this view, agents formed expectations of inflation precisely because they believed that the Federal Reserve System would accommodate those expectations rather than permit a recession; these inflationary expectations then became self-fulfilling. Chari, Christiano, and Eichenbaum argued that if the Federal Reserve Board had been given less discretionary power, the situation that Burns described could have been avoided.

THE VOLCKER RECESSION AND THE REMOVAL OF INFLATION

Burns' term as chairman of the Federal Reserve Board ended in October of 1979 when Paul Volcker took over. Under Volcker's chairmanship, the Federal Reserve Board reduced U.S. inflation by lowering the rate of monetary growth. In effect, the Federal Reserve Board engineered a leftward shift of the aggregate demand curve. Initially, the policy of lowering the monetary growth rate was perceived as a temporary shock that shifted the aggregate demand curve to the left. But firms and workers did not expect this policy to continue, and a lower expected inflation rate was not built into contracts. As a consequence, the reduction in aggregate demand resulted in a recession.

Figure 18.10 illustrates the behavior of key economic variables from 1977 through 1983. Panel A illustrates the growth in M1, and panel B indicates the behavior of the interest rate. The money growth rate slowed from 9% in 1978 to 5% in 1981, while the interest rate on six-month loans increased from 7% in 1978 to a peak of 14% in 1981. Undoubtedly, the Federal Reserve Board could have prevented the increase in the short-term interest rate by allowing narrow measures of money to grow at a faster rate. Minutes of the Federal Reserve Board meetings from the period indicate that it chose not to. Instead, the Federal Reserve Board allowed a sharp rise in the interest rate because it wanted to lower the inflation rate.

Panel C of Figure 18.10 indicates an initial consequence of the reduction in the monetary growth rate—a sharp recession as GDP growth went from 4% in 1978 to –2% in 1982. The current interpretation of these events is that households and firms did not expect the Federal Reserve Board to tighten the rate of money growth when they negotiated their wage contracts. As a consequence, the inflation rate in the early 1980s was lower than the rate that firms and workers had anticipated. The Federal Reserve System's monetary contraction caused a movement down the aggregate supply curve, leading to a loss of

FIGURE 18.10

Removing Inflation from the Economy

These graphs illustrate the behavior of money growth, inflation growth, and the rate of interest over the period from 1977 to 1983.

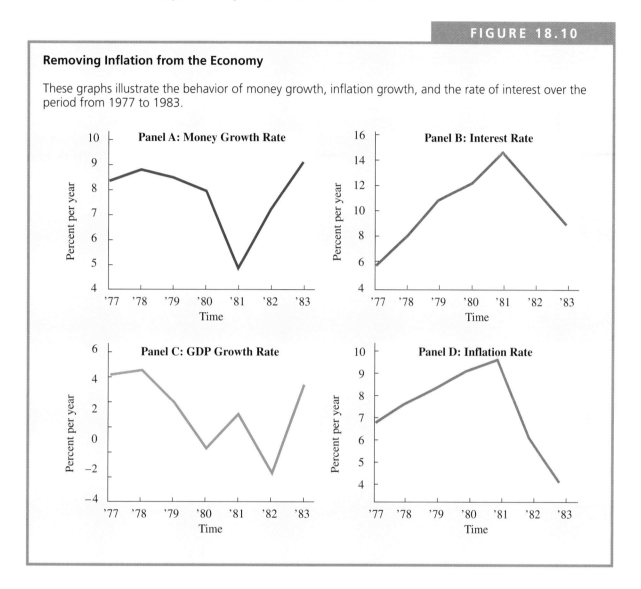

output in the short run. The payoff did not occur until 1982–1983, when the inflation rate finally fell from a peak of almost 10% in 1981 to 4% in 1983 (panel D).

MONETARY POLICY UNDER ALAN GREENSPAN

Most economists believe that the disinflation of the early 1980s was costly in terms of delayed output; it took time for households and firms to build a lower expectation of inflation into contracts. Because it is costly to remove inflation from the economy, the Federal Reserve Board is constantly alert to the possibility that inflationary expectations are building up.

Monetary policy under Alan Greenspan, 2001 chairman of the Federal Reserve Board, is best viewed as a balancing act between the use of monetary policy to offset adverse shocks to the economy and the exercise in caution over monetary policies that may be too expansionary. Expansionary monetary policy might lead to a buildup of inflationary expectations in a way that becomes self-fulfilling.

Under Greenspan's chairmanship, the current view of policymakers is that discretionary monetary policy is an important means of offsetting shocks that occur elsewhere in the economy. For example, the FOMC believes that toward the end of 2000, the economy began to enter a recession, perhaps caused in part by the steep increase in oil prices that occurred during that same year. As a consequence, the Fed sharply lowered the interest rate, reversing an earlier policy of raising rates. The Fed believes that a negative supply shock, like the oil price increase, will tend to raise the price level temporarily and lower GDP growth. If the Fed is able to observe the shock in time and react to it with an offsetting monetary disturbance, then the impact of the supply shock on GDP growth could be completely compensated for. In practice, the Fed lowered the interest rate by providing extra liquidity to the system (increasing the money supply). They tried to shift the aggregate demand curve up at the same time the aggregate supply shifted upward, which they believed occurred because of the increase in the price of oil. The Fed policy will likely result in temporarily higher inflation than would otherwise have occurred, but hopefully it will ameliorate the effect of the oil shock on unemployment and growth.

The danger of using discretionary policy in this way is that the Federal Reserve Board may not be able to recognize adverse supply shocks in time to take the correct action. As a consequence, an attempt to run discretionary policy may actually exacerbate problems in the business cycle. In addition, if the Federal Reserve System stimulates the economy too often, it may contribute to an increase in inflationary expectations that could be difficult to remove without a costly recession in the future.

CONCLUSION

A complete dynamic model of aggregate demand and supply can be used to explain the joint determination of inflation and GDP growth in both the long run and the short run. According to the dynamic new-Keynesian theory, the short run is a period over which expectations of future inflation are fixed. The long run is the period over which expectations adjust. In the short run, monetary policy has real effects because expectations have already been written into wage contracts. Over longer periods, wage contracts change to reflect new expectations, and increases in the supply of money are totally absorbed by price increases.

The Phillips curve is a stable relationship between wage inflation and unemployment when expectations are fixed. The Phillips curve does not work when expectations of inflation are determined endogenously. The modern theory of aggregate demand and supply explains why the Phillips curve appeared to be stable before 1970 and why that apparently stable relationship disappeared in the 1970s and 1980s. The theory argues that the Phillips curve shifted when policymakers tried to exploit the unstable relationship by raising growth above its natural rate. As inflation became anticipated, it was built into expectations, and the Phillips curve shifted upward. Policymakers are now aware of the importance of preventing the buildup of inflationary expectations. This awareness causes them to be cautious in using monetary policy to offset the effects of adverse supply shocks on employment and growth.

KEY TERMS

Discretionary monetary
   policy
Excess money growth
Expected value

Nonaccelerating inflation rate of unemployment
   (NAIRU)
Real wage inflation
Stagflation

QUESTIONS FOR CHAPTER 18

1. Describe the history of inflation in the United States, decade by decade, since 1949. What was the highest value of inflation during this period? What was the lowest? When did each occur?

2. What happens to the Phillips curve relationship between wages and unemployment when there is a change in the expected price level? Explain your answer using the new-Keynesian wage equation and a graph of the Phillips curve. Discuss a period in U.S. history during which the behavior of wages and unemployment were consistent with an increase in the expected price level.

3. What is the role of the parameter c in the neoclassical wage equation? Prove that as c gets very large, the neoclassical and classical models are the same.

4. Assume that the expected inflation rate is 4%, the natural rate of output growth is 5%, and the natural rate of unemployment is 6%.

   a. If a 1% increase in unemployment above its natural rate decreases nominal wage inflation by 2%, find the Phillips curve equation.

   b. Using your answer to part (a), predict the rate of unemployment that is consistent with 4% wage inflation.

   c. Assume that the short run aggregate supply curve has a slope of 1. If the growth rate of GDP is 4% when unemployment is at the rate you calculated in part (b), what is the inflation rate?

   d. Can the situations described in part (a), part (b), and part (c) persist forever? What will happen in the long run?

5. Explain the *nonaccelerating inflation rate of unemployment (NAIRU)*. What factors might change the NAIRU? Is the NAIRU directly observable? Why is this a problem for the Fed when formulating discretionary monetary policy?

6. What is meant by the *natural rate of employment?* How does the natural rate of employment differ from the natural rate of unemployment? What are the factors that determine each of these concepts? Can you think of circumstances under which the natural rate of unemployment and the natural rate of employment would both increase?

7. Define *rational expectations*. Does rational expectations imply that expectations are always correct or that mistakes cannot be made? Explain why or why not.

8. Suppose that an economy begins in a long-run equilibrium. The central bank then decides to increase the money supply. Discuss the short-run impact of this action on wages, inflation, unemployment, and output. Explain in detail the process by which the economy returns to a long-run equilibrium. Provide the appropriate dynamic aggregate demand and supply graphs to illustrate this process.

9. Suppose that the Federal Reserve thinks that the natural rate of unemployment is 5%, when in fact the natural rate of unemployment is 6%. If expectations are rational, what will be the impact of a discretionary monetary policy that attempts to sustain 5% unemployment? Explain.

10. Suppose that expectations are not rational but instead are equal to last year's actual inflation. That is, $\left(\frac{\Delta P}{P}\right)_t^E = \left(\frac{\Delta P}{P}\right)_{t-1}$ Show that it is possible to design a monetary policy for which unemployment is permanently below the natural rate.

11. Discuss two ways in which the Phillips curve relationship in Equation 18.1 differs from that in the traditional Keynesian model. What impact do these two differences have on the ability of a central bank to use monetary policy to control unemployment? Explain.

12. Quoting from Milton Friedman's "The Role of Monetary Policy" (*American Economic Review,* 1968):

> *. . . the monetary authority controls nominal quantities—directly, the quantity of its own liabilities. In principle, it can use this control to peg a nominal quantity. It cannot use its control over nominal quantities to peg a real quantity . . .*

> a. Explain how this claim is at direct odds with the traditional Keynesian notion of the Phillips curve. What does this statement imply about the trade-off between inflation and unemployment?

> b. Given Friedman's statement, does this mean that targeting nominal interest rates is an acceptable policy for the Fed to follow? Explain why or why not.

13. Discuss two criticisms of using discretionary monetary policy to stabilize output.

14. Read the article "Formulating a Consistent Approach to Monetary Policy" by Gary Stern, president of the Federal Reserve Bank of Minneapolis. This article is available on-line at http://woodrow.mpls.frb.fed.us/pubs/ar/ar1995.html. Answer the following questions:

a. How is inflation related to long-run growth?

b. Which central banks have recently announced low inflation targets? Why?

c. Why does Stern believe that the Federal Reserve Board should not "act aggressively in most circumstances" to stabilize business cycles?

d. Briefly summarize Stern's three proposals for running monetary policy on a day-to-day basis.

CHAPTER 19

What We Know and What We Don't

Introduction

Economists have a unique approach to social problems that sets them apart from most other social scientists. This approach, called "methodological individualism,"[1] begins with the assumption that societies consist of large numbers of individuals, each of whom makes choices over what to produce and what to consume. The defining aspect of the economic approach is that the preferences of individuals can be taken as fixed for the purposes of analyzing economic questions. Economic choices are made to achieve a goal—either for the maximization of profits, as in the case of firms, or for the maximization of utility, as in the case of households.

---

1. Not all economists subscribe to this approach, although it attracts a much greater consensus in economics than in other social sciences.

WHAT WE KNOW

THE CAUSE OF ECONOMIC GROWTH

We learned in Chapter 1 that U.S. GDP per person has grown at roughly 1.9% per year for the past 100 years. But a number of countries (among them Japan, South Korea, and more recently China) have achieved much more rapid rates of growth.

Probably the most useful thing to remember is that technology advances at different rates in different countries. The history of the world is a history of leaders and followers, and currently the United States is at the very forefront of the production of knowledge. It is much easier to grow by catching up with the world leader than by pushing forward the frontier. The main reason for the recent rapid growth of the East Asian countries is their ability to emulate the organization and production techniques already in place in the West. China is now undergoing a very rapid change from a rural economy to a modern industrial economy, and along the way it is developing a market economy and a modern trading system. This reorganization is in part responsible for the rapid growth in the Chinese economy over the last two decades.

Until very recently, we did not really know what causes growth in advanced industrialized economies. Economic theory predicts that GDP per person cannot grow unless technology improves each year. We must continually discover newer and more-productive ways of producing commodities in order to avoid the stagnation that comes from diminishing returns to capital. For over 200 years, the advanced, industrialized countries have been discovering new technologies at a rate permitting increases in their standard of living of 1.9% per year, but only recently have we begun to collect data on growth across different countries, which allows us to understand why some countries have grown faster than others.

The data set collected by Alan Heston and Robert Summers has caused a burst of intellectual activity among economists who argue that growth is the result of externalities stemming from the acquisition of knowledge. If these economists are right, the immediate future looks very promising: The invention of the computer and the construction of the Internet are the most significant advances in the technology of knowledge production since the printing press. The invention of movable type was, arguably, the single most important cause of the industrial revolution. There are many signs in the current world economy that suggest we will soon enter a similar period of rapid economic growth.

Market capitalism can deliver growth, but there are alternative ways of organizing social and economic policies within a capitalist society. The western European economies, for example, have grown at about the same rate as the United States, but they have chosen, at least so far, a greater degree of government intervention in markets. In the mid-twentieth century, the economies of the former Soviet Union and its satellite nations in eastern Europe have achieved relatively rapid industrialization under a centrally planned system. But the comparative performance of East and West Germany suggests that the communist model was much less successful at delivering sustained increases in the standard of living of its citizens than the market capitalist model. When the Berlin Wall fell in November of 1989, it quickly became apparent that the standards of living in East and West Germany, a single country with a single culture and comparable infrastructure only 45 years earlier, had diverged dramatically. China has grown rapidly by adopting a market system; whether this will inevitably lead to a democratic political system remains to be seen.

STUDYING BUSINESS CYCLES

The main advances in business-cycle theory over the past two decades have been theoretical. We have begun to understand how to use the tools of supply and demand analysis to study dynamic problems, and for the first time in a very long while, a consensus is developing among macroeconomists. Textbooks on macroeconomics that were written as recently as 10 years ago divide macroeconomists into different schools of thought: monetarists and Keynesians, classicals and neoclassicals, and real business cycle economists and new Keynesians. Currently, and at research meetings throughout the world, these divisions have become a thing of the past. Progress is slow but discernible, and these days there is far more consensus than conflict.

How has this consensus developed? First and foremost, the dominant method of analyzing contemporary problems in macroeconomics is to apply the microeconomic tools of supply and demand. The problems that we face are often more complex than the problems of a single industry or a single market, but the methods we use are the same. Economies are conceptualized as collections of rational thinking human beings who interact in markets. The simplest way of applying this idea is to assume that households and firms can trade as much of any commodity as they wish at a given price: perfect competition. But more-complicated models have also been studied. Firms might be modeled as monopolists that can influence the price at which they sell by restricting quantity. Markets might involve search or random matching of buyers and sellers. By constructing model economies based around the paradigm of the rational participant, economists can look at what causes business cycles. By constructing simulations of economic models and checking the predictions of the models for other observable facts, we ask whether the explanation given by the model is the correct one.

THE CAUSES OF BUSINESS CYCLES

Although economists broadly agree as to the right method for analyzing business cycles, there is still tremendous disagreement about their causes. One school of economists, led by Edward Prescott at the University of Minnesota, argues that 70% of post–World War II business cycles have been caused by random shocks to technology. More recently, these findings have been challenged by a group of economists motivated by Keynes' view that animal spirits might partly be the cause of fluctuations in both the pre- and postwar periods.[2] What differentiates this recent debate from arguments between macroeconomists of the 1960s is that today's arguments are couched in the same language, the

---

2.   Quantitative research on animal spirits as a cause of business cycles is relatively recent, and there is still no easily accessible source. For the adventurous, a collection of research papers in the *Journal of Economic Theory* (no. 63, 1994) deals with quantitative applications of economic models in which animal spirits are the main cause of business fluctuations.

language of demand and supply, and these alternative theories can therefore potentially be resolved by confrontation with scientific evidence.

A modern theory of the business cycle consists of a system of difference equations that models the propagation mechanism together with a hypothesis about the nature of the impulse. Real business cycle economists and their opponents disagree about both of these components. These disagreements are relevant to policymakers because if business cycles are caused by shocks to productivity, and if the propagation mechanism that causes persistence operates through the equalization of demand and supply in competitive markets, there is probably no reason for governments to intervene in the economy in order to stabilize the cycle.

If, on the other hand, business cycles arise from the animal spirits of investors, perhaps the Federal Reserve Board should act in ways that prevent wild fluctuations in beliefs from being transmitted to employment and GDP. These questions are hard to analyze because no one can tell whether or not wild swings in beliefs are justifiable until after the fact. A good example of this is the current activity in the stock market. The market has realized high real returns in recent years, mainly as a consequence of beliefs that there will be very high future profits. At the end of the 1990s, the ratio of the price of a stock to the average dividend paid by a stock reached historically high levels. Because investors in the stock market are buying claims to future dividends, the market was betting that these dividends would themselves become very large, and very soon. If they are wrong, the average value of stocks could fall dramatically, and that, in turn, could have repercussions for employment and growth.

Economists agree that business cycles are caused by shocks to aggregate demand and supply, and that these shocks persist for long periods of time, in part because households try to smooth their consumption through saving. But there is considerable disagreement over what percentage of business fluctuations is caused by demand shocks, what percentage is caused by supply shocks, and whether or not the market mechanism causes shocks to persist for longer than they should.

THE CAUSES OF INFLATION

In Chapter 1, we pointed out that the trend rate of inflation has been quite a bit higher since 1945 than before 1945. The cause seems clear. In the period before 1945, the world inflation rate was limited by discoveries of gold because currencies were tied to gold and to each other at fixed rates under the gold standard. In 1948, with a move to the gold-exchange standard, currencies became tied to the U.S. dollar, and the link to gold gradually eroded. This move from a commodity-based monetary system to a purely fiat system allowed governments throughout the world to choose their rates of monetary expansion without limit. As different countries chose to expand their money supplies at different rates, the gold-exchange standard itself collapsed, and since 1973 we have lived in a world of floating exchange rates in which the only check on inflation is the conservative nature of central banks.

The consensus among economists as to the cause of inflation is relatively new. In the 1970s, an influential "cost-push" school argued that the main cause for inflation was the growth of strong trade unions. It was relatively controversial for Milton Friedman to argue in the 1950s that inflation is caused by excessive creation of money, largely because the

WEBWATCH

How To Find Economic Sites on the Net

Throughout this book, we have given interesting Web sites that you can use to supplement the material in the book. But Web sites are constantly being built, updated, and changed. One site that will probably have a degree of permanence is Bill Goffe's Resources for Economists on the Internet, at: http://www.econwpa.wustl.edu/EconFAQ/EconFAQ.html.

Resources for Economists on the Internet is the most comprehensive list of economic resources available. It lists university departments and institutions, teaching tools, and research material. If it's available and economic, the address is probably somewhere on Bill Goffe's site.

quantity theory of money had been discredited by the observation that the propensity to hold money is not a constant. Proponents of the utility theory of the demand for money did not argue that the propensity to hold money is constant, but that it is a stable function of the interest rate, and the incorporation of this idea into modern macroeconomics has led to a consensus that money growth is essential to the maintenance of a sustained increase in the general level of prices. Friedman coined the then-controversial phrase, "inflation is always and everywhere a monetary phenomenon." Today this statement is accepted as scientific fact.

The most recent episode of inflation in the United States was relatively mild on a worldwide scale, but is was important enough to cause significant disruption in economic activity and was partly responsible for the downfall of the Carter presidency. Inflation began to build up in the late 1960s and reached a peak of 10% in the 1980s. It was caused by a monetary policy in which the Federal Reserve Board was committed to keeping interest rates low during a period in which fiscal deficits were increasing. This low interest rate policy forced the Federal Reserve System to monetize government debt at an increasing rate, leading to an excessive monetary expansion and an eventual collapse of the policy itself as inflationary expectations fed into the capital markets.

HOW INFLATION IS RELATED TO GROWTH

Perhaps the most difficult and least understood area of macroeconomics is the relationship of money to growth. It is widely believed that maintaining a low inflationary environment in order to promote growth is important, largely because we know that countries with very high inflation rates, like Argentina, Brazil, and Bolivia, suffer from systemic employment problems stemming from the disruption of financial markets by the erosion of their currencies. There seems to be some evidence from the United States in the 1960s and from the United Kingdom over the last century that low inflation rates are associated with low unemployment and high growth. Modern explanations of this phenomenon suggest that inflation causes growth in the short run through mistaken expectations on the part of households and firms. For this reason, the Federal Reserve System no longer tries to stimulate GDP on a short-run basis through monetary expansion. The exact connection between the short run and the long run is a subject of modern research in macroeconomics, and the natural-rate hypothesis, which we examined in Chapters 17 and 18, is itself once more under attack.

THE RESEARCH FRONTIER

What are the "hot topics" these days in universities and research institutes? If you were to study macroeconomics in graduate school, what kinds of things would you learn, and how might you contribute to the advancement of knowledge?

RESEARCH ON GROWTH THEORY

A recent topic of study is the endogenous theory of growth. To see why, take a look at the article "Making a Miracle" by Robert E. Lucas, Jr.,[3] in which he analyzes the potential increase in social welfare that could be brought about in a country like India or Ghana if it were to emulate the experience of Hong Kong or Japan. Up until the seventeenth century in Europe, growth in GDP resulted in growth in population. As more goods were produced, more people were born, but most of these people lived a miserable existence relative to the average citizen of an advanced industrialized nation in the 1990s. It was only with the onset of the Renaissance in sixteenth-century Europe that this began to change, and the world economy has not looked back.

How is knowledge disseminated? What is the difference between the process of discovery and the process of innovation whereby new discoveries are applied? How does investment in research and education influence the production of knowledge? Should research be left to the private sector, or should it be actively encouraged through government grants or government research institutions? These are the questions that are being asked of modern growth theory. As new data emerges that allows us to compare the results of social experiments, such as the development of a market economy in China, reliable answers are increasingly likely. The theory of economic growth has been the single most important research topic in macroeconomics in the last two decades, and it is likely to occupy the minds of many of our best researchers for several decades to come.

RESEARCH ON BUSINESS CYCLES

For the 25 years following World War II, most macroeconomists were occupied with attempts to reconcile Keynes' book, *The General Theory of Employment, Interest, and Money,* with the microeconomic paradigm of supply and demand. Initially, the ideas in *The General Theory* seemed to work, and many economists believed that the problem of understanding business cycles had been solved. But the shifting of the Phillips curve in the 1970s and 1980s led to a reevaluation. To paraphrase Robert Lucas, many economists began to feel that as practical advisors to policymakers, they were "in over our heads."

---

3.   Robert E. Lucas, Jr. "Making a miracle," *Econometrica*, Vol. 61, no. 2, pp 251–272.

The arrival of the idea of rational expectations in the 1970s changed all of that. Macroeconomists began to question the foundations of the Keynesian model and searched for explanations of business cycles that were more firmly rooted in the microeconomic foundation of supply and demand. The culmination of this was the real business school, which in its strongest form denies the need for active government intervention. By this time, the pendulum had swung the other way, and academic economists completed a transformation from being interventionists with cures for all social ills to being introverts who, in political circles, were not really sure that they belonged at the party.

The rational expectations revolution has been a healthy development for macroeconomic science. It has forced us to make sure that our economic theories are internally consistent and to adopt the view that the microeconomic model of behavior should also be used to explain the macroeconomy. Not surprisingly, the early models of this idea were crude and could not capture the rich complexity of the real world. But more recently, research that combines explicit dynamic models with supply and demand analysis has been much more widely embraced; economists have realized that the method itself permits many explanations. The static Keynesian analysis that guided policy advisors in the 1960s is dead. But the combination of Keynesian insights into the role of market failures and the discipline of the demand and supply model of the RBC school is likely to prove very fruitful in the next few years.

INFLATION, GROWTH, AND THE MONETARY TRANSMISSION MECHANISM

One of the more interesting areas under study today is the monetary transmission mechanism. We know that an increase in the rate of monetary expansion leads to lower unemployment in the short run and to higher inflation in the long run. Theories suggest that there is a natural rate of unemployment that is independent of policy, but evidence is accumulating from the European experience and from a long series of observations in the United States that the natural rate of unemployment can change substantially from one decade to the next. It is a short step to ask whether the natural rate is itself a function of monetary policies that influence the long-run rate of inflation.

At present, many economists are researching why an increase in the monetary growth rate lowers unemployment in the short run. This can only happen in our theoretical models if the nominal wage (or some other nominal price) is slow to respond to monetary changes. But understanding why rational economic agents choose to engage in behavior that seems destined for bad societal outcomes in the short run is not easy to explain. Several competing theories are currently being analyzed, and perhaps in the coming years an academic consensus on this issue can provide an alternative model to policymakers that can improve the dynamic demand and supply model.

THE FUTURE

The study of macroeconomics is more exciting today than ever. Because economists are unable to conduct experiments, we are forced to search for regularities in data that contains many different variables that are changing at the same time. Only relatively recently, and with the invention of the personal computer, has the analysis of huge amounts of data become practical. When A.W. Phillips wrote his seminal article on wage inflation and unemployment in the 1950s, he analyzed his data with a hand calculator. Today, an analysis that would have taken weeks of painstaking calculations just 30 years ago can be carried out in seconds by an undergraduate using a laptop computer. The invention of the personal computer is doing for economics what the invention of the telescope did for astronomy.

Along with the ability to analyze data has come an extensive collection of economic statistics. Before World War II, very few countries collected national income data in a comprehensive way. Today, we have amassed 30 years' worth of data on every country in the world, and the quality of the data is constantly improving. As we accumulate better data on economic time series, we will get a much better feel for the way that economies work. We cannot design experiments, but politicians often conduct them for us. As countries experiment with different economic and social policies, and as we observe and measure the results, we will naturally accumulate a wealth of observations that will enable us to discriminate between different hypotheses. We are indeed living in interesting times.

OBS	Real GDP	GDP Price	Private Consumption	Private Investment	Government Consumption	Government Investment	Exports	Imports	Net Exports
1890	260.4224632	5.460121261	155.2551678	55.06986733	23.76400978	5.501365132	11.55064154	14.81386887	-3.263227
1891	271.8747874	5.371890861	166.406569	53.74864289	25.37037545	5.873238574	12.81117813	16.11831639	-3.307138
1892	298.5142561	5.171674732	174.2730614	64.23674407	27.2357992	6.305083927	14.91526465	17.04638092	-2.131116
1893	283.9067353	5.283660046	175.1375111	55.41889827	26.60681985	6.15947529	13.07757722	16.94550276	-3.867926
1894	276.0453132	4.951098318	169.9508129	51.27141614	26.15244205	6.054286889	14.27794232	14.70915099	-0.431209
1895	308.6807515	4.88322862	191.21627 57	59.44375538	28.46839275	6.59042917	13.07132385	15.87964885	-2.808325
1896	302.150284	4.750882605	190.6976059	54.51315188	28.07657057	6.499722387	15.40481975	17.41841931	-2.0136
1897	331.427296	4.771243722	205.6525858	62.0378928	30.43859003	7.046529582	16.7480677	18.12683657	-1.378769
1898	338.2635369	4.927343819	209.1103847	59.74868835	31.97136959	7.401367849	18.31323712	15.29866184	3.014575
1899	369.8854305	5.083444333	233.8336464	61.39071693	36.55100051	8.461551801	18.0099185	15.79555656	2.214362

OBS	Real GDP	GDP Price	Private Consumption	Private Investment	Government Consumption	Government Investment	Exports	Imports	Net Exports
1900	379.3184232	5.327775246	235.9947706	67.11179584	35.6097169	8.243644771	19.49946694	17.15568255	2.343784
1901	423.2970498	5.283660046	264.9538359	73.84656629	38.98222592	9.024380163	21.05266945	17.22451762	3.828152
1902	427.1691593	5.460121261	267.2014052	77.87846647	38.46532798	8.904718358	18.78565878	17.71184321	1.073816
1903	448.4950623	5.527991375	283.1937248	81.19995493	40.40260257	9.353197171	18.94366956	19.46783743	-0.524168
1904	442.9518434	5.592467276	286.9108585	73.7172969	40.82809264	9.451698067	19.72907	19.64759062	0.081479
1905	476.0747963	5.704452173	303.335403	84.24393491	42.90011796	9.931371654	20.1679217	20.65742517	-0.489503
1906	531.1168427	5.860553103	336.8760517	96.53740525	46.80791692	10.8360266	21.85397104	22.92455202	-1.070581
1907	539.0391245	6.104884016	343.1865346	98.62097161	47.20675868	10.92835841	22.58002236	25.62929114	-3.049269
1908	495.008707	6.060768816	321.5752919	82.03663566	45.01986643	10.42209315	22.76724827	22.49156582	0.275682
1909	555.849612	6.257591148	356.758395	98.61620616	49.68448334	11.50195135	20.04649235	21.9883074	-1.941815
1910	570.8812929	6.434051947	363.3282128	105.5088692	50.56101393	11.70486806	20.67080613	25.14294912	-4.472143
1911	589.3773127	6.359395487	380.8765419	103.0767383	51.9981615	12.03756754	23.28926002	25.4535706	-2.164311
1912	618.6661797	6.624087934	390.8177136	114.6976381	53.81556435	12.45829606	24.34654257	25.94983908	-1.603297
1913	624.3703071	6.596940055	403.6980143	108.109825	54.67547362	12.65736494	27.47237192	28.64888308	-1.176511
1914	601.2545255	6.729285653	398.6842059	98.34566139	52.91928244	12.25080691	26.07724691	29.07858333	-3.001336
1915	594.4014944	7.034699502	391.7686083	94.08580565	52.32600418	12.11346307	29.22083339	26.19549865	3.025335
1916	639.0884387	7.872891625	427.1246014	89.34488289	54.48595336	12.61349102	50.25656155	38.82371269	11.43285
1917	649.5706505	9.708767684	417.8749895	94.56047718	63.7778268	14.7645585	47.75611732	36.01743517	11.73868
1918	750.8607953	10.62161585	415.9732001	87.7467228	147.7266363	34.19869684	42.04017768	29.28559638	12.75458
1919	703.1210342	12.48803359	434.3859789	20.43475788	166.3387383	38.507396	47.32821613	32.03105917	15.29716
1920	658.0894006	14.49019155	455.6514418	64.09150861	82.77299437	19.16193729	41.43919584	39.23061409	2.208582
1921	613.2426406	11.80933661	484.783397	20.79498391	78.78336538	18.23833871	26.76124678	27.16411729	-0.402871

OBS	Real GDP	GDP Price	Private Consumption	Private Investment	Government Consumption	Government Investment	Exports	Imports	Net Exports
1922	704.805146	10.96096476	502.677506	80.60920413	75.88291065	17.56688382	24.85542906	31.0150674	-6.159638
1923	761.7710279	11.40211759	548.3204506	89.4535706	78.65378706	18.20834134	25.94822418	36.10736478	-10.15914
1924	787.1893151	11.23244355	588.949587	75.24614988	79.18334267	18.3309334	29.38822382	35.03408447	-5.645861
1925	847.3577045	11.4699877	571.7470377	125.6426994	83.29990409	19.28391682	31.8551351	37.86448009	-6.009345
1926	895.7561777	11.30031283	618.513767	126.9244781	87.42634199	20.23918665	30.76951399	40.99869756	-10.22918
1927	900.1733289	10.99490023	632.4314073	118.1327699	87.47373066	20.25015712	32.41214562	39.75088345	-7.338738
1928	909.4109588	11.13063879	641.2487944	113.1736402	88.79821203	20.55677439	35.96450581	38.21537373	-2.250868
1929	980.7744812	10.91076203	682.4830455	129.6071429	94.83866637	27.29695784	34.5613457	42.83180593	-8.27046
1930	893.7722182	10.56161798	640.0201689	90.92857143	99.913359	32.20427748	28.60385588	37.80754717	-9.203691
1931	825.0296895	9.601470588	616.6348166	57	102.1254538	33.7378145	23.70856511	33.91374663	-10.20518
1932	715.7099737	8.46675117	561.9869406	21.20535714	101.2422033	29.44391006	18.81327434	27.63342318	-8.820149
1933	700.6725455	8.292179144	550.6635069	22.5625	106.9833065	19.62927467	19.10123262	28.7638814	-9.662649
1934	754.9743694	8.990468081	567.5255767	34.86160714	122.1089109	21.26504594	21.40489886	29.39191375	-7.987015
1935	813.0952227	9.252326536	600.1419892	55.30357143	126.6355594	21.46951832	22.94067636	39.06361186	-16.12294
1936	928.3821719	9.252326536	657.7438044	76.25446429	110.5163087	29.13720344	24.28448167	33.18436658	-13.89988
1937	968.3626357	9.776042614	682.6061263	90.25	138.3385827	27.50143022	30.61956384	42.45498652	-11.83542
1938	929.5756186	9.514184159	667.3441069	59.29017857	149.0479596	28.11484542	29.46773072	33.28571429	-3.817984
1939	1003.330623	9.426898562	699.9605193	79.22321429	154.7890629	34.55570014	31.38745259	35.29541779	-3.907965
1940	1081.262692	9.601470588	732.5769318	103.3125	162.6278714	34.14675927	35.99478508	35.67708895	-0.682304
1941	1277.704015	10.2124731	774.5474852	126.7232143	224.0135731	88.1272578	37.53056258	45.59514825	-8.064586
1942	1533.459638	10.73619001	773.8090004	69.04464286	386.1998108	241.4809601	25.2443426	46.97681941	-21.73248
1943	1838.50461	10.91076203	796.7020295	45.37946429	587.8010174	342.79663	21.40489886	63.30566038	-41.90076

OBS	Real GDP	GDP Price	Private Consumption	Private Investment	Government Consumption	Government Investment	Exports	Imports	Net Exports
1944	1993.055955	10.99804846	826.1183411	50.72321429	668.838972	370.2980544	23.61257901	67.19946092	-43.58688
1945	1912.617648	11.60905097	879.5354091	70.0625	622.3581167	271.6405059	31.48343869	71.21886792	-39.73543
1946	1518.183521	14.57677874	958.9225262	165.8258929	265.1949589	31.48862609	64.0227244	50.4938054	13.52892
1947	1495.15	16.32250067	976.4	168.625	209.8816151	29.34167582	75.925	46.6	29.325
1948	1559.925	17.2625	998.05	215.35	219.2661162	42.93903664	59.8	54.375	5.425
1949	1550.9	17.265	1025.35	164.3	233.9500869	58.68335164	59.225	52.45	6.775
1950	1686.55	17.4125	1090.85	232.5	243.5554134	65.32867874	51.825	62	-10.175
1951	1815.075	18.5975	1107.15	233.2	324.5933343	105.3028756	63.525	64.425	-0.9
1952	1887.275	18.9825	1142.4	211.1	361.8001347	143.0278801	60.575	70.125	-9.55
1953	1973.875	19.24	1197.25	220.95	381.5627497	147.4240227	56.55	76.725	-20.175
1954	1960.5	19.4475	1221.85	210.75	353.6301052	137.404911	59.3	72.925	-13.625
1955	2099.525	19.735	1310.35	262.1	354.4029262	123.398093	65.6	81.7	-16.1
1956	2141.1	20.415	1348.75	258.6	353.6300715	126.4656834	76.475	88.325	-11.85
1957	2183.825	21.125	1381.8	247.4	372.5094864	130.7595917	83.1	92.1	-9
1958	2162.775	21.6425	1393.025	226.5	374.0551622	140.2675166	71.75	96.425	-24.675
1959	2318.975	21.88	1470.7	272.85	380.1274865	133.9289	72.4	106.6	-34.2
1960	2376.675	22.185	1510.725	272.8	385.4730416	127.5546175	87.425	108.025	-20.6
1961	2432.025	22.43	1541.275	271	401.8989721	139.7616068	88.9	107.275	-18.375
1962	2578.9	22.74	1617.325	305.325	434.7843485	146.2146831	93.65	119.475	-25.825
1963	2690.375	22.995	1683.95	325.725	455.8402652	146.3332867	100.725	122.65	-21.925
1964	2846.45	23.3375	1784.85	352.6	473.2687748	148.3646211	114.175	129.2	-15.025
1965	3028.575	23.7725	1897.575	402	497.0166117	149.5234383	116.475	142.95	-26.475

OBS	Real GDP	GDP Price	Private Consumption	Private Investment	Government Consumption	Government Investment	Exports	Imports	Net Exports
1966	3227.425	24.45	2006.075	437.275	547.8002088	165.093343	124.275	164.2	-39.925
1967	3308.325	25.205	2066.25	417.175	601.3873221	173.7874494	127.025	176.15	-49.125
1968	3466.075	26.29	2184.225	441.275	639.3258324	169.9460949	136.325	202.4	-66.075
1969	3571.4	27.5875	2264.775	466.925	652.8866876	161.1419421	143.7	213.95	-70.25
1970	3578.025	29.05	2317.475	436.225	661.9496154	153.9392353	159.275	223.05	-63.775
1971	3697.65	30.5175	2405.2	485.8	678.2598487	144.0328323	160.425	234.95	-74.525
1972	3898.375	31.8125	2550.475	543	703.3299248	145.6243981	173.475	261.3	-87.825
1973	4123.425	33.595	2675.925	606.55	709.9513075	147.2307678	211.45	273.425	-61.975
1974	4099.05	36.605	2653.75	561.725	723.6390227	156.7513585	231.575	267.275	-35.7
1975	4084.45	40.0275	2710.875	462.225	740.7140548	161.267934	230.025	237.55	-7.525
1976	4311.725	42.295	2868.875	555.475	751.9312178	156.9861546	243.625	284	-40.375
1977	4511.75	45.015	2992.075	639.4	772.5605894	150.0614168	249.725	314.975	-65.25
1978	4760.575	48.2275	3124.675	713	784.7937104	159.7113428	275.85	342.25	-66.4
1979	4912.125	52.24	3203.125	735.4	794.374864	169.2104823	302.375	347.925	-45.55
1980	4900.9	57.0525	3193.05	655.275	822.7713106	175.850065	334.825	324.825	10
1981	5020.925	62.3675	3236.025	715.6	840.832937	171.4174622	338.625	333.375	5.25
1982	4919.375	66.2575	3275.475	615.25	863.2908499	169.4116876	314.65	329.225	-14.575
1983	5132.35	68.8725	3454.275	673.75	890.1565559	178.2968312	306.95	370.7	-63.75
1984	5505.125	71.4375	3640.6	871.45	925.7970498	195.0163162	332.6	460.95	-128.35
1985	5717.025	73.695	3820.85	863.4	976.178313	215.4761901	341.625	490.725	-149.1
1986	5912.4	75.3225	3981.2	857.675	1021.058062	229.9790253	366.775	531.95	-165.175
1987	6113.25	77.5725	4113.375	879.275	1048.800909	237.5676105	407.95	564.175	-156.225

OBS	Real GDP	GDP Price	Private Consumption	Private Investment	Government Consumption	Government Investment	Exports	Imports	Net Exports
1988	6368.3	80.2175	4279.45	902.825	1060.602762	232.0759721	473.5	585.65	-112.15
1989	6591.825	83.27	4393.675	936.5	1083.773333	237.3601859	529.4	608.775	-79.375
1990	6707.9	86.53	4474.525	907.3	1115.958203	249.3270905	575.675	632.2	-56.525
1991	6676.425	89.6625	4466.625	829.475	1132.229681	245.7246807	613.25	629.025	-15.775
1992	6880.1	91.845	4594.475	899.825	1140.387675	242.9066228	651	670.775	-19.775
1993	7062.65	94.0525	4748.9	977.875	1139.90809	234.839802	672.725	731.8	-59.075
1994	7347.725	96.0075	4928.15	1107.025	1148.111471	234.8721594	732.825	819.375	-86.55
1995	7543.825	98.1025	5075.625	1140.6	1155.812633	242.7608603	808.2	886.6	-78.4
1996	7813.125	100	5237.5	1242.7	1171.769593	250.1558683	874.175	963.125	-88.95
1997	8144.875	101.9125	5417.225	1385.775	1199.871326	253.2713238	983.075	1095.225	-112.15
1998	8495.65	103.1125	5681.85	1547.4	1222.92512	260.5785962	1004.575	1222.175	-217.6
1999	8848.225	104.5525	5983.6	1637.75	1274.128707	284.8518136	1042.35	1365.4	-323.05
2000	9156.6	105.86	6225.2	1724.2	NA	NA	1077.7	1454.8	-377.1

Absence of arbitrage opportunities A situation in which there are no opportunities to profit by buying commodities or financial securities in one market and selling them in another. *Chapter 13*

Animal spirits The idea that mass psychology can be an independent cause of economic fluctuations. *Chapter 6*

Appreciation (of a foreign country's currency) A decrease in the number of foreign currency units that can be purchased for a dollar in a flexible exchange rate system. (*See also* **Devaluation**; **Depreciation**; **Revaluation**.) *Chapter 13*

Balance of payments The change in the foreign exchange reserves of the government. *Chapter 13*

Balance of trade The difference between the values of exports and imports of goods and services. *Chapter 2*

Balance sheet accounting A system for measuring the assets and liabilities of an economic unit, such as a household or a firm. *Chapter 2*

Banknote A paper claim to assets on deposit at a financial institution that is transferable from one individual to another. *Chapter 10*

Barter economy An economy in which all trade must be accomplished through bilateral exchange of commodities. *Chapter 5*

Base year The year whose prices are used to value goods and services in the construction of real GDP. *Chapter 1*

Boom (expansion) A period of time during which the growth rate of real GDP is above trend. *Chapter 1*

Budget constraint An inequality that describes the combinations of commodities that can be purchased and the labor that can be supplied, given a household's wealth and given the wage and the price of commodities determined in the market. *Chapter 4*

Budget deficit An excess of expenditures over revenues. *Chapter 2*

Business cycles The tendency of many economic time series to display coherent, persistent swings from one period to the next. *Chapter 1*

Capital elasticity The percent increase in output for a 1% increase in capital employed in production. (*See also* **Labor elasticity**.) *Chapter 15*

Capital market The set of financial institutions that channel savings from households to firms. *Chapter 2*

Capital stock The stock of machines, factories, houses, and unsold goods. *Chapter 9*

Central bank An institution that controls a nation's money supply. In the United States the central bank is the Federal Reserve System. *Chapter 10*

Circular flow of income The idea that GDP and income for the whole economy are different ways of measuring the same thing. *Chapter 2*

Classical aggregate demand curve A curve that illustrates all combinations of GDP and the price level for which the quantity of money demanded equals the quantity supplied. *Chapter 5*

Classical theory of aggregate demand A theory that asserts that the aggregate quantity of goods and services demanded at a given price depends only on the quantity of money in circulation. *Chapter 5*

Classical theory of aggregate supply A theory that asserts that the quantity of output produced is determined only by preferences, technology, and endowments. *Chapter 4*

Closed economy An economy studied in isolation from the rest of the world. *Chapter 2*

Cobb-Douglas production function A formula that describes how much output can be produced for given amounts of labor and capital. $Y = AK^{\alpha}(LQ)^{1-\alpha}$ where Y is output, K is capital, L is labor, A and α are constants, and Q measures labor productivity. *Chapter 15*

Coherence A measure of the degree to which two variables move together over time. (*See also* **Persistence**.) *Chapter 1*

Competitive equilibrium allocation A list of the quantities of commodities and labor demanded and supplied by every household and firm in a competitive equilibrium. *Chapter 4*

Competitive equilibrium A property of a model economy in which the quantities of all commodities demanded (including labor) equal the quantities supplied. *Chapter 4*

Compound growth A process of growth by which a variable increases each period by a fixed percentage of its level. *Chapter 3*

Conditional convergence hypothesis The proposition that per capita incomes of countries that have the same characteristics should grow closer together over time. *Chapter 16*

Constant returns to scale A property of a production function whereby if all inputs are multiplied by a positive number, output produced is multiplied by the same number. *Chapter 15*

Consumer Price Index (CPI) A measure of the cost of a standard bundle of consumer goods in a given year. *Chapter 1*

Consumption goods Commodities used to meet immediate needs. *Chapter 2*

Consumption smoothing The process of borrowing and lending in the capital market in order to distribute consumption more evenly through time. *Chapter 6*

Contract theory The theory that nominal wages are set by labor contracts and are changed infrequently. *Chapter 8.*

Contraction (recession) A period of time during which the growth rate of GDP is below trend. *Chapter 1*

Convergence hypothesis The proposition that per capita incomes of countries should grow closer together over time irrespective of national characteristics. *Chapter 16*

Corporate bond A promise by a firm to make a series of fixed payments over time. *Chapter 9*

Correlation coefficient A measure of the strength of association between two variables. *Chapter 3*

Countercyclical variable One that tends to decrease when real GDP increases and increase when real GDP decreases. *Chapter 1*

Coupon The fixed periodic payment by a firm to the owner of one of its bonds. *Chapter 9*

Cycle (*See* **High frequency component**.) *Chapter 3*

Deficit An excess of expenditures over revenues. (*See also* **Surplus**.) *Chapter 10*

Demand for money An equation that shows how much money the household would like to hold each week as a function of income and (in some theories) the interest rate. *Chapter 5*

Demand management Active government intervention—through fiscal or monetary policy—designed to maintain a steady rate of economic growth. *Chapter 9*

Depreciation (of a foreign country's exchange rate) An increase in the number of foreign currency units that can be purchased for a dollar in a flexible exchange-rate system. (*See also* **Appreciation**; **Devaluation**; **Revaluation**.) *Chapter 13*

Depreciation (of capital) The portion of gross investment devoted to replacing worn out capital. *Chapter 2*

Detrending The process of separating a time series into two components—a trend and a cycle. *Chapter 1*

Devaluation (of a foreign country's exchange rate) An increase in the number of foreign currency units that can be purchased for a dollar in a fixed exchange-rate system. (*See also* **Appreciation; Depreciation; Revaluation**.) *Chapter 13*

Difference equation An equation that relates the current value of a variable to its own past values. *Chapter 1*

Differencing The process of calculating the changes in a time series variable from one period to the next. *Chapter 3*

Diminishing returns The idea that as more and more labor is added to a fixed quantity of capital, the additional output that can be produced increases at a diminishing rate. *Chapter 4*

Discount rate The interest rate charged by the Federal Reserve System on loans to financial institutions. *Chapter 10*

Discretionary monetary policy A policy (not based on a predetermined rule) whereby the central bank adjusts monetary variables on a day-to-day basis in an attempt to influence the economy. *Chapter 18*

Disposable income National income minus taxes plus transfers. *Chapter 11*

Domestic economy The economy of a single country of interest. *Chapter 2*

Domestic expenditure Expenditure on goods and services produced in the domestic economy. *Chapter 2*

Double coincidence of wants A situation in a barter economy in which the goods that one person wants to sell are the same as those that another wants to buy. *Chapter 5*

Dynamic (economic) analysis The study of how the economy evolves from one period to the next. (*See also* **Static (economic) analysis**.) *Chapter 14*

Dynamic theory of aggregate supply A theory that explains how the growth of GDP is related to wage and price inflation. *Chapter 17*

Economic model An artificial economy represented by a graph or a set of equations. *Chapter 1*

Efficiency units A way of measuring labor input that takes account of skill. An hour of time supplied by a surgeon contains more labor measured in efficiency units than an hour supplied by a laborer. *Chapter 15*

Efficiency wage theory The theory that firms pay workers more than their marginal product to induce them to work hard. *Chapter 7*

Employment rate The fraction of the adult population that is employed. *Chapter 3*

Endogenous growth theory The theory that explains growth of per capita income using the assumption that productivity improves each period for reasons that are explained endogenously within the model. (*See also* **Exogenous growth theory**.) *Chapter 15*

Endogenous variable A variable that is explained within an economic model. (*See also* **Exogenous variable**.) *Chapter 4*

Endowments The quantity of resources available to an economy (including the time of its people). *Chapter 4*

ex ante **real interest rate** The nominal interest rate minus the *expected* inflation rate. *Chapter 11*

Excess GDP growth The amount by which GDP growth exceeds growth in total factor productivity. *Chapter 17*

Excess money growth The amount by which the money growth rate exceeds the natural rate of output growth. *Chapter 18*

Excess wage inflation The amount by which wage inflation exceeds the natural rate of output growth. *Chapter 17*

Exchange controls Limits on the amount of a foreign currency that an individual or firm can buy or sell at a point in time. *Chapter 13*

Exchange services The flow of benefits a household gains by holding money because it is generally acceptable in exchange. *Chapter 5*

Exogenous growth theory A theory that explains growth of per capita income using the assumption that productivity improves each period for reasons that are exogenous to the model. (*See also* **Endogenous growth theory**.) *Chapter 15*

Exogenous variable A variable that is not explained within an economic model. (*See also* **Endogenous variable**.) *Chapter 4*

Expected value The value that would be obtained by averaging a random variable over many repeated observations. *Chapter 18*

Expenditure method A method of measuring GDP by adding up all expenditures on final goods and services. *Chapter 2*

ex post **real interest rate** The nominal interest rate minus the *actual* inflation rate. *Chapter 11*

Factor services Services of the factors of production that households supply to firms in exchange for income. *Chapter 2*

Feasible choice A combination of labor demanded and output supplied that is possible, given the available technology. *Chapter 4*

Federal Open Market Committee The body responsible for determining and implementing U.S. monetary policy. *Chapter 10*

Federal Reserve System The central bank of the United States. *Chapter 10*

Fiat money Money that is backed by laws requiring it to be accepted in all legal transactions. *Chapter 10*

Final good One sold directly to the final user. *Chapter 2*

Financial asset A claim to resources that will be delivered in the future. *Chapter 2*

Financial liability An obligation to deliver resources in the future. *Chapter 2*

Firm An economic organization that produces commodities. *Chapter 4*

Fixed exchange-rate system A world monetary system in which the rate that each national currency trades for any other currency is fixed and regulated by the nation's central bank. (*See also* **Floating (flexible) exchange-rate system**.) *Chapter 13*

Flexible trend The low-frequency component that results from decomposing a time series into a trend and a cycle using a flexible detrending method. Flexible detrending is computed using a formula that lets the trend vary slowly over time. *Chapter 3*

Floating (flexible) exchange-rate system A world monetary system in which the value of one national currency in terms of another is freely determined by demand and supply. (*See also* **Fixed exchange-rate system**.) *Chapter 10*

Flow (variable) A variable measured per unit of time. (*See also* **Stock**.) *Chapter 2*

Frictional unemployment Unemployment that results from labor turnover. *Chapter 7*

Fully-funded pension A pension plan in which contributions are invested in stocks or bonds and in which retirees earn claims to the income streams from their invested assets. *Chapter 6*

GDP accounting identity An identity linking the components of GDP: $Y = C + I + G + NX$. *Chapter 2*

GDP deflator A price index computed as the ratio of nominal GDP to real GDP. *Chapter 1*

Gold standard A world monetary system in which each nation's currency is convertible to gold at a fixed rate. *Chapter 10*

Gross domestic product (GDP) The value, at market prices, of all final goods and services produced within a nation's borders during a given time period. *Chapter 1*

Growth The increase in real GDP over time. *Chapter 1*

Growth accounting A method of calculating the shares of growth in per capita GDP that are attributable to growth in capital, labor, and productivity. *Chapter 15*

High-frequency component (cycle) The part of a time series that remains after removing a linear or a flexible trend or after differencing the series. *Chapter 3*

Household A group of individuals who live together and make collective economic decisions. *Chapter 2*

Human capital The stock of accumulated knowledge. *Chapter 15*

Hyperinflation A period of very rapidly increasing prices. *Chapter 1*

Income method A method of measuring GDP by adding up all the income earned by the factors of production. *Chapter 2*

Indifference curve A curve showing combinations of commodities demanded and labor supplied that make a household equally happy. *Chapter 4*

Inflation rate The rate of change of the price level from one year to the next. *Chapter 1*

Intermediate good A good produced by one firm and used as an input by another. *Chapter 2*

International Monetary Fund An organization that acts as an international central bank. *Chapter 13*

Intertemporal budget constraint An equation that describes combinations of present and future household consumption that are feasible at each stage of life by borrowing and lending in the capital market. *Chapter 6*

Intertemporal indifference curve A curve showing combinations of present and future consumption that make a household equally happy. *Chapter 6*

Intertemporal production possibilities set Those combinations of current investment and future production of commodities that are feasible given the state of technology. *Chapter 6*

Intertemporal trade Exchange of commodities at different points in time mediated by borrowing and lending. *Chapter 16*

Intertemporal utility theory A theory that asserts that households allocate their consumption through time in order to maximize their utility. *Chapter 6*

Investment demand curve A curve that shows the quantity of investment goods demanded by firms at different real interest rates. *Chapter 6*

Investment goods Commodities that add to the stock of capital. *Chapter 2*

IS curve A curve that shows all combinations of the nominal interest rate and income at which saving equals investment. *Chapter 11*

IS-LM equilibrium A situation in which the nominal interest rate and income are simultaneously determined at the intersection of the IS and LM curves. *Chapter 12*

Isoprofit line A line showing all combinations of commodities supplied and labor demanded that yield the same profit. *Chapter 4*

Keynesian aggregate demand curve A curve showing all combinations of the price level and real GDP that are consistent with IS-LM equilibrium. *Chapter 12*

Knowledge function A function that describes how the productivity of an individual worker depends on the stock of capital in society. *Chapter 16*

Labor demand curve A curve showing the quantity of labor that firms are willing to hire at different real wage rates. *Chapter 4*

Labor elasticity The percentage increase in output for a 1% increase in labor employed in production. (*See also* **Capital elasticity**.) *Chapter 15*

Labor force All individuals who are either working or looking for work. *Chapter 3*

Labor force participation rate The fraction of the civilian population over the age of 16 that is in the labor force. *Chapter 3*

Labor income The income earned by supplying labor services. *Chapter 2*

Labor supply curve A curve showing the quantity of labor that households are willing to supply at different real wage rates. *Chapter 4*

Learning by doing Acquisition of knowledge through the act of production. *Chapter 16*

Lender of last resort The central bank's role in lending money to banks that are short of reserves. *Chapter 10*

Linear cycle The component of a time series that remains after removing a linear trend. *Chapter 3*

Linear detrending The process of decomposing a time series into trend and cycle by drawing the best straight line through the data. *Chapter 1*

Liquid assets Assets that pay a lower rate of return than similar assets of equal risk because they are themselves generally acceptable in exchange or because they can quickly be converted into other assets that are generally acceptable in exchange. *Chapter 9*

Liquidity preference A theory of why households and firms hold money when they could be earning interest by holding bonds. *Chapter 9*

LM curve A curve that shows all combinations of the nominal interest rate and income at which the quantity of money demanded equals the quantity supplied. *Chapter 9*

Low-frequency component (trend) A slowly moving component of a time series. *Chapter 3*

Macroeconomics The study of the working of the economy as a whole. *Chapter 1*

Macroeconomic variable An economic concept, pertaining to the aggregate economy, that can be measured and that can take on different values. *Chapter 1*

Marginal product (of a factor) The additional output produced by a one-unit increment in a factor of production, holding constant the inputs of all other factors. *Chapter 15*

Market A collection of traders who exchange commodities with each other. *Chapter 4*

Market rate of interest The rate of interest at which households and firms can borrow and lend in a competitive capital market. *Chapter 6*

Menu costs The costs of rewriting price lists in response to an ongoing inflation. *Chapter 8*

Microeconomics The study of the behavior of individual producers and consumers in markets. *Chapter 1*

Monetary base The liabilities of the Federal Reserve System. *Chapter 10*

Monetary policy The direct manipulation of the quantity of money or the nominal interest rate by the Federal Reserve System in order to alter one or more economic variables. *Chapter 9*

Money A commodity or financial asset that is generally acceptable in exchange for goods or services. *Chapter 5*

Money supply The quantity of money in circulation in an economy. *Chapter 5*

Money supply multiplier The ratio of the money supply to the monetary base. *Chapter 10*

National Income and Product Accounts (NIPA) A set of data on GDP and its components, published by the U.S. Department of Commerce. *Chapter 2*

Natural (output) path A list of values of output each period when the (output) growth rate equals the total factor productivity growth rate. *Chapter 17*

Natural (real wage) path A list of values of the real wage each period when the (real wage) growth rate equals the total factor productivity growth rate. *Chapter 17*

Natural rate of output The quantity of commodities supplied when unemployment is at its natural rate. *Chapter 12*

Natural rate of unemployment The unemployment rate that occurs in a search equilibrium. At the natural rate of unemployment, no firm or worker can profitably offer to trade at a higher or lower real wage. *Chapter 7*

Neoclassical growth model An exogenous theory of growth developed from the neoclassical theory of distribution. *Chapter 15*

Neoclassical synthesis The idea that the Keynesian theory of aggregate demand and supply holds in the short run and the classical theory of aggregate demand and supply holds in the long run. *Chapter 5*

Neoclassical theory of aggregate supply A dynamic theory of aggregate supply in which output growth may differ temporarily from its natural path. *Chapter 17*

Neoclassical theory of distribution The proposition that each factor of production is paid the value of its marginal product. *Chapter 15*

Neoclassical wage equation An equation used to explain the Phillips curve that relates wage inflation to expected price inflation and unemployment. *Chapter 17*

Net domestic product (NDP) The maximum output that is available for consumption without running down the stock of capital. *Chapter 2*

Net investment The portion of gross investment that contributes to increases in the capital stock. *Chapter 2*

Net worth The value of assets (real and financial) of an economic unit minus the value of its financial liabilities. *Chapter 2*

Neutrality of money The idea that if the money supply is increased (decreased) all nominal variables will increase (decrease) in the same proportion, and all real variables will remain unchanged. *Chapter 5*

Nominal exchange rate The number of units of a foreign currency that can be purchased for each unit of domestic currency. *Chapter 13*

Nominal GDP GDP measured using current prices. (*See also* **Real GDP**.) *Chapter 1*

Nominal interest rate The interest rate on loans expressed in dollars. (*See also* **Real interest rate**.) *Chapter 6*

Nominal rigidity A situation in which a nominal price or wage rate does not adjust quickly in response to disequilibrium. *Chapter 8*

Nominal wage The wage measured in dollars per period of time. *Chapter 4*

Nonaccelerating inflation rate of unemployment (NAIRU) Another name for the natural rate of unemployment. *Chapter 18*

Okun's Law The empirical regularity that real GDP falls 3% below trend for each 1% increase in the unemployment rate. *Chapter 8*

Open economy An economy that trades with the rest of the world. *Chapter 2*

Open market operations Federal Reserve purchases or sales of bonds in the capital markets in an effort to influence the money supply. *Chapter 10*

Opportunity cost (of holding money) The opportunities, in terms of goods and services foregone, that are given up by the decision to hold money. *Chapter 5*

Peak The point in a business cycle at which the difference of real GDP from trend begins to decline. *Chapter 3*

Per capita production function A function that expresses the output per unit of labor that can be produced from a given input of capital per unit of labor. *Chapter 15*

Perfect capital mobility A property of a model of being able to borrow and lend at the same real interest rate in any country in the world. (*See also* **Zero capital mobility**.) *Chapter 16*

Perfect competition A market in which all traders are able to buy or sell as much of any commodity as they desire at a given price and in which no individual trader is able to influence that price. *Chapter 4*

Perpetuity A bond that promises to make coupon payments forever. *Chapter 9*

Persistence The tendency of a time series to be highly correlated with its own past values. (*See also* **Coherence**.) *Chapter 3*

Phillips curve A negative relationship between unemployment and wage inflation that was first found to hold by A. W. Phillips in U.K. data. *Chapter 17*

Portfolio allocation An allocation of wealth among different kinds of assets. *Chapter 9*

Preferences The factors that cause households to choose one combination of goods over another. *Chapter 4*

Present value The value today of a specific amount of resources to be delivered at a future date. *Chapter 6*

Price deflation A situation of a falling price level (negative price inflation). *Chapter 17*

Primary deficit A measure of how much government expenditures plus transfer payments exceed revenues. The primary deficit *does not* include interest payments on outstanding debt. (*See also* **Reported deficit**.) *Chapter 14*

Private production function (private technology) The production function that faces an individual firm, holding constant the factors of production used by all other firms in the economy. (*See also* **Social production function**.) *Chapter 16*

Procyclical variable One that tends to increase when real GDP increases and decrease when real GDP decreases. *Chapter 1*

Production function The outer boundary of a production possibilities set. *Chapter 4*

Production possibilities set Those combinations of labor supplied and commodities produced that are feasible, given the state of technology. *Chapter 4*

Product method A method of measuring GDP by summing the value added by every firm in the economy. *Chapter 2*

Profit The income earned by supplying capital services. *Chapter 2*

Propensity to hold money The ratio of money to nominal GDP. *Chapter 5*

Purchasing power parity The idea that the real exchange rate should equal 1.0 in the long run. *Chapter 13*

Quantity equation of money An equation that links the price level to the quantity of money, the level of GDP, and the propensity to hold money. *Chapter 5*

Quantity theory of money (classical theory of the price level) A theory that asserts that the price level is determined by the combination of the classical theories of aggregate demand and supply. *Chapter 5*

Rational expectations The idea that agents will learn to forecast future prices and incomes without making systematic errors. *Chapter 12*

Real business cycle model An economic model in which all fluctuations in real GDP are explained in terms of random fluctuations in technology and in which the quantity of labor supplied equals the quantity demanded at every point in time. *Chapter 4*

Real exchange rate The value of a basket of foreign goods relative to a basket of domestic goods. *Chapter 13*

Real GDP GDP measured using base-year prices. (*See also* **Nominal GDP**.) *Chapter 1*

Real interest rate The interest rate on loans expressed in commodities. (*See also* **Nominal interest rate**.) *Chapter 6*

Real money balances The value of money measured in units of commodities. *Chapter 9*

Real wage The wage measured in units of final output per time period. *Chapter 4*

Real wage inflation The percentage rate of increase of the real wage. *Chapter 18*

Recession The period from the peak of a business cycle to the subsequent trough. *Chapter 3*

Reconstruction hypothesis The hypothesis that Japan and Germany grew rapidly after World War II because they needed to replace capital that was damaged during the war. *Chapter 16*

Relative purchasing power parity The idea that the relative values of the GDP deflator between different countries should not change systematically over time. *Chapter 13*

Reported deficit A measure of how much government expenditures plus transfer payments exceed revenues. The reported deficit *does* include interest payments on outstanding debt. (*See also* **Primary deficit**.) *Chapter 14*

Representative agent economy A model in which a single family makes all economic decisions. *Chapter 4*

Required reserve ratio The minimum ratio of reserves to deposits that commercial banks are required to hold by law. *Chapter 10*

Reserves The portion of customers' deposits that private banks retain in their vaults or keep on deposit with the Federal Reserve System. *Chapter 10*

Retained earnings Profits used to purchase new capital rather than being returned to shareholders as dividends. *Chapter 2*

Revaluation (of a foreign country's exchange rate) A decrease in the number of foreign currency units that can be purchased for a dollar in a fixed exchange-rate system. (*See also* **Appreciation**; **Depreciation**; **Devaluation**.) *Chapter 13*

Ricardian equivalence A theoretical proposition that it is irrelevant whether the government finances its expenditures by borrowing or by raising taxes. *Chapter 14*

Risk aversion A preference for a steady income over one that fluctuates. *Chapter 9*

Saving The decision not to consume. *Chapter 9*

Saving supply curve A curve showing the quantity of saving supplied by households at different real interest rates. *Chapter 6*

Scatter plot A graph in which each point represents an observation on two different variables at a given point in time. *Chapter 3*

Search theory An economic model of the process by which workers and firms are matched up over time. *Chapter 7*

Social production function (social technology) The production function that faces society as a whole if all firms simultaneously alter their inputs of factors of production. (*See also* **Private production function**.) *Chapter 16*

Solow residual (total factor productivity) The quantity of output produced per unit of factors of production when each factor is weighted by its share of national income. *Chapter 15*

Solution (to a model) A list of values of the endogenous variables of a model as functions of the exogenous variables. *Chapter 4*

Stability A property of the steady state of a difference equation. If a steady state is stable then solutions that begin near the steady state will converge towards it over time. *Chapter 14*

Stagflation A situation of simultaneously high inflation and high unemployment. *Chapter 18*

State variable A variable that is used to summarize how the economy changes through time. In dynamic economic models, other endogenous variables are expressed as functions of the state variables. *Chapter 14*

Static (economic) analysis The study of the economy at a point in time. (*See also* **Dynamic economic analysis**.) *Chapter 14*

Steady-state solution A solution to a difference equation that is the same in every period. *Chapter 14*

Stock (variable) A variable measured at a point in time. (*See also* **Flow**.) *Chapter 2*

Substitution effect The change in the quantity of labor supplied that results from increasing the real wage, holding fixed the household's wealth. *Chapter 4*

Surplus An excess of revenues over expenditures. (*See also* **Deficit**.) *Chapter 10*

Technology A method for transforming the factors of production into finished goods. *Chapter 4*

Time series A sequence of numbers that measures an economic variable at consecutive dates. *Chapter 1*

Total factor productivity (*See* **Solow residual**.) *Chapter 15*

Trend (*See* **Low-frequency component**.) *Chapter 3*

Trough The point in a business cycle at which the difference of real GDP from trend begins to increase. *Chapter 3*

Uncovered interest rate parity The idea that the expected real interest rate, measured in units of domestic goods, should be the same on bonds issued in all world currencies. *Chapter 13*

Unemployment rate The fraction of the labor force that is unemployed. *Chapter 3*

Utility function A mathematical formula used to represent preferences. *Chapter 4*

Utility theory of money An economic theory that asserts that households hold money to obtain the utility flowing from the services of real money balances. *Chapter 9*

Velocity of circulation The ratio of nominal GDP to the nominal money stock; the number of times per period that the average dollar is spent on GDP. *Chapter 9*

Volatility Rapid up-and-down movements of a variable measured by its standard deviation. *Chapter 6*

Wealth The sum of the values of money and bonds held by a household. *Chapter 9*

Wealth effect The effect on the quantity of a commodity demanded or supplied as a consequence of an increase in household wealth. *Chapter 4*

World supply of capital curve A curve showing the quantity of funds supplied to a domestic economy by the rest of the world at different values of the real interest rate. *Chapter 6*

Zero capital mobility A property of a model in which it is assumed that households and firms cannot borrow or lend abroad. (*See also* **Perfect capital mobility**.) *Chapter 16*